European History
1848–1945

T. A. Morris

Gor Blimey
Chief!

UNWIN HYMAN

Published by
UNWIN HYMAN LIMITED
15–17 Broadwick Street
London W1V 1FP

First published in 1985 by
University Tutorial Press Ltd

Reprinted 1987, 1988, 1990

ISBN 0 7135 2794 3

Printed in Great Britain by
Butler & Tanner Ltd, Frome and London

Acknowledgements

The publishers would like to thank the following for use of tables: a table from A. Adamthwaite, *The Making of the Second World War*, by permission of George Allen & Unwin (page 274); 2 tables from *European Political Facts*, by C. Cook and J. Paxton, and 2 tables from *Industrialization of Russia*, by M. E. Falkus, by permission of Macmillan, London and Basingstoke (pages 92 and 117); a table from G. A. Craig, *Germany 1866–1945*, © Gordon A. Craig, 1978, 1981, by permission of Oxford University Press (page 211); a table in abridged form from Alec Nove, *An Economic History of the U.S.S.R.* (Pelican Books, Revised edition 1982), p. 94, © Alec Nove 1969, original sources: *Sotsialisticheskoe Stroitel'stvo SSSR* (1934, pages 2–3; Gladkov, Sovetskoe narodnoe Khozyaistvo (1921–25) (Moscow 1964), pages 151, 316, 357, 383; E. Lokshin: *Promyshlennost' SSSR*, 1940–63 (Moscow 1964), page 32; *Nar. Khoz.*, 1932, page 8 (page 190); a table from M. Ferro, *The Great War 1914–18* by permission of Routledge and Kegan Paul (page 172); 2 tables from T. G. Charman, *Modern European History Notes*, by permission of Telles Langdon Publications (pages 175 and 290).

Preface

The teaching of History at A Level and in Higher Education has been in a state of flux for some years now with the introduction of new teaching media and of new document based techniques. Two elements, nevertheless, remain essential to students of the subject at these levels. A sound, comprehensive narrative of events is the first necessity for all who are tackling a period with which they are not already familiar. All too often academic textbooks, in their eagerness to illustrate a particular thesis or interpretation assume familiarity with the narrative where none exists. Secondly, and especially in more advanced study of the subject, it is important to understand that there have been many interpretations of specific historical events and that these interpretations have often been influenced by the contexts in which they have been written. The student who is forced to resort to the 'concise notes' variety of textbook for a comprehensible narrative will invariably fail to understand the nature and the variety of historiographical interpretations.

European History 1848–1945 has thus been written to combine these important elements of historical study. The student embarking for the first time upon advanced study in this subject will find here a narrative of events that is at once detailed, but presented in such a way as to make the inter-connection of events and their annotation as easy as possible. Also, for the first time in a school or college textbook, the student will find a concise guide to the various ways in which these events have been interpreted by the writers of the past and by the historians of the present. Consequently *European History 1848–1945* provides those essential bases without which the student cannot hope to derive full benefit from the modern techniques now available.

Contents

1
Europe 1815-48: Themes and Problems

The century between 1848 and 1945 formed in many respects an organic whole. Certainly the dramatic era of the French Revolution and of the Napoleonic conquests had drawn to a close in 1815, but the major political and ideological issues at stake in Europe in the following three decades were still very much those of the revolutionary period. The aspirations of liberal conspirators and of conservative politicians alike were the same that had motivated them and their predecessors in the years since 1789. Only in the years after 1848 did a new generation come to power that had not experienced at first hand the traumas of 'Great Revolution'. Only then did the economic development of the major European states truly depart from the conditions of the eighteenth century. 1848, therefore, marked a significant stage in the development of problems that were not fully played out until the end of the Second World War, if then. It is impossible, nevertheless, to aspire to any real understanding of the Europe of 1848 without an outline of the events and forces which shaped that Europe. Many of these continued to influence the political, economic and philosophical development of the continent for many years thereafter.

(a) The Vienna Settlement

The political shape of Europe at the beginning of 1848 was predominantly the result of the great international settlement reached by the major powers, Britain, Russia, Prussia and Austria upon the collapse of the Napoleonic Empire in 1814–15. Although only the latter stages of their deliberations were held in the Austrian capital, the earlier stages held on French soil before the temporary return of Napoleon from Elba are often combined with them under the general title of the 'Vienna Settlement'. The statesmen present had as their primary task the huge labour of providing for the political future of France and of those territories conquered by France, of re-establishing the balance of power shattered by the Napoleonic

campaigns, and of attempting to ensure against any similar disruption in the future.

The cornerstone of the settlement was bound to be the fate of France herself. Although forcing the French to accept a restoration of the Bourbon monarchy deposed in 1792, the attitude of the allies in 1814 was one of wisdom and forbearance. They appreciated that harshness now would only store up trouble for the future. Only after substantial French support for Napoleon during his last campaign in the 'Hundred Days' in 1815 did France lose those territories that she had occupied between 1790–92, and suffer the imposition of a large war indemnity, and an army of occupation for three years. After the payment of the indemnity (1818) France was admitted to the alliance of the major powers, now the Quintuple Alliance, and became once more a full member of the diplomatic community. Even so, suspicion of a future revival of French ambitions remained a constant feature of European diplomacy until her definitive defeat in 1870. The governmental settlement of France was also inspired by the need to ensure her future stability. With both republican and Napoleonic forms of government generally unacceptable to the victorious allies, France was to undergo a restoration of the Bourbon dynasty deposed in 1792. That dynasty, in the person of Louis XVIII, was not to be restored unconditionally to all its former powers, however. At the behest of the allies the Bourbon monarchy was to be transformed into a constitutional regime, adhering to a 'Charter' which guaranteed the maintenance of many of the primary achievements of the revolutionary and Napoleonic years.

The wider territorial settlement achieved by the allies may be divided into three sub-sections. Firstly, the allies sought to prevent future French expansion by the creation of a cordon of relatively strong states around her borders. To this end, a new United Kingdom of the Netherlands was created, consisting of the old Dutch Republic and the Austrian Netherlands (now Belgium). The Italian border state of Piedmont was strengthened by the addition of Nice and Savoy, taken from

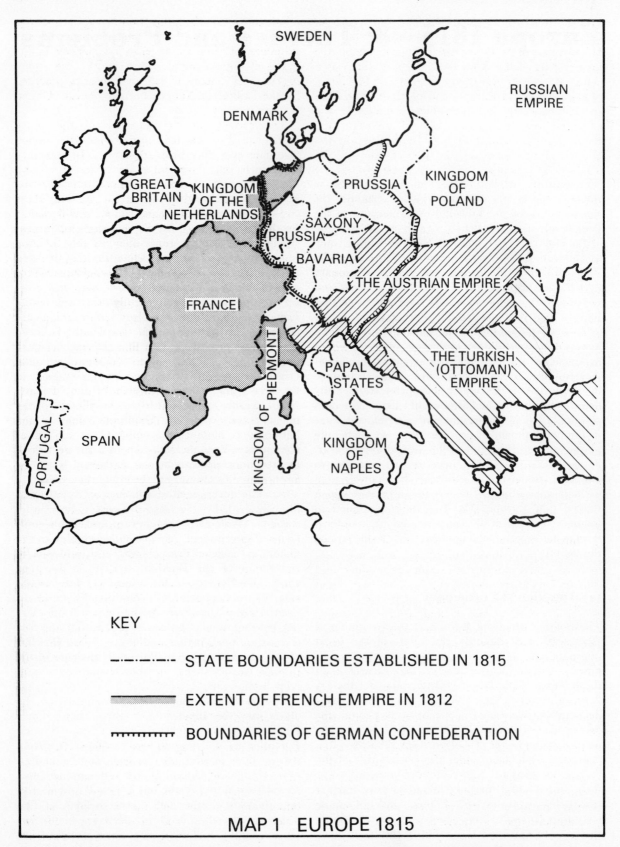

MAP 1   EUROPE 1815

France, and the formerly independent port of Genoa. To the east, Prussia was awarded the task of front-line protector of Germany by gaining the greater part of the Rhineland. In part, this was a compensation for the disappointment of her hopes of gains in central Europe, and partly it arose from the reluctance of the other allies to undertake the expensive and dangerous task of guarding the Rhine frontier against France. In this respect the Rhineland settlement was, in the words of A. J. P. Taylor, 'a practical joke played by the Great Powers on the weakest of their numbers'. Reluctant though Prussia was in her turn to take on the responsibility for the industrial areas of the Rhineland, impregnated with liberalism and catholicism, their gain had the greatest significance for the future, both of Germany and of Europe.

Secondly, this cordon was backed and supported by another. In Germany, a loose union of 38 states known as the German Confederation (Deutscher Bund) was established to compensate for the collapse of the old Holy Roman Empire, and to ensure that the mass of small German states would be less easy prey for a future expansionist power. Likewise, in Italy, behind the enlarged state of Piedmont a strong Austrian influence was maintained. This was based upon direct possession of Lombardy and Venetia, and upon the reign of princes related to the Austrian House of Habsburg in the duchies of Tuscany, Parma and Modena. Farther south, the restoration of the Pope to his temporal power and of the Bourbon family to rule in Naples, all aimed to counteract the strong French influence sown in Italy over the last two decades.

Thirdly, and largely independent of the fate of France, other territorial adjustments were necessary to satisfy the ambitions of certain of the allies, and thus to bind them more securely to the settlement as a whole. The most important were those concerning Saxony and Poland, which threatened at one time to precipitate war between the allies themselves. The peace conference ultimately agreed to the transfer of 40% of Saxon territory to Prussia, further strengthening her German power and leaving an independent 'rump' state. Also a generally unsatisfactory settlement was agreed whereby Poland became a kingdom under the rule of Tsar Alexander of Russia, nominally independent but in all essentials subject to Russian control, as the next century was to show. Lastly, largely upon the initiative of Great Britain, the victorious powers pledged themselves to further regular meetings with a view to diplomatic consultations upon whatever new causes of tension might arise in European politics. With France

admitted to it in 1818, this 'Concert of Europe' was perhaps the most lasting achievement of the statesmen of 1814–15. It earns comparison in the eyes of some commentators with the more sophisticated systems of collective security practised by the League of Nations in 1919, or the United Nations in 1945.

The success, or the morality of the peace settlement has excited deep emotions among historians ever since its establishment. In a century in which the principles of liberalism and nationalism attracted wide support, the Vienna settlement was much criticised for ignoring those concepts. The criticism made in an English radical pamphlet of 1821 was much repeated in the next century, and is still heard today: 'Public opinion was disregarded. National feeling was despised and the expression of it harshly repulsed. Whole countries were transferred from one Prince to another, without any consideration for their wishes or habits.' That these comments are less frequently heard today is due to two factors. Firstly, study of the settlement indicates that liberal principles were not invariably sacrificed to conservative ones. Constitutions were established or maintained in France, Spain, the Netherlands and Poland. Germany was a good deal less divided in 1815 than it had been in 1789. The shortcomings of the settlement were not in the terms that it laid down, but in the type of governors who, for the next three decades had perforce to be entrusted with the application of those terms. Secondly, the experience of two world wars, and of a failed peace settlement in 1919 has led historians to a much rosier view of the treaties that kept Europe at peace for forty years. Conscious now of the political weaknesses of liberalism, and of the potential disruptiveness of nationalism, many would stress that the Congress was justified in its search for stability. They would echo the words of Sir C. Webster: 'The primary need of Europe, once the Napoleonic tyranny was overthrown, was a period of peace; and this the statesmen of Vienna undoubtedly secured in a far greater degree than the publicists of the time dared to hope.'

(b) Conservatism

For all their startling successes before 1815, and despite their more modest achievements after that date, the liberal, constitutional and national ideas of the French revolutionaries were defeated and in opposition for most of the first half of the nineteenth century, and in some states for the whole century. In Europe as a whole the dominant political ideas of the period were those of the conservatives whose triumph was represented by the Vienna settlement.

European conservatism was based upon three main principles or group interests. The first of these was the principle of hereditary monarchy, a principle so powerful that the French revolutionaries had hesitated three years before abolishing it, only for Napoleon to re-establish it throughout western Europe as the best guarantee of social and political stability. For some, the principle of monarchy was synonymous with the concept of 'legitimacy', the view that in any one state, one family alone was directly entrusted with power by God. Subsequent Russian tsars would not have differed much from Paul I (1796–1801) when he defined his absolute power as follows: 'Know that no one in Russia is important except the person who is speaking to me; and that, only while he is speaking'. Such notions of legitimism, however, were not widely held even by the statesmen who served such monarchs. In the view of Metternich, who was often regarded as the personification of post-1815 conservatism, monarchy was desirable, not because it was the will of God, but because it seemed to offer the best hope of continuity and stability in human affairs. His view attracted widespread support. 'Monarchy', concludes D. Thomson, was at this time 'to most people the most natural form of government in the world'.

Behind the monarchy in most European states stood the two groups who had suffered most, or had been most threatened by the upheavals of the last 25 years, the landowning nobility and the Church. In both cases the group had been transformed by the French Revolution from the rivals of the monarchy, mistrusting its centralising influence, into its close ally, aware now of far greater threats to their interests. The role of the landowner is best illustrated in Prussia, where the feudal Junker class formed the staunchest support of the monarchy, or in Russia where, before the emancipation of the serfs (1861), the local control of the landlord formed the perfect complement to the central authority of the Tsar. In France the pre-revolutionary authority of the landowner had not survived intact. His place had often been taken by richer tenant farmers or by Napoleonic functionaries profiting from the break-up of the great estates. The events of 1848 well illustrate, however, that the new landowners had fully inherited the conservative interests of the old. The Catholic Church had not only suffered assaults upon its property, but upon its doctrines too. In France, in Italy, in Spain, along with its Orthodox 'cousin' in Russia, it now ranged itself on the side

of conservative principles throughout the century. The maintenance of the temporal power of the Pope was to remain an emotive issue, and the philosophical clash between the rationalist ideas of the 'Rights of Man' and the view of man as a sinful creature wholly subject to the will of God, formed one of the fundamental intellectual conflicts of the period.

Two theoreticians of conservatism may be chosen to represent its main branches. For the Frenchman Joseph de Maistre (1753–1821), the supreme facts of human life were Original Sin, and man's consequent inability to create a good society by means of his reason. 'Mankind', he proclaimed, 'is not progressing, it is groping back towards lost realms of light'. Monarchy was thus divinely ordained, in partnership with the Church, for the guidance of man, and the horrors of the French Revolution clearly showed how man lost his way when he rejected that guidance. Ultimately, because the authority of the monarch derived from God, it was subordinated to that of God's main delegate on earth, the Pope. In the final analysis, de Maistre's Catholic conservatism owed a great debt to the medieval concept of universal Christendom.

Far more modern, and thus far more influential, was the conservatism of the Englishman Edmund Burke (1729–97). In his *Reflections on the Revolution in France* (1790) he laid his stress, not upon abstractions or mysticism, but upon the importance of experience as the chief guide in government. 'It is with infinite caution', he wrote, 'that any man ought to venture upon pulling down an edifice, which has answered in any tolerable degree for ages the common purposes of society'. For Burke, the tragedy of the Revolution lay in the failure of questionable rationalist principles to take the place of institutions developed steadily through the experience of centuries. His was not necessarily an argument against change, merely against changing too fast and without due caution. In the hands of British Tories in the 19th century, Burke's was a philosophy of cautious advance, although elsewhere it was too often felt that any change at all was dangerous as tending to release anew the forces of revolution.

(c) Liberalism

In the first half of the 19th century the main rival to these conservative principles, and the other major governmental philosophy throughout the century, was liberalism. Although the concept of liberalism received coherent definition in Britain during these years, notably in the writings of Jeremy Bentham and John Stuart Mill, it remained a much broader one on the continent. The army officer in revolt against absolute monarchy in Spain in 1820, the intellectual supporting the Decembrist revolt in Russia in 1825, the German student participating in the demonstrations of the 'Burschenschaften', would all have found many points upon which to dispute with one another. They were united, however, by a variety of factors: by their common negative aim to revise or undermine the conservative system of 'Vienna Europe'; by common features of liberal political programmes; and by certain common philosophical bases to their thought.

European liberalism drew much of its philosophical inspiration from the rationalist thought of the 18th century and from the early years of the French Revolution. From the former it inherited its primary point of contention with conservatism. This was the conviction that man is essentially good and that to allow him individual freedom will lead, not to anarchy and lawlessness, but to the ordered and rational progress of society. From the latter came the classic statement of liberal preconceptions on society and on politics, the 'Declaration of the Rights of Man and the Citizen' (26th August 1789). Essentially an expression of middle class individualism, the declaration begins by establishing the 'natural and imprescriptible rights' of 'liberty, property, security and resistance to oppression'. It goes on to expand them into a full doctrine of equality of rights and equality before the law. Herein are to be found the elements that recur in every set of liberal demands presented in the next century. The first demand was for a constitution. Indeed, as C. Breunig has pointed out, 'the word "constitution" took on an almost mystical significance for liberals in some German and Italian states, who assumed that by its mere existence such a document would solve all their problems'. Within such a constitution would be found requests for a consistent set of individual freedoms: freedom of speech, of worship, of assembly, and of the press; freedom from arbitrary arrest, imprisonment and taxation; equality of opportunity. Parallel to these demands, especially in the states with more advanced economies, ran the request for the freedom that critics such as Marx felt to be the end-product of all liberal thought, the freedom of trade and economic enterprise.

It will be clear that what 19th century liberals drew from the French Revolution was the principle of 'liberté' rather than that of 'egalité'. In general, they were willing to accept material inequalities with the excuse that by equality of opportunity and the principle of 'self-help' any worthy man could aspire to material prosperity. The familiar slogan of British liberalism was that 'poverty is the divinely ordained consequence of a misspent life'. Thus European liberalism quickly ceased to be a radical political doctrine in the 19th century. 'We must preserve the political work that is the fruit of the Revolution', wrote Chateaubriand, 'but we must eradicate the Revolution from this work'. Similarly, Alexis de Tocqueville, in his influential work *Democracy in America* (1835–40), praised the American achievement precisely because it had created democratic institutions without degenerating into mob rule. Although aspiring to constitutional monarchy or parliamentary rule as an ideal, liberals were increasingly resigned to accept more undemocratic regimes, as in Russia or Prussia. They were also resigned to limit themselves to detailed practical work on specific problems, such as legal procedures, or the improvement of living and working conditions. The essentials of the Vienna settlement were thus in only limited danger from liberalism. A more real threat was posed by the other great middle class philosophy of the era, nationalism.

(d) Nationalism: Mazzini

In many cases in Europe in the 19th century, liberal political principles frequently went hand in hand with the desire for a free national state. This was because the conservative power that offended liberals was a foreign power. It is easy to appreciate how, to an Austrian governor in Italy, or to a Russian governor in Poland, the terms 'liberal' and 'nationalist' could appear to be almost interchangeable. However authoritarian and illiberal nationalism may have become in the 20th century, it was still reasonable in the 1830s and 1840s to equate the two ideals.

At this point in European history we may define nationalism as follows: it is the belief that the natural division of mankind is the nation, as opposed for example to the social or economic class. A nationalist believed that, in the words of E. Kedourie, 'the only legitimate type of government' for each division 'is self-government'. In this form nationalism had its roots, like liberalism, in the Rationalist thought of the 18th century. It also had roots in the French Revolution, which had declared in the 'Declaration of the Rights of Man and the Citizen' that 'the source of all sovereignty resides in the nation'. The nation, in this sense had no necessary racial connotation. It was not necessarily based upon a common language or common ethnic characteristics, but upon the factors identified by another French thinker, E. Renan, a century later (1882). 'A nation is a great solidarity, created by the sentiment of the sacrifices which have been made and of those which one is disposed to make in the future. It presupposes a past; but it resumes itself in the present by a tangible fact; the consent, the clearly expressed desire to continue life in common'. In this French tradition nationalism is not an excuse for aggression, for the division of man from man, but a bond uniting them in a spirit of fraternity.

The greatest exponent of this form of nationalism was in fact an Italian, Guiseppe Mazzini (1805–72). Born in Genoa of prosperous, intellectual parents, he developed a lasting sympathy for the causes of Italian unity and liberty in his mid-teens. A member of the conspiratorial society, the Carbonari, from 1827, he was sufficiently aware of their shortcomings by the early 1830s to develop his own movement. He drew its ideas and its name from the clandestine journal 'Young Italy' ('La Giovine Italia'). Central to the principles of Young Italy was the conviction that the binding together of the shattered Italian people would be the means of that people's moral and religious regeneration. Mazzini, like all Romantic thinkers, accepted Rousseau's argument of the natural goodness of man, and of his corruption by an evil and selfish environment. He thus viewed the effects of fraternal union within the nation in a way similar to the hopes of the Utopian socialists (see section **j**) for fraternal union within a reformed economic system. For Mazzini, too, educational reform and other forms of social improvement were essential adjuncts to his form of nationalism.

The second essential element in the beliefs of Mazzini and those he inspired concerns the relationship between the 'new' Italy and the other nations of Europe. 'Nations', as he vividly expressed it, 'are the citizens of humanity as individuals are the citizens of the nation'. The achievement of Young Italy would, by its imitation throughout the continent, lead to a 'Young Europe' in which nations would become morally and spiritually enriched. She would have no cause to attack her neighbours. Europe had received from 'old' Italy the cultural stimulus of the Roman Empire and the spiritual stimulus of the Roman Church. Now it would receive from Young Italy the example of the destruction of clerical and feudal privilege, and of all restrictions upon the fulfilment of human potential.

Unfortunately, Mazzini was wholly unable to realise these ideals. His nationalism was based upon a thorough reading of romantic philosophy and literature, and not at all upon a realistic assessment of contemporary politics or economics. His reliance upon conspiracy, insurrection and guerilla warfare as means of rousing the nation to action proved utterly ill-founded. He could not conceive that apathy or ignorance might blind the Italian peasant to his appeal. 'Like so many nationalists', writes H. Kohn, 'Mazzini in the fire of his apostolate misread history'. It would nevertheless be a grave error to underestimate his influence upon future generations. By that very fire and dedication he did more than any other European to keep alive a cause with very little material foundation, until the circumstances of great power politics had shifted in its favour. He was, in J. Bowle's phrase, 'a secular saint; a propagandist of the first order. He was a brilliant writer, the selfless indefatigable creator of a myth'.

(e) Nationalism: Germany

'I abhor', wrote Mazzini in 1847, 'the usurping and monopolising nation, conceiving its own grandeur and force only in the inferiority and poverty of others'. Unfortunately, even as he wrote this, other currents in nationalist thought had led the movement very much in that direction. German nationalism was to show in 1848 some very different characteristics from those of its French counterpart. Partly, this was due to the social and political circumstances of Germany, the weakness of her middle classes and her greater political diversity. Also there was a large contrast between her cultural fruitfulness and her political impotence in the age of Beethoven, Goethe and Schiller. These characteristics found their expression in the writings of three dominant intellectual figures.

The first of these was a Lutheran pastor from Germany's most easterly provinces, Johann Gottfried von Herder (1744–1803). Reacting against what he felt to be the excessive dependence of German intellectuals upon French thought and fashion, Herder developed his theory of the uniqueness of each national group and of each set of national characteristics. Each was created by God with its own 'spirit' or 'genius' ('Volksgeist') which it should preserve, cherish and develop, rather than slavishly imitate and pay homage to a foreign genius. For Herder a major role of nationalism was the development of a nation's awareness of its own unique culture, such as was undertaken by the brothers Grimm in their famous collection of German folktales compiled between 1811–29. It must be stressed that Herder showed no interest in claiming the superiority of any one of these national cultures over the others. 'No nationality', he specifically states, 'has been solely designated by God as the chosen people of the earth; above all we must seek the truth and cultivate the garden of the common good'. His work had, however, instituted a radical development in the concept of 'the nation' by replacing the consenting community of French thought with the broadly racial concept of the 'Volk'.

Such generosity as Herder's towards other nations could not survive the trauma of Napoleon's invasion of Germany and the humiliating defeat of the Prussian army at Jena (1806). The development of the thought of the Saxon university professor, Johann Gottlieb Fichte (1762–1814), was characteristic; admiration for the ideals of the French Revolution turning to revulsion when those ideals were imposed upon a defeated German nation. In his *Addresses to the German Nation* ('Reden an die Deutsche Nation', 1807–08), Fichte moved German nationalism away from its liberal origins by two important stages. Firstly, he stressed not merely the diversity between peoples, but the superiority of the German national 'spirit'. Adulteration of the national spirit, by imitation of or contact with foreign cultures, caused degeneration. Thus, by avoiding foreign domination since Roman times, the Germans had preserved their language, their culture and their whole national identity in a much purer form than had the French, the Italians or the Slavs. It was a case taken up with enthusiasm by a younger generation of agitators such as Friedrich Jahn or Ernst Arndt, who proclaimed unequivocally in 1818, 'let us hate the French strongly, and let us hate our own French who dishonour and ravage our energy and our innocence'. Here, as an alternative to Mazzini's views, was a nationalism specifically directed against neighbouring states.

Fichte's second innovation was to stress, in reaction to the political weakness that surrounded him, the importance of the state for the protection and development of the individual and of the national identity. This element was to be developed much further by his successor at the University of Berlin, Georg Wilhelm Friedrich Hegel (1770–1831). Although Hegel was primarily concerned with developing a general philosophical system, and not with the politics either of nationalism or of socialism, his influence upon both movements was profound. His greatest contribution was his development of the theory of Dialectic. According to this theory, all change and progress in history results from the clash of opposite ideas and forces.

From such clashes between a 'thesis' and its diametrically opposed 'antithesis', there results an end product, a 'synthesis'. It contains elements of both original ideas or forces. This synthesis will eventually come into conflict with its own opposite, and so change progresses. As an example, the French Revolution might be seen as a clash between a thesis (absolute monarchy) and antithesis (radical democracy), producing the synthesis of Napoleonic paternalism. The influence of this theory upon a Europe soon to receive Charles Darwin's message of scientific evolution was enormous, and the influence of Hegel upon Karl Marx's views of economic progress was especially important.

For Hegel, however, the ultimate outcome of this dialectical development was not the victory of the working classes, but the emergence of the nation state. Sharing Herder's view that man's creative ability was limited when he acted as an individual, Hegel preached that only as part of the organic state could man truly fulfil himself. All this might still have placed him nearer to Mazzini than to Fichte, had it not been for two factors. Firstly Hegel was convinced of the special destiny reserved for Germany in this development, and of the role to be played by the Prussian monarchy in this respect. Secondly, he strongly implied that the conventional notion of legality and right in relations between states had little meaning if the positions of the nations represented inevitable stages in the dialectical process. His reminder that 'men are foolish to forget the Truth that lives in power' rings ominously through the history of 19th and 20th century Germany. Two generations of thought thus made nationalism in Germany a doctrine centred upon a sense of cultural superiority, a sense of duty to the national state and an unhealthy admiration of power. Such features were not unique to Germany in the 19th century. Panslavism, especially, imitated some of them (see Chapter 6, section **j**). The combination of these philosophical convictions with the growing political and economic power of Prussia was to make this German nationalism a particularly potent and dynamic force in the history of the next century.

(f) The Fate of the Vienna Settlement: The Balance of Power

In assessing the long-term success of the Vienna Settlement, one is confronted with conflicting evidence. If its primary aim was to achieve ideological unity among the governors of Europe, then the Settlement failed. Britain never accepted the validity of, or the necessity for conservatism of the Russian or Austrian variety. Unanimity was further undermined by the triumph of the principle of popular sovereignty in France in 1830. But the balancing of roughly equal power blocs against each other, so that no one power could henceforth achieve the kind of supremacy that France had enjoyed before 1812, proved remarkably durable. This 'Balance of Power' proved to be the greatest achievement of the Vienna statesmen, and the most prominent diplomatic feature of the years 1815–48.

At first, repression played a significant role in the preservation of this stability. The Holy Alliance, which was contracted between the rulers of Russia, Austria and Prussia in September, 1815, was a remarkably abstract entity, 'perhaps the vaguest document ever to trouble European diplomacy' (A. Sked). It was subscribed to subsequently by most other European rulers, but rejected on grounds of political principle, religion or fear by the King of England, the Pope and the Sultan of Turkey. The Alliance was ostensibly an agreement to renounce war and to commit the rulers of Europe to friendly coexistence as Christian brothers. This nature it took from the unstable mysticism of its founder, Tsar Alexander I. To a more hard-headed conservative, such as the Austrian Foreign Minister Klemens von Metternich, the scheme was a 'high-sounding nothing'. Metternich, nevertheless, was to give the Alliance a more practical application. Through him it became a weapon for direct military intervention in the affairs of the lesser states, in the interests of political counter-revolution and of legitimate monarchy. This principle of armed intervention was laid down, despite British opposition, at the Congress of Troppau (1820). It was successfully applied against liberal risings in Naples, Piedmont (1821), and Spain (1822). Thus, the Holy Alliance and its interventionist policy destroyed the ideological unity of the five major powers, yet preserved the territorial settlement established in 1815.

The policy of intervention did not long survive its early triumphs. By the mid-1820s, old territorial differences between the major powers had resurfaced sufficiently to make the prospect of Austrian armies marching into southern Italy, or Russian forces entering the Turkish Empire, too unattractive to be tolerated as a general principle. Instead, the major powers fell back upon the principle of consultation and co-operation that had been established at the Congress of Vienna. From 1820 onwards, the causes of nationalism and liberalism won some notable victories. These successes came only with the co-operation of the major powers, in cases where they were convinced

that the triumph would not endanger the general European equilibrium. Thus, the rebellion of some of Spain's American colonies in 1822 succeeded because the economic interests of Great Britain, and the desire of the United States for domestic security, made these great maritime powers hostile to the idea of counter-revolutionary intervention by more conservative powers. The revolt of the Greek nationalists against their Turkish overlords (1821–29) was ultimately successful because powerful emotional forces and influential opinions made it impossible for the powers to maintain their initial pro-Turkish stance. Metternich's view that massacred Greek rebels 'hanged, impaled or with their throats cut, hardly count' as long as the Turkish bloc was maintained, was widely countered by other forces. In Russia, the Orthodox Church urged support for their co-religionists, and some politicians failed to resist the tempting vision of a pro-Russian Greek satellite on the Mediterranean. In the west, an influencial pro-Greek (Philhellenist) movement grew up among an educated class raised on the glories of classical Greece. Western governments, furthermore, could not tolerate the risks of unilateral Russian action. A complicated combination of diplomacy and anti-Turkish force brought about a settlement whereby Greece not only became independent from Turkey, but whereby a future position of neutrality vis-à-vis the other powers would be assured. The Belgian revolt against Dutch rule (1830), which eventually brought about the only major change in the boundaries of western Europe during this period, succeeded for similar reasons. Great Britain traditionally disliked the prospect of a large stretch of Channel coastline controlled by one state. Therefore Belgian independence, together with an international guarantee of neutrality (1839) suited the interests of Britain, and ultimately those of France. Belgian neutrality ensured that no power could henceforth attack France's northern borders without the most severe international implications.

The most severe threat both to the Balance of Power, and to the peaceful co-operation of the major powers came from the re-opening of the Eastern Question, of which the Greek War of Independence was part. At the basis of this problem was the patent decline of the Turkish Empire. Britain, France and Austria, especially, feared that Russia might fill the vacuum caused by such a decline. Having failed to secure any material advantage from the Greek question, Russia made more blatant attempts to gain advantage in the eastern Mediterranean following the attack upon the Sultan (1832) by his nominal vassal, the

Khedive of Egypt, Mehemet Ali. In return for Russian support the Sultan agreed to the Treaty of Unkiar Skelessi whereby Russia gained greater security behind the closed Dardenelles, and effectively established a form of unofficial protectorate over the Sultan. Russia's advantage was challenged only in 1839, when the death of Sultan Mahmud left the Ottoman Empire exposed once more to the power of the Khedive, now openly backed by the French. The dual threat of Russian intervention and of the domination of the Turkish Empire by a friend of France sufficed to drive the powers to the conference table once more. There the isolation of France eventually produced the Straits Convention (1841), which preserved the integrity of the Ottoman Empire, and the existing middle-eastern interests of the great powers. That it had not definitively solved the Eastern Question was to be proved a decade later by the outbreak of the Crimean War.

By 1848, great power rivalry was firmly re-established over several issues. Russia's ambitions in eastern Europe distanced her even from her Austrian neighbour, and her governmental ideology distanced her from increasingly liberal regimes in Britain and France. Colonial rivalry, and British distrust of French actions in Belgium and in Spain guaranteed that the 'Entente Cordiale' reached by the two states in the 1830s would never develop into a firm liberal 'bloc'. Yet the territorial system established at Vienna, and the balance of power, survived with only minor modifications. Initially war-weariness and the absence of any great, outstanding territorial issues explained this permanence. Subsequently, the fear of the social and political forces, nationalism, liberalism and socialism, that might surface if the diplomatic mud were stirred too vigorously, caused the leaders of the powers to desist from such action. This consistent restraint is one of the most striking features of the years 1815–48. The abandonment of such restraint in the era of Napoleon III, of Bismarck, and of Cavour sets the years that followed 1848 firmly apart from the preceding epoch.

(g) The Fate of the Vienna Settlement: France

Perhaps the greatest failure of the European settlement of 1815 concerned France. There the Vienna statesmen had sought to guarantee future political stability and to provide her with a regime which would 'heal the wounds of the revolution' without recourse to the international adventures of the previous two decades. As has already been stated, the restoration of the Bourbon dynasty was, in theory, a substantial compromise. Louis XVIII was restored as a constitutional monarch. He was committed by the 'Charter' to maintain such fundamental elements of the revolutionary and Napoleonic period as the Civil Code, the sale and redistribution of noble and ecclesiastical estates, and the principles of equality before the law, equality of taxation and careers open to talent. The preamble added by Louis himself, however, made it abundantly clear that he viewed these freedoms not as natural rights of the people, but as gifts granted by a monarch whose only superior was God.

Although Louis' personal feeling was that the Charter was a reasonable price to pay for his restoration, the compromise was subjected to the most severe strains between 1815–30. The government proved unable, and probably unwilling, to prevent an epidemic of counter-revolutionary vengeance. Its name, the 'White Terror', recalled the unbridgeable gap created between the social classes by the earlier, revolutionary terror. In public life, too, a strong 'Ultra'-royalist party profited from sympathy at the highest political levels, notably from Louis' brother and heir, Charles, Duc D'Artois. Although such politicians as the Duc de Richelieu sought to maintain the spirit of the constitution, it is generally agreed that the murder of Artois' son, the Duc de Berry (February 1820), began a consistent descent into reaction. The succession of Artois as Charles X (1824) merely made the descent official government policy.

The measures of Charles' reign embraced the restoration of clerical influence, especially in education, and the re-institution of press censorship. Also the National Guard, cherished by the bourgeoisie as their safeguard against the forces of the monarchy, was disbanded. In 1829 and 1830, elections showed the level of discontent among the enfranchised classes by returning large liberal majorities. Then Charles sought a return to personal government in defiance of what most conceived to be the spirit of the Charter. Attempts to dissolve the Chamber, and to influence the election of its replacement by a further reduction of the electorate precipitated the outbursts of July 1830, which ended the Bourbon monarchy for ever.

The popular disturbances which shook Paris at this time also proved that discontent was not limited to the enfranchised classes. They threatened a return to the republican excesses of 40 years earlier, which would have undermined the whole work of the Vienna statesmen. Louis Philippe, the

Duc d'Orleans, was rapidly elevated to the position of 'King of the French' (a significant acknowledgement of popular sovereignty) by prominent members of the bourgeoisie and of the Assembly. He owed this to the fear of what the alternatives might be if revolutionary actions continued. Similar motives caused his general recognition by the European powers, which foreshadowed their recognition of Louis Napoleon Bonaparte two decades later. Constitutionally, Louis Philippe was to govern France until the great economic crises of the late 1840s under much the same terms as Louis XVIII. The revised Charter of 1830 differed in only a few respects from its prototype of 1815. The major difference was that the King now recognised it as representing the inalienable natural rights of the people, and publically at least, did not baulk at a throne 'surrounded by republican institutions'.

The experience of the French governments between 1815–30 made it clear once more that the major advances of the revolutionary and Napoleonic period were irreversible. No subsequent French administration was seriously to consider governing without reference to the interests of those conservative classes, notably the bourgeoisie and the peasantry, that had benefited most from the revolution. The events of 1830 also provided a potent reminder of another force in French politics. 'We did not know the people of Paris', Rémusat was to write, 'and we did not realise what they could do'. The potential for proletarian revolt was not only to be an occasional inspiration to radical leaders until the Commune of 1871, and beyond, but also a powerful agent for the co-operation of conservative and moderate schools of political thought in France throughout the rest of the century. Louis Philippe's reign confronted a problem that could still be evaded by many of his contemporaries; how to adapt to economic and social developments without harming the fundamental propertied interests upon which his regime rested. His answer was to make his government a 'bourgeois monarchy', a 'government of the elite, and a meeting point of all the aristocracies, whether of birth, wealth or intelligence' (J. Droz). Ultimately that basis, although wider than the basis upon which the Bourbon monarchy had rested, was too narrow (see Chapter 2, section **b**). His successors, both Imperial and Republican, were going to have to pretend to considerably more extensive support. Also the questions of French domestic stability, and of France's place in the European balance of power, were to continue to haunt the statesmen of Europe.

(h) The Fate of the Vienna Settlement: Central Europe

It has long been fashionable to refer to the years between 1815–48 as the 'Age of Metternich'. Against this has been raised the objection that the control of the great Austrian diplomat over the European events of that era was extremely limited, that Russia, Britain and, after 1830, France, went very much their own way. Nevertheless, across a great swath of territory in central Europe, across the Austrian Empire itself, across neighbouring Italian states, and across the German Confederation, the principles of Metternich remained dominant throughout these years. These principles had been formed in direct reaction to the liberal ideas of the early phases of the French revolution, which had degenerated into domestic terror and into two decades of international conflict. From this degeneration Metternich concluded that monarchical government alone guaranteed the security of the continent. It alone, based on the consent of the aristocracy and of the other estates of the realm, guaranteed authority and stability. Any departure from this time-honoured format, however moderate and apparently reasonable, was in fact merely the thin end of the revolutionary wedge. His conservatism fell somewhere between that of de Maistre and that of Burke (see section **b**). He was an intensely practical politician, unimpressed by romantic notions of 'divine right', but strictly opposed to any gradual concessions to modernism. Liberalism, to Metternich, was a manifestation of the selfish material interests of the 'agitated classes' rather than of enlightened ideals. It was thus to be resisted by direct attacks upon the media most frequently used by the liberals, by censorship of the press, by resistance to demands for direct political representation, and by a complex system of surveillance and other police activities.

In opposition to these principles, the receding tide of the Napoleonic invasions left behind in central Europe many substantial pools of liberal and nationalist sentiment. Within the Austrian Empire itself the greatest obstacle to monarchical centralisation lay in the historical separatism of Hungary, and particularly in the powers of the Hungarian Diet. Without the consent of the Diet laws made in Vienna had no validity in Budapest. As is shown elsewhere (see Chapter 2, section **i**) Hungarian ambitions represented only the most striking element in a bewildering variety of national aspirations. In Italy, too, although the Austrian controlled provinces of Lombardy and Venetia were less troubled than most of the other states, Austrian ideals were constantly challenged by radical movements drawing their inspiration from the days of the French occupation (see Chapter 2, section 1). Similarly, in Germany, the undercurrent of liberal and national demands was persistent. In the years immediately after the defeat of Napoleon it manifested itself mainly in the restricted, yet noisy, context of student organisations, the 'Burschenschaften'. They were generally given to romantic, but sterile gestures such as the 'Wartburg Festival' (October 1817), celebrating the 300th anniversary of Luther's stand against foreign religious forces. They occasionally descended into violence and even, in the case of the reactionary poet Kotzebue (1819), to political assassination. In the ensuing decades the liberalism of the students tended to give way to the liberalism of the professors. This occurred as the political theorists of the south German universities shared with the merchants of the Rhineland the leading places in the demand for recognition of the great liberal freedoms in the government of the German states.

These challenges Metternich faced less with a reactionary 'system', as most contemporaries and some subsequent historians have seen it, than with a formidable array of expedients. In Germany he benefited from the conservatism of the princes, and from the willingness of such as the King of Prussia to be guided by him on constitutional problems. More important still, Austria's presidency of the German Confederation put the machinery of that body at the disposal of his cause. Thus Metternich was able to answer the disruption of the Burschenschaften with the Karlsbad Decrees (1819), and the disturbances inspired by the events of 1830 in France by the Six Articles (1832). The combined effect was to gag the liberal press, to impose control over academic syllabuses, to remove unreliable teachers, and likewise to strangle 'progressive' ideas at their source. Perhaps the greatest success of the conservative cause was the abolition of the Hanoverian constitution in 1837. In Italy, similarly, Metternich could operate through Austria's direct control of Lombardy and Venetia, her dynastic links with the duchies of Modena, Parma and Tuscany, and the habitual reliance of other Italian rulers upon Austrian aid 'in extremis'. Paradoxically, it was within the Austrian Empire itself that Metternich had to improvise most. His projects for administrative and financial reform to streamline the government of this vast conglomerate were consistently frustrated by an Emperor who took too literally his role as an autocrat. He insisted that all major issues should receive his personal attention which frequently

reduced administration to chaos. The succession of the weak-minded Ferdinand in 1835 merely substituted court intrigue for personal interference. Increasingly Metternich came to rely upon the most disreputable methods to contain problems that he could not solve. He dominated the state police system, exercised direct control over press censorship, maintained a complex spy network, and distributed bribes and subsidies where they might aid his work. Few major Hungarian leaders escaped substantial periods of imprisonment. All possible allies were exploited. The Catholic Church received enthusiastic backing and the literary and cultural aspirations of lesser nationalities who might also regard the Hungarians as a threat were sometimes tolerated and encouraged. Even Austria's economic backwardness was seen as an advantage, for 'the labours to which [the peasants] are obliged to devote themselves are too continuous and too positive to allow them to throw themselves into vague abstractions and ambitions'.

Yet how successful was this great conservative, this 'rock of order'? It is easy to construct a list of failings. In Italy, although he preserved the native rulers from the wrath of their liberal and nationalist subjects, he himself bemoaned his failure to persuade them to undertake such administrative reforms as might have strengthened their rule in the long term. In Germany, Austria's leadership failed on two important counts. Her economy was unable to provide adequate commercial leadership. Thus it was Prussia who headed the Customs Union (Zollverein) formed in 1834. Metternich accurately foresaw that 'the links which bind Austria to the other states of the German Confederation would gradually become loosened and in the end break entirely, thanks to this barrier'. Secondly, Austria's financial degeneracy left her army 'so run-down, demoralised and ill-led that it could scarcely be described as battle-worthy' (A. Sked). Austria's failure to provide Germany with decisive military leadership in the international crises of 1830 and 1840 foreshadowed her ultimate failure in this respect in the next two decades.

Yet, if Metternich could not defeat nationalism in Hungary, Germany and Italy, and if he could not definitively silence constitutional demands, he prevented these forces from making any significant progress in central Europe for three decades. It was a colossal conservative achievement, and the force of the outburst in 1848 bore witness to the frustration caused by his success. More important, Metternich created one of the distinctive international features of the 1815–48 period. He was in large part responsible for the essential governmental stability of the great territorial mass of central Europe which served as a barrier to the ambitions of France and Russia alike. Able to resist foreign encroachment, yet too incoherent ever to take the offensive, this 'bloc' thus made a fundamental contribution to the maintenance of the balance of power and of international peace. At the centre, both literally and figuratively, of the international history of the 1848–1945 period is the fact of Austrian decline and disintegration, and the attempts of France, Prussia, Piedmont, unified Germany and Italy, and ultimately of Soviet Russia, to take advantage of that fact. The watershed of 1848, between an 'Age of Metternich' and a 'Post-Metternich Europe' is thus a real and significant one.

(i) Population, Industrialisation and Urbanisation

Important as were the ideological and material disputes created or amplified by the French Revolution, the development of Europe in the early 19th century was as much the result of a second revolution. Although the British industrial revolution is often spoken of as an 18th century phenomenon, the achievement of that century was really only to produce a firm basis, in terms of technological development and the reorganisation of production, for the great economic 'take off' that occurred in the three decades after the Napoleonic wars. The revolutionary modifications made to the steam engine by James Watt and their application to textile manufacture, the development of new techniques for iron smelting and coal mining and the foundation of railway technology most recently, not only provided Britain with a formidable power base, but blazed an experimental trail for continental Europe to follow. Perhaps the real revolution in continental terms was the population revolution. Between 1750–1850, the population of Europe nearly doubled, from 140 million to about 266 million. The staggering impact of this increase may be gauged from the estimate that the previous doubling of the continent's population had taken nearly twelve centuries, while the increase for the century 1650–1750 had been a mere 3%. The rate of increase was, of course, uneven. France experienced only a 30% increase in the 75 years after Waterloo, while the number of Germans and British doubled. Russia felt the pressure most keenly of all, doubling her population in the first half of the century alone. The main explanation for this phenomenon lies in the sharp fall in the death rate, attributable to a variety of factors. Among

them are the considerable advances made in medical science, especially those contributing to the fall in infant mortality, the growth of public order and stability, and the improvements achieved in food production throughout this period. D. Thomson is not alone in seeing in this population 'explosion' a prime cause of the discontent, instability and international competition that characterised the 19th and 20th centuries. 'Against this tide', he wrote, 'no social and political order could stand intact'.

The effects of technical and social change were felt unevenly across the continent, generally spreading eastwards from their origins in the west. Belgium, fortunate in her natural resources and in the enlightened and coherent policy of her government after independence, was an early imitator of Britain's example. A national railway system was completed between 1834–44 and Liege and southern Hainault became leading areas of coal and iron production. France made a slower start, but the reign of Louis Philippe (1830–48), with his deliberate identification with bourgeois interests, brought consistent government support for industrial development. Two thousand miles of railway track were laid between 1837–48 (compared with a 6000 mile system in Britain by 1850) and an important law concerning road improvements was passed in 1836. Industrial areas developed in Alsace, Normandy and the Nord, where textiles predominated, and in Lorraine where an important metallurgical industry was developing. Two qualifications must be noted, however. Firstly, technology remained relatively primitive, with nine blast furnaces out of every ten still fuelled by charcoal rather than coke. Secondly, it must not be forgotten that, with only 400 000 Frenchmen employed in factories in 1848, France remained both economically and culturally a predominantly agricultural nation.

Beyond the Rhine, industrialisation was in a less advanced state by 1848. In Germany, political diversity was a major factor in slower and more piecemeal growth, but foundations had been established. Prussia by 1848 was only 25% behind France in terms of railway mileage. Heavy industry, however, remained scattered, and operated mainly by small plants relying upon traditional means of production. Even the Krupp works at Essen, the industrial giant of the later 19th century, employed only 140 workers in 1846. German iron output, at 200 000 tons per annum, was only 10% of Britain's total in 1850. The agricultural basis of German society died hard, as was the case in France. Not until 1900 were 50% of all Germans town dwellers. Nevertheless, the

1830s saw one major step taken towards the future economic strength of Germany. Based in part upon the foresight of such economists as Friedrich List, and partly upon the desire of the Prussian state for economic predominance in Germany, a customs union (Zollverein) was established in 1834, uniting a number of smaller free-trade unions and comprising all of the major German states with the exception of Austria. In Russia and in much of the Habsburg Empire, the beginnings of true industrialisation still lay some way in the future.

A major result of this industrial growth was the development of large concentrations of urban population. The French textile town of Roubaix experienced a population increase from 8000 to 34000 between 1831–41 alone. The population of Paris rose from 550000 to just over one million between 1800–50. and the total number of European cities with a population of more than 100000 rose from 22 to 47 in that same period. Neither were the new industrial cities of the continent spared the dreadful problems of disease and overcrowding that characterised the British industrial revolution. Nine out of every ten young Frenchmen conscripted into the army from urban areas in 1840 were rejected as physically unfit, and the spectacular cholera epidemic in Paris in 1831–32 killed 18400 victims in the course of six months. With a working day of 13 hours standard in Germany, and 14–15 hours common in France, outbreaks of urban violence were frequent.

While these problems predominated in the towns, the rural population also felt the effects of the technological and demographic upheavals. In the countryside too a society, relatively stable for centuries, was reshaped by pressure of increased population, pressure upon food supplies, and increased competition for suitable farming land. A measure of this pressure may be gained from the fact that 236000 Germans emigrated from their homeland between 1841–50. Although details obviously differed from state to state, and from locality to locality, the 1830s and 1840s were characterised generally for large numbers of peasants and artisans by the uprooting of their traditional ways of life and livelihood, and by their transplantation to unfamiliar environments with unfamiliar problems.

Lastly, alongside the growth of a new form of urban proletariat, industrialisation also began the transformation of the urban middle class, nourished by the profits of the new forms of production. As the pace of development varied from country to country, so the development of this class varied. In Russia the pace of modernisation was so slow as to make a minimal impact upon the influence of the old governing class until the end of the century, while in Berlin in 1848 only 700 out of a population of 400000 were classified as belonging to the capitalist mercantile class. The potential development of that class was even then being shown in France, however. There the prosperity of that middle class is indicated by the fact that, although the wealth qualification for the vote remained at the same high level throughout the reign of Louis Philippe, the number thus qualified to vote increased from 160000 in 1830 to 240000 in 1846. Embryonic though they might still be in many parts of the continent, it was clear that powerful rivals to the existing governing classes were in the process of formation.

(j) Socialism: the Utopians

The newest challenge of the 19th century, both to the old hierarchy of the landowner and to the new one which the bourgeoisie sought to construct, came from that scattered group of intellectuals who called themselves 'socialists'. Socialism, even in 1848, was not yet widely influential. It was little known among the working classes that it sought to serve, especially among the peasantry, and lacked any true concensus of means and aims. The basis had already been laid by then, however, for movements that were to transform European politics and society in the subsequent decades.

Diverse as the term 'socialist' undoubtedly was, those movements that claimed it as their title had certain common bases for their views. One was their common dissatisfaction with the system of industrial production currently developing in Europe. Its main fault was, as Robert Owen put it, that it laid too great a stress upon the production of goods, and too little upon their distribution. The result was that, despite the vast industrial resources and agricultural fertility of the continent, millions of its population 'are but imperfectly supplied with some, and are entirely destitute of most, of the necessities and comforts of life'. Secondly, socialists shared a highly optimistic view of human nature and of man's capacity for virtue and co-operation in his social existence. They rejected the opinion of conservative thinkers, such as de Maistre, that man was necessarily sinful, and had in many cases, in the words of Proudhon 'lost faith in God and found it in humanity'. From these bases proceeded the conclusion of a number of early 19th century socialist writers that the reformation of society was possible only by turning one's back upon those societies formed for personal profit, and constructing instead communities based upon co-operation and mutual respect. Such projects were generally termed by their critics 'Utopian' in reference to Sir Thomas More's great 16th century social fantasy.

Perhaps the most famous of these Utopian experiments was that of the Welsh socialist Robert Owen (1771–1858). Believing strongly in the corrupting nature of the modern industrial environment, he sought to demonstrate in his New Lanark Mills in Scotland that industry could function without exploitation and squalor, that co-operation could replace competition in society. The success of the New Lanark venture was insufficient to encourage other manufacturers to follow Owen's example, and subsequent ventures in America ended in failure. Nevertheless, in his views on the potential of human nature, and on the importance of environment and education, Owen exercised a substantial influence on several of the future mainstreams of socialism, especially on trade unionism and on the co-operative movement.

With the exception of Owen, utopian socialism had its strongest roots in French thought, with Henri de Saint-Simon (1760–1825) possessing a strong claim to be considered the first modern socialist. Saint-Simon did not reject the concept of a hierarchical society, but wished to see it adjusted so that society should reflect the importance of scientific and industrial advance and its potential for improving the lot of the masses. Prominent in the new hierarchy would be, not the decorative but useless courtiers of the 'ancien regime', but the intellectual elite and the captains of industry, capable of providing for the needs of the unpropertied classes. It became the purpose of the state to serve the interests of the population in general and not merely those of a privileged minority. Saint-Simon's tolerance of the principle of property made his views relatively widely acceptable in France in the 1830s and 1840s, and he had considerable influence over some of those surrounding the throne during the Second Empire.

Like Owen, Charles Fourier (1772–1837) believed that man's future happiness depended upon a radical reorganisation of capitalist methods of labour and production. Human 'passions' or instincts, he believed, were presently misdirected and corrupted by the faults in man's living and working environment. His hope was to create a number of small, self-contained communities ('phalanges'), in which labour would be shared and distributed according to the individual talents and interests of the workers, with frequent rotation of tasks to ensure variety and maintain enthusiasm. Like Saint-Simon, Fourier saw no cause to attack the concept of private property, his principle

concern being to increase the satisfaction of the working life, not to redistribute wealth. Economic restrictions and his own eccentricity meant that Fourier's new communities remained a dream. His writings exercised a substantial influence, however, as a systematic exposure of the faults and abuses within the existing capitalist system.

The next generation of French socialists was dominated by Louis Blanc (1811–82) and Pierre-Joseph Proudhon (1809–65). Blanc differed from his predecessors mainly in the importance that he attached to the state. He felt that only when governmental power was in the hands of those sympathetic to the working classes could the worker be freed from the curse of periodic depression and unemployment, and enjoy his basic right, the right to work. His view that such a government should establish what he called 'social workshops', co-operative units of production, was seen as the key to wider social co-operation and harmony. It had great influence upon the policies of the republican government in France early in 1848. Proudhon's main point of departure from earlier writers lay in his attitude to private property. In his best known work, *What is Property?* (1840), he answered his own question with the famous phrase that 'property is theft'. The abolition of capitalist property, and the gradual replacement of the state by a system in which universal fraternal co-operation replaced monolithic authority, lay at the basis of his socialism. 'In him', M. Salvadori had concluded, 'the anarchist component of socialism prevailed over the collectivist'. In the work of Blanc and of Proudhon, therefore, it is possible to discern important points of contact with later trends in socialist thought. Proudhon's anarchism can be detected in the establishment of the Paris Commune in 1871 and, thereby, in the Russian Soviets of 1905 and 1917. Both still apparently failed to grasp some of the fundamental realities of industrial and political power. It was by incorporating these realities into socialist thought that the leading figures of German socialism in the 19th century were to make the most important contributions to the political thought of that century.

(k) Socialism: Marxism

1848 saw the greatest single development in the history of socialism with the publication in London of a concise work entitled *The Communist Manifesto*. Of its two authors, one was Friedrich Engels (1820–95), son of a prosperous manufacturer with interests in Manchester and in the Rhineland. His co-author and lifelong friend was the greatest and most influential thinker that socialism has produced, Karl Marx (1818–83). He was a Rhinelander by birth, and thus much more closely associated than the utopians with industrial society, and a member of a family converted from Judaism, and thus directly acquainted both with oppression and with messianic philosophy. He was already a prominent figure in exiled radical communities in Paris. Marx and Engels, both deeply influenced by the dialectical philosophy of Hegel, had already engineered (1846–47) the foundation of the Communist League. Now they presented the outline of communist economic and political philosophy, which Marx was subsequently to expand in such major works as *Capital* (Das Kapital 1867).

The achievement of the *Communist Manifesto* was that it undertook to place the contemporary experiences of the working classes in the widest historical context, replacing the ill-founded hopes of the utopians, and the reckless conspiracy of the desperate, with a coherent view of history. It explained the origins of the workers' plight, and deduced the logical development of their economic situation. 'It set the day-to-day experiences of the working class', wrote N. MacKenzie, 'against the background of history and gave them meaning'. It preached the hard doctrine of the need to use force to destroy a social system based upon exploitation, and told the working classes squarely that their fate lay in their own hands.

The starting point of the Marxist argument was that history consists of a constant struggle between the social-economic classes, with political power and control of the state at any given time lying with that class that controls the means of economic production. The latest stage of this struggle had seen the steady triumph of the merchant and industrialist class, the bourgeoisie, whose victory over the landowning aristocracy was marked out by such great events as the English Civil War and the French Revolution. By the very growth of its industrially based power, however, capitalism created the tools of its own destruction. Firstly, capitalism strove towards monopoly, making competition and the defeat of one company by another an essential, self-destructive feature of the system. Secondly, it transformed the working classes by concentrating them in large numbers, by exploiting their labour in a naked and obvious fashion, and by provoking them to unite against these abuses. This exploitation he summarised in his 'theory of surplus value'. This stated that the value of a product derived primarily from the labour expended on its production. Yet the wages received by the worker were always lower than the market value of the finished product. The balance had passed to the capitalist in the form of profit. In effect the profit of the capitalist amounted to the theft of the worker's labour. The development of capitalism also had important international implications. Competition for limited resources and markets between company and company would be reflected by similar rivalry between state and state. Thus capitalism, that appeared so strong in Marx's own day, would steadily manufacture the crisis that would destroy it.

Marx's other great contribution to socialist development was to stress the importance of working class political organisation to ferment and to exploit this crisis, and to promote class-consciousness among fellow workers. In his view only the Communist Party could fulfil this role, by virtue of its more comprehensive historical view, and more logical grasp of social and economic realities. The victory of the working class in the resultant revolutionary struggle would be followed by a historical stage referred to as the 'dictatorship of the proletariat'. The machinery of state, now controlled by the workers, would be turned against the defeated classes, to eliminate them. Only when this stage was completed could a truly 'communist' society, with public ownership of land and all other means of production, with a heavy and progressive income tax, and with public control of all financial resources, come into being. The machinery of state, since its sole purpose was class exploitation and repression, would have no role in a classless society, and would 'wither away'.

It must be stressed that the *Communist Manifesto* had virtually no practical impact upon the events of 1848. Its influence thereafter grew steadily on socialist thought, especially with the establishment of the International Working Men's Association in London in 1864. This was indirectly controlled by Marx. Although challenged in the later 19th century by 'revisionists', notably the Germans Lassalle and Bernstein, who believed in the peaceful triumph of the proletariat by means of the ballot box, the 20th century triumphs of men and movements professing to be his disciples have made Marx's doctrines the official philosophy of half the modern world. Ironically, these movements have had the most success in the least industrialised parts of the globe. The debate on the correctness of the Marxist analysis is of course deeply entangled in the continuing debate between capitalist and communist powers. The official view of the latter largely reiterate the claims made by Engels at Marx's graveside that 'as Darwin discovered the law of evolution in organic matters, so Marx discovered the law of evolution in human history'. Western liberal and conservative writers have attacked the Marxist analysis on many fronts. They pointed out that the success of mixed economies in the west contradicts the theory of inevitable class warfare. They have drawn attention to the success of liberal and democratic socialist governments in levelling inequalities, raising living standards and guaranteeing basic economic security by reform rather than by revolution. Above all they have refused to see economic factors as the only agents of historical change. G. Craig speaks for several generations of liberal historians when he writes that 'the question of causation is too complicated to permit us to claim that any single factor is always more important than others in determining the course of history'.

Progress Paragraphs

Answer the following questions in about 150 words

By what means did European statesmen in 1815 seek to prevent a future major war?   Section (**a**)

Was the Vienna Settlement a success?
Sections (**a, f, g & h**)

How did the conservatism of Burke differ from that of the 'legitimists'?   Section (**b**)

What were the prime demands of European liberals in the early 19th century, and why did they later become more conservative?   Section (**c**)

How did the nationalism of Fichte and Hegel differ from that of Mazzini?   Sections (**d & e**)

What did 'Utopian' socialism seek to achieve?
Section (**j**)

In what ways did the socialism of Marx differ from that of the Utopians?   Sections (**j & k**)

What was the importance of population changes in 19th century Europe?   Section (**i**)

2
The Revolutions of 1848

(a) The General Crisis

Although the traditional forms of European society had been under pressure from economic and demographic changes as well as from political opposition for some time before 1840, the years between 1845–47 formed a particularly severe phase in the crisis. Indeed, one of the most helpful contributions to the understanding of 1848 was that made by the French historian, C. E. Labrousse, in his explanation that the revolts resulted not from one crisis, but from a conjunction of several. A particularly acute agricultural crisis coincided with a newer kind of economic crisis, an industrial slump. The infant industrial economies of Europe had less experience of this and it gave special urgency to the longer lived political problems of the individual European states.

The agricultural crisis became acute in 1845. The potato blight of that year had its most dramatic manifestations in Ireland, where it eventually accounted for the loss of up to a million human lives, but the failure of the crop also cut a swath of hunger and suffering across Europe, in Belgium, Holland, Germany and Poland. The following year, the unusually hot, dry weather caused the failure of the grain harvest, and as the failures continued it became impossible to make good the shortfall from the surplus of the previous harvest. Throughout Europe the crisis was reflected in sudden and steep price rises. In Hamburg the price of wheat rose 51.8% between 1841–47, 70% of that increase occurring in the period 1845–47. In Switzerland, the price of rye doubled in the same two years, and bread prices doubled in the one year 1846–47. Lastly it should be remembered that, even when imports of foreign grain were possible, the incomplete state of most European railway systems made its passage to many parts of the continent impossible.

The same years 1845–47 saw the most severe of the industrial crises that had hit Europe at intervals of roughly ten years since the end of the Napoleonic Wars. Partly it was a crisis of overproduction, in which producers, finding that they had saturated the markets available to them cut back production, thus creating unemployment or reducing wages. In France production in the iron and coal industries fell by 30% and 20% respectively in 1847. Similarly in Germany, the amount of spun yarn exported by the member states of the Zollverein fell by 40% between 1844–47. In part, the crisis also resulted from the impact of factory production in some parts of Europe upon older forms of production in other areas. The hostility shown by skilled craftsmen and artisans to factories, mills, railways and their owners in 1848 clearly indicated their views as to the origins of their hardships. Thirdly, the industrial crisis was linked to the agricultural crisis, for in many localities the need to use government or bankers' funds to buy large quantities of foreign corn left little or nothing available for investment in industry. Bankruptcies multiplied and business confidence reached a new low ebb. The impact of all this upon living conditions was naturally most severe. The coincidence of high food prices with declining wages caused great and widespread hardship, especially in the towns. Here, three elements of discontent came together; the unemployed and hungry artisan, the peasant fleeing from the rural ills of land-hunger and semi-feudal oppression, and the middle classes with their liberal or nationalist opposition to the existing regimes. Cologne was far from unique in having one in four of its inhabitants receiving some form of public assistance in 1847. Meanwhile, the numbers of central Europeans seeking relief in emigration to the USA rose between 1840–46 from 34 000 a year to 93 000.

It can be seen that the violence of 1848 occurred, not at the height of the European crisis, but during the steady improvement after it. It resulted from the steady accumulation of frustration during the previous two and a half years of hardship. 'The wave of high prices', wrote Labrousse, 'had spread over the country like a flood, and, like a receding tide, it left behind it a ruined population'.

Nevertheless, the increasing prosperity of 1848–49 goes far to explain the withering of rebellion in most European states after such promising beginnings. Thus, the immediate trigger to the outbursts of February and March 1848 must be sought in the political circumstances and disputes of the various states. In describing these it is important not to generalise, for the resemblance between the affairs of one state and those of its neighbour was merely superficial. The views of the revolutionary leaders were usually much more diverse than the common distress that briefly provided them with a rank and file following. As a whole, wrote C. Pouthas of these leaders, 'the same vocabulary, the same programme, concealed dissimilar situations'.

(b) France: the Crisis

Substantially agricultural, yet experiencing the stirrings of industrialisation especially in northern and some central regions, France provided a classic example of the conjunction of economic crises. A dreadful harvest in 1846 sent corn prices soaring. In Normandy they more than doubled between mid-1846 and mid-1847. A better harvest in 1847 did not fully counteract the rise, and the year went down in folklore as 'the year of dear bread'. Already that year there were cases of rural unrest in western France. Peasants tried to prevent the transport of scarce grain to the towns, and elsewhere rioters sought suspected hoards of grain from earlier harvests. The fall in the purchasing power of the peasantry combined with the wider recession to produce a spectacular industrial slump. In 1847 one third of the working population of Paris was supported by charity. Railway building, after rapid progress in the previous few years, slowed almost to a halt, and the gold reserves of the Bank of France sank so low that the Bank was forced to negotiate a one million pound loan from the Bank of England.

On the face of it, these crises assaulted a government with a better claim to public support than any other in continental Europe. Louis Philippe had ascended the throne as the result of popular revolution in 1830, he governed with the aid of a constitution and an elected assembly, and he claimed the middle classes as his main source of support. His, in short, was a government such as would have delighted most German or Italian liberals. Such an appearance, however, was deceptive. The government of Louis Philippe was not based upon the semi-religious claims that supported the Bourbons, nor upon the glamorous conquests of a Napoleon. It was based upon the principle that Guizot, first minister in 1847, had recently defined. 'Let us not talk about our country having to conquer territory, to wage great wars, to undertake bold deeds of vengeance. If France is prosperous, if she remains free, rich, peaceful and wise, we need not complain'. When suddenly France was no longer prosperous, the faults of her government became more obvious. In foreign affairs its policy had provided a sorry contrast with past glories. In the 1830s France had abandoned advantageous policies in Belgium and in the Near East in the face of pressure from the other powers. By 1846 she found herself isolated by a rift with Britain over the marriage of one of Louis Philippe's sons to the royal house of Spain. Social policy had failed to meet the needs of embryonic industrialisation. A Factory Act (1841) restricting child labour in larger enterprises stood almost alone on the statute book, and even that was badly enforced. Meanwhile, those well enough informed could read convincing arguments on social improvement in the works of Louis Blanc (see Chapter 1, section **j**) or of Louis Napoleon Bonaparte (see section **d**). Persistent demands for the extension of the electoral franchise had been rejected. While Louis Philippe was willing to acknowledge the principle of government, to an extent, for the people, he remained unwilling actually to allow the people to govern. As a result, only about 240 000 of France's population of 32 million were entitled to vote under the electoral law introduced in 1831.

Lastly, as the suffering of many Frenchmen became more acute, so the aura of corruption that hung about French public life became even more objectionable. Guizot's systematic use of bribery to gain support for his policies lent credence to stories of speculation by public figures at a time of national hardship. Isolated sensations, such as the murder of his wife by the Duc de Choiseul-Praslin took on undue political significance. It was not that the government of Louis Philippe was a bad government. It was not, however, a distinguished one, and men were increasingly able to think badly of it. 'The feeling of instability', as de Tocqueville remarked to the Assembly in the last weeks of 1847, 'that feeling that is the precursor of revolutions, exists to a remarkable degree in this country'.

(c) France: Success

For all this accumulation of tension and discontent, the fall of the French government in February 1848 occurred almost by accident. The moderate opposition in the Assembly was led by A. Thiers. In order to stay strictly within the law at a time when political meetings were banned they chose the tactic of holding a series of banquets at which after-dinner speakers could, under a thin veil of legality, put forward their views on political reform. The government's decision (20th February) to ban even this essentially middle class form of protest precipitated popular demonstrations in the streets of Paris. Louis Philippe's nerve was already sufficiently shaken for him to dismiss his chief minister, Guizot, when (23rd February) a clash between troops and demonstrators led to the shooting of between 40 and 50 of the latter. The following day, with much of the working population of Paris in outraged rebellion, and with the National Guard refusing to perform its peacekeeping duties, Louis Philippe abdicated and made his way in confusion to exile in England.

The monarchy had not been toppled by a coherent opposition party or coalition. Indeed, it had not been toppled at all. Its forces had not been defeated, so much as abandoned by their commander. The events in Paris found an echo in some other outbursts, in Lyon, Limoges and Rouen for instance. In the rest of France, as R. Price has written, 'the Revolution must have presented a somewhat artificial and imposed character . . . accepted . . . because there was no agreed alternative'. The Provisional Government formed on 25th February to fill the vacuum was, like the king it replaced, a compromise. The essentially liberal body envisaged by the poet-cum-politician, Alphonse de Lamartine, was expanded to include more radical elements in order to avoid the risk of the Parisian insurgents forming a rival administration. The uneasy coalition between the intellectuals who had spearheaded the ideological struggle and the workers who had risked their lives on the barricades appointed Lamartine to the foreign ministry, L. Garnier-Pagès to the control of the nation's finances, with radicals such as A. Crémieux at the Ministry of Justice and A. Ledru-Rollin at the key post of Minister of the Interior.

The policies of this administration, like its composition, struggled to compromise between the satisfaction of the radicals' demands, and the reassurance of the bourgeoisie. In foreign policy, its priority was to reassure the powers of Europe that the events of 1848 would not have the international repercussions of 1792. Lamartine's grandiose 'Manifesto to Europe' sought to convince them that they were dealing with a much more peaceful France than that which had given way to the temptations of conquest under the Napoleonic Empire. The statement that France no longer felt bound by the treaties of 1815 concluded by the Bourbons did much to lessen Europe's sense of reassurance. However, within a few days most of the powers had more pressing problems on their hands than the question of revolution in France. The financial policy of the Provisional Government was mainly conciliatory. In an attempt to maintain business confidence, no attack was made upon the Bank of France, and all debts of the monarchy were officially honoured. This moderate policy represented one of the administration's greatest failures. It failed to arrest the slide in share prices and the drain in gold reserves that had marked the last two years. The government's attempt to strengthen its financial position by imposing a 45% tax on direct income caused widespread resentment. It was especially objectionable to the many small farmers to whom, in the absence of the feudal survivals that characterised agricultural communities elsewhere in Europe, the government had very little to offer.

In terms of domestic political reform, on the other hand, the Provisional Government broke radical new ground. The very decision to found a republic, rather than accept the regency envisaged in Louis Philippe's abdication, recalled the more extreme phases of the 'Great' revolution. It owed much, like the other domestic reforms, to the pressure of Parisian radicalism. It was followed (2nd March) by the introduction of universal manhood suffrage, which instantly raised the electorate from about 240 000 to some nine million. Most controversial were the measures taken by the administration to alleviate the prevailing social distress. The establishment of the Luxemburg Commission, an assembly of workers' delegates charged to survey social problems and to suggest solutions, was an eloquent gesture. The establishment of 'National Workshops' to provide work for the substantial number of unemployed could have been more than an eloquent gesture. Ostensibly the embodiment of Louis Blanc's theories on state intervention to guarantee the 'Right to Work', they turned out to be a poor imitation. Few projects of importance were entrusted to the Workshops for fear of the damage that they might do, with their cheap labour, to competing private businesses. They served little purpose other than the performance of minor public works such as the levelling of the Champs de Mars in Paris. Nevertheless, they attracted the bitter opposition and resentment of middle class opinion, because they represented a dangerous alternative to normal employment relationships, and seemed to be consuming inordinate amounts of public money without obvious result.

(d) France: Failure

The elections to the Constituent Assembly of the Republic, held on 23rd April 1848, provided the mass of Frenchmen with their first opportunity to comment upon the events of the past two months. Their response was an unmistakably conservative one. Of 880 seats, radical and socialist candidates secured about 100. Candidates supporting the ideal of monarchy secured three times that number. Why was counter-revolution succeeding revolution so rapidly? Certainly, the influence of the conservative clergy was far stronger in the localities, as the radicals rightly complained, than that of the Provisional Government. However it is unlikely that they persuaded many to vote against their better judgement. Karl Marx's classic explanation was couched in terms of class warfare; that February 1848 saw a temporary alliance of middle and working class interests against a common enemy, which soon began to disintegrate once that enemy had fled. Although happy to see the back of Louis Philippe, the bourgeoisie had no desire to see the end of the society that he represented. More recent writers, although agreeing that the February coalition quickly fell apart, have not seen the causes in such clear cut terms. G. Duveau has stressed the diversity of the political views of different elements of the Parisian working classes, and has warned against treating them as a single unit. The American, P. Amann, saw the violence of early 1848, not as a statement of coherent class interests, but as a general outburst of anger with many causes. The Banquet Crisis, he states, 'unleashed a wave of violence that sought to redress social grievances, which had nothing to do with revolutionary ideology'. Common to all these interpretations is the picture of the French merchant and peasant proprietor, aware of the sudden danger to their material interests, salvaging what they could from the wreck of the monarchy.

A major clash between radicals and conservatives was foreshadowed in April and May. After a number of demonstrations against the elections to the Assembly, which many of the radicals felt were being held before the electorate had been sufficiently 'educated', a mob demanding French support for the rebels in Poland invaded the Assembly (15th May). The decisive confrontation came with the outbreak of violence in Paris known as the 'June Days'. The immediate cause of this crisis was the decision of the government (21st June) to expel unmarried men from the National Workshops and to make plans for their closure. In response to a blatant attempt to 'pervert' the revolution, barricades were raised in many parts of Paris. Four days (23rd–26th June) of bitter fighting raged between insurgents and their opponents before troops under General Cavaignac won the first great conservative victory of this French revolution. The rebellious quarters of Paris were reduced street by street, with the loss of some 1500 Parisian lives. The defeat of the insurgents represented the defeat of the radical element in the revolution. Over 11 000 people were prosecuted, and Paris remained under martial law until mid-October. Much of the work of the February revolution was deliberately undone. The National Workshops and all political clubs were dissolved, censorship of the press was reimposed, and such clauses as that concerning the 'right to work' were deleted from the existing draft of the constitution.

The triumph of conservatism in France was confirmed in December in the elections for the Republic's first President. Of the six candidates, five had played some role in the events of the year, and their election performances clearly showed the limitations of their achievements. General Changarnier received 5000 of the 7.5 million votes cast. Lamartine, whose tenure of the Foreign Ministry had lasted little more than a month, achieved 18 000. F. Raspail (37 000 votes) and A. Ledru-Rollin (370 000) were both too tainted in the public view by their contact with radicalism to attract many votes outside the capital. Cavaignac who was second in the election with 1 448 107 votes, appealed to many as the champion of public order, yet in general attitudes to the 'butcher of June' were ambiguous. Another man, who had not even been present in France for the first four months of the revolution, had the dual advantages of being free from association with either radical or reactionary events earlier in the year. He also bore a name automatically linked in the minds of many Frenchmen with domestic stability and international prestige. Louis Napoleon Bonaparte had already been elected to the Assembly by four Departements in June upon his return to France. Now he polled an overall majority by receiving 5 434 226 votes to become the first, and only President of the Second Republic.

(e) France: Louis Napoleon Bonaparte

The most obvious recommendation of the new President was, indeed, his name. Born (20th April 1808) the son of Louis Bonaparte, the Emperor's brother, he was thus the nephew of the great Napoleon. Superficially, there did not seem to be a great deal else to suit him for such high office. He had lived much of his earlier life in Italy. Possibly, although it has never been conclusively proved, he was involved in the conspiracies of radical political societies. With the death of Napoleon's only legitimate son, the Duc de Reichstadt (1832), he assumed the leadership of the Bonaparte dynasty. Attempts to pursue what he clearly believed to be his, and France's destiny ended in humiliating failure. Attempts to raise revolt at Strasbourg (October 1836) and Boulogne (August 1840) led, first to flight, then to imprisonment in the fortress of Ham on the Belgian border, and finally (1846) to further exile in England. His image, when he returned to his native city upon the fall of Louis Philippe, was not an attractive one. Yet the mediocrity of his earlier career was one of the negative factors that aided him at this fateful moment. His success in 1848 owed much to the support of established politicians who felt that they had little to fear from this 'mini-Napoleon', but that they might exploit his name for their own ends. 'He is a cretin', commented Thiers both unkindly and inaccurately, 'whom we will manage'. Secondly, his very lack of any successful connection with the politics of the mid-1840s was, at this time, a recommendation. Louis Napoleon's hands were clean.

If he had achieved little by practical action Louis Napoleon had shown his worth as a propagandist. Two works written in exile had already sold some half million copies in France by 1848. *The Napoleonic Ideals* ('Des Idées Napoleoniennes') written in 1839, and *The Extinction of Pauperism* (1844) jointly propounded the theory that the social and political problems of France, her economy, her international status and her domestic divisions had only been effectively tackled in the last half century by one regime, that of the Emperor. Only he had been able to reconcile the just principles of the revolution, with the national desire for stability and order. *The Napoleonic Ideal*, he proclaimed, 'means to reconstitute French society, overthrown by fifty years of revolution, to conciliate order and liberty, the right of the people, and the principles of law. It replaces the hereditary system of the old aristocracies by a hierarchical system, which, while securing equality, rewards merit and secures order. It disciplines democracy, and renders her an element of strength and stability'. An electoral manifesto in December 1848 that pledged Louis Napoleon to the reduction of taxation, the increase of employment, the expansion of private economic enterprise, the freedom of the press, and the protection of the educational rights of the Church drew largely on *The Napoleonic Ideals* and had the widest possible appeal to the new electorate.

The brief political history of the Second Republic further illustrates the triumph of social conservatism in France. At home, the new elections to the Assembly (May 1849) returned some 500 conservatives against some 250 republicans. The most notable domestic legislation of Louis Napoleon's presidency was the so-called 'Falloux Law' (March 1850), giving the Church powers of supervision over education in the localities. This concession to conservative, Catholic opinion, had a notable parallel in foreign policy in the military expedition that overthrew the radical Roman Republic (see section **n**), restored the Pope to his capital, and left a French garrison as his guardian. Such measures were merely the prelude to a more lasting form of conservatism, that of the Second Empire.

(f) Germany: the Crisis

The complex of states that made up Germany felt the impact of the economic crises of 1846–47 to an even greater extent than France because their own economies were generally less advanced. Agrarian discontent in the months before March 1848 took different forms in states that had not yet made the advance from feudalism accomplished in France in 1789–92. Land hunger and the persistence of semi-feudal oppression gave rise to demands for the abolition of feudal dues, for the curbing of the feudal privileges of the nobility and, where possible, for the division amongst the peasantry of the large feudal estates. The economic crisis in the German towns displayed two distinct characteristics. The first was the material distress that resulted from the failure of the harvests in the countryside. Already in 1847 there were bread riots in Stuttgart and in Ulm, and substantial violence in Berlin triggered by the shortage of potatoes. The distinctive features of German urban distress were not so much those associated with oppressed factory workers, but rather those associated with artisans, already under pressure from the growth of mechanised production before the depression of 1846–47 hit them. The early months of 1848 witnessed such acts of 'Luddism' as the burning of mills in Dusseldorf, demonstrations by weavers in Chemnitz, and assaults by wagoners in Nassau upon the newly constructed railways. Factory production, too, experienced severe difficulties as investment and demand declined, as was illustrated by strikes for higher pay and shorter hours in Berlin, Leipzig and Dresden. The combination of all these economic factors was in some cases catastrophic. Twenty-five per cent of the population of Cologne received some form of public assistance in 1847, while in Berlin between 1841–50 the sums spent on poor relief rose twice as fast as the population.

Politically, too, much remained to be done in the German states that had been achieved in France a generation earlier. A. Ramm reminds us that Germany before 1848 'was a country where to have a political opinion was difficult, to express it almost impossible, and to join with others to promote it, conspiracy punishable by the heaviest prison sentences'. A. J. P. Taylor has dwelt with only a little overstatement upon the personal unfitness of the rulers of many of the German principalities. 'Ceaseless inbreeding, power territorially circumscribed, but within those limits limitless, produced mad princes as a normal event . . .; and of the utterly petty princes hardly one was sane'. It is certainly true in this context that one of the immediate causes of discontent in Bavaria, second largest of the German states, was the irresponsible infatuation of the unbalanced King Ludwig for an exotic dancer with the stage name of Lola Montez.

As so much of the fate of Germany during and after 1848 was to hinge upon the Kingdom of Prussia we should perhaps consider the political crisis of the 1840s in that state in greater detail. Superficially, Prussia seemed to conform to A. J. P. Taylor's general pattern. The accession of Friedrich Wilhelm IV in 1840 had brought to the throne a vague romantic, ostensibly interested in the cause of German unity. In reality he never yielded on the principle of the Divine Right of Kings, and was only truly interested in leading Germany himself in the fashion of a paternalistic medieval Emperor. In 1847 he had temporarily raised the hopes of German liberals by summoning the Prussian assembly (Landtag). He had then shown that he viewed that body much as a medieval king viewed his Estates General, meeting not to govern, but to advise and to co-operate with their lord. The other mainstay of Prussian conservatism, the landowning Junker class, also found itself in an unaccustomed position in the years immediately before 1848. Their desire for the construction of an Eastern Railway (Ostbahn), linking their agricultural estates in East Prussia with markets in the major cities, had temporarily placed them in the unusual position of supporting the summoning of an assembly which alone could grant the necessary funds. Strange and perturbed as the political scene in Prussia might have seemed in 1846–47, and real as the economic distress was, it must be stressed how little scope for true governmental crisis existed. The administration was soundly organised and in many cases, in economic matters for instance, was pursuing far-sighted and logical policies. The finances of the state were sound, far sounder than those of the Austrian Empire. The army was well-trained, reasonably well-equipped and wholly loyal. Especially in the context of improving harvests and falling food prices in 1848, it was likely to take more than a temporary loss of nerve on the part of the government to achieve any permanent revolution in Prussia.

(g) Germany: Success

In the German states, as in much of central Europe, the news of the February revolution in Paris was the trigger that turned long-term resentment into actual political confrontation. 'It is impossible', declared a leading Berlin newspaper, 'to describe the amazement, the terror, the confusion aroused here by the latest reports from Paris crowding on each other almost hourly'. And if the political society of Prussia's capital seemed shaken, what hope was there for such minor entities as Mecklenburg–Strelitz? By the second week of March the leaders of most German states had despaired of surviving where the King of the French had perished, and had begun the wholesale granting of constitutional demands. In Bavaria, King Ludwig abdicated and saw his successor, Maximilian II, accept the principles of a representative assembly, ministerial responsibility, a jury system and a free press (9th March). In Baden, all feudal obligations were abolished (10th March) and in Württemberg the king renounced his hunting rights. Even Prussia could not escape. At first Friedrich Wilhelm seemed to preserve his political position by ordering his troops not to fire upon demonstrating crowds, and by putting his name to the usual list of concessions. An outbreak of street fighting on 18th March broke his nerve and he sought to save himself by ordering the withdrawal of the army from Berlin and, as a virtual prisoner of his people, appointed a liberal ministry led by Rhineland businessmen, L. Camphausen and D. Hansemann.

Liberal reforms were only one of the elements in what seemed a remarkable victory for the insurgents. On the face of it, the most spectacular concession of the rulers of Prussia, Bavaria, Baden and Württemberg was their agreement to participate in the organisation of a German national Parliament, a vehicle for the unification of the nation. At the height of the liberal success, the first steps towards such a body were already being taken. A group of enthusiasts, mainly academics and predominantly from the southern states, resolved at a meeting in Heidelberg (5th March) to summon a Preliminary Parliament (Vorparlament) which would in turn supervise elections to a German Representative Assembly. Thus this Assembly had its origins not in the exercise of any state's power, but in the absence of power, in a vacuum characteristic of March 1848. The Vorparlament, in its five day session, decided that elections should be by universal male suffrage and proportional representation, with one delegate for every 50 000 Germans. The Assembly that finally gathered in St. Paul's Church in Frankfurt (18th May) was predominantly elected by those middle classes preoccupied with constitutions and parliaments, and was the classic illustration of Sir L. Namier's characterisation of 1848 as 'the revolution of the intellectuals'. Of 830 delegates who sat there at one time or another 275 were state officials, 66 were lawyers, 50 were university professors, and another 50 were schoolmasters. Only one came from a truly peasant background, and only four from the artisan classes. Relatively united in social origins and in their view of the Germany they did not want, they were to discover like most revolutionaries that the construction of a new state and society is a process fraught with difficulties.

(h) Germany: Failure

The German liberals who dominated the Frankfurt Parliament have perhaps been more harshly treated by historians than any comparable group in the 19th century. Historians of the left have followed Marx and Engels in condemning them for not taking violent actions to overthrow existing power structures. The 'Prussian' school of historians in the period following unification such as von Treitschke, have blamed them for their opposition to Germany's 'best hope', the Prussian monarchy. Foreign commentators, such as Namier and Taylor, have seen them as ideological frauds, ultimately interested only in German power. Indeed, the failure of the Frankfurt Parliament was almost total not because it failed to use its opportunities, but because the opportunities of 1848 were illusory.

The first set of difficulties faced by the men who hoped to create a German state concerned the eventual nature of that state. What would be the constitutional framework of the united Germany? For a majority of deputies, it was of great importance to recruit the princes as supporters of a monarchical Germany, rather than risk the radical politics that accompanied republicanism. From this, two other issues followed. Which of Germany's royal houses should predominate, and what should

be the relations of the Parliament with older authorities within Germany? Conservatives preferred to see the constitutional decisions of the Assembly implemented by the princes in their individual states, while more radical spirits wished to see princely authority overridden by that of the Assembly. In June under the influence of its President von Gagern, the Assembly took the decision to claim executive power, superior to that of any state or to that of the Federal Diet. They also decided to entrust the leadership of Germany to the greatest of the German families, the Habsburgs, in the person of the Archduke John. The Assembly was thus moving towards a 'Greater Germany' (Grossdeutschland) including all German speakers, rather than a 'Lesser Germany' (Kleindeutschland), without the Germans of the Habsburg territories. That ambition was to be thwarted by the recovery of Habsburg authority in the Austrian Empire in October and November 1848.

A second set of problems arose from the fundamental weakness of the Frankfurt Assembly, its total lack of material power. Lacking an army of its own, it was bound to depend upon the goodwill of the major German princes for the most basic functions of government, such as the collection of taxation. Like other constitutional bodies set up in 1848, the Assembly was only ultimately able to survive if the regimes that it sought to replace voluntarily handed over their power. In particular, the Assembly was helpless in the face of two challenges. Firstly, various nationalities laid claim to territory seen by the Assembly as part of the Fatherland. In March 1848, Denmark occupied Schleswig and Holstein, an event closely followed by Palacky's declaration that Bohemia belonged to the Czech nation, and by a rising of Polish nationalists in Posen. The initial sympathy of the Assembly for the aspirations of other nationalists evaporated when those aspirations seemed to threaten German power. Seeing no other alternative to the diminution of Germany, the Assembly applauded many of the selfish actions of their erstwhile enemies. The victory of the Austrian army in Prague, and the suppression of the Poles by the Prussian army both received widespread applause. When the Prussian army in action against the Danes was forced by foreign pressure to accept a disadvantageous armistice (August 1848), the Assembly, for all its harsh words, could only confirm its impotence by accepting the settlement.

The other challenge came from the embryonic and relatively incoherent working class movement which, in the last months of 1848, was beginning to react to the failure of the Frankfurt Parliament to solve working class problems. While the Assembly devoted itself to the abstract task of drawing up a constitution, separate and independent workers' assemblies met in Hamburg and in Frankfurt itself, making economic demands quite against the interests of the bourgeois delegates in St. Paul's Church. They requested the limitation of factory production, restrictions upon free economic and industrial growth, and the protection of the privileges of the old artisan guilds. When barricades went up in Frankfurt (18th September) and disturbances ensued in Baden, Hesse-Cassel, and Saxony, the Assembly's only recourse was once more to the use of Prussian and Austrian troops.

The emergence of the national issue and the growing fear of working class violence were two of the factors that paved the way for the triumph of conservatism in Germany. The third factor was the steady recovery of nerve by the King of Prussia. By August the radicalism of Prussia's own parliament in abolishing the feudal, legal, and financial privileges of the Junker class had brought that class into open opposition to the liberals. Encouraged by their support and by increasing evidence of the army's reliability, Friedrich Wilhelm dismissed his liberal ministers and ordered the army back into Berlin. In December, he first banished and then dissolved the Prussian parliament. Next it was the turn of the Frankfurt Parliament. The anti-nationalist stance of the Austrian Habsburgs in March 1849, gave the Assembly little alternative but to offer the crown to the only other German powerful enough to wear it. Friedrich Wilhelm's refusal to 'pick up a crown from the gutter' sealed Frankfurt's failure. Much has been written about the motives of the King of Prussia. Certainly his distaste for constitutional monarchy was genuine, but there is also evidence that he harboured a neo-medieval belief in Austria's divinely ordained leadership of Germany and her princes. With the withdrawal of Prussian and Austrian delegates from Frankfurt, the National Assembly was already a shell when it moved to Stuttgart to await its dispersal by Prussian troops (June 1849). Although permanent agrarian reforms survived from the events of 1848–49, the liberal, constitutional revolution had achieved nothing. Indeed, we may even accept the judgement of A. J. P. Taylor that there was in no realistic sense a political revolution at all in Germany in 1848: 'There was merely a vacuum in which the liberals postured until the vacuum was filled'.

(i) Austria: the Crisis

Nowhere was the conjunction of different economic and political crises so dangerous as in the Austrian Empire, for the Empire was threatened in 1848–49, not merely with a radical constitutional change, but with the very collapse of its complex, multinational structure.

The period of Austrian history between 1815–48 has been described by H. Kohn as 'an era of stagnation'. Those years had witnessed some half-hearted attempts by Metternich at political and fiscal reform, thwarted by the conservatism of the Emperor. Latterly the political scene had been dominated by rivalry and jealousy, notably between Metternich and his rival Count Kolowrat. The accession in 1835 of the Emperor Ferdinand, physically sick and mentally abnormal, merely ensured that the political malaise spread to the very pinnacle of the state system. Economically, the Austrian Empire had produced nothing to rival Prussia's policy of tariff reform and industrial modernisation. Austria and Hungary together produced 710 000 tons of coal in 1845, compared with 5.6 million tons produced by the Zollverein states, and had made only modest and halting progress in railway construction. Although Austrian cities were as yet spared the horrors of industrialisation, they had little to offer the peasants driven from the countryside by agricultural depression. A. J. P. Taylor has stressed that the urban unrest in Vienna or in Budapest owed more to the lack of industrial employment than to the hardships that such employment entailed. Thirdly, the government imposed, or attempted to impose, an intellectual straitjacket upon the Empire. 'I do not need scholars', an earlier Emperor had informed his schoolteachers in 1821, 'but obedient citizens. Whosoever serves me must teach what I command'.

The rise of nationalism gave the Austrian crisis a distinctive flavour of its own, for in a state of such racial diversity, such doctrines were always likely to be explosive. Although Germans dominated the politics and commerce of the Empire, they constituted only a little less than a quarter of its population. Of the total, a little less than 20% were Hungarians, about 7% were Italians, 6% Rumanians, and 45% Slavs. This last section then subdivided into a bewildering variety that included Czechs, Slovaks, Serbs, Ukrainians, Poles and Croats. The question of national identity and the awareness of national cultures were of relatively recent growth. At the beginning of the century, vernacular languages were largely confined to the peasant populations, with the business of the Provincial Assemblies or Diets conducted in Latin. In 1840 Hungarian nationalists succeeded in replacing Latin by Magyar as the official language

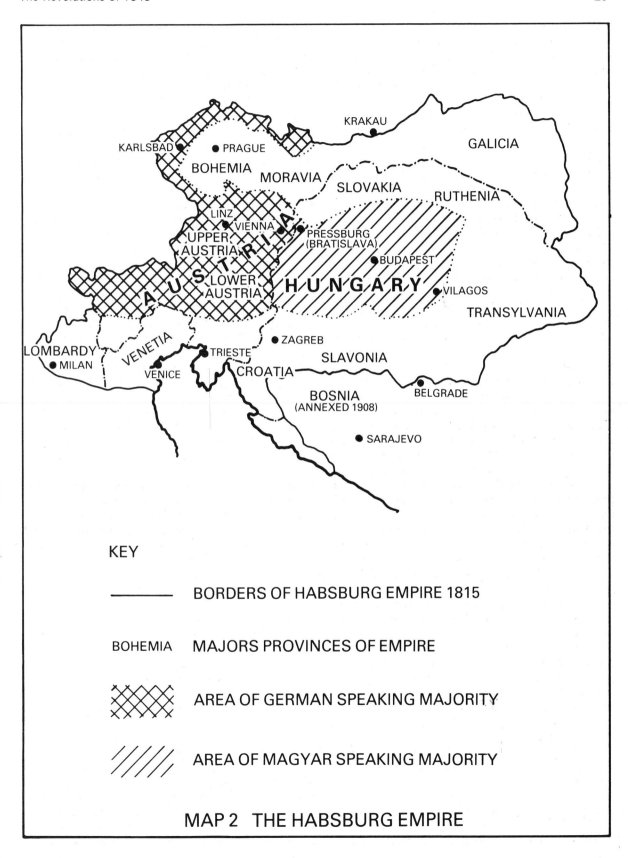

KEY

——————— BORDERS OF HABSBURG EMPIRE 1815

BOHEMIA MAJORS PROVINCES OF EMPIRE

AREA OF GERMAN SPEAKING MAJORITY

AREA OF MAGYAR SPEAKING MAJORITY

MAP 2   THE HABSBURG EMPIRE

of their Diet, and over the next four years Magyar also became established in legal and educational use. Other languages made headway in literary contexts, as in the publication of Jungmann's Czech dictionary, Palacky's history of the Czechs, and Preseren's Slovene poetry. Otherwise, the aims of these national minorities varied. Some aimed for improved status within the Empire, as did the Czechs. Others, such as the Italian nationalists, hoped to secede from the Empire to form part of a larger independent nation. In Hungary, a significant increase in political tension occurred in the late 1830s and early 1840s with the rise of a radical nationalist journalist, Lajos Kossuth. Where moderate nationalism, under Count Szechenyi, had previously aimed at cultural and economic advance within the Empire, Kossuth demanded far more. His aims were administrative autonomy and parliamentary rule for Hungary. His method was to win the support of the Hungarian gentry for the revival of the old Hungarian state by appealing to their anti-Slav interests and prejudices.

(j) Austria: Success

As was the case in Germany, the news of the February revolution in Paris ignited the tinder of political revolt in Austria. Middle class liberals, student radicals and elements of the Viennese working class joined together in street demonstrations and the presentation of petitions to the Emperor in the first weeks of March. On 13th March clashes with regular troops led to loss of life and the Emperor, who had already lost his wits, now lost his nerve. Later that day, the 1848 revolutions gained their most notable 'scalp' with the resignation of the Imperial Chancellor, Klemens von Metternich. Two elements seem to have combined in the fall of the great champion of European conservatism. Some historians, such as the Frenchman M. Pouthas, have seen fear as the main motive within the Austrian court. They portray Metternich, like Guizot in Paris, as a sacrifice to save the rest of the establishment. For the Austrian, G. von Poelnitz, the personal antipathy of such rivals as Kolowrat played a greater role, and the popular disturbances provided an opportunity for the pursuit of personal vendettas. The difference of interpretation is important, for what could be seen as the most sensational event of early 1848 takes on far less significance if it was merely the result of temporary divisions in the governing elite of the Empire.

With the departure of Metternich into exile, Ferdinand, like Friedrich Wilhelm, preferred concessions to flight. In April he conceded freedom of the press, and gave permission for a constitution for the German speaking areas of the Empire. The following month he promised a constituent assembly based upon universal manhood suffrage, and accepted the arming of a volunteer National Guard in Vienna.

It was inevitable that the collapse of Imperial will-power would encourage opposition in the provinces of the Empire. Indeed, the Hungarian Diet meeting at Pressburg (now Bratislava), had begun the formulation of its demands ten days before the fall of Metternich. These demands crystallised into the so-called March Laws, a mixture of classic liberal demands with more specifically nationalist ones. Freedom of the press, equality of taxation, equality before the law, and freedom of religion vied with the demand for the removal of all non-Hungarian troops from Hungarian territory. In the countryside, all remnants of serfdom were to be abolished, as was the practice of 'robot', the compulsory labour due owed by many peasants to their landlords. Further, it must be understood that when Kossuth and his supporters spoke of 'Hungary', they envisaged not merely a state embracing those areas populated by Magyar speakers, but all those territories that had been part of the medieval Kingdom of Hungary. Transylvania, Croatia and Ruthenia could thus expect no Hungarian sympathy for their own cultural or national aspirations. On 11th April, Ferdinand conceded all the demands of the Hungarian Diet and effectively accepted the establishment of an independent Hungarian state.

In the second great centre of nationalist unrest, Prague, confidence in national strength was less pronounced. The Pan-Slav Congress assembled there (2nd June) chose, not the path of national independence, but that which became known as 'Austro-Slavism'. This centred upon the view that the best course for the Slav peoples of the Empire lay within a reformed Habsburg Empire. Outside, they would merely fall prey to the selfish desires of the Germans and the Russians. Indeed, Palacky's refusal to accept a seat at the Pan-German Frankfurt Parliament was a landmark in the Czechs' claim for the recognition of their own national identity. 'If the Austrian Empire did not exist', he had concluded, 'it would be necessary to create it', for the safety of the minor Slav nationalities. Thus, the demands that emanated from Prague were for linguistic equality of Czech with German, for the abolition of the 'robot', and for what Palacky called the 'peace, the liberty and the right of my nation', but not for the independence of the Czech state. Austro-Slavism represented an impossible paradox. It depended upon the weakness of the Viennese government for its success, upon the voluntary dismantlement by the Habsburgs of their Imperial absolutism, and yet trusted in Habsburg strength for protection against German or Russian domination. While it illustrates the high hopes of 1848, it also provides a classic example of the chronically weak foundations upon which these hopes rested.

(k) Austria: Failure

The first major success of the counter revolution in 1848 occurred in Prague. As even the Czechs seemed convinced of their own weakness it is scarcely surprising that those commanding the undefeated Austrian forces in the north moved towards the same conclusion. In reaction to renewed radical and student violence in the city (13th June), General Windischgrätz, Imperial governor of Moravia, took the decision to bombard Prague. Within three days it was in his hands. Not only was the resistance of the insurgents ineffectual, but they found themselves largely without sympathy in the outside world. The hostility of the German National Assembly was repeated in the violent language of radicals in Vienna. 'The victory over the Czech party in Prague', rejoiced the journal *Friend of the People,* 'is and remains a joyful event'. The events in Prague serve well to illustrate the fatal isolation of each of the 1848 risings from all of the others.

The revolution in Vienna suffered from a steady decline rather than from a sudden collapse. By the time of Windischgrätz's triumph, the Viennese radicals had some notable triumphs to their credit, the formation of a constituent assembly, the formation of a National Guard, and there were more to come. In September, the assembly struck at the social basis of rural Austria by its abolition of the 'robot' and of the hereditary rights of the nobility in local administration. These should perhaps be seen as the major lasting changes wrought by the 'Year of Revolutions' in the Empire. The end of the practice of 'robot' had a ruinous effect on the lesser gentry who lost a valuable source of cheap labour. This breaking of the power of the local landlords, although it was not the direct aim of the assembly, was to confirm the subsequent dominance of the central authority of the Imperial government.

Fatal weaknesses were already becoming evident in the position of the revolutionaries. The dynasty remained in power, and continued to be served by ministers of the 'old school'. The Imperial army was not only undefeated, but actually victorious in the provinces. Worse, divisions began to appear in the ranks of the revolutionaries themselves. Some elements among the German speaking radicals favoured the cutting of links with the non-German provinces of the Empire, and aimed at a greater German unity with other states represented at the Frankfurt Parliament. Others wished to see the territorial preservation of the Empire and applauded the victories of Windischgrätz and Radetzky. The discussion of a constitutional settlement aggravated the divisions. Many liberals remained content with a constitutional monarchy of the sort recently overthrown in Paris, while stricter radicals sought a republic. The emergence of workers' organisations in Vienna revived memories of the 'June Days' in Paris, with demonstrations in August broken up by the middle-class National Guard. The government's decision (3rd October) to declare war on the Hungarian rebels brought matters to a head. Radical demonstrations in favour of Hungary, in which the Minister of War was lynched, emboldened the conservatives to treat Vienna as Prague had been treated. The task was harder and bloodier, but by the end of the month and at the cost of 3000 to 5000 lives, Generals Windischgrätz and Jellacic had reconquered Austria's capital.

The regeneration of conservative government was steadily consolidated. In November, a new government under Count Schwarzenberg took office. In December, as the living symbol of regeneration, the eighteen year old Franz Josef ascended the Imperial throne upon his uncle's abdication. The new administration was firmly based upon realism and upon power politics for, in A. J. P. Taylor's words, 'Schwarzenberg was too clever to have principles, Franz Josef too blinkered to understand them'. The fate of the constituent assembly well illustrates the methods of Austria's new masters. Since October it had lingered in exile in the Moravian town of Kremsier deliberating over an Austrian constitution. By the completion of its task (1st March 1849), Schwarzenberg felt strong enough to do without an assembly, but not without a constitution. Within three days of the formulation of the 'Kremsier Constitution' he had dissolved the assembly and allowed the Minister of the Interior, Count Stadion, to introduce an Imperial constitution of quite a different tenor. While it permitted a Parliament based upon universal manhood suffrage, it stressed strongly the indivisible nature of the Empire. Although Hungary received recognition of its linguistic separatism, she and all other regions of the Empire could expect only direct government from Vienna.

An important factor leading the government to grant constitutional concessions was the need to maintain general support while Hungary remained undefeated. From October 1848 the policy of the Imperial government towards Hungarian autonomy had been one of open hostility. Three methods of attack suggested themselves. Firstly, tacit support for the Slav minorities alienated by Kossuth's 'March Laws' became active and overt. The advance of the Croat General Jellacic into southern Hungary was, however, short-lived (September 1848) and unsuccessful. Secondly, the hope that Windischgrätz might win a third counter-revolutionary success with Austrian troops proved ill-founded. He moved slowly against a divided Hungarian leadership and was eventually defeated at Isaszeg in early April 1849. A week later, in response to Schwarzenberg's constitution, an Hungarian Republic was proclaimed, and the Viennese government was forced into the extreme measure of appealing for foreign aid. Russia's response to the Austrian appeal owed as much to fears that the Hungarian example would be imitated in Poland as it did to conservative principles, but it proved decisive. The three-pronged attack of Jellacic, Windischgrätz and 140 000 Russians ended the life of the Hungarian Republic at Vilagos (13th August 1849) and opened a period of bloody repression and retribution. The official annulment of the Hungarian constitution in 1851 put the final touch to the conservative triumph in the Austrian Empire.

(I) Italy: the Crisis

If the initial outbreak of violence in France came as a surprise, the contemporary disturbances in Italy were wholly predictable. The political and economic crises in the Italian states had roots going back to the restoration of 1815 and, in many cases, far beyond. Economic hardship in Italy was the result, not merely of a temporary, cyclical crisis, but of long-standing backwardness. The commerce for which the city states of the Renaissance had been noted had long given way to ownership of land as the main source of wealth and prestige, and the handicaps in the way of trade in the early 19th century were enormous. Customs barriers proliferated not only between states, but within states. Piedmont alone had had nearly 500 such barriers before the French Revolution. Italy's major navigable river, the Po, was cut into 22 sections by customs barriers. Travel between state and state was unwelcome to most rulers, many of whom

would have shared the view of the Duke of Modena who declared that 'all travellers are Jacobins', and forbade stage-coaches to cross his territories. Thus 90% of Italy's population in the first half of the 19th century was dependent upon the land. The conditions of agricultural production were primitive and inefficient. About half the peasantry in the north still owed contractual labour to their landlord and the proportion was much higher in the south. Such semi-feudal conditions made Italian corn subject to huge fluctuations in price, and the abnormal shortages of 1846–47 were already contributing to urban rioting in Rome and Livorno as early as February and March 1847.

The restoration of Italy's political divisions in 1815 meant that the peninsula suffered not from one political crisis, but from a whole collection. Between them, the restored princes represented all that was worst in European conservatism. In Piedmont, sometimes also referred to as the Kingdom of Sardinia, Victor Emmanuel I had marked his return to power by the abolition of both the civil and the commercial codes of law, and by the systematic rejection of all innovations, such as vaccination and street-lighting, introduced by the French. In Naples, where tension continued unabated between the mainland territories and the island of Sicily, the constitution of 1812 was revoked, and personal government restored. The Pope, restored to his temporal rule in central Italy, continued to limit participation in the administration of the Papal States to members of the clergy, and maintained a form of government that even the arch-conservative Metternich considered to be 'both detested and detestable'. Throughout Italy, the conservative influence of the Catholic Church stifled economic enterprise and political or philosophical change.

Essential to the whole conservative structure was the direct influence exercised by Austria through her control of Lombardy and Venetia, and her indirect influence over Parma, Modena and Tuscany. To protect her vested political interests and for ideological reasons, Austrian policy was consistently, as Metternich put it, 'to extinguish the spirit of Italian unity and ideas about constitutions'. Worse still, for Italian liberals and nationalists, Austrian territorial possessions in Italy made the maintenance of the Italian 'status quo' a central part of the whole European settlement established at Vienna in 1815. Lastly, conservatism derived strength from the lower levels of society, from the differences of dialect that hindered communication between Italians, from the parochialism of most Italians and their preoccupation with local affairs. As a Neapolitan historian explained in the 1850s, 'the patriotism of the Italians is like that of the ancient Greeks, and is the love of a single town, not of a country; it is the feeling of a tribe, not of a nation'. Both the map of Italy and the political nature of its regimes, therefore, remained frozen by a formidable combination of economic backwardness, political apathy, Austrian power, the acquiescence of the major powers, and the power of the Catholic Church.

Against these obstacles, in the thirty years before 1848, was ranged a variety of liberal and nationalist movements, differing in their methods, their aims, and the measure of their success. Between 1815–31, the radical stage belonged to those groups, of which the so-called 'Carbonari' were the most prominent, who viewed conspiracy and selective revolt as the best means of provoking general rebellion. In 1820–21, in Naples, Sicily and Piedmont, in 1831, in Parma, Modena and the Papal States, the Carbonari engineered radical risings and army mutinies. In each case the aims of the rebels were parochial, concerned only with changes in their own state. In each case they encountered considerable popular apathy, or else fought shy of courting popular support, and in each case they found no answer to the might of the Austrian army. By 1831, five of the six main rulers in Italy, Piedmont being the exception, had called in Austrian troops to support them. This was a further indication of how essential the defeat of the Habsburg forces would be to the advancement of the Italian national cause.

With Giuseppe Mazzini and the 'Young Italy' movement, the parochialism of the Carbonari was swept away. Mazzini's views, methods and weaknesses have already been described (see Chapter 1, section **d**). It is sufficient here to stress his insistence upon a unitary state, rather than a federal arrangement, upon a republican form of government, and upon tireless propaganda work. It was a combination which naturally rendered his policy unacceptable to all crowned heads in Italy and throughout Europe. Little as he achieved in the 1830s and the 1840s, it is due to Mazzini more than to any other Italian leader that an Italian cause in any form still existed in 1848. Hopelessly romantic as he was, he succeeded, in D. Mack Smith's words, in 'defining the goal and arousing enthusiasm among more practised soldiers and statesmen'. Mazzini's radicalism and republicanism were also unacceptable to a more moderate school of reformers and nationalists who began to put forward their views in literary form in the 1840s. Cesare Balbo, in his *Of the Aspirations of Italy* ('Delle Speranze d'Italia') and Massimo d'Azeglio, in his

Of the Recent Events in the Romagna ('Degli Ultimi Casi di Romagna'), written in 1844 and 1846 respectively, both recognised the need for political force at the head of the Italian cause. They both viewed the King of Piedmont as their best hope. Practically, many moderates also laid great stress upon the promotion of social amenities, such as savings banks and schools, and upon the encouragement of industry. The cheese industry at Gorgonzola and the Chianti wine industry are largely the results of this interest. For Vincenzo Gioberti, however, the future of Italy lay, not with Piedmont, but with the Papacy. Abruptly, in 1846, it seemed that Gioberti might have hit upon the right path.

(m) Italy: Success

It is perhaps misleading to refer to the events in Italy as 'the revolutions of 1848' for that particular phase of Italian history had begun in 1846, with the sensational election of Cardinal Mastai-Ferretti as Pope. Under his chosen title of Pius IX he was to be one of the key figures of the events of the next two years.

Gioberti, in his work *Of the Moral and Civil Primacy of the Italians* ('Del Primato Morale e Civile degli Italiani') had portrayed the Papacy and the Catholic Church as the chosen agents of Italian national revival. Gioberti condemned revolutionary means towards unity, made no specific mention of the expulsion of the Austrians from the peninsula, and desired a confederation of Italian states under the presidency of the Pope. The scheme certainly had the merits of preserving the local status of the individual princes, and of placing the Austrians in the potentially embarrassing position of opposing the head of their own church. On the other hand, the prospects of finding a Pope willing to play the role designed for him by Gioberti and his 'Neo-Guelph' supporters seemed remote. The election of Pius in June 1846 changed all that. In his initial burst of political reform he amnestied political prisoners and accepted a measure of non-clerical participation in government. In 1847 he put forward the suggestion of an Italian customs union. When Austria, thrown off balance by this 'Liberal' Pope, dropped the broad hint of establishing a garrison at Ferrara (July 1847) within Papal territory, Pius protested so vigorously that he became a national hero for such an anti-Austrian gesture. For all his subsequent failure to lead the Italian cause to success (see section **n**), Pius' election had an enormously stimulating effect upon Italian politics. 'It must have seemed', wrote G.

Berkeley, 'as if the chief anti-national stronghold of [the nationalists'] opponents had suddenly hoisted their own tricolour'.

The second key figure of these years in Italy was Charles Albert, King of Piedmont since 1831. Nationalist historians in the intervening century have created a 'legend of Charles Albert', gallantly sacrificing his own interests, even his own throne, in the national cause. It is more acceptable today to view him either as 'a romantic without the willpower to transform his visions into reality', as does the Italian A. Omodeo, or like D. Beales, as a thorough conservative, opportunist enough to take advantage of European chaos to increase the power of Piedmont, to 'use, but not surrender to ideology'. Certainly, even before the rising in Paris, events seemed to be running against Italian conservatism. In January 1848, in protest against Austrian rule in Lombardy, patriotic middle-class Italians staged a 'tobacco strike'. They gave up smoking in order to deprive the Austrians of the revenue from their tobacco duty. On 12th January Palermo, in Sicily, rose in revolt against the government from Naples. In February and March, the rash of new constitutions began to affect Italy too. Tuscany received one from its Duke (11th February), and Naples from its King. Even the Pope could not avoid the fashion (4th March). Also in March Austrian troops were expelled from Milan and Venice after several days of street-fighting. Charles Albert did not stop at the granting of a constitution. Less than three weeks later he committed Piedmont to war against the apparently disintegrating Austrians, in support of the risings in Lombardy and Venetia. With reluctant initial support from Naples and the Papacy, Charles Albert had at least the superficial appearance of leading the greatest bid in modern Italian history for freedom and nationhood.

(n) Italy: Failure

For all the themes and theories of the previous years, the chance for nationalist action in Italy had been provided by the disruption of the European 'status quo', and especially by the distraction of the Austrian armed forces. The return of European stability, and the recovery of the Austrian government spelt the doom of Italian freedom. A month after the triumph of Windischgrätz in Prague, the Piedmontese army met the forces of Marshal Radetzky at Custoza (25th July 1848). The Papacy and the Kingdom of Naples had already withdrawn their contingents of troops, and defeat badly undermined Piedmontese morale.

Although the army survived substantially intact, the pessimism of the generals and Charles Albert's own fears of radical activity at home led to a precipitate retreat from Lombardy. Renewed pressures upon the King only led to another defeat at Austrian hands at Novara (23rd March 1849). The price paid this time was the permanent removal of Charles Albert from political life through his abdication in favour of his son, Victor Emmanuel. In addition, Austria imposed an indemnity of 75 million lire upon Piedmont. That she retained her territorial integrity was due mainly to the European objections that would have been raised to any tampering with this important 'buffer' zone on France's borders. Charles Albert's proud boast that 'Italy will do it herself' (Italia fara da se) had proved altogether empty.

The war had also served to demonstrate the limitations of Pius IX as a leader of the national cause. Leading a confederation of Catholic states was one thing. To lead one Catholic state against another was quite a different matter. Pius' confidante, G. Montanelli, put the kindest interpretation upon the Pope's motives. 'As an Italian he wanted to see the foreign invaders driven out of his country, but as Pope—as the universal Father he could never declare a war of independence against Austria'. A more recent historian, E. L. Woodward, has interpreted the whole pretence of liberal-national leadership as a piece of confused thinking. 'How could the Sovereign Pontiff become a constitutional ruler? Who could be responsible for the actions of the Vicar of God on earth?' Nevertheless, Pius continued to work with his constitutional government until November. Then he despaired of constitutionalism and fled Rome for the safety of Naples. With his flight died the last hope of the Papacy fulfilling the role that Gioberti had mapped out for it.

'The royal war is over', declared Mazzini in a national appeal in August 1848; 'the war of the people begins'. The flight of the Pope foreshadowed a second, equally unsuccessful phase in the struggles of 1848–49, the republican phase. In February 1849 a Roman Republic was proclaimed to fill the vacuum left by Pius. With Mazzini providing its political inspiration, and Giuseppe Garibaldi conducting its military defence, it represented the pinnacle of radical aspirations. Its decrees calling for the distribution of Church lands to the peasantry, and for the public housing of the poor, could not offset its weaknesses. It was ravaged by inflation, starved of support from other quarters of Italy, and subjected to the combined hostility of France and Austria. After a heroic defence, the Republic was defeated in June 1849, and the presence thereafter of a French garrison amplified the foreign interest in the future of Italy.

Meanwhile, with the defeat of Piedmont, Venice and Tuscany had both gone their respective ways. Under the leadership of Daniele Manin Venice once more declared herself a Republic, as she had been until the Napoleonic invasion. She resisted Austrian siege warfare, with its horrors of bombardment, cholera and starvation, until late August 1849. Tuscan radicals expelled their Grand Duke in February 1849, but could not do the same to the Austrian forces that came to restore him in April.

The combination of circumstances in Italy in 1848–49 made those years seem especially auspicious for the cause of Italian freedom. Yet what did it all achieve? Firstly we find the famous judgement of G. M. Trevelyan that 1848 was 'the turning point at which modern history failed to turn'. Then we have the judgement of the patriot, Settembrini, that 'this generation made Italy', that the example of 1848 was 'the point at which we became Italians, felt ourselves united and gathered together under a single standard'. We must conclude that, although the rebels of 1848 achieved nothing material in Italy, except for the Piedmontese constitution, the future course of Italian history was significantly altered. The refusal of Pius IX to put himself at the head of the national cause, and his conservative response to the events in Rome, killed the hopes of Gioberti and the Neo-Guelphs. The author himself renounced them and exhorted patriots to look instead to Piedmont. The failure of radical republicanism demonstrated anew its various faults; the failure of its various advocates to co-operate with one another, and their impotence in the face of opposition from a major power. Leopold II, Grand Duke of Tuscany, and Ferdinand of Naples had shown their true colours by refusing to co-operate with Charles Albert, and much of northern Italy was more firmly than ever under the control of Austria. The one exception to this catalogue of gloom was the state of Piedmont, whose King had embraced a constitution, and staked his soldiers' lives and his own crown upon the Italian cause. Italian nationalists were not likely to forget these factors. The future of Italy, as the next two decades were to prove, lay with Piedmont.

(o) Historiography

The most striking feature of the revolutions of 1848–49 is their very great complexity. Each national rebellion raised its own set of historiographical problems. Questions such as the role of Piedmont in the events in Italy, or the achievement of the German liberals have been investigated in the relevant sections of this chapter. Here we are primarily concerned with the views taken of the 1848 phenomenon as a whole.

Firstly, what justification is there for regarding the outbursts in various states as parts of one great event? For much of the 19th century they were not in fact so regarded. Events in Italy were usually interpreted as part of the wider history of the Risorgimento, those in Germany as part of that nation's route to unity, and those in France as part of the unfinished business of the Great Revolution. The tendency to view these events as part of a general European crisis has arisen from the work of two main groups of historians. Firstly, those interested in liberal and liberal-national ideas traced many common features in the events of 1848–49. Within a decade of the revolutions an English commentator, E. Stillingfleet Cayley (*The European Revolutions of 1848*, 1859), had noted these similarities. Many historians have since agreed with the great Italian, B. Croce, that 'it seemed as though one and the same daemon were agitating the entire mass of Europe'. The distinguished list of authorities who have seen in 1848 primarily the clash between liberal ideas and those of the conservative restoration of 1815 has included V. Valentin (*1848: Chapters of German History*, 1940), F. Meinecke (*The Year 1848 in German History*, 1948), and G. P. Gooch (*The Centenary of 1848 in Germany and Austria*, 1948). Sir Lewis Namier produced an important variation on this theme when he stressed (*1848: Revolution of the Intellectuals*, 1944) how liberal principles were actually subordinated to nationalist ambitions by the so-called 'liberals' of 1848.

The main alternative to this liberal interpretation also has a pedigree reaching back to the middle of the 19th century. To Karl Marx (*The Class Struggles in France*, 1850) and to Friedrich Engels (*Revolution and Counter Revolution in Germany*, 1851–52), the true meaning of the events of 1848 was as the beginning of the great proletarian revolution, and the social and economic factors behind the revolts were of far greater importance than the theories of 'old women' and 'humbugs' such as the Frankfurt liberals. Despite, or perhaps because of their claims, these social and economic factors remained largely disregarded for a century. New respectability was given to these elements by C. E. Labrousse (*1848–1830–1789. How Revolutions are Born*, 1949) with his conclusion that the upheavals of 1848–49 resulted from the coincidence of several crises, political and economic. Since then, important work has been done on social questions in individual states, such as that by G. Quazza (*Social Struggle in the Risorgimento*, 1951) and J. Droz (*The German Revolutions*, 1957). It would now be widely accepted that, for a full explanation, political, social, ideological and economic factors must all be taken into account. As T. Hamerow (*Restoration, Revolution, Reaction*, 1958) has written, 'the Revolution was the expression not only of ideological forces like nationalism and liberalism, but also of deep-seated popular dissatisfactions engendered by the transition from agrarian manorialism to industrial capitalism'. Modern historians still differ, however, in the stress to be laid upon any one of these factors.

Secondly, what if anything did the revolutions of 1848 achieve? Probably the most famous judgement upon them is that of G. M. Trevelyan that '1848 was the turning point at which modern history failed to turn'. More recent commentators have sometimes agreed, like P. Robertson (*The Revolutions of 1848: a Social History*, 1952), that the 'Year of Revolutions' produced no worthwhile social or political change. Such a judgement is only valid if the events are regarded from a liberal viewpoint. It is true, although Valentin and Meinecke would disagree, that liberalism gained very little from its exertions. The same is not true of nationalism, however. It can scarcely be doubted that, in the cases of Italy and Germany, the events of 1848 did much to bring to the fore those forces that were eventually to influence the unification of those states most profoundly; the power of Piedmont, the power of Prussia, and the ambitions of Louis Napoleon. In fact the greatest transformation wrought by 1848 was wrought upon European conservatives. These men had clearly demonstrated to them the weaknesses and divisions in those political forces that they had feared for decades. The age of Metternich, of timorous conservatives regarding co-operation as the only guarantee against anarchy, gave way to the age of Bismarck. Confident conservatives were certain that, with a strong army and prosperous economy behind them, they could not be harmed by mere ideas. 'Our world begins in 1848'. So wrote the Franco-American historian, A. Guérard, in 1943. If, by that, he meant the world of power politics and national egoism, which had just erupted into a second world war, his claim was perfectly justified.

Progress Paragraphs

Answer the following questions in about 150 words.

Why was 1845–47 a period of extraordinary economic hardship in Europe?   Section (**a**)

What were the weaknesses of Louis Philippe's position in 1848?   Section (**b**)

How radical, and how popular was the French Provisional Government?   Section (**c**)

Explain the triumph of conservatism in France by mid-1848.   Section (**d**)

Account for the popularity of Louis Napoleon Bonaparte with the French electorate in 1848.
Section (**e**)

To what extent was Prussia in a state of political crisis in 1846–48?   Section (**f**)

What had German liberals achieved by May 1848, and how?   Section (**g**)

What were the limitations upon the powers of the Frankfurt Parliament?   Section (**h**)

Account for the recovery of Prussia in 1848–49.
Section (**h**)

How severe was the threat of nationalism to the Habsburg Empire in the 1840s?   Section (**i**)

Contrast the demands of nationalists in Hungary and Czechoslovakia in 1848.   Section (**j**)

Why did 1849 end in failure (a) in Vienna and (b) in Hungary?   Section (**k**)

In what ways was Italy economically and politically backward in the 1840s?   Section (**l**)

What handicaps faced Italian nationalists in the 1840s?   Section (**l**)

Assess the motives in 1846–48 of (a) Pius IX and (b) Charles Albert.   Section (**m**)

Why did Pius IX and Charles Albert achieve so little in 1848?   Section (**n**)

Did the events of 1848–49 change anything in Italy?
Section (**n**)

3
The Second French Empire, 1852-70

(a) The Weakness of the Second Republic

The essential weakness of the Second Republic in France lay in the incompatibility between the nature of its President and the nature of the constitution under which he was bound to govern. The vast majority of the votes cast for Louis Napoleon Bonaparte in 1848 were votes for permanence, for stability and for order (see Chapter 2, sections **d** & **e**). By 1851 Louis Napoleon had set himself at the centre of a formidable conservative coalition. The elections of May 1849 had returned an Assembly in which the 'Party of Order', the coalition of Legitimists, Orleanists, and Bonapartists, held 64% of the seats, as opposed to 34% in the previous Assembly. The support of the French Catholics was assured, not only by their fear of the 'Reds', but by appreciation of the French military intervention to suppress the Roman Republic, and of the Falloux Law of 1850.

The President remained saddled with a constitution specifically designed by its authors in 1848 to obstruct a man such as he, and to prevent the emergence of a dominant Imperial figure. The President was limited to a tenure of office of only four years, and he was not thereafter eligible for re-election to the post. Inevitably 1852 held the twin prospects for the President of a return to political oblivion, and for the propertied electorate of a return to the political battles, and perhaps to the street fighting of 1848.

(b) The Coup d'État

Clearly, Louis Napoleon never seriously considered relinquishing power to return to obscurity at the end of his four year term. There is some truth in the charges of his enemies, that his personal debts made it impossible for him to turn his back upon the fruits of office. More important was the mission of the restoration of French stability and prosperity, laid down in the *Napoleonic Ideal*, which would have to be abandoned with the abandonment of

office. There is only rough justice in the view propagated by Victor Hugo that Louis Napoleon had cynically sworn his oath to the Republican constitution the better to destroy it, and the better to plunder the state. Although the President undoubtedly desired the extension of his powers, he originally hoped to achieve this by working within the constitution he had sworn to implement. J. P. T. Bury points out that forceful action was very much the last resort of a man who had consistently resisted the suggestions of those who tried to tempt him into a 'coup d'état' earlier in his term of office. Besides, Louis Napoleon had no wish to repeat the experience of earlier 'coups'. Ignoring the advice of bolder spirits such as Persigny, Louis Napoleon attempted to persuade the Assembly to amend the constitution by legal means to allow the re-election of the President. Such a change, however, required a 75% majority, the support of some 540 deputies. By July 1851 it was clear that Louis Napoleon would not overcome this constitutional obstacle, and by the last month of that year the choice lay between yielding to the letter of the constitution or overthrowing it.

The groundwork for the eventual 'coup' and the preparation of public opinion were thorough. By use of his presidential powers Louis had removed potential opponents, like the commander of the Paris garrison, and replaced them with reliable allies. Saint Arnaud now commanded the troops in Paris, Maupas was Prefect of Police, and Morny, the President's illegitimate half-brother, was Minister of the Interior. A series of provincial tours in the late summer and autumn allowed Louis Napoleon to gauge public support. The date chosen was 2nd December, a great 'Napoleonic' date for it was the anniversary of the great victory at Austerlitz in 1805. The code name, 'Operation Rubicon', also had Imperial overtones. Seventy-eight police officers, unaware that they were part of a concerted plot, each arrested a prominent member of the opposition. The dissolution of the Assembly was announced, and enforced next day by Saint Arnaud's troops. The casualty list by 4th December stood at 215, and 27000 arrests had been made, of whom some 9000 were eventually sentenced to deportation, mainly to Algeria.

The effect of the 'coup d'état', therefore, was twofold. In general, it went smoothly, and was easily accepted. 'If the "coup d'état" of December 2nd was a crime', F. A. Simpson has concluded, 'then France was its accomplice rather than its victim'. This was borne out by the results of the plebiscite held on 21st December, when 7.5 million out of 8 million voters cast a 'Yes' vote in approbation of Louis Napoleon's action. Louis was delighted and relieved. 'More than 7 million votes have just absolved me', he told the committee that had organised the plebescite, 'by justifying an act that had no other aim than to spare our country, and perhaps Europe from years of trouble and misfortune'.

In Paris, however, the figures proved that a centre of opposition had been created that Louis Napoleon would never overcome. There, the margin in favour of the President was only 133 000 with 80 000 abstaining.

(c) The Authoritarian Constitution

Having destroyed the constitution of the Second Republic, the first concern of the transformed President was to dictate to the French a new constitution free from the obstructions of 'Parliamentarianism'. It was indeed a Napoleonic constitution for, as Louis Napoleon himself explained: 'I have taken as a model the political institutions which have, since the beginning of the century, and in similar circumstances, consolidated a society which has been disturbed, and raised France to a high degree of prosperity and greatness.... Why should we not adopt the political institutions of that period?'

The constitution granted the President absolute power for a period of ten years. Although he was 'responsible before the French people', and, therefore, not 'absolute' in the old monarchical sense, he alone could initiate legislation, or conclude treaties of peace or war. He commanded the armed forces and the civil service, and could, if the occasion demanded, govern by decree. He alone appointed or dismissed ministers, and these ministers had no collective responsibility to the legislature. This latter consisted of three bodies, all effectively subject to the power of the President. The Council of State (Conseil d'État) was directly appointed by the President from among the ranks of the senior civil servants. Its main task was the drafting of legislation, although it had, of course, no powers to initiate any such legislation. The

Senate, the upper house of the Assembly, consisted of 'notables', perhaps generals or retired administrators, appointed for life by the President. They were the prime illustration of Louis Napoleon's confession that he didn't 'mind being baptised with the water of universal suffrage', but 'refused to live with his feet in it'. The Legislative Body was indeed elected, for a period of six years, by universal male suffrage, but the 260 deputies were limited to the role of accepting or rejecting legislation proposed by the government. They could not initiate their own projects, and could not question ministers on points of their policies. Their debates, furthermore, could not be attended by the public.

This stiffling of public political life, a basic principle of the new regime, was further reflected outside the Assembly. Political parties and the political press, already severely handicapped by the deportations and arrests that followed the 'coup d'état' were further shackled. Political meetings could now only be held in the presence of government officials, and the Press Decree of 1852 gave the government extensive powers to suspend and suppress publications. In Paris, for example, only four political journals survived the year.

This was effectively an Imperial constitution, and Louis Napoleon had made little attempt to conceal the fact. It needed but a short step to transform the authoritarian President into an Emperor and emboldened by the popularity of his moves in 1851, Louis Napoleon began once more to 'test the water' of popular opinion by means of a series of provincial tours in the autumn of 1852. Upon his return, the Senate predictably produced the legislation necessary to create an Empire in name as well as in form. Appealing to the people once again by plebescite in November, Louis Napoleon received another overwhelming popular ratification, this time by eight million votes in favour of the Empire, with a mere 250 000 standing out against it. Upon this evidence of popular support Louis Napoleon claimed to base his Second Empire, but it was noted that he chose as his Imperial title 'Napoleon III', as though the Duc de Reichstadt, the only legitimate son of the first Napoleon had succeeded his father in spirit, and as though his own claim to power was at least as much dynastic as it was democratic.

(d) The Enforcement of the Constitution

Popular though it undoubtedly was at the time of its creation, the strength of the Second Empire, like that of the First, lay in the effective administrative machine that it operated. The ministers, firstly, depended very strictly upon the approval and support of the Emperor. Napoleon III drew his ministers from three main sources. Some were members of the dynasty. Prince Jerome was his cousin, and Morny (Minister of the Interior and later President of the Legislative Body) was his half-brother, the illegitimate offspring of one of his mother's extra-marital relationships. Walewski (Ambassador to London 1851–55, and Foreign Minister 1855–60) was an illegitimate son of Napoleon I. Others, like Persigny (Minister of the Interior and then Ambassador to London) had served the dynasty faithfully in exile. Most were survivors of the previous regimes. Morny himself had served under Guizot, but without reaching the highest ranks and unduly dirtying his hands. Many others, Fould, Magne, Billaut, and Rouher, for instance, had similar histories. This helps us to conclude that, although the principles of the regime were Bonapartist, the personnel was not. Nor could it be, for the 1830s and the 1840s had seen the development of no Bonapartist party nor hierarchy in France. 'The change', wrote Lhomme, 'was not in the governing class, but in the governing team'.

In the country at large, the influence of the government operated through the Prefects and the Mayors, themselves creations of the First Empire. The major tasks of the former were to keep the Emperor informed of the state of public opinion in the departments and to serve the Emperor's interests in local affairs. At elections, in particular, they were under specific instructions to aid government candidates and to do all that they could to hinder those of the opposition. Their efficiency in this task was reflected in the fact that only nine opposition candidates were successful in the 1852 elections.

Although the Second Empire was a distinctly centralised and authoritarian state, it was not in any real sense a military or a police state. J. P. T. Bury points out that although the Emperor made many concessions to the army to retain its support, such as the reconstitution of the Imperial Guard, the institution of decorations for gallantry, and of improved pensions, it was at no stage after the 'coup d'état' used as an instrument of government. The police, too, seem to have played the part of tools in the hands of the Prefects. The Church was a much closer and more direct ally, able to exercise a more subtle influence over the populace, and gaining in return more important concessions, such as an increase in government aid for the repair of churches and for the payment of clerical stipends, greater control over education,

after the precedent of the Falloux Law of 1850, and the presence of the religious orders in France.

(e) First Domestic Measures

The new regime's first moves were aimed at the cementing of its power and at the removal of all alternative sources of influence and authority. The National Guard, for example, was suppressed. It had long been regarded as the safeguard of the bourgeoisie against the military tyranny of the monarchy, and a good case could now be made for regarding it as redundant, given that the champion of the bourgeoisie was firmly in power. Similarly, in a measure reminiscent of future dictators, the Emperor demanded an oath of allegiance from all government servants and officials. This was not to the state or to the nation, but to himself as Head of State.

The most controversial of these early measures was that contained in the decree of January 1852, which confiscated the estates and possessions of the Orleans family. Many led by Victor Hugo saw it as a greedy and vengeful act by one whose life the Orleans had spared, and others looked askance at the seizure of private property by one who posed as its protector. To others, these have seemed harsh judgements, given that the exiled Orleans retained 100 million francs worth of property elsewhere. Also, of the 300 million that now came into the Emperor's hands, very substantial sums were reserved for causes of which the radicals of 1848 would have been proud. The improvement of workers' dwellings in the industrial towns, the establishment of mutual benefit societies, of pension funds, of orphanages, and of agricultural projects were all financed out of the liquidation of the Orleans' regime.

(f) The Economic Aims of the Empire

The most important and lasting achievements of the Second Empire were those in the related spheres of French commerce and industry. Hostile commentators, nevertheless, have tended to claim that these achievements were overshadowed and devalued by the Emperor's destruction of political liberty. As recently as the 1950s, J. M. Thompson passed the judgement that Napoleon III aimed 'to award economic prosperity as a consolation prize for loss of political liberty'. J. P. T. Bury is more inclined to set that judgement in reverse, and see political authoritarianism as a means to the real domestic end of the reign, the drive to realise France's true economic potential.

Much was made of the similarity between the policy of Napoleon III and the principles of the Saint Simonians. They were the followers of Comte Henri de Saint Simon (1760–1825), and stressed the prime importance of economic production, and the primacy of those involved in this vital area (see Chapter 1, section **j**). There is little evidence that the Emperor ever aimed systematically to implement such a philosophy. He was not a sophisticated thinker in either philosophical or economic terms, but they accorded well enough with the policies of his uncle's regime. The new Emperor was well enough read in contemporary economic and political thought to give a wide freedom to men, such as the Périere brothers, de Lesseps, and Chevalier, who can be shown to have been more specifically and directly influenced by Saint Simon.

(g) The Commercial Revolution

The Second Empire opened under the most favourable economic circumstances. The steady decline in world prices that had prevailed from 1815 to 1850 and which had exercised a generally depressing effect upon trade, was sharply reversed by a dramatic increase in the gold supply. The major 'strike' in California in 1849 was followed by the equally spectacular 'gold rush' in Australia in 1851, the two together roughly doubling the world's supply. The Emperor's detractors made much of these circumstances to belittle the economic achievement of the Second Empire. Nevertheless, the French derive credit from the fact that no other European country made comparable advances in the 1850s under such favourable circumstances.

The major obstacle to the modernisation of the French economy was the conservatism of the French banking system. Wealthy and highly developed though it was, it lay largely in the hands of such families as the Rothschilds, old established bankers with strong links with conservative dynasties, and with equally conservative economic policies. With the aid of the more progressive Péreire family, the government set about outflanking these staid bastions. The Crédit Foncier, a mortgage bank established in 1852, and the Crédit Mobilier, an industrial credit institution founded in the same year, both offered shares for sale to the public. They thus tapped the vast private wealth that was, perhaps, France's greatest economic advantage. With these huge funds, they could make loans to finance public works undertaken by private contractors, without placing an undue burden upon government finances. Thus outmanoeuvred, the older establishments had little choice but to expand their own range of investments to engage themselves more deeply in industrial finance. The appearance of the Société Générale de Crédit Industriel et Commercial (1859) and of the Crédit Lyonnais deposit bank (1863) completed 'a financial revolution' (J. M. Thompson) which, whatever difficulties were experienced by the new institutions in the less favourable climate of the 1860s, was not to be reversed.

(h) The Industrial Revolution

French industrialisation was a long and continuous process, and the bases already existed at the time of the foundation of the Second Empire. The progress made during its twenty year lifespan was, nevertheless, most striking. Communications constituted a priority, for no other industry could thrive without ready access to its sources of raw materials and to its markets. The first work on French railway construction had been begun under Louis Philippe but, consisting mainly of short stretches of track dictated mainly by local needs, it scarcely formed a viable basis for a national system. The financing of new, more comprehensive development was usually a joint undertaking between public and private finance. By 1870, the State had invested some 634 million francs in railways, usually in paying for the 'infrastructure', the necessary land and so forth, and for shares to maintain their interest in the company. The companies themselves paid for the 'superstructure' of the lines, the buildings, track, rolling-stock, and so on, and were granted long-term concessions, up to 99 years, for the exploitation of their new investments.

With the consolidation and rationalisation of the system, from 42 smaller enterprises into six main companies, the railways effectively transformed the social and economic life of France. The average cost of transporting a ton of produce dropped from 25 centimes to 5 in the course of 20 years. Thus total traffic increased (from 6.2 billion km/tons in 1852 to 11.82 billion in 1869) and prices dropped. The telegraph network, a vital tool for the centralised administration, increased from 2000 to over 70 000 km in the course of the reign. By linking the major economic centres of France with Belgium, Spain, Germany and Italy, the railway system was also the key to French international commerce. Lastly, not only did the railway 'boom' provide a vast new demand for the products of

	1845	1848	1855	1860	1865	1870
Railway track (Thousand km)	—	2.2	5.5	10.0	13.6	16.9
Freight carried (Million tons)	—	2.9	10.6	27.9	34.0	44.0
Mineral fuels (Million tons)	4.2	—	7.5	8.3	11.6	13.3
Miners employed (Thousands)	34.8	—	54.3	65.6	77.9	82.7
Iron ore (Million tons)	2.5	—	3.9	3.0	3.0	2.6

Table 3.1

heavy industry, consuming 7.2% of their total product between 1855–64, but it opened the way to new markets and new sources of raw materials. Table 3.1 illustrates both the growth of the French railways, and also the related growth of other areas of French heavy industry.

(i) Agriculture

Nevertheless, France, the land of the peasant smallholder, remained a country where agricultural interests continued to play the major role. In 1866, 51.5% of the population continued to find its livelihood from the land. The improvement of agricultural production in France was a vital area of government concern, where, although its methods were similar, the results were less uniformly striking. Some impressive figures can, nevertheless, be quoted. By irrigation and drainage, 1.5 million hectares of new land came under cultivation, making the total area of cultivated land in France at the end of the Second Empire 26.5 million hectares, the highest figure in the country's history. The area given over to the cultivation of wheat was 33% greater in 1862 than in 1840, and the increase in the area of sugar beet production stood at a huge 137%. Spectacular improvements, however, tended to be local rather than national, and 'success stories' tend to be offset by cases where no substantial change in production or agricultural methods took place at all. Modernisation occurred, but irregularly, and most frequently upon the large estates. France boasted 9000 mechanical harvesters in 1862, but they were spread between 3.6 million cultivators of land.

(j) Public Works

The clearest physical imprint of the Second Empire was that left upon the fabric of its capital city. In the first year of his reign, Napoleon III had given notice of his concern with the material state of Paris by the completion of his uncle's great avenue, the Rue de Rivoli, and the construction of Les Halles as a central market for the city. The following year, the appointment of Baron Haussmann as Prefect of Paris provided a man of sufficient energy and determination to cut through the web of vested interests and allied complications that stood in the way of the transformation of the medieval city into an Imperial showpiece to rank with London, Vienna, or St. Petersburg. The process was long and difficult. The debts incurred were not finally paid off until 1929, and Haussmann made many enemies for himself and for the regime through his cavalier attitude to finance. Enemies claimed that the main purpose of the Emperor and of his Prefect was to replace the easily barricaded revolutionary rabbit-warren of 1848 with vistas that were as suitable for artillery fire as they were pleasant to the visitor's eye. Doubtless the strategic advantages were not lost upon Napoleon III, but they do not seem to have been uppermost in his mind. The records of his intense personal interest in the project bear out Persigny's judgement that 'his main aim throughout was to carry out great works in Paris, to improve the living conditions of the working classes, to destroy unhealthy districts, and to make the capital the most beautiful city in the world'.

Most aspects of modern Paris bear witness to the 'great works' of the Second Empire. The modern boulevards, the railway stations, the open spaces at the Parc Monceau and the Bois de Boulogne date from this period. Gas lighting was introduced throughout the city, and a vast new system of sewers was constructed (although these failed to save the city from further outbreaks of cholera in 1866 and 1867). The second stage of the project saw the construction of residential suburbs for the workers displaced from the centre. Numerous other towns and cities, among them Lyon, Rouen, Le Havre, Bordeaux, and Marseilles, experienced similar public works schemes upon a smaller scale.

The impact upon the foreign visitor was much as desired. The great English social reformer Lord Shaftesbury, as he viewed the new developments, could imagine that with such a ruler, the French worker could be excused for exclaiming, 'Long Live Despotism! Down with Free Governments!'

(k) The Empire and its People

Clearly, however, substantial sections of the French population were reacting with much less gratitude and enthusiasm towards the Imperial reforms by the mid-1860s. Was this merely ingratitude, or did it reflect a deep rooted failure on the part of the government to transform society as the Emperor's early writings had promised? Once more, the answer is complicated by vast diversity between region and region, and between industry and industry. It is by no means possible in the 1850s and 1860s to speak of a homogeneous working class in France with one set of interests and reactions.

The Parisian worker remained the steadfast opponent of the regime, from the plebiscite of 1851 to the legislative elections of 1863, when the opposition made a clean sweep of the Parisian constituencies and beyond. The discontent was partly ideological, partly material. The problem of poverty in the first years of the Second Empire was enormous. Research based upon the wills of urban workers suggests that 70–80% of the population of Paris was too poor to bequeath any property in 1847. The figure scarcely descended below 70% over the next two decades. The rebuilding of Paris,

impressive as it was in the eyes of visitors, in the long run merely changed the location of the slums. The worker found it impossible to return to the rebuilt centre of the city, where rents had advanced far beyond his capacity to pay, and had to be content with the new suburbs where, in the phrase of L. Lasare, higher rents and immigration from the provinces had created 'a red belt enclosing, besieging the centre of the city'.

The textile industry is another example that must be borne in mind when considering the generally optimistic statistics of the Empire's economic growth. Not only was it one of the worst sufferers from increased British competition after 1860 (see section 1), but was savagely hit by the 'cotton famine' that resulted from the civil war in the USA. In 1860, 365 000 bales of cotton entered France through Le Havre, compared with only 31 000 bales in 1862. Thus, although 'real' wages showed a distinct increase under the Second Empire, factors such as these, and price fluctuations beyond the control of any government (such as those caused by bad cereal harvests in 1853, 1855, 1861 and 1867) meant that in local cases, no real improvement in living conditions would be noticed.

Nevertheless, statistics can be quoted to suggest some substantial improvements in the lot of the 'average' Frenchman. Consumption per head of all major foodstuffs was higher in the decade 1865–74 than in the decade 1845–54, sometimes, as Table 3.2 shows, by a substantial margin.

Perhaps the most spectacular social developments were those brought about in education. The work of Rouland (1856–63) and Duruy (1863–69) at the Ministry of Education made great inroads into the problems of illiteracy and lack of instruction, leaving only 312 French communities without a school in 1867, compared to 2690 in 1850. By 1866, 68% of French children between 5 and 14 years of age were attending school, compared to 51% in 1851 and between 1856 and 1881 the estimated rate of illiteracy fell from 31% to 15%. J. Rougerie has concluded that 'there was still real misery, but there is no doubt that the worker of the 50s and 60s lived better than his predecessor of the 40s'.

Consumption per head of (in grams per week)	Bread	Potatoes	Fruit/Veg	Sugar	Meat/Fish	Milk/Cheese	Butter
1845–54	714	107	245	10	78	168	17
1865–74	763	254	265	20	100	208	21

Table 3.2

(I) The Liberalisation of the Empire: Commerce

The most important factor in reaching a conclusion as to the nature of the regime of Napoleon III is, as T. Zeldin has emphasised, the interpretation that one gives to the steady relaxation of authoritarianism, and to the liberalisation of the government of France that took place in the last ten years of the Empire. To the enemies of the Emperor the explanation was simple. He was forced into concessions by mounting opposition, in an attempt to retain his power. Napoleon III had always spoken of repression, however, as a purely temporary expedient. In *The Napoleonic Ideals* he had used the comparison that: 'Liberty is as a river; in order that it may bring fertility and not devastation, its bed must be hollowed out deep and wide'.

Indeed, in 1851, he had given himself 10 years of absolute power for the accomplishment of this task. It seems reasonable to accept the argument that pressures such as those provided by the economic recession of 1857–58, and by the limited success of the Italian campaign in 1859, did not create the policy of liberalisation, but merely dictated its timing.

The policy of economic liberalisation had been advocated by the Emperor since 1853, but had been strenuously resisted by the Legislative Body. Napoleon III still regarded the principle of freer trade as essential, both as a foundation of the future economic expansion of France, and as the cornerstone of the understanding with Great Britain which he considered a vital element of foreign policy. British suspicion of French policy in Italy in 1859 rendered rapprochement more urgent than ever. The free trade treaty signed with Britain in 1860 known, after the chief negotiators as the 'Cobden–Chevalier' Treaty had such distinct political overtones that Cobden described it as 'nine-tenths political rather than politico-economical, with a view to cement the alliance with this country'. All the same, its economic consequences were far reaching. Import duties on British coal, textiles, iron and steel were to be lowered by 25% over five years, and French wines, silks and fancy goods would enter Britain at substantially reduced rates. It was the tip of a 'laissez faire' iceberg, being followed by reciprocal trade treaties with Belgium (1861), the Zollverein (1862), Italy (1863), Switzerland (1864), Spain and the Netherlands (1865), and Austria and Portugal (1866).

This was not, however, a policy guaranteed to bring stability and calm. The beneficial effects of free trade were always envisaged as being in the long term. In the present lay mainly the opposition of conservative businessmen and financiers, and the unrest of workers whose industries found immediate competition with the industrial might of Great Britain extremely difficult. Stability and calm could only reasonably be expected from political reform.

(m) The Liberalisation of the Empire: the Constitution

This took two forms; reform of the laws governing the political activities of the working classes, and relaxation of the limitations upon Parliamentary liberty. Movement towards the first goal began in 1859 with the amnesty offered to political exiles. Only Ledru-Rollin, the extreme republican, was excluded, although a number of others refused the gesture of conciliation. In 1862, the government subsidised the visit of a workers' delegation to the International Exhibition in London, allowing a degree of contact with foreign workers that would have seemed highly dangerous a few years earlier. Thereafter, reform proceeded with great rapidity. Peaceful strikes were legalised in 1864, and the theory of equality of employer and worker before the law was recognised. The legality of trades unions was fully established by 1868, and proposals to abolish the 'livret', a form of workers' passport without which a man could not be employed, were before the legislature when war broke out in 1870.

At first the attitude of the government to constitutional reform was highly ambiguous. In 1860, came the grant to the Legislative Body of a package of concessions in the vital area of finance. The Emperor renounced the right to borrow money elsewhere when the Legislative Body was in recess, and agreed that the budget should be voted by sections rather than as a whole, thus giving the deputies more chance to attack any unpopular section. For the first time, furthermore, their debates could be observed and reported by journalists.

The legislative elections of 1863 saw the return of 32 opposition candidates where there had been only five before, a compliment to the freer political atmosphere in France had not Napoleon subsequently dismissed Persigny from his post as Minister of the Interior for failure to secure better results. Thus the government contradicted itself by granting greater freedoms and then reacting uneasily when those freedoms revealed opposition to the regime. Why? One reason seems to be that the ministers generally found it hard to accept the new course chosen by the Emperor. The political limitations of the 50s left the Emperor with a very limited range of politically experienced men from whom to choose a new generation of ministers. Of the older generation, most, like Rouher who was christened the 'Vice Emperor' for his domination of domestic politics from 1863–69, were bitterly opposed to any relaxation of Imperial control. Some commentators, notably the American N. N. Barker, have also been convinced of the strong conservative influence of the Empress Eugenie upon her husband. Lastly, no account of the last years of the Second Empire will make consistent sense without the knowledge that, at least from the middle of 1865, when a stone in the bladder was diagnosed, the Emperor was acutely ill and often in severe pain. 'I find a sick man', commented the Empress in 1866, 'irresolute, exhausted . . .. He can no longer walk, no longer sleep, and scarcely eat'.

Perhaps the decisive domestic stimulus to reform was the formation, in 1866, of the 'Third Party'. This was a group of 40 members of the government majority in the Legislative Body who broke away, not to oppose the government, but to press for further reform within the constitutional framework. The amendment proposed by their leaders, Adolphe Thiers and Emile Ollivier, to the address from the throne summarised the attitude of much of the apparent opposition of the time. 'France, firmly attached to the dynasty that guarantees order, is no less attached to the liberty that she believes to be necessary for the fulfilment of her destinies'. Other pressures, such as those caused by the failure of the Mexican expedition (see section **r**) and the virtual collapse of the Périere banking empire, came from farther afield.

The new elections of 1869 finally galvanised the government into action at a realistic pace. To the government's credit, they were the freest held under the Second Empire, and they were the closest. The margin in the government's favour was now 4.5 million votes to 3.3 million. J. M. Thompson regards this as the crisis point for the Empire, remarking that 'perhaps even France never so closely as in the autumn and winter of 1869 resembled a people in disintegration'. However of the 270 opposition members, 116 belonged to the essentially loyal 'Third Party'.

The mandate for substantial reform was clear, and Napoleon III chose the moment to establish the 'Liberal Empire' at which his policies had been hinting. Accepting the resignation of Rouher, he called to office Emile Ollivier. He was prominent in the 'Third Party' and a representative of just that

new generation of politicians which had been conspicuous by its absence until very recently. He then, in the words of J. P. T. Bury, 'adopted the reforming programme of the 116 as his own'. Under the new laws of September 1869, the Legislative Body could propose legislation, elect its own officers, and debate and vote on the budget. At last, the Emperor had touched the pulse of the nation. Share prices rose and journals previously hostile to the regime acclaimed its transformation. The plebiscite called in May 1870 to ratify the measures returned a favourable majority, with 7.3 million saying 'Yes', 1.57 million 'No', and 1.9 million abstentions. This was comparable with the results of 1851–52.

It can never be clearly established whether this was a temporary expedient which the Emperor aimed to reverse at the earliest opportunity or whether, as T. Zeldin claims, it was a genuine 'attempt to break the vicious circle of revolution and reaction in which France had been caught since Louis XVI'. Before that question could be answered, the Second Empire had been destroyed by quite different factors. What may be safely concluded is that, by May 1870, the Empire was quite safe from internal disintegration. Perhaps it always had been, for what opposition there was, was much more opposition to the Authoritarian Empire than to the idea of Empire itself. Thus the causes of its sudden collapse must be sought further afield.

(n) Foreign Policy: Aims and Principles

The ideas laid down in *The Napoleonic Ideals* on the subject of foreign policy were considerably vaguer than those on domestic policy. His uncle, Louis Napoleon had declared, had aimed 'to substitute, among the nations of Europe, the social state for the state of nature . . . to found a solid European association, by resting his system upon completed nationalities and satisfied general interests'. Did this mean that the foreign policy of the Second Empire was to be a pursuit of the romantic doctrine of nationalities, or was that merely a cover for a general attack upon the autocratic interests that upheld the Vienna Settlement?

The best answer is provided by a rare moment of honesty in diplomacy. In February 1863, the Empress Eugenie discussed with the Austrian ambassador a far-reaching plan for the settlement of current European disputes (this was at the moment of the revolt in Poland) and the logical resettlement of the map of Europe. She did this possibly to test his reactions and those of his government. The Polish question would be settled by the creation there of an independent state and, as compensation, Russia would be free to expand into Armenia and the Caucasus at the expense of the Turkish Empire. The other great questions, those of Italy and Germany, would be dealt with by similar 'give and take'. Austria would surrender Venetia to Italy, thus completing the business of 1859, and would find compensation in the annexation of Silesia, and in influence over that part of Germany south of the River Main. The gain of Hannover, and hegemony over Germany north of the Main would make this palatable to the other great German power, Prussia. She would thus be able to release the Rhineland, which could form an independent 'buffer state' under the rule of the King of the Belgians. His obsolete kingdom could then be partitioned between France and the Dutch. Historians disagree as to quite how serious these suggestions were. A. J. P. Taylor does not pay any great attention to them, but W. E. Mosse and N. N. Barker are among those who consider them genuine.

Of course, the scheme was far too grandiose, and touched upon far too many sensitive areas to get further than the theoretical stage. Yet in the light of previous and subsequent events it is not fanciful to see it as a statement of the 'ideal' outcome of Second Empire foreign policy. It incorporated the realisation of national ideals, but only to the extent that best served French interests. Thus there would be two Germanies and three Italian states, where full unification would create powerful neighbours on France's borders. It also betrays the ideal extent of desired French expansion. This was expansion to the 'natural' frontiers of the Scheldt, the Alps, and perhaps the Rhine, with friendly and relatively weak 'client' states beyond these borders, and keeping the potential enemies, Austria, Russia, and perhaps Prussia at a safe distance.

The one element that is not shown clearly enough in the plan of 1863 is the element that Napoleon III undoubtedly regarded as the cornerstone of his policy. Above all he felt that it was the opposition and economic power of Great Britain that had defeated his uncle. As in the case of the 1860 commercial treaty, the friendship of Britain was to be retained at all costs. Initially, however, the distrust of all the powers, not least of all that of Great Britain, limited Napoleon III's freedom of diplomatic action. The editor of the *Times* in 1853 was convinced 'that in order to retain his precarious hold upon the French people, and especially upon the army, Louis Napoleon was resolved upon a forward policy'.

(o) The Crimean War

For 10 years after the foundation of the Second Empire, the attention of French foreign policy centred upon the Mediterranean. Firstly, attention was concentrated, as so often in the past, upon the 'Eastern Question'. The factors that led to this latest revival of an old controversy were ostensibly religious. Having recently (December 1852) restored the rights of the Catholic Church in the Holy Places in Palestine, Napoleon III now saw those rights withdrawn again as a result of the mission of Prince Menshikov, the envoy of the Tsar, to Constantinople in March 1853. Palmerston was correct when he observed that 'The Greek and Catholic Churches are merely other names for Russian and French influence'.

The Menshikov mission put forward further significant demands such as that for a Russo-Turkish defensive alliance, and for Turkish recognition of Russia's right to act as the protector of all Orthodox Christians within Turkish territories.

The contemporary English historian of the Crimean War, A. L. Kinglake, was the founder of a persistent thesis that from this stage Napoleon III aimed for war with Russia. This was based upon traditional English mistrust of the French in general and the Bonapartes in particular. Certainly, a variety of tempting motives presented themselves; the chance to cement his popularity with the Catholic voters; the chance to erase the blot of 1812 from the Napoleonic record; the chance to protect important commercial interests in the Levant; the chance to work in harness with Britain, and thus consolidate an important friendship. All of these objectives could equally be gained by diplomacy. Thus, the Russian occupation of Wallachia and Moldavia in July 1853, to exert a protective influence over the local Christians, was met by the so-called Vienna Note rather than by war. By the Vienna Note France joined Austria and Britain in attempting to pacify the Tsar by a confirmation of the Treaty of Kutchuk–Kainardji, and there was a Turkish guarantee of goodwill towards Christians within the Empire. As late as January 1854, Napoleon III was still proposing a four power conference to steer events away from their violent path. That war ultimately broke out was the responsibility of the Turkish Sultan. Emboldened by the evidence of widespread international support, he decided upon military action against the invaders of his northern territories. His land victory at Oltenitza was offset by the destruction of his fleet at Sinope, necessitating allied action to prevent the anticipated Russian naval domination of the Levant.

In a war fought by inexperienced generals and untried troops in unfamiliar terrain, it was difficult for any country to emerge with honour. France, however, probably had most cause for satisfaction among the major powers involved. The campaign centred upon the siege of the naval base of Sebastopol, without which the Russians would be unable to maintain a significant fleet in the Black Sea. The French contingent could claim the two most important blows that encouraged the Russian evacuation of their positions after a siege of exactly a year. The destruction of the Russian supplies at Kertch, and the successful assault upon the Malakoff fortress in early September 1855, supplied his allies with the 'great success' that Napoleon III had promised them.

The cost was high, however. Combined allied casualties totalled 115 000 by the time Sebastopol fell, and the siege was estimated in its last stages to be costing the equivalent of £2.75 million per week. With all the major French interests already served, and with Russo-phobia never so high in France as it was in England, it was time to resort to diplomacy again.

There can be little doubt that the Treaty of Paris that concluded the war in 1856 marked the high point of Napoleon III's diplomacy. It achieved most of the points that France could ever seriously have hoped for. The independence and integrity of the Turkish Empire were guaranteed by the contracting powers. Russia's influence was restricted by the clauses that forbade her to build fortifications on the shores of the Black Sea, and which reaffirmed the Straits Convention of 1841. For the satisfaction of the Catholic interests, the Sultan acknowledged that his Muslim and Christian subjects enjoyed equal rights, and Russia's claim to protect Greek Orthodox subjects was rejected. Perhaps most important of all, in contrast to decades of isolation and diplomatic impotence, Paris had become the centre of the first major resettlement of Europe since 1815, and her Emperor could with justification pose as the arbiter of Europe. If anyone could claim truly to have won the Crimean War it was surely France.

(p) Italy

It was equally clear that the real loser in the Crimean War was the major non-combatant, Austria. By refusing to extend help, or even sympathy to Russia so soon after Russia's important intervention in Hungary in 1849, she had lost her major ally, and found no substitute. 'You did not conciliate Russia', Eugenie criticised the Austrian ambassador to Paris. 'You did not regain your influence over Germany, and you cannot count upon the gratitude of France and England'.

The main factor that denied French and British gratitude to Austria was the Italian question. The Piedmontese delegation had left Paris, nevertheless, disappointed and despondent. For all his past experience of Italian romantic conspiracy, it scarcely seemed possible in 1856 for the French Emperor to free his hands in order to 'do something for Italy'. The concern of French Catholics for the temporal powers of the Pope; the general unpopularity of war in France, even a victorious one; the inadvisability of causing further offence to the legitimist powers so soon after the Russian war; all these were factors that seemed to prove in 1856 that the opportunity had not yet arisen.

The turning point came in one of the most bizarre episodes even of Napoleon III's colourful administration. In January 1858 an assassination attempt was made upon the Imperial couple by an Italian patriot, Felice Orsini. Innocent bystanders were killed and injured, but Napoleon and Eugenie emerged unharmed. Orsini was captured and condemned to death. Surprisingly, however, the Emperor allowed his would-be murderer to transform his outrage into a martyrdom. From the death cell Orsini was allowed to launch a final appeal to the Emperor to act in support of the Italian cause, his neglect of which had caused Orsini to seek his death. 'The present state of Europe makes you the arbiter of whether Italy is free or the slave of Austria and other foreigners. . . . The happiness or unhappiness of my country depends on you . . .'. Recent writers have differed in their interpretations of Napoleon III's actions in the case of Orsini. J. M. Thompson, seeing the Emperor's whole approach to the Italian intervention as tentative and uncertain, sees his sympathy for Orsini merely as the sentiment of one soldier of fortune for another. W. H. C. Smith sees more controlled opportunism in the affairs of 1858–59, and interprets the Imperial attitude to Orsini as the calculated exploitation of a most welcome opportunity. 1858 was a year of careful cultivation of Franco-Piedmontese relations, with one unmistakable aim. The key meeting took place on 20th July between the Emperor and Cavour, at the fashionable spa of Plombières in the Vosges. Negotiations were secret and personal, and lasted only 4 hours, but a clear programme for French intervention in Italy emerged. It was imperative that France appear the protector, rather than the aggressor, and it was proposed that a union between the tiny principality of Massa-Carrara and Piedmont be used as the bait to provoke Austria into a belligerent ultimatum to Piedmont. As to the extent of the intervention, the French force should comprise 200 000 men to supplement 100 000 Piedmontese, and this joint force was committed to sweep the Austrian presence from Lombardy and Venetia. It would, however, limit its operations to northern Italy, leaving the Pope undisturbed. The result would be an Italy of four separate, independent sections, the enlarged Piedmont, a Kingdom of Central Italy headed by the Duchess of Parma, the Papal territories, and the Kingdom of Naples. In return, France would be enlarged by the transfer of Savoy, and perhaps Nice, from Piedmont. In the first month of 1859, a formal military alliance between France and Piedmont demonstrated to the world the closeness of serious action by the French against Austria.

Nevertheless, war was not inevitable. As late as April 1859 it seemed that British pressure might bring the powers involved to the conference table. The immediate cause of the war was Austria's incredible blunder in presenting Piedmont (19th April) with an ultimatum demanding unilateral disarmament or war. This occurred when international negotiations seemed to be stripping France of any credible pretext for intervention. Austria's declaration of war three days later thus provided Cavour and Napoleon III with precisely the allocation of rôles that they had envisaged at Plombières.

The French campaigns of May and June 1859 lacked the dash and romance of those of the first Napoleon, but they achieved results. The battle at Magenta (4th June) was 'a battle without plan or co-ordination' (J. M. Thompson), but was a victory in as much as it left the road to Milan open to the French. The Battle of Solferino (24th June) was equally confused and twice as costly. The two engagements cost the French 2300 casualties to add to the 4500 dead of disease. These were considerations serious enough for a humane Emperor reduced by the sight of the field of Solferino to 'a half fainting, half vomiting mass of misery' (L. C. B. Seaman). Other considerations were more serious still. A further advance into Venetia would involve a campaign against the Quadrilateral, a formidable formation of Austrian fortresses, and Cavour's annexation of Tuscany (see Chapter 4, section g) left many French Catholics in severe doubt as to the Pope's prospects in the new Italy. Most serious of all, Prussia's mobilisation in the Rhineland left France exposed and vulnerable with her main forces committed to a lengthy campaign in the south.

It is no surprise that Napoleon III chose this moment to meet the Austrian Emperor at the conference table at Villafranca (11th July 1859). By the armistice concluded there, and ratified at Zurich in November, Austria surrendered Lombardy to France (a much less embarrassing expedient than a surrender to Piedmont) and retained Venetia. Only in the short term, and from a strictly French point of view, was Napoleon III's Italian venture a success. The Emperor had shown energy and industry, if little military skill, and had withdrawn 'as soon as the destiny of his country seemed to be imperilled'. He had added the names of two new victories to the Napoleonic Canon. Eventually in March 1860, he succeeded in negotiating the acquisition of Nice and Savoy, thus completing the first substantial push towards France's 'natural' frontiers. He had left many loose ends, however, and these were to form a complex knot. The Italian question remained unsolved, with an Austrian presence maintained in Venetia. Villafranca ensured the future suspicion of Italy towards France, without disposing of Austrian resentment. Prussian and British suspicions of Napoleonic ambitions were revived so that, in effect, France was as isolated in 1860 as Austria had been the previous year. Lastly, the continued instability of Italian politics gave Napoleon III no chance to withdraw from the thankless, expensive and dangerous task of protecting the Pope from his radical enemies.

(q) Colonial Expansion

In many respects, the Second Empire presided over the regeneration of French imperialism. The colonial empire in 1850 was a scattered and shabby thing. It consisted largely of the pieces of the 18th century empire that had been preserved from British annexation, and with a total population of about 659 000. The Emperor's motives in encouraging colonial expansion ran, as J. P. T. Bury points out, parallel to his motives in domestic politics and economics. Economic concerns held a narrow lead over the hope of gratifying the army by presenting them with easy conquests, and the Catholics by conversions to the faith.

In keeping with the general Mediterranean orientation of French foreign policy in the 1850s, the most striking colonial efforts were made in North Africa. Building upon firm foundations laid by the July Monarchy, the development of Algeria was impressive both in terms of physical extent and of modernisation. By 1857, French control extended as far inland as the edge of the Sahara, and even the traditionally troublesome Berber tribesmen were effectively tamed. As in metropolitan France, while political liberties were suppressed, especially in view of the Republican exiles deported there in 1851–52, railways and telegraphs proliferated. The Emperor's cherished ideal of humane civilian government, however, came to nothing. Partly this was the result of factors beyond his control, such as the locust plague of 1866, the drought of 1867 and the cholera epidemic of the following year. Partly, it was due to the later apathy of an Emperor beset by increasing European difficulties.

Farther east, the limitation of French ambitions to 'informal empire' ensured that Egypt would provide one of the great successes of the Second Empire. French strategic ambitions in the Mediterranean combined with Saint-Simonian economic ideals in the project of Ferdinand de Lesseps, a cousin of the Empress, for the construction of a canal linking the Mediterranean and the Red Seas through the isthmus of Suez. The opening of the Suez Canal in 1869, after ten years' work, was a monument to the vision and industry of the Second Empire. But in practical terms it badly damaged relations with Turkey and Great Britain, both of whom naturally saw the project as a serious threat to their interests in a most sensitive area.

Similar industry and vision manifest themselves in other areas of French colonial expansions, although the results were never again so spectacular. In Senegal, the appointment of the enlightened and energetic General Faidherbe as governor (1854) was to be a guarantee of success. Not only did it mark the beginning of a systematic penetration inland, but also that of a successful and peaceful economic development, typified by the creation of the port of Dakar (1857) as a base for the export of local produce.

In the Far East too, 'formal' and 'informal' empire went hand in hand. In China there was substantial co-operation with the British to secure further European trading rights, but it was that very British presence that frustrated French hopes of the establishment of a major economic base such as that enjoyed by the British at Hong Kong. In Indo-China, on the other hand, Napoleon III allowed himself to be influenced by the reports of French missionaries which assured him that direct intervention against the unpopular ruler of Annam, Tu-Duc, would bring rich benefits to the Church and to France alike. As has so often proved to be the case since, especially in Indo-China, the ruler proved to be more popular and able than expected.

France found herself engaged in a lengthy and distant conflict between 1857 and 1860, before the capture of Saigon finally wrung concessions from Tu-Duc. France then gained, by the Treaty of Saigon, control over the three eastern provinces of Cochin China, and guarantees for the free exercise of Catholic faith all over Annam. By then, however, the French government was becoming far too preoccupied with its involvement in Mexico to be able effectively to exploit its advantages on the opposite side of the globe. Only by the energy of local French administrators did French influence penetrate to Cambodia (1863) and to the Mekong Valley (1870). Generally, French colonial expansion demonstrated the same tendencies as her political and economic record in Europe. The dynamism and impressive achievement of the 50s gave way to a slowing pace, and sometimes to confusion or stagnation in the 60s.

(r) Mexico

The limitations upon French success in their Asian and African enterprises paled by comparison with the spectacular failure of the Emperor's daring intervention in the New World. In terms purely of results, the Mexican venture was Napoleon III's most misbegotten piece of opportunism in a career characterised by opportunism. In terms of its original conception, however, the scheme was no worse than dozens of 19th and 20th century interventions by European countries in protection of their threatened financial interests. It could even be seen as a visionary attempt radically to revise the balance of power in the Americas in France's favour.

The independence of Spain's South American colonies in the 1820s had benefited two major powers in particular. The United States found herself able to reserve to herself almost total political influence in the continent, and Britain alone possessed the naval strength effectively to exploit the economic potential of the region. Other powers traded with, and invested in the former colonies very much as 'poor relations'. The events of 1856–61 created a situation ripe for the revision of this state of affairs. Firstly, Mexican politics plunged into a period of renewed anarchy. After having 46 heads of state in its 29 years of independence (1821–50), renewed civil war now broke out between the forces of Benito Juarez, an economic liberal and anti-clerical, and the conservative President Miramon. Established in office by 1861, Juarez suspended the payment of interest on all Mexico's international debts. This came at a time when the civil war in the United States dimmed the prospects of any American intervention in the south.

However sound in conception, the expedition soon got out of hand in practice. Firstly, what was to have been an international intervention became a purely French one in 1862 when Spain and Britain developed severe reservations about the possible reaction of the Americans. Then, in May 1863, the defeat of a French column at Puebla stung France into deeper and more costly commitment involving 30 000 troops. The true tragedy of the scheme, however, sprang from that part of it that was entirely of the Emperor's conception. Possibly under the influence of the Empress, he proposed the cementing of Mexican stability by the establishment there of a European dynasty. The choice fell upon the Archduke Maximilian, brother of the Emperor of Austria, and thus had the agreeable side-effect of repairing Franco-Austrian relations. By the Convention of Miramar in 1864, Maximilian accepted the proposal, and agreed to pay France 270 million francs once he was established, as repayment of Mexico's original debt, and to cover French military expenses.

Not only was the expedition, in the words of the new Empress of Mexico, 'a gigantic experiment', but it was being carried out at the worst possible time. By 1864, the civil war in the USA was drawing to a close, and the United States were extending encouragement and aid to Juarez, to repel the unwelcome European intervention. By 1866, France had far more urgent need in Europe for the forces tied down in Mexico. Long before Maximilian had had the time to win the hearts of his new subjects, his French forces began to be evacuated. The process was complete by February 1867, and within four months, the capital was once more in the hands of Juarez. Gallantly refusing to flee his adopted country, Maximilian was executed by firing squad on 19th June. 'None', observed Rouher to the Legislative Body, 'could calculate the passions of the Mexican nation'. It was a poor excuse for a failure that cost France 6000 men and the equivalent of £45 million.

(s) The Development of Diplomatic Isolation

Between the conception of the Mexican expedition and its final fiasco, a series of events began to work a revolution in European diplomacy. For a decade the Mediterranean had been the focus of diplomatic attention. Now a succession of crises turned this attention almost totally towards the north. The details of the revolt in Poland (Chapter 6, section **h**), of the Schleswig-Holstein affair (Chapter 5, section **h**), and of the general collapse of Prussian-Austrian relations (Chapter 5) are described elsewhere. What concerns us here is their impact upon French diplomacy.

French interests were involved directly neither in Poland nor in Schleswig-Holstein. Domestic tension, and the diversion of a substantial force to Mexico would have made intervention difficult even if that had not been the case. Such sympathy as existed in France for the 'underdog' did not go as far, the Emperor was constantly reminded from the provinces, as a demand for war. Denmark could not even appeal to the liberal traditions of the 'Napoleonic Ideal'. Thus Schleswig-Holstein was also 'a question that did not touch the dignity of France'. Reasonable as such an attitude was, the most ominous feature of the events of 1863 and 1864 was the wall of distrust that met the Emperor's attempts to organise a diplomatic solution to the Polish question. These efforts have been interpreted by the Franco-American historian A. L. Guérard in the most favourable light. '. . . in 1863 he was perhaps the last genuine European who stood in a place of authority, a successor to Metternich, a precursor to Woodrow Wilson'. Intervention in Italy, and now in Mexico, ensured that French projects for conciliation totally failed to dispel the conviction that France merely hoped to pick up further pieces from European collisions. From being the focal point of Europe in 1856, the Emperor found himself isolated and burdened with embarrassing commitments as the greatest threats to the interests of his state emerged.

(t) The Biarritz Conference and the Austro-Prussian War

The Convention of Gastein (August 1865) that seemed to patch up relations between Austria and Prussia (Chapter 5, section **h**) seemed another alarming step towards France's complete isolation. It must have been with great relief that Napoleon III heard of Bismarck's willingness to meet him privately at Biarritz in October 1865.

The secrecy that surrounded the Biarritz interviews makes it impossible to this day to state with certainty what took place between the two great opportunists. J. M. Thompson is quite specifically of the opinion that Bismarck revealed his plans for an armed confrontation with Austria, and secured French neutrality with vague promises of compensation in the Rhineland. J. P. T. Bury maintains that, throughout, Napoleon III's prime concern was with Venetia which would, in the event of any future hostility, be prised away from Austria to complete France's 1859 undertaking of Piedmont.

As Austro-Prussian relations deteriorated, French policy was based upon an assumption that any future war between them would be long and evenly-matched, leaving France perhaps as arbiter, or as holder of the balance of power in Europe, presumably with a bill to present for her services in either case. France settled her stance (June 1866) by an agreement with Austria that she would maintain her neutrality in return for Austria's promise to surrender Venetia, whatever the outcome of the war. At the beginning of July 1866, it seemed highly unlikely that the German question could be resolved without the co-operation and blessing of France.

On 3rd July that view was totally discredited by the engagement at Sadowa in Bohemia, where the Austrian army was routed. The initial response to the receipt of the news in Paris was one of satisfaction at the discomfiture of autocracy, and at the liberation of Venetia. This was quickly soured by the realisation of the wider implications of Prussia's triumph. 'We felt', reported La Gorce, 'that something in the soil of old Europe had just crumbled. Among the people, uneasiness. In the sovereign's circle, bitter complexity'. The situation might still have been saved, however. It is possible that the real error in French policy was not committed at Biarritz, but at the meeting of the Council of State at St. Cloud on 5th July. At the very last minute, the proposals of the Foreign Minister and of the Minister of War to mobilise 50 000 men with a view to action against the Rhineland, was reversed by the Emperor. Why did France remain inactive? The strongest argument against military demonstration had been that it would imply support for Austria, and would thus ruin France's long-term cultivation of her relations with Italy. Furthermore, the agricultural depression, the policy of the ministry of finance for greater economy in the military budget, and the knowledge of the peaceful disposition of the people, were all inhibiting factors.

(u) The Policy of Compensation

The official reaction of the French government remained calm, stressing that the 1815 settlement had been overturned, Venetia liberated, and the cause of national self-determination advanced 'without the movement of a single French soldier'.

Unofficially it was clear that French prestige, too, had been mauled at Sadowa, and that Prussia could overturn the present balance in central Europe whenever she so wished. The Empress Eugenie spoke for many when she remarked to Prince Reuss that 'with such a nation as a neighbour, we run the risk of seeing you at the gates of Paris one fine day before we scarcely realise it. I shall go to bed French and wake up Prussian'. Napoleon III's government was left with two means to redress the balance. It could accept the growth of Prussian power, and use conciliatory diplomacy to build up a system of alliances that might guarantee French security, or it could launch itself upon a unilateral search for territorial compensation to re-establish national prestige. The two courses were incompatible yet, in the years that remained to the Second Empire, French policy was to pursue them both.

From July 1866, the French ambassador in Berlin was pressing Bismarck on the subject of compensation, mentioning the frontier of 1814, Luxemburg, and the Rhineland. Early the following year, the Emperor broached the project that came closest to success. His approach to the King of the Netherlands with the offer to purchase from him the Grand Duchy of Luxemburg contained many promising elements, not least the financial embarrassment of the Dutch King. The Dutch agreement to the deal was made, however, conditional upon the agreement of Prussia, whose troops garrisoned the Duchy. Bismarck raised no official objection to the transaction but German national reaction to the Luxemburg proposals was perfectly predictable. In early April, Bismarck replied to a question in the Reichstag, that he was officially committed to the maintenance of all 'German' territories. The Luxemburg deal was dead. This fact was confirmed in May 1867, when an international conference in London, although depriving Prussia of her rights of garrison, declared the Grand Duchy a neutral and independent state.

The failure of what Bismarck dismissed as a 'Policy of Tips' turned the screw a little more tightly upon the French government. It was left in no doubt by the icy response of the Legislative Body to the news of the Luxemburg check, that it could ill afford any further fall in its stock. If it continued to speak of peace it showed that it recognised the possibility of war by attempting to construct an anti-Prussian alliance. Austrian and Italian responses in the course of 1867 were, however, cautious. The Austrian Emperor was understandably reluctant to suffer further defeats. The price demanded by Italy, which was the withdrawal of French troops from Rome, was too high to be acceptable to Catholic opinion in France. The year 1868 opened, therefore, with France still in a position of total diplomatic isolation.

(v) The Hohenzollern Candidature and the Ems Telegram

The new challenge that 1868 posed to the international prestige of France came from an unexpected source. The circumstances whereby the throne of Spain came to be offered to a branch of the Hohenzollern family, the ruling house of Prussia, are described elsewhere (Chapter 5, section **o**). Our prime concern here is with the French reaction when, on 2nd July 1870, the French foreign office received official confirmation of the move that would threaten them with a diplomatic encirclement. Feeling that justice was wholly on her side this time she made it clear, especially through a fiery speech by Gramont the Foreign Minister (6th July) that this was considered sufficient grounds for war with Prussia. In the face of such threats, the Prussians rapidly denied any knowledge of, and of course any support for, the candidature. By 12th July, Hohenzollern hopes of the throne of Spain were as dead as those of Napoleon III for Luxemburg.

No sooner had the French government ensured that the error of 1866 would not be repeated, than it committed a new one. The day after the withdrawal of the candidature, the French ambassador 'button holed' King Wilhelm at the spa resort of Bad Ems, 'to ask me in an importunate way that I should authorise him to telegraph at once that I pledged myself never again for the future to give my consent, if the Hohenzollern renewed their candidature'. The implied lack of faith in the Prussian monarch, and the attempt to rub Prussia's nose in her own diplomatic defeat were ill-timed, and far more likely to cause offence in Germany than the remote trans-Pyrenean defeat itself. Bismarck's release to the press of the skilfully edited text of the King's telegram to him about the incident, the 'Ems telegram', created the desired uproar in Germany and acted, as Bismarck intended it to, as 'a red rag upon the Gallic Bull'.

France now had to gauge her reaction to the German outcry. At first, a plan was produced for another international conference but, as public opinion had not been ready in 1864 or in 1866 for war, so now it was not ready for conciliation. The wife of the Austrian ambassador observed that 'Paris was given over to unrestrained enthusiasm, and cries of "On to Berlin!" . . . don't let them try to tell me today, as they like to do, that nobody in France wanted war; everybody wanted it'. Just as, in domestic policy, the Emperor's 'Napoleonic Ideal' combined with public pressure to produce the Liberal Empire, so, in foreign policy, the same factors combined to produce the Franco-Prussian war. War credits were voted on 15th July, the French ambassador was withdrawn the following day, and on 19th July, France declared war.

(w) The Franco-Prussian War

How well was the French army prepared for this, its greatest trial? Some improvements had been made since the 1859 campaigns. The recruitment law that finally passed in 1867, increased the number of men with military training by cutting the period of training to 5 years, and establishing a period of a further 4 years' service in the Reserve. By 1870, most of these men were equipped with the 'Chassepot' rifle, a splendid weapon with a range double that of the German 'Needle Gun', but the weaponry did not necessarily compensate for other defects. 'I am afraid', commented the writer Mérimée, upon hearing the news of war, 'that the generals are not geniuses'. Nor had they the experience of European wars that the Prussian commanders had recently acquired. Bourbaki had seen successful action, but only in Algeria. Bazaine, in Mexico, had not even had a record of unambiguous success. MacMahon and Canrobert, likewise, had yet to be weighed in the balance. Most ominously, the French mobilisation was disjointed and, at times, simply chaotic. Finally, the French were outnumbered, with 275 000 troops covering a 250 km front, while 450 000 Germans held a narrower 160 km line.

Within three weeks the shape of the war had been established by a series of German attacks in Alsace. At Spicheren (4th August) and at Forbach and Froeschwiller (6th August) the forces of Bazaine and MacMahon were surprised and forced into a retreat. Bazaine's retreat took him towards the fortress town of Metz. His fate was sealed by a major engagement between the villages of Gravelotte and St. Privat (18th August). There, from good defensive positions, with their 'Chassepot' rifles, the French inflicted heavy casualties. One Prussian regiment lost 8000 men in 20 minutes at one point, but Bazaine failed to take advantage of the situation by means of a counterattack. Instead the timid commander chose to fall back on the supposed safety of Metz, where he was besieged by the reinforced enemy,

MAP 3
FRANCE AND THE
FRANCO-PRUSSIAN WAR

SEDAN

BEAUMONT
METZ
TO PARIS
GRAVELOTTE
SPICHEREN
WISSEM-
BOURG
NANCY
WÖRTH
SAVERNE
STRASBOURG
BELFORT
R. RHINE

BELGIUM

LORRAINE
STRASBOURG
ALSACE

PARIS

NANTES

DUCHY
OF
SAVOY

KINGDOM
OF
ITALY

LYON

BORDEAUX

COUNTY OF NICE

NICE
MARSEILLES

SPAIN

KEY

- - - - - - - - FRENCH FRONTIERS IN 1870

- - - · - - · - - FRONTIERS ADJUSTED BETWEEN 1859–71

⟶ MAIN DIRECTIONS OF PRUSSIAN OFFENSIVE, 1870

and was able to emerge only at the end of October, in order to surrender.

The second French army, commanded by MacMahon and accompanied, or encumbered by the sick Emperor, moved to the relief of Metz. The slowness of its progress and the indiscretion of the French press, from whom the enemy learned of the army's whereabouts, allowed the invaders to surprise MacMahon some 15 miles from Sedan, to which the French fell back for the decisive action of the brief war. There, on 3rd September, the French were submitted to a murderous bombardment, ended only by the Emperor's personal decision to surrender. One hundred and four thousand men, 6000 horses, and 419 guns were handed over to the German forces, and although the war was to survive Sedan by some months, its outcome could no longer be in doubt. Partly in the hope that this could be passed off as a dynastic war, which had been decided by the surrender of one of the warring dynasties, the Legislative Body, on 4th September 1870, declared the Second Empire at an end, and the Republic re-established. For the second time, the Bonaparte dynasty which offered France glory in many different fields, failed to survive a major reverse on the field of battle.

(x) Historiography

The circumstances of the fall of Napoleon III, amidst national humiliation, and the distrust of all major European powers, ensured that the immediate historical judgements upon him and his regime would be harsh ones. The tone was set during the Empire itself by two brilliant polemicists, with fundamental political objections to the Napoleonic regime, Victor Hugo and Karl Marx. Their chief weapon, demonstrated by Hugo in *Napoleon the Little* (1852) and by Marx in *The 18th Brumaire of Louis Napoleon* (1852), was ridicule. They held the view that Louis Napoleon was a petty adventurer, rising on the reputation of a man who he could not hope to emulate. Although great in other fields, neither man could pretend to be an objective historian and, as their publication dates reveal, their judgements are judgements upon the ideology of the Second Empire, and not upon its record of achievement.

So too, the judgements reached by the earlier French commentators also bore the flavour of political outrage. Indeed, in his own country, a Parliamentary republic for all but five years since 1870, Napoleon III has never fully lived down the 'guilt' of his destruction of the Second Republic. Taxile Delord (*History of the Second Empire*, 1869–75) set the republican trend with a violent indictment

in the early days of the Third Republic, and Albert Thomas (*The Second Empire*, 1906) contributed a socialist interpretation and condemnation. Abroad, an Englishman, Arthur Kinglake (*The Invasion of the Crimea*, 1863–80), and a German, Hermann Oncken (*The Rhine Policy of Napoleon III*, 1926), fully established the view of the Emperor as an irresponsible and dangerous expansionist in his foreign policy. Relatively recent French works such as Pierre Renouvin's *History of International Relations* (Vol. 5, 1954) preserve some of this earlier flavour.

Time and geographical distance have tended to soften judgements on the Second Empire. The ideas of the 'revisionist' school have even extended to France itself. Pierre de la Gorce, for example, was not kind to the Emperor in his monumental, seven volume *History of the Second Empire* (1894–1905), but in his old age, in *Napoleon III and his Policy* (1934), he began to revise his verdict. 'He was indeed nefarious. But no sooner have I written this, than I would wish to soften this judgement; for he was also good, and at times, enlightened'. The major works of the 'revisionist' school have, however, been produced by British and American writers. F. A. Simpson, in *Louis Napoleon and the Recovery of France* (1923), stressed that, especially in terms of domestic achievements, the Second Empire was more important than the First and considerably more fruitful than its immediate forerunners. Albert Guérard extended this understanding (*Napoleon III*, 1943) to what he saw as the farsighted conception of his foreign diplomacy. Lynn M. Case, in his important work on French public opinion, and the government's means of keeping in touch with it (*French Opinion on War and Diplomacy during the Second Empire*, 1954), has demonstrated the very real influence that opinion exercised upon the policy making of the Empire. Perhaps the most valuable recent contribution to this school has been the work of Theodore Zeldin, whose works on *The Political System of Napoleon III* (1958) and *Emile Ollivier and the Liberal Empire of Napoleon III* (1963), have largely illuminated the internal workings of the French government, and revised views on the nature and origins of the liberal phase of domestic policy. Of the English writers most readily accessible to the student today, the most critical is J. M. Thompson. His *Louis Napoleon and the Second Empire* (1954) draws parallels between the Emperor and Hamlet, men not great enough for the tasks that they had set themselves. G. P. Gooch (*The Second Empire*, 1960) and J. P. T. Bury (*Napoleon III and the Second Empire*, 1964) are both more sympathetic, the former dwelling upon the personal qualities of the Emperor, and the latter upon the consistency with which he applied his ideas.

Progress Paragraphs

Answer the following questions in about 150 words

Why did Louis Napoleon resort to a 'coup d'état' in 1851? What evidence is there of the popularity of his action?   Section (b)

What was authoritarian about the 'Authoritarian Empire'?   Section (c)

What means were available to Louis Napoleon for the enforcement of his rule, and how did he use them?
Sections (c & d)

What were the motives behind Napoleon III's economic policy, and how did he hope to finance it?
Sections (f & g)

In which sections of the economy did the policies of the Second Empire have greatest effect?
Sections (h, i & j)

How fair would it be to claim that the economic policies of the Second Empire substantially improved the standard of living of the French worker?
Section (k)

What reasons did some sections of the French population have for opposing the Imperial regime in the early 1860s?   Section (k)

What motives have been suggested for the liberalisation of the Imperial regime in the 1860s?
Section (l)

What forms did the liberalisation of the Empire take?
Sections (l & m)

Why, in view of the liberalisation of the regime, was there still so much opposition to the regime in 1869?
Section (m)

What motivated the foreign policy of the Second Empire?   Section (n)

In what respects could the Crimean War and its outcome be seen as the high point of the diplomacy of the Second Empire?   Section (o)

Why were the years 1859 and 1862 especially auspicious for French intervention in Italy and Mexico respectively?   Sections (p & r)

In what ways was France's diplomatic position weakened by her policies in Italy and Mexico?
Sections (p & r)

What successes and what failures were experienced in French colonial policy during the Second Empire?
Section (q)

Why did France play no part in the European crises of 1863–66? What were the effects of her non-intervention?   Sections (s & t)

Why did France go to war over the Ems Telegram when she had accepted the events of 1866?
Sections t, u & v)

Suggest reasons for France's defeat in the Franco-Prussian war.   Section (w)

4
The Unification of Italy

(a) Piedmont and Victor Emmanuel II

After the nationalist failures of 1848–49 Italy presented a panorama of military occupation, restored political reaction, and suppressed constitutions. There was only one exception to this rule. That exception was the buffer state of Piedmont in the north-west angle of Italy. Although decisively defeated at Custoza and at Novara, she retained her constitution, the integrity of her territory and her freedom from Austrian occupation. Her monarchy had effectively usurped the place previously held by Pius IX in the hearts of nationalists by its willingness to lead the cause in 1848. The ruler to whom Gioberti and others now looked after the abdication of Charles Albert in the aftermath of Novara was his son, the 29 year old Victor Emmanuel II.

The 'official' view of Victor Emmanuel propagated by Italian historians for many years after unification was that of the saviour of Piedmont and the Piedmontese constitution from the victorious Austrians, the champion of Italian constitutional monarchy, and the eventual father of his country. The contemporary view of the King of Piedmont was less spectacular. He was sufficiently vague in his political views for the Austrians to consider him a cautious conservative, while the British thought him a cautious liberal. He was probably just cautious. In his personal life, he generally justified his popular nickname, 'The Gentleman King' ('il re galantuomo'). He showed courage and good sense, although also a laziness and coarseness that led the diarist Greville to dismiss him as 'the most debauched and dissolute fellow in the world'. D. Mack-Smith concludes rather more reasonably that he was the sort of man 'always happiest in either the barracks, the stables, or the hunting field'.

Victor Emmanuel's background was an odd one for a nationalist and liberal. He was educated and trained to be heir to an autocracy. His mother and wife were both members of the Austrian House of Hapsburg. Furthermore, his meeting with the Austrian commander Radetzky at Vignale cannot be seen as 'saving' the Piedmontese constitution. Mack-Smith points out that a moderate settlement was equally important for Austria for at least three reasons: to save the Piedmontese monarchy from dangerous criticism from its own radical subjects, to preserve stability in the rest of Italy, and to prevent Piedmont turning for assistance to France, a tactic she would exploit ten years later. Besides, the importance of the Piedmontese constitution (il Statuto) was mainly symbolic and its democratic nature should not be exaggerated. Of the two chambers, the upper one was directly appointed by the King, and the literacy qualification for voting limited the electorate to 2.25% of the population. Under its terms, the King retained several powers of the greatest importance such as the command of the army and the powers to appoint and dismiss ministers.

Like his first essay in foreign relations, Victor Emmanuel's first domestic actions were not exactly those of a liberal. His first task was to ensure his control of the kingdom by means that included the shelling of Genoa to win it back from the radicals that remained entrenched there. His first administration included several of the 25 military men who were to hold ministerial office during his reign, although by the end of 1849 the administration was in the hands of a group of moderate conservatives under the leadership of Massimo D'Azeglio. The first major policy of the ministry, nevertheless, concerned one of the great liberal principles of the 19th century, the contest for power and influence between the Church and the State. Neither King nor minister wished to tolerate the considerable influence of a body that had set its face so firmly against them both in 1848. The batch of measures produced in 1850, known as the Siccardi Laws, was a substantial first move in a decade of Piedmontese anti-clericalism. Church courts and other ecclesiastical privileges incompatible with Parliamentarianism were abolished, the number of holy days was limited, and the senior Piedmontese churchman, Archbishop Fransoni, was imprisoned when he ordered his clergy to ignore these measures. Such

MAP 4   THE POLITICAL DIVISIONS OF ITALY 1815–59

SAVOY   1
2 MAGENTA
3
CUSTOZA
NOVARA
SOLFERINO
VENICE
4
TURIN
5 BOLOGNA
GENOA
MASSA
AND
CARRARA
NICE
FLORENCE
6
7
CORSICA
(French)
MENTANA
ROME
TEANO
8
NAPLES
SARDINIA
1
ASPROMONTE
PALERMO
MARSALA
SICILY
8

KEY

1 KINGDOM OF PIEDMONT   5 DUCHY OF MODENA

2 LOMBARDY   6 DUCHY OF TUSCANY

3 VENETIA   7 PAPAL STATES

4 DUCHY OF PARMA   8 KINGDOM OF NAPLES

determined measures were rare from D'Azeglio, who Mack-Smith describes as 'an amateur in politics, a painter and a novelist by profession, and a statesman only by accident'. Having found a parliamentary majority hard to come by in the first place, he found it undermined in 1852 by an opportunistic alliance between the leader of the 'middle class party', Rattazzi, and his own finance minister, Camillo di Cavour. Their opposition, and the refusal of the King to accept the next stage of D'Azeglio's anti-clerical legislation (a bill enforcing civil marriage) brought about the fall (May 1852) of the ministry, and the advent to power of the most influential figure in the history of 19th century Italy.

(b) Cavour: Personality and Aims

Born in August 1810, into a family of the Piedmontese nobility, Cavour's personal background was as much French as it was Italian, and wide open to the broader influences of western Europe. His father had served as an official in the Napoleonic administration, and his mother had been born in Geneva and brought up a Calvinist. The reading of the young Cavour had included many of the most progressive names in political and economic theory, Smith, Bentham, Ricardo, and the conventional army career of the young nobleman had proved undistinguished and unfulfilling and had lasted only five years (1826–31). The next sixteen years were spent largely in three types of pursuit. His foreign travels, in France, Britain and Switzerland shaped both political and economic views. Meetings with de Tocqueville in France and indirect contact with the men who were dictating the shape of industrial Britain helped to turn him into a broad-minded conservative with views broadly comparable to those of his greatest political 'hero', Sir Robert Peel. Secondly, in his administration of the family estates and business interests in Piedmont, he put into practice the policy of modernisation and development that he had learned abroad. His ventures included the formation of the Lake Maggiore Steamboat Co. and the foundation with others of the Bank of Genoa, and the Bank of Turin. Thirdly, he turned to journalism, a natural means for the propagation of his ideas. Writing predominantly on social, economic and scientific questions, he made his greatest journalistic impact in 1847 with the foundation of *The Resurgence* ('il Risorgimento'). This was a liberal journal immediately popular in Piedmont, and with the Italian refugees who flocked into Piedmont from other parts of the peninsula. Only with the first Piedmontese constitutional elections (June 1848) did the chance to take an active part in politics present itself. Elected to the Assembly, Cavour supported D'Azeglio in the conclusion of the armistice with Austria, and in the maintenance of the constitution, and served him as Minister of Industry and Commerce from the summer of 1850, before succeeding him in 1852.

Such is the consistent 'good press' that Cavour has received since his death, not only from Italian writers, as the most influential figure in the modernisation, liberation, and unification of Italy, that it is extremely important to understand the nature of his 'liberalism' and his 'nationalism' correctly. Of the former M. Salvadori writes as follows: 'Cavour believed in liberty, in responsibility, and in the ability of the educated individual to act responsibly on the basis of his own decisions'. Yet this man achieved his aims in part by bribing newspapers, betraying colleagues like D'Azeglio, and rigging elections. Every major step in his diplomatic career was taken without consultation with Parliament. It is perhaps easier to consider what Cavour did not want. As early as 1835 he had written that '. . . I am persuaded that the 'juste milieu' is the only policy right in the circumstances, capable of saving society from the two rocks which threaten to break it—anarchy and despotism'. We shall understand his 'liberal' policies best if we see them as a means of avoiding the main dangers that he felt threatened Piedmont, and perhaps Italy. These were the tyranny of the traditionalist, autocratic state and the dogmatism of a reactionary church, and on the other hand, the dangerous extremism of Mazzini and the other left-wing radicals active in Italian politics.

The question of Cavour's nationalism has produced even greater controversy, with historians divided between the view that the unification of the whole of Italy was his aim from the beginning of his career, and the claim that he was primarily, perhaps exclusively interested in the expansion and consolidation of his own state, like Bismarck. A. J. Whyte represents the former position in writing that 'Cavour's ultimate aim was the deliverance of Italy from Austria and the formation of an Italian kingdom'. Mack-Smith, on the other hand has maintained that, as late as 1858, 'he still could not accept Mazzini's idea of a united Italy. So long as he obtained Lombardy and Venice he would dominate the peninsula, and that was enough'. The answer is perhaps that it is wrong to see Cavour's attitude as being rigid and consistent throughout his career, and we perhaps find a clue in the letter written by Manin to Pallavicino (September 1856) concerning the attitude of his National Society to the policy of the Piedmontese minister. 'We must work incessantly to form public opinion, because as soon as opinion is clear and forceful, Cavour I am sure will follow it. I think Cavour to be too intelligent and too ambitious to refuse the Italian enterprise if public opinion demands it strongly enough'. Thus, we may best understand the attitude of Cavour to the question of Italian national unity if we view him not as a man in control of events, directing them towards his preconceived goal, but as a practical politician with aims, originally limited, but modified and expanded by the development of factors over which he had little control.

(c) Cavour: Domestic Policy

Cavour's domestic administration of Piedmont between 1852–59 had as its aim therefore the creation of a state stable and prosperous enough to dominate Italy. In some respects the element of stability was achieved by methods that would not have been approved by the English liberals he so much admired. Mazzinian democrats were persecuted, the Mazzinian press was suppressed, and Parliament was blatantly overridden when it did not serve the purposes of the Prime Minister. For example, in 1857 when the elections returned an unexpected right-wing majority, Cavour seized upon a series of dubious technicalities to unseat a number of successful candidates and reduce the right wing to manageable proportions. In January 1855, Cavour held all of the three main posts in the administration, Prime Minister, Foreign Minister, and Finance Minister. Other policies making for stability were of a more typically liberal nature. A string of administrative reforms, in the financial departments (1852), in the foreign office (1853), and those of La Marmora in the army increased efficiency and removed those conservative elements hostile to Cavour. Further anti-clerical measures, notably the suppression of 152 monasteries and 1700 benefices in 1855, further restricted the influence of the Church, but also added an extra £145 640 to the state's income.

The most spectacular achievement of the decade was the laying of the foundations for Piedmontese commercial and industrial prosperity. Already, as Minister of Finance and Commerce, Cavour had concluded a string of free trade treaties. These were with Belgium, with France and with Britain, and had the dual purpose of forging international links with the more advanced states of western Europe, and of attracting into Piedmont the raw materials

and machinery necessary for her development. In the same capacity he had floated large internal and foreign loans to pay off the war indemnity owed to the Austrians as well as to finance the industrial projects of the government. The level of government expenditure on such projects, as well as the long term effects of the policy, may be judged from the fact that the public debt of Piedmont rose between 1847–59 from 120 million lire to 725 million. It would, of course, be misleading to refer to Piedmont in 1859 as a 'modern industrial power,' but she had produced a number of impressive projects to advertise her status at the head of the Italian states. Of Italy's 1798 km of railway track in 1859, Piedmont had 819 km. 1855 saw the production of Italy's first steamship, the *Sicilia*, in Genoa, and of Italy's first home-produced railway locomotives. Further schemes were in progress for the construction of the Mont Cenis tunnel through the Alps, and for the modernisation of the port of Genoa. In the course of the 1850s, Piedmont's trade trebled in value. In material terms, therefore, as well as in terms of constitutions and of military leadership, Piedmont had effectively claimed the first place in Italy by the end of the 1850s.

(d) Piedmont and the Crimean War

In terms of the liberation of Italy, Cavour's most important contribution was that he was able to place the 'Italian Question' firmly into the general context of European diplomacy. This was the forum in which the 1815 settlement had been shaped, and the only forum in which that settlement could really be revised. It was not until the outbreak of the Crimean War in 1854 however that a real opportunity presented itself. It was a bold step for a minor power such as Piedmont to intervene in a European conflict such as this, and it is not surprising that some historians have seen this as a master stroke by Cavour, supported by Victor Emmanuel. A. J. Whyte argues that Cavour's first great diplomatic achievement was to overcome the reluctance of Britain and France who would have preferred the assistance of Austria, and naturally doubted that Austria would agree to fight alongside the Piedmontese. M. Salvadori and D. Beales have laid the stress rather differently, seeing much more of the initiative coming from the allies who felt that Austria would be much more likely to send troops to the Crimea if she were assured that Piedmont was committed there too, and was thus unable to attack her in the rear. D. Mack-Smith, characteristically, moves even further from the traditional interpretation, viewing the plan for intervention as primarily the brainchild of Victor Emmanuel who, fretting at the constitutional restraints imposed upon him, saw war as a good opportunity to reassert his royal powers.

Whatever the process by which the decision was reached, by the end of 1854 Piedmont had concluded an agreement with the allies by which 18 000 Piedmontese troops would travel to the Crimea and by which Piedmont would, of course, be entitled to a place at the congress at which peace would eventually be made. Neither the military intervention nor the Congress of Paris was the success for the Italian cause that Italian historians have sometimes imagined them to have been. La Marmora's troops gave a good account of themselves at the Battle of the Chornaya (August 1855), and in their own eyes did something to restore the prestige lost at Custoza and Novara, but the official line that 'about 2000 of them were killed or died of disease' conceals the fact that not more than 30 of that number actually died of their wounds.

Similarly, Cavour travelled to Paris for the peace conference in 1856 still greatly inexperienced in the ways of 'Great Power' diplomacy, and with hopes that were never really likely to be realised. His first aim was for territorial compensation for Piedmont's efforts, possibly in the shape of the Duchy of Parma. Such a measure never seems to have been seriously considered by the congress. Secondly, he hoped to obtain some commitment from the powers on the subject of the Austrian presence in Italy. He could not hope to obtain this from France who had troops of their own in Rome, and could not contemplate renewed war so soon after their Russian campaign. The British representative, Lord Clarendon, however, attacked Austrian excesses and Papal and Neapolitan misgovernment in far harsher terms than Cavour could have used. It was a measure of Cavour's inexperience, however, that he should have imagined that Clarendon might be speaking for his government, and the British were soon to make it clear that they had no intention of intervening actively in so controversial a continental matter. In the context of 1856 Cavour had failed to achieve a diplomatic initiative and had not created the conditions necessary for a military solution to the problem of the Austrian presence. The future of northern Italy remained extremely uncertain.

(e) The Pact of Plombières

One result of the events in Paris in 1856 was a significant increase in Piedmontese confidence in her dealings with Austria. Cavour's feelings were, doubtless, that the sympathy of France and Britain would at least be sufficient to deter Austria from any threatening ambitions. So it seemed, for Austrian policy in her provinces of Lombardy and Venetia from 1856 was much more conciliatory. The policy of confiscation of the property of exiles was relaxed, and an amnesty for political prisoners was announced in 1857. Victor Emmanuel's famous speech of January 1859, in which he declared that he could not stop his ears to the 'cry of grief' ('grido di dolore') that came from the neighbouring provinces, must have tested Austrian nerves to breaking point. It may have been instrumental in making them blunder into war later that year.

Another undoubted effect of the 'grido di dolore' speech was to cement relations between the Piedmontese government and the nationalist exiles. One such exile, the Neapolitan Massari, recorded that 'Senators, deputies, spectators sprang to their feet and broke forth in deafening cheers; the French, British and Prussian ministers gazed in emotion. We poor exiles applauded frantically'. Relations between Cavour and the exiled nationalists had been ambiguous since the Crimean War. The latter had formed the National Society in the mid-1850s whose main figures were La Farina, Pallavicino, and Manin, the hero of the former Venetian Republic and which boasted a membership of some 8000. They were further convinced by the intervention in the Crimea that Piedmont represented Italy's best hope, but still entertained severe reservations about the sincerity of the leadership, and especially about that of Cavour. 'Convinced', Manin had written in 1855, 'that above all Italy must be made, that this is the first and most important question, we say to the house of Savoy: "Make Italy and we are with you. . . . If not, we are not"'.

On the other hand, nothing was more likely to damage relations with France, certainly the most important factor in Cavour's calculations, than the assumption by Napoleon III that Piedmont was really serving the interests of a band of radicals. Although Cavour tried hard to consolidate the friendship of the Crimea all was very nearly ruined by Orsini's terrorist attack of January 1858. As shown in Chapter 3, the Orsini affair was an obscure and mysterious business, but there seems little doubt that Napoleon III's first reaction was one of great bitterness towards a Piedmontese government that had allowed Orsini to avoid arrest and reach France. At this stage it seems to have been Victor Emmanuel, rather than Cavour, who performed one of his periodic services to Italy by presenting a brave reply to the attacks of the

Emperor. He presented Piedmont as the best guarantee in Italy against the excesses of the radicals. These claims, combined with Napoleon's long standing, if somewhat vague desire to 'do something for Italy', calmed the Emperor. A visit of his confidante, Dr. Conneau, to Turin (June 1858) first raised hopes of direct co-operation between the two states against Austria. Thereafter, progress was rapid, culminating in the secret meeting between Cavour and Napoleon III at Plombières in July, where plans for a four part confederacy of Italy under the presidency of the Pope were agreed (see Chapter 3, section **p**). It is impossible to escape the conclusion that the terms of the Plombières agreement represent the views of Napoleon III rather than those of the anticlerical Cavour. One is led once more to the view of Cavour as an opportunist willing to accept conditions of this sort to achieve what he had long known to be an essential precondition of the liberation of northern Italy, namely the military intervention of France.

(f) The War of 1859

The war which first undermined Austrian authority in northern Italy has already been examined from the viewpoint of the French Empire (see Chapter 3, section **p**). For many years, the traditional view from the Italian side was of a war of national liberation, cunningly contrived by dedicated Italians and finally betrayed at Villafranca by a cynical foreigner. Instead examination of the Piedmontese and Austrian war efforts should show how absolutely essential the part played by the French forces was to the achievement even of the limited success of 1859.

Italian reaction to the outbreak of war sheds some interesting light upon the extent of Italian enthusiasm. The Piedmontese mobilisation was half-hearted. Not only was there a tendency to leave the hard work to the French, but also a distinct reluctance on the part of conservative army officers to arm large numbers of men at a time when Piedmont was full of dangerous radical exiles. Where there was enthusiasm, it was not always nationalist. Victor Emmanuel was as keen on the war as Cavour, but as D. Mack-Smith argues, his main motive was that the constitution allowed him, as commander-in-chief, far greater powers and more direct political influence in war than in peace time. He felt himself, writes Mack-Smith, 'a new man, powerful again, and free from interfering civilians'. Indeed, relations between King and Prime Minister were rarely worse than at this time

when Victor Emmanuel directed affairs at Turin. For one reason or another, the numbers of the Piedmontese army fell 40% short of the number agreed at Plombières, and they were not supplemented by a flood of patriotic volunteers from other parts of Italy. Victor Emmanuel had boasted of 200 000 such volunteers rallying to his cause, but only about 10% of that total materialised.

Fortunately, the Austrian campaign was also faulty in several respects. The command of their forces was left by the Emperor to the 'courtier soldiers' Grunne and Gyulai, rather than to the more able Benedek or Hess. Their mobilisation was carried out at the pace of the Napoleonic Wars, allowing the French ten days to move their troops into Piedmont by rail. The mobilisation could not be more than partial, given the need to leave substantial bodies of troops in other parts of the Empire, especially in Hungary, in anticipation of possible trouble there. The force of 90 000 that eventually assembled in Italy was considerably smaller than the Franco-Piedmontese force that faced it. The main engagements of the campaign that followed, at Magenta (4th June) and at Solferino (24th June), were predominantly French engagements. Indeed, not a single Piedmontese soldier lost his life at Magenta, although on the day of Solferino the Piedmontese army was involved nearby in a significant subsidiary engagement at San Martino. It was, therefore, logical and perfectly in keeping with the previous history of the 'Italian Question' that peace should be made when and how the convenience of the intervening power dictated.

The armistice concluded at Villafranca on 11th July 1859 emphasises once more the extent to which the fate of Italy was dependent upon wider European considerations. Not only were the negotiations limited to the rulers of France and Austria, but the main factors motivating Napoleon III were distinctly non-Italian, (see Chapter 3, section **p**). It seems very likely, however, that he was also motivated to an extent by perfectly logical misgivings about Piedmont's conduct of the war. It seemed unlikely that the small kingdom would be able to fulfil her promise to pay France's campaign expenses if the war continued for much longer; Piedmont's commanders had virtually no plans nor much equipment for the prolonged siege warfare that would now be necessary if the line of Austrian fortresses on the borders of Venetia were to be attacked; it was becoming increasingly clear that Cavour had plans for the central Italian duchies that went far beyond the terms of the Plombières agreement. The terms of the armistice transferred Lombardy, minus the important border fortresses of

Peschiera and Mantua, to France on the assumption that they would transfer the territories to Piedmont. The rulers of Tuscany and Modena, who had fled at the news of Magenta, were to be restored, and the principle of a confederacy under Papal leadership was confirmed. Venetia, of course, remained in Austrian hands. The attitude of Victor Emmanuel to the settlement was ambiguous; that of Cavour was not. Meeting his monarch for the first time in weeks, he railed against the terms of the armistice, called the King ' "traitor" and worse', and advised in absolute desperation that Piedmont should fight on alone. When the King wisely rejected the foolish advice, Cavour resigned his office.

(g) Cavour and the Central Duchies

Even as these events were taking place, however, it was becoming increasingly clear that the terms of Villafranca could never be implemented in full. The major difficulty would be the restoration of the rulers of central Italy. In his main piece of direct co-operation with the National Society, Cavour had connived at the establishment of provisional administrations in the central Italian territories, in the name of 'Italy and Victor Emmanuel'. By taking such action in an area designated at Plombières as strictly beyond Piedmontese control Cavour was clearly violating the agreement and reinterpreting it in a fashion much more favourable to his own state. The King seems to have had no prior knowledge of the operation and regarded it as madness to risk the alienation of his ally at such a vital stage in the campaign.

Cavour's resignation after Villafranca left his 'commissioners' in Tuscany, Parma and Modena in an awkward and advanced situation, faced with the alternatives of acting on their own initiatives, or abandoning their positions. They did the former. Luigi Farini had himself elected dictator in Parma, Modena and Bologna, which he declared united under their old Latin title of Emilia. In Florence, the capital of Tuscany, a provisional government under Ricasoli played the same role. It declared that it would never tolerate the return of the former rulers and that it was its intention to 'make part of a strong Italian Kingdom under the constitutional sceptre of King Victor Emmanuel'. Further reforms in both Emilia and Tuscany brought the currencies and customs of those territories into line with those of Piedmont. A. J. Whyte declares of Farini and Ricasoli that 'these two men saved Italy'. Their actions were indeed brave and valuable for the Italian cause, but the

judgement once again does scant justice to Napoleon III. Not only were his armies indirectly responsible for the original flight of the rulers of Tuscany, Parma and Modena, but it was he, in the negotiations at Zürich that formalised the terms of Villafranca, who insisted that no force should be used to implement the terms relating to central Italy. This ruled out the dangers of Austrian or French intervention on behalf of the former rulers, but made it hard for Piedmont to enforce her own union with the territories. The answer lay in the combination of this piece of unfinished business with another. The section of the Plombières agreement whereby France would receive Nice and Savoy as repayment for her military aid had been ignored at Villafranca as France's obligations, to clear the Austrians from Lombardy and Venetia, remained unfulfilled. Now it was resurrected in a Franco–Piedmontese agreement concluded in Turin in March 1860. It was decided that Savoy and Nice on the one hand, and Emilia and Tuscany on the other should hold plebiscites to decide their future allegiances. In both cases the result was decisive. In Emilia the voting was 426 006 to 1506 in favour of annexation by Piedmont, and in Tuscany the margin was 366 571 to 14 925, although a total of 153 000 abstentions served as a reminder of Tuscan jealousy of their separate historical and cultural traditions.

The events of 1859–60 therefore represented neither complete success nor complete disappointment for Piedmont. Her area and population were doubled as a combined result of war and diplomacy. Both of these methods of expansion, however, had depended crucially upon the aid of France. Also, few of the declared tasks, either of the Piedmontese government or of the nationalists, had been achieved. Both Austrian and French troops remained on Italian soil, and some major tasks in the process of creating an Italian nation remained to be undertaken.

(h) Garibaldi: Personality and Aims

That the Italian cause progressed so rapidly from the apparent deadlock of early 1860 was very largely the responsibility of one very remarkable man. Giuseppe Garibaldi was born in Nice (4th July 1807) and was associated from about 1834 with the romantic and conspiratorial nationalism of Mazzini's 'Young Italy' movement. His first efforts in the Italian cause, participation in an unsuccessful rising in Genoa, were rewarded with the death sentence passed in his absence and with flight to South America, where he established his reputation as a guerrilla fighter and leader of genius. In 1848 he found the Piedmontese wary of employing a known radical, but made an international reputation by his defence of Mazzini's Roman Republic. After further exile in America, and on his island home of Caprera off the coast of Sardinia, he fought in 1859 for Piedmont, or as he always saw it, for Italy against Austria. His aims for Italy were simple. With a fine disregard for the constraints imposed by international diplomacy or by economic backwardness, he worked for a free and unified state, preferably a republic, but a constitutional monarchy if necessary. His political views were confused, so confused that men as far apart as the great English Liberal W. E. Gladstone and the Fascist dictator Benito Mussolini could claim him as a kindred spirit. The obituary of Garibaldi published in the 'Times' (5th June 1882) passed an accurate judgement upon him. 'In politics, as in arms, his mind lacked the basis of a rudimentary education. He rushed to conclusions without troubling his head about arguments. His crude notions of Democracy, of Communism, of Cosmopolitanism, or Positivism, were jumbled together in his brain and jostled one another in hopeless confusion'.

His fame and achievement, however, rest upon his actions rather than his thought. His fame in Italy and abroad rests upon the fact that his contribution to the unification falls halfway between those of the other two great Italian figures, Mazzini and Cavour. Mazzini kept the flame of Italian nationalism burning at the time of greatest adversity, but in material terms achieved very little. Cavour achieved much, but had to dirty himself and his reputation in the murky waters of European politics to do it. Garibaldi seemed to many, to have avoided both these traps. His greatest admirer among historians, G. M. Trevelyan, wrote that his work should be 'an encouragement to all high endeavour amongst us in a later age, who, with our eyes fixed on realism and the doctrine of evolution, are in some danger of losing faith in ideals, and of forgetting the power that a few fearless and utterly disinterested men may have in a world where the proportion of cowards and egoists is not small'.

(i) The Sicilian Expedition

No event in the eleven year period (1859–70) during which the modern Italian state was effectively created has so caught the imagination as Garibaldi's invasion of Sicily and subsequent overthrow of the Neapolitan state. Certainly, his

tactical expertise and personal charisma were major factors in the success of the Sicilian adventure, but like all historical events, the roots of this success were more complicated.

Firstly, Garibaldi did not initiate events in Sicily. The rising in Palermo, the chief city of the island that took place on 4th April 1860, owed nothing to him and nothing to Cavour. It was the work of a group of Mazzinian Republicans led by Francesco Crispi and Rosalino Pilo. As republicans, they had refused to identify with the Piedmontese monarchy's war in the previous year, and now Cavour returned the compliment by virtually ignoring their approaches to him. The support that the rising received in Palermo was due to a combination of national and local factors. It was in part a result of the excitement generated by the events of 1859, but a more important cause was the disappointment felt at the continued conservatism of the young King Francis II, newly succeeded to the throne of Naples. The major difference between this outburst and most of its Mazzinian forerunners was that the Palermo revolt was quickly taken up in the countryside by the peasantry. Their motives were entirely derived from local affairs, and their violent protests were directed as much against the landlords who raised their rents and charged them for the privilege of grinding their corn, as against the Neapolitan troops sent to restore order.

Encouraged by these circumstances, Garibaldi began to prepare for the passage to Sicily. With just over one thousand volunteers, mainly of middle class and professional origins and very few of them from further south than Tuscany, he sailed from Genoa and landed them from two ancient steamers at Marsala on 11th May. In so doing he was greatly aided by the presence of a squadron of ships of the Royal Navy, actually concerned with the safety of local British property, but wrongly supposed by the patrolling Neapolitan navy to be allies of Garibaldi. The arrival of these forces proved too much for the harassed Neapolitan troops. On the 15th, Garibaldi gained a substantial success at Calatafimi. Palermo fell to him on the 30th May, and shortly afterwards agreement was reached with the Neapolitan commanders for the withdrawal of their troops across the straits to the mainland.

(j) The Conquest of Naples

The gallant and romantic Sicilian adventure now took on a succession of more sinister international implications. If Garibaldi followed the fleeing troops on to the Neapolitan mainland, why should he not beat them again? If he did so, what was to prevent him from crossing the border from Naples into the Papal States? If he did that, what was to stop a major international crisis involving the French garrison and possibly other Catholic powers? None of these considerations was very attractive to the government of Piedmont, whose attitude to the Sicilian expedition as a whole has been the subject of fierce controversy. Naturally, the 'nationalist' interpretation has been that Cavour and his government gave to Garibaldi all the help they reasonably could without raising a storm of international, diplomatic protest. La Farina wrote that 'Cavour's friends helped the expedition with every possible means'. Nothing would now seem, as D. Mack-Smith stresses, to be further from the truth. Garibaldi received so little help from the government that some would-be volunteers had to be sent home for lack of funds to feed them, and the very ships that transported the 'Thousand' to Sicily had to be stolen. The government even refused the release of 12 000 of Garibaldi's own guns stored in a police arsenal in Milan.

Why then, if it did not support Garibaldi, did the government allow the expedition to gather on Piedmontese soil and to sail from a Piedmontese port? The answer seems to be provided by Cavour in a letter to Nigra the day after the expedition had landed in Sicily. 'I could not stop his going, for force would have been necessary. And the ministry is in no position to face the immense unpopularity which would have been drawn upon it had Garibaldi been prevented'. Cavour's ministry did, indeed, face a major cabinet revolt at that time in protest against the cession of Nice and Savoy to France. Thus, torn between his dislike for Garibaldi's radicalism and the dangers of international objections, and the danger of offending the many Italians who loved and admired Garibaldi, the pragmatic Cavour kept his mouth shut and his options open and waited upon the outcome of the expedition. The astounding success of the 'Thousand' forced Cavour's hand. A successful Garibaldini invasion of Naples would at best lead to a prestigious, radical regime in the south disputing the leadership of Italy with Piedmont, and at worst might precipitate a further international war in Italy over the status of the Papacy. Writing to Nigra once more, Cavour clearly outlined the dangers of the moment. 'If Garibaldi passes over to the mainland and seizes the Kingdom of Naples and its capital, as he has done with Sicily and Palermo, he becomes absolute master of the situation. King Victor Emmanuel loses more or less all his prestige; in the eyes of the great majority of Italians he is no more than Garibaldi's friend. . . . With the resources of a kingdom of 9 000 000 inhabitants at his disposal, surrounded as he is by irresistable popular prestige, it is impossible for us to struggle against him'.

Cavour's first attempts to avert such disaster went sadly wrong. Agents were sent into the Kingdom of Naples to stir up a pro-Piedmontese revolt that would preempt Garibaldi, but they only encountered the general apathy that had bedevilled generations of Italian revolutionaries. On the 22nd August 1860, Garibaldi finally crossed the Straits of Messina and landed in mainland Naples. With the general population showing no serious inclination to protect him against the invader, Francis II abandoned Naples on 6th September, and it was occupied by the Garibaldini the following day. Cavour rose to the occasion with perhaps the greatest piece of opportunism of his career. On 12th September he informed the European powers that Piedmont had no option but to intervene in the Papal territories to restore order. Opposition from Papal forces was brushed aside six days later at Castelfidardo, and by 1st October the Neapolitan forces between the two sets of invaders had ceased to resist. At a dramatic meeting at Teano, north of the city of Naples, on 26th October, Garibaldi faced the choice of acknowledging the precedence of the King of Piedmont or fighting him. He chose to hand over his conquests to Victor Emmanuel, and to retire voluntarily to his island home of Caprera. Plebiscites were held with the now customary haste and by the end of 1860 these had sanctioned the union, not only of the Kingdom of Naples, but also of the Papal territories of Umbria and the Marches with Piedmont, signified by the new title of the Kingdom of Italy.

(k) The Difficulties of the New Kingdom: Economic

The new kingdom of Italy, officially in existence from March, 1861, had to face the future without the talents of the man who had done more than anyone else to establish it, and to ensure that Piedmont would dominate it. Cavour died unexpectedly on 6th June 1861, exhausted by the problems and tensions of the last few years. His aims had undoubtedly been very different from those of Mazzini and of Garibaldi, and his relations with his king had rarely been better than cool and suspicious. By his masterly flexibility in the face of great political and emotional forces that he could not directly control, however, he fully deserved the place with which he was credited by the English poet Meredith in the creation of Italy:

'We think of those
Who blew the breath of life into her frame:
Cavour, Mazzini, Garibaldi: Three:
Her Brain, her Soul, her Sword; and set her free
From ruinous discords . . .'.

Unfortunately, Italy was very far from being 'free from ruinous discords'. She had been formed hastily, imperfectly, and against the will of many, and now had to face the cost of Cavour's policies. In Cavour's place followed a succession of men, Ricasoli (1861–62), Rattazzi (March–December 1862), Farini (1862–63), Minghetti (1863–64) and La Marmora (1864–66). None of these was of the calibre of their great predecessor, and most of them had been kept relatively ignorant of the details of government by Cavour's virtual monopoly of the major cabinet posts.

Of the three prime difficulties that faced these men, the most glaring was the state of the Italian economy. Not only did the new kingdom have to cope with the huge deficit of 2450 million lire incurred by Cavour to carry through his policies of 1856 (which cost 50 million lire) and 1859 (which cost a further 250 million), but it also inherited the debts of the smaller regimes that he had helped to oust from other parts of Italy. It was assumed that a modern state would need certain trappings, such as new roads, railways, and military equipment. The construction of a sizeable modern navy, especially, was a foolish luxury when Italy's most likely enemy, Austria, was only a very moderate naval power. The result was heavy and unpopular taxation, such as Sella's flour tax proposed in 1865, and the negotiation of large foreign loans often on humiliating terms. By the middle of the 1860s, more than a third of Italy's government bonds were in foreign hands and most Italian railway shares were owned by non-Italians.

Italy faced these problems with a main industry, agriculture, so deeply in debt that 30% of each year's product was estimated to be eaten up in repayments, and so archaic in its methods that the economist Nassau Senior considered that cereal production in the south had scarcely increased its output since the days of the Roman Empire. Furthermore, it proved impossible to extend Cavour's principles of financial and industrial modernisation to the rest of Italy. Conservative attitudes in central and southern Italy included a distrust of paper money and a condemnation of financial borrowing and lending as immoral. Agriculture so dominated the lives of the working classes that the census of 1861 indicated only 3 million people employed in industrial production,

of whom 80% were women or children sharing their time between this and agriculture. The textile industry and the production of some chemicals, such as sulphur, had potential, but in an age dominated by coal Italy lacked sources of energy until the development of hydro-electric power enabled her to exploit her considerable water resources.

(I) The Difficulties of the New Kingdom: The Southern Question

The greatest rival in severity to Italy's economic problems was the 'Southern Question', the difficulties that arose from the social, economic and political diversity of the Italian regions. The huge majorities recorded in favour of unity in 1860–61 proved to convey a dangerously misleading impression. They constituted a vote against a number of things, the tyranny and incompetence of previous rulers and the lawlessness of rebellious peasants, for example. They probably also represented a considerable degree of electoral malpractice. An observer of the Nice plebiscite, for instance, noted that the slips necessary for a 'no' vote were often in short supply and sometimes missing altogether, and this was probably true in many cases in the south. What those who voted 'yes' were really voting for was not absolutely clear. United Italy could take one of at least two forms, a federal state, in which the regions retained much of their local autonomy, or a centralised one, wholly governed from one national capital. Cavour seems to have considered both, but in the last months of his life had firmly set his face against the federal solution. The reasons are not altogether clear. It is true that federalism seemed to have failed in the world's greatest federal state, the USA, which stood on the verge of civil war in 1861. It is difficult to avoid the conclusion that above all federalism threatened the domination of Piedmont within Italy, and that Cavour's decision was taken to impose a rapid solution upon a problem that he had not expected to arise so suddenly.

Italy thus became 'Piedmontised' at an almost indecent rate. The legal system of Naples, for example, was revolutionised by the passage of 53 decrees in only two days in February, 1861. 'Piedmontism' involved the division of the Kingdom into 53 provinces on the model of the French departments, each governed by a prefect. Customs, coinage, weights, and measures were standardised in theory, although the illegal use of old coinage and measures persisted at least until the end of the century. The Italian constitution was, in effect, an expanded version of the Piedmontese constitution. There were 443 members of the assembly elected by a mere 150 000 voters who fulfilled the dual qualification of paying 40 lire per year in taxes, and being literate. Thus, on average, each deputy was elected by about 300 voters.

'Piedmontism' had two great drawbacks. One was the daunting degree of ignorance that existed in all parts of Italy about the other parts. In particular, the ignorance of the north about conditions in Naples and Sicily applied to all levels of government. Cavour himself, although he had visited France, Britain and Switzerland, had never travelled further south than Tuscany. The policy thus resulted in a bizarre series of misconceptions and mistakes. Compulsory education was prescribed for southern Italy and in Sicily, where 90% of the population was illiterate, but it could not be paid for without attacking the property of the Church. The dissolution of 2382 monasteries and convents by 1866 provided some funds, but outraged local religious feelings, and deprived the localities of charitable institutions run by the monks and nuns, long before the state could afford to replace them. The jury system was introduced throughout the south despite the protests of local authorities that Mafia activity would make the corruption and intimidation of juries a simple matter.

Allied to ignorance, the second drawback was a simple lack of resources, both financial and human. The south, it was fondly imagined by men who had never been there, was rich in minerals. Instead it proved a drain upon the resources of the north, and Piedmont, unlike Prussia in the case of German unification, had neither the income nor the trained manpower effectively to administer its new territories. One important effect was explained in detail by Pasquale Villari, a Neapolitan professor of history, writing in 1866. 'In schools, for instance, the provincial governments in Sicily and Naples . . . made elementary education compulsory; but teachers, administrators and inspectors were all lacking and had to be improvised in a hurry. So the Piedmontese elementary teacher became a headmaster . . . and sometimes he who at Turin had been an excellent teacher, in southern Italy now became a bad headmaster or inspector. This one example was multiplied a hundred times'.

'The imposition of the Piedmontese administrative system', concludes D. Mack-Smith, 'reinforced the impression that one region had virtually conquered the rest'. Predictably the southern regions reacted as they had done against earlier injustices. What the national government referred to as 'campaigns for the suppression of brigandage' amounted in fact to a full scale civil war in the south, which was not effectively settled in the central government's favour until 1865, and which claimed more Italian lives than all the battles of the 'Risorgimento' put together. In 1863 alone, the government committed 90 000 troops to peacekeeping operations in the south, far more than had ever taken the field against the Austrians.

It was not realistic to expect that such deep rooted difficulties would be solved within a mere decade. The processes of road building, agricultural reform and educational improvement were still far from complete by the outbreak of the First World War. It is, therefore, not surprising that the official utterances of the Italian government attempted to concentrate public attention as far as possible upon the third of the new kingdom's outstanding problems.

(m) The Difficulties of the New Kingdom: The Venetian Question

The government of Victor Emmanuel in 1861 owed much of its continued prestige to the opportunism that had identified it with the national cause through its intervention in Naples. It was thus very difficult, especially at a time of such extreme domestic difficulties, for that government to ignore the fact that in the eyes of the nationalist there were still two important pieces missing from the Italian 'jigsaw'. Upon taking office, Ricasoli was quick to assure Italians that 'we claim Rome as our natural capital and Venetia as an integral part of our national soil'. Rome and Venice, however, were not Naples. To gain either of them would mean dealing with one or more of the great powers at a time when nearly half of the Italian army was fighting its reluctant compatriots in the south.

The first moves towards a solution to the 'Venetian Question' were thus made by men to whom such diplomatic niceties were of little concern, by Garibaldi and his 'Party of Action'. Assuming that what had worked in Naples would work in Venetia, they were active in 1862 attempting to engineer an armed rising, and again in 1864 pinning their hopes this time upon risings elsewhere in the Hapsburg Empire which would draw Austrian troops out of Italy. In both cases the protests of foreign diplomats when news leaked out, caused the Italian government to intervene to scotch Garibaldi's plans.

Instead, like all the other component parts of the 'Italian Question', except Naples, the Venetian Question had to wait for a solution until the general mood of European politics was ready. The decline of Austria's relations with Prussia in the course of the Schleswig-Holstein affair in 1864 alerted both Prussians and Italians to the common ground in their foreign policies, and to the common benefits that might result from action against Austria. Italian enthusuasm was not absolute. Victor Emmanuel continued to believe, in Mack-Smith's words, that 'the important thing was to have a war, and as soon as possible'. To his anti-constitutional motives of 1859 he now added the desire to distract attention from the problems in the south. La Marmora, however, recalled the pitfalls of playing the role of junior partner to a major power. Hence his offer to purchase Venetia from an anxious Austrian government for 1000 million lire. When the initial enthusiasm of the Emperor was overridden by the military faction in Vienna, the Italian government had little option but to enter into closer negotiations with Prussia. By April 1866, General Govone's mission to Berlin had concluded a military agreement by which both sides undertook not to conclude a separate peace, thus hoping to avoid another Villafranca, and by which Italy was to receive Venetia as the reward for her role.

On 20th June, four days after Prussia, Italy formally declared herself at war with Austria once more.

(n) The War of 1866

After the great gains of 1859–60, Italians' expectations were high and the King himself was, according to one of his ministers, 'quite drunk with over confidence'. In theory, the confidence was quite justified. Italy could expect to put some 250 000 men into the field against the 130 000 that the divided Austrian army could spare for its southern front. The fleet, too, after the recent spending 'spree', could count twelve ironclad battleships of the most modern design, to Austria's seven. In reality these advantages were to be outweighed by other factors. The Italian General Staff 'was not notable for military skill and experience' (Mack-Smith), and many, like the fleet's commander Admiral Persano, owed their positions primarily to influence and corruption at court. In any case, it was conveniently overlooked that it was not these men, but guerrillas and Frenchmen who had won the great battles of the

'Risorgimento'. Even below the highest levels of command, organisation was so bad and planning so rudimentary that only about 25% of the army ever reached the front. Once there, the unfortunate troops found strategy paralysed by bitter personal rivalries between prominent officers, and by the presence of a monarch who insisted upon taking overall personal command despite the opinion of General Cialdini that 'the king is wholly ignorant and incompetent'.

Thus the confidence did not last long. On 24th June, La Marmora's and Cialdini's forces fought an indecisive action against a strong Austrian defensive position at Custoza, close to the 1848 battlefield, but then disintegrated due to panic and to confused orders, which seem to have been in no small part the fault of Victor Emmanuel. The engagement wrecked the reputations of La Marmora and Cialdini and burst the 'bubble' of Italian military pride. A month later, Persano's fleet engaged the Austrian fleet off the island of Lissa in the Adriatic, and in the midst of similar confusion lost three major ships including the *Re d'Italia*, the pride of the Italian navy. It was claimed at Persano's court martial that the fleet had fired 1450 shells without scoring a major hit on the enemy. Neither battle was a serious defeat in military terms, and casualties were low, 750 at Custoza and 600 at Lissa. These factors allowed nationalist and monarchist historians such as Volpe and Monti in subsequent years almost to represent the war as a success. Indeed, the crushing defeat inflicted by the Prussians upon the Austrians at Sadowa (3rd July) brought about an armistice (26th July) by which Italy gained Venetia after all. At the time, however, it was impossible to see the war as anything other than a miserable failure. Almost all the aims of the government had been frustrated. It had brought none of the glory or heroism necessary to weld the disparate parts of the country into a nationally conscious whole, it had done great harm to the prestige of both the army and the monarchy, and Venetia had only come into Italian hands, just as Lombardy had done in 1859, through the triumph of a foreign army. Once again there had been no Venetian uprising in support of the Italian forces, and the blindest of patriots could hardly have failed to notice that the huge majority recorded in the subsequent plebiscite in favour of union with the rest of Italy (641 000 votes to 69) hardly squared with Venetian apathy during the war itself. 'Above all', concluded Pasquale Villari, 'the war destroyed many illusions as well as destroying our unlimited self-confidence. Never again can we look at ourselves quite as we used to do'.

(o) The Continuing Problem of Rome

The failures of 1866 rendered even bleaker the Italian government's prospects of establishing its capital in Rome. In the five years since Garibaldi had been checked on the Pope's frontiers, two main methods had been pursued for gaining access to Rome, with little success.

The first solution, of course, had been that of the 'Party of Action'. Dismissing the power of the Papacy as a 'tottering shanty', Garibaldi seems to have regarded Rome as an easier target than Naples had been. In this judgement he was wrong on three counts. Firstly, he would be forced to confront the French garrison as well as the small Papal army. Secondly he would probably have to face the army of his own government, who could not permit 'banditry' to prejudice their diplomatic relations with France, and could not contemplate the humiliation of acquiring their capital city from a revolutionary. Thirdly, he was once more badly mistaken in hoping that his actions might spark off a popular revolt within the Papal territories. The Church, A. J. Whyte observes, was at the heart of the region's economy, and was unlikely to be attacked by the populace that it supported. 'The Church amused them, employed them and fed them, and to her they looked alike for consolation in trouble and material help in times of stress'.

Nevertheless, the idealism of Garibaldi and the highly ambiguous attitude of the King and some of his ministers twice tempted the 'Party of Action' into projects that caused the government acute embarrassment. Firstly, in August 1862, an expedition that could easily have been intercepted had the Italian fleet had clearer orders, landed at Aspromonte in Calabria. It had to be checked by government troops. Five years later, in October 1867, the provisional withdrawal of the French troops gave Garibaldi another opportunity. At Mentana (3rd November), however, his forces were defeated by the Papal troops, reinforced at the last moment by the hurriedly returning Frenchmen.

The second possible solution was by means of diplomacy. It seemed unlikely, however, that the Italian government, after a decade of pronounced anti-clericalism, would achieve much by direct negotiation with the Church. Throughout the 'Risorgimento' the reaction of the Papacy to changing social and political circumstances was, in the words of A. J. Whyte, 'to bind her medieval robe more closely around her'. This process of restating her inflexible position culminated in the publication, in December 1864, of the encyclical *Quanta Cura* which listed a 'Syllabus of Errors' of 80 points. Among the 'errors' were the principle of liberty of conscience, of state education, of liberalism, of constitutional government, and of opposition to the Temporal Power of the Pope. It was an attack upon most of the progressive ideas of western Europe in the 19th century, and as such most embarrassing to all progressive Catholics. It was also a manifesto of opposition to most of the professed ideas of the Italian government.

Negotiations with France were rather more fruitful. Napoleon III had long regretted the expense and political inconvenience involved in protecting a stubborn and reactionary Pope, but could not agree to abandon him to the 'bandits' who had set up the Roman Republic in 1849. After 1862 it was possible to claim that the encounter at Aspromonte indicated that the responsible Italian government effectively had Garibaldi under its control. By 1864, therefore, the French were willing to enter into highly secret negotiations which resulted in the so-called Convention of September. This was an agreement whereby France consented to remove her garrison from Rome in return for an Italian undertaking to protect Papal territory from all external attack. A number of sympathetic commentators have been tempted to admire a move by which, in A. J. Whyte's words, 'the wolves were set to guard the fold'. D, Mack-Smith opposes this view, too, by pointing out that the Italian diplomats must either have been lying deliberately to the French, or else deliberately breaking their promises to the Italian electors concerning Rome.

(p) The Acquisition of Rome

Whatever the motives behind it, the Convention of September did not bring the Italians any closer to making their capital in Rome. The withdrawal of French troops in December 1866 was reversed by the Mentana fiasco less than a year later, and the situation remained one of stalemate and confrontation until 1870. Then, as usual, Italy's problems were resolved by European factors quite beyond Italy's control. The drift of France towards war with Prussia offered two openings to Italy. The first was diplomatic when, in May 1870, Napoleon III sought a basis for an anti-Prussian alliance. For all the doubts about fighting against her most recent ally, Italy suggested Rome as the price of her co-operation. For the French Catholics, the price remained too high. The outbreak of war, however, presented Italy with an opportunity that public opinion would not permit her to miss. France's Roman garrison could no longer be spared and, by 19th August, the evacuation was complete. The Prime Minister, Giovanni Lanza, still acted

D

with great caution, waiting until the defeat of France at Sedan, the formal agreement of Spain, Austria, and the Catholic German states, and the arrest of Mazzini ensured that there would be no unfortunate side effects. The modest Papal army was overcome in a brief engagement on 19th September 1870, as a result of which Rome was at last occupied by the Italian army.

The usual plebiscite (2nd October) produced the usual result, indicating a huge majority in favour of union with the rest of Italy (133 681 to 1507). Again the result contradicted the previous indifference of the population, and a French officer in the Papal army, the Comte de Beaufort, published a detailed account of alleged dishonesty at the polls. This included the absence of 'No' voting slips, intimidation, plural voting, and the introduction of non-qualified voters. His account is, perhaps, a fair representation of the plebiscites of the 'Risorgimento'.

It was one thing to win Rome, and quite another to win the Church's acceptance of the fact. Stripped of his temporal power, for instance, Pius IX made his supreme act of defiance in July 1870 by declaring the doctrine of Papal Infallibility. In May 1871 by the Law of Guarantees, the Italian government made a further gesture of conciliation as it sought to define the position of the Pope within the Kingdom of Italy. The full spiritual jurisdiction of the Pope was recognised, freedom of communication with the Church throughout the world was confirmed, along with liberty of appointment to all ecclesiastical offices, and liberty of teaching. The Pope received an annual grant equivalent to £129 000, remained free of Italian taxation, and retained the full use of the Vatican and of Castel Gandolfo. Typically, Pius IX chose to remain a 'prisoner in the Vatican', and not until 1929 was the Italian state formally recognised by the Papacy.

(q) Historiography

The historiography of the 'Risorgimento' is affected by problems just the opposite of those posed by the study of Napoleon III. Whereas the failures of the French Emperor prejudiced most early, and some later accounts of his work, the success of the movements for the unification of Italy led to the obscuring of many less palatable aspects of the story, and the undue glorification of other aspects and individuals. Two 'schools' of historians were prominent in this process. The first was the 'official' or nationalist Italian historians such as D. Zanichelli, (*Politics and History: Discourses and Studies*,

1903), A. Monti (*Figures and Characters of the Risorgimento*, 1939), and A. Oriani (*Quartet*, 1923). The dates of publication of the last two works will serve to indicate that this school of thought enjoyed a new lease of life in Fascist Italy, again for reasons of nationalism. For Zanichelli the Risorgimento was 'the most important fact of the 19th century', while Victor Emmanuel benefited especially from this adulation, being hailed by Oriani as 'the grandest and most glorious sovereign in the history of Christian Europe'.

The second very sympathetic 'school' consisted of those historians of western Europe and the USA who saw in the unification of Italy the triumph of liberalism and modernism. Most notable among these was perhaps the great Italian Benedetto Croce (*A History of Italy, 1871–1915*, 1929), and the Englishman G. M. Trevelyan (*Garibaldi and the Making of Italy*, 1911). While Trevelyan laid substantial stress upon the role of Garibaldi, A. J. Whyte (*The Political Life and Letters of Cavour*, 1930) and the American W. R. Thayer (*The Life and Times of Cavour*, 1911) emphasised the contribution of the great Piedmontese statesman. Thayer, in particular, was extremely hostile towards Mazzini, whose activities he saw as a major hindrance to the process of unification.

The rise of fascism in Italy in the 1920s, and the considerable political difficulties of the country since World War II have, however, caused a great diversification of views on its earlier history. Indeed, it is interesting to note that A. J. Whyte's view in *The Evolution of Modern Italy* published in 1944 was already less sympathetic. Above all, republican and socialist writers have done much to draw attention to the positive achievements of Mazzini. Luigi Salvatorelli (*The Thought and Action of the Risorgimento*, 1944) has pointed out the role that Mazzinians such as Orsini played in the development of the events of the 1850s and 1860s, and Adolfo Omodeo (*The Political Work of Cavour*, 1945) stressed that Mazzini's role as radical 'bogey man' provided Cavour with an important tool in his dealings with the great powers. The communist view of the Risorgimento may be represented by Antonio Gramsci who, writing in prison during Mussolini's rule (*The Risorgimento*, 1949) attacked all the major leaders, including Mazzini, for neglecting the rural discontent in which lay the potential for a true social and economic revolution.

Catholic historians constitute another group that has, of course, taken a hostile view of the pragmatism and anti-clericalism of the Italian and Piedmontese states. E.E.Y. Hales, for instance, (*Pio Nono; a Study in European Politics and Religion in the 19th Century*, 1954) defends the attitude of Pius IX towards the Italian state by pointing to the repeated bad faith of Italian and Piedmontese politicians.

In recent years the debate on the unification of Italy has been dominated by the work of Denis Mack-Smith. His main contribution to the argument has been to discredit any idea of Cavour operating to a master plan for unification and to stress the element of improvisation in his policies, to stress the consistent hostility between Cavour and Garibaldi (*Cavour and Garibaldi, 1860*, 1954), and to combat the myth of Victor Emmanuel as an idealistic patriot and father of his country (*Victor Emmanuel, Cavour and the Risorgimento*, 1971).

Progress Paragraphs

Answer the following questions in about 150 words.

Why did so many Italian liberals look to Piedmont for leadership after 1848?   Section (**a**)

In what sense should Cavour be regarded as a liberal?
                                                                                        Sections (**b & c**)

In what sense should Cavour be regarded as a nationalist?   Section (**b**)

By what means did Piedmont achieve the economic leadership of Italy?   Section (**c**)

Why did Piedmont participate in the Crimean War, and why did she gain from her participation?
                                                                                        Section (**d**)

What were the main developments in Piedmont's relations with (a) Austria and (b) France between 1856–59?   Section (**e**)

To what extent was Piedmont dependent upon France for the successes of 1859?   Section (**f**)

By what means did Cavour extend Piedmontese control over the Central Italian Duchies?
                                                                                        Section (**g**)

Why has Garibaldi been such a popular figure among writers on Italian unification?   Section (**h**)

Why did Garibaldi undertake the Sicilian expedition of 1860?   Section (**i**)

Why did Cavour eventually intervene in Naples following Garibaldi's invasion?   Section (**j**)

What were the economic consequences for the Kingdom of Italy of its unification? Section (**k**)

What were the origins of Italy's 'southern question'?
                                                                                        Section (**l**)

By what means was Venetia eventually added to the Kingdom of Italy?   Sections (**m & n**)

Why could the Kingdom of Italy not acquire Rome as its capital until 1870?   Sections (**o & p**)

What position did the Papacy choose to take up within the Kingdom of Italy in 1870?
                                                                                        Section (**p**)

5
The Unification of Germany

(a) 1850: Erfurt to Olmutz

Viewed in terms of constitutional change, or of lasting social development, the events of 1848–49 had made as little lasting impression upon Germany as upon Italy. In the short term, however, the revolutionary events appeared to have had one notable consequence. The prestige of the Prussian state was at a higher level than for many years following her role in recent German affairs, while Austria was still engaged elsewhere with her Imperial affairs. Also, the German Confederation could be regarded as defunct following the recent constitutional eruptions. How could the vacuum in princely German politics be filled without risking the revival of radical, nationalist ideas? This was the question that Baron J. von Radowitz, adviser to the King of Prussia on federal reform for more than twenty years, tried to answer in a set of proposals put to a representative assembly of the German states at Erfurt in March 1850. These included a union of the North German states under the presidency of the King of Prussia, and under the protection of the victorious Prussian army. For Friedrich Wilhelm, the great advantage of such a plan was that Prussian influence would be based upon sound monarchical principles and not, as the offer of the German crown had been in 1849, upon the principle of popular sovereignty. In general, Austria would be excluded from this 'Erfurt Union', although von Radowitz also proposed a compromise. This was that Austria might be linked to the Union by a second, wider union, based upon free trade and perhaps also upon a common foreign policy.

In effect, von Radowitz was moving too far too fast. The only real basis for the Erfurt Union was the fear of the German princes at the prospect of renewed liberal onslaught. He and Friedrich Wilhelm, as A. J. P. Taylor has put it, 'thought the princes converted [to the idea of a "Kleindeutsch" union] when they were merely frightened'. In fact, it was already evident that many of the 'middling' German states feared Prussian hegemony as much as, if not more than, liberal revolt. Hence the refusal of eleven states, including Hanover, Bavaria, Saxony and Wurttemberg, to send representatives to Erfurt. The insuperable weakness of the proposals was that they arose from an Austrian withdrawal from German affairs that was only temporary. By late 1850, with the Hungarian and Italian revolts under control, the Austrian premier F. von Schwarzenberg was able to declare that 'we shall not let ourselves be thrown out of Germany', and began to insist upon the reconstitution of the Confederation as it had existed before 1848.

A constitutional conflict in the small duchy of Hesse-Cassel, which formed the vital link between the two blocks of Prussian territory, provided the test of nerves between the two German powers. With the alternatives of seeking aid from the Erfurt Union, or from the Confederation, Hesse-Cassel turned to the latter. For a while, Prussia seemed willing to fight to defend her new found prestige, but Russian support for Austria, as demonstrated against the Hungarians, proved the decisive factor. 'Only the Tsar is sovereign', wrote Karl Marx at the time. 'In the end rebellious Prussia will bow to his command'. So indeed, at a meeting at Olmutz (November 1850), Friedrich Wilhelm gave in once more to his doubts and to the doubts of many of the Prussian conservatives, agreeing to abandon the Erfurt Union in favour of the revival of the German Confederation under Austrian presidency. By the so-called 'Capitulation of Olmutz', Prussia abandoned the leadership of Germany for a decade and a half. Prussian reactions to the fact ranged between conservative satisfaction and the abandonment of a dangerous innovation, to patriotic humiliation. All were aware that German leadership remained beyond Prussia's reach until a change in the military balance of Germany, and in the European system of alliances took place.

(b) Prussia and Austria, 1850–60

The political life of Germany in the 1850s has been dismissed by A. Ramm as a period of 'sterile parliamentarianism within the states and sterile

MAP 5   GERMANY AND CENTRAL EUROPE 1815–66

SCHLESWIG

HOLSTEIN

MECKLENBURG
SCHWERIN

EAST
PRUSSIA

HANOVER

PRUSSIA

● BERLIN

ESSEN ●
● COLOGNE

MINOR
STATES

PRUSSIA

HESSE
CASSEL

MINOR
STATES

SAXONY

BRESLAU ●

LUXEMBURG

HESSE
DARMSTADT

PRAGUE ● ✕ SADOWA

OLMUTZ ●

ALSACE-
LORRAINE

BADEN

WURTEMBERG

BAVARIA

MUNICH ●

VIENNA ●

● MILAN

● VENICE

KEY

LIMITS OF GERMAN CONFEDERATION 1815–66

SOUTHERN BORDER OF NORTH GERMAN CONFEDERATION
1866

KINGDOM OF PRUSSIA (1865)

AUSTRIAN EMPIRE

diplomacy without'. The charge of sterility is certainly true in the sense that all formal initiatives for a further constitutional development of Germany, like those of 1850, came to nothing.

Between 1851–53, Austrian statesmen attempted to consolidate and exploit the position of supremacy in German affairs manifested at Olmutz. Firstly, Schwarzenberg proposed the extension of the Confederation to include Austria's non-German territories, thus forming an 'Empire of 70 millions' indisputably under Austrian control. When this was rejected by the German princes assembled at Dresden (mid 1851), Austrian proposals switched to an economic tack. A. Bach, Minister of the Interior, and Baron von Bruck, the former Rhineland liberal in charge of Austrian finances, proposed the linking of the Prussian dominated Zollverein (see section **d**) with the Empire to produce a vast central European (Mitteleuropa) economic union. The Austrians, however, were overplaying their hand. Olmutz had restored the balance between Austrian military power and Prussian economic power upon which the independence of the lesser princes depended. These princes had no intention of seeing Austria upset that balance, and their independence, again. She had, therefore, to be content with a commercial treaty with Prussia, acting as spokesman for the Zollverein, signed in February 1853.

It cannot be said, however, that this decade was sterile in the sense that no development took place at all. In Germany, as in most of Europe, the Crimean War acted as a great catalyst to political change. Despite the debt that his state owed the Russians since 1849, the foreign minister Buol believed that Austria should conclude an alliance with the western powers, as a safeguard against nationalist action in Italy. He also had no desire to see Russia in control of Moldavia, Wallachia and the mouth of the Danube. This line necessitated an understanding with Prussia to ensure that she would not seek to benefit in Germany from Austria's preoccupation as she had done in 1850. Prussian opinion, however, was bitterly divided, with conservatives favouring a pro-Russian policy, while the liberals favoured France and Britain. In the end, Friedrich Wilhelm followed the least controversial line, that of neutrality. Thus neither of the German powers played a military role in the war, although Austria maintained a highly benevolent attitude towards the allies. The events of the Crimea did, however, effect a number of subtle changes in the German 'status quo'. Firstly, Austria's concerns had been shown to be purely Imperial, rather than German. Her diplomacy had been dominated by thoughts of Moldavia, the

Danube, and Italy, and her aims had been caricatured by Bismarck as being 'to procure a few stinking Wallachians'. Secondly, her failure to repay her debt to Russia had ruptured forever the 'Holy Alliance' between the two great legitimist powers, leaving Austria isolated in European diplomacy. Prussia, although also neutral, owed Russia no such debt, and her neutrality had at least granted Russia security on her Polish borders. In German terms, as A. Ramm stresses, the Crimean War was a depressing episode, proving her remoteness from the great decisions of European politics, and confirming her 'international nullity'. H. Bohme prefers to judge it in Prussian terms, as a period of great advance in prestige within Germany, as Austria's national and international prestige sank.

The Italian War of 1859 continued the process of Austrian humiliation. In H. Bohme's words, 'Austria now buried her plans for a Customs Union, her German policy and her economic policy on the battlefields of northern Italy'. As a legitimist, the Prussian regent Prince Wilhelm inclined towards aid for Austria, but Austria's alienation of all the other European powers made this a dangerous course to take. In the event, Prussia delayed mobilisation of her forces until Austria's defeat was virtually assured (July 1859). She then mobilised in concert with the South German princes, and with a view to protecting the Rhine frontier against further French expansion. Thus Prussia appeared to be making a gesture for the protection of Germany at a time when it was becoming increasingly difficult to believe in Austrian protection. 1860, furthermore, with Napoleon III's annexation of Nice and Savoy, brought further cause for the princes to believe in the need for protection against French aggression. When Napoleon visited Baden Baden in an attempt to dispel this anxiety (June 1860) he found himself faced with a phalanx of rulers, from Bavaria, Hanover, Saxony and Wurttemberg, united in their apprehension. In general, the European events of 1856–60 marked the beginning of German confidence in Prussia's military capacity in addition to her undoubted economic capacity.

(c) The Prussian Army

In 1850, the prospect of far-ranging conquests by the Prussian army seemed remote. That army still rested very heavily upon the tactics and traditions of the Napoleonic Wars. Indeed, as W. McElwee has stated 'to the outward eye the Prussian army in 1859 was as clumsy and antiquated an instrument as any of the others'. The mobilisation of that year seemed to confirm as much, but in fact, at that very point, the Prussian military establishment was in the midst of a process of transformation.

The key date in the process was perhaps 1857, the year in which Helmut von Moltke was appointed as Chief of Staff. Von Moltke was an unusually cultured and humane man to lead a great national army. 'Every war', he wrote later in his life, 'even one that is victorious, represents a great national misfortune'. Even the great triumph of 1870 was for him 'a step backwards into barbarism'. Politically, his brand of romantic patriotism was closer to that of King Wilhelm than to the realism of Bismarck. He was not primarily, however, a political animal. 'For Moltke', wrote G. Ritter, 'politics was an acquired interest rather than a congenial preoccupation and he was deeply concerned with it only when it directly touched the military sphere'.

In terms of numerical strength, the reforms of 1862 (see section **e**) put Moltke's army squarely on terms with that of Austria. Thereby 63 000 men were called up each year, for a total period of seven years, three of them in the standing army and four in the front line reserve, liable to instant recall in an emergency. This gave a standing army of 180 000, with a fully trained reserve of 175 000. In 1866, therefore, Prussia could mobilise 370 000, including some 'Landwehr' units. As they had far fewer security commitments on other frontiers, they were able to outnumber their enemy on the Bohemian front by 278 000 to 271 000.

As important as numbers was the superior organisation of the Prussian army. The Prussian General Staff had its origins in the War Academy founded by the great military theorist C. von Clausewitz in the Napoleonic era. Not only did it produce officers of great expertise and professionalism, but guaranteed a uniformity of practice and doctrine in all branches of the army. At Moltke's insistence, for example, all senior officers devoted much attention to the adaptation of modern transport and industrial methods to military needs. By comparison, the Austrian army remained dominated by such senior commanders as Gyulai and Wimpffen, who owed their rank more to influence at court than to proven ability, and was riddled with inefficiency. Out of a theoretical force of 600 000 men in 1866, bad reserve training and the practice of allowing the well off to buy themselves out of military service reduced the fighting force to about 350 000. Basic training in the standing army, furthermore, was so bad that it was estimated that two troopers out of three at the start of the 1859 Italian campaign were unable to load and fire their muskets.

Finally, the Prussian army undoubtedly led Europe in the application of industrial developments to military purposes. Not only were Prussian railways specifically planned with a view to swift transit from one distant frontier to another, but the General Staff operated a special department dedicated to the study of transport by rail. In both 1866 and 1870 this swift concentration of troops was a vital factor. In 1866, Prussia's five railway lines assembled her troops on the Bohemian frontier in 25 days against 45 days taken by the Austrians. In 1870, it proved possible to transport some units from East Prussia to Lorraine in only 36 hours. In terms of armament, the Prussian infantry was synonymous for some years with the Dreyse Needle Gun. First issued in 1848 and in general use by 1864, it fired at five times the rate of the old muzzle loader, and its effect at Sadowa caused the 'Times' correspondent to declare that 'the Needle Gun is king'. Nevertheless, it had its limitations in range and in accuracy, and the victory of 1870 owed more to the Prussian artillery. Equipped by the mid-1860s with a new Krupp breech loader, with cooled steel barrel and a breech sealed against escaping gases, the techniques of this branch of the army were perfected in the new School of Gunnery founded in swift reaction to the superior performance of the Austrian gunners at Sadowa.

(d) The Prussian Economy

Above all, two main factors coincided to ensure that Prussia's economy would become predominant among the economies of the German states. Firstly, Prussia was blessed with remarkable natural resources, supplemented by the gain in 1814–15 of the richly endowed territories of the Rhineland. Through the Ruhr Valley and west and south west across the Rhine lay substantial deposits of coal and iron ore. Rich coal resources were also available in the Saar Valley, in Prussian Silesia and in Upper Silesia, where zinc and iron deposits were also worked. Secondly, although private and foreign capital was prominent in the early promotion of these industries, Prussia was remarkable for the degree of government interest and involvement in their subsequent development. Although recent commentators, such as K. Borchardt, have stressed the haphazard and partial nature of government intervention, it undoubtedly affected some important areas. The contribution of F. von Motz, finance minister from 1825–30, included tax reforms and a road building programme. P. Beuth, head of the Department of Trade and Industry from 1815–45, did much to foster technical education. A sound Prussian banking system owed much to C. von Rother's reorganisation of the Bank of Prussia in 1846.

The greatest monument to this interest was the establishment of the German Customs Union (Zollverein) in 1834. This unit, with an area of 160 000 sq. miles, and a population of 23.5 millions, was the culmination of the process of creating smaller unions throughout the 1820s. Prussia benefited from the creation by securing the effective union of her eastern and western territories, and by establishing her economic influence above that of Austria in German affairs. Her leading position in the Zollverein was recognised by those clauses in the establishing treaty that accepted her tariffs as the norm for all, and which recognised the right of the Prussian government to negotiate on behalf of the Zollverein as a whole. This leadership was, indeed, effective, as witnessed by a dramatic rise in customs revenue from 14.5 million (1834) to 27.4 million thalers (1845). Also a string of treaties won favourable trading terms for the Zollverein with Piedmont, Holland (both 1851), Belgium (1852) and France (1862).

Prussia also took the leading role within Germany in the development of those branches of heavy industry vital to the modern and militarised state. Her iron and coal industries benefited substantially from the introduction of new technology. The number of steam engines operative in Prussian industry rose from 419 (1837) to 1444 (1848) at a time when the next best figure was Saxony's 197 (1846). Twenty-four new deep level mines were opened in the Ruhr coalfield between 1841–49, while new sources of zinc (Dortmund, Bonn), lead (Aachen) and blackband iron (Dortmund) were discovered and exploited in the late 1840s and early 1850s. Due also to rapid conversion from charcoal-smelting to coke-smelting, Prussia's output of iron rose sharply from 0.5 million to 1.29 million tons between 1852–57. Although private capital was once more of prime importance, government legislation once again played a helpful role in Prussia, as in the Mining Laws of 1851 and 1860 which freed mine owners from strict state supervision and halved taxes upon output. The laws subsequently did much to free mine labour from old guild restrictions upon mobility.

The rise of the Prussian steel industry may be measured by the rise of its greatest unit, the Krupp factories in Essen. Based upon a successful method of producing cast steel, Alfred Krupp's enterprise grew between 1826 and 1861 from a single foundry employing seven men to a vast complex employing 2000. In the next three years alone, thriving on military orders from the Prussian government, especially for modern artillery, the workforce trebled again. In all, Prussian steel production was seven times greater in 1864 than in 1848. The rate of economic growth within the Zollverein boundaries may be gauged from Table 5.1.

Although both Bavaria (1835) and Saxony (1837) were ahead of Prussia in the foundation of German railways, and although the Prussian government was no less suspicious about the new method of transport than were other states, the 1840s and 1850s saw a rapid transformation in their attitude. Appreciating eventually the advantages of east–west communications for economic and strategic purposes, Prussia was behind only Saxony in the foundation of a state owned line (1847), and then sought consistently to extend state influence over the system. Consequently, by 1860 55% of Prussian railways were worked by the state. Quite apart from its economic significance, the growth of the German rail system as a whole naturally played a considerable role in the process of 'shrinking' Germany and in stressing the insignificance of the lesser states. At every turn, therefore, in the examination of Prussian and German economic growth in the 1850s and 1860s, one is reminded of the famous judgement of J. M. Keynes that 'the German Empire was not founded on blood and iron, but on coal and iron'.

	1820	1840	1850	1870	
Railways	—	549	5822	18 560	kms.
Coal	1.0	—	6.9	29.4	million tons
Pig Iron	0.046	0.17	0.53	1.4	million tons

Table 5.1

(e) The Prussian Constitutional Crisis of 1860–62

The period between 1858–62 saw a transformation of Prussian domestic politics that turned a decade of sterility into a period of crisis that threatened to bring down the monarchy. The first element in this change was a change of monarch. In October 1858, the mental illness of Friedrich Wilhelm necessitated the appointment of his brother, Prince Wilhelm, as Regent. He succeeded to the throne upon his brother's death in 1860. Wilhelm was already 61 years old in 1858, his first political memories dating from the Napoleonic Wars. By 1848 he had the reputation of a strict conservative, but that was an oversimplification. He was, indeed, deeply attached to the principle of legitimate monarchy and to the traditions of Prussian military glory, but had been convinced of the need to adapt in the face of modern forces. As a man of honour, his attitude towards his brother's constitution was one of respect, 'not' as G. Mann has written, 'because he liked it, but because a king must stand by his sacred word'.

The second major development was the revival of the German national movement in the last years of the 1850s. The national question, in A. Ramm's words 'barely retained public interest' in the early 50s. In a negative sense, the absence of any German influence over events in the Crimea played a role in its revival. More positively, the partial success of Italian nationalism in 1859 also had an impact north of the Alps. Also of importance were the consistent efforts of the lesser German princes to reform the Confederation with a view to increased influence in foreign affairs. The revival culminated in the formation (1859) of the National Association (Nationalverein), directly inspired by the Italian National Society. The Association was banned in all major German states, but continued to look to Prussia for leadership, as Italians had looked towards Piedmont. Their reasons were similar too. The journalist J. Froebel wrote in 1859 that 'The German nation is sick of principles and doctrines, literary greatness and theoretical existance. What it demands is power, power, power. And to the man who offers it power it will offer honour, more honour than he can imagine'.

Thirdly, whether as a cause or result of the nationalist revival, came a marked resurgence in liberal political activity. In Prussia it manifested itself especially in the emergence of the Progress Party (Fortschrittpartei). Raised upon the anti-Austrian, anti-Russian and theoretically anti-militaristic foundations of traditional Prussian liberalism, it enjoyed great success in the first elections of the new decade. In the elections to the Landtag in January 1862 it won 83 seats in an assembly that contained only 16 conservatives. Three months later its strength rose to 136 seats while the conservatives fell to 11 and the 'old' Liberals fell from 95 to 47.

Such was the political temper of the Landtag that had to consider the proposals of the King and of his War Minister, A. von Roon, for the reform of the Prussian Army. These proposals were also in part a result of the crisis of 1859. The government's prime concern was with the size of the army for,

while the Prussian population had doubled since 1814, the annual intake of recruits had remained static at 40 000. Von Roon now proposed to increase this to 63 000, with 53 new regiments. He also hoped to transform the nature of the army by limiting the role played by the reserve militia (Landwehr). This was composed of part time soldiers who had finished their three years training and who, in his view, and on the evidence of the 1859 mobilisation, 'lacked the genuine soldierly spirit and had no firm discipline'. To the Liberal majority, however, the Landwehr had the advantages of being freer from the detested spirit of Junker militarism and of costing them far less in taxes. It also recalled fond memories of the 1813 'people's war' against Napoleon. Thus, von Roon was not only fighting a technical battle, but a class battle too.

By 1862 the dispute was already two years old, and the assembly has twice been deceived by the government into making temporary grants of money for the army. Angry and alienated, they now refused to sanction the national budget, leaving Willhelm to contemplate the possibility of abdication. Only as a desperate measure, and at the urgent prompting of von Roon, did he take the most important political decision of his life. He summoned to office a man closely identified with the far right of Prussian politics, the ambassador to Paris, Otto von Bismarck-Schonhausen.

Bismarck was not the man to be impressed by abstract principles, whether of Legitimism or of Constitutionalism. Nevertheless, his first attempts were to find grounds for compromise with the Landtag. Only when that failed did he take the determined course of adjourning their sitting (October 1862) and proceeding to collect and to spend the national budget whether they liked it or not. As theoretical justification, Bismarck exploited the 'Gap Theory' ('Luckentheorie'). He claimed that the constitution made the budget the joint responsibility of the two houses of the Assembly and the monarch, but failed to cater for the event of a disagreement between them. In that event, he claimed without much justification, the executive power reverted to the King. More important than any theory, however, was the knowledge that real power rather than moral rectitude lay in the hands of the government and with its 53 new regiments. 'The great questions of the day', he told the Landtag in his first and most famous speech of his ministerial career, 'will not be decided by speeches and the resolutions of majorities—that was the great mistake of 1848 and 1849—but by iron and blood'. For four years and through two wars, Bismarck was to direct Prussian affairs without a constitutionally approved budget, and in the face of continued parliamentary opposition.

(f) Bismarck

The new Minister President of Prussia was a man of 47 without any ministerial experience, and with extremely limited experience of government administration. Otto von Bismarck, greatly though he stressed his origins among the Prussian feudal aristocracy, was no ordinary Junker. His middle class mother had insisted upon an education in Berlin and at the University of Gottingen. Here he derived a veneer of student liberalism and literary radicalism, even if his swordsmanship and riotous living were more in line with typical Junker behaviour. From his Berlin schooldays came close acquaintance with members of leading Prussian families, even with the royal family, which would later serve him well. A. J. P. Taylor has attached great importance to Bismarck's psychological reaction against the middle class trappings of his early life. 'He was the highly educated sophisticated son of a highly educated sophisticated mother, masquerading as his slow witted father and living down his middle class origin by an exaggerated emphasis on the privileges of his class'. By nature he was intensely ambitious, rightly convinced of his superiority over the narrow minded conservatives that made up the Junker ranks, and intolerant of criticism to an extent that often brought on physical illness. From the time of his marriage (1847) he professed a simple, personal Protestant faith, but was able totally to divorce personal from political morality to an extent that was to alienate many of his early allies among Prussian conservatives.

This strange semi-Junker gained his first political experience almost by accident at the age of 32, sitting in the Prussian assembly in 1847 only as a substitute for a sick member. From this experience, and from the revolutionary events of 1848–49, he derived an intense hostility to radicalism. This was matched by a disdain for parliamentary 'talking shops' and a contempt for policies based upon abstract romanticism, whether of the Right or Left wing varieties. Having gained a powerful reputation on the extreme right of Prussian politics, he bitterly opposed the Erfurt Union as a 'shameful union with democracy'. He rejoiced when the Austrian pressure at Olmutz succeeded in maintaining the 'status quo'.

The 1850s constituted a crucial period in Bismarck's personal and political development. From 1850–58 he sat as Prussian representative in the Federal Assembly (Bundestag), apparently ideally suited to aid a reconciliation between the two great conservative forces in Germany. Indeed, contrary to his later autobiographical claims, his stance remained pro-Austrian until 1854. Many commentators have interpreted the transformation as deriving primarily from Bach's and Bruck's attempts to change the German 'status quo' in Austria's favour. For A. J. P. Taylor it is rather that the advent of the Crimean War convinced Bismarck of Austria's inability to perform the vital service that he required of her, namely the protection of conservative interests in Germany. Indeed, Bismarck wrote at the time 'I should be very uneasy if we sought refuge from a possible storm by hitching our trim and sea-worthy frigate to that worm-eaten old Austrian man-of-war'. It was not only his views that changed, but perhaps also the whole nature of his approach to political questions. For T. S. Hamerow, the main effect of these years was in 'converting a narrow-minded Junker into a skilled and subtle diplomat'.

By 1859, Bismarck was so out of sympathy with Austria that he could advise General von Alvensleben to 'march southwards with our whole army with boundary posts in our soldiers' knapsacks and drive them into the ground, either at Lake Constance or where Protestantism ceases to prevail'. His view was so out of keeping with Prince Wilhelm's concern for legitimacy that his reward was to be packed off as ambassador, first to St. Petersburg (1859) and then to Paris (1862).

Thus, Bismarck's beliefs and motives upon his advent to power may be sorted into three categories. Firstly, his political instincts were conservative, although his intellect taught him that conservative ends could now only be attained by harnessing more modern notions, such as industrialism and nationalism. Secondly, his allegiance was to Prussia. Not to 'the people' or to 'the nation' as that of the German nationalists was, but to the monarchical, Junker dominated state, which he valued as 'an organ of power, . . . a principle of order and authority'. Only when that state became nominally a German state did Bismarck's allegiance become German. Thirdly, Bismarck believed unswervingly in his own superior claim to exercise political power. 'He claimed', writes A. J. P. Taylor, 'to serve sometimes the King of Prussia, sometimes Germany, sometimes God. All three were cloaks for his own will'.

(g) The Bases of Bismarckian Foreign Policy

The British statesman Benjamin Disraeli recounted in later years a conversation that he claimed to have had with Bismarck in 1862. According to Disraeli, the then Prussian ambassador to Paris laid down a clear programme. 'As soon as the army shall have been brought into such a condition as to inspire respect, I shall seize the first best pretext to declare war against Austria, dissolve the German Diet and give national unity to Germany under Prussian leadership'. Recent historians' reactions to this have either been to dismiss the conversation as an elaboration by Disraeli, or to minimise it as the barest outline of long term aims by a man as yet unaware of the complexities of politics at the highest level. The subjection of Austria, at least in northern Germany, and the destruction of the Confederation probably represent Bismarck's ultimate hopes well enough. In power, however, he found repeatedly that a masterplan was impossible, and that the only means of progress was the piecemeal exploitation of external events. In the 1860s he became the supreme realist and pragmatist, learning to declare in later life that 'man cannot create the current of events. He can only float with it and steer'.

Neither, despite the outbreak of three wars in his first eight years of power, should Bismarck be seen as a warmonger. He followed Clausewitz in believing that 'war is the continuation of politics by other means'. Yet generally he regarded these 'other means' as dangerous and to be avoided wherever possible. 'War', as A. J. P. Taylor has defined it, 'deprived him of control and left the decision to generals whose ability he distrusted'. The first essential, therefore, was to secure Prussia's German and European position as favourably as events would allow.

Her position with regard to her major European neighbour was improved by factors arising from the Polish revolt of January 1863. The reaction of the Prussian government was to send General von Alvensleben to St. Petersburg (February 1863) to offer a convention whereby Russian troops would be allowed to pass through Prussian territory in pursuit of Polish rebels. It was not a startling concession, considering what Prussian Junkers had to lose from a peasants' revolt, but it contrasted favourably with France's pro-Polish stance, and with Austria's Crimean 'betrayal'. The reward for the Alvensleben Convention may be seen in Russia's future acquiescence in Prussia's upsetting of the central European balance of power. There was to be no Olmutz in the 1860s.

Two further issues cemented Prussia's position within Germany. By signing a trade agreement with France in mid-1862, Prussia technically violated existing Zollverein treaties. This gave Austria the chance, her last as it happened, to make alternative economic proposals to the princes. Their rejection of these overtures, their acceptance of the Franco-Prussian agreement, and their conclusion of a renewed Zollverein treaty, excluding Austria (1865), constituted a triumphant confirmation of Prussian economic leadership in Germany. As regards political leadership, however, Austria seemed to be on firmer ground. The Emperor's decision (August 1863) to summon an Assembly of Princes (Furstentag) to discuss reform of the Confederation, seemed likely to confirm her position and maintain the duality of power in Germany. At Bismarck's insistence, the Prussian King refused to acknowledge Austrian leadership by attending, and refused to accept the reform proposals drafted there. As events were to prove, this was the last attempt to unite Germany by princely consent. Thus Austria's traditional claim to speak and act for the princes as a whole was open to acute doubt at the moment when the next crisis of German nationalism erupted.

(h) Schleswig-Holstein

The issue of the two duchies on the borders of Germany and Denmark was an old one, and had last come to a head in 1848. The problem arose from a mixed population and from a confusion of dynastic and semi-feudal claims. Schleswig, to the north, was predominantly Danish, while Holstein had a substantial German majority and was actually a member of the German Confederation. The territories were technically subject to the King of Denmark, but enjoyed a large degree of legal and administrative independence from Copenhagen. The crisis of 1848 had arisen from the support of middle-class, nationalist Holsteiners for the claims of the Duke of Augustenburg, whose son continued the family's bid for power in the early 1860s. The pre-1848 status of both Schleswig and Holstein was confirmed by the major powers in 1852 by the so called London Protocol. This left both parties dissatisfied by confirming both Danish overlordship, and the liberties of the duchies.

The decision of the new King of Denmark, Christian IX, in 1863 to regulate the situation in his country's favour precipitated a renewed crisis. The mood of German nationalists at this initiative is well illustrated by the declaration of the Prussian Liberal K. Twesten that he 'would rather suffer the Bismarck ministry for some years longer than allow a German land to be lost to us'. Bismarck, too, had a number of benefits to derive from intervention. In the first place he could not tolerate the increase in the prestige of the German Confederation that would result from her easy victory over Denmark. It seems clear, too, that he always had the ultimate annexation of the duchies in mind. This was not necessarily as a piece of crude land hunger, but predominantly as a sop to confirm his position in the eyes of King Wilhelm. At no stage did Bismarck pretend to be acting on behalf of nationalism, writing that 'it is no concern of ours whether the Germans of Holstein are happy'. Nor is it seriously maintained any longer that this was a cynical trap to lure Austria into military commitment and to lay the basis for future tensions. The alliance by which the two German powers agreed upon joint action (January 1864) was necessary to avoid Austrian jealousy, to prevent her leading a Confederation force, and to minimise the fears and resentments of the other signatories of the London Protocol.

The war itself was a one-sided affair, concluded by the treaty signed in Vienna, in October 1864, under which King Christian renounced both Schleswig and Holstein. After years of wrangles in which the Confederation had put forward the German viewpoint, that body was now totally excluded from the settlement. The claims of the Duke of Augustenburg were also conveniently ignored, and the newly acquired territories were placed under the joint administration of Prussia and Austria. Their ten months of joint rule were marked by squabbles, accusations and threats of war. Rather than precipitate a confrontation, Bismarck accepted the conciliatory Convention of Gastein (August 1865) which formally divided the administration. Prussia took responsibility for Schleswig and Austria for Holstein.

As matters stood at the close of 1865, Bismarck had great cause for satisfaction. Quite apart from influence over Schleswig, his actions had demonstrated once more the impotence of the Confederation. Also, so far from opposing him, Austria had been a party to that demonstration. For the first time in German political affairs in that century, Prussia had led while Austria followed. Bismarck might also have been entitled to suppose that he had done something to lessen the hostility of liberals to him within Prussia. As a result, O. Pflanze has claimed, of the blow struck apparently for the German cause, 'almost overnight the Bismarck cult was born. Its devotees began to reinterpret their hero's actions during the preceding four years. They excused his infringements of the constitution in view of what they presumed to have been his hidden purpose'. Others, such as G. Mann, do not accept that Prussia's liberals were won over so easily. There is little doubt, however, that within the next year, Bismarck was to score

remarkable triumphs over all his opponents within Germany.

(i) The Austro-Prussian War

It has already been pointed out that it is no longer widely maintained that the Schleswig-Holstein question was a trap deliberately laid by Bismarck to lure Austria into war. W. M. Simon speaks for the majority of recent commentators in pointing out that in 1864 and early 1865, war still posed too great a risk for Bismarck happily to contemplate it. Late 1865 and early 1866, however, saw several of the outstanding uncertainties resolved in a manner satisfactory to Prussia.

The first such uncertainty was the attitude of France. Bismarck's meetings with Napoleon III at Biarritz and St. Cloud (October–November 1865) left him confident of French neutrality in the event of an Austro-Prussian conflict. It is far from certain that any promises of territorial compensation for France were made (see Chapter 3, section **t**) and it may be that the most important outcome was Bismarck's realisation that Napoleon's main desire was to remain at peace. Secondly, the attitude of Italy was clarified. A trade treaty with the Zollverein (December 1865) had not fully won Italy over to the Prussian camp, but the failure of her friendly approaches to Austria had decided her course by April 1866 (see Chapter 4, section **m**). By the military alliance then concluded, Italy agreed to fight with Prussia against Austria, with Venetia as her reward. This was on the condition that the war began in the next three months. By this diplomacy Bismarck had ensured that he would only fight on one front, while Austria fought on two. He had also ensured that the issue would be decided by war. In May, as a last peace bid, Austria actually agreed to acknowledge Prussian supremacy in northern Germany, but demanded the retention of Venetia, forcing Bismarck to reject the offer because of his commitment to Italy.

Ostensibly, the war that began with the Prussian invasion of Holstein in June was about the administration of the duchies. Prussia accused the Austrian authorities of violating their mutual agreements by sheltering refugees from the harsh Prussian rule in Schleswig. Clearly, too, when Austria referred this dispute to the Confederation, she was in breach of the Gastein Convention. These were obviously convenient excuses. The war was really the trial of Prussian strength, postponed in 1850, against Austria and against the Confederation, which was Austria's main power base in Germany. It was apt that Prussia also went to war with Saxony, Hanover, Bavaria, Wurttemberg, Baden, Hesse Darmstadt, Hesse Cassel and Nassau. In a very real sense it was a war for the conquest at least of northern Germany.

In the war itself, the German states proved to be ineffectual allies. Their forces failed to make any effective links with those of Austria. Also, in a series of engagements conveniently ignored by subsequent nationalist historians, at Langensalza, Dormbach, Kissingen and Rossbrunn, they were eliminated from the conflict. On the all-important Bohemian front the decisive action was fought at Sadowa (Königgrätz) on 3rd July. Superior Prussian infantry tactics and armaments ensured heavy Austrian losses (roughly 20 000 to Prussia's 9000) and left open the road to Vienna. The rapid conclusion of an armistice at Nikolsburg three weeks later was the result of compelling factors on both sides. The Austrian Emperor was motivated by nationalist 'rumblings' in Bohemia and Hungary. Bismarck himself had reason to fear the attitudes of France (see Chapter 3, section **t**) and Russia to Prussia's extraordinary triumph. In combating the strong desire of King Wilhelm and his generals for territorial gain, Bismarck was thinking not only of foreign jealousy and the future balance of power, but also of the danger of the conservative Prussian state and administration overreaching itself. 'Our power finds its limits', he wrote at the time, 'when the supply of Junkers to fill official posts gives out'.

(j) The Treaty of Prague

Prussia's defeat of Austria, which was enshrined in the Treaty of Prague (23rd August 1866), caused a greater disruption to the European state system and balance of power than any other event since the defeat of Napoleon. The contemporary German historian Gregorovius captured the importance of the event with only a little exaggeration. 'The entire Prussian campaign has no parallel in the history of the world. . . . The consequences of the Battle of Sadowa are at least as follows: the unification of Germany through Prussia, the consummation of Italian independence, the fall of the temporal power of the Papacy, the deposition of France from the dominion she has usurped over Europe . . .'.

In more sober detail, the treaty allowed Prussia to annex Hanover, Hesse Cassel, Nassau, Frankfurt, and Schleswig-Holstein. By recognition of her right to form all German territories north of the line of the River Main into a new North German Confederation, Prussia encompassed the death of

the old German Confederation. A seven week military campaign had thus untied the knot that had defied decades of diplomatic wrangling. Apart from Venetia, Austria suffered no territorial loss. Instead, she surrendered to Prussia the only prize that Bismarck really desired, her prestige and status within Germany. Nevertheless, the defeat had profound long term effects upon the Austrian Empire. At a stroke, she was banished from the political affairs of both Germany and Italy. The only direction in which she could now seek prestige and expansion was towards the south-east, towards the Balkans. This was a factor that was to have grave consequences by 1914. For the time being, she turned in on herself. She reassessed her internal strength, and revised her internal organisation. The most important product of these processes was the Compromise (Ausgleich) of 1867, under which Hungary was recognised as a constitutional monarchy, free from Austrian interference in her internal affairs and united to her only through the person of her King. From 1867 to 1918 the Austrian Emperor was also King of Hungary, and his monarchy acquired the title of the Dual Monarchy.

(k) The 'Surrender' of the Prussian Liberals

The events of 1866 also provided Bismarck with a notable domestic triumph. The Prussian Liberal movement had to decide upon its reaction to the partial achievement of the unification of Germany. They had sought unification for decades but consistently condemned the means by which it was achieved. Many were intoxicated by Bismarck's success. 'I bow before the genius of Bismarck', wrote a previously consistent critic, von Schering. 'I have forgiven the man everything he has done up to now, more, I have convinced myself that it was necessary'. J. Miquel insisted that his fellow Liberals should now be practical. 'Today more than ever before politicians must ask, not what is desirable, but what is attainable'. Bismarck chose the moment perfectly to approach the Landtag with an admission that he had acted illegally over the past four years, and a request for their pardon in the form of an Act of Indemnity. He was duly pardoned by 230 votes to 75. The Progress Party split on the issue and there emerged from the disagreement a new party, the National Liberals. They were still devoted to the principles of the rule of law and of free trade, but were for the present on common ground with Bismarck in their enthusiasm for a strong German state power.

Did Prussian liberalism 'sell out' to Bismarck?

The answers of historians have tended to depend upon their views of liberalism, or of the German state founded by Bismarck. To H. von Sybel, a patriotic contemporary, the Act of Indemnity was an act of enlightened and moderate compromise. More recently, O. Pflanze has accused the Liberals of surrendering to success. They were the victims, he claims, 'of their own limited ends, their lack of genuine popular support, and their lust for national power'. W. M. Simon, however, accuses the Liberals not of cowardice in 1866, but of lack of realism earlier. He agrees with Miquel that 1866 represents not a loss of nerve, but an awakening to reality.

(l) The North German Confederation

The greatest reality of the new North German Confederation, envisaged by the Treaty of Prague, was that it rested upon a basis of military conquest by Prussia. The true nature of Prussian domination was clearly illustrated by the cases of Hanover, where a long established dynasty was deposed and the fortune of its king confiscated, and of Schleswig-Holstein, where Prussia continued to ride roughshod over the Augustenburg claims. Of the 23 states that associated themselves by treaty in the North German Confederation, Prussia supplied five sixths of the total population. The constitution of the Confederation, however, was a compromise. It was a synthesis between Bismarck's original, rigidly conservative ideas, and Liberal attempts to preserve some measure of parliamentary liberty. Why, given the power of his position, did Bismarck compromise? G. A. Craig and W. M. Simon answer that he deliberately attempted to create a viable parliament so as to play it off against the separatist tendencies of the governments of the member states. E. Eyck adds to this that he wished, through concessions to the Liberals, to make future membership more inviting to the southern states.

Thus, the North German Parliament (Norddeutscher Reichstag) enjoyed voting by secret ballot, election by universal manhood suffrage, freedom of speech, and free publication of debates. The Liberals also succeeded in forcing the administration to submit the budget, which was nearly all for military expenditure, for the Reichstag's approval every four (later every seven) years. On the other hand, Bismarck retained substantial freedom of action. Most taxes were indirect, from Zollverein customs and duties, and were therefore beyond Reichstag control. The Federal Chancellor (himself) was the only 'responsible' minister, and it was far from clear to

whom he was 'responsible'. Indeed, there were no other federal ministers to impede Bismarck. Finally, the initiation of legislation was in the hands of the Federal Council (Bundesrat) made up of appointed representatives of the states' governments. It was effectively the old Federal Diet, but now firmly under the presidency and control of Prussia.

(m) The Question of the Southern States

It is probable that Bismarck had no clear plans for further action at the end of 1866. He was exhausted by a year of crisis. 'There is nothing more to do in our lifetime', he had written to his wife. Yet the problem of the southern German states remained, their position problematical and paradoxical. Strong separatist forces survived south of the Main. Of the four states, only Baden, whose Grand Duke was son-in-law to the King of Prussia, showed real enthusiasm for union with the north. In Hesse, popular enthusiasm was offset by governmental hostility to the idea, while in Bavaria and Wurttemberg opposition to the north was more general. A strong Democratic Party in the latter kingdom remained hostile to Prussian absolutism, while in Bavaria, dynastic jealousy and staunch anti-Protestantism combined with widespread dislike of Prussian militarism. As late as 1869, the election of a large Catholic majority to the Bavarian assembly seemed to confirm the strength of separatism.

Why, then, could the south not be left alone? In part, there was the danger of what allies they might find if they were not the friends of Prussia. The Austrian Emperor, for instance, had given clear notice that he did not necessarily regard the Treaty of Prague as a final and irreversible settlement by appointing the former Saxon premier, F. von Beust, as his foreign minister. France, too, was tentatively to seek friends south of the Main. Secondly, pressure for further progress came from the liberal nationalists in the north who, like J. Miquel, refused to see the River Main as more than 'a preliminary stop where the engine has to refuel and rewater in order to continue the journey'. Most important, the separate existence of the southern states was a sham. Unable to translate into reality the vague phrases of the Treaty of Prague concerning a southern union, mainly because of the mutual jealousy of Wurttemberg and Bavaria, the southern states were effectively dependent upon Prussia in both military and economic terms. Already members of the Zollverein, the southern states had little option after 1866 but to accept Prussian proposals for a

'Customs Parliament' that would add political links to the existing economic ones. Still, by electing a majority of separatist sympathisers, the southern states continued to keep their distance. The most effective link between the new Confederation and the south was, therefore, the string of military treaties that Bismarck had concluded with the southern states in August, 1866. These placed Prussia in the position recently vacated by Austria as their protector. Already, by the end of 1866, war remained the most likely cause of further German unification.

(n) Germany and France: the Luxemburg Question

The key diplomatic questions raised by the events of 1866 were those concerning future German relations with France. In his memoirs which were published after his fall from office, Bismarck professed to have believed that a conflict with France was an inevitable step along the path to further national unity. In fact, his view at the time was certainly less clear than that. It was based upon the assumption that Napoleon III could not simply accept the changes of 1866, but was uncertain as to the shape or timing of the Emperor's initiative. 'Napoleon III', he wrote at the time, 'has recently lost more prestige than he can afford. To recover it he will start a dispute with us on some pretext or other. I do not believe he personally wishes war, . . . but his insecurity will drive him on'.

After initial probes in the direction of Belgium or of the Rhineland, Napoleon's 'policy of compensation' settled upon the Grand Duchy of Luxemburg as its object. The French proposals concerning Luxemburg have already been described (Chapter 3, section **u**). What concerns us here is the German reaction to those proposals. It does not seem possible to maintain any longer that Bismarck trapped or tricked the French Emperor over the Luxemburg question. On the contrary, most recent commentators have agreed that he was quite content to cede the territory and its fortifications to France as the price of placating her and preserving the stability of his new North German creation. What he would not do was to commit himself publicly to that policy at a time when he badly needed the support of liberal nationalists in the Reichstag. The insistence of the King of Holland that he would not sell Luxemburg without the specific agreement of Prussia was thus the factor that killed the deal. Bismarck did not initiate the nationalist outcry that now condemned

the loss of any 'ancient German land', but he was powerless to act against it. Prussia effectively gained nothing from the international conference (May 1867) that agreed to the neutralisation of Luxemburg and to the removal of the Prussian garrison. France was not placated, and the strategic position of Germany was not strengthened. Increased unease in the southern states at French ambitions was Bismarck's only consolation. When E. Eyck wrote that 'the Luxemburg affair was the turning point in Bismarck's development from a Prussian to a German statesman', he meant it not in the sense that the Chancellor had undergone a conscious conversion, but in the sense that he had for the first time lost the initiative. He had been carried along further than he wished by a force that he had previously confidently exploited.

(o) Germany and France: The Hohenzollern Candidature

The peace of western Europe survived the Luxemburg crisis with some ease, only to perish three years later over a most unlikely dispute. In September 1868, revolution in Spain overthrew the ruling house of Bourbon. By the beginning of 1869, the Spanish throne had already been rejected by a number of candidates who placed too high a value on the quiet life. Then the candidature was taken up of Prince Leopold von Hohenzollern-Sigmaringen, a member of the Catholic branch of the Prussian ruling house. By the following February, Spanish representatives were busy overcoming the misgivings of the prince, and of the Prussians, who stressed that the candidature should by no means be seen as part of official Prussian policy. With King Wilhelm's permission grudgingly given (June 1870) the project seemed able to go ahead as long as speed and secrecy presented the French with a 'fait accompli', and outflanked their obvious objections at the installation of a monarch with Prussian sympathies on their southern borders. That hope, however, was thwarted by misunderstanding and delay in Madrid. In early July, before the Spanish parliament could formally decide upon their king, the French ambassador received official confirmation of the rumours that he had already heard.

The reaction of the French foreign ministry (Chapter 3, section **v**) was strong enough, and had sufficient backing elsewhere in Europe, to kill the Hohenzollern candidature. Clumsy French attempts, however, to extract a promise from King Wilhelm that the project would never be renewed, seemed to call into question the royal and the national honour. This gave Bismarck the chance to snatch from the Spanish affair greater advantage than had ever seemed possible. By releasing to the press an edited version of the telegram in which the King reported his conversation with the French ambassador at Bad Ems, which gave the impression of a blunt exchange of diplomatic insults, Bismarck once more took control of the nationalist forces that had served him so well in the past. Faced with the choice of retreat or further confrontation, France declared war (19th July) over the Spanish question, initiating a conflict in which a united German state was to be forged.

In his memoirs, Bismarck was eager to convey the impression of total detachment from the Hohenzollern affair, and to charge the disruption of European peace to the insolence and instability of the French regime. Recent research, especially by G. Bonnin and E. Eyck has, however, shown Bismarck's close links with the candidature. These were from the initial distribution of bribes in Madrid, through the difficult process of convincing King Wilhelm of the strategic advantages of the project, to the final affair of the 'Ems Telegram'. It is difficult to doubt that Bismarck engineered the candidature, but that is not necessarily to say that he did so with a view to precipitating war. Indeed, as Λ. Ramm has pointed out, it was only by accident that the French government found out about the candidature in time to react at all. Is it not better, therefore, to see Bismarck's aim as being to outmanoeuvre and surround France in such a way as to force her to accept further Prussian aggrandisement without a fight? The thwarting of the plan, rather than the plan itself, left him with no other means than war for the purpose of creating stronger links between the northern and the southern German states. He could have had unity without war, but only by the means of war, could he guarantee that that unity would rest upon a basis of Prussian military domination. This was the only basis acceptable to Bismarck and to those he served.

(p) 1870: The Completion of German Unity

The series of military factors by which the Franco-Prussian War was won and lost is described in Chapter 3, section **w**. Of greater importance here is the series of political developments that accompanied the war, and by which a unified German Empire was formed.

At the outbreak of war, a powerful combination of factors ensured that the southern states would honour their treaty obligations to Prussia. Not least among these was the popular enthusiasm which Karl Marx dismissed contemptuously as 'south German beer patriotism'. Much pressure also came from the leaders of the National Liberals, especially E. Lasker, who organised persuasive propaganda campaigns south of the Main, and from the Crown Prince of Prussia, Friedrich, a consistent advocate of unity and of the Hohenzollerns' claim to the Imperial German crown. Although once more events were moving beyond Bismarck's control, he too played his role by the well timed publication of France's earlier compensation proposals, a frightening revelation for the southerners.

While the generals, to the chagrin of the Chancellor, kept the conduct of the war closely under their own control, Bismarck's prime concern was to negotiate a settlement with the southern states that would turn a wartime alliance into a permanent union. In this task three main obstacles presented themselves; the respective separatisms of Wurttemberg and Bavaria, and the determination of King Wilhelm not to accept a 'popular' crown, nor to see the Prussian crown diminished by becoming a wider German one. In the long run, the position of the major southern states was hopeless. They could not rely on each other, could not risk an isolated existence outside an otherwise united Germany, and could scarcely resist growing nationalist enthusiasm within their own boundaries. Continued separatism, as King Ludwig of Bavaria conceded, 'would be completely impossible politically because of opposition from the army and the people, as a result of which the Crown would lose the support of the country'. German unity without Austria was assured in November 1870, when a mixture of threats and bribes from Prussian state funds persuaded Ludwig to sign a treaty accepting unification. Baveria and Wurttemberg kept a number of symbols of independence. They had control over their posts and railways, and over their armies in peacetime. This was a small price for Bismarck to pay for an assurance that the offer of the German crown would come to Wilhelm from the princes, and not from the Reichstag which, in the event, was merely asked to approve the offer. This it did with enthusiasm. For all his reservations and regrets about the transformation of his beloved Prussian kingdom, Wilhelm could console himself that the assembly that proclaimed him 'German Emperor' (not 'Emperor of Germany', for that would have offended Bavarian feelings, and would have raised awkward questions about the extent of Germany) at Versailles on 18th January 1871, was an assembly of his fellow monarchs. He had not 'picked up a crown from the gutter'.

Bismarck's great achievement by 1871 was not that he had created a united German state. Many other forces, nationalism, industrialism, had given him invaluable aid in that. His great achievement had been to bring about German unity without the elements traditionally associated with it, elements hateful to his Junker class; without parliamentary rule and without true democracy. From the point of view of Prussian ideology, the triumph was a great one. It was a triumph over both radicals, who had wanted a different Germany, and over conservatives, who had been reluctant to take Prussia into any kind of Germany. From the point of view of Germany's political future, however, the consequences of this achievement were grim. The founding of the German Empire in this fashion, as T. S. Hamerow has concluded, 'represented the triumph of the mailed fist over the libertarian principle in the life of Central Europe'.

Progress Paragraphs

Answer the following questions in about 150 words.

Why was Prussia unable to maintain the Erfurt Union?
Section (**a**)

In what ways did Prussian prestige within Germany advance at the expense of Austrian prestige in the 1850s? Section (**b**)

What factors made the Prussian army such a formidable force by the mid 1860s?
Section (**c**)

What were the greatest strengths of the Prussian economy between 1830–1860? Section (**d**)

Why did Keynes consider that 'coal and iron' formed the true basis of the German Empire?
Section (**d**)

In what respects did the German and Prussian domestic political scenes change between 1855–60?
Section (**e**)

Why did the Prussian government seek army reforms in 1860–62, and why did the Landtag oppose their proposals? Section (**e**)

In what did Bismarck believe? Sections (**f** & **g**)

In what ways had Bismarck strengthened Prussia's German and international status by the beginning of the Schleswig-Holstein dispute? Section (**g**)

What was the Schleswig-Holstein dispute about?
Section (**h**)

Why did Bismarck feel ready to confront Austria in 1866? Sections (**h** & **i**)

What were the consequences for Germany, and for Europe, of the Treaty of Prague? Section (**j**)

Why was the attitude of Prussian liberals to Bismarck so changed by 1866? Sections (**h** & **k**)

What was liberal and what was illiberal about the constitution of the North German Confederation?
Section (**l**)

Why did the southern states enjoy a separate political existence for so short a time after 1866?
Sections (**m** & **p**)

Account for the failure of Napoleon III's attempt to purchase the Grand Duchy of Luxemburg.
Section (**n**)

What role did Bismarck play in the affair of the Hohenzollern Candidature for the Spanish throne? Why did this affair lead to war with France?
Section (**o**)

Why did the southern German states join Bismarck firstly in the war against France, and secondly in a permanent political union? Section (**p**)

6

The Consolidation of Russian Conservatism, 1848-94

(a) The Political Legacy of Nicholas I

The reign of Tsar Nicholas I, from 1825-55 represented the highest development of autocratic monarchy in Russia, yet like all high points, it contained in itself the main elements that caused its subsequent decline.

The most influential factor in establishing the themes of his reign was the dramatic Decembrist revolt that marked his accession. This unsuccessful attempt by liberal intellectuals and army officers in St. Petersburg to place his brother Constantine at the head of a constitutional monarchy, filled Nicholas with horror. Despite the defeat of France in 1815, and of this blasphemous attempt to undermine the Tsar's God-given authority, he felt revulsion at the spread of radical ideas in Europe. This revulsion was renewed and revivified at regular intervals; by the deposition of Charles X by the French in 1830; by the Polish revolt of 1831; and by the European revolutions of 1848. His pretension to act as the 'Gendarme of Europe' in Wallachia (1848) and Hungary (1849) typified the role that he felt compelled to play throughout his reign, that of the defender of the old paternalist discipline against the influences of 'rotten, pagan France'.

In domestic politics, therefore, Nicholas' reign may be characterised quite accurately by the slogan coined by Uvarov, his Minister of Education from 1832-49: 'Orthodoxy, Autocracy, Nationality'. Throughout the 19th century, the Orthodox Church, with its message of faith in God and unquestioning submission to God's will, was the major support of the Tsarist regime. It endorsed the regime's claim that its power was an expression of the Divine Will. Numerous other religious groups existed, indeed, a commission set up in 1859 reported 9.3 million non-Orthodox Christians in Russia. However, for most of the 19th century it was contended, with varying degrees of coercion, that only members of the Orthodox faith could really be true and reliable subjects of the Tsar.

The autocracy of the Tsar is a more complex concept to grasp. It involved not only authority, but also paternal responsibilities towards his subjects. 'The Tsar is a father', explained a senior police official, 'his subjects are his children, and children ought never to reason about their parents'. To allow children to make decisions about the future of the family would be a dereliction of responsibility by the father. Government in Russia, therefore, remained strictly in the hands of the Tsar, and was exercised by a complex and unwieldy machinery. The main tool of government was His Imperial Majesty's Private Chancery. The Third Section of this Chancery was in charge of state security, standing at the centre of a complex web of censorship and surveillance. The work of the censors extended from the strict limitation of any reporting of events in western Europe, to the banning of any criticism of social conditions in Russia. It also involved the control of any careless or dangerous expression in any form of literature. In the reign of Nicholas I, the Third Section shadowed some 2000 persons, and dealt with some 15 000 security cases annually.

At the root of the concept of 'Nationality' in Uvarov's slogan lay another conviction that dominated Russia's 19th century history. This was that Russian social organisation, religion, government, culture and philosophy were, by their very isolation from the mainstreams of European development, superior. It was thus the duty of all Russians to protect these blessings against all external (i.e. western) threats. Over the last century and a half, the great philosophical debates in Russia had centred around the struggle between 'Westernisers', who desired the spread of some western technical and philosophical ideas, and the 'Slavophils', who wished to preserve and consolidate the essentials of Slav culture, and to spread that culture to the non-Slav parts of the Empire. The visible manifestation of this concept of 'Nationality' was the general tendency towards the expansion of Russian influence over neighbouring territories. To the west, although Nicholas made no attempt to imitate Alexander I's grandiose project for a Holy Alliance, he showed in 1848 that he shared his brother's deep concern for the political tendencies of his western neighbours. Of particular concern was the effect of western liberalism and nationalism upon Poland. The revolt of 1831 was ruthlessly suppressed, and resulted in the abolition of many important elements of Polish national identity. The constitution was withdrawn, the universities closed and the Russian language more rigorously imposed in Polish public life. To the south, a consistent 19th century theme was the attempt to convert the declining Turkish Empire into a client of the Russian Empire. Although held in check by the suspicion of the other major powers, Nicholas' continued concern for influence over the Sultan's Orthodox Christian subjects precipitated the Crimean War in 1854 (see Chapter 3, section **o**). To the east and the south east occurred the most spectacular Russian expansion of the century: the acquisition of Persian Armenia (1828), influence over Dagestan and the Caucasus consolidated in the 1830s and 1840s, control over the Uzbeks and the Kazakhs in the same decades, and establishment of Russian influence in the Far East, typified by the foundation of the aptly named Vladivostok (Lord of the East) in 1861.

(b) The Social and Economic Legacy of Nicholas I

The prime social problem of Nicholas' Russia was that of serfdom, meaning the legal institution that recognised the ownership of one man, woman, or family by another, and the total subjection of the serf to the will of his owner. It had been recognised, but swept under the carpet for more than half a century. 'There is no doubt', Nicholas told the Council of State in 1842, 'that serfdom in its present situation in our country is an evil, palpable and obvious for all, but to attack it now would be something still more harmful'. In 1858, 31% of Russia's population of 74 millions, that is some 22.5 million persons, were serfs. In addition, over 19 millions were 'state peasants', tied to lands owned by the crown. The authority of their owners, sometimes delegated to the elders of the peasant commune (the 'mir'), was almost absolute. It extended over the allocation of land, labour dues, taxes, and corporal punishment, to the actual sale of the serf to a new master. Under Nicholas I legislation did away with some of the most inhuman aspects of the institution, forbidding the splitting up of families by the sale of individuals (1833), and banning the auction of serfs (1841). The tentative reforms did very little to still the peasant discontent that had been a constant feature

of Russian politics for a century. Seven hundred and twelve outbreaks occurred between 1826 and 1854, half of them in the last ten years of that period. Yet two compelling reasons militated against the abolition of serfdom. One was that the monarchy scarcely dared to go against the vast vested interest of the nobility and landowners, whose financial and social status depended upon the number of 'souls' they owned. Secondly, the monarchy itself derived great benefit, not only as the owner of 'state peasants', but also because of the allegiance of the serf to the landowner. This was combined with the allegiance of the landowner to the Tsar, and constituted the whole political hierarchy upon which the stability of Russia seemed to depend. 'The landowner', commented Nicholas' Chief of Police, 'is the most faithful, the unsleeping watchdog guarding the state; he is the natural police magistrate'.

A further negative result of serfdom, essentially although not exclusively a rural institution, was the restriction it placed upon the development in Russia of an urban middle class, or of an urban workforce. In 1833, the total urban population was about 2 million, out of nearly 60 millions. Even so, most towns and cities were market and administrative, rather than industrial centres, and Russia lacked the basis for any serious industrial development on the scale of western Europe. The Soviet historian P. A. Khromov estimates a total of only 67 000 people employed in textile manufacture in 1830, and only 20 000 in the iron and steel industries. Russia's cotton industry in 1843 had only 350 000 mechanised spindles to compare with 3.5 million in France, and 11 million in Britain. Her share of world iron production dropped, as the industry developed faster abroad, from 12% in 1830 to 4% in 1859. The classic indication of Russia's industrial backwardness was the slow growth of her railways. The first, a short line for the use of the Imperial family from St. Petersburg to the summer residence at Tsarskoe Selo, was built in 1837. The first train did not run between St. Petersburg and Moscow before 1851.

(c) The Legacy of 1848 and of the Crimea

The last years of Nicholas' life were dominated by two great crises: the shock of the European revolutions of 1848, and the collapse of much of the regime's prestige in the Crimean War. The main result of the events of 1848 was the destruction of any remaining positive elements in Nicholas' paternalism. His plans for intervention in the affairs of other European states were paralleled by stern reaction against any hint of liberalism in Russian domestic affairs. The campaign against any freedom of thought or expression was typified by the formation of the Buturlin Committee to supervise and regulate the work of the existing censors, and by the attack (April 1849) upon the intellectual circle of M. V. Petrashevsky. This circle was influenced by the works of the French Utopian Socialists, and included in their ranks the young writer, F. M. Dostoevsky. As usual, a changed attitude to such matters involved the appointment of a new Minister of Education, and P. Shirinsky-Shikhmatov proceeded to raise school fees, to reduce the numbers of university students (from 4600 in 1848 to 3600 in 1854), and to suppress the study of such dangerous subjects as philosophy and European constitutional law.

As the justification for such measures was the defence of Slav culture and society from western infection, it was inevitable that the conflict in the Crimea should, from the Russian point of view, have wider implications than those directly related to foreign policy. As L. Kochan writes, 'what began as a military trial of strength rapidly developed into a trial of the regime's strength'.

In both trials, Russia was found wanting. Allied troops landed on Russian soil at Eupatoria (14th September 1854) and had laid siege to Sebastopol within two weeks, after Menshikov's failure to check their advance at the Battle of the Alma. The year long siege showed both facets of the Russian military machine. The gallantry of the common soldiers defied all efforts to take the town, but weaknesses of strategy and supply contributed to the defeat of a number of relief operations, at Balaclava (October 1854), at Inkerman (November 1854) and at the Chornaya (August 1855). In the midst of these failures, Tsar Nicholas died on 2nd March 1855, apologising to his son for the state in which he left his empire.

A superficial consideration of the peace terms concluded in Paris in 1856 suggests that the results of the defeat were not too severe for Russia. Despite the neutralisation of the Black Sea and the loss of her influence in the Rumanian principalities, Russia was never threatened with the destruction of her 'great power' status as France was in 1815. The nature and causes of her defeat, however, had more serious implications for the continuation of the Tsarist regime. Russia's vast military strength had proved to be an illusion. Partly because of the need to maintain forces on other frontiers (lesser actions did indeed take place in the Gulf of Finland and in Siberia), but largely because of the lack of a modern system of communications, Russia was never able to muster more than 60 000 of her one million soldiers in the Crimea. Worse still, Russian industry proved largely incapable of equipping these troops properly. It could provide no more than one musket for every two men at the start of the war, and could equip only 4% of Russian troops with the newer, long-range percussion rifle, when 33% of French troops and 50% of British troops used this weapon. Quality, like quantity, was wanting. The Warsaw armoury produced 1500 new rifles in 1854, of which only 10 were found upon delivery to be in perfect working order.

As the autocracy justified itself on the grounds that it guaranteed Russian stability and greatness, the defeat in the Crimea seemed to justify comments such as that passed by the government censor A. V. Nikitenko: 'The main shortcoming of the reign of Nikolai Pavlovich consisted in the fact that it was all a mistake'.

(d) Alexander II: Aims and Character

The accession of Alexander II is comparable to the election of Pope Pius IX in terms of the hopes that it raised for an end to blank and sterile political and social reaction. The anarchist Kropotkin recorded that 'at this time in the streets of St. Petersburg intellectuals hugged one another, telling each other the good news'. The first actions of the new Tsar, like those of the new Pope in 1846, seemed to justify the hopes. Political prisoners were released, among them surviving Decembrists and members of the Petrashevsky circle. Censorship was relaxed, tax arrears cancelled, and some of the liberties of Poland and of the Catholic Church were restored. Yet Alexander's motives, like those of Pius, were not in any real sense liberal. Coming to the throne at the age of 36, as undisputed heir, he had had a much more thorough preparation for power than his father. He was less of a soldier, less of a disciplinarian, more aware of the faults in the social and governmental systems of Russia, but had no serious doubts about the system of autocracy. W. E. Mosse and H. Seton-Watson both see Alexander II standing at the crossroads between traditional autocracy and modern constitutional and social development. Both, too, see him recoiling from the dramatic step of abandoning the former, and failing mainly because he sought to reach an unrealistic compromise between the two. P. Dukes is rather less kind in his assessment of Alexander's personality. 'As Tsar, Alexander II was idle rather than tolerant, weak willed more than liberal. He admired his father's system of government, but lacked the energy and persistence to maintain it'. Alexander's accession, therefore, marked the opening of a period of reform in Russian domestic affairs, without any real willingness to recognise the implications of many such reforms.

(e) The Emancipation of the Serfs

This pseudo-liberal Tsar was, nevertheless, the man who introduced the most spectacular social reform of the 19th century. Speaking in April 1856 to the nobility of Moscow, and referring both to the failures of the Crimean War and to the renewed peasant disturbances, Alexander used the famous phrase that the 'existing order of serfdom cannot remain unchanged. It is better to abolish serfdom from above than to wait for the time when it will begin to abolish itself from below'.

The lapse of five years between this first reference and the Edict of Emancipation of February 1861 reflected the complexity of the task undertaken. Generally, the 232 000 serfowners were not sufficiently scared to co-operate unreservedly with the Tsar, and only the Lithuanian nobility accepted his invitation to submit plans for the process of emancipation. The greatest problem was the question of land. To liberate the serfs without land would merely have been to have created a vast and dangerous mass of destitute third class citizens. To grant them land, on the other hand, came dangerously close to admitting the truth of the radical doctrine that the land truly belonged to those who worked it.

Ultimately, the Edict of Emancipation gave to the serfs their personal freedom over a period of two years, and the land which they had previously worked. Thus 'Household Serfs', domestic serfs who did not work on the land, received no land and formed a new social problem. For State Peasants the period of transition to freedom was five years. The landowners were not expected, however, to surrender land freely and thus bear the brunt of the measure. In compensation for the land that they transferred to the peasants, they received payment in the form of government bonds. To recoup their losses, the government charged the peasants Redemption Dues, in the form of regular payments over a period of 49 years.

How great a reform was the Emancipation? H. Seton-Watson stresses its scope and achievement by a valuable comparison with the less peaceful and less successful emancipation of the American negro slaves at the same time. L. Kochan, on the other hand, dismisses the Emancipation as a 'fraud'. On the one hand, the reform ended an era of Russian social history, and on the other it had a host of implications that detracted from its overall value.

In many respects it would be more accurate to say that serfdom had been abolished rather than that the serfs had been emancipated. Firstly, the process was slow, dictated by the needs of the individual landowner. Secondly, the land settlement made upon the ex-serfs was usually unsatisfactory. The areas granted were usually too small, resulting in an average holding of about 9 acres, and landlords rarely hesitated to compensate themselves for the loss of free serf ·labour by inflating the estimated value of the land. Many peasants thus found themselves saddled with redemption payments far greater than the actual productive value of the land they farmed. Thirdly, many peasants were convinced that the land was theirs by right in the first place, and greatly resented the purchase by redemption payments of their own 'property'. Lastly, although freed from the landowner, the peasant often remained bound to the commune, the 'mir', which continued to exercise many irksome restrictions upon travel, freedom of enterprise, and so on.

In the shorter run, too, emancipation did not seem to solve the twin problems of rural unrest and industrial backwardness. Four hundred and ninety-nine outbreaks of violence were recorded in 1861, the worst of which was at Bezdna, in Kazan Province, where 70 peasants were killed by troops. The inadequacy of peasant land holdings ruled out the rapid rise of a prosperous class of peasant consumers. As late as 1878, it was estimated that only 50% of the peasantry farmed allotments large enough for the production of surplus goods, and this proportion failed to increase largely because of a dramatic 50% rise in the rural population of Russia between 1860–97. Nor did the government's reforms help to create a landowning class with the funds for substantial agricultural or industrial investment. So deeply in debt were the majority of landowners before emancipation that L. Kochan estimates that 248 million of the 543 million roubles paid to them by the government by 1871 was used merely to pay off existing debts and mortgages.

(f) Further Administrative Reform

One inescapable consequence of the emancipation was that the direct government of the localities by serf-owning landlords was broken forever, and needed urgently to be replaced. The intended remedy for this ill was the establishment of the zemstvos. These were rural district and provincial assemblies, whose functions included the administration of primary education, public health, poor relief, local industry and the maintenance of the highways. Potentially, such elected assemblies, supplemented from 1870 by similar urban assemblies, were as radical a measure in an autocracy as the emancipation itself. It is clear, however, that Alexander saw them as props to the autocracy, rather than as a step away from autocracy. Thus the hopes of Russian liberals were dashed almost before they were raised. Both the system of voting and their established local reputations made it easy for the conservative nobility to dominate the assemblies, and at provincial level they occupied 74% of all zemstvo seats between 1865–67. Furthermore, when zemstvo bodies had the temerity to suggest that delegates from each assembly should gather to form a central, national body, they were sharply reminded by the Tsar of the limitations upon their powers. This was the point, states H. Seton-Watson, where Alexander stood at the crossroads between autocracy and liberal reform. Having whetted the appetite for the latter, he chose the former.

The emancipation of the serfs also necessitated substantial reform of the Russian legal system, now that the summary justice of the landlord could no longer be so easily applied in the localities. From 1865 onwards measures were introduced to ensure that legal proceedings were conducted in public, that legal procedures were uniform for all classes of society, that a jury system prevailed for the trial of all serious charges and that judges were independent of the government. These were remarkable reforms, ensuring that, in Seton-Watson's words, 'the court room was the one place in Russia where real freedom of speech prevailed'.

If all these reforms were directly or indirectly a response to the military disasters of the Crimea, then it was only logical that the bases of the Russian military establishment should also be re-examined. Army life, too, had generally reflected the state of Russian society, with privileges for the noble officer and savage penalties for the peasant soldier. The task of bringing greater equity and efficiency into this system fell to the Minister of War, D. A. Milyutin. He was perhaps the leading liberal figure in Russia in the 1860s, and hailed by Florinsky and other Russian historians as one of the few outstanding statesmen of imperial Russia. During his tenure of office Milyutin reduced the term of service in the army from the 'life sentence' of 25 years to a period of six years. He also introduced universal military service (1874) to which all males were now liable at 20 years of age, without the loopholes that had frequently allowed the nobility and richer classes to escape the obligation to serve their country. The abolition of more brutal forms of punishment, of military service as a form of punishment for criminal offences, and of the 'military colonies' to which the sons of long-term recruits had been sent to be trained as the next generation of soldiers, all went far to humanise conditions in the Russian army.

Lastly, education, always an accurate barometer of the philosophy of the Tsarist governments, was re-liberalised. The Minister of Education, A. S. Norov, reversed most of the repressive measures of the previous reign. The numbers of university students were allowed to rise again (1855) and lectures were permitted once more on European government (1857) and on philosophy (1860). A new University Statute (1863) gave the universities more autonomy in the conduct of their affairs than at any previous point in their history.

(g) The Growth of Radical Opposition

Yet the reforms of Alexander II, so far from strengthening and stabilising the regime and earning universal acclaim for the 'Tsar Liberator', drew fierce criticism from most sections of the political spectrum. The Tsar suffered the classic fate of those who try to enjoy the best of both worlds, and became trapped in a crossfire of criticism. Conservatives resented the loss of influence and privilege, and liberals became frustrated at the Tsar's refusal to take his reforms to their logical conclusion. Many governmental departments became the scenes of bitter personal and political rivalries, such as that between Milyutin and P. A. Shuvalov at the Ministry of War. The disappointment of conservatives and liberals alike, however, was muted by the need to rally against the more radical and revolutionary forms of opposition that developed. This opposition was fuelled by a fierce ideological hatred of the regime, and encouraged by the freer political atmosphere created by the Tsar's reforms.

The most important names on the Russian left in the 1850s and 1860s were probably those of A. I. Herzen, N. G. Chernyshevsky and D. I. Pisarev. Herzen, already an exile from Russia by 1848, had moderated his stance as a result of the revolutions of that year, and became more willing to accept and applaud reforms, even if they came from Tsarist government. His journal *The Bell* ('Kolokol') was published from London and regularly reached influential persons in Russia by unofficial channels.

Chernyshevsky took the reverse path. Originally

part of the literary radicalism of the 1850s, and enthusiastic about the emancipation of the serfs, he came to realise that further worthwhile reform was impossible without a fundamental alteration of Russia's political and economic bases. Thus he stands on the threshold of the new generation of Russian radicals who paved the way for the philosophy of the 1917 revolution. Chernyshevsky himself, however, was largely deterred from the further development of his views by the increasing use of violence by those who claimed to be his disciples. Nevertheless, his novel *What is to be Done?* (1862) inspired the next generation and provided the title for one of Lenin's most important works.

To a very limited extent, Pisarev supplied an answer to Chernyshevsky's famous question. Rejecting revolution as impossible for the present, Pisarev advocated a thorough examination and revision of the moral and material bases of society, in order to provide a better future basis for justice and equality. His followers were advised not to 'accept any single principle on trust, however much respect surrounds this principle'. From this desire to accept nothing of the existing society without question, the novelist Turgenev named this philosophy 'Nihilism' (from the latin 'nihil'— 'nothing'), a term which Pisarev liked and accepted.

Many young radicals were reluctant, however, to wait for revolution as Pisarev thought necessary. Broadly, they envisaged two possible answers to the question 'What is to be done?' One of these was Populism, a movement that dominated Russian radicalism in the mid-1870s. The founders of Populism, N. K. Mikhailovsky and P. L. Lavrov, viewed the Russian peasantry as a force of great revolutionary potential, but which needed thorough re-education. Thus, in 1874–75, some 3000 young radicals invaded the countryside to open the eyes of the rural population to their plight and to the sources of their salvation. This movement 'To the People' was a depressing failure. H. Seton-Watson notes that 'some peasants listened with sympathy, many were hostile, and most understood hardly anything of what they heard'. Over 1600 of these Populists were arrested between 1873–77, often handed over to the police by the very peasants, blindly loyal to the Tsar, who they sought to help. Learning from these failures, a breakaway group calling itself 'Land and Liberty' ('Zemlya i Volya') made some progress in the following years with a revised plan that involved living with the peasants for longer periods, the better to learn their mentality. Perhaps the most lasting legacy of Populism, however, was the foundation by members of 'Land and Liberty' of the first unions

for Russian industrial workers in Odessa (1875) and in St. Petersburg (1878).

For those with equal conviction but less patience, the more attractive alternative was that of conspiracy and terrorism. The first attempt on the life of the Tsar came in 1866, when a student named Karakozov shot at him in the streets of St. Petersburg. The best claim to be the founder of the conspiratorial activism that triumphed in 1917 belongs, however, to S. G. Nechayev. Apparently motivated by a mixture of idealism and ambition, he created a complex system of revolutionary cells up to 1869, by ruthless methods. This system collapsed when internal arguments caused him to murder a fellow conspirator, and the resultant trial gave full publicity to the unsavoury aims and methods of Nechayev.. The real 'heyday' of terrorism as a means towards political change followed a split in 1879 in the ranks of 'Land and Liberty'. While one wing, led by G. V. Plekhanov and P. B. Akselrod, and calling itself the 'Black Partition' ('Chorny Peredyel'), favoured further peaceful work among the peasants, an opposing group named 'The People's Will' ('Narodnaya Volya') advocated violence as the trigger to general revolution. Although other government officials were among their early victims, their chief target was always the Tsar himself. Within a period of a year, Alexander survived another attempt to shoot him (April 1879), an attempt to dynamite the royal train, which blew up the wrong train (December 1879), and an explosion in the banqueting hall of the Winter Palace (February 1880). Although by the end of 1880 the radical opposition within Russia had achieved nothing of worth, and was to achieve nothing for another quarter of a century, many of the methods and preconceptions of the 1917 revolutionaries can be seen in the process of formation in the reign of Alexander II.

(h) The Polish Revolt, 1863

The bitter disillusion felt by Alexander II at the reaction to his role as the 'Tsar Liberator' was not only fed by the troubles that followed the Emancipation, but also by the great rebellion of his Polish subjects in 1863. Poland had fallen under the power of the Tsar as a result of a compromise made at the Congress of Vienna in 1815. Rather than allow the former independent kingdom to become part of the Russian Empire, the allies had preserved her nominal independence, but allowed the Tsar to rule as King of Poland, thus effectively combining the two states. The special status of Poland, and the vague liberalism of Alexander I had combined to give Poland rather freer institutions than existed elsewhere in eastern Europe. Poland had a constitution, a parliament, and the use of Polish as an official language, for example. The first Polish rebellion (1830) had, however, resulted in the suppression of many of these liberties by Nicholas I. Nevertheless, Poland, like other parts of the empire, had reason to greet the accession of Alexander II with optimism. His conciliatory gestures included the filling of the vacant Catholic Archbishopric of Warsaw (1856), the foundation of a medical school in that city (1857), and the formation of a new Agricultural Society (1857) to promote new techniques of cultivation.

On the surface it appeared that, as in the rest of the empire, the question of land reform was the most pressing Polish problem. Unlike the rest of the empire, however, the demand for such reform was directly connected with the desire to re-establish Polish nationhood, a desire to which no Tsar could accede. It was the nationalist demonstrations in Warsaw that set off the train of events in February 1861. In April the Agricultural Society was dissolved on account of its links with the nationalist unrest, and in the resultant demonstrations up to 200 were killed. In May 1862, the Tsar's brother Constantine, who was a conciliatory liberal man, was appointed viceroy in an attempt to defuse the situation, and came close to assassination in his first month in office. A series of further concessions was proposed, including the emancipation of Polish Jews, and the opening of a university in Warsaw, but a proposal for the conscription of Poles into the Russian army nullified any calming effect, and armed rebellion broke out in January 1863.

It was largely a rural rebellion, with most of the landowners more or less favourable to the rebels, but with the attitude of the peasants remaining highly ambiguous. It took nearly a year to control and was not properly over until August 1864. In that year, agrarian reform was at last carried through, giving freehold tenure to 700 000 peasant families, without any redemption payments to the Russian government. Although H. Seton-Watson sees the reform mainly as an attempt to separate the peasants from the nationalist landowners, it was in the tradition of relatively liberal treatment used by Russia towards Poland between 1855–63. Its general failure was naturally seen by the Tsar as evidence of ingratitude and of the futility of conciliatory gestures, for as R. F. Leslie points out, it had the effect of making the peasant smallholder as Polish as the gentleman landowner had been. In reality it showed the impossibility of reconciling such beliefs as Polish nationalism and Tsarist

autocracy. Henceforth, Russian policy towards all the other nationalities of the Empire would be one of russification.

(i) The Death of Alexander II

By the beginning of the 1880s, Alexander II was, in the words of W. E. Mosse, 'isolated from the Russian people, unpopular with the educated public, and cut off from the bulk of society and the Court. His fate had become a matter of indifference to the majority of his subjects'. Largely, this was the result of vacillation between two policies, but even at court he was increasingly unpopular as a result of his embarrassing passion for the much younger Princess Dolgoruky. She bore Alexander a number of illegitimate children, and he married her with indecent haste upon the death of his first wife in 1880. W. E. Mosse suggests that this passion contributed to the further confusion of Imperial policy in the last years of Alexander's life. While the Tsar grew more and more disillusioned and conservative, the princess remained the friend and patron of a number of liberal politicians. Thus the government's reaction to the violence of 1879–80 was a mixture, once again of repression and concession. Executions took place, but the major political event was the appointment as Minister of the Interior of M. T. Loris-Melikov, a member of Princess Dolgoruky's liberal circle. Despite the misgivings of the Tsar, Loris-Melikov had, within a year (January 1880–February 1881), abolished the Third Section, replaced the reactionary D. A. Tolstoy as Minister of Education, and steered the Tsar to the verge of the most fundamental reform of his reign. By February 1881, plans were prepared for the calling of a national assembly, partly of nominated members, but partly of elected representatives of the zemstvos and town councils. It was thus a limited body, but a logical and significant step away from total autocracy. The Soviet historian P. A. Zaionchkovsky concedes that 'in the conditions of an increasingly complex situation it might . . . have been the beginning of the establishment of a parliamentary system in Russia'. The Tsar had just given his personal approval to the measure, however, when the luck of the 'People's Will' changed on 13th March 1881, and Alexander was killed by the second of two bombs thrown at his sledge in a St. Petersburg street.

(j) Alexander III and the Return to Reaction

The heir to the throne was Alexander's son by his

first marriage, who succeeded as Alexander III. The death of his father did not initiate the conservatism of the son, but the horrible circumstances of that death, and the cruel irony of its timing confirmed it most strongly. 'Alexander III', wrote H. Seton-Watson, 'was a true Russian. He knew his people. He would not sacrifice the truly Russian principle of autocracy'. The greatest influence on the views of the new Tsar came from his former tutor and trusted advisor, K. P. Pobedonostsev. Pobedonostsev's sympathies lay with autocracy against democracy, with Orthodoxy against all other sects, and with Russians against all other nationalities of the Empire. For him universal suffrage was 'a fatal error'; the principle of the sovereignty of the people was 'among the falsest of political principles'; parliamentarianism was the 'triumph of egoism'; and the freedom of the press 'one of the falsest institutions of our time'. As Pobedonostsev also served the new Tsar as tutor of his eldest son, Nicholas, his influence stretched unbroken from 1881 to the turmoil of 1905.

Although of less direct influence, another major 'prophet' of the new temper in Russian thought, and especially in Russian foreign policy, was N. Y. Danilyevsky. In his most influencial work, *Russia and Europe* (1871), he rejected the enthusiasm of the westernisers for western philosophy and technology, and argued that as Russia had a quite different history and development, she should ignore the Roman and Germanic worlds and concentrate upon her Slav nature and inheritance. This view differed from the old Slavophil notions in that it was more aggressive, preaching a union of all the Slav nations under Russian leadership stretching from the Baltic to the Adriatic. To this regeneration of aggressive, autocratic nationalism was given the name Pan-Slavism.

It was scarcely surprising that the bomb that destroyed Alexander II also destroyed the careers of his more liberal ministers and the policies that they advocated. Loris-Melikov was replaced as Minister of the Interior by N. P. Ignatiev, who later gave way to D. A. Tolstoy. At the heart of the new policy lay the hope of restoring the Russian nobility to the position of strength and influence that it had held before the Emancipation. In July 1889, the office of Justice of the Peace in local government was abolished, and a new office, that of Land Commandant (Zemsky Nachalnik) was created. The essential qualification for this office was membership of the nobility, and the office enjoyed senior administrative and judicial power in the locality, over-riding the powers of the zemstvos. The partly elective zemstvo became a prime target for the reactionaries.

Laws of 1890 and 1892 revised the franchise in rural and urban assembly elections in order to restrict the popular vote. In St. Petersburg, the combined effect of the laws was to reduce the electorate from 21 000 to 7000. Furthermore, the assemblies frequently found their most apolitical proposals obstructed and undermined by the objections of a government fundamentally opposed to the very principle of elected assemblies.

Naturally, educational policy also felt the impact of the revision of government thinking. The Minister for Education from 1882 to 1898 was I. V. Delyanov, a man essentially opposed to any 'dangerous' advance in education such as had been promoted by the reforms of Alexander II. Policies towards the universities included the limitation of their administrative autonomy (1884) and the raising of their tuition fees (1887). The raising of fees was also a useful method in primary and secondary education to ensure that the 'children of coachmen, servants, cooks, washerwomen, small shopkeepers, and persons of similar type . . . should . . . not be brought out of the social environment to which they belong'. Only parish elementary schools, safely under the influence of the local clergy, were allowed any real expansion during Delyanov's term of office. Consequently, by the end of the 19th century Russia presented a bizarre educational paradox. Her elite contained some of the most famous figures of the century: scientists (Pavlov, Mendeleiev), writers (Chekhov, Tolstoy, Gorky), historians (Klyuchevsky), musicians (Tchaikovsky) of world repute. Yet this brilliant surface of Russian society hid a substructure of rottenness and ignorance represented as late as 1897 by a staggering illiteracy rate of 79%.

(k) Russification

Referring specifically to Poland, the conservative writer and publicist Y. F. Samarin had described nationalism in the 1860s as 'a dissolving agent as dangerous, in a different way, as the propaganda of Herzen'. The policy of russification, that is of attempting to suppress the local characteristics of various areas within the Empire, and to spread Russian characteristics to all the Tsar's subjects, was not originally introduced by Alexander III but was, as part of his renewed emphasis upon autocracy, applied with fresh vigour and determination.

The Russians were, in fact, in a minority within their vast Empire, 55% of the total population belonging to other racial groups. The largest groups within the population were, according to the census of 1897, as shown in Table 6.1.

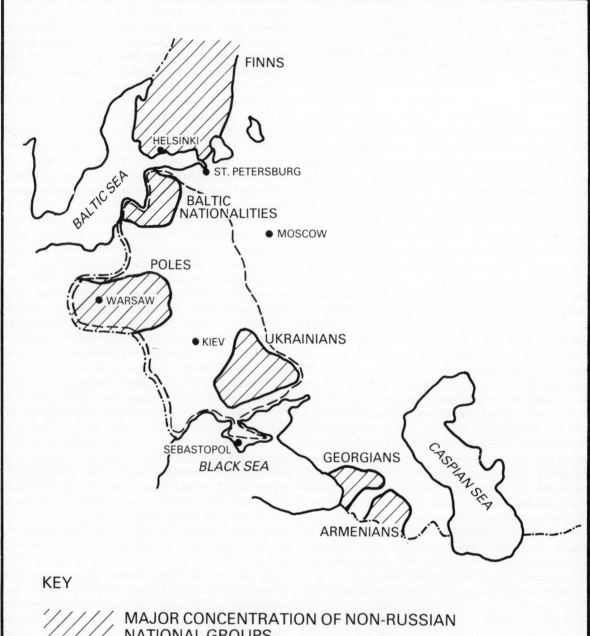

KEY

//////// MAJOR CONCENTRATION OF NON-RUSSIAN
         NATIONAL GROUPS

–·–·–·– BOUNDARIES OF RUSSIAN EMPIRE 1815–1917

––––––– JEWISH PALE OF SETTLEMENT

MAP 6   EUROPEAN RUSSIA 1815–1917: THE DISTRIBUTION OF NATIONAL MINORITIES

Great Russians	55.6 m	Tartars	3.4 m
Ukrainians	22.4 m	Germans	1.8 m
Poles	7.9 m	Armenians	1.2 m
White Russians	5.8 m	Georgians	0.8 m
Jews	5.2 m		

Table 6.1

The total population of the Empire at that time was a little over 125 million. J. N. Westwood has divided these racial groups into three main categories, which he labels 'mainly loyal, mainly disloyal, and the Jews'.

In the 'disloyal' category it was of course the Poles who, after the nationalist outbreak of 1863, could most expect to be the subject of rigid russification. The measures taken by the subsequent governors of defeated Poland, F. F. Berg (1864–74), and P. Kotzebue (1874–80) set the pattern for future similar policies elsewhere. The property of the Roman Catholic Church was seized (1864) and Warsaw's university was closed (1869). Russian replaced Polish as the administrative language, and more and more Russians replaced Poles in the ranks of the administrators. Similar measures were passed in the Ukraine, but there, as there had been no comparable nationalist demonstrations, they were mainly directed against a small group of radical intellectuals. The other main components of the 'disloyal' group were the Tartars and the Georgians. In both cases, the Orthodox Church played a leading role on behalf of the state, converting an estimated 100 000 Tartars by 1900, and fighting a fierce conflict that went as far as political assassination in some cases against the Georgian Church. Islam and the Georgian Church both put up fierce resistance, however, and the problem of separatism among the Tartars and the Georgians was still very much alive in 1917.

Much more damaging to the autocracy of the Tsar were the counter-productive efforts to 'russify' areas whose loyalty to the Tsar had not previously been in doubt, notably Finland, Armenia and the Baltic territories of Estonia, Latvia and Lithuania. The Finns had been especially well treated under Alexander II, and had even had the use of their own language not merely permitted, but actually made compulsory in local administration. Now disadvantageous trade tariffs were imposed, Russians and their language intruded more and more into Finnish government, and the process culminated in 1903 with the suspension of the Finnish constitution, a direct breach of the terms upon which Alexander I had absorbed Finland into the Empire in 1815. Armenians, too, were

essentially well disposed to Russian rule which had done much to protect them from their major enemies, the Turks. Their reward, under Alexander III, included the confiscation of the property of the Armenian church, and the suppression of the Armenian language. Similarly, the Baltic Germans had enjoyed privileged treatment at the hands of the last two Tsars, several of whose chief ministers came from that region. Now, in contrast, the construction of the great Orthodox cathedral in Riga (1885) and the increasing proportion of Russian students at the famous University of Dorpat (now officially known by its Russian name of Yuriev) constituted symbols of uncompromising Russian domination.

Characteristically, the worst blows fell upon the shoulders of the Empire's long-suffering Jewish population. Even the Jews had known some relaxation of their conditions during the previous reign. Recruitment of Jews into the army had been placed on the same basis as that of Russians and the laws forbidding settlement beyond the 'pale' or official area of Jewish settlement established by Catherine the Great had been somewhat relaxed. Now, however, Alexander III's regime combined in effect the 'official' religious anti-semitism of the Orthodox Church with crude popular hostility that arose from the Jews' economic role. Associating the Jews in official propaganda with the Polish rebellion and with the assassination of Alexander II, but also happy to use them as scapegoats on which popular discontent could be vented, the government permitted and even encouraged 'pogroms'. These were riotous attacks on Jews and their property in which robbery, violence, and even murder were commonplace. An estimated 215 such disturbances occurred between the first outbreaks in May 1881, in the Ukraine, and the 'great' pogrom of 1905 in Odessa in which nearly 500 Jews were killed. As Minister of the Interior, however, D. A. Tolstoy was less keen to countenance such actions, not out of any concern for the victims, but out of a general uneasiness at the idea of civil disorder. In its place he instituted a series of less violent, but equally discriminatory measures. No new Jewish settlers were allowed in rural areas, even within the Pale of Settlement. Jews were forbidden to trade on Christian holidays which, as they already closed on Jewish holidays, made it hard for them to compete with non-Jewish rivals. Strict quotas for Jews were set in schools and universities which never rose above 10% even within the Pale. In 1886 in Kiev, and in 1891 in Moscow all 'illegal' Jewish settlers were expelled, which provided a useful opportunity to harass 'legal' settlers as well.

Apart from emigration, which was perhaps generally easier for Jewish traders than for some others, the Jewish reaction to these hardships provides a good illustration of the effects and failure of this policy of 'russification'. Two other courses presented themselves for Jews who had had enough of such treatment. One was militant nationalism which, in this case took the form of the Zionist movement. The other was revolutionary agitation, as seen in the formation of the Jewish socialist 'Bund' in 1897, which was to play an important part in the development of revolutionary socialism in Russia in the next two decades. Thus, in the long run did the policy of 'russification' prove to be an even more dangerous 'dissolving agent' than the nationalism that it originally set out to combat.

(I) Foreign Policy: Western Europe

Just as the end of the Crimean War signalled a turnabout in domestic policy, with substantial reform taking the place of rigid reaction, so an equal but opposite change came about in the foreign policy of the Russian Empire. The defeat, the evidence it provided of Russian weakness, and the preoccupation of the government with domestic changes all limited the one-time 'gendarme of Europe' to a largely passive role from 1856 until the early 1870s.

Nevertheless, Russian diplomacy did have one major aim during this period. It was an uncharacteristic one, for the defeat in the Crimea had transformed the greatest conservative power into a revisionist power, eager especially to revise the Black Sea Clauses of the Treaty of Paris that placed such humiliating restrictions upon her naval power in that area. Between 1856–63 the best means of achieving this end seemed to be to cultivate' the friendship of France with a view to gaining a diplomatic agreement at some future date. Thus at the Paris conference (May–August 1858) which formed Wallachia and Moldavia into an effectively independent Rumanian state, Russia co-operated eagerly with the French 'line'. In March 1859, she even agreed to remain neutral in the event of French action in northern Italy, a very stark contrast to her attitude to disruption in the Austrian Empire just 10 years earlier. By the early 1860s, however, the French 'entente' was on its last legs. French interference with the 'legitimate' regimes of Italy was more than Alexander II could tolerate, and the breaking point came with the evidence of French sympathy for the liberalism and the Catholicism of the Polish revolt in 1863.

For 10 years from 1863 Russia was almost wholly isolated in European diplomacy. The sole exception was in her relations with Prussia which were improved by General von Alvensleben's mission in that year to offer aid against the Polish rebels. It was beneath the Imperial dignity to use the forces of a lesser power to control her own subjects, but the gesture was in contrast to French, Austrian and British hostility, and Russia extended benevolent neutrality towards Prussia in her anti-Austrian adventures of the 1860s. Indirectly, Prussia's adventures led to the achievement of Russia's main ambition. With Europe preoccupied with the Franco-Prussian War from July 1870, Russia sensed the moment to renounce the Black Sea Clauses. The Foreign Minister, A. M. Gorchakov, informed the powers in November 1870 that Russia no longer accepted this section of the Treaty of Paris. Although the action was condemned in principle at a conference in London two months later, the powers were content tacitly to recognise that no retaliatory action could be taken.

In the longer term, the main result of the Franco-Prussian War was that Russian diplomacy had to come to terms with a more powerful neighbour than she had ever known before, in the shape of the new German Empire. The conclusion of the League of the Three Emperors between the rulers of Russia, Austria and Germany in 1873 (see Chapter 7, section **j**), gave a false air of stability to the politics of eastern Europe. Behind its facade, a series of factors kept alive Russian resentment at rising German power and at Austrian pretensions in the Balkans. The settlement engineered by Bismarck at the Congress of Berlin (see Chapter 7, section **k**) which limited Russia's gains from her conflict with Turkey, struck a bad blow at Russo-German relations. Meanwhile, in 1883, Rumania formally associated herself by treaty with Germany and Austria. A measure of the tension between Russia and Austria is gained from the refusal of Alexander III (April 1887) to renew the Three Emperors' Alliance, as the League had become in 1881. The Reinsurance Treaty concluded with Germany alone two months later (see Chapter 7, section **m**) maintained the facade of stability. It was a dubious piece of opportunism, partially at odds with Germany's undertakings towards Austria, but provided an encouraging indication of Germany's desire to maintain good relations with Russia. Thus, the refusal of a new German Kaiser to renew the Reinsurance Treaty in 1890 (see Chapter 10, section **e**) seemed a specific rejection of Russian friendship, and a stark renewal of her international isolation.

The result was a revolution in Russian

diplomacy, whereby she turned towards republican France, different in every important aspect of recent history and culture, but well placed strategically to the west of Germany. The process by which France and Russia passed from financial to military understanding is described elsewhere (see Chapter 8, section **p**). Russian approaches to Germany in 1893 have suggested to some authorities that the exercise may have been viewed by some in St. Petersburg as a lever to force Germany into warmer relations. There being no favourable reaction from Berlin, an 'Entente' with France became the mainstay of Russian foreign policy 'faute de mieux'.

(m) Foreign Policy: The Balkans

The emergence of a great and concentrated power 'bloc' in central Europe restricted Russian ambitions to two main theatres in the 1870s and 1880s. The first of these was in the Balkans, where the renunciation of the Black Sea Clauses of the Treaty of Paris gave Russia a new lease of life. Her policy there continued to be motivated by the familiar blend of concern for national security, and the search for prestige in the face of domestic difficulties, with an extra spice added by the doctrine of Pan Slavism (see section **j**).

In the early 1870s, Gorchakov's policies in southeast Europe were conducted more in a spirit of cautious realism than of abstract Pan Slavism. In 1875, however, a series of revolts began among the Serbian and Bosnian subjects of the Turkish Sultan, which set off much Pan Slav agitation for the despatch of Russian aid. The brutal suppression of an associated Bulgarian revolt in 1876 further excited both Russian feelings and foreign suspicions. Gorchakov quietened Austrian misgivings by an agreement concluded at Reichstadt (July 1876), whereby Russia would regain Southern Bessarabia, lost in 1856, and Austria would receive part of Bosnia and Herzegovina in the event of a successful Russian clash with Turkey. Such a war was brought closer, as it had been in 1854, by the inflexible attitude of Turkey. In the first three months of 1877 the Sultan rejected proposals for reform from several of the major European powers, and Russia formally opened hostilities in April of that year.

The war was fought on two fronts. In the Caucasus the Turks used the tactic of stirring up local rebellion to keep the Russian forces occupied, and not until late in the year did the latter win decisive successes, winning a major victory at Aladja Dag (October) and capturing their main objective, the fortified town of Kars (November). In the European theatre the initial Russian advance was checked at Plevna, which held out against it from mid-July to early December 1877. The fall of that town paved the way to a victory that Russia sealed at the decisive battles of Plovdiv and Shipka (January 1878). It had been, as L. Kochan has noted, 'a war between the "one-eyed and the blind"—so many errors of strategy and judgement were committed'.

Nevertheless, Russia briefly enjoyed considerable gains. The Treaty of San Stefano (3rd March 1878) ignored her Reichstadt undertakings to Austria and created a large Bulgarian state wide open to Russian influence. The diplomatic hostility caused by such success forced Russia, however, to agree to a revision of the treaty formulated at an international congress in Berlin (see Chapter 7, section **k**). The size of Bulgaria, and thereby the extent of Russia's Balkan influence, was reduced. Russia, nevertheless, was left with southern Bessarabia and the Caucasian gains of Kars and Batum. It was a clever settlement, but left Pan Slavs and Russian nationalists bitterly offended, especially with Bismarck whose 'honest broker' stance seemed to them to hide anti-Russian and pro-Austrian intent. In the development of Russian relations with her central European neighbours, therefore, the events of 1877–78 foreshadowed greater conflicts to come.

(n) Foreign Policy: Asia

If the aftermath of the Crimean War left Russia badly placed to take positive initiatives in European affairs for several decades, no such restrictions existed along her eastern frontiers. 'These', L. Kochan has written, 'were the happy hunting-grounds of Russian imperialist adventurers, dubious carpet-baggers, and pseudo-viceroys'. Some voices were indeed raised in St. Petersburg against the risks and costs of such unbridled expansion, but they proved unable to check the ambitions of provincial generals and their followers. Motivated by chauvinism, by a sense of a civilising mission, and often by pure greed, Russian control spread steadily into the Caucasus, across the Caspian Sea, and into Siberia. Turkestan was penetrated by stages that included the taking of Tashkent (1865) and of Samarkand (1868), and the Khanate of Bokhara acknowledged indirect Russian rule in 1875. The integration of these areas into the Empire proper was slowly effected by such means as settlement by Russian peasants, especially during Stolypin's period as premier, and by a number of ambitious communication projects, such as the construction of the Transcaspian Railway between 1886–98. The spreading of Russian influence in Siberia was a longer process. Substantial territory was gained from China by the treaties of Aigun (1858) and Peking (1860), and the foundation of Vladivostok in 1861 was a tangible symbol of Russian penetration to the shores of the Pacific itself. Here too, great feats of communication were undertaken. The first work on the great Trans-Siberian Railway, one of the great engineering feats of the 19th century, was begun in 1892.

The sale of the colony of Alaska to the USA in 1867 defined the limits of Russia's eastward expansion, which constituted the most successful example of European territorial expansion in the 19th century.

(o) Economic Development 1855–94

Although, as has already been stated, the great social reforms of the 1860s did not stimulate general economic growth, the reigns of Alexander II and Alexander III did form a period of overall industrial development. This development was, however, uneven and fluctuating. In the 1860s, the difficulties of the Emancipation and the 'Cotton Famine' resulting from the Civil War in America were retarding factors. In the 1870s, however, the Russian economy benefited from the increase in railway building, and from a policy of low tariffs which facilitated the import of raw materials. Of the former, A. Gerschenkron has written that Russia's 'greatest industrial upswing came when . . . the railway building of the state assumed unprecedented proportions and became the main lever of the rapid industrialisation policy'. The development of Russia's railways was not only substantial in quantitative terms, but also possessed much greater economic logic than the earlier lines had displayed. Lines such as those between Moscow–Kursk, Moscow–Voronezh and Moscow–Nizhni Novgorod linked major markets to areas of industrial production, while the Kursk–Odessa and Kharkov–Rostov lines linked these, and areas of agricultural production, to the ports of the Black Sea. Similarly the Baku–Batum railway (1883) linked the Caspian with the Black Sea, and hugely increased oil production. The steady growth of the Russian railway system is illustrated in Table 6.2.

Following the initial policy of freer trade, tariffs began steadily to rise as it became clear that liberal tariffs were causing a heavy influx of foreign goods

Date	Kilometres constructed
1861–65	443 kms
1866–70	1378 kms
1871–75	1660 kms
1876–80	767 kms
1881–85	632 kms
1886–90	914 kms

From M. E. Falkus, *Industrialisation of Russia,* Macmillan.

Table 6.2

and creating a substantial trade imbalance. The first major increase came in 1877, followed by further acts in 1881 and 1882, and culminating in the great protective tariffs of 1891, which especially affected iron, industrial machinery and raw cotton. The beneficial effect on domestic coal and pig-iron production is shown in Table 6.3.

Date	Coal (poods)	Pig-iron (poods)
1860–64	21.8 mil	18.1 mil
1865–69	28.4 mil	18.9 mil
1870–74	61.9 mil	22.9 mil
1875–79	131.3 mil	25.9 mil
1880–84	225.4 mil	29.2 mil
1885–89	302.6 mil	37.6 mil
1890–94	434.3 mil	66.9 mil
1895–99	673.3 mil	120.9 mil

1 pood=36 lbs=16.3 kg

From M. E. Falkus, *Industrialisation of Russia,* Macmillan.

Table 6.3

In judging the level of Russian industrial development one certainly sees the truth of Lenin's judgement (1899) that 'if we compare the present rapidity of development with that which could be achieved with the modern level of technique and culture, the present rate of development of capitalism in Russia really must be considered slow'. In the longer term, nevertheless, one can also appreciate the judgement of a later economic historian, W. O. Henderson: 'If the Russian economy was still backward in some respects, it was also true that vigorous state action, foreign capital and foreign machinery had given Russia a powerful impetus on the road to industrialisation'.

Progress Paragraphs

Answer the following questions in about 150 words.

Explain the guiding principles of Russian government under Nicholas I. Section (**a**)

What were the advantages of serfdom for the Russian government and in what ways was serfdom disadvantageous? Section (**b**)

What were the effects of the defeat in the Crimea (a) upon Russia's international status and (b) upon the prestige of her government? Section (**c**)

What motives lay behind Alexander II's reformist programme? Section (**d**)

In what ways did the Emancipation of 1861 fail to satisfy the hopes of the serfs? Section (**e**)

In what ways did the Emancipation of the serfs pave the way for reforms after 1861? Section (**f**)

How did A. I. Herzen and D. I. Pisarev differ in their views of the reform of the Russian social system? Section (**g**)

What was Populism and why did it fail to achieve its aims? Section (**g**)

What role did the Polish Revolt of 1863 play in turning Alexander II away from his programme of reforms? Section (**h**)

What factors caused Alexander III to revert to a policy of reactionary autocracy? Section (**i**)

What forms did Alexander III's reaction take? Section (**j**)

Why did Russia pursue a policy of Russification in the late 19th century, and how successful was it? Section (**k**)

Account for the instability of Russia's system of foreign alliances during this period. Section (**l**)

What factors caused Russian involvement in the Balkans at this time, and what factors limited her success there? Section (**m**)

Comment upon the extent of Russia's Asiatic expansion during this period. Section (**n**)

How advanced was Russian industry by the death of Tsar Alexander III? Section (**o**)

7

Germany under Bismarck 1870–90

(a) The Treaty of Frankfurt

The outcome of the Franco-Prussian War and the ultimate shape of the German Reich were decided simultaneously by the terms of the treaty signed at Frankfurt on 10th May 1871. France was compelled to pay a war indemnity of five billion francs over a period of three years. Territorially, too, France was not to escape as lightly as Austria had in 1866. German nationalist claims to Alsace had flickered in 1815, among the student societies of the 1820s, and in 1848–49, and now that desire was supplemented by power, annexation was perhaps inevitable. 'This territory', wrote the historian H. von Treitschke, 'is ours by the right of the sword, and annexation follows from the right of the German nation to prevent the loss of any of its sons'.

Northern and eastern Lorraine, with the great fortress of Metz, also became German territory. There was far less justification for regarding these as German lands, and for many years the standard view on this point was that Bismarck bowed reluctantly to the pressure of the army, the King, and the nationalists; that he was, as A. J. P. Taylor put it, 'the prisoner of German public opinion as he had been over Luxemburg in 1867'. More recently, headed by the research of W. Lipgens, it has appeared that Bismarck may have had some role in the formation of that public opinion. His motives, however, are unlikely to have been ideological. On a practical level G. A. Craig points out that French bitterness was likely to be just as great, whatever the terms of surrender, and Bismarck himself wrote in similar vein to his ambassadors abroad. 'We cannot look to the French temper for our guarantees. . . . What the French nation will never forgive is their defeat as such. . . . In German hands Strasbourg and Metz will take on a purely defensive character'.

(b) The Constitution of the Reich

In theory, the German Empire created in 1871 was a voluntary association of German states, governed by as free a constitution as existed anywhere in Europe. In practice, behind each article of that constitution lurked the power and influence of Prussia. The Empire was a federal state, consisting of the four kingdoms of Prussia, Bavaria, Wurttemberg and Saxony, of eighteen lesser states, three free cities, and the Imperial Territory (Reichsland) of Alsace-Lorraine. Each of these, with the exception of Alsace-Lorraine retained a great deal of autonomy in terms of its own domestic administration. Of these constituent parts, however, Prussia was by far the largest. It comprised something over 60% of the Reich's area (134 000 out of 208 000 sq miles) and of its population (24.7 million out of 41 million).

The basis of the parliamentary constitution was adapted directly from that of the North German Confederation. The Imperial Assembly (Reichstag) was elected by universal manhood suffrage, but was beset by a host of limitations which prevented its growth into a true parliamentary body. It had the power to question the Chancellor (whose office fell of course to Bismarck) and to initiate debate upon points of his policy, but neither he nor any other minister was responsible to the assembly for his actions. It had theoretical control over any alteration to the military budget, but largely sacrificed this weapon by agreeing in 1874, largely through fear of precipitating a new constitutional conflict, to approve that budget for a period of seven years. It repeated this process in 1881 and 1887. This 'loss of the full right of budget approval', argues H. Holborn, 'blocked the growth of a parliamentary system in Germany'. Furthermore, the bulk of the remainder of Reich income, from indirect taxes, posts, and from the contributions of the member states, lay beyond the control of the Reichstag.

In reality, therefore, political power lay outside the Reichstag. In part it lay with the upper house, the Bundesrat, but for the most part it lay with the Prussian hierarchy. To the Bundesrat, which was the body representing the independent interests of the states, belonged the power to initiate legislation. Also with the assent of the Emperor, it had the power to de lare war and to determine disputes between th tes. With the interests of the Reich and of the individual states thus balancing each other out, real power lay with the King of Prussia and his ministers. He was by hereditary right German Emperor, with full powers over the appointment and dismissal of ministers who were responsible only to him. He also had full control over foreign affairs, and the right to the last say in any dispute over the interpretation of the constitution. By virtue of her size, Prussia possessed 17 of the 58 seats in the Bundesrat, at a time when 14 constituted a veto. The balance of forces in the German constitution was such, therefore, as to indicate very clearly that it was designed to block and to prevent any major change or development in the future.

(c) Political Parties and Philosophies

The parties that competed for seats in the Reichstag, with the varying degrees of success indicated in the table below, were very different organisations from their English counterparts. Pressure groups representing the sectional interests of one part or another of the diverse German nation, they remained in A. Ramm's phrase 'social phenomena rather than instruments for winning the struggle for power'.

On the right wing of the Reichstag stood two major groups, the Conservatives (from 1876 the 'German Conservatives') and the Imperial Party ('Reichspartei'). The former had its strength in Prussia itself, among Protestant, aristocratic landowners. Concerned at, and sometimes openly hostile towards Bismarck's flirtations with liberalism and nationalism, they remained a moderate force

in the Reichstag, but a major one in the Prussian Landtag, which they dominated by means of their local influence. The Reichspartei enjoyed a broader geographical basis of support, among landowners and industrialists alike, and their support for the Imperial Chancellor was much more consistent, in admiration of his great achievement in the foundation of the Reich.

The Centre Party (Zentrum), founded in 1870, still tends to be described as the party of Germany's large Roman Catholic minority. In fact it was more than that, primarily dedicated to the defence of the interests of the Catholic Church. It also attracted others with a partisan objection to the recent work of Bismarck, such as the Protestant Hanoverian 'Guelphs', who were supporters of the deposed King George. Particularly strong in Bavaria and in the Rhineland, the party was led in the Reichstag by a Catholic Hanoverian, Ludwig Windthorst. One of the few great parliamentarians of the 'Bismarck Era', greatly respected even by those who loathed his views, Windthorst has been characterised by G. Mann as 'a sly idealist, a devout fox, a man of principles and a very clever politician, dignified and cunning'.

In the National Liberals Bismarck had in the 1870s his most enthusiastic supporters, at one with him in their enthusiasm for a centralised state, if increasingly at odds with him in their support for progressive social and constitutional legislation. To their left stood the Progress Party, diminished but unbowed by the liberal split of 1866, sharing the National Liberals' enthusiasm for free trade and the rule of law, but opposed to the centralism and militarism of the Bismarckian state. In E. Richter and E. Lasker they, too, had effective parliamentary leaders, the latter so consistent a critic of the Chancellor as to be described by him as 'even more of a vile louse than Windthorst'.

	1871	1874	1877	1878	1881	1884	1887	1890
German Conservatives	57	22	40	59	50	78	80	73
Reichspartei	37	33	38	57	28	28	41	20
National Liberals	125	155	141	109	47	51	99	42
Progress Party	46	49	35	26	60	—	—	—
Centre Party	61	91	93	94	100	99	98	106
Social Democrats	2	9	12	9	12	24	11	35
Guelphs	9	4	10	4	10	11	4	11
National Groups i.e. Alsatians, Poles, Danes.	14	30	30	30	35	32	29	27

Total seats—397 (1871–382)

Table 7.1

Two smaller groupings are also worthy of note. German socialism in 1871 was as yet a modest force, based upon F. Lassalle's General Workers' Association (Allgemeiner Arbeiterverein) founded in 1863, and the Social Democratic Workers' Party formed by W. Liebknecht and A. Bebel at Eisenach in Saxony in 1869. Its day was, however, shortly to come (see section **h**). A less successful future awaited the three substantial national minority groups, the Poles (3.5 million), the Alsatians (2 million) and the Schleswig Danes (150 000) whose candidates nevertheless contested Reichstag elections consistently from 1874.

(d) The Consolidation of the Reich

The first seven years of Bismarck's government of a united Germany, from 1871–78, are frequently described as his 'Liberal Era'. While Bismarck was by no stretch of the imagination a true liberal, he found it most convenient during this period to co-operate in the Reichstag with the National Liberal Party. In the first place, they were the dominant party in an assembly where the Chancellor had no party of his own. Secondly, the spirit of conciliation that had motivated the indemnity of 1866 (see Chapter 5, section **k**) remained alive. They remained broadly sympathetic towards Bismarck as the architect of their major policy aim, national unity. Most important, their immediate aims coincided on the questions of the consolidation of that national unity and the centralisation of the administration of the Reich.

The state created by Bismarck was still a curiously disunited entity. It lacked religious unity and unity of economic interests, and contained national minorities with little or no desire to be part of a German Empire. There is thus much truth in A. J. P. Taylor's description of the Reich in 1871 as merely 'a wartime coalition'. Such were the separatist feelings of the states, for instance, that Germany had no national flag until 1892 and no national anthem until after the First World War. For Bismarck, with his desire for closer political control, and the National Liberals, with their enthusiasm for national unity, it was vital that this situation be improved. Thus the first session of the Reichstag saw the passage of over 100 acts to this end. The currencies of the states were united into a national currency, all internal tariffs were abolished, and a uniform body of commercial law was introduced. The Prussian State Bank became the Reichsbank, and Germany adopted the gold standard. Uniformity of legal procedures was achieved by 1877. A National Appeals Court was established by 1879, although the codification of German civil law did not come into effect until long after Bismarck's tenure of power (1st January 1900). To conservative critics it might have seemed as if the National Liberals were bearing Bismarck further to the left. In fact it is clear that the Chancellor gave his 'supporters' nothing that involved any real power. The Press Law (May 1874) provided little protection for editors against government prosecution. Reichstag attempts to limit Junker influence in Prussian local government achieved little of practical value, and we have already seen (section **b**) how the Reichstag failed to any serious degree to maintain control over the vital area of government military expenditure.

After administrative separatism, the second major area of disunity was constituted by the question of the national minorities within Germany's borders. For twenty years, by a mixture of coercion and conciliation, Bismarck attempted to tie these minorities more closely to the German state. He had no significant degree of success. In Alsace-Lorraine the decision to allow French or pro-French elements to leave the territories resulted in the migration of 400 000 people between 1871–1914. The remainder found themselves governed by Prussian civil servants, with the German language imposed in schools and in local administration. From 1874 they were represented in the Reichstag, and the choice of governors for the territories showed some tact and common sense. E. von Manteuffel (1879–85) was a humane and conscientious administrator. His successor, Prince Chlodwig von Hohenlohe, was a south German Catholic and had more in common with the Alsatians than had most of his protestant Prussian underlings. The consistency with which the people of Alsace returned to the Reichstag deputies in favour of separation from the Reich showed, however, that such attempts at conciliation were largely unsuccessful.

In the case of the Poles, conciliation was much less in evidence. The Polish clergy were hard hit during the Kulturkampf. Their leader, Cardinal Ledochowski, was imprisoned and his seat left vacant for twelve years. The use of the Polish language was outlawed in education and in the law courts. State funds were used to finance the purchase of lands in Polish hands for the purpose of settlement by Germans, although the Poles were rather more successful in raising funds for the reverse purpose. It is scarcely surprising that, given these tactics, the Polish problem remained unsolved. Finally, the problem of the Schleswig Danes was largely ignored. In 1879, on the eve of the Dual Alliance, Austria agreed to allow

Germany to abandon the plebiscite in North Schleswig promised by the Treaty of Prague in 1866. It took a world war to revise the status of North Schleswig and of Alsace-Lorraine, and two to resolve the problems of Germany's Polish subjects. This shows the extent of Bismarck's failure to solve this aspect of the problem of national consolidation.

(e) The Kulturkampf: Motives

Much of the first decade of the domestic politics of the Reich was dominated by the clash with the Catholic Church branded at the time as the 'struggle for civilisation' ('Kulturkampf'). It is difficult for us to grasp today, in a generally more tolerant age, the feelings aroused by this legal assault upon Germany's substantial Catholic minority. We shall miss its significance altogether unless we accept that, as E. Eyck tells us, 'in those years many of the most enlightened and highly educated men believed that the future of mankind was at stake'.

The roots of the Kulturkampf went deep into German history, certainly back to Prussia's acquisition of the largely Catholic Rhineland in 1815, possibly to the Reformation. As it occurred in the early 1870s the struggle was really made up of two separate clashes. For Bismarck's allies, the German liberals, the offence of the Catholic Church is best seen in Pius IX's *Syllabus of Errors* published in 1864 (see Chapter 4, section **o**). By condemning as erroneous every major principle for which Italian and German liberals stood, Pius had declared moral war. For the liberals the battle truly was one for the future of human thought, centring upon the vital question of the control of education. The very term 'Kulturkampf' was first coined by the liberal R. Virchow, one of the most prominent members of the Progress Party.

For Bismarck the issue was less abstract. Nor, despite his Protestantism and that of the Prussian Junkers, was his battle a doctrinal one. 'It is not a matter of a struggle between belief and unbelief', he declared. 'It is a matter of the conflict between monarchy and priesthood. What is at stake is the defence of the state'. For him the origins of the Kulturkampf lay in the events of 1866–70, which had turned tens of thousands of German Catholics from sympathetic 'Grossdeutsch' supporters of the Habsburg Monarchy into reserved followers and subjects of Prussia. Also its origins lay in the recently declared doctrine of Papal Infallibility (July 1870). By aiming to tie Catholic loyalties directly to the Papacy, instead of to the national

state, that decree was a clear challenge to state power. Despite initial opposition from German bishops and from German Catholic intellectuals, the majority seemed ready to place religion before national allegiance. Among those who jumped onto this 'bandwagon' were the Poles, who demanded use of their language in schools, and the Catholics of Alsace-Lorraine. The launching of this struggle offered Bismarck certain other political advantages, such as closer ties with Italy, with Russia (themselves greatly troubled by Catholic Poles), and with the National Liberals. However, his major motive was probably the desire to combat those whom he felt quite genuinely to be 'enemies of the Empire' ('Reichsfeinde'). The Catholics were thus the first of many minority groups to play this role in 'united' Germany.

(f) The Kulturkampf: Results

The spearhead of the attack upon the Catholic Church was formed by the legislation framed, under Bismarck's instructions, by A. Falk who was the Prussian Minister of Religious Affairs. Firstly, in 1872 came the severance of diplomatic relations with the Vatican (May) and the expulsion of the Jesuit order who were sympathetic to the Papacy, from German soil (July). In the following year came the major onslaught in the form of Falk's notorious 'May Laws'. The education of clergy, clerical appointments and the inspection of Church schools were all brought under state control. Appointments to German ecclesiastical positions were limited to those educated in Germany, and priests were forbidden to use the threat of excommunication as a means to coerce opponents. In a further series of measures civil marriage, strenuously opposed by Bismarck in 1849, became compulsory in the Reich, and most religious orders in Germany were dissolved (1875).

In 1874–75 Church and state remained locked in conflict. Eight of the twelve Catholic bishops in Prussia were deprived of their offices and more than a thousand priests were suspended from their posts. The desired political effect was not, however, achieved. Spiritually the Church thrived upon this 'martyrdom', and politically the increase in the Centre Party's representation in the Reichstag (see section **c**) frustrated Bismarck's hope of a quick surrender. Other unhappy side effects arose. Good foreign relations with Austria were made difficult by this anti-Catholic stance and the danger of an Austro-French understanding grew. Prussian conservatives, although staunchly Protestant, disliked the liberals' hostility to all religious instruction in schools and distrusted Bismarck's liberal 'alliance' in general. Indeed, the price demanded by the liberals in terms of free trade and ministerial responsibility for their further support, seemed to Bismarck himself to be becoming unreasonably high.

The death of Pius IX (1878) and the election of the more conciliatory Leo XIII was an opportunity that Bismarck seized with enthusiasm. With the repeal of the bu!' of the 'May Laws' (1878) and the symbolic dismissal of Falk (July 1879), the Kulturkampf came to an abrupt end. Of the great 'struggle for civilisation' only the laws on civil marriage, state supervision of schools and those against the Jesuits remained.

Did Bismarck, therefore, lose the Kulturkampf? Certainly the struggle did much to damage his earlier work of unification, and made the majority of German Catholics more sympathetic to Papal authority than they had been before. Perhaps, however, we should see 1878–79 as a tactical withdrawal from a dangerous battlefield rather than as a defeat. Reconciliation did at least largely transform the Centre into a purely religious party. If we see Bismarck's aim as the preservation of his state in the longer term, then perhaps we should accept the long-standing verdict of C. Grant Robertson that 'Bismarck deliberately sacrificed victory in the Kulturkampf to victory in other issues, more important in his judgement'.

(g) The Move to Economic Protectionism

The tactical withdrawal that ended the Kulturkampf provided Bismarck with the opportunity to make some sweeping changes in his system of domestic political alliances and to introduce a note of greater conservatism into his domestic policies. These changes have often been interpreted as opportunist, but they can also be seen, as by A. Ramm, as a 'coherent and systematic revision of policy in relation to the economic, social and financial needs of the Reich'.

The first of the needs that Bismarck now felt compelled to meet was the growing demand for measures of economic protectionism. While free trade remained an essential principle of the National Liberals, demands for higher protective tariffs increased from other quarters. While their origins can be traced back to the slumps in the Berlin and Vienna stock markets in 1873, these demands began to receive urgent support from the chiefs of the iron and steel industries from 1875 in the face of British competition. Also in the mid-1870s Prussia's Junker landowners began to change

their traditional free trade stance. Instead of aiming at free access to the markets of Britain and France, they now found themselves vulnerable at home and abroad to the cheap grain arriving from the United States. The adoption of protective tariffs by France, Russia and Austria-Hungary over this same period seemed to make it all the more desirable for Germany to follow suit. Apart from this impressive array of industrialist and Junker opinion, the government itself had pressing motives. Protection would aid the growth of national self-sufficiency in the event of a future crisis, and tariffs provided it with a valuable source of income independent both of the Reichstag and of the member states. From 1876, the path chosen by Bismarck became clearer. In April of that year he accepted the resignation of R. Delbrück, head of the Chancellor's Office and architect of the earlier free trade policies. In early 1878, the refusal of the liberal leaders to join Bismarck's cabinet unless they were given substantial undertakings on ministerial appointments and policy decisions, sealed their fate in Bismarck's eyes. When the new tariff laws were enacted in the Reichstag (July 1879) they laid duties of between 5–7% upon imported food, and of 10–15% upon imported industrial goods. An amendment proposed by Freiherr zu Frankenstein limited Bismarck's triumph by fixing an upper limit of 180 million marks in tariff income to be retained by the Reich, any surplus being distributed among the states. If this provided those states with some little satisfaction, there was none for German liberalism. A substantial step had been taken back to the path of convervatism, and the 'Liberal Era' in the history of united Germany was effectively at an end.

(h) Bismarck and Socialism

The second compelling motive for Bismarck's change of course was his desire to combat what he saw as the menace of socialism within Germany. Although the weakness of the socialists in the Reichstag might have seemed to make them unlikely candidates for the label of 'Reichsfeind', Bismarck, like most European statesmen, was genuinely shaken by recent events such as the Paris Commune (see Chapter 8, section **b**). The 'Eisenach' socialists had, after all, refused their support for the war of 1870. Many remembered Bebel's claim in the Reichstag (May 1871) that 'before many decades pass the battle cry of the proletariat of Paris will become that of the whole proletariat of Europe'. It seems probable that if Bismarck's opposition to Catholicism was not primarily ideological, his opposition to socialism was. In A. J. P. Taylor's words, he 'genuinely believed in the turnip-ghost which he conjured up.'

Bismarck's opportunity came in mid-1878 when two attempts upon the life of the Kaiser gave him the chance to raise the cry of 'the Fatherland in Danger', to dissolve the Reichstag and to hold new elections. Although neither assailant had any clear association with the Social Democratic Party, the mood of the electorate was patriotic and conservative. 'The Emperor has the wounds', commented a liberal observer, 'the nation the fever'. The Social Democrats had few seats to lose and the real losers in the election were the National Liberals. A majority of deputies were returned in favour of Protection, the repeal of the 'May Laws', and the passage of Bismarck's anti-socialist measures (Sozialistengesetz). The law (19th October 1878) did not directly ban the Social Democratic Party, but savaged their organisation by banning any group or meeting aimed at the spread of socialist doctrine, outlawing trade unions, and closing a total of 45 newspapers. It was originally in operation, thanks to a liberal amendment, for only two and a half years. It was nevertheless renewed regularly until 1890.

It was clear to Bismarck that socialism could not be conquered by oppression alone. The second string of his anti-socialist policy was thus a programme of 'state socialism'. This meant a series of measures, reminiscent of Junker paternalism, to improve the conditions of the German workers. In 1883, medical insurance and sick pay were introduced. Although these were largely financed by the workers themselves, the employers were responsible for the funding of the scheme of insurance against industrial injuries introduced the following year. Finally, in 1889, old age pensions were introduced, some two decades before their appearance in Britain. Historians have differed in their estimates of 'state socialism'. Some, like E. Eyck, have seen the policy as a fraud. It was pursued for short term political advantage. They point out how much more advantageous it would have been to relax the restrictions upon trades unions to allow the workers to fight their own battles. They note that old age pensions were paid only to those who reached the age of seventy. This was a ripe old age indeed for an industrial worker. G. A. Craig, however, believes that it is possible to trace such paternalism in Bismarck's policies right back to 1862. He feels that 'state socialism' was based upon genuine conviction. Whatever its motives, concludes W. N. Medlicott, the effects of the policy were so laudable as to constitute Bismarck's 'greatest claim to statesmanship in the last decade of his career'.

Was Bismarck then more successful against socialism than he had been against Catholicism? Certainly he gained enthusiastic support from 'academic socialists' ('Kathedersozialisten') such as Brentano and Weber. He horrified some liberals who accused him of attempting to found communism in Germany. Certainly, he failed to check the growth of the Social Democratic Party, for whom Engels claimed an increased membership from 550 000 in 1884 to 1 427 000 in 1890. The workers, claims W. M. Simon, saw 'state socialism', as a fraud and gave their electoral support to the left. A. J. P. Taylor, however, recalls how subservient the German working class was to government policy in the years leading up to 1914 and concludes that Bismarck's policy had at least defused the threat of working class opposition to the state. 'The workers seemed to have received social security as the price of political subservience, and they drew the moral that greater subservience would earn a yet greater reward'.

(i) The Principles of Foreign Policy

Before 1870 Bismarckian policy had aims, more or less specific, that were pursued and eventually achieved by the skilful exploitation of external events. After 1871 the essential principles of foreign policy underwent a substantial change. In the eyes of Bismarck the 'little German' settlement of that year was final and Germany was a 'satiated' state, without further territorial ambitions. As he himself remarked, 'when we have arrived in a good harbour, we should be content to cultivate and hold what we have won'. It was now Bismarck's primary aim to prevent external events from disrupting the settlement that he had created. In this undertaking he was to achieve far less success than he had enjoyed in the first decade of his diplomatic career.

The prime obstacle to his desired stability was, of course, France. No French government between 1871–1918 was willing openly to accept the loss of Alsace-Lorraine as permanent, thus leaving open the possibility of a future war of revenge (Revanche). Equally, no French government was so rash as to believe that France could reverse the judgement of 1871 single-handed. A key consideration was France's ability to contract alliances (Bundnisfähigkeit). The situation in this respect in 1871 was ambiguous. On the one hand, France was separated from Russia by a vast ideological rift, and from Austria-Hungary by bitter memories of 1859. On the other hand, Russia and Austria-Hungary were bound to be concerned at the great upsurge of German power between 1866–71, and to fear what the British statesman Disraeli called the 'German Revolution' which had destroyed the old European balance of power. Voices as diverse as those of the conservative Swiss historian J. Burckhardt and Karl Marx declared that the ultimate result of 1871 would be war between Germany and Russia, between the new and the old dominant powers of Europe. To complicate matters further, relations between the Empires of Russia and Austria-Hungary continued to be strained, especially over their rival claims in the Balkans. Also the possibility had to be considered of one of them seeking French aid against the other. Realising as much himself, Bismarck described to von Bülow the delicate balancing act that he needed to perform. 'The pivot of our position is our relationship with Russia. I believe that if the Prussian and the Cossack ever come to blows, Europe will become republican. The ticklish factor in our connection with Russia is of course Austria. We cannot let Austria be overrun and shattered. But just as little can we let ourselves be dragged into war by her'.

(j) The Dreikaiserbund

For some years after 1872 the mainstay of Bismarck's delicate diplomatic balance was the understanding between the rulers of Germany, Russia and Austria-Hungary known as the League of the Three Emperors (Dreikaiserbund). First projected at a meeting of the monarchs in 1872, it was confirmed the following year (22nd October 1873). It was given more concrete form by a series of bilateral military agreements promising aid to any party attacked by a fourth party.

In concluding this very general and formless agreement, Bismarck probably had three main motives, although authorities disagree as to the placing of the main emphasis. Firstly, the Dreikaiserbund represented a natural union of conservative ideals against disruptive forces such as nationalism and the socialism of the Paris Commune. Secondly, as E. Eyck stresses, the League ensured that neither Austria-Hungary nor Russia was available as an ally for France. A. J. P. Taylor, on the other hand, prefers to emphasise the third potential benefit to Germany from the League. 'Its object', he writes, 'in so far as it had one, was to prevent a conflict between Austria-Hungary and Russia in the Eastern Question'. In short, preoccupied by domestic issues for much of

the decade, Bismarck sought to ensure that Europe remained quiet by ensuring that he directed a combination of three of Europe's five main powers.

(k) The Crises of 1875 and 1878

Behind the superficial unity of the Dreikaiserbund lay a basis of self-interest and mutual suspicion that was always likely to undermine it. Two crises in the 1870s demonstrated the instability of the League. The first, the so called 'War in Sight' crisis of 1875, was the result of Bismarck's first major diplomatic miscalculation. He had estimated, since 1871, that his purposes were best served by the survival of a republican government in France, as this would strengthen Russian and Austrian suspicions of France and keep that country in isolation. He even went so far as to dismiss and humiliate his ambassador in Paris, H. von Arnim, when the latter disagreed and promoted royalist interests. Now in 1875, political developments in France indicated a rise in royalist support (see chapter 8, section **c**) and displayed disturbing signs of military preparation. Bismarck's reaction was to allow threats of preventive war, which he certainly never intended to fight, to circulate from unofficial sources. These came to a head with an article in the *Berliner Post* (9th April 1875) entitled *Is War in Sight?* Far from leading to the desired French embarrassment and retreat, the article caused France to appeal to the other powers to prevent a further German assault upon her. In the interests of peace and of the balance of power, Britain and Russia led the protests to Berlin. The crisis ended as suddenly as it had begun, with a German withdrawal. There was much personal bitterness between Bismarck and the Russian premier Gorchakov, who posed flamboyantly as the saviour of European peace. The limits of Russia's confidence in Germany had been starkly illustrated.

The second crisis, the Eastern crisis of 1875–78, was not of Bismarck's making. It arose from the general revolt of the South Slav peoples, with Bulgarian support, against their Turkish overlords in 1875–76. Pan Slavism and practical political interests encouraged successful Russian intervention (see Chapter 6, section **m**) and resulted in the Treaty of San Stefano (3rd March 1878). By this treaty European Turkey was substantially reduced by the creation of sizeable Russian client states in Bulgaria, Rumania, Serbia and Montenegro. Bismarck had eloquently disclaimed any interest in the Eastern Question, using the famous phrase that no Balkan issue was 'worth the healthy bones of a single Pomeranian musketeer'. Even so, he could not fail to be concerned at the prospect of a clash between Russia and Austria-Hungary, who now saw her only remaining sphere of influence threatened. The only alternative to war was a conference of the great powers, and this met in Berlin (June–July 1878) under the presidency of Bismarck. He was in his role as the 'Honest Broker', aiming not for personal profit, but for a peaceful settlement between his 'clients' Russia and Austria-Hungary. The interests of the other major powers, including Britain, ensured that Russia would not be able to maintain the San Stefano settlement. Instead, Serbia and Montenegro were limited in size by being refused any part of Bosnia or Herzegovina, which territories were occupied by Austria-Hungary to ensure her continued influence in the Balkans. Most important, the large Bulgarian state was divided, with nominal Turkish rights preserved there.

Superficially, the Congress of Berlin marked a highpoint in Bismarck's diplomatic career. In the short term, he had indeed preserved peace and confirmed Berlin as the axis around which European diplomacy turned. E. Eyck, on the other hand, is one of those who prefer to see the congress as the beginning of the end of the Bismarckian system. Although they kept their substantial Asian gains from Turkey, Russian opinion was bitter at the loss of Slav territory won at the cost of Russian blood, and Alexander II was not alone in seeing the Congress of Berlin as 'a European coalition against Russia under the leadership of Prince Bismarck'. The introduction of protective tariffs against Russian agriculture in 1879 only confirmed this impression. Quite apart from the chill that entered into Russo-German relations, the Dreikaiserbund was further undermined by the installation of Austria-Hungary in Bosnia and Herzegovina against the will of the local population. Not only did that move increase the likelihood of Austro-Russian tension in the short term, but in the long term of course lit the fuse that was to lead to the explosion of 1914.

(I) The Dual Alliance

Anti-German feeling in Russia after the Congress of Berlin was the result of thwarted Pan-Slav ambitions and of the wounded pride of Gorchakov, rather than of any deliberate reorientation of German policy. It had great long-term importance in that it confirmed Bismarck in the impression that he had already derived from the events of 1875–78. This was that the time had come to put Germany's relations with Austria-Hungary on a

surer footing. His motives were undoubtedly complex, but were dominated by the desire to avoid diplomatic isolation, and perhaps by the hope of frightening Russia back onto better terms with Germany by the prospect of her own isolation. It was also certain that a clear commitment to Austria would be the most popular of the diplomatic options within Germany, especially at a time when his own domestic policy relied so heavily upon Conservative support. As Bismarck wrote to the reluctant Wilhelm, 'German kinship, historical memories, the German language, all that makes an alliance with Austria more popular in Germany than an alliance with Russia'. Nevertheless, it was only with great difficulty that the Emperor's scruples about the 'betrayal' of Russia and of his fellow monarch were overcome.

In Austria, on the other hand, the prospect was greeted with great enthusiasm. The wounds of 1866 had been largely closed by more recent scares concerning Russia, and by the replacement as Prime Minister of the anti-Prussian Beust by the conservative Hungarian aristocrat, Count Andrassy. He remembered Hungary's debt to Prussia from 1866, and was reported to have 'jumped for joy' at news of the German proposals. The Dual Alliance between the two states was thus concluded in October 1879, although its terms remained secret for nearly a decade. Both powers committed themselves to aid the other in the event of a Russian attack, but only to neutrality if the attack came from another power. In short, Austria was not committed to aid Germany in hostilities against France, an inequality that drew further criticism from the Kaiser. Not for the first time Bismarck had to resort to the threat of resignation to coax his master into a step that the latter felt to be disadvantageous and almost, in the context of the Dreikaiserbund, immoral.

In the following years, the Dual Alliance became the centre of a system of German diplomacy that has been alternatively interpreted as the salvation of European peace in the 1880s, and as confused and contradictory. In May 1882, the alliance became a Triple Alliance through the association of Italy with Germany and Austria-Hungary. This extension of the Bismarckian system had substantial advantages for Germany in that her mutual undertakings with Italy were specifically anti-French. This provided her for the first time with a committed ally against that country. On the other hand, Bismarck had earlier admitted that Austria's alliances with Serbia (June 1881) and Rumania (October 1882) draw Germany even deeper into areas where she had absolutely no direct stake or interest.

Meanwhile, what of Russia? The Dual Alliance was a success in that Russia applied to Germany for a renewal of the Dreikaiserbund in response to it, and perhaps to Bismarck's brief flirtation with Great Britain, who was Russia's great rival in the Eastern Question. This was indeed concluded (June 1881) on a more formal basis than before. The three powers agreed to remain neutral in the event of one of their number going to war with a fourth power. Also Russia and Austria-Hungary acknowledged each other's spheres of influence in the Balkans. Russia acknowledged Austria-Hungary's right to annex Bosnia-Herzegovina whenever she chose to do so, while Austria-Hungary withdrew her objections to the reconstitution of 'Big Bulgaria'. Concluded for a period of three years, Austro-Russian relations remained good enough for the Dreikaiserbund to be renewed in 1884. It met its end, however, in the aftermath of renewed crisis over Russian influence in Bulgaria in 1887.

(m) The Reinsurance Treaty

The crisis that arose over Russia's virtual deposition of Bulgaria's independent minded King Alexander (August-September 1886) raised the likelihood of an Austro-Russian clash more starkly than at any time since 1878. The resultant collapse of the Dreikaiserbund threatened the whole basis of Bismarckian diplomacy. In an attempt to plug the gap and to retain some influence over Russia's actions, the Chancellor was able to conclude (June 1887) a bilateral, completely secret agreement with Russia, known as the Reinsurance Treaty. By its terms both powers agreed to remain neutral in a dispute with a third power. Also Germany recognised Russia's preponderant interest in Bulgaria. As these terms did not apply in the event of a German attack on France, or of a Russian attack upon Austria-Hungary, Bismarck did in fact gain a means of preventing the latter eventuality.

Much controversy has centred upon the question of the compatibility of the Reinsurance Treaty with the terms of the Dual Alliance. Was this the last great trick of a great diplomatic juggler bent upon European equilibrium and peace, as J. Langer has argued? Or is E. Eyck nearer the truth in his view of Bismarck's judgement faltering in old age, clouded and confused by basic conservative prejudices? In the letter of the two agreements there was in fact no contradiction. They did put Germany in the position of having to decide, in any Austro-Russian clash, who was truly the aggressor. On that question would hang the

decision as to which treaty Germany honoured. There was the achievement of Bismarck in the Reinsurance Treaty, that it maintained Germany's power to arbitrate between Russia and Austria-Hungary. In A. Ramm's words, 'Bismarck kept the peace of Europe, but kept it on Germany's terms'.

Unfortunately, within three years, Germany was to face the task of maintaining the delicate balance without the services of this consummate diplomat. What was Bismarck's diplomatic legacy? J. McManners has concluded that, by his commitment to Austria-Hungary, he bequeathed potential political disaster: 'Two years before Bismarck's fall from office, his system was shaking and the shadow of a Franco-Russian alliance was creeping into the horizon'. This is perhaps too harsh in that it attaches too little importance to the forces driving Bismarck in his decision in 1879, and underestimates the Reinsurance Treaty. It was, after all, Wilhelm II who allowed the treaty to lapse in 1890 when Russian enthusiasm for its renewal remained high. Nor did Bismarck create the Eastern European tensions that erupted in 1914. We could conclude with A. J. P. Taylor that, although neither Bismarck nor any other statesman could exercise full control over the political forces and currents of the continent, 'without him the great war of all against all—of class against class, nation against nation—would have got under way sooner'. His greatest fault did not lie in his system of alliances. It lay in the fact that his neurotic monopolisation of power meant that the diplomatic and political future of Germany would inevitably lie in the hands of lesser and less experienced men.

(n) The Beginnings of German Colonialism

In the mid-1880s the otherwise consistent if complex course of German foreign policy took a quite unprecedented twist. Bismarck gave his government's support to the formation of a far flung but substantial body of German colonial possessions. This contrasted with the fact that in 1871 he had refused to annex French colonial possessions in place of Alsace-Lorraine, and as late as 1881 had declared that 'so long as I am Chancellor we shall pursue no colonial policy'.

Germany's part in the 'Scramble for Africa' was concentrated in the years 1884–85 and took the form of the official establishment of sovereignty in areas where German trading interests had been developed by private firms over the past decade or so. In April 1884, the state agreed to 'protect' the strip of territory at Angra Pequena, in what is now

Namibia. It had been secured from the Nama tribesmen by the Bremen merchant, A. Lüderitz. Within the year, to the deep concern of British interests in southern Africa, this had grown into the colony of South West Africa. In July of the same year, the government accorded the official status of German Consul-General in Togoland and the Cameroons to G. Nachtigal. He had previously been acting in that area for a group of Hamburg businessmen. In February 1885, K. Peters, a businessman and adventurer of deservedly dubious reputation, acquired most of German East Africa (now Tanzania) for the Reich by a series of shady deals with local chiefs. Further afield, the establishment of Imperial control over northern New Guinea (May 1885) and subsequently over the western part of the Samoan Islands in the Pacific (1899) completed the shape of the German colonial empire.

The reasons for this abrupt departure from tradition have exercised historians ever since, and there is still no general agreement as to Bismarck's motives. The traditional view of nationalist historians was that Bismarck had always hoped for colonial greatness and was merely awaiting his opportunity. This cannot any longer be accepted in the face of so much evidence of Bismarck's indifference. In its place, the most widely accepted explanation is that, as I. Geiss puts it, 'the German Chancellor had to conform to dominating trends in German society'. Such trends were indeed manifold. German industry, for example, was now powerful enough (see section **o**) to seek new outlets and new sources of raw materials abroad. It was perhaps natural that, after the introduction of protective tariffs in 1879, many businessmen should seek similar protection from the state for their interests abroad. This enthusiasm found expression in the formation and success of such pressure groups as the German Colonial Union (Deutscher Kolonialverein, 1882) and the Society for German Colonisation (Gesellschaft für Deutsche Kolonisation, 1884). Nationalist feeling also proclaimed that the German state, having established its European position, now had to make its power felt in the wider world. This was needed especially at a time when France, Britain and Belgium were carving out empires for themselves. Lastly, Bismarck might have been influenced by the argument of the political conservatives. They saw foreign adventures as a welcome distraction from domestic tension at a time when the struggle against the 'Reichsfeind' of German socialism was in full swing.

At least two other interpretations are worthy of note, which see colonialism, not as an aberration, but rather as another trick on Bismarck's part in pursuit of his traditional policies. For A. J. P. Taylor, Bismarck was still primarily concerned with European politics. Colonialism, with its resultant tensions between Germany and the British Empire, was part of a strategy that aimed to improve German relations with France by drawing the two states into a common anti-British cause. His encouragement of French ambitions in North Africa and in the Far East (see Chapter 8, section **o**) supports this thesis, but we would have to conclude in that case that the policy failed with the spectacular collapse of the Ferry government and its colonial policy in 1885. For E. Eyck, the Chancellor's concerns lay even closer to home. His main aim was to separate the Crown-Prince Friedrich, a colonial enthusiast, from his liberal supporters in the Reichstag while liberal feeling was generally hostile to the principle. Friedrich was surely soon to succeed to the throne as Wilhelm was 87 years old in 1884. Anti-British feeling, furthermore, might diminish the influence of Friedrich's English wife Victoria. She was no friend to the Chancellor and his policies.

Whatever the rationale behind it, the German colonial policy was generally sterile. Bismarck had hoped that colonisation would not become a financial burden upon the Reich, but would be financed by private enterprise. 'I do not wish to found provinces', he told the Reichstag in 1884, 'but to protect commercial establishments in their development'. These hopes were ill founded. By 1913, colonisation had cost the German taxpayer over a thousand million marks in direct government aid. Only Togoland and Samoa had proved to be self-supporting. In almost every respect the results of thirty years of imperialism had been a disappointment. The total German population of its colonies was only 24 000, most of them salaried officials. Only South West Africa, where diamonds were discovered in 1907, fulfilled hopes of valuable natural resources. The native populations, poor and under-developed, had been unable to play the role of consumers of German industrial produce. Worst of all, the limited colonial experiment of 1884–85 was to provide a basis for German pretensions to a 'World Policy' in the next decade. It thereby played no small role in the events that led to war in 1914.

(o) German Economic Development

The unification of the Reich in 1871 provided a number of direct stimulae to an economy which already possessed a substantial basis for prosperity.

Alsace-Lorraine, for example, contained Europe's largest deposits of iron ore. Production increased rapidly under German control, from 684 000 tons in 1872 to 1 859 000 tons in 1882. The injection of part of the French indemnity payments into the national economy caused a spectacular if short lived boom between 1871–73. This was felt especially in the building and railway industries. Lastly, as shown in section **d**, unity provided the opportunity for a burst of legislation designed further to unify the economic life of the Reich.

In terms simply of output, the 'Bismarck Era' provided further dramatic advances for the German economy. Coal production soared, steel production increased by some 700% and the German merchant marine advanced from virtual non-existence to the position of second largest in the world. Table 7.2, by contrasting German development with that of Great Britain and France, gives an impression of her advance as a world industrial power. Apart from the doubling of the railway network, it is also important to note the extent of nationalisation that took place during these decades. Twenty-four thousand out of Prussia's 28 000 kms of track passed into state ownership between 1879–84.

	1870		1890
Population	41 m.	Germany	49 m.
	32 m.	Britain	38 m.
	36 m.	France	38 m.
Coal (m. tons)	38	Germany	89
	118	Britain	184
	13	France	26
Steel (m. tons)	0.3	Germany	2.2
	0.6	Britain	3.6
	0.08	France	0.6
Iron Ore (m. tons)	2.9	Germany	8
	14	Britain	14
	2.6	France	3.5

Table 7.2

In these respects the two decades merely formed part of a steady and consistent development. What was unique to this period was the development of two important features of the direction of the economy. Firstly, the post war boom provided a considerable stimulus to the German banking industry. By the mid-1870s Germany had a remarkably well endowed system. Apart from the

Reichsbank there were six other banks which dominated the commercial and industrial scenes with a combined capital of 2500 million marks. These included the so-called 'D-banks', the Deutsche Bank, the Dresdener Bank, the Darmstadter Bank, and the Discontogesellschaft. They participated widely in the arrangement of private loans to industry and public loans to the state, in the direction of mergers and cartels, in the encouragement of new industries such as electricity and chemicals, and in the development of foreign and colonial ventures. With their representatives sitting on the boards of many leading companies, the co-operation of industrialists and bankers known as 'Finance Capitalism' reached a high stage of development during this period. Such bankers could also provide great services for the state. F. Stern has recently drawn attention to the role played by Bismarck's own banking advisor, G. Bleichröder, in the financial management of some of the Chancellor's major projects. He it was who financed the expensive military projects of 1863–66 at a time when state reserves had fallen from 21 million thalers to 4 million during the constitutional crisis. Also he stage-managed the policy of railway nationalisation in the 70s and 80s.

The second distinctive feature of contemporary economic development was the growth of 'Cartels'. These were groupings or agreements made between different companies in the same industry aimed at avoiding the dangers of competition by such measures as price fixing, agreements on the level of production, and the sharing of markets. Four such Cartels existed in 1865, and only eight a decade later. Harder times made such arrangements more attractive and Germany boasted 90 in 1885 and 210 five years later. The largest Cartels, such as the Rhenish Steel Syndicate and the Ruhr Coal Syndicate, and the men at their heads, such as Krupp, Stinnes and Thyssen, exercised enormous influence over the economic, and sometimes over the political development of the Reich. Their demands for higher tariffs in the 1870s and their later campaigns for naval and colonial development show this very clearly. A further result of these Cartels was that safe home markets enabled German industrialists increasingly to break into foreign markets by 'dumping' goods cheaply. This was subsidised by guaranteed domestic profits.

Therein lay the ultimate failure of Bismarck's conservative system. For all his fears of Catholics or Socialists, the greatest danger to Junker, Prussianised Germany lay in the increasing demands and ambitions of German financiers and industrialists.

(p) Education and Culture

It was common throughout Europe in the 1870s to explain Germany's phenomenal recent successes in terms of her educational system. Indeed, there is little doubt that in terms of elementary education, to the age of ten, she led the world. The success of her system may be gauged from the startling statistic that the national rate of illiteracy in the 1870s was a little over 1%, compared with 33% in Britain, about 50% in France and over 75% in Italy. Although the elementary schools (Volksschulen) formed the basis of a complex and successful educational system, a number of factors ensured that working class literacy did not lead to high social mobility. The fees charged by the grammar schools (Gymnasium), the habit of recruiting largely from private preparatory schools, and a drop out rate of nearly two thirds between the ages of ten and eighteen ensured that university was the preserve of the wealthier classes. In 1900, only 1% of university students were working class. This was a tenfold increase since 1890.

Limited as they were in their intake, German universities continued to enjoy a high reputation in the 'Bismarck era'. Each state jealously protected the reputation of its own institutions and vied to attract the most prestigious teachers. These men constitute an impressive list in at least two main disciplines. In the natural sciences Germany claimed leading figures in most fields. Among them were the mathematician K. Gauss (1777–1855), the chemist J. Liebig (1803–73), and the biologists R. Koch (1843–1910) and R. Virchow (1821–1902). Fascination with the process and achievement of unification also gave renewed impetus to the study of German history. The doyen of the 'Prussian school', L. von Ranke, was still alive and 75 years old in 1871. The 'school' was revivified by such as H. von Sybel and H. von Treitschke, both deeply concerned with the phenomenon of the rise of the nation state (see section **q**). On a broader basis, the great classical historian T. Mommsen, and the Swiss born historian of the Italian Renaissance, J. Burckhardt, remain authorities in their fields.

In general, the first decades of political unity were years of cultural sterility relative to an earlier age when political impotence had contrasted with the enormous fertility of Schiller, Goethe, Beethoven, Herder, Kant and many others. The monumental canvasses of 'court' painters such as A. von Werner and A. von Menzel, the mock-gothic or mock-Renaissance styles of public architecture, and much of German literature lacked originality. They imitated the empires of the past while celebrating the one that had just been founded. An American visitor a generation later remarked that 'a visit to the National Gallery of Berlin makes me gnash my teeth. The sight of so much misspent labour, of the acres of canvas deluged with dirty, bad paint, raises my bile'.

Two figures stand out above this mediocrity. The first is that of the composer Richard Wagner (1813–83). He was a democrat and a cosmopolitan in his earlier life, but became increasingly committed to Germany and its culture from the late 1860s. He believed in the superiority and originality of German language and musical creativity. This showed itself in his theoretical writings such as *What is German?*, in his attack upon Jewish musical influences in *Judaism and Music*, and in his profound use of German legend and myth, notably in his great cycle of operas *The Ring of the Nibelungs*. 1872 saw the beginning of his project for a theatre at Bayreuth. This was not merely for the production of his own work, but in G. Mann's words as 'a temple of German art, a centre of the national community'.

The second 'giant' of the age was the philosopher and philologist Friedrich Nietzsche (1844–1900). To a large extent, the thoughts and writings of Nietzsche were negative, a fierce and systematic criticism of the bases of the society in which he lived. He despised the modern tendency towards 'popular' culture and all that pandered to the tastes of the 'masses'. He regarded the newly-founded national state with distrust and distaste. Above all, he rebelled against the 'slave morality' of Christianity, with its emphasis upon meekness and equality. In his most famous work *Thus Spake Zarathustra* (1883–85), he declared that 'God is dead', and that the future belonged to the 'Superman' ('Übermensch'). This was the man with the courage, the spirit and the will to transcend himself and realise his full human potential. It is probable that Nietzsche meant this in terms of the individual, rather than in any political sense, of a strong leader dominating the state. He was certainly bitterly opposed to racism and described himself politically, not as a nationalist, but as 'a good European'. His work was largely neglected in his lifetime but was most popular when, like Wagner's, it was adopted and adapted by a later generation to justify the striving for power of autocratic leaders and of the German race.

(q) Historiography

With the exception perhaps of Napoleon Bonaparte, no 19th century figure has attracted the attention and controversy that surrounds the life and achievement of Otto von Bismarck. It was estimated in the mid 1970s that some 6000 works on him and on the Germany of his time had been published, and still the arguments on the subject are far from exhausted. Some broad themes of opinion may, nevertheless, be distinguished among this complexity.

The success of Bismarck's work in unifying part of Germany gave rise in his own lifetime to a German historiography that portrayed him as the master statesman leading Germany to its rightful destiny. A generation of historians agreed broadly with H. von Sybel (*The Founding of the German Empire by Wilhelm I*, 1889–94) that here was 'a politician of great stock who sacrificed everything to the interests of the state'. Prominent in this school of thought was the great Prussian academic H. von Treitschke, whose monumental *German History in the 19th Century* (1879–94) traced the inevitable rise of Prussian mastery with Bismarck as the chosen instrument of fate. Naturally, there were differences over detail, notably over the question of the defeat of Austria. This was a 'tragic inevitability' to some southern writers but joyfully accepted by the Prussian Treitschke. In general, German work was, like the unfinished biography begun in 1902 by E. Marcks, 'designed as a thanks offering to a man who willed` everything, accomplished everything, embodied everything', who made Germany 'strong and manly'.

For major dissent from this thesis, one had either to look to countries that had suffered at Bismarck's hands, or to wait until the events of 1914–18 and 1933–45 had proved that the Chancellor's work had more sinister implications. The picture of Bismarck as a Machiavellian and immoral power politician was given great emphasis in the memoirs of the French politician E. Ollivier (*The Franco-Prussian War and its Hidden Consequences*, 1912). It was subsequently seen by some foreign authorities as the basis for the disastrous era of German Nazism. H. Kohn (*Rethinking Recent German History*, 1952) saw Bismarck as being directly responsible for Hitlerism. 'The Prussian victories of the 1860s, and the transformation which they wrought in the minds of most Germans, laid the foundations for the defeats of 1918 and 1945'. For other writers, such as G. Barraclough, (*Origins of Modern Germany*, 1947) his responsibility was indirect. By crippling the development of democratic institutions in Germany, he had laid the country open to future dictatorships.

In general, German enthusiasm for Bismarck's work survived the First World War, but was severely damaged by the bombing and invasion of 1944–45. German liberals such as E. Eyck (*Bismarck: Life and Work*, 1941–44) and the veteran academic F. Meinecke (*The German Catastrophe: Reflections and Recollections*, 1960) have led the attack upon his repression of political freedom after 1870. They did not have any great criticism of his earlier work towards unification. It has been left to the German-American historian O. Pflanze (*Bismarck and the Development of Germany*, 1963) to defend the argument that unification itself was an artificial movement. It was 'a fiction of nationalistic historians', not broadly desired by public opinion and engineered mainly to serve Bismarck's own political ends. German conservatives have continued to argue, led by G. Ritter (*Europe and the German Question*, 1948) that Bismarck should not bear the responsibility for later developments. They also argued that his semi-feudal conservatism, his religion, and his 'Little German' views, all distanced him greatly from the principles of Nazism. As H. Rothfels (*Bismarck and the State*, 1954) put it, 'we may criticise Bismarck for paving the way to some fatal trends of our day, but . . . we cannot very well overlook the fundamental fact that Hitler . . . did precisely what the founder of the Reich had refused to do'.

The most important development of recent decades in the study of Bismarck's Germany has been to move away from the study of diplomacy and of 'Grand Policy' ('Grosse Politik'), to diminish the role played by great men such as Bismarck, and to stress instead the wider context in which they played their roles. In a negative sense A. J. P. Taylor (*Bismarck: The Man and Statesman*, 1955) has portrayed Bismarck 'warts and all', as a brilliant but unstable neurotic, driven less by great principles than by overwhelming personal ambition and egoism. More positively, W. E. Mosse (*The European Powers and the German Question*, 1958) has stressed the conducive diplomatic circumstances which facilitated Bismarck's tasks. 'If he played his hand with great skill, it was a good one in the first place'. Leading in this field at present is H. Böhme who, in *Germany's Path to Great Power Status* (1966), concentrated upon the social and economic development of contemporary Germany. He saw in the development of her economic life the true current of German greatness, on the waves of which Bismarck merely rode and steered.

Progress Paragraphs

Answer the following in about 150 words

Why did Germany annex Alsace-Lorraine in 1871?
                                    Section (**a**)

In what senses was the German constitution not truly democratic?   Section (**b**)

How did Prussia ensure her influence over the constitution of united Germany?   Section (**b**)

What attitude was taken to Bismarck and his policies by (a) the German Conservatives, (b) the Centre Party, (c) the National Liberals?   Section (**c**)

In what senses was Germany still disunited after 1871? How successfully did Bismarck promote fuller unity?   Sections (**d, e, f**)

How similar were the motives of Bismarck and the German liberals in opposing the Catholic Church in the Kulturkampf?   Section (**e**)

What motives had Bismarck for terminating the Kulturkampf?   Sections (**f, g, h**)

From whom did the demand come for economic protectionism?   Section (**g**)

For what reasons and with what success did Bismarck pursue an anti-socialist policy after 1878?
                                    Section (**h**)

In what ways was German foreign policy changed by unification?   Section (**i**)

What were Bismarck's main reasons for participation in the Dreikaiserbund?   Section (**j**)

What events weakened the cohesion of the Dreikaiserbund after 1875?   Section (**k**)

What did Bismarck hope to gain from the Dual Alliance?   Sections (**k, l**)

Summarise Germany's relations with Russia between 1878–90.   Sections (**k, l, m**)

Why did Germany pursue a colonial policy after 1884?   Section (**n**)

What was the impact of unification upon the German economy in terms of output and organisation?
                                    Sections (**d, o**)

What impact did unification have upon the cultural life of Germany?   Section (**p**)

8
The French Third Republic to 1914

(a) The Heritage of the Republic: War

The events of 4th September 1870 in Paris revolutionised both the nature of the French regime and the nature of the war with Germany. On that day, undermined by the news of the defeat at Sedan and the captivity of Napoleon III, the Empire collapsed and a republic, the third in French history, was proclaimed by the people of Paris at the Hotel de Ville. As had happened on the two previous occasions, the provinces were generally content to follow the lead of the capital. The most pressing business of the Provisional Government that now established itself, with J. Trochu as its premier and J. Favre in charge of foreign affairs, was the war. Brief hopes that the fall of the Bonaparte dynasty might quickly terminate a conflict attributable to dynastic ambitions were quickly disappointed. Encouraged by great popular support in Paris, the government declared itself the Government of the National Defence and declared its intention to wage 'war to the death' ('la guerre à outrance').

The next four months of republican warfare were to salvage for France a little of her self respect, but also to poison Franco-German relations for the next eighty years. At the centre of the bitter struggle was the siege of Paris which lasted from 20th September 1870 to 28th January 1871. It entailed the starvation and bombardment of Europe's greatest city. Elsewhere the Germans were harassed by guerillas and by three armies raised with the object of relieving the capital. All three had their initial successes, but lacked the reinforcements to make good their casualties. By the time of the surrender of Paris, all three had suffered irreparable damage, General Chanzy at Le Mans (13th January), General Bourbaki at Héricourt (17th January) and General Faidherbe at St. Quentin (18th January). The unfortunate Bourbaki was even unsuccessful in his subsequent attempt to commit suicide.

Considering the position of France in late January 1871, with no troops to speak of, with war weariness growing in the provinces, and with revolt imminent in her conquered capital, the terms of the Treaty of Frankfurt (10th May 1871) were harsh but not crippling. The loss of the provinces of Alsace and Lorraine was bitterly resented, but predictable (see Chapter 7, section **a**). On the other hand, the important border fortress of Belfort which had been undefeated after a siege of over three months, remained in French hands. The war indemnity charged by Germany was still an enormous sum, although reduced from six billion to five billion francs. Only by paying it could the government, which was no longer provisional since the February elections, clear the national soil of German troops. It was perhaps one of the greatest achievements of the Republic that it had cleared its territory of the Army of Occupation by September 1873, and had still managed to balance the national budget by 1875. It drew upon the large reserves of private wealth in France.

The heritage of the Third Republic was an economic millstone of vast proportions. The war had cost France 150 000 lives and the equivalent of £695 million, to say nothing of the mines and 1.5 million inhabitants of Alsace-Lorraine. By the time of the conclusion of peace, the very stability and existence of the state had been called into question anew.

(b) The Heritage of the Republic: The Commune

Within three weeks of the German entry into Paris, France was further shaken, and further humiliated in the eyes of the world. This was by the outbreak of civil war that followed the establishment in Paris of the radical administration known as the Commune. The nature of the Commune has been the cause of much controversy among historians. Karl Marx quickly claimed it as the first great proletarian uprising, directed against capitalism by predominantly working class leaders. This view had generally dominated the view of Marxist writers since. Most more moderate writers have drawn attention to the other strands of radicalism represented in the Commune, such as Anarchism, or the Jacobinism of the first French revolution. They also acknowledged the fact that while 25 of the Commune's elected administrators were workers, the other 65 came from the middle and professional classes. In the views of D. Thomson and of T. Zeldin, the Commune had its roots in a purely French radical tradition. It has since had a mythology woven about it to serve a more modern revolutionary movement. In fact, leaderless and largely incoherent, the Commune was, as F. Jellinek describes it, 'fertile in examples of every revolutionary hypothesis'.

In the long term, the origins of the Commune lay in the peculiar urban social problems, and in the tradition of active communal politics that had made Paris a revolutionary battleground in 1789, 1830 and 1848. Its shorter term causes can easily be found in the disastrous defeat of 1870–71, and in the severe hardships of the siege by the Prussian Army. In the aftermath of their humiliation and suffering, the staunchly republican Parisians now saw a largely monarchist Assembly returned by the elections of 8th February. Within a month the Assembly confirmed fears that it would strike at the interests of the poorer Parisians despite their earlier heroism. A series of acts in early March suspended the pay of the near mutinous Parisian National Guard, and ordered the immediate payment of rents and commercial bills 'frozen' for the duration of the war. Thus, in Sir D. Brogan's phrase, 'the Assembly . . . threatened a great part of the population of Paris with bankruptcy or eviction or both'. Still, the Commune was not the result of any general uprising. A government attempt to remove artillery from the city was thwarted by National Guardsmen, and two unpopular generals were lynched (18th March). Thiers and his government responded by withdrawing the administration entirely from Paris to conservative Versailles. The Central Committee of the National Guard found itself in charge of Paris with neither programme nor tactics. This was not because of any action of their own, but for want of any other government.

The Commune was to govern Paris for 73 days (18th March–28th May 1871), and for most of that time was doomed to failure, having failed to pursue the government to Versailles and to widen its support. In all, it was far more important for what it was than for what it did. Preoccupied for most of its life with its defence against the Versailles government, the Commune nevertheless passed some laudable legislation. It created co-operative workshops, abolished the system of fines for the breaking of petty workshop rules, and introduced the principle of free, compulsory education for both sexes, as an antidote to the influence of the Church. On the other hand, it made little coherent assault upon capitalism, leaving the Bank of France and all forms of private property largely untouched. Its importance lies in the fact that, for the first time since 1792, state power in a European capital lay in the hands of an elected committee composed mainly of working and middle class elements. Europe saw no such democracy again until 1917.

The Commune made its most lasting impression by the nature of its suppression. The entry of government troops into Paris (21st May) began the so-called 'bloody week' as the city was recaptured street by street. While the 'Communards' executed 56 hostages and killed about 1000 troops, as many as 20000 citizens died, sometimes in battle, sometimes in summary executions without trial. In the aftermath over 13000 Parisians were imprisoned and 7500 were transported to penal settlements in the colonies. A total of 40000 suffered for their involvement.

The results of the Commune, like its causes, have been the subject of much dispute. France's international prestige sank to a new low ebb, and the Republic became burdened with a great legacy of radical and socialist bitterness. J. P. T. Bury, on the other hand, stresses that the long standing problem of Parisian insubordination had been tackled deliberately and successfully by Thiers. Also, 'the proscription and exile of so many extremists enabled the new Republic to attain constitutional legality and to develop in a peaceful and orderly fashion during its first formative years'. Thiers himself has received a mixed 'press'. T. Zeldin accuses him of creating the Commune, by his evacuation of Paris, with the deliberate aim of crushing Paris as a force in French politics. For D. Thomson, Thiers is a more statesman-like figure who, like Abraham Lincoln, had to fight a civil war to protect the very unity of France, which was already defeated and vulnerable. Whether primarily patriotic or Machiavellian, we must conclude that Thiers' treatment of the crisis of the Commune had been energetic, decisive and totally successful.

(c) The 'Provisional' Republic 1871–77

For two years after her defeat France lived, in the words of a foreign observer, 'under a provisional government run by an old gentleman of 74'. Adolphe Thiers was architect of the Orleanist monarchy in 1830, and moderate critic of the Second Empire. He was not even a Republican, but rather a supporter of constitutional monarchy. He maintained, as his handling of the Commune had shown, a profound disgust for the politics of the masses. The government over which he presided as 'Chief of the Executive Power' remained vaguely republican. This was mainly out of a general desire to avoid questions of ideology so soon after the outbreak of civil war, and largely because, in Thiers' own words, 'the Republic divides us least', at a time when the nation seemed in genuine danger of disintegration. The future of the Republic and of the nation remained nevertheless in severe doubt.

What options existed for the future government of France? Superficially, a restoration of the monarchy seemed most likely, with some 400 monarchists among the 700 deputies returned in the elections of February 1871. These were bitterly divided between the supporters of the Houses of Bourbon and Orleans. An obvious compromise suggested itself in that the Bourbon claimant, the Comte de Chambord who was grandson of Charles X, was childless. He might ascend the throne, therefore, on the understanding that he would be succeeded by the Orleanist claimant, the Comte de Paris or his children. Enmity between the two houses might have thwarted this plan, but the immediate obstacle was a bizarre decision by Chambord. Having accepted the principles of parliamentary government and universal suffrage, he then decided to abandon the tricolour as the national flag, and to revert to the royalist white flag. His determination not to let 'the standard of Henri IV, of Francis I, of Jeanne d'Arc be torn from my hands' only served to show how far his 40 years' exile in Austria had distanced him from reality. Such was the attachment of the nation to the flag of the revolution, and of the great Napoleonic victories, that Chambord's stubborn repetition of this condition effectively made a restoration impossible.

With Bonapartism crippled by the death of the former Emperor (1873), popular support for republicanism increased. Above all, the original monarchist vote had been a vote for peace and stability. It was steadily undermined by the failure of the monarchists to agree upon a king, and by increasing evidence of the conservatism of Thiers' brand of republicanism. In addition to the enormous achievement of paying off the war indemnity, he had pleased the middle classes by refusing proposals for an income tax, and by favouring a return to economic protection. He had also appealed to the patriotism of the nation by a new Army Law (August 1872) which introduced conscription for a term of five years' service as the basis for reconstruction of the army. As Sir D. Brogan put it, many now asked themselves 'What could a king do that M. Thiers could not do as well or better'?

The resignation of Thiers (July 1873), forced upon him by those who disliked his increasing attachment to republicanism, threw the future of the Republic into renewed doubt. From 1873–77, France was governed by what D. Halévy has christened 'the Republic of Dukes'. She was under the presidency of Marshal MacMahon. He had been created Duc de Magenta by Napoleon III, and was served in high office by six other dukes, de Broglie and Decazes being the most prominent. The administration's main aim was to give the government a form and institutions which would guarantee its conservative nature and eventually, if Chambord ever saw reason, could equally form the basis of a constitutional monarchy. In November 1874, MacMahon's period of office was fixed at seven years. What now was to be his title? The proposal by the deputy, Wallon, that it be 'President of the Republic', was adopted by only one vote (February 1875). Only by 353 votes to 352 did the Chamber accept the status of Republic, and then without any guarantees against future change.

The additional laws that made up the so-called 'Constitution of 1875' were designed specifically to strengthen the electoral chances of the conservative parties. The President became eligible for re-election at the end of his term, unlike the president of the Second Republic, and retained important powers such as the power to dissolve the Assembly. An upper chamber (Senate) was instituted, with one third of its members chosen for life and the remainder elected for nine years. Lastly, election was to be by single member constituencies (Scrutin d'Arrondisement). This was opposed to the earlier method of electing the deputies for a department 'en masse' from party lists (Scrutin de liste), which had always seemed to favour the superior organisation of the Left. Its main task completed, the 'provisional' Assembly dissolved itself (December 1875) in anticipation of new elections. These frustrated every hope of the conservatives by returning 340 Republicans against 200 right wingers and 75 Bonapartists. Even conservative hopes for the Senate proved ill-founded, with 57 of the 75 life members proving to be Republicans. The monarchist President found himself faced with a Republican Assembly with which co-operation was impossible.

(d) The Consolidation of the Republic, 1877–85

The future of the Republic was assured by the crucial election campaign of 1877. Faced with an intolerable political deadlock, MacMahon acted within his constitutional powers by appointing an unrepresentative administration under the Duc de Broglie, and dissolving the Assembly. He stretched those powers to the limit, however, by his dismissal of 70 Prefects, 226 Sub-Prefects, and 1743 mayors in an attempt to secure maximum local influence in favour of right wing candidates. Leading republicans such as Gambetta, Thiers and Grévy retaliated by fighting one of the most energetic election campaigns of the 19th century, to which the death of Thiers in mid campaign added an emotional touch. The Republican victory by the huge margin of 326 seats to 207 sealed the fate of the 'Republic of Dukes'. MacMahon had failed to impose the authority of the President over that of the Chamber, and failed to impose the influence of the French aristocracy over the people, and gave way to Jules Grévy, a republican acceptable to the majority of deputies. 'It was not only a political turning point', remarked Λ. Cobban, 'it was a more decisive social revolution than anything that had occurred in 1830, 1848 or 1871'.

Such a judgement can be accepted in the sense that the men who dominated the next decade and a half of republican politics were of a very different social stamp from those who went before. Leon Gambetta (Prime Minister 1881–82) was the son of an Italian grocer, dedicated to the replacement of aristocratic influence by that of what he called the 'new social stratum', meaning the lower middle classes. For Gambetta, states T. Zeldin, the Republic 'meant the opening of doors and the breaking down of barriers'. Jules Ferry (Prime Minister 1880, 1883–85) came from a more solid legal, bourgeois background, but was equally dedicated to the principle of eventual equality of rights and dignity in society. In this process, he attached the greatest importance to universal primary education, and spent a little over four years as Minister of Education. Thirdly, Charles-Louis Freycinet (Prime Minister 1879, 1882, 1886) was a Protestant, something still largely unacceptable in the upper levels of French society. His political career was based, not upon the fire and oratory of a Gambetta, but upon his unobstrusive ability as a political manager and conciliator. 'Small, dapper, aloof, subtle, insinuating', wrote A Cobban, he 'was for a whole generation to run up and down the corridors of the Third Republic like a little white mouse'.

On the other hand, confirmed in power by republican appointments in the army, in the judicature, and by great electoral success at a local level, these men still adhered to the principle of Thiers that 'the Republic will be conservative or it will not be at all'. By abandoning the radicalism for which Gambetta was noted a decade earlier, they became branded as the 'Opportunists'. Their early legislation contained much that was of a predominantly symbolic nature; the return of the Assembly to Paris from Versailles (1879); the amnesty extended to surviving Communards (1879–80); the observance of 14th July—Bastille Day—as a national holiday, and the adoption of the revolutionary 'Marseillaise' as the national anthem (1880).

These were closely followed by a series of political reforms of real liberal and democratic content. In 1881 a new Press Law was introduced which removed the possibility of prosecution for the expression of a political opinion. In 1883 all local communities, with the exception of Paris, acquired the right to elect a mayor, rather than having one imposed upon them by the Prefect. At the same time the Senate was democratised by the abolition of life membership. 1884 saw the introduction of competitive examination for offices in the Civil Service, and the legalisation of trades unions for the purpose of protecting the workers' economic interests. Simultaneously, the transformed Republic acquired a reputation to rival that of the Second Empire in the performance of great public works. The Paris International Exhibition of 1878 was followed by the transformation of Marseilles and Le Havre into modern, international commercial ports, by the modernisation and nationalisation of France's inland waterways (1879), and by the doubling in size of the French railway system.

(e) Politics in the Third Republic

The Third Republic presents a startling paradox with apparently contradictory elements of progressiveness and conservatism, and of stability and instability. It triumphed spectacularly over the rule of the aristocracy in 1877, yet made surprisingly few fundamental changes in the social structure thereafter. It saw 108 different ministries installed between 1870–1940, with an average life of eight months, yet the 'constitution' of 1875 lasted for 65 years, longer than any other French constitution to date, until violently overthrown by foreign aggression.

The resolution of this paradox lies in the realisation that this French parliamentary democracy differed greatly from its European counterparts, in that a deliberate attempt was made to ensure that the legislative power (the Chamber) should be considerably more powerful than the executive power (the government). Too often in the past a powerful man or influential group had come to dominate and overthrow republican democracy. The Chamber, therefore, was dominated not by the Presidents, but by the deputies. These had at least three main weapons at their disposal to keep the government in check. The practice of 'interpellation', of questioning ministers often on points of minor detail, could delay government business, and often force the resignation of the government. As many as 4000 interpellations might take place annually. Secondly, the deputies used their power to initiate legislation to swamp the government with projects. In the parliament of 1893–98, for example, 3328 bills were proposed, 1112 of them by private members, often on matters of purely local interest. Lastly, deputies participated in permanent commissions before which all government legislation had to pass. Gambetta, for instance, played a major, if negative role as head of the Commission for Finance between 1877–81.

The results of this system were many. The principle of republicanism was rarely backed by complex programmes of reform as governments despaired of ever getting them past the Chamber. Party loyalties remained, moreover, extremely vague and changeable as deputies became preoccupied with their local interests and their personal projects for legislation. The deputies themselves, on the other hand, became professionals. They were usually drawn from the professional and middle classes, enjoyed a salary equivalent to that of a colonel or a judge (whereas their British counterparts had to wait until 1912 for a much more moderate salary) and a pension if they served as long as 30 years. Naturally enough they became primarily concerned, not with great issues of state, but with the relatively minor interests of their constituents, attention to which kept them in their agreeable positions. So agreeable was the position that elections were frequently marked by various forms of corruption, from falsified registers to the straightforward purchase of votes. The continuity within the regime was also supplied by these deputies, for most parliaments had about 150 members with twenty years' experience or more. Continuity was also given by the civil service, and by the President, who was no longer the dominant figure he had been in 1848, but a valuable element of stability. Therefore a few major themes at least could run from government to government.

(f) Church and State: The Policy of Ferry

Perhaps the most persistent of these themes was the contest between the Republic and the Catholic Church for the hearts and minds of the French people. The conservative era of the Second Empire and the 'Republic of Dukes' had been a flourishing one for the Church. Between 1851–78 membership of religious orders had soared, from 3000 to over 32 000 for men, and from 34 000 to about 128 000 for women. Their combined wealth was estimated at 421 million francs, or £16.8 million in contemporary values. Worst of all in the eyes of republicans, their future seemed assured by the grip upon education allowed them by the Falloux Law of 1850. In 1878 some 40% of French education was conducted by Church schools.

On the other hand, the defeat of 1871 polarised views among the anti-clerical opposition to the Church. It was regarded as significant that the defeat had been at the hands of protestant Prussia, where such an important social role was played by the teachers of the state schools. To many, as to the contemporary historian Edgar Quinet, the defeat of MacMahon at Sedan was the defeat of 'Bonapartism, caesarism, catholicism, jesuitism', of all that was corrupt and sterile in France. The writings of Auguste Comte were also influential in the formation of intellectual anti-clericalism. In his *Système de Politique Positive* (1852-54) he had argued that all aspects of human life and consciousness pass through three stages of development, the theological, the metaphysical, and the highest stage, the scientific or 'positive'. Modern society, now clearly in the third stage in material terms, was thus bound to throw off the constraints of theology and spiritualism. This 'Positivism' provided a tempting philosophical basis for the political views of many intellectual republicans.

In common with the leaders of the German 'Kulturkampf' and with the liberals of the Kingdom of Italy, the leaders of the consolidated French Republic felt it impossible to develop the principles by which they hoped to govern while the population remained subject to the enormous pressure and influence, essentially conservative, of the Church. Indeed, the force of the anti-clerical campaign owed much to the fact that it constituted a rare area of agreement between all shades of republican opinion. Its radical attractions were not offset, as in many other cases by the disadvantage of high cost and taxation. 'The most urgent of all reforms', declared Gambetta, 'must be the liberation of universal suffrage from every sort of tutelage, obstacle, pressure and corruption'. From 1879, therefore, the government waged a far more genuinely ideological 'struggle for civilisation' than Bismarck had attempted. Its key area of attack was education, its primary aim 'to tear away the soul of the youth of France' from the Church. Its key figure was Jules Ferry, Minister of Education from 1879–83.

By one of the most far-reaching and progressive laws passed under the Third Republic (1882) primary education, from the age of six to thirteen years, became compulsory and was provided free. Equally important to Ferry, it was to be wholly free from the influence of the Church. Teachers in these schools were to be laymen, were employees of the state (1886) and were subject to state examination. To meet the demand created by the disqualification of 40 000 clerical teachers, each department was charged (1879) with the creation of a college for the training of female primary school teachers. The Jesuit order, with others, was first banned from teaching and then (1880) expelled from France. Beyond the primary level, the attack upon clerical influence was part of a wider programme of educational reform. This included the closing of the Catholic universities, the revision of the traditionally classical secondary school syllabus, and the establishment (1880) of the first state secondary school for girls. Beyond the sphere of education altogether, the position of the Church was assaulted by the legalisation of divorce, the introduction of civil marriage (both 1884), and by the repeal of the law of 1814 forbidding Sunday working (1879).

(g) Church and State: The Final Separation

Between the two spasms of bitter Church–State rivalry in France lay the period of conciliation known as the 'Ralliement'. From the viewpoint of the Republic, the end of the 1880s marked for it a point of unprecedented strength. The centenary of the Revolution was marked in 1889 by the lavish International Exhibition, of which the new Eiffel Tower was the 'star', and to which 25 million visitors thronged to be impressed by the wealth and resources of the nation. From such a position of stability the state could afford a more conciliatory attitude towards its clerical enemies, and in 1890, largely at the prompting of Pope Leo XIII, the Church responded. The logic of the argument broached to French conservatives by Cardinal Lavigerie, the Primate of Algeria, was that, unable to change the political settlement in France, the Church merely suffered unduly from its opposition. After initial conservative resistance to this line, the Pope explicitly instructed the French Catholics (1891) to accept the authority of the Republic.

It is true that the Ralliement had its enemies among Catholics and republicans alike, but it might have survived had not the Dreyfus Affair (see section **j**) once more polarised conservative and radical views. When the ministry led by R. Waldeck-Rousseau (1899–1902) took office with the specific aim of uniting all elements of republican support, it was always likely that it would realise that, in J. P. T. Bury's words, 'anti-clericalism was the cement that bound the different elements of the republican bloc together'. The death of Leo XIII in 1903 heightened the possibility of a clash. His successor, Pius X, was of an altogether more dogmatic stamp.

Moderate though he was, Waldeck-Rousseau provided the weapon for the final assault upon the Church. This came in the form of the Association Law (July 1901), whose terms forbade the existence in France of any religious body or community without the specific authorisation of the government. In essence this was a defensive measure, which was transformed into an offensive one by Waldeck-Rousseau's successor, E. Combes. The new premier, remarked Sir D. Brogan, 'shared all the ideas, prejudices, hates, principles of the small-town anti-clerical'. Under his enforcement of the Association Law 54 male and 81 female congregations were banned from France (1902), while the five authorised congregations were ordered to abandon all teaching activities within ten years (1904).

1904 also witnessed the final crisis of relations between Rome and the Republic. The Pope precipitated the crisis by his protest at the visit of President Loubet to the King of Italy in Rome, the first visit by the head of a Catholic state since the loss of the Pope's temporal power in 1870. The reaction of the French administration was to break off diplomatic relations with the Vatican (November 1904) and to introduce a bill which realised the dream of generations of anti-clericals by proposing the final separation of church and state in France. By its passage (9th December 1905), the state guaranteed freedom of worship, but ceased officially to recognise or to subsidise any specific religion or cult. The land and assets of the Church were to be handed over to lay parish corporations (Associations Cultuelles), although ultimately all such property was sequestered by the state. This left the clergy simply as tenants of 'buildings needful for worship'.

Bitter as provincial opposition to so radical a measure was, there is much truth in J. P. T. Bury's judgement that 'the momentous separation of 1905 was probably beneficial to both sides'. Although the new and sudden poverty of the Church hit recruitment badly, reducing the annual rate of ordinations from 1563 in 1905 to 704 in 1914, the same factor probably had a beneficial effect upon the quality of the recruits. Quantity, too, began to increase in the 1920s. Better still, the Church now found itself wholly free from state interference in appointments and other matters, such as had operated since the Napoleonic Concordat with the Vatican in 1801. The same could not be said of its conservative ally, the army, whose appointments were so strictly controlled by L. André, War Minister from 1900–04, as to cause a scandal over his use of spies to enquire into the political views of candidates for promotion. If Bury's opinion is open to doubt, it is in the sense that Separation removed the best area of common ground between the diverse members of the governmental Radical Bloc. 'Separation', in the words of M. Rebérioux, 'had marked the end of a common struggle'. From 1905, therefore, the government found itself subjected to a new series of threats from a different point of the political compass (see section **m**).

(h) The Republic in Danger: Boulangism

By the time of the 1885 elections the Republic was about to enter a period of renewed trial. A serious agricultural depression had hit France in the 80s, the result of cheap grain imports from America. Its results were compounded by the ravages of the vine disease, phylloxera, which reduced wine production by more than two thirds between 1875 and 1889. In addition, the collapse of the Union Génerale Bank (1882) ruined many small farmers. Economic hardship coincided with political outrage, especially over the collapse of Ferry's colonial policy at Tonkin (see section **o**) in 1885. Already in 1882 the nationalist P. Déroulède had formed the 'League of Patriots', which became a powerful right wing force by 1885, with 182 000 members. It was formed in protest against a policy that seemed to ignore the question of Alsace-Lorraine.

The 1885 elections were the first under the Third Republic to be held by the method of 'Scrutin de Liste' (see section **c**). The aim was to improve the standard of elected deputies and to rescue the Republic from the welter of trivial and obstructive interpellations in the Assembly. The surprise result was a dramatic revival of the Right, increasing its share of the vote from 25.9% in 1881 to 43.9%. The reign of the Opportunists seemed endangered. The response of the Prime Minister, Freycinet, was to pass stringent measures against all members of former royal families, expelling them from France (1886). Also he appointed to the key post of War Minister a distinguished soldier of proven republican sympathies, General Georges Boulanger.

The succeeding months witnessed the transformation of the little known general into a national 'cult'. His reputation as the long-awaited military saviour of France began with a series of modest but useful reforms in the army, and continued with the magnificent impression that he made upon the public at the 'Bastille Day' parade at Longchamp. It reached its peak in 1887 with the 'Schnaebele Affair'. The arrest of a French official on the Alsatian border by Germans (April 1887) brought threats of war from the minister, to the horror of the government and the delight of the nationalists. The subsequent release of Schnaebele was interpreted as evidence of Bismarck's fear. Bismarck's use of 'Boulangism' to gain an increased army grant that year only further convinced French chauvinists that they had found 'General Revenge' who would soon win back for them Alsace and Lorraine.

The attempts of a frightened government to rid themselves of an apparently 'Napoleonic' figure failed due to Boulanger's enormous personal popularity. Also there was a further scandal (November 1887) when the son-in-law of the President was brought to trial for the illegal sale of state honours for private profit. With the resignation of President Grevy, with both socialists and nationalists staging huge demonstrations, and with the general winning a string of by-elections, it seemed that France was on the verge of a new 'coup d'état' with Boulanger in the role of Louis Napoleon. That this did not happen was due to Boulanger's dramatic refusal to play that role when Paris seemed at his feet after his latest electoral success (27th January 1889). Instead, he panicked and fled to Brussels to avoid arrest. He committed suicide there, after the death of his mistress in 1891.

Historical judgement upon Boulanger has varied between harshness and limited sympathy. To J. P. T. Bury he was 'a broken reed, a man who had no real political ideas or political courage.' To M. Baumont he failed to act in 1889 because 'instead of being the saviour of France he preferred to save his own skin.' A. Cobban has been a little kinder, however, seeing in this lack of action a genuine regard for political legality and belated common sense. However that may be, we must conclude that the movement was of greater importance than the man. Firstly, it represented the temporary union of all those forces hostile to the Republic. Nationalists, royalists, Bonapartists and even radical leftists saw in Boulanger a tool with which to wreck a regime which they hated. Secondly, the failure of Boulangism allowed the Republic to reconsolidate its position with an overdue burst of legislation. 'Scrutin d'arrondisement' was restored and the practice of standing for several constituencies at once was abolished. Lastly, the affair transformed Republicanism into an even more conservative creed, determined now to defend the 'constitution' of 1875 against the extra-parliamentary agitation for which the 'Boulanger Affair' had set a dangerous and lasting precedent.

(i) The Republic in Danger: The Panama Scandal

To the great frustration of the Boulangists, no sooner had they lost their leader than the Republic was struck by a new scandal. In 1891 the Panama Canal Company, headed by the great engineer F. de Lesseps, went bankrupt. It had been formed ten years earlier to repeat the success of Suez, but had run into insurmountable engineering obstacles in Central America which had steadily drained its substantial private capital. Its last hope had lain with a grant of public money by the Assembly (1888), secured by the liberal distribution of bribes to deputies, as was common in such business. The grant failed to do more than postpone what was France's worst financial disaster for two centuries. The legal action taken by disappointed shareholders led to a complex variety of charges against public men. The suspicious death (November 1892) of Baron de Reinach, a Jewish banker accused by the anti-semitic press of having distributed the bribes, triggered off a witch hunt.

It emerged from the investigations of the courts and of the hostile press that nearly one third of the company's capital of 1000 million francs had been used in bribes. Among those indicted were five former ministers, including a former premier, C.-T. Floquet, five members of the Senate and a former Governor of Algeria. Although the charges in general could not be made to stick, the suspicions did. The career of M. Rouvier, the Minister of Finance, was blighted for a decade, as was that of the controversial Radical leader G. Clemenceau.

In a sense, there was much that was insubstantial and transient about the Panama Scandal. The elections of 1893 indicated no popular outrage against a 'corrupt' Republic. The conservative opposition actually lost a substantial amount of support and a large majority of the suspected deputies were re-elected. In three notable senses, however, the scandal transformed French politics. The prestige of the accused Republicans never recovered, and a new generation, young men like R. Poincaré, L. Barthou and T. Delcassé,

stepped into their place. They were less marked by the passions of the foundation of the Republic, and more ready than the founders to reach working compromises with other political groups. Secondly, with many working class voters convinced that a capitalist republic must always be corrupt, the 1893 elections saw the first substantial presence of socialist deputies in the Chamber. There were 49 where 12 had sat before. Lastly, the anti-semititic element in the scandal, fanned by the journalism of such as the fanatical E. Drumont, established a relatively new factor in French politics. This was soon to flourish even more strongly with the emergence of an 'affair' that dwarfed all its predecessors.

(j) The Republic in Danger: The Dreyfus Affair

For a decade from 1896, the public life of France was dominated by an issue which split the politically aware sector of the nation and illustrated starkly that the fundamental divisions within the Republic had survived intact for the first quarter century of its life. The origins of the issue lay in the discovery (September 1894) of a sheet of paper containing a list of secret documents evidently communicated to the German intelligence service by someone within the French General Staff. On the thin evidence of handwriting, charges were brought against one Alfred Dreyfus, one of the few Jewish officers in the army. He was convicted (December 1894), largely on the evidence of Major Henry of the Intelligence Bureau, and sentenced to life imprisonment on the penal colony of Devil's Island.

That a 'Dreyfus Affair' arose from such a conviction was largely the work of Lieutenant Colonel Picquart, appointed head of the Intelligence Service in March 1896. Alerted by the continued passage of material to Germany, and by evidence implicating one Count Esterhazy, who was a personal friend of Henry, he re-opened the case. His suspicions were brushed aside by the army, but by communicating them to the vice-president of the Senate and to the Dreyfus family, he ensured that the matter would become more than a military concern. The two sides in the conflict now became more clearly defined. The army reaffirmed the correctness of their verdict with the aid of 'conclusive' evidence provided by Henry. This was subsequently proved to be a forgery. On the other hand, increasing doubts about the whole conduct of the case erupted with the famous open letter from the writer Emile Zola to the President of the Republic, under the title of 'J'Accuse'. In it he made specific allegations of perjury and corruption against individual officers, and was himself tried and sentenced. The case was now a matter of public concern.

The bitter dispute that now divided politicians, intellectuals and private families was only to a very limited extent about Dreyfus himself. On both sides there were idealists who sincerely wished to see a miscarriage of justice rectified, or who were convinced of Dreyfus' guilt and wished to see him duly punished. Many others were merely fighting on the old battle lines of French politics. Many 'Dreyfusards' saw in the Affair only a convenient stick with which to beat the army officers and their allies the churchmen. Among the 'Anti-Dreyfusards' were conservatives and monarchists aiming to discredit the Republic. Also there were nationalists who believed that the honour of the army, the instrument of France's future resurgence, must be maintained at all costs. Anti-semitism became a more powerful force in France than it had ever been before, fuelled by the journalism of Drumont. Many saw in the attempts to clear Dreyfus' name the machinations of a Jewish conspiracy against the nation. Incidents were many, from public insults to the President of the Republic, to an attempted 'coup d'état' by the nationalist Déroulède (February 1899).

The turning point was reached in late 1898 when a new Minister of War, General Cavaignac, re-opened the case in an attempt finally to prove Dreyfus' guilt. Instead, he came to realise the strength of Picquart's assertions. The arrest, confession and subsequent suicide of Colonel Henry, and the flight of Esterhazy, wrecked the case of the 'Anti-Dreyfusards'. A retrial of Dreyfus produced another absurd verdict of 'guilty but with extenuating circumstances' (August 1899), before the government stepped in to issue a full pardon. Not until 1906 was the matter finally settled by Dreyfus' rehabilitation into the army and decoration with the Legion of Honour.

What were the results of a decade of scandal and controversy? To a large extent they were negative. Social questions in France had been obscured by what J. Guesde called a 'civil war of the bourgeoisie'. The rift between state and Church, and between republican and conservative which the 'Ralliement' had seemed to close (see section **g**) now gaped wider than ever. On the other hand, there was a sense in which the Dreyfus Affair confirmed the steady advance of Republicanism. The forces of the Church and the army, by stubbornly defending an increasingly hopeless position, had suffered a further defeat. A purge of the compromised officers made even the latter body more sympathetic to the Republic. The administration formed by R. Waldeck-Rousseau in 1899 thus had as its prime motive the regeneration of the Republic after more than a decade of sterile dispute.

(k) Economic Development

Economically, as in political and diplomatic terms, the Third Republic inherited a disaster. The cost of the war, the loss of raw materials, especially iron ore in Alsace-Lorraine, and the temporary decline of Paris as a commercial and financial centre during the siege and the Commune, were all sad blows. In the short term, they were blows from which France made a remarkable recovery. Writing in 1878, an English commentator, S. Bourne, could declare that 'France is of all the European nations the one of the most growing prosperity. We saw her wealth in the ease with which she provided for the German indemnity and in the rapidity with which she is recovering from disasters enough to have paralysed and destroyed nations even stronger than she'. In the longer run, the 1880s and 1890s were to produce factors (see sections **h** and **i**) which were to slow that progress dramatically. France was never again to aspire to a position higher than fourth among the great industrial powers of the world, significantly inferior to Germany in all important industrial respects. In purely domestic terms, on the other hand, French industry maintained a comfortable and steadily increasing degree of prosperity.

The traditional heavy industries made steady progress, although handicapped, by comparison with Germany or Britain, by relative lack of resources. They improved their output spectacularly in the years immediately before the outbreak of war. The output of iron ore is especially impressive, based upon the fortunate factor that a substantial part of the Lorraine ironfield, mainly discovered and exploited after 1871, still lay within French territory. In the newer industries, born at the turn of the century, France's performance gave less ground for satisfaction. Although individual French scientists were responsible for a number of major developments, such as the work of the Curies on radium, and that of Pasteur in microbiology, the chemical and electricity industries were slow to grow in France. French investment in electricity in 1913 was only one third of the equivalent figure in Germany. An exception to this rule was the French motor industry which, by building more than 107 000

	1870	1880	1890	1900	1910
Coal	13 330	19 362	26 083	33 404	38 350
Iron ore	2614	2874	3472	5448	14 606
Steel	84	389	683	1565	3413
(figures indicate thousands of tons)					

From C. Cook & J. Paxton *European Political Facts* Macmillan.

Table 8.1

vehicles by 1914, stood second only to that of the USA.

Throughout the period, government economic policy moved away from the 'laissez faire' attitudes of the later years of the Second Empire, to offer greater protection to French industries often at a disadvantage in competition with their neighbours. Freycinet's intervention to modernise railways, inland waterways and harbour installations has already been mentioned (section **d**), but one should also refer to the consistent protectionism of J. Méline as Minister of Agriculture (1883–85) and as chairman of the Assembly's Tariff Commission. His work culminated in the so-called Méline Tariff of 1892. This imposed duties of 25% on most agricultural imports and upon most manufactured and semi-manufactured goods, while allowing free entry to those raw materials necessary to French industries.

In considering the effects of these developments upon the living standards of the average Frenchman, we perhaps find the key to the great paradox of the Third Republic, its steady survival in the face of almost constant political opposition. For we find that the forty years or so before the World War were a period of steady improvement in the French standard of living. In the second half of the 19th century the average Frenchman's consumption of wine and potatoes rose by 50%, that of meat and beer by 100%, that of spirits by 200%, and that of sugar and coffee by 300%. The research of M. Lévy-Leboyer indicates a 300% rise in the gross national product since 1800, with an annual rate of increase between 1900–14 of 1.6% (Britain 2.1%, Germany 2.8%). Whatever abstract and philosophical objections might therefore be raised against the Republic, its economic performance kept it safe from those most potent agents of political change, hunger and deprivation.

(l) A Cultural Golden Age

Whereas in Germany after 1870, national victory and solidity produced very few cultural achievements of lasting value (see Chapter 7, section **p**), an age of defeat and political uncertainty in France coincided with a period of artistic brilliance rarely paralleled in modern Europe. To speak of this as an achievement of the Third Republic would, however, be misleading on two counts. Firstly, its roots lay in the period before 1870. 'The fall of the Second Empire', as A. Cobban has noted, 'was not a date in artistic, literary or scientific history'. Secondly, artistic greatness was often achieved in the face of fierce 'official' opposition. The works of those now regarded as France's greatest painters were referred to by a leading functionary as 'the paintings of democrats, of people who do not change their underwear'. The historian E. Lavisse could place those same artists in 1889 among the enemies of the Republic along with 'the decadent people, the incoherent people, and General Boulanger'.

Undoubtedly the greatest product of this period was the school of painting known as 'Impressionism'. Its roots were in the realism of such earlier artists as Courbet and Millet, famous for their unsentimental treatment of peasant scenes. The movement advocated that art should be less concerned with mere outline, and concentrate instead upon fleeting effects of light and motion, as in Monet's early work *Impression— The Sun Rising*. Add to Monet's name those of Cézanne, Pissarro, Sisley, Degas, Gauguin and Renoir, and one still has an incomplete list of the major French artists embraced by the term 'Impressionists'. The subsequent influence of Impressionism was also huge, being evident in the 20th century schools known as Expressionism and Cubism. Fauvism, which took its name from a critic's insult (Fauve—wild animal), owes a negative debt to Impressionism, by rejecting orthodox treatment of light and perspective. Nor was the influence of the movement limited to painting. The greatest sculptor of the century, Rodin, called himself an Impressionist in the sense that he tried in his work to catch a moment and a mood rather than merely to reproduce a form, with a similar result in terms of official hostility.

French literature, too, moved away almost as vigorously from the romantic traditions of the earlier 19th century, producing its own catalogue of immortal names. Literary Realism, pioneered by Flaubert in his *Madame Bovary* (1857) and *L'Education Sentimentale* (1869), gave way gradually to its more brutal variety, Naturalism. Zola's series of *Rougon-Macquart* novels (1871–93) form a classic example of this. The same period saw de Maupassant establish himself as the master of the short story, and the flowering of the Symbolist school of poets led by Verlaine, Baudelaire and Mallarmé.

French music, like French politics, lived for much of this period in the shadow of Germany. The music of Offenbach, Bizet and their immitators, popular though it was, was far too frivolous and lightweight to rival the impact of Wagner upon French audiences. Only in 1902, with the appearance of Debussy's opera *Pelléas et Mélisande* which was based upon the Symbolist play of that name by Maeterlinck, did a French musical school of comparable note begin to take shape. It was to be developed in the succeeding decade by Ravel, Fauré, Dukas and Satie.

As a footnote, not treated so seriously by contemporaries, but of considerable significance in the light of subsequent development, we should observe the origins of the French cinema in this period. Within ten years of the first projection in Paris by the Lumière brothers (December 1895), the cinema had begun to win acceptance as more than a sideshow. This was largely due to the work of G. Méliès in the fields of scenery and production techniques. Two other prominent names in the French industry before the war are still household names in the modern cinema. C. Pathé built up France's first major film company between 1903–09, with a capital of 35 million francs. L. Gaumont, builder of a 5000 seat auditorium in Paris, provided Europe with the prototype of the modern, purpose-built cinema.

(m) The Resurgence of French Socialism

The roots of French socialism were already planted deep by 1900. They went back to the traditions of 1848 and beyond, to the ideas of the French utopian socialists (see Chapter 1, section **j**). These ideas had created a broad basis of sympathy, especially among the peasants of the south, long before the advent of widespread industrialisation. The 'coup d'état' of 1851 with the punishment of those who opposed it, the conservatism of the Second Empire, and the savage repression of the Commune (see section **b**), had all dealt cruel blows to French socialism. That it became a major political force once more in the years before 1914 was largely due to the influence of three men.

Jules Guesde (1845–1922) played the greatest role in the introduction of Marxism into France, although in the course of his political career he departed some way from Marxist orthodoxy. He was an unattractive man, and as such only partly successful as a politician. He was a strict enthusiast, to the extent that his enemies dubbed him 'Pope Guesde' or the 'Red Jesuit'. Nevertheless he had the great strengths of being, in T. Zeldin's words 'an outstandingly persuasive, enthusiastic and impressive orator, a vigorous, unsuppressible journalist, a tireless organiser'. He founded (1881) the French Workers' Party (Parti Ouvrier Français or P.O.F.). It was based mainly upon well organised pockets of support in the industrial regions of the north, boasted 16000 members by 1898 and attracted 294000 votes in the general election of that year. Guesde's main rival for the first place among French socialists in this period was Jean Jaurès (1859–1914). Less impressed by the doctrines of Marxism, Jaurès was of a more independent frame of mind. He disliked and distrusted Guesde's strict party discipline and the rigidity of his political doctrines. Detesting violence, whether in a national or a class context, he envisaged the achievement of proletarian power 'by the methodical and legal organisation of their own forces under democratic law and universal suffrage'. It was his unswerving faith in the preservation of peace by the co-operation of French and German workers that led to his murder by a crazed nationalist on the eve of the World War. Nine years earlier, under pressure from the Second Socialist International, these two major tendencies in French socialism had come together to form the S.F.I.O. (Parti Socialiste, Section Française de l'Internationale Ouvrière). Its predominantly Marxist manifesto represented a major political defeat for Jaurès.

Neither man could claim as much influence upon the political events of the first decade of the century as Georges Sorel (1847–1922), the founder of Syndicalism. His doctrine, propounded in his *Reflections on Violence* (1906), rejected the bourgeois democratic state and advocated direct action by politically motivated trades unions (Syndicat-Union). They were to use the general strike as their main weapon if necessary. There was much in this doctrine that appealed to anarchist and anti-parliamentary traditions in French socialism. The movement had already been deeply divided over the appointment of a socialist, A. Millerand, in Waldeck-Rousseau's cabinet (1899). It had accepted the decision of the Amsterdam Congress of the International (1904) that socialists should withdraw their support from 'bourgeois' administrations.

Since 1895 and the foundation of the C.G.T. (Confédération Generale du Travail), French unionism had possessed a suitable organ to co-ordinate direct action. There were 2399 unions affiliated to it by 1906. The acceptance by the C.G.T. of the principle of the general strike as a political weapon in the so-called 'Charter of Amiens' in that year confirmed the tone of French domestic politics during the last decade of European peace.

(n) The Republic and the Social Question, 1904–14

The period of unusual ministerial stability from 1899–1905, when Waldeck-Rousseau and Combes led the so-called 'Radical Bloc', seemed to promise that at last the Republic would be able to address itself to the neglected problem of social reform. After years of struggle with conservatism, a French premier could declare that he recognised 'no enemies on the left'. He could, for the first time in European history, include a socialist, A. Millerand, in his cabinet. It was not to be, however. The union of radical and socialist groups could not survive the decision of the socialist Amsterdam Congress to ban co-operation with capitalist governments. The so-called Radicals who now dominated Republicanism found themselves forced back into a position of preserving the Republic, but this time from the left wing threats to social order and stability.

Strike activity escalated quite suddenly in 1904 to unprecedented levels. The total for that year of 1026 strikes was double the total for 1903. The new level was subsequently maintained, often with a specifically political content. On Mayday 1906, the C.G.T. launched a campaign with the aim of securing an eight hour working day, which set the tone for a number of disruptions in key sectors of the economy. There were strikes in Marseilles, Paris, Le Havre and other major centres (1907–08). A widespread strike in the south caused disruption in the wine industry (1907), and railway workers (1908) and post office workers (1909) caused considerable dislocation by their actions.

There was some irony in the fact that the task of dealing with this new threat fell to the ministries of G. Clemenceau (1906–09), a fierce radical critic of earlier administrations, and of A. Briand (1909–10), formerly a prominent socialist. Their policies showed the truth of T. Zeldin's assertion that the Radicals 'could never work up a fighting enthusiasm for social reform'. Although Clemenceau entered office with a programme of seventeen proposed reforms, only one was passed. This was a measure for some railway nationalisation. Although in the last years of peace an act providing for old age pensions (1910) and a codification of labour legislation (1912) were pushed through the Assembly, an impressive array

of proposals was killed by that body. Among its victims were measures for a minimum factory wage, better factory inspection, and the introduction of an income tax. This innovation was rejected 65 times by parliaments between 1872–1907.

Instead, the great achievements of the ministries lay in their vigorous counter measures to the strike agitation. Clemenceau did not hesitate to use the army to oppose the strikers, often on such a scale as actually to outnumber them. Not infrequently military action led to deaths among the demonstrators, as at Courrières (1906), Raon-l'Etape (1907) and Draveil (1908). The reputation of the premier by the time he left office was that of 'Clemenceau the Killer'. Briand proved an apt pupil, breaking a railway strike in 1910 by mobilising the army reservists, a move that had the effect of putting many of the strikers in uniform and subject to military law.

By 1914 the greatest positive achievements of the Third Republic lay in the past. Perhaps its major achievement had been the creation of the broad concensus of support that had enabled the regime to survive so far for 44 years. It still did not seem to preside over a united nation. On the eve of war, the General Staff still estimated that as many as 13% of men of military age might refuse to be conscripted. That the eventual figure for refusals was as low as 1.5% shows what success the Republic had in fact achieved against its enemies. In the final analysis, the Third Republic had made great headway as regards two of its inherited problems. Domestically, it had taken great strides towards the creation of a secular state. In foreign policy it had, belatedly, revolutionised France's status as a European power.

(o) Foreign Policy: Colonialism

Together with the assault upon the Church, colonialism is one of the key themes that runs through the history of the Third Republic. Two bursts of colonial activity saw the expansion and consolidation of a French Empire that was in fact to outlive the Republic itself. Unlike the struggle with the Church, colonial expansion was by no means widely popular within the Republican ranks. Its achievement owed as much to private initiative as to concerted government policy.

The motives that set this course were diverse and are subject to controversy. In his work *Tonkin and the Motherland* ('le Tonkin et la Mère Patrie', 1890) Jules Ferry put forward the view that 'colonial policy is the daughter of industrial policy', that an industrial country graduated naturally to Imperialism to win safe resources and markets. This is likely to have been a justification of an unpopular policy after the event rather than an explanation of original motives, for French industrialists had shown little enthusiasm for colonisation. Even as late as 1914, French industry derived ten times as much raw materials from non-colonial as from colonial sources. Rather, it is likely that colonial adventures represented to many the only arena in which France could pursue greatness at a time when the politics of Europe seemed so unfavourable. Prévost-Paradol wrote at the time that a Mediterranean empire would be for France 'not only a satisfaction to our pride, but certainly . . . the last resource of our greatness'. There can be no doubt that in this respect Ferry's government received quite explicit support from Bismarck, who saw colonialism as a valuable distraction from concerns over Alsace-Lorraine. Lastly, A. Cobban has stressed the Catholic element in French colonialism, noting that of 4500 missionaries outside Europe in the 1880s, 75% were French.

For whatever reason, from 1878, the year of her re-emergence into the diplomatic world at the Congress of Berlin, France began to add in a piecemeal and chaotic way to her overseas empire. In May 1881 a military campaign extended French influence in North Africa by forcing the Bey of Tunis to accept a French protectorate in the Treaty of Bardo. Between 1882–85 French representatives established a further protectorate over Madagascar, and created a French territory in the Congo, based upon the explorations of Brazza. Also the reconquest of Tonkin and Annam in Indo-China, was completed, which de Broglie in 1874 had not thought worth the cost of a garrison.

There were many in the 80s who shared de Broglie's view. The colonial question bitterly divided French political opinion, and split Republicans profoundly. While Ferry saw Imperialism as the key to future greatness, socialists saw it as an immoral spin-off of capitalism, while radicals and conservatives joined in condemning it as a waste of men and money that would be better spent seeking revenge against Germany. The nationalist, P. Déroulède, protested that to offer colonies as a consolation for Alsace-Lorraine was like offering 20 servants to a couple that had lost two children. Clemenceau went so far as to describe government policy as 'high treason'. These objections led in 1882 to the sacrifice of French interests in Egypt because the Assembly refused to finance French co-operation with Britain, and eventually destroyed the Ferry government. A minor reverse at Langson in Tonkin (March 1885)

led to the rallying of all Ferry's opponents and those of the Republic to force him out of public life. Some genuinely feared that Tonkin might become another Mexico, but many merely wished to see the back of Ferry.

Ferry fell, but Tonkin and the French empire did not. The Assembly granted the reinforcements that they had denied to Ferry to his successor a few weeks later. By 1887, Cochin-China, Cambodia, Annam and Tonkin were united as French Indo-China. Stimulated perhaps by the knowledge that growing friendship with Russia (see section **p**) increased France's European security, French colonialism enjoyed renewed vigour in the 1890s. French influence in Africa was substantially increased by the conquest of Dahomey (1890), the colonisation of the Ivory Coast (1893), the occupation of Timbuctoo (1894) and the annexation of Madagascar (1896).

In European terms, French expansion seemed to be having one of the effects that Bismarck hoped for, the growth of jealousy and rivalry between France and Great Britain. All over the globe agreements were patched up that avoided open conflict; in the New Hebrides, where a joint administration was agreed in 1887; in Egypt, where the Suez Canal was neutralised by the Constantinople Convention (1888); in the Niger Valley where spheres of influence were established in 1890. Tension remained such, however, that the Fashoda crisis of September 1898 nearly brought the two countries to war. A confrontation between a French expeditionary force and Kitchener's British force at Fashoda in the Sudan led to British demands for French withdrawal. Public opinion in France was ready to fight over such an affront, but Delcassé, the Foreign Minister, was realistic enough to know the strength of the British navy and the damage that a lengthy colonial conflict could do to France's European position. Thus Fashoda decided that France's African influence was to be limited to the west. Anglo-French relations remained bitter and hostile, but only for a relatively short time before other factors worked a transformation upon them.

(p) Foreign Policy: The Russian Alliance

In 1871 the international status of France was as desperate as at any time in her history. Bordered by a united Germany of 41 million inhabitants to France's 37 million, and by a united Italy, her international isolation was complete. Her eligibility as an ally was at a low ebb, she was humiliated in war and riven with civil strife. Nearly two decades later, in 1889, those in charge of her foreign affairs had achieved little improvement. Foreign reaction to the 'War in Sight' crisis of 1875 had reduced the immediate threat of German aggression (see Chapter 7, section **k**). Also attendance at the Congress of Berlin (1878) had marked an overdue return to the diplomatic community, but these events had gained France no reliable friends. By the Triple Alliance and the Reinsurance Treaty, Austria-Hungary, Italy and Russia remained tied to the Bismarckian system of alliances, which had as its very cornerstone the isolation of France. The chances of improvement seemed slight. Relations with Russia were soured by the rift between republican democracy and Tsarist autocracy, and by Russian contempt for French political instability. In the words of the Tsar's foreign minister, Giers, the Republic was merely 'a mass of rottenness'. As regards Italy, her entry into the Triple Alliance (1882) and the declaration of the French protectorate over Tunis, where Italy also had historic ambitions, led to a decade of bitterness. This was fanned by the anti-French economic policies of the then premier, G. Crispi.

The remarkable transformation of French foreign relations from 1890 must be explained largely in terms of certain steps in German diplomacy, although credit is due to the exploitation of those steps by two outstanding foreign ministers, G. Hanotaux (1894–95, 1896) and T. Delcassé (1898–1906). They dominated the Quai d'Orsay at this crucial period. The refusal of Wilhelm II to renew the Reinsurance Treaty (see chapter 10, section **e**) compounded Bismarck's uncharacteristic error in 1887 in refusing to sanction German loans to Russia, and left Russia herself in a state of isolation. The progress of the two isolated powers towards one another was slow, and marked by much Russian reticence, but France had much to offer. An agreement to curtail Russian nihilist activity in France was followed by the more important step of opening the French money market to Russian loans. This was a move worth over £400 million to Russia within a decade. Slowly, between 1891–94, the military understanding all important to France took shape. The visit of a French naval squadron to Kronstadt (July 1891) resulted only in a very general agreement to 'consult together on every question that endangers general peace' (August 1891). In the following year, however, meetings between the respective Chiefs of Staff, Boisdeffre and Obruchev, resulted in an agreement on joint military action. The Tsar finally consented to regard this as the basis of an official Franco-Russian alliance (January 1894). By this Russia undertook to attack

Germany if that country attacked France, or aided Italy in an attack on France. France was similarly committed if Germany attacked Russia, or aided Austria-Hungary in such an attack.

France had carried off one of the great diplomatic 'coups' of the 19th century, overcoming immense difficulties to break the nation's crippling isolation. The popularity of the alliance was enormous, by stark contrast to public indifference to colonial successes. Public demonstrations on the occasions of the Russian fleet's visit to Toulon (1893), or the visit of the Tsar to Paris (1896) left little doubt that Russia had become 'the first love of the Third Republic'. Only a few detached voices pointed out, like those of more recent commentators such as Sir D. Brogan, that the alliance committed Russia to no action on behalf of Alsace-Lorraine. However, it might well embroil France in eastern European questions which had been, hitherto, none of her business.

(q) Foreign Policy: Italy and Great Britain

Remarkable as it was, the Russian alliance only formed one factor in the achievement of French diplomacy at the turn of the century. Within eight years a new relationship had also been forged with Italy. The key to these developments lay in the fall of the anti-French administration of G. Crispi following Italy's colonial catastrophe against Abyssinian tribesmen at Adowa in 1896. Italian disillusion with African adventures diminished the importance of the dispute over Tunis, and Delcassé was able to conclude a series of agreements on spheres of influence in North Africa. These recognised French rights in Tunis (1896) and those of Italy in Tripolitania (1900). In November 1898 he also concluded a new Franco-Italian trade treaty to replace the one renounced by Crispi in 1887. The significance of such developments should not be exaggerated. Italy was still a member of the Triple Alliance, a status she confirmed in 1902, although assuring France at the time that she would never go to war with her under the auspices of that alliance. Clearly then, if Italy remained betrothed to Germany, she was intent upon serious flirtations with other suitors.

In 1898, for all her diplomatic success elsewhere, France stood on the verge of war with Great Britain over the Fashoda crisis (see section **o**). In subsequent years French hostility to British policy in South Africa, and British hostility to the policy of France's great ally, Russia, in the Far East, seemed to hold little promise of warmer relations. This gap was also largely bridged by courtesy of

German errors. Her decision to enter into naval rivalry with Britain, her tactless support of the Boers, and Britain's own increased sense of isolation after the Boer War, all provided the basis for an Anglo-French 'rapprochement'. The keys to improved relations were provided by mutual concessions on the subject of influence in North Africa, and by the tactful diplomacy of two men. These were Paul Cambon, ambassador to London from 1898 to 1920, and Britain's new monarch, Edward VII, whose visit to Paris in 1903 did so much to break down popular antipathy to Britain. April 1904 saw the conclusion of a comprehensive agreement on outstanding colonial questions. France recognised Britain's predominant interest in Egypt, while Britain conceded to France a 'free hand' in Morocco. Lesser disputes concerning Newfoundland, Siam, Madagascar and the New Hebrides were also settled. This so-called 'Entente Cordiale' had strict limitations. It contained, for example, absolutely no military commitment by either side. However, it did conclude a remarkably fruitful decade for French diplomacy, at the end of which the Republic could face any political development within Europe with greatly increased confidence.

(r) Historiography

The two most obvious and impressive features of the French Third Republic were its long duration by comparison with other French regimes, and the abject nature of its eventual collapse in 1940. These features, suggesting initial success and gradual stagnation, have imposed an unusual uniformity upon recent historical interpretations of the period. D. Thomson's *Democracy in France Since 1870* (1969) may be taken as a clear statement of the dominant view on the Third Republic. Its success, claims the author, was due to the regime's ability to combine conservative political institutions with a set of radical social aims. Its ultimate failure and collapse may be attributed to the unwillingness of subsequent governments to change a formula that had worked in the past. A range of recent French writers have laid their stress upon various aspects of this theme. J.-P. Azéma and M. Winock (*The Third Republic*, 1970) have concentrated upon the 'narrow, fearful self-interest' of the French bourgeoisie as the main cause of the stagnation of the Republican system. Meanwhile, F. Goguel (*Party Politics Under the Third Republic*, 1946) saw the period as a contest between policies of 'Movement' and those of 'Established Order'. The gradual triumph of the latter resulted in what G. Wright has labelled the 'Stalemate Society'.

Serious divergences from this central theme have been relatively few, and have usually reflected a particular political sympathy. J. Chastenet (*History of the Third Republic,* 1952–63) has put forward a much more sympathetic view of the policies of the Opportunists and of the later Radicals. He saw in them, not political timidity, but praiseworthy political moderation. Marxist writers, on the other hand, have taken their lead from Karl Marx himself (*The Civil War in France*, 1871) in viewing the Republic as a wholly conservative institution, springing from the blood of the suppressed Communards. H. Guillemin (*Origins of the Commune*, 1956–60) could be taken as a more recent representative of this viewpoint.

As has been the case with a variety of other historical periods and problems, a recent tendency has been to avoid writing the history of the Third Republic in terms of the development of parties and policies. E. Weber (*Peasants into Frenchmen: the Modernisation of Rural France*, 1976) has seen the real significance of the Third Republic as being that it witnessed the breakdown of long-standing localism and parochialism. This aided the growth, through developments in communications, education, military service, and so forth, of a true sense of French nationhood. Meanwhile the major publication on the period has undoubtedly been T. Zeldin's monumental *France 1848–1945,* (1973–77), which has turned its back upon any attempt at general summary of the era. It concentrates instead upon detailed and intimate examination of the social and psychological roots of the contemporary French society.

Progress Paragraphs

Answer the following questions in about 150 words.

How serious were French losses at the end of the Franco-Prussian War?   Section **(a)**

What caused the establishment of the Paris Commune?   Section **(b)**

Why did the Paris Commune achieve so little?
                                                      Section **(b)**

Why did France become a Republic after 1871?
                                                      Sections **(c, d)**

How did the political nature of the Third Republic change in the late 1870s?   Section **(d)**

What features of the political life of the Third Republic militated against radical political change?
Section (**e**)

Account for the hostility of Republicans towards the Church.
Section (**f**)

By what means did Republican politicians seek to diminish the powers of the Church? Sections (**f, g**)

Who were attracted by 'Boulangism', and why?
Section (**h**)

What do the Panama Scandal and the Dreyfus Affair tell us about the contemporary divisions in French society?
Sections (**i, j**)

How economically advanced was France during this period?
Section (**k**)

In what respects was this period a 'golden age' of French culture?
Section (**l**)

What were the principal theories and aims of the French left between 1880–1910?
Section (**m**)

How did the government combat social unrest between 1900–14?
Section (**n**)

Account for the upsurge of French colonialist activity under the Third Republic.
Section (**o**)

What factors enabled France to construct a strong system of foreign alliances between 1890–1910?
Sections (**p, q**)

9

The Crisis of Russian Autocracy: 1894–1914

(a) Nicholas II: Personality and Aims

The death of Alexander III from nephritis in October 1894 brought to the throne his 29 year old son, Nicholas. As has often been the case, a determined and dominant father had produced a shy and less assertive successor. There is a rare unanimity among historians that the new Tsar was not equal to the tasks that confronted him. He was, in the judgement of R. Charques, 'a negative character, commonplace in mind, weak of will and fatalistic in temperament. . . . a man transparently immature and of patently insignificant interests'. In an attempt to achieve a fair and balanced assessment, many commentators have drawn attention to his personal qualities, especially those as husband and father, but as J. N. Westwood has responded, 'family happiness has never yet saved a dynasty'.

For all this, influences such as the assassination of his grandfather in 1881, and his education at the hands of K. P. Pobedonostsev, made the new Tsar utterly determined upon one thing. This was the maintenance of the autocracy of his predecessors. His marriage in the year of his succession, to Princess Alice of Hesse-Darmstadt, only compounded the difficulties. Alexandra, as she became upon conversion to the Russian Orthodox faith, shared her husband's political ineptitude. Being a stronger character and equally devoted to the principle of autocracy, she was better able to resist the good advice of those who might yet have saved the monarchy.

The probable course of the reign was indicated at an early stage. Meeting representatives of the zemstvos and the town councils in January 1895, Nicholas dismissed their hopes 'for public institutions to express their opinion on questions which concern them' as evidence that they were 'carried away by senseless dreams'. To the horror of those who hoped for some relaxation of the oppression of his father's reign he pledged himself to 'uphold the principle of autocracy as firmly and as unflinchingly as my late unforgettable father'. In terms, however, of the social and economic development of Russia, and of the development of foreign affairs, Nicholas was on the verge of a very different world from that that Alexander III had known.

(b) The Russian Economy

The early years of Nicholas' reign saw little respite for the peasantry and for many of the smaller gentleman landowners from the problems that had beset them since the emancipation. The official government policy of low bread prices meant a low income for the farmer even when harvests were good, and harvest failures were frequent in these years, notably in 1891, 1892, 1898 and 1901. The steady increase in the population of European Russia also increased the pressure upon peasant holdings that had often been inadequate to begin with. It has been estimated that the average peasant holding shrank from 35 acres in 1877 to 28 acres in 1905 due to subdivision within the growing family. The result, quite apart from frequent outbreaks of agrarian violence, was that arrears in taxation and in redemption payments accumulated rapidly. Motivated by concern for its own income and for the future of the landed gentry and nobility, the government attempted two major solutions. One was the formation of an improved Land Bank in 1896 equipped with funds and with reserves of land, much of it former state land, to encourage the purchase of viable holdings that might overcome the pressing 'land hunger' of the agricultural classes. Within two years of its formation the interest rates charged by the bank upon its loans were as low as four per cent. The second attempted solution was to exploit a larger proportion of Russia's vast land resources by encouraging settlement on 'virgin' lands in the east. In 1896 the government founded its Resettlement Bureau to encourage migration to Siberia. As a further encouragement, and to improve the public image of Siberia, the shipment of criminals there was suspended in 1900. Neither method was wholly unsuccessful, but neither could hope to do more than scratch the surface of an enormous problem. It is true that the total amount of land in peasant hands increased substantially, by over 26 million hectares between 1877 and 1905, but that in the hands of the nobility declined by nearly 21 million. Equally the fact that 750000 peasants migrated to Siberia in the last four years of the century needs to be set against the huge total peasant population of nearly 97 million returned in the 1895 census.

By the revolutionary year of 1905, several insuperable obstacles remained between the peasant and a lasting solution to the land question. One was the continuing existence of the peasant commune (the 'mir') to which many were still bound by the legislation of 1861, and which imposed restrictions upon travel and freedom of enterprise that rendered government encouragement pointless. Secondly, the consistent lack of direct financial investment in agriculture meant that the Russian peasant was still usually bedevilled by primitive farming methods totally outdated in western Europe. The magnitude of Russian agricultural production was a reflection of her land resources, and not of the efficiency with which they were exploited. In 1898–1902, for example, an average acre of Russian farmland produced 8.8 bushels compared to 13.9 in the USA and 35.4 in Britain.

The fact, therefore, that Russia became the world's largest supplier of wheat to foreign markets in 1913 by exporting 3.33 million tons, hides the truth that much of this was what came to be called 'starvation exports'. These were exports undertaken despite the domestic need for the product, to pay for the industrial raw materials and machinery upon which the government, by the late 1890s was staking the future of Russia.

(c) The Russian Economy: the Policy of S. J. Witte

For all the political shallowness of Nicholas II, he was served by two ministers who might, given the right circumstances and consistent support, have saved the monarchy. The first of these was Sergei Witte, who became Minister of Finance in August 1892 and held the office until 1903. Witte was of Dutch origin, but his family had achieved noble status by service to the state, and he had risen to his high office by the unusual route of outstanding service in railway administration.

Witte did not regard himself, once in office, as a narrow financial specialist. Self-confident and dynamic, he regarded the ultimate aim of his

policies as being the salvation of Russia and the creation of a strong modern state. In this respect his political views were confused and uncertain. Although he professed himself dedicated to the maintenance of the autocracy, he cannot wholly have failed to foresee the effects that the economic transformation of Russia would have upon that autocracy. This curious mixture of energy and miscalculation naturally made Witte a controversial character among contemporaries and historians alike. Contemporary political opponents accused him of extravagance and of unpatriotic concessions to foreign capitalists. A number of recent historians have criticised him for being insufficiently aware of the need for substantial agrarian reform. Others, nevertheless, are impressed by the extent of his vision and by his practical political ability. To T. H. von Laue he was attempting 'to rally both government and people to one common, almost superhuman effort'. To H. Seton-Watson, Witte was 'one of the outstanding statesmen of the 19th century'.

To Witte, the key to Russia's future greatness lay in industrialisation. The only alternative to this was that Russia become a 'European China', a vast market unable to supply its own needs and thus 'the eternal handmaiden of states which are economically more developed'. His view was not original, being largely that of the previous Minister of Finance, I. A. Vyshnegradsky (1887–92), and also being influenced by Bismarck's policies in Germany. His real contribution was the coherent programme that he proposed in the 1890s to achieve this desired industrialisation. The basis of the policy was the strengthening of protective tariffs to guard infant Russian industries against the destructive competition of stronger European economies. But how was Russian industry to develop when the vital investment capital was lacking, when the total amount of capital lying in Russian banks amounted to a mere 200 million roubles? How would foreign powers react to the restriction of so valuable a market? Witte's answer was to invite these powers to continue to participate in the Russian economy, but by investing capital in it rather than by off-loading their consumer goods onto it. Thus the capital would be provided for the development of Russian industry. Industrial development would also safeguard the government against social unrest by providing fuller employment, and in the long run higher wages and cheaper goods. Protective tariffs, the attraction of foreign capital, and the placing of the Russian currency on the Gold Standard (January 1897) in order to inspire greater foreign confidence, were thus the three prongs of the policy to which Witte trusted for the creation of a great industrial Russia.

(d) The Russian Economy: Industrial Development

At the time of the outbreak of the First World War Russia was still a modest industrial power by comparison with much of Europe and with the USA. For example, she produced in 1912 only 5.6% of the world's pig-iron and only 3.66% of its steel. In 1910 only 30% of Russia's total national production was industrial, compared to 75% in Britain, 73% in the USA, 70% in Germany, and even 47% in Austria-Hungary. In purely Russian terms, nevertheless, progress had been rapid. An annual industrial output valued at 1502 million roubles in 1890 had increased to 5738 million by 1912. It should be borne in mind that this period included a major economic slump (1899–1902) and very serious foreign and domestic disruptions (1904–06). Development differed from area to area and from industry to industry. Industrial production was largely concentrated in four regions: in St. Petersburg and the northern shores of the Baltic, in Moscow and the provinces of Nizhni Novgorod and Vladimir, in Poland, and in the Donbas and Krivoi Rog regions in the south. As to industries, textile production continued to dominate accounting in 1910 for 40% of Russia's industrial output. Table 9.1 shows that, although they may not have compared so favourably with their more developed world rivals, other industries made impressive advances.

Certainly, those industries detailed in Table 9.1 were among those that benefited most from the influx of foreign capital in response to Witte's policies. No recent study exists of the exact extent to which foreign powers and individuals involved themselves in Russian industry, but older studies permit us to see that the extent was vast. The estimates of P. Ol, a very early Soviet commentator, showed 214.7 million roubles of foreign capital invested in Russia in 1890, 280.1 million in 1895, and then a very substantial upsurge to reach 911 million in 1900, and 2000 million before the outbreak of war in 1914. About half of this went into the mining and metallurgical industries of the south, and it is possible that by 1900 90% of the financing of these sectors of the economy was done by foreign capital. Oil production and banking were the next largest recipients of foreign funds. The greatest financial friend to Russia was her closest political ally, France, whose investment was about 33% of the total in 1914. The other most important suppliers of capital were Great Britain (23%), Germany (20%), Belgium (14%) and the USA (5%).

The development of Russian railways also produced some impressive growth statistics which pale somewhat by comparison with more advanced countries. The rate of railway construction that had produced less than 5800 kms between 1861–90 accelerated to produce a national system of 59 616 kms by 1905, and the imagination of the world was captured by the vast engineering feat of the construction of the Trans-Siberian Railway linking European Russia to its most easterly outpost of Vladivostok between 1891–1904. The greatest years of industrial expansion, however, saw a tailing off of railway building. The five years between 1908 and 1913 saw the slowest rate of growth in the railway system since the 1880s, and although Russia boasted the world's second largest railway network in 1913, the gap between her and the only state of comparable size was substantial. Her network totalled 62 200 kms compared to 411 000 kms in the USA. Other forms of communication in Russia remained wholly inadequate. Only the major inter-city roads of European Russia matched up to general European standards, and the merchant marine was remarkably small, nearly all of Russia's substantial foreign trade travelling in foreign ships.

The last major feature of Russia's pre-1914 industrialisation was, indeed, the dramatic increase in her foreign trade. Table 9.2 indicates the steady increase in that trade in both directions. It should be remembered, however, that while the balance remained favourable to Russia, her exports consisted very largely of agricultural produce. The balance in industrial goods remained very much to Russia's disadvantage. Russia was most heavily

	Coal	Petroleum	Iron ore	Steel
		In thousands of tons		
1880	3290	382	—	307
1885	4270	1966	—	193
1890	6010	3864	1736	378
1895	9100	6935	2851	879
1900	16 160	10 684	6001	2216
1905	18 670	8310	4976	2266
1910	25 430	11 283	5742	3314

From Cook and Paxton, *European Political Facts, 1848–1918*. Macmillan 1978.

Table 9.1

	Imports (million roubles)	Exports (million roubles)
1904	651.4	1106.4
1906	800.6	1094.8
1908	912.6	998.2
1910	1084.4	1449.1
1912	1171.7	1518.8

Table 9.2

involved with Germany to whom she exported 453 million roubles' worth of goods in 1913 and from whom she received 652 millions' worth. Great Britain held second place in both respects.

(e) Growth of the Urban Proletariat

The steady industrialisation of the Russian economy accentuated, of course, the breakdown of the traditional social structure already begun in 1861. It combined with the continuing agrarian problems to accelerate the drift of consistent numbers of workers from the impoverished countryside into the developing centres of industrial production. Some 2.5 million workers were employed in factory or workshop production in 1900. Taking into account their families and dependents, this probably meant between 10 and 13 million Russians were now economically dissociated from the land and reliant upon an industrial wage. This was a relatively small proportion of Russia's total population (1895) of 116.5 million, but was probably three times the figure that had applied in 1880.

Of equal importance was the increase in the size of the units of production. Table 9.3, indicating an increase of about 30% in the number of factories while the workforce doubled, makes it clear that the average factory's workforce grew substantially. Indeed, nearly half of Russia's industrial workforce in 1902 worked in factories employing 1000 men or more.

	Factories	Workers
1887	30888	1318000
1890	32254	1434700
1897	39029	2098200
1908	39856	2609000

Table 9.3

The results of these changes were typical of the early stages of industrialisation elsewhere in Europe. The dramatic rates of growth of the major towns between 1867–97, such as Moscow (197%), Warsaw (253%), Baku (702%) and Lodz (872%), suggest the problems of urban overcrowding that developed. The conditions of living and of employment are suggested by the trickle of social legislation wrung from a reluctant government by a wave of strikes at the turn of the century. The employment of children under 12 was forbidden (1892), female labour was banned in mines (1892), and an 11 and a half hour working day was legally instituted (1896) although usually ignored by employers, and factory inspectors were finally instituted in 1903. Nevertheless, major problems such as overcrowding in factory barracks, and the illegal payment of part of the worker's wages in kind, persisted. Strikes, although illegal until 1905, were frequent. Sixty-eight were recorded in 1895, 125 in 1900, culminating in 14000 in the revolutionary year of 1905.

(f) The Growth of Opposition: Marxism

The greatest success of Russian Populism, the murder of the Tsar in 1881, proved to be its swansong. The romanticism, the lack of realism, the violence of Populism drained much of its public sympathy and created a temporary void which might be filled by other ideas. That the arguments of the German socialist thinker Karl Marx (see Chapter 1, section **k**) came to fill part of the gap was partly due to the enthusiasm of G. V. Plekhanov, and partly to the curious leniency of the Russian censors. Plekhanov, originally a Populist prominent in the 'Land and Liberty' movement, became convinced by the growth of Russian industry that Marx, and not those who concentrated upon the Russian peasant and his commune, held the key to Russia's revolutionary future. Vera Zasulich and P. B. Akselrod were other figures who formed a bridge between Populism and Marxism in Russian thought. By 1894 Plekhanov's writings had given Russian readers their most coherent exposition of Marx's thought. That they were able to read it at all was largely due to censors who admitted Marxist works in the belief that they would weaken the terrorist threat of Populism. *Capital* was thus available in a Russian translation as early as 1872. J. Lawrence has also pointed out how easily Marxist ideas of the future society might be grasped by those used to the teaching of the Orthodox Church. 'In Marxism the Saviour becomes the Proletariat, the Church becomes the Party and the universal triumph of Communism takes the place of the Second Coming'.

Nevertheless, it is only with hindsight that the earliest Marxist groups in Russia can be seen as important political entities. A number of very small cells existed from 1889 in St. Petersburg, Moscow, Vilna and Kiev, but their main claim to fame was that one of the St. Petersburg groups was joined in August 1893 by a young lawyer from Simbirsk named V. I. Ulyanov, who was later to take the 'cover' name of V. I. Lenin. Not until March 1898 did representatives of the various groups meet secretly in Minsk to found the Russian Social Democratic Labour Party (RSDRP). Even then the immediate arrest of 8 out of the 9 delegates rendered Marxism a very modest force in Russian politics at the turn of the century.

As regards tactics, the Russian Marxists rejected the use of terror as counterproductive and chose to concentrate instead upon industrial agitation and propaganda. Marxists were active alongside other opposition groups in the industrial disturbances in St. Petersburg in 1895, 1896 and 1897. The most important development in the latter sphere was the foundation in 1900 in Germany, by V. I. Lenin and J. Martov of the journal *The Spark* ('Iskra'). In addition, Lenin was a prolific writer and publicist, elucidating Marxist theory and laying down his strong views on how the future struggle of Russian socialism should be organised. In 1902 he published what H. Seton-Watson calls 'his greatest contribution to political theory, and . . . perhaps the most significant single document in the history of communism'. *What is to be Done?*, which used the title of Chernyshevsky's earlier novel, rejected the arguments of those who would have socialists limit themselves to legal economic activities and of those who continued to place their faith in the peasantry, and stressed instead the need for a 'party of a new type'. This was to be a tight knit, disciplined and dedicated group of professional revolutionaries. By rejecting reliance upon the eventual good sense of workers and peasants, by rejecting the aid of well-meaning but amateurish intellectuals, and by rejecting terrorism, *What is to be Done?* represented a substantial break with the past traditions of the Russian Left.

Such an organisation, however, was unacceptable to many who wished for a broader, more popular basis to the party, and who distrusted Lenin's tendency towards autocratic leadership. At the 2nd congress of the RSDRP in London in 1903, the party split into the 'Men of the Majority' ('Bolsheviki'), favouring the views of Lenin, and the 'Men of the Minority' ('Mensheviki'), favouring the alternative view now championed by Martov. The terms are misleading, as Lenin's group had actually been outvoted by the end of the congress, but the names coined by him stuck firmly to the factions whose divisions further weakened the short term effectiveness of the RSDRP.

(g) The Growth of Opposition: Others

Given the ultimate success of the Marxists it is perhaps natural that a number of western historians should have followed the lead of their Soviet counterparts in emphasising their importance in the years before the outbreak of war in 1914. Other commentators, however, among them the German E. Oberlaender, have tried to dispense with the wisdom that comes with hindsight and to stress that in the context of the time at least two other opposition movements had far greater support and played a far more positive role in the events of the years between 1900–14.

The first of these was the Socialist Revolutionary Party founded in 1901. The SRs, as they came to be called, were essentially second generation Populists, their cause revived by severe agrarian distress in 1891 and by the release of some earlier leaders from exile in Siberia. They followed a path recognisable to the earlier generation, but modified to meet changed circumstances, such as the undeniable development of Russian capitalism. It is common for historians to refer to the Socialist Revolutionaries as 'the Party of the Peasants'. L. Kochan and H. Seton-Watson, however, stress the breadth and relative looseness of their views and their membership. The various groups established in Saratov, in Moscow and in the Ukraine in the 1890s placed a common emphasis on the need to propagate their views among the urban workers, but placed varying degrees of confidence in the peasantry and in terrorism as a revolutionary weapon. The development, especially in the Ukraine in 1902, of widespread agrarian discontent in which SR agitation was prominent, served greatly to amplify the role of the peasantry in party theory. When party policy was officially formulated, therefore, the peasantry was placed in the role of the army which would follow the vanguard of the urban proletariat. The main plank of the party's platform was the redistribution of agricultural land to the peasantry on the basis of how much each could profitably use.

The terrorist branch of the SRs also achieved spectacular if sterile successes. The deaths of the Minister of Education, Bogolepov (1901), the Minister of the Interior, Sipyagin (1902), his successor, Plehve (1904), and the governor of Moscow (1905), were all the work of its members. The apparent success of peasant agitation and terrorist conspiracy thus made the SRs a party of action, while the Marxists seemed to remain a party of faction and theory. 'More than any other party', wrote R. Charques, 'it was the party of youth'. This immediate, superficial appeal made it the most popular of the radical opposition groups until 1917.

Secondly, came the diverse groups that constituted Russian liberalism. Prominent among these were the 'zemstvo' members, some of whom, led by P. N. Shipov, persisted in their hopes for a representative assembly to provide some form of consultation between the Tsar and his people on the lines of the old 'Zemsky Sobor'. Many 'zemstvo' politicians, supported by a more radical liberal group known as the 'Third Element' expressed less interest in political institutions than in practical reforms within the existing social system. Among their demands were the abolition of corporal punishment and of the power of the Land Commandants over the peasantry, and the introduction of universal primary education. In the light of the events of the decade between 1905–14 these liberals might claim to have been the most successful of the opposition groups in Russia.

Until 1905, however, the two courses of action proposed by liberals had borne little fruit. For a while it had seemed that direct representations to the government might work. The then Minister of the Interior, I. L. Goremykin, seemed willing to introduce 'zemstvo' institutions into Lithuania, Byelorussia and other areas where none existed. By 1902, however, he had lost both the debate on the subject within the council of ministers and his official post. The other course, common to many opposition groups, was to found a party and a journal in the safety of foreign exile. The establishment of the newspaper *Liberation* ('Osvobozhdenie') and the Union of Liberation (Soyuz Osvobozhdeniya) was complete by 1903.

The dramatic realisation of a number of liberal demands was, however, to be brought about by foreign affairs of a quite different nature.

(h) The Origins of the Russo-Japanese War

The Russo-Japanese War, to a far greater degree than the First World War, was the direct result of two sets of Imperialist ambitions attempting to expand into the same power vacuum. Russian economic activity in the Far East had a long history (see Chapter 6, section **n**). The development of Vladivostok dated from the 1860s but, although important, that port was of limited use as it was closed by ice for three to four months of the year. The decision to begin the Trans-Siberian Railway in 1891 represented a substantial commitment in that area. Between that year and the turn of the century, furthermore, Russia gained substantial advantages from the steady decline of the Chinese Empire. The construction of the Chinese Eastern Railway across Manchuria (1897) brought valuable political and economic penetration of that region, and in 1898, to offset German gains in China, Russia demanded and received a 25 year lease on the ice free port of Port Arthur and on its hinterland, the Liaotung Peninsula. When Chinese resentment of foreign encroachments made itself felt in the Boxer Rebellion (1900), Russian troops were most prominent in the protection of European lives and interests, creating a dangerous confidence in their ability to defeat any mere oriental foe.

Japan watched Russian progress with apprehension and with resentment. Her recent modernisation and westernisation contrasted starkly with China's decay, and she had taken advantage of that decay to prosecute long-standing territorial claims. The Chinese–Japanese War of 1894–95 had established Japanese control over Korea, Port Arthur and the surrounding Manchurian territory, only for her to be forced to relinquish her conquests by pressure from the European powers established in China. Russia's subsequent acquisition of much of this territory was naturally a source of great nationalist indignation in Japan.

Two years of efforts (1901–03) by Japan to reach an understanding about spheres of influence in Manchuria and Korea failed, largely due to Russian apathy. When, in February 1903, Russia failed to remove her 'temporary' garrison from Manchuria, it looked suspiciously as if she had ambitions to dominate both regions. There is little evidence to suggest a deliberate desire for aggression on Russia's part, but many factors left her inclined to accept a military solution if the necessity arose. The so-called 'Bezobrazov Theory' or 'Scapegoat Theory' whereby Russian arrogance in the Far East was largely due to the work of an adventurer of that name with strong connections at court, is no longer widely held. G. Katkov, for example, has helped to show that the government was more closely connected with eastern financial adventures than was originally thought, and that the blame placed upon Bezobrazov and his like was partly a campaign by prominent politicians, including Witte, to distract attention from their own role. Nevertheless, influential figures did have

MAP 7   THE FAR EAST AT THE TIME OF RUSSO–JAPANESE WAR

large financial vested interests in economic ventures such as the Russian Timber Company of the Far East. Furthermore, the Tsar received considerable personal encouragement for adventures in the east, notably from the German Kaiser, happy to see Russian attentions diverted from eastern Europe by a cultural 'crusade' against the 'Yellow Peril'. Last, but not least, the domestic political tensions in European Russia made the Tsar and his ministers wish for a foreign distraction. There were doubtless many in high places who shared Plehve's famous judgement that 'to stem the tide of revolution, we need a successful little war'.

Nevertheless, in the words of A. Mazour, 'the Russo-Japanese War was declared by the admirals and not by the diplomats'. In February 1904, their patience exhausted, and aware of the lack of Russian preparation, the Japanese fleet launched an attack on Port Arthur without a formal declaration of war and laid mines to blockade the Russian fleet in the port.

(i) The Course and Results of the Russo-Japanese War

The general assumption that Russia could expect a quick and easy victory over a minor power such as Japan should not have survived intelligent and detailed examination. Although Russia's population was three times that of Japan and her territory vastly greater, Japan enjoyed much easier access to the theatre of war. Russian communications were dependent upon the Trans-Siberian Railway which operated on a single track for much of its length and which still had a gap of 100 miles in it in the region of Lake Baikal. Russian forces in the Far East totalled only 100 000 men at the beginning of hostilities, which the railway could only reinforce at a rate of 35 000 per month. Political developments in the west later made it desirable to keep large numbers of experienced and reliable troops available for action there, and naval reinforcements posed even greater problems with the Black Sea fleet effectively 'locked in' that sea by the terms of the Straits Convention of 1841. Lastly, the Russian command structure was crippled by the rivalries between the regular army commanders and the court favourites who directed political affairs in the Far East. Japan, on the other hand, had the capacity to put 180 000 men into the field immediately and to reinforce them by a short sea route. For all the endurance and bravery that they showed, the Russian soldiers never fought with the nationalistic and semi-religious fanaticism that the Japanese soldiers frequently displayed.

On land, the Russian forces quickly found themselves unable to contain the numerically superior Japanese and by May 1904 Port Arthur was cut off. The land campaigns then centred upon the respective needs to take or to relieve that port. The eventual surrender of Port Arthur in January 1905 followed a siege of 156 days and cost the Russians 17 200 casualties. Japanese casualties, however, totalled 110 000. As stores and ammunition remained in fair supply, the surrender resulted in a subsequent charge of treason against the commander, General Stoessel. Russian hopes of regaining the vital port faded after the Battle of Mukden (February–March 1905), a larger battle than any in the 19th century, involving 600 000 men.

Even so, as Russia still had the potential for reinforcement while Japan's resources were now stretched to their limits, the truly decisive factor in the war must be sought in the naval campaign. Without command of the sea, Japan would have been unable to supply or reinforce her forces on the Korean mainland, but Russian attempts to wrest the initiative from her were spectacularly unsuccessful. In April 1904 the most popular and able of the Russian commanders, Admiral Makarov died when his flagship, the 'Petropavlovsk' struck a Japanese mine. Only twice afterwards did the fleet venture out of harbour before the surrender of Port Arthur. In May 1905 the powerful Baltic fleet arrived in eastern waters having completed an epic voyage around the globe, without rest at anchor, and refuelling the huge coal-burning battleships at sea. To reach the theatre of war was a great achievement in itself, but it was the fleet's only achievement. On 27th May 1905, attempting to pass the Straits of Tsushima to reach Vladivostok, it encountered the Japanese fleet under Admiral Togo and lost 25 of its 35 ships in battle, most of the survivors being interned in neutral ports.

The Russians had lost largely as a result of numerical and strategic disadvantages, but partly because once more the incompetence of officers and administrators contrasted, as it had done in the Crimea, with the bravery and sacrifice of the common soldier. The greater effectiveness of Japan's modern equipment caused J. N. Westwood to ask 'which of the two belligerents was western and which oriental'. Despite these factors, Europeans' conviction of their own racial superiority rendered the outcome of the war stupifying and astounding.

On the face of it the peace settlement arrived at through American mediation at Portsmouth, New Hampshire (August 1905), let the Russians off lightly. Port Arthur and the Liaotung Peninsula were ceded, of course, to Japan. Through Witte's tough negotiation, Russia paid no war indemnity, kept half of the island of Sakhalin and retained her dominance in Manchuria. The Treaty of Portsmouth, however, marked a turning point in the foreign policy of Tsarist Russia. Russian interests in the Far East were not ended, but strict limitations were placed upon them. The result was that for the first time in nearly 25 years the foreign prestige of the Russian Empire depended predominantly upon developments in Europe.

(j) The 1905 Revolution: Origins

Military failure and humiliation added to the revolutionary pressure already upon the Tsarist government at the end of 1904. Most of the ingredients for a conflagration were now present. Peasant unrest had recurred sporadically since 1902, industrial strikes had occurred between 1902–04 in most cities, and several explosions of student unrest had occurred in Moscow and St. Petersburg in the same years. The spark that set them all off was provided by the 'Bloody Sunday' massacre of 22nd January 1905.

'Bloody Sunday' marked the spectacular failure of a daring experiment in the control of revolutionary elements. S. V. Zubatov, Chief of Police in Moscow, had proposed the concept known as 'police socialism' in 1902. It consisted of official encouragement of moderate workers' organisations, aiming at genuine improvements in wages and conditions, in the expectation that members would thus refrain from more dangerous political demands. Of these organisations, one of the largest was the Assembly of Russian Factory Workers, founded in 1903 and boasting 8000 members within a year. Its leader was the Orthodox priest G. A. Gapon, a controversial and enigmatic figure. After 1905, left wing suspicion of his motives was so bitter that he was 'executed' by SR agents (1906). Definite evidence of treachery has never been uncovered and it is perhaps more likely, as J. N. Westwood judges, that the misguided man 'rather fancied himself in the role of saviour'. Strict control over the activities of the society was difficult, however, and the plan to present a loyal petition for redress of grievances to the Tsar in St. Petersburg carried Gapon along with it. The demonstration by more than 150 000 people in front of the Winter Palace was perhaps the last time the Russian people genuinely approached the Tsar in his traditional role as the 'Little Father' of his people. The panic that led the Imperial troops to fire upon the crowd, killing an estimated 1000, killed 'Police Socialism', mortally wounded the reputation of the autocracy and triggered the 1905 revolution. 'It did more than perhaps anything else during the whole of the reign', writes R. Charques, 'to undermine the allegiance of the common people to the throne'.

(k) The 1905 Revolution: Spontaneous Revolt

Gapon's subsequent denunciation of the Tsar encapsulated the hatred felt by much of the Russian population. 'The innocent blood of workers, their wives and children lies forever between you, the murderer of souls, and the Russian people. . . . May all the blood that must be spilled fall on you, you hangman'. In Russian industry, this anger was reflected in an unprecedented strike movement. Four hundred thousand workers went on strike in February, and the total exceeded 2.7 million by the end of the year. No strike had greater effect than that of the railway workers in October, whereby the Russian cities were in imminent danger of starvation and the Russian economy of collapse. No major city in European Russia escaped the dislocation of its fuel supplies, and its administration.

The relatively small size of Russia's urban proletariat made its revolt, although serious, a problem that might be contained. A general revolt of the peasantry, however, was a much more serious prospect. The first such revolt broke out in the Kursk Province in February and by April had spread to most of the prime agricultural regions of European Russia. The peasant unrest was originally spontaneous, but subsequently exploited by the radical political parties. Thus the All-Russian Peasant Union, formed by regional delegates in May 1905, put forward views very similar to those of the SRs. At a local level, however, demands and actions were far less coherent, inspired by hatred of past wrongs and the hope of present gain, especially in the form of land. Three thousand, two hundred and twenty-eight such disturbances were serious enough to require the intervention of troops and an estimated 29 million roubles' worth of damage was inflicted upon Russian landowners in the course of the year.

The key to the success of the revolution lay in the attitude of the armed forces. Thus a most ominous element of the 1905 disturbances was the sporadic outbreak of mutinies in army units, but more especially in the navy. Rebellions occurred at Kronstadt in the Baltic and at Sebastopol on the Black Sea, but the most famous was the mutiny on board the battleship 'Potemkin' also in the Black Sea in June. Rebelling against the squalor of their conditions of service and the harshness of their officers, the crew seized control of the ship, killed some of the officers and bombarded Odessa. The prospect of general mutiny posed a grave threat to the regime's survival, but it did not materialise. The 'Potemkin' was forced to seek asylum in a Rumanian port, and mutinies on other ships were suppressed. The larger part of the army remained loyal. Despite a number of cases of fraternisation between troops and rioters the Imperial Manifesto published in December, promising better pay and fairer treatment had the desired effect upon troops mainly of peasant origin. By clever use of non-Russian troops against Russian mutineers, and vice-versa, the government had largely restored military discipline by the end of the year.

The separatist desires of national minorities within the Russian Empire provided a fourth factor threatening to dissolve that political entity. Socialist and Nationalist tendencies combined to produce a rash of nationalist parties and groups, including the Ukrainian 'Enlightenment' group (1905), the Ukrainian Social Democratic Party (1905), the White Russian Community (1903), the Moldavian Democratic Party (1906) and the All-Estonian Congress (1905). Their demands and activities varied from the publication of books and journals in their native tongues, through the desire for a representative assembly within the Empire, to the demand for complete independence.

(l) The 1905 Revolution: Political Crystallisation

The summer of 1905 encouraged a rapid crystallisation of opposition groups as each came to believe that its hour had come. Two main liberal groups appeared. The Union of Liberation, supported by some of the 'zemstvo' politicians, established in October the Constitutional Democratic Party, soon known from the abbreviation of its title as the 'Kadets'. Its demands included an assembly elected by direct and universal suffrage and the restoration of ancient national rights to Poland and Finland. They were thus rather more radical than the Union of Unions formed in February by representatives of a number of professional bodies.

The Russian Left was caught largely unawares and in a state of disarray by the events of 1905. The emergence in October of a Council ('Soviet') of Workers' Deputies in St. Petersburg was not the work of established socialist leaders, but a direct action by politically conscious workers to co-ordinate their strike action. Its 400–500 members represented 5 trade unions and 96 factories and, once the established leftist groups stirred themselves to tap the potential of the organisation, it mainly represented the 'Menshevik' tendency of the RSDRP, with 'Bolsheviks' and SRs in a distinct minority. Of those who returned from exile, none made a greater impact than L. D. Trotsky, an associate of Lenin's but more sympathetic at this point with the more democratic 'Menshevik' views. His intellectual and oratorical skills made him briefly one of the leading figures in the political chaos of the Russian capital.

How much importance should one attach to this first 'Soviet'? To the historians of the USSR its significance is of course huge as a 'dress rehearsal' for 1917, and the official *Historical Transactions* has concluded that 'the formation of "soviets" in the course of 1905–07 was the greatest historical achievement of the working class of Russia'. On the other hand, the 'Soviet' lasted only 50 days. It was not responsible for the huge strike of October and the second general strike it called in November petered out into anti-climax. An American commentator, A. Mazour, has written that 'the soviet entered inconspicuously, as if by chance, and departed ignominiously'. It is true that its importance outside St. Petersburg was negligible, but it draws its significance from the lead it gave to later revolutionaries and from the brief influence it enjoyed in the capital where in October, according to H. Seton-Watson, 'it is arguable that the soviet exercised more authority . . . than the Imperial government'. Evidence exists of over 550 other 'Soviets' throughout Russia, but none with the influence of the St. Petersburg prototype.

(m) The 1905 Revolution: the October Manifesto

Frightened by his government's loss of control, by the possibility of further military disobedience, and by the actuality of peasant rebellion which was the oldest fear of the Russian nobility, the Tsar had the choice of two courses of action. In early October he seemed ready to resort to outright military dictatorship, but faced with the objections of most senior ministers and some prominent members of the royal family, he finally recognised the need for concessions. The October Manifesto (30th October 1905) was, superficially, a recognition of most of the classic liberal demands. It granted freedom of person, of speech, of religion, of assembly and of organisation. Above all it confirmed the proposal made in August for the summoning of an elected assembly or 'Duma'.

In direct response to the agrarian unrest, a further set of concessions in November cancelled redemption payments and called for the peasants in return 'to preserve peace and order, and not violate the laws and rights of others'. Neither the November nor the October Manifesto really touched upon the true nature of Russia's social and political problems. The former made no concession to the peasants' desperate need for land and the latter set no real limitation upon the autocratic power of the Tsar. Russia faced the last nine years of peace with a liberal facade resting uneasily upon incompatible absolutist foundations. 'A constitution is given', remarked Trotsky, 'but the autocracy remains'.

(n) Stolypin and Repression

In another of his characteristically vivid phrases Trotsky described the October Manifesto as 'the whip wrapped in the parchment of a constitution'. Indeed, the government had sufficiently recovered its nerve to set about the restoration of its authority by the dual policy of consistent repression and inconsistent reform. In November, both the members of the St. Petersburg Soviet and those of the Union of Peasants were arrested. In December, a last desperate insurrection in Moscow was crushed by regular troops with the loss of about 1000 rebel lives, while loyal troops suppressed mutinous veterans of the eastern war along the route of the Trans-Siberian Railway. The efforts of the government were aided by the activities of extreme right wing groups hostile to the liberalisation of 1905. A legal political party, the Union of the Russian People (October 1905), was supplemented by terrorist gangs known as the 'Black Hundreds' which attacked known reformists and specialised in anti-semitic 'pogroms'.

In the course of the next few years, however, counter terror became a longer term government weapon in the hands of P. A. Stolypin. A newcomer to the Council of Ministers in 1906, he was appointed its chairman in 1907. His credentials as the ruthless governor of the Province of Saratov during the revolutionary year were perfect for his new task, and he has been widely regarded as the second of the two men, after S. J. Witte, who might have saved the regime had the Tsar had the wit to listen to his advice. Stolypin's plans for the regeneration of Russia had two facets. The first was the waging of an unrelenting war against violent political opposition, a tactic made more necessary

than ever by the resurgence of revolutionary violence in the summer of 1906. In 1907, an estimated 1231 officials and 1768 private citizens died in terrorist attacks. To this Stolypin replied with terror of his own. His 'field courts martial', operating under Article 87 of the Fundamental Laws (see section **p**), carried out 1144 death sentences in the nine months preceding May 1907. The bases of radical politics were also attacked through pressure upon unions and upon the press. Six hundred of the former closed between 1906–12, and 1000 newspapers ceased to publish during the same period. Ostensibly, the policy was a success. In 1908 the number of political assassinations had dropped to 365. From A. I. Guchkov, leader of the Octobrists in the Duma, was drawn the grudging compliment that 'if we are now witnessing the last convulsions of the revolution, and it is undoubtedly coming to an end, then it is to this man that we owe it'.

(o) Stolypin and Reform

Stolypin, however, was not such a reactionary as to consider that counter terror alone could restabilise the Tsarist regime. Reform, too, was essential and where Witte had set himself the task of modernising Russian industry, his successor turned to the more deep rooted problem of the peasantry. The key to Stolypin's agrarian policy was his belief that the surest basis for the regime was the support of a prosperous and contented section among the peasantry. To achieve this without damaging the landlords he sought primarily to free the peasant from the Communes created by the 1861 Emancipation. Acting again through the government's emergency powers he formulated a law (November 1906) by which any peasant had the right to withdraw himself and his land from the Commune. A further law (June 1910) dissolved all communes where no redistribution of land had taken place since the Emancipation. These laws were the culmination of a programme that had also granted to peasants equal civil rights in local administration (October 1906) and had transferred substantial amounts of state land to the Peasants' Bank (September 1906) in an attempt to satisfy 'land hunger'.

The subsequent growth of private peasant ownership was substantial. An estimated 20% of the peasantry enjoyed hereditary ownership of their land in 1905, while the proportion had risen to nearly 50% by 1915. Consolidation of scattered strips of land into viable farms was a slower process, and less than 10% of peasant holdings had been thus improved by the latter date. Three million cases, however, were awaiting the attention of land officials when the advent of war slowed their work almost to a halt. The lowering of interest rates in the Land Bank and the offering of migration facilities to 3.5 million peasants in Siberia between 1905–15 bear further witness to the concern of the Tsar's senior ministers with the agrarian problem.

The greatest weakness of the Stolypin reforms, like those of Witte, was that they did not enjoy the complete support of the Tsar. Strongly influenced by extreme right wing factions, resentful of any such changes, Nicholas was probably on the verge of dismissing Stolypin when the latter was assassinated in Kiev in September 1911. The murderer, Bogrov, was linked with both the SRs and the secret police and the confusion that has always surrounded his motives for his crime is a measure of how Stolypin's 'enlightened conservatism' had drawn upon him the hatred of both political extremes.

(p) The Dumas: Formation

Outwardly Russia entered 1906 with a radically revised and modernised constitution. In effect, each element in that constitution was little more than a sham. The revived Council of Ministers, presided over at first by S. J. Witte, had the appearance of a cabinet. In fact, the ministers were entirely dependent upon the Tsar for appointment, direction, and dismissal, and thus merely continued to serve the autocracy. The upper house of the assembly, the Council of State, was half elected, by zemstvo, church, noble and university bodies, but

was also half appointed by the Tsar. The lower house, the State Duma, was wholly elective but was tied hand and foot by a series of limitations upon its powers from its birth in February 1906. It had no control over military expenditure, nor over the Tsar's household finances, and in any case an enormous French loan of 2250 million gold francs (April 1906) rendered the crown financially independent. It had no means of controlling or even of censuring ministers. Most important of all, Article 87 of the Fundamental Laws (April 1906), drawn up without consultation with the Duma, left the Tsar with the power to govern by decree whenever the assembly was not in session.

The representative nature of the Duma was further limited by the decision of all major left wing groups to boycott the first set of elections. Thus the elections in early 1906 were mainly contested by the 'Kadets' (see section 1) and two other groups. The 'Octobrists' were moderate conservatives, taking their name from their acceptance of the October Manifesto. The Labour Group (Trudoviki) was a faction largely reflecting the views of the SRs, despite the fact that the SRs were not officially involved in the contest.

The relative fortunes of these and other groups in the elections to the four Dumas that met between 1906–17 are reflected in Table 9.4.

The changes in composition from Duma to Duma reflect two factors. One was the eventual decision of groups on both political extremes to participate in elections, if only to change the nature of the assembly. The more important factor was that election was by indirect 'college' voting, whereby communities of differing sizes nominated a delegate to exercise a single vote for them. This has been variously interpreted as an administrative

	1st Duma	2nd Duma	3rd Duma	4th Duma
Social Democrats	—	65	14	14
Socialist Revolutionaries	—	34	—	—
Trudoviki	94	101	14	10
Progressives	—	—	39	47
Kadets (also known as the Party of the People's Liberty)	179	92	52	57
Non-Russian National Groups	121	—	26	21
Centre Party	—	—	—	33
Octobrists	17	32	120	99
Nationalists	—	—	76	88
Extreme Right	15	63	53	64

Table 9.4

necessity, given Russia's vast size, and as a cynical trick to 'rig' election results. Certainly, it gave the government the chance to limit or increase the influence of sections of the population by changing the size of the community exercising one vote.

(q) The Dumas: Achievement

The task facing the Dumas was nearly impossible. They faced, in G. Fischer's words, 'the dilemma of attaining complex, specifically western objectives in an illiberal, underdeveloped society'. Much compromise would have been needed, and very little was forthcoming. The Tsar was never more than coldly formal in his attitude towards the Duma, and a number of historians, including G. Fischer and R. Charques, have laid blame upon the liberal majority in the early Dumas for their inflexibility and their insistence upon unrealistic demands.

The 1st Duma (April 1906) was unmistakably hostile to the government in its major demands, for land reform and for an amnesty for political prisoners, and was dissolved after only 73 days. The 2nd Duma (February 1907) suffered from a transfer of influence from the centre to the extremes. The 'Kadets' were greatly reduced in numbers after their irresponsible and impulsive 'Vyborg Manifesto' (July 1906) in which 120 of their members broke the law and disqualified themselves from future elections by calling for civil disobedience against the government. On the other hand both extreme right wing and extreme left wing groups now decided to participate in the elections and proceeded to use the Duma for their own forms of propaganda. The 2nd Duma, therefore, amounted to little more than three and a half months of continuous uproar.

The longer lives of the 3rd and 4th Dumas (November 1907 and November 1912) resulted from P. A. Stolypin's dual decision to work with a suitably conservative assembly, and to revise the electoral laws to that end. While the electoral law of 1905 had blatantly favoured the conservative forces of landowners and peasants, the new one (June 1907) even further manipulated the electoral 'colleges'. In effect it left some 50% of the final votes in the hands of the landowners (up from 31%), 23% in the hands of the peasantry (down from 42%), while the growing urban proletariat exercised only 2% of the votes (down from 4%).

The result was two assemblies that 'hovered between two worlds' (R. Charques), those of reform and reaction. Historians are consequently divided as to whether or not they should be seen as successes. Certainly the 3rd and 4th Dumas were thwarted on many important reformist issues. Bills for the extension of the zemstvo system into Poland and for religious toleration were defeated in the Council of State. When Stolypin used his emergency powers to pass the former measure it was a triumph for the Fundamental Laws rather than for the Duma. On the other hand, the hated Land Commandants (see chapter 6) were replaced by reinstated Justices of the Peace, compulsory health insurance for industrial workers was introduced (June 1912) and, with much local co-operation from the 'zemstvos', much progress was made in Russian education. Universal primary education within ten years was adopted as an official policy (May 1908) and by 1914 was 50% of the way towards completion, involving 7.2 million children. Figures for attendance at secondary schools (510 000) and at universities (40 000) in 1914 do not, unfortunately, reflect a uniform advance.

As H. Seton-Watson points out, however, the achievement of the Dumas should not only be estimated in terms of measures passed. It had not become a truly representative assembly, because the government had never wanted such an assembly, but by 1914 political parties were legally established and, while rebellion was punished, open political discussion was tolerated and allowed to appear in the press. All of these factors represented advances scarcely dreamed of before 1905.

(r) The Russian Regime on the Eve of War

Perhaps more than any previous period in Russian history, the 'Stolypin Era' has provoked controversy among historians. Two questions predominate. How should Stolypin's work be evaluated, and how far had his reforms and those of Witte set Tsarist Russia on a survival course by 1914?

Assessments of Stolypin's work have often followed partisan political lines. Soviet historians, of whom A. Y. Avrekh is notable, have concentrated upon the suppression of revolution, upon the 200 000 political prisoners in 1908, and the 5000 death sentences passed between 1907–09. To Avrekh the 'Stolypin course' was 'the inescapable situation of reaction, the historic destiny of the rotten regime', for revolution was still the only logical outcome of the social and economic forces at work. Western appraisals have usually been kinder ranging through those that excuse his use of terror by reference to the revolutionary terrorism with which he was faced, to the Russian-American emigré L. I. Strakhovsky, who views Stolypin as a most positive reformer and as the brightest hope of the Tsarist regime. Avoiding the bias of both extremes it is sound to view Stolypin as an enlightened and positive conservative, implacably hostile to liberal and revolutionary challenges to the autocracy, but lucidly aware of the inadequacy of mere entrenched reaction.

On the broader question of the adequacy of Russian modernisation, commentators have divided into 'optimist' and 'pessimist' schools, respectively confident and doubtful of Tsarist Russia's prospects had she avoided the European War. The 'optimists', for whom the economic historian A. Gerschenkron has been a prominent spokesman see the increasing economic maturity of Russia, based upon industrial development and sound agrarian reform, as a guarantee of peacetime stability. 'One might surmise', he concludes, 'that in the absence of war Russia could have continued on the road of progressive westernisation'. This view is questioned not only by Soviet writers, but by westerners such as T. H. von Laue, E. H. Carr and W. E. Mosse. They draw attention to the limitations of Stolypin's reforms over Russia in general and stress the possibility that his sacrifice of the weaker peasant to 'the sober and the strong' would, in the end, only have added to the ranks of the revolutionary proletariat.

The evidence is inconclusive. On the one hand, the years 1910–14 saw another 13 000 peasant outbreaks, a major outburst of violence in the Lena goldfield (1912) and 1.5 million industrial workers on strike in the last six months of peace. On the other hand, education and literacy were spreading at an unprecedented rate and the revolutionary parties were paralysed by internal dissentions and by the regular exposure of police agents in their midst. The combined membership of these groups in 1910 was only ten per cent of the 1905 total, and Rosa Luxemburg could refer to the RSDRP in 1914 as 'a handful of fighting cocks living abroad... and to expect anything from these cocks is pure delusion'.

Possibly, the decisive factor in the controversy is that stressed by D. W. Treadgold who emphasises the implacable hostility towards change of much of the Russian ruling class and especially of the Tsar who regarded good government as 'not an ideal to be sought but an irrelevance compared to . . . the maintenance of the loyalty of the Russian people to his own person'. Perhaps in the final analysis progress towards a more modern Russia might still have been blocked by a narrow-minded and reactionary autocracy.

(s) Russian Science and Culture on the Eve of War

The attention of the 'optimistic' school of historians has not been limited to political and economic affairs. 'Not only the body of Russia but the soul as well', comments the 'optimist' emigré M. Karpovich, 'was growing stronger in the decade which preceded the World War'. Indeed, considering the narrowness of Russia's educated stratum and the limitations of her higher education facilities, her contribution to science and technology in the twenty years before 1914 is quite remarkable. In most scientific fields Russia produced men of genius. I. I. Mechnikov was a leading figure in the study of infection and immunisation, running the Pasteur Institute in Paris and winning a Nobel Prize in 1908. An earlier Nobel Prize (1904) went to perhaps the most famous of all Russian scientists, I. P. Pavlov, whose work on digestive enzymes and conditioned reflexes in dogs still makes him a household name today. In chemistry D. I. Mendeleyev evolved the Periodic Table and described a number of new elements, while in agricultural science K. A. Timiryazev was the foremost soil scientist of his day.

In applied technology Russia suffered rather more from her material backwardness, but led the world in two important respects. A. S. Popov's work on Radio communications ran parallel to, and sometimes ahead of that of Marconi, while Russia's contribution to aerodynamics was of the greatest importance. The work of N. Y. Zhukovsky and S. A. Chaplygin on airflow, important as it was, cedes precedence to that of K. E. Tsiolkovsky whose developments in the fields of design and fuel make him one of the most important figures in the history of rocket technology.

In most of the arts, a golden age had just passed in Russia by 1914. The major exception to this rule was in the performing arts. In ballet S. Diaghilev's *Ballets Russes* (1909) held its primacy for decades. In its choreographer, M. Fokine, its dancers, V. Nijinsky and A. Pavlova, and its primary composer I. F. Stravinsky, it boasted the world's best. The Moscow Arts Theatre, with K. Stanislavsky as its major director, and Russian opera, with F. Chaliapin as its leading performer, also raised Russia to a level of unprecedented cultural brilliance. The greatest Russian writers of the age, however, were recently dead. These were A. P. Chekhov in 1904 and L. N. Tolstoy in 1910. Although not primarily political writers, both were obsessed in their last works, as in Chekhov's *Cherry Orchard* and Tolstoy's *Resurrection*, with the stagnation and sterility of Russian society. Their successor was A. M. Peshkov who, writing under the pen-name 'Gorky' (meaning 'bitter') had already produced a stream of novels and plays by 1914. These were more specifically political than those of his predecessors, exposing the squalor and hopelessness of society's 'Lower Depths'. L. Kochan describes Gorky as 'the first consciously proletarian novelist', and these works were to make him the doyen of Soviet literature in the 1920s and early 1930s.

(t) Historiography

The enduring importance to the modern world of the events that shaped Russian history between 1856–1917 has combined with the closed nature of past and present Russian society to ensure that a large proportion of the historical commentaries on the period have been written from a partisan point of view. Russian writings on the period, from before or since the Revolution, have always clearly reflected an official standpoint. At first this took the form of official court biographies such as those by Shilder (*The Emperor Nicholas I, his times and reign,* 1903) and S. S. Tatishchev (*The Emperor Alexander II, his times and reign,* 1903). These naturally accepted the Tsarist view of government and society and viewed the events of the reigns in that light.

Since the Revolution Russian historians have inevitably interpreted events in a Marxist sense, stressing the hopelessness of attempts to save a rotten regime by social and economic reforms, and treating the period 1905–17 as one of recurring revolutionary crisis that could only have one logical conclusion. The Soviet writer is also bound to accept as truths a number of opinions published during the period by V. I. Lenin. Thus the role of the Bolshevik Party and the correctness of Lenin's interpretation of events between 1905–17 tend to be stressed while the roles of the Mensheviks, the SRs and, of course, the conservatives are diminished. This is evident in official publications directly sponsored by the government (*History of the Communist Party of the Soviet Union,* 1960) and in more strictly academic works such as that of A. M. Pankratova (*The Revolution of 1905–07 in Russia. Documents and Materials,* 1955–61), A. Y. Avrekh (*Stolypin and the Third Duma,* 1968) and A. B. Shapkarin (*The Peasant Movement in Russia, June 1907–July 1914,* 1960).

In general, western historians have not accepted the thesis of 'inevitable' revolution, but have viewed the period immediately before the war as one open to various possibilities. This has led to the debate between 'optimists' and 'pessimists' referred to in section (**r**). A. Gerschenkron (*Economic Backwardness in Historical Perspective,* 1962) and T. H. von Laue (*Why Lenin? Why Stalin?,* 1964) have already been mentioned as leading proponents of the respective cases. To the 'optimist' school should also be added those liberals, Russian and foreign, whose sympathy with parliamentary democracy and the rule of law convinced them that the Dumas were following the correct road when war intervened. P. Miliukov, a leading Kadet politician (*History of Russia,* 1932) and S. Pushkarev (*The Emergence of Modern Russia 1801–1917,* 1963) provide good examples of the arguments of Russian exiles, while B. Pares (*Russia and Reform,* 1907 or *My Russian Memoirs,* 1931) provides a classic statement of the problem viewed from a Victorian-liberal bias.

Virtually no serious apology for the Tsarist regime has been attempted, except in the memoirs of certain leading government figures, such as those of S. J. Witte (*The Memoirs of Count Witte,* 1921) and K. P. Pobedonostsev (*Reflections of a Russian Statesman,* 1898).

Of the many English and American works of recent years, attempting to reach a balanced synthesis of both western and Soviet research on the period, by far the most detailed and authoritative is that by H. Seton-Watson (*The Russian Empire, 1801–1917,* 1967).

Progress Paragraphs

Answer the following in about 150 words.

How well suited was the personality of Nicholas II to the task of governing a state in flux such as Russia?

Section (**a**)

What factors prevented a solution to Russian agrarian problems during this period?   Section (**b**)

In what ways was Russia industrially backward during this period, and how did S. J. Witte hope to remedy this backwardness?   Section (**c**)

Assess the industrial development achieved by Russia during this period.

Section (**d**)

What were the results (a) in material terms and (b) in social terms of Russian industrialisation?

Sections (**d and e**)

What factors promoted the growth of Marxist views among the Russian Left during the 1880s and the 1890s?   Section (**f**)

On what points did Bolsheviks, Mensheviks and Socialist Revolutionaries disagree?
                                    Sections (**f** and **g**)

What caused the Russo-Japanese War and why did Russia lose it?   Sections (**h** and **i**)

How did (a) urban, (b) agrarian and (c) military unrest show itself in 1905?   Sections (**j** and **k**)

What role did the radical political parties play in the 1905 Revolution?   Sections (**k** and **l**)

How was the Tsarist government able to survive the 1905 Revolution?   Sections (**k** and **m**)

What were the aims of P. A. Stolypin and how did he attempt to achieve them?   Sections (**n** and **o**)

In what ways did the Dumas fall short of being true representative assemblies?   Section (**p**)

In what ways and for what reasons did the 3rd and 4th Dumas achieve more than the 1st and 2nd Dumas?   Section (**q**)

In what ways, if any, was the Tsarist regime more stable in 1914 than it had been ten years earlier?
                                    Section (**r**)

What signs were there of cultural and scientific health in Russia between 1900 and 1914?
                                    Section (**s**)

10
Germany and Austria in the Wilhelmine Age 1888–1914

(a) Kaiser Wilhelm II

The long reign of Wilhelm I ended in March 1888, in the Kaiser's 92nd year. His son, now briefly Kaiser as Friedrich III, had only months to live. He has suffered for a year from cancer of the throat, which had already deprived him of the faculty of speech, and which ended his life in June. The Imperial throne of Germany thus passed to his own son, and the thirty year reign of Wilhelm II began.

The personality and psychology of the new Kaiser, now 29 years of age, have been a source of unwaning fascination for historians. His relationship with his parents, especially with his English mother, was tense and uneasy, and his personal sensitivity was undoubtedly increased by an accident at birth which left him with a withered arm and partially deaf. At Bonn University he had shown far less interest in systematic study and learning than in the company of sycophantic student aristocrats, and discovered the true passion of his youth in his years as an officer in the Potsdam Guards. It was an ominous but fair indication of his future character that he gained such satisfaction from the superficial glamour and excitement of military life. Dismissed by his own father as 'inexperienced, immature and presumptuous', Wilhelm has not been much more kindly treated by historians. Some, such as K. S. Pinson, have shown a relatively sympathetic understanding of his weaknesses: 'Under the mask of the proud Emperor there was an essentially sensitive, insecure, timid and nervous individual'. Others, such as G. A. Craig, find more to blame in his personality: 'Wilhelm had as much intelligence as any European sovereign and more than most, but his lack of discipline, his self-indulgence, his overdeveloped sense of theatre, and his fundamental misreading of history prevented him from putting it to effective use'. The age of the young Kaiser was also significant. He belonged to a new, confident generation unaware of the dangers that German conservatism had narrowly survived in 1848 and in 1862. As Golo Mann has put it, 'his memories began in 1870. He regarded the position which he owed to brilliant manoeuvres and clever acts of violence as the gift of God, as the natural order of things'.

What did this mean for the conduct of the German government? Firstly, it meant that Wilhelm II would not be content with the passive role played by his grandfather. He believed passionately in the Divine Right of Kings and, from this outmoded thesis, derived a notion of the mystical link between the ruler and his people that resembled the views of Friedrich Wilhelm IV (see Chapter 2, section **f**). Not for him a reign based upon the narrow interests of Junker landowners, or dictated by the advantage of Prussia alone. Wilhelm, in the words of A. J. P. Taylor, 'desired an absurdity—to be Emperor of all the Germans'. In a state built by Bismarck upon division and confrontation the prospects of harmonious relations between monarch and Chancellor were dim.

Strong though he was on principle, the mode of government of the new Kaiser was hectic, spectacular and shallow. He travelled obsessively, rarely spending as much as half the year in his capital and earning the nickname of 'Der Reise-Kaiser' (the travelling Emperor). He had views on everything, but rarely bothered to back his 'inspiration' with hard information. 'He just talks himself into an opinion', remarked Kiderlen-Wächter in 1891, while Wilhelm's biographer M. Balfour has remarked that 'his fluency in speaking meant that he approached all questions with an open mouth'. It was a fair summary of the man and the monarch that he openly boasted that he read neither the newspapers nor the German constitution. The outcome was a thirty year reign of great spectacle, constant motion, but little positive content. It amounted in the words of the future Weimar minister W. Rathenau, to a 'dilettante foreign policy, romantic conservative internal policy and bombastic and empty cultural policy'.

(b) The Fall of Bismarck

For all the monumental achievements of the past

three decades, Bismarck's position as Chancellor of the Reich had remained theoretically dependent upon the goodwill of the monarch. That position had appeared for some years to be threatened by the prospect of the succession of Crown-Prince Friedrich, with his allegedly liberal sympathies, and his English wife, the Crown-Princess Victoria. The death of Friedrich saved Bismarck from one challenge to his authority only to confront him with another. If the political sympathies of Wilhelm were less liberal, he differed fundamentally with his Chancellor as to methods of government.

The issues that divided the two men between 1888–90 were, in reality, merely symptoms of their different interpretations of the Reich and of the role of the Kaiser. A strike by miners in the Ruhr (May 1889) gave Wilhelm the chance to display his brand of benevolent paternalism towards the German working class. While he prepared a programme of social reforms, including a ban on Sunday working, Bismarck rejected the principle of conciliation and concession and aimed to continue a policy of hostility and confrontation. His plans to make permanent the renewable Anti-Socialist Laws (see Chapter 7, section **h**) not only provoked a clash in the royal council (January 1890), but had severe repercussions in the Reichstag elections in the following month. Bismarck's coalition of Conservatives and National Liberals lost 85 of their 220 seats, and the Social-Democrats nearly doubled their share of the vote. Deprived of the support of both monarch and Reichstag, Bismarck had only intrigue to fall back on. His attempts to force through a 'package' of measures to revise the constitution, to facilitate his political control, forced the Kaiser's hand. Wilhelm chose the path of conciliation, demanded Bismarck's resignation, and received it on 18th March 1890.

For all his earlier achievement, Bismarck bequeathed to Germany a legacy of tension and troubles. By the concentration of power in his own hands he had consistently obstructed the growth of truly representative institutions in Germany. As Max Weber commented, 'Bismarck left behind him as a political heritage a nation without any political education . . . a nation without any political will, accustomed to allow the great statesman at its head to look after its policy for it'. Undoubtedly, Bismarck had governed with great shrewdness, but the sad result of his political egoism was that his great power now passed into the hands of an irresponsible and unstable monarch. Wilhelm, furthermore, inherited a variety of thorny problems, especially in colonial and foreign policy, which Bismarck had allowed to develop for reasons of short-term political

advantage. Despite his famous announcement upon Bismarck's resignation that 'the ship's course remains the same. "Full steam ahead" is the order', Wilhelm's fundamental misunderstanding of recent German and European history was to guarantee the destruction of most of the essential principles of Bismarckian Germany within the next thirty years.

(c) German Economic Growth

The years of Wilhelm II's reign down to 1914 saw German industry build upon its Bismarckian foundations (see Chapter 7, section **o**) to take its place among the foremost industrial economies of the world. In this respect, the character of the country matched that of the Kaiser. It was young, dynamic, and outwardly confident. At the basis of Germany's economic acceleration was a continued rapid growth in population, providing native industries at once with a greater labour force and with more consumers. Between 1870 and 1890 Germany had experienced a population rise of 21%, from 40.9 to 49.5 million. In the next two decades, the rate of increase was half as great again, leading to a total of 65 million Germans.

In the traditional heavy industries of the Reich the years from 1890 saw no fundamental deviation from the paths followed between 1870–90, but did witness a spectacular acceleration in the pace of output. Coal production was challenging that of the British coal industry by the outbreak of the World War, while steel output had surpassed that of Great Britain in 1900, and was nearly double that of her rival by 1910.

The necessary corollary of these increases in German production was the expansion of her communications system. As regards rail transport the Wilhelmine period saw a steady continuation of the growth that was a central feature of economic expansion since the foundation of the Reich. A system that extended 11 600 miles in 1870, and 26 136 miles in 1890, had grown to 36 894 miles by

	Coal & lignite	Pig iron	Steel	Foreign exports	Foreign imports
	(m. tons)	(m. tons)	(m. tons)	(£m.)	(£m.)
1890	89.1	4.66	3.16	170.5	213.65
1900	149.8	8.52	7.37	237.65	302.15
1910	192.3	14.79	13.15	373.74	446.71
1913	279.0	—	—	504.83	538.52

Table 10.1

1910. More novel, however, was the spectacular development of a German merchant navy. The total tonnage of steamships registered at Hamburg rose from 99 000 in 1880 to 746 000 in 1900, while the figures for Bremen in the same period were 59 000 and 375 000. Germany's total merchant marine in 1914 amounted to 3 million tons, only a quarter of the British total, but nearly three times that of the USA.

Nor was German expansion limited to traditional industries. By the outbreak of the World War, she had established a substantial lead over all other European powers in the new chemical and electrical industries. In the former, Germany came to produce 75% of world output of chemical dyes by 1914, and played a prominent role in the development of agricultural fertilisers, of pharmaceutical products and of the industrial uses of sulphuric acid, sodium and chlorine. The latter field to which Werner von Siemens had already contributed the electric dynamo (1867) and important work on electronic traction (1879 onwards), saw the development of the two biggest electricity combines in Europe. These were Siemens/Halske, and AEG (Allgemeine Elektrizitäts Gesellschaft—General Electricity Company). In fact, by 1913 half of the world's electro-technical trade was in German hands. 'Beyond question', Sir J. Clapham has concluded, 'the creation of this industry was the greatest single achievement of modern Germany'. Such household names as Daimler and Diesel also attest to German achievement in the engineering industry.

The total wealth of the German Reich increased in the peaceful years of the Wilhelmine era, according to the contemporary economist, K. Helfferich, from 200 000 million marks to 300 000. Table 10.2, produced by H. Holborn and relating to Prussia alone, indicates the increase in the number of great personal fortunes in this period. Other evidence suggests that the increase in German prosperity was more generally felt. 'Per Capita' income doubled, for example, in the course of 40 years. It rose from 352 marks per annum (1871–75), through 603 pa (1896–1900) to 728

marks pa in 1911–13. The dramatic decrease in the rate of emigration, from 134 200 in 1880–89, to 28 000 between 1900–10, also indicates the relative rise in German living standards by the latter decade.

It should be noted, however, that this overall prosperity was not shared by German agriculture. Although scientific methods of cultivation had spread rapidly since 1870, German grain producers could not compete adequately with American imports, especially when large ocean-going steamers and low freight charges cheapened imports further. By 1900, it was cheaper to import grain from America than to transport it 250 miles within Germany. Grain prices dropped and heavy internal tariffs were necessary to keep the Junker farmers of East Prussia solvent. Economically, therefore, the Germany of Wilhelm II presented a subtly contrasted picture of modern dynamism and embattled conservative interests.

(d) Caprivi and the 'New Course': Domestic

Bismarck's successor as Chancellor of the Reich and as Prime Minister of Prussia was General Leo von Caprivi. He brought to these offices the prestige of high military rank, personal honesty and modesty, but none of the political experience or deviousness necessary to master the complexities and contradictions of the Bismarckian state. 'The primary problem of the Caprivi Era', in the opinion of its prime historian, J. Alden Nichols, 'was how to handle a complex political creation that had finally escaped from the control of its creator'. The new Chancellor, like the Kaiser, desired greater conciliation and less confrontation in domestic politics. He refused to regard any political grouping as a 'Reichsfeind' and was willing to accept the assistance of any group in furthering his projects. Both men claimed not to be inaugurating a 'New Era', an indication of how little they understood of Bismarck's rule.

In fact, the years 1890–94 saw systematic inroads made into the domestic system established by Bismarck. The Anti-Socialist Laws were allowed to lapse, and attempts were made to win the working classes over to the Reich with a series of reforms that included a ban on Sunday working, the limitation of working hours for women and children, and the establishment of courts for industrial arbitration. Confrontation with national minorities in Posen and in Alsace-Lorraine was eased by the relaxation of rules governing the use of German in administration and education. A

Total fortune of:	1895	1911
Between 100–500 000 RM	86 552	135 843
Between 500 000—1m. RM	8375	13 800
Between 1–2m. RM	3429	5916
Over 2 million RM	1827	3425

Table 10.2

moderate reduction was sought in the privileges of Prussia within the Reich. Prussia's independent foreign ministry was abolished, her tax system reformed and a graduated income tax introduced. Of much more direct offence to the Prussian Junkers was Caprivi's new economic course. In the interests of increased trade and of cheaper food, he abandoned Bismarckian protectionism, that great guarantee of the Junkers' agricultural prosperity. A series of bilateral trade treaties, with Austria-Hungary and Italy in 1892, with Belgium, Switzerland and Rumania in 1893, and with Russia a year later, greatly stimulated Germany's industrial progress but involved as their price the reduction of German agricultural tariffs. The unfortunate coincidence of these measures with the increase in cheap American corn exports drove not only the Junkers, but most farmers into opposition to the government. The Federation of Agriculturalists (Bund der Landwirte), founded to organise this opposition (February 1893), boasted 250000 members within the year and constituted one of several new conservative forces in German politics.

The fate of two pieces of projected legislation illustrated the deterioration of Caprivi's political position. A bill by the Prussian Ministry of Education, proposing religious segregation of schools, and closer control by the Churches of religious education (1892), was defeated by the vociferous opposition of all liberal groups in the Reichstag. The defeat occasioned Caprivi's resignation as Prime Minister of Prussia, which further weakened his political base. More surprisingly, a new Army Bill, proposing to enlarge the army by a two year service period instead of three, and to request the renewal of the Military Budget every five years instead of seven, also ran into severe opposition. Presented to the Reichstag in 1892, it was only passed after a dissolution and new elections in which the conservative parties and the Social Democrats prospered at the expense of the Liberals.

Four years in office served to convince Caprivi that he had underestimated the selfishness of the various political interests in the Reichstag. In the same period, the initial, superficial 'liberalism' of the Kaiser had faded like that of Alexander II or Pius IX. Wilhelm accepted his Chancellor's resignation in October 1894. He was disillusioned at the failure of the workers to desert the Social Democrats and rally to him, perturbed at the resurgence of political violence evident especially in the assassination of the French president by anarchists, and perplexed at the rift between the government and Junker conservatism. In terms of

positive achievements, we must accept A. J. P. Taylor's judgement that Caprivi was 'never an important figure nor even a significant one'. His four years in office are, nevertheless, of negative significance as a last attempt to achieve a domestic concensus in Germany, before subsequent governments sought that concensus by methods more dangerous for the peace of Europe.

(e) Caprivi and the 'New Course'; Foreign Policy

It is a more complex matter to decide whether Caprivi departed from the traditional Bismarckian course in handling Germany's foreign affairs. Certainly he presided over the destruction of a central element in the Bismarckian diplomatic system when (March 1890) he refused to renew the Reinsurance Treaty with Russia (see Chapter 7, section **m**). In this, he acted from no essentially anti-Russian motive, and hoped to maintain friendly relations with the great eastern power. He was influenced by personalities in the foreign office, such as F. von Holstein whose general leanings were anti-Russian. Their convincing arguments concerned the incompatability of sections of the Treaty with German undertakings to Austria and to Rumania, and the undoubted fact that its terms gave far greater advantages to Russia than to Germany. In short, Caprivi acted honestly where greater deviousness might have served better. The result of his action was the almost immediate confirmation of Bismarck's nightmare, a diplomatic understanding between Russia and France (see Chapter 8, section **p**). Also, by agreeing to the renewal of the Triple Alliance with Austria and Italy in 1891, he made a substantial contribution to the formation of hostile camps in Europe that eventually undermined her peace.

Caprivi remained Bismarckian, however, in the sense that he continued to resist the considerable pressures within Germany for a 'World Policy'. He saw little realistic future in the acquisition of colonies, and the essence of his policy remained European, to consolidate and improve Germany's position in Central Europe. This aim was served by his system of economic agreements with Germany's neighbours (see section **d**) and also by the confirmation of the Triple Alliance. It had its most controversial manifestation, however, in the Anglo-German treaty of July 1890. By this treaty Germany transferred to Great Britain all rights to the island of Zanzibar, and to substantial areas of the adjacent African mainland, in return for the strategic North Sea island of Heligoland. If, however, as G. A. Craig has suggested, the Zanzibar agreement was an opening move in a plan to tempt Britain into closer relations with Germany in place of the Russian alliance, it was a failure. Caprivi underestimated the reluctance of the British to get involved in binding continental commitments. He also found that his concept of Germany's continental future was not widely popular at home. The Pan German League (Alldeutscher Verband), which took form between 1891–94, was a deliberate attempt to encourage the Reich to pursue a more energetic, prestigious and cosmopolitan foreign policy. Thus, although Caprivi rejected some of the methods most dear to Bismarck, the brief span of his government did represent the last attempt to limit Germany to European commitments before his opponents launched her on the flamboyant and ultimately disastrous course of 'World Policy'.

(f) Government in Wilhelmine Germany 1894–1914: The Chancellors

The German Reich was to have three more Chancellors between the fall of Caprivi and the outbreak of war in 1914. The first of these was a Catholic, Bavarian aristocrat, Prince Chlodwig von Hohenlohe-Schillingfurst (1894–1900). After a lifetime in state service, he reached the highest office at the age of 75, and was frankly a stop-gap. His conservative views on domestic matters and his pro-Russian sympathies recommended him to the German right, and his lack of any coherent programme of his own fitted in well with Wilhelm's ambitions of personal government. Primarily, in the words of Friedrich Naumann, Hohenlohe was 'an artist in the avoidance of catastrophe', and his years in office constituted in retrospect a lull before the diplomatic storm of the new century.

Hohenlohe's resignation in 1900 was precipitated by the Kaiser's persistent failure to consult him on important policy matters. His successor, however, was to be a prime accessory in Wilhelm's irresponsible dilettantism. Bernhard von Bülow (1900–09) was a more cosmopolitan and, it was felt, more modern man than Hohenlohe. Having risen through the Foreign Office, where he had been Minister since 1897, he was closely identified with German colonial expansion and seemed to share the Kaiser's enthusiasm for a 'world role'. He had a reputation for brilliance, but superficial polish was not backed by firm principles or broad vision, and he deserved the nickname bestowed upon him by Kiderlen-Wächter of 'the eel'. There was too much of the flattering courtier about

Bülow for him to have been a safe moderating influence on the Kaiser as Hohenlohe had been, and H. Holborn has laid upon him much of the blame for Germany's diplomatic irresponsibility during the period. The circumstances of Bülow's fall are thus ironic. Although his resignation in June 1909 was ostensibly due to the defeat in the Reichstag of his project for a tax on inherited wealth, the real cause of his downfall was, like Bismarck's, the loss of the monarch's confidence. This arose from Bülow's carelessness the previous year in allowing the publication of an interview given by Wilhelm to the British *Daily Telegraph*. Characteristic irresponsibility on the Kaiser's part led to utterances offensive to Britain and to Russia and highly embarrassing to Germany, and an enormous outcry in the Reichstag brought Wilhelm to the verge of a nervous breakdown and ended the 'golden age' of his personal government. In the long run, as many foreign observers have pointed out, the Reichstag missed the opportunity for long-term constitutional change afforded by the *'Daily Telegraph* Incident', and Bülow alone paid a high price for the affair.

The last peacetime Chancellor of Imperial Germany was Theobald von Bethmann-Hollweg (1909–17). A conscientious administrator, and a man of personal courage and honour, he seemed from the point of view of domestic affairs, an ideal choice. However, his crippling disability was his total inexperience in foreign or military affairs. However much this might have recommended him to a Kaiser who desired supremacy in those fields, it was part of Germany's tragedy that such a man led the government at the time when the fate of Europe depended upon such matters.

In an important sense such changes in personnel were of secondary importance. Of greater significance in the years between 1894–1914 was the erosion of the overall power of the Chancellor, perhaps the most important of all the departures from Bismarck's system of government. In part, this was due to what R. Flenley has called an 'invasion from above', to the Kaiser's consistent desire for personal rule. Historians have been divided as to the extent of Wilhelm's personal influence, but J. G. Röhl has made a strong case for regarding 1897 as a crucial stage in its development. Between that time and the crisis of the *Daily Telegraph* interview, he claims, Wilhelm 'dictated policy to an amazing extent . . .: all appointment, all bills, all diplomatic moves were made on his orders'. At the same time the power of the Chancellor was eroded from below, by the loss of control over various, previously subordinate ministries. Caprivi had allowed far greater freedom to other departments than Bismarck had ever tolerated, and Tirpitz, at the Naval Ministry, provided a good example of an independence of action inconceivable before 1890.

(g) Government in Wilhelmine Germany 1894–1914: The Army

The decline of the Chancellor's office, the personal unreliability of the monarch and the failure of the Reichstag to seek fundamental political change, were different elements in the severe weakening of civil government in Germany. The most important result of this was that the German army occupied a status unparalleled in Europe. It owed this status in part also to the role that it had played in Germany's growth. In A. J. P. Taylor's phrase, the nation suffered from a 'Sadowa-Sedan complex', based on the memory of the great victories of the past. Glorification of war and virile conquest was commonplace in contemporary German thought and writing. 'The whole nation', remarked the socialist Bebel, 'is still drunk with military glory and there is nothing to be done until some great disaster has sobered us'.

Two illustrations may help to indicate the independence of the army from German government. In November 1913, a series of disturbances broke out in the garrison town of Zabern (Saverne) in Alsace. They were evidently triggered by the arrogant behaviour of garrison troops, and resulted in arbitrary arrests, the use of force to disperse crowds, and the declaration by the military authorities of a state of siege. Fearful for public order, the civil authorities sought to discipline the soldiers involved, but were directly overruled by the Kaiser himself. Escalating, the 'Zabern Affair' caused an outcry in the Reichstag comparable with that over the *Daily Telegraph* interview. The vote of censure against the government and its support of the military authorities was carried by 293 votes to 54. Yet the matter ended there. As in 1908, the Reichstag hesitated to take further action, and the Kaiser and his ministers firmly maintained their support of the army. The failure to take any effective action against military excesses finely illustrated the virtual immunity of the army from political control.

A similar point is made by a study of the contemporary development of military strategy. Under Count von Schlieffen, Chief of the General Staff from 1891–1906, the army command had come to terms with the problems of war on two fronts. Their definitive strategy, formulated in 1897, the 'Schlieffen Plan', called for a rapid outflanking movement through Belgium and Luxemburg to eliminate France from the war before Russian mobilisation was completed. Sections of that force could then be transferred to the eastern front to meet the Russians. It was a daring plan militarily, yet was politically indefensible, as Germany was among those nations who guaranteed Belgium's neutrality. Yet, the strategy became the basis of German military planning for the next 15 years. Gerhard Ritter, who sees in the growth of unrestrained military independence in Germany one of the main causes of the disaster of 1914, has outlined the reason for this. 'To raise political objections to a strategic plan worked out by the General Staff would have appeared in the Germany of Wilhelm II unwarranted interference in a foreign sphere'. In the years preceding 1914, as in that year itself, the German military establishment differed from those of other European powers, not in the degree of its preparedness for war, but in the degree of its independence from civil governmental restraint.

(h) The Government of Wilhelmine Germany: Domestic Politics

For many years after the collapse of the German Reich in 1918, it was usual for historians to conclude that the policies of Wilhelmine Germany had been shaped primarily by foreign aims and ambitions. In recent years, however, a younger 'school' of German historians has insisted upon the 'primacy of domestic affairs'. They argue that domestic struggles were the prime preoccupation of German politicians, and that even the great adventure of Weltpolitik was in truth only a foreign means to a domestic end. In the words of H.-U. Wehler who is a leading representative of this 'school', the true theme of Wilhelmine, and indeed of Bismarckian politics was 'the defence of inherited ruling position by pre-industrial elites against the onslaught of new forces—a defensive struggle which became even sharper with the erosion of the economic foundations of these privileged leading strata (and) also created ever more dangerous tensions because of the success it achieved'.

Certainly, the years of Caprivi's Chancellorship had seen the vested interests of the Junker class threatened by the vaguely benevolent attitude of the Kaiser towards social problems, and by the sympathy of the Chancellor for industrial economic interests. The fall of Caprivi, largely the work of the Junkers themselves, forced future Chancellors to seek new tactics against the dual threats of socialism and industrialism. The first tactic was repression. After 1894, the expressed desire of Wilhelm II to be 'King of the Beggars' was rarely in evidence. Instead, the Kaiser pointedly withdrew his original instructions to Lutheran pastors to concern themselves with social questions, and the five years between 1894–99 witnessed a stream of anti-socialist and anti-union legislation proposed in the Reichstag, mostly without success. The period earned the nickname of the 'Stumm Era' in honour of the prominent industrialist Stumm–Halberg, whose employees were strictly forbidden to join any political or social organisation. The refusal of the Reichstag, in which conservative representation dropped 21% between 1893–98, to support a policy of repression, forced a change of tack. Under Bülow's administration, the government embraced a principle defined in 1897 by J. Miquel as 'Sammlungspolitik'. In other words, it sought to 'gather together' behind a common policy all the major propertied and conservative interests in the Reich. If the antipathy of Junker and industrialist could be bridged, a formidable front could be presented to Social-Democracy. Bülow's policy had two 'prongs'. One was his reorientation of economic policy evident in 1902 when he abandoned Caprivi's system of trade treaties, to replace them with a set of high tariffs protecting agriculture, and certain key German manufactures from foreign competition. Russian corn, incidently, was largely excluded thereby from the German market, to the relief of the Junkers. The discontent of German heavy industry, meanwhile, had already begun to be relieved by the inauguration of Germany's massive naval construction programme. Aptly this conciliation of conservative economic interests became known as the 'Alliance of Rye and Steel'. Meanwhile, the wider policy of Weltpolitik played the same role. Bülow's explanation of his policy in 1897, while superficially declaring the 'primacy of foreign affairs', in fact betrayed the true nature of Weltpolitik. 'I am putting the main emphasis', he declared, 'on foreign policy. Only a successful foreign policy can help to reconcile, pacify, rally, unite'.

A lesser, but nevertheless significant, feature of the domestic politics of 1894–1914 was the reversal of Caprivi's conciliatory policies towards national minorities within the Reich. In Prussia, for example, Bülow rigorously enforced the laws banning the use of Polish in education, and passed a law in the Landtag (1908) allowing the expropriation of Polish estate owners for the settlement of German farmers. It is true that in 1911 Alsace and Lorraine received a new constitution integrating them more closely into the normal political system of the Reich. The 'Zabern Incident' of 1913 (see section **g**) showed clearly, however, that the brutal mentality of military occupation still predominated.

(i) The Government of Wilhelmine Germany: The Social Democrats

If one were to judge merely by the results of Reichstag elections held during the administrations of Bülow and of Bethmann-Hollweg, one would conclude that 'Sammlungspolitik' had failed to secure the state against the threat of socialism. As Table 10.3 shows, the temporary lapse of Social-Democrat support in 1907 was reversed so effectively that by 1912 the party was the most powerful in the Reichstag. Their triumph certainly had an effect upon the Kaiser and his government. 'The German parliamentarian', Wilhelm declared in 1913, 'becomes daily more of a swine'. Yet how much of a threat did Social-Democracy pose to the Imperial system of government? For all its Marxist origins, the German socialist movement by 1912 was broadly committed to the 'revisionism' proposed by Eduard Bernstein in 1898 in his work,

	1890	1893	1898	1903	1907	1912
Conservatives	93	100	79	75	84	57
National Liberals	42	53	46	51	54	45
Left Liberals	76	48	49	39	49	42
Centre	106	96	102	100	105	91
Social Democrats	35	44	56	81	43	110
Poles, Danes, Alsatians, etc.	38	35	34	32	29	33
Anti-Semites	5	16	13	11	21	13

Table 10.3

The Presuppositions of Socialism and the Tasks of Social Democracy. Bernstein's conclusion was that Marx had been mistaken about the approaching crisis of capitalism, as the rising living standards of German workers proved, and that change should not be sought through revolution. From 1906 onwards, leading Social Democrats were willing to make electoral pacts with the Liberals to forward desirable social policies. They were willing in general to subscribe to an Imperial foreign policy which they interpreted as primarily opposed to reactionary Tsardom, and even supported the financial provisions of the Army Bill in 1913, because they proposed a property tax. In short, there can be little doubt that G. A. Craig is justified in his judgement that 'neither the working class nor the political class that represented it was a force bent on the destruction of the existing political system'.

Nevertheless, it is possible to understand the apprehension of the ruling classes at the electoral success of Social-Democracy. That success destroyed the conservative 'Bülow Bloc' of parties, and replaced it with a bloc effectively able to resist any unpopular government legislation. The 1912 elections, wrote W. J. Mommsen, thus created the 'stalemate of the party system'. The Zabern Incident, although it eventually demonstrated the weakness of the Reichstag's initiative, also provided a frightening illustration of how massive anti-government feeling could now be mobilised within the assembly. The Social-Democratic party, furthermore, did possess an active left-wing. It was led by such as Liebknecht, Luxemburg and Mehring, it maintained an orthodox Marxist line, and was to show its mettle in 1918. Lastly, we should not ignore the fact that the prospect of power in the hands of industrial workers appeared outrageous and highly dangerous to many conservatives, quite regardless of the uses to which those workers might turn their power. With or without logical justification, therefore, the election results of 1912 ensured that domestic political tensions were as high as ever as the conservatives of the German government and General Staff approached the international crisis of the last years of peace.

(j) Weltpolitik: Origins

In the years that followed the fall of Caprivi, a revolutionary new factor came to dominate the foreign policy of the Reich. Departing from the essentially European concerns of Bismarck, that policy came more and more to demand a world role for Germany. By enlarging her interests in non-European affairs Germany was to claim the status of a 'World-Power' ('Weltmacht'). The reasons for this fundamental change were complex and varied, yet on the whole this 'World Policy' ('Weltpolitik') must be seen as an external reflection of internal German developments.

Firstly, it undoubtedly reflected the mentality and personality of the Kaiser. Weltpolitik consisted of a headstrong and incoherent insistence that Germany should have a say in all major issues, just as Wilhelm intruded his half-formed opinions into all aspects of domestic government. As I. Geiss has put it, 'German foreign policy during this time bore the personal stamp of the Kaiser. He found it more or less congenial and in keeping with his personal ambitions and his style of behaviour'. Certainly, Wilhelm made a direct practical contribution to this policy by his appointment to high office of its enthusiastic supporters. In 1897 alone, the promotions of J. von Miquel to the Vice-Presidency of the Prussian Ministry, of A. von Tirpitz to the Naval Ministry and of B. von Bülow to the head of the Foreign Ministry provided the core of the Weltpolitik 'crew'.

Weltpolitik was not merely a result of the Kaiser's whim. The expansion of German industry had renewed and increased the national sense of power, and many leading figures expressed the fear that existing resources and markets would soon prove insufficient and that emigration to the USA might rob Germany of her most dynamic sons. 'Our vigorous national development', claimed Bülow himself, 'mainly in the industrial sphere, forced us to cross the ocean'. The historian Treitschke and the statesman Delbrück publicised a variation upon this theme. Since German unification the colonial expansion of other powers had cancelled out Germany's advance in status. Germany was faced with the choice of colonial expansion or stagnation as a major power. This theme of world expansion as a logical sequel to unification was most eloquently expressed by the great sociologist Max Weber in his inaugural lecture at Freiburg University in 1895. 'We have to grasp', he stated, 'that the unification of Germany . . . would have been better dispensed with because of its cost, if it were the end and not the beginning of a German policy of World Power'.

Lastly, many recent historians concentrating upon the domestic affairs of the Reich have interpreted Weltpolitik as essentially an element in the solution of Germany's internal political problems (see section **h**). At a time when the apparent factional divisions in German politics were widening, it provided a means of uniting national opinion and neutralising the disruptive opposition of the Social Democrats. In this last respect, the patriotic stance of the Social Democrats in 1914 certainly suggests that Weltpolitik succeeded where the reform programmes of Bismarck and of Caprivi had failed. I. Geiss speaks for this school of thought in concluding that 'Weltpolitik came into existence as a red herring of the ruling classes to distract the middle classes and working classes from social and political problems at home'. Where Bismarck in 1890 and Wilhelm in 1894 had toyed with the idea of a *coup d'état* as the answer to domestic pressures, Germany now turned to the glamour and excitement of Weltpolitik.

(k) Weltpolitik: Manifestations

In the last four years of the 19th century the mentality of Weltpolitik manifested itself in all those quarters of the globe subject to European penetration. In Africa it took the form of a pretentious masquerade as protector of the Boers in their confrontation with British imperialism in the Transvaal under President Kruger. After the thwarting of an ill-organised British-backed coup, Wilhelm dispatched his famous 'Kruger Telegram' congratulating the Boers on maintaining their independence 'without having to appeal to friendly powers for assistance'. With German naval power in its infancy, it was an empty and rhetorical gesture, whose only lasting effect could be to cause offence to a potentially friendly European power. The first tangible reward of Weltpolitik was reaped in China in 1897. There, alarmed at the extent of Japan's success in her war against China (1894–95), Germany acted in concert with Russia and France to modify the original Japanese gains, and to ensure that China remained open to European penetration. Her own private gain was a 99 year lease of the port of Kiaochow as a trading and naval base. The following year the small groups of Pacific Islands, the Carolines and the Marianas, were purchased from Spain. In 1899, Germany declared dissolved her condominium with Britain and the USA over the islands of Samoa, and assumed possession of the eastern portion of the islands. Patently trivial as such gains were, the extension of German interests in the Middle East had more serious international implications. As early as 1888, the Deutsche Bank had agreed with the Turkish government to finance the projected railway from Baghdad to the Persian gulf. It was clearly a region sensitive to both British and Russian interests. While Bismarck had specified at that time that German money implied no direct

German political interest, Wilhelm II showed none of his restraint. In a typically pretentious speech (1898) he referred to himself as 'the protector of 300 million Muslims', and openly referred to 'my railway'. The compensation for strained relations with Britain and Russia was the steady attraction of the Turkish Empire into the German orbit, yet the First World War was to prove Turkey an ally of doubtful worth.

Yet the most spectacular and damaging manifestation of Germany's new ambitions was the growth of her naval power. The development of a mighty battle fleet, like Weltpolitik itself, served several purposes. For many, like its founder Admiral von Tirpitz, it was an assertion of the nation's new status. 'The fleet', he declared, 'is necessary to show that Germany is as well born as Britain'. In so saying, he betrayed the essential feature of naval development. It was aimed at, and bound to offend, Great Britain. She was the one major European power with whom Germany had no potential continental argument, and whose friendship might have offset the Franco-Russian alliance. Equally, the decision to develop the fleet provided a huge new outlet for German heavy industry. It was no mere coincidence that so great an industrialist as Alfred Krupp was a leading member and backer of the Naval League (Flottenverein), founded in 1898. To the politically minded middle-classes, furthermore, the fleet represented a national weapon relatively free from the influence of Prussian Junkers. Hence the judgement of I. Geiss that 'the battle fleet was an instrument of the German middle class'. It 'represented the massive economic interests and social aspirations of the most prosperous and dynamic elements of German society'. The first great Naval Bill, of March 1898, envisaged an eventual force of 19 battleships, 12 heavy cruisers and 30 light cruisers. These estimates were doubled in 1900, and when the launching of the British battleship 'Dreadnought' (February 1906) rendered much of the existing British fleet obsolete, further German bills in 1906, 1907 and 1908 signalled the beginning of a serious naval arms race.

With the exception of the new battle fleet, the physical results of Weltpolitik were meagre, even absurd. By 1914, Germany possessed a colonial 'Empire' of only about a million square miles. Total German investment in those colonies in 1912 was only 505 million marks. The colonies were, furthermore, dotted about the globe, almost indefensible and totally vulnerable to the attack of an enemy, as their fates in 1914 were to prove. In terms of Germany's overall diplomatic position, the decision to move towards 'World Power' was of enormous negative importance. It completed the destruction of the Bismarckian European balance, and prepared the way for Germany's isolation and encirclement. Bernadette Schmitt has summarized the error of Weltpolitik as follows. 'A policy of naval expansion, the development of an African empire, commercial and financial penetration of the Near East could each be justified. But to pursue all three courses at the same time was the worst possible policy, for it kept alive the distrust and suspicion of the Entente powers, convinced them of the dangerous reality of German militarism, and made them more anxious than ever to act together'.

(I) Germany and Europe 1894–1905

The weakening of the Bismarckian system of alliances left Germany's European diplomacy with two central themes in the decade after the fall of Caprivi. The first of these was the desire to maintain friendly relations with Russia in the hope of detaching her from her newfound friendship with France. 1894 provided two sources of hope in this respect, with the replacement of Caprivi by the more conservative and 'Bismarckian' Hohenlohe, and with the accession of Nicholas II. A cousin of the Kaiser, the new Tsar enjoyed friendly personal relations with his fellow Emperor, and was susceptible to Wilhelm's entreaties to pursue a civilising mission against the 'Yellow Peril' in eastern Asia. The 1890s saw common action against excessive Japanese gains from China, but the logical outcome of Russia's commitment was her embroilment in the Russo-Japanese War in 1904 (see Chapter 9, section **h**). Well though such distractions suited Germany's purposes, the conviction in St. Petersburg that such a war had always been the German goal merely compounded the damage done by the cancellation of the Reinsurance Treaty. Nevertheless, Wilhelm came close to success in a final effort to separate Russia and France. In a meeting at Björkö (July 1905) he persuaded the Tsar to conclude an agreement whereby both states undertook to aid the other in the event of an attack by another European power in Europe. The success was, however, merely superficial. The Tsar had undertaken more than his ministers would allow him to fulfil. The implications of the loss of French economic aid alone were so serious that they refused to endorse the agreement, and the Treaty of Björkö remained a 'dead letter' from the moment of its signature.

A logical response to the growing intimacy of Russia and France would have been to cultivate relations with Great Britain more closely. German attitudes to Britain, nevertheless, remained highly ambiguous. The Ambassador to London, von Hatzfeldt, consistently hoped and believed that Britain might be drawn into the Triple Alliance, and consistently condemned Weltpolitik as a tactless means of alienating a valuable ally. The Kaiser himself was certainly attracted to certain elements of British society, but had an intense dislike for others, such as her constitutional monarchy. 'It was a love', comments H. Holborn, 'unfortunately shot through with unruly jealousy'. Such ambiguity was mirrored in the diplomatic history of the 1890s. The promise of the agreement over Heligoland and Zanzibar contrasted with the lively hostility created by the 'Kruger Telegram'. Germany's official, and vaguely benevolent, neutrality during the Boer War (1899–1900) was offset by the violently anti-British propaganda of the Pan German League and the Naval League. Thus, when a Conservative government in Britain abandoned the isolationism of the Liberals and put out feelers for a formal alliance, the opportunity was missed. The first British approach (March 1898) failed because of German fears that a treaty might fail to achieve parliamentary ratification, and that relations with Russia might be strained to no avail. The second approach (January 1901) was killed by a series of miscalculations by the German Foreign Office. In the first place, senior officials remained convinced that a German alliance was Britain's only option. Speaking of British hints of an approach to France, Bülow himself declared that 'in my opinion we need not worry about such remote possibilities'. Secondly, therefore, Germany set excessively strict conditions upon an understanding with Britain. She was to tie herself, not simply to Germany, but to the Triple Alliance as a whole. Finding the prospect of commitment to the maintenance of Austria-Hungary quite unacceptable, Britain had within three years informally associated herself with the Franco-Russian 'Entente'.

The so-called 'free hand' policy of the German Foreign Office, by rejecting British overtures, and by overestimating the significance of the Björkö agreement, had left Germany by 1905 isolated but for her partners in the Triple Alliance. Given the vacillations of Italy, and her closer relations with France (see Chapter 8, section **q**), this effectively meant reliance upon Austria-Hungary as Germany's sole reliable ally. To appreciate more fully the implications of this fact, a brief summary is necessary of the development of that power since her defeat by Prussia in 1866.

(m) Austria-Hungary:
The Compromise and the Dual Monarchy

The defeat suffered by Austria at the hands of Prussia in 1866 ended the roles played by the Empire as a German power and as an Italian power. It was possible that the defeat would bring about the collapse of her multinational structure and thus end her role as a great European power altogether. That this did not happen was the results of timely concessions granted to the one nationality capable of destroying the integrity of the Empire, the Hungarians, and to the moderate realism of certain Hungarian leaders. 'We must not over-rate our strength', Ferenc Deak warned some of the more headstrong nationalists, 'and must confess that on our own we are not a great state'. Hungarian leaders were thus content to seek concessions within the Habsburg Empire, which entered upon a new lease of life as Austria-Hungary, or the Dual Monarchy.

The political form of this new entity was laid out in the Compromise (Ausgleich) negotiated in March 1867, mainly between F. F. von Beust, the Empire's Saxon born Foreign Minister, and Gyula Andrassy, spokesman for the Magyar nobility. By its terms, Hungary became a separate kingdom, linked to its Austrian neighbour in a variety of ways. In the first place, the Hungarian crown was to be worn by the Austrian Emperor. The unity of the Dual Monarchy was not merely personal, however, for the states were to share a common foreign policy and common armed forces. By paying only 30% of the expenses of the latter, indeed, Hungary ensured her national security at a remarkably economic rate. Other matters of common interest to the two states, such as customs, the monetary system, and interlinking railway communications, were to be governed by agreements renewed between the two partners at intervals of ten years. The Compromise, therefore, was a unique document. It was neither an international treaty, nor a confederation.

At the centre of his new constitutional arrangement stood the Emperor-King, Franz Josef. Having originally come to power in the difficult and dangerous circumstances of 1848, he was a man of many qualities. He tackled his 'God-given' duties with a devotion and Spartan sense of duty that entailed long hours of work and minute attention to the details of government. On the other hand, he lacked the imagination or flexibility to continue the process of constitutional adaptation and development into the 1870s. True, he accepted the Austrian constitution of December 1867, which ended his absolutism by recognising such principles

as ministerial responsibility and the independence of the judiciary, and which recognised in theory the equality of the different national groups within the Austrian territories. True, he seemed ready between 1868–71 to make concessions to the Czechs in Bohemia that might have established a 'Triple Monarchy'. Dissuaded from this, however, by Magyars and Austrian Germans jealous of their dominant positions in the Dual Monarchy, Franz Josef became content to regard the 1867 Compromise as a definitive and final constitutional settlement to be defended and upheld by any expedient at his disposal. This did not quite make Austria-Hungary, in H. Kohn's phrase, 'an Empire without an idea', but ensured that its central idea, the power partnership of Germans and Magyars, would be unacceptable to a large proportion of Franz Josef's subjects. A principle feature of the Compromise was that it was concluded without reference to any of the other nationalities of the Empire and sacrificed their political and cultural interests to the co-existence of the two leading national groups. While conciliatory gestures were made to the minorities under Austrian rule (see section **n**), the Hungarian constitution offered little consolation to those minorities governed from Budapest (see section **o**). The aspirations of these national minorities were to be a consistent source of instability and disturbance within the Dual Monarchy. What judgement, ultimately, is to be passed on the Compromise? In the context of 1867, it was a shrewd and successful move which did much to facilitate the survival of the Habsburg Empire as a major power bloc. In R. A. Kann's words, 'the Compromise gave the Danube peoples the chance to live peacefully for nearly two generations and to work hopefully for a longer lasting settlement'. The tragedy of the Compromise was that its initial flexibility gave way to doctrinaire rigidity on the part of the Emperor-King, and to shortsighted egoism on the part of the governing classes of Hungary. In the long run, therefore, it built up a new set of challenges for the Dual Monarchy which it did not ultimately survive.

(n) Austria-Hungary:
The Government of Austria

In the aftermath of the constitutional upheavals of 1867, the Liberal party representing in the main German middle class interests maintained an ascendancy in the Austrian parliament. Franz Josef thus found himself obliged to co-operate with them, and Austria entered upon a decade of unprecedented liberalisation. As happened in other states, the Catholic Church found itself under attack. It lost control over education and was forced to accept the legalisation of civil marriage (1868). In 1870, in the face of Pius IX's declaration of Papal Infallibility, the Concordat concluded with Rome in 1855 was cancelled. Other reforms included the provision of free and compulsory elementary education (1869), and various measures to liberalise the civil and legal status of Jews. It was an impressive programme, but was not matched by the Liberal's record on the question of nationalities. A project to give the Czechs in Bohemia equal footing with Germans and Magyars in a 'Triple Monarchy' was brought to nothing by the vested interests of those two dominant national groups. The conservative Emperor, in any case, was always a reluctant ally of the Liberals and broke with them without regret in 1879 when they opposed the outcome of the Congress of Berlin, and especially Austria's growing control over Bosnia and Herzegovina.

The Emperor now turned to the support of a minister whose conservatism he found much more attractive. Count Edward Taafe, an aristocrat of Irish origins governed the Empire longer than any other minister between the fall of Metternich and the collapse of the Habsburg regime. His survival was due in part to the bond of trust between himself and the Emperor, but also to the powerful alliance that he established with Polish, Slovene, German and Bohemian conservative landowners. This, he declared, was his 'Ring of Iron' around the German Liberals. His allies were paid for their support by various national concessions. The Polish language was permitted in various branches of the administration. The Czechs gained a new electoral law (1882), that gave them a majority in the Bohemian Diet, and the wider use of Czech in legal administration. Also in 1882, the University of Prague was divided into two sections, one now taught and administered in Czech. In the short term, Taafe's policies enjoyed considerable success, but they aimed merely to preserve an unsatisfactory and problematical 'status quo'. Thus, while A. J. P. Taylor can claim that 'Taafe's system gave Austria a stability and calm such as she had not enjoyed since the days of Francis I', it is equally true to claim, as C. A. Macartney has, that 'Taafe not only did not produce an answer to the riddle of the monarchy, he did not even look for one'.

The relative calm in Austrian domestic politics, furthermore, did not last beyond 1893. Thereafter opened a new era of political bitterness and agitation. An important element in this was the emergence in Austria of a vociferous if disorganised

Pan German movement, led by Georg von Schönerer. It was the violent opposition of the Pan Germans to the policy of concessions to the national minorities that precipitated the fall of Taafe in 1893 amidst controversy so violent that Prague had to be placed under martial law. Four years later, the attempts of his successor, Badeni, to extend the use of the Czech language led to demonstrations and riots that paralysed the functions of parliament and threatened the stability of the state. Schönerer's organisation was only one element in the new political atmosphere, however. The period also witnessed the rise of the Christian Socialist Party, led by Karl Lueger. The element of paternalist reform in this Catholic party was sincere and, as Mayor of Vienna between 1897–1907, Lueger presided over an impressive programme of urban improvement. Equally prominent, however, was the party's anti-semitism, fed by the economic problems of the bourgeoisie at a time of industrial depression. It is worthy of note that both Schönerer and Lueger exercised some influence over the political development of the young Adolf Hitler. Thirdly, the introduction of universal manhood suffrage (January 1907) furthered the development of an Austrian Social Democratic Party, founded twenty years earlier by Viktor Adler. Like its German counterpart it was Marxist in its theories, but increasingly parliamentarian in its practice. It had made substantial progress in the cities of the Empire by the outbreak of war, winning 87 seats in the elections of 1907, to the disquiet of the middle classes.

For all these problems and divisions, it is easy to overestimate the weaknesses of the Empire in 1914. The economic coherence of the state, with Hungary supplying agricultural produce to the industrial areas of Austria, was an element of strength. So too was the enduring alliance between Crown, Church, Army and bureaucracy. Even in the midst of party disputes, and the claims of the nationalities, as A. J. P. Taylor has stated, 'no party on either side seriously desired the break-up of Austria-Hungary'. In the event, for all its apparent weakness, it took four years of fierce, concentrated fighting to bring the Dual Monarchy to its knees.

(o) Austria-Hungary:
The Government of Hungary

The Compromise of 1867 represented a triumph for the aggressive Hungarian nationalism manifested in 1848–49. It permitted Hungarian domination over the domestic affairs of a territory similar to that of the old Kingdom of Hungary, yet still enabled

Hungarians to enjoy the security of membership of the Habsburg Empire. Yet only in a very limited sense did it create a Hungarian state. Hungarians, or Magyars, constituted less than half the population, 6 million out of 13.5 million in 1867, and even then political power lay predominantly in the hands of a limited land-owning stratum of Magyar society. From these factors arose the two dominant features of Hungarian politics. By comparison with its Austrian counterpart, Hungarian political life rested upon a narrowly restricted franchise. To limit the influence of poorer Magyars and non-Magyars alike, the Electoral law of 1874 allowed only 800 000 inhabitants to participate in the election of the Hungarian House of Deputies. Secondly, domestic policy was dominated by a strict and thorough policy of Magyarisation, aimed at weakening the national cultures, Rumanian, Slovak, Croat, Serb and Ukranian, that had threatened Hungarian interests in 1848–49. Ninety-five percent of all state officials were Magyar, as were 90% of all judges. Eighty percent of all newspapers were printed in the Magyar language, which also dominated the legal and educational systems, and even the railway timetables. Only the Croats, with a separate Diet, their own schools and police force, and a bloc of 40 representatives in the House of Deputies effectively maintained an active cultural identity. The fate of the other minority cultures may be represented by the decline in the number of Slovak-speaking schools in the Kingdom, from 1805 in 1875 to 241 in 1905. It should also be noted that Hungarian nationalism played no small part in determining the foreign attitudes of the Dual Monarchy. The links of Polish and Ukranian minorities with Poles and Ukranians in the Russian Empire naturally stimulated Hungarian suspicions of Russian Pan Slavism and provided Habsburg foreign policy with a strong anti-Russian impulse. Thus rigid Hungarian attitudes stored up trouble for the future and made almost impossible a satisfactory settlement of the nationalities problem. Nevertheless, under the long premiership of Kalman Tisza (1875–90), official Hungarian enthusiasm for the terms of the Compromise ensured stable and harmonious relations between Austria and Hungary. Tisza, furthermore, presided over the centralisation and improvement of Hungary's communications system, and over a period of modest commercial and industrial prosperity.

By the late 1880s, however, a new generation of nationalists was proposing a new view of the Compromise. Tisza's Liberal Party found itself challenged by a National Party, under the leadership of Albert Apponyi, and latterly by the Independence Party of Ferenc Kossuth, son of the great nationalist rebel of 1849. Kossuth's stress, in particular, fell upon the limitations imposed upon Hungary's national independence by continued partnership with the Habsburg monarchy. Such nationalist sentiments were fed by the death and funeral of Lajos Kossuth (1894), by the millenium of the original Magyar invasion of Hungary (1896), and by a cultural renaissance which produced as its greatest figures the composers Bartok and Kodaly.

Tension with Austria centred upon two issues, the maintenance of a joint army commanded in German, and Hungarian participation in the Austrian monetary and customs system. Franz Josef's reasonable conviction that a separate military establishment would hinder the military efficiency of the Dual Monarchy precipitated a confrontation with the radical Magyar nationalists in 1905. The defeat in that year's elections of Istvan Tisza, the son of Kalman Tisza and also an enthusiast for the Compromise, led Franz Josef to undertake the forceable dissolution of the House of Deputies, and to propose the introduction of a system of universal manhood suffrage in Hungary. By that proposal, he threatened instantly to put non-Magyars and the Magyar peasantry into a majority in Hungarian government. The threat worked, and Kossuth and his followers agreed in 1906 to withdraw their economic and military claims. Unfortunately, it had only been a threat. Franz Josef had had in his hands a weapon for the solution of the nationality problem in Hungary, but had refused to use it. The exclusive partnership between Germans and Magyars was continued. Under successive premiers Hungary loyally honoured the 1867 Compromise, but made little or no progress on the issues of social reform, or of concessions to the national minorities. On the contrary, 1912 witnessed the suppression of the Croat constitution, while a general strike in the same year bore witness to the level of labour unrest. By solving neither of these problems before 1914, the Hungarian governments had, in the judgement of the American commentator A. J. May, 'muffed an opportunity for which they, their Hungary, and the Dual Monarchy would one day pay the penalty'.

(p) Austria-Hungary: Foreign Policy and The Balkans

Between 1859 and 1871 the foreign policy of the Habsburg Empire was reduced to a Balkan policy. In that period Imperial influence was excluded from Italy, while Bismarck's definitive victory over France confirmed that hopes of renewed Austrian influence over Germany were unfounded. In the hands of the Magyar aristocrat, Gyula Andrassy, Austro-Hungarian foreign policy became increasingly pro-German and anti-Russian. Fearing Russian expansion, he saw the future of the Empire as depending upon economic penetration of the Balkans, and to this end promoted the construction of important railway links between Austria-Hungary, Constantinople and the Aegean port of Salonika. From the Austro-Hungarian point of view, therefore, it was perfectly logical that the League of the Three Emperors (see Chapter 7, section **j**) should eventually develop into a defensive alliance with Germany against Russia, the Dual Alliance (see Chapter 7, section **l**). Imperial interests in the Balkans, after all, were not merely a matter of expansion and prestige. Control of the River Danube and access to the Adriatic coast were questions of fundamental economic importance to the Empire, and the rise of Slav nationalism could never be a matter of indifference to a state with so large a Slav population.

Three distinct stages may be identified in Austrian political involvement in the Balkans. The first of these was begun by the Congress of Berlin (see Chapter 7, section **k**), under the provisions of which Austria was permitted to occupy and administer the Turkish provinces of Bosnia, Herzegovina and Novibazar. These remained under the nominal suzerainty of the Ottoman Empire, but in reality gave Austria-Hungary a substantial stake and influence in Balkan affairs. This state of affairs survived the crisis of 1885–87, when Russia attempted unsuccessfully to replace King Alexander of Bulgaria with a more amenable monarch, but these years saw a hardening of attitudes and the visible formation of armed camps. Three diplomatic developments provided testimony to Austrian determination to preserve her 'great power' status in the Balkans. Two of these were the renewal of the Triple Alliance (February 1887) with Germany and Italy, and the publication (February 1888) of Germany's commitments to Austria-Hungary under the Dual Alliance. In addition March 1887 saw the conclusion of a Mediterranean agreement between Austria-Hungary, Italy and Britain, to preserve the 'status quo' around the shores of that sea.

The second stage was opened by a severe blow to Austrian aspirations in the Balkans. In 1903 King Alexander of Serbia, of the pro-Austrian Obrenovic dynasty was assassinated, and the accession of the pro-Russian Karageorgevitch faction signalled a radical change in Serbian policy. King Peter I and his foreign minister, Pasic, quickly made it clear that they favoured a policy of 'South Slavism' (Yugoslavism), whereby Serbia aspired to economic, and perhaps eventually political leadership of the Balkan Slavs, including those under Austrian control. The customs union concluded in 1904 between Serbia and Bulgaria showed that these plans were more than idle rhetoric. Indeed, they badly compromised the ambitions of Austrian 'trialists', who hoped that the Slavs might eventually be admitted to a three-cornered partnership with the Germans and Magyars in running the Empire, and encouraged the view in Vienna that Serbia was 'the Piedmont of the South Slavs'. Furthermore, at the instigation of Hungarian economic interests, the Empire imposed prohibitive tariffs upon Serbian agricultural produce, especially livestock. Between 1904–08, the so-called 'Pig War' helped to maintain an atmosphere of hostility and mistrust between Serbia and the Dual Monarchy. Only at the latter date did the formal annexation by Austria-Hungary of the provinces of Bosnia and Herzegovina (see Chapter 11, section **e**) lead her Balkan policy into its third and fatal stage.

Progress Paragraphs

Answer the following questions in about 150 words.

What elements in the personality of Wilhelm II threatened the continued existence of the Bismarckian system of government?   Section **(a)**

Over what did Wilhelm and Bismarck disagree?
                                                             Sections **(a, b)**

What were the main features of German economic expansion in this period?   Section **(c)**

What were the main aims of Caprivi's administration?
                                                             Section **(d)**

In what ways did Caprivi depart from the governmental methods and policies of Bismarck?
                                                             Sections **(d, e)**

What were the strengths and shortcomings of Caprivi's successors as Chancellor?   Section **(f)**

Account for the prominence of the Army in German politics in this period.   Section **(g)**

By what means did the governments of Wilhelmine Germany seek to heal the divisions in domestic politics? Sections (**h, j**)

Were the Social-Democrats a serious threat to the governing classes of Wilhelmine Germany? Section (**i**)

What was 'Weltpolitik' and why did Wilhelmine Germany pursue it? Section (**j**)

What did Germany gain and what did she lose by Weltpolitik? Section (**k**)

Summarise Germany's position in European diplomacy by 1905. Section (**l**)

What concessions did Austria make to Hungary by the Compromise of 1867? Section (**m**)

What elements of instability were there in domestic Austrian politics in this period? Section (**n**)

In what ways did Hungarian domestic politics threaten the future of the Dual Monarchy in this period? Section (**o**)

What caused the degeneration of Austro-Serbian relationships between 1903–08? Section (**p**)

11
The First World War: Causes and Course 1905-18

(a) The Status Quo in 1905

In retrospect, it is possible to see in the process of formation in 1905, those armed camps that clashed so violently in the First World War. In the previous decade and a half, several factors had undermined the stability of the Bismarckian system of alliances. By virtue of her own refusal to renew the Reinsurance Treaty with Russia (see Chapter 10, section **e**) Germany was no longer 'à trois in a Europe of five powers'. By virtue of her own decision to pursue a 'World Policy' (see Chapter 10, section **j**), and above all by her decision to construct a battle fleet, she could no longer count as Bismarck had done upon the benevolent neutrality of Great Britain in continental matters. Nor could Germany count upon the isolation of the other powers from each other. Apprehension over German ambitions had enabled France and Russia to sink their ideological differences, as France and Britain sank their colonial differences (see Chapter 8, sections **p** and **q**), in the Entente that formed the embryo of their 1914 wartime alliance. Over what, however, were two alignments of European powers to clash? France's cautious new friends were unlikely to back her in a reconquest of Alsace-Lorraine, and a series of international agreements had put the old bugbear of the Eastern question, in A. J. P. Taylor's phrase, 'on ice'. Two factors between 1903–05, however, suggested that European attention might soon concentrate once more upon the Balkans. Firstly, the advent of a pro-Russian regime in Serbia (see Chapter 10, section **p**) placed obstacles in the way of Austrian ambitions in that region. This was the only area, after her diplomatic and military disasters since 1850, in which the Dual Monarchy could still seriously entertain ambitions. Secondly, the traumatic defeat of Russia in her war with Japan (see Chapter 9, section **i**) meant that she too had largely to renounce other ambitions, and concentrate upon an eastern European role. From 1905, therefore, the Balkans represented the last hope for the 'great power' status of both the decaying 19th century autocracies.

Yet this is not to say that a general European war was in any way inevitable in 1905. On the contrary, many factors stood in the way of such an eventuality. Even within Germany's alliance with Austria-Hungary, the firmest element in European diplomacy, it was far from certain that Germany would back her partner unequivocally in an adventure in the Balkans. Within the Triple Alliance between Germany, Austria-Hungary and Italy the attitude of Italy was extremely ambiguous. The so-called Triple Entente between Russia, France and Great Britain, furthermore, was an extremely loose arrangement. As late as 1911 the relations between the three partners were so uncertain that A. J. P. Taylor has considered the Entente to be virtually 'in the process of disintegration'. The Russo-Japanese War, if it had turned Russian attention more firmly back to European affairs, had also cast severe doubts upon her value as an ally. If her army could not defeat the Japanese, what value could it have in a war with Germany? Colonial disputes, notably in Persia, soured Britain's relations with Russia. Also, the Franco-British Entente, while representing a great improvement in the relations between the old rivals, contained no element of military commitment whatsoever. If the atmosphere of European diplomacy remained uneasy in 1905, therefore, many more errors and miscalculations were still required to lead the continent to the catastrophe of 1914.

(b) The 'New Imperialism': Economic Interpretations

Despite the factors outlined above, the most startling element in international relations in the three or four decades before 1914 was the rebirth of European colonialism. This 'New Imperialism' was striking for two main reasons. Firstly, it represented the resurrection of a fashion that had seemed long dead, killed by the steady decay of earlier empires, such as those established by Britain and Spain in the Americas. Secondly, it surprised contemporaries

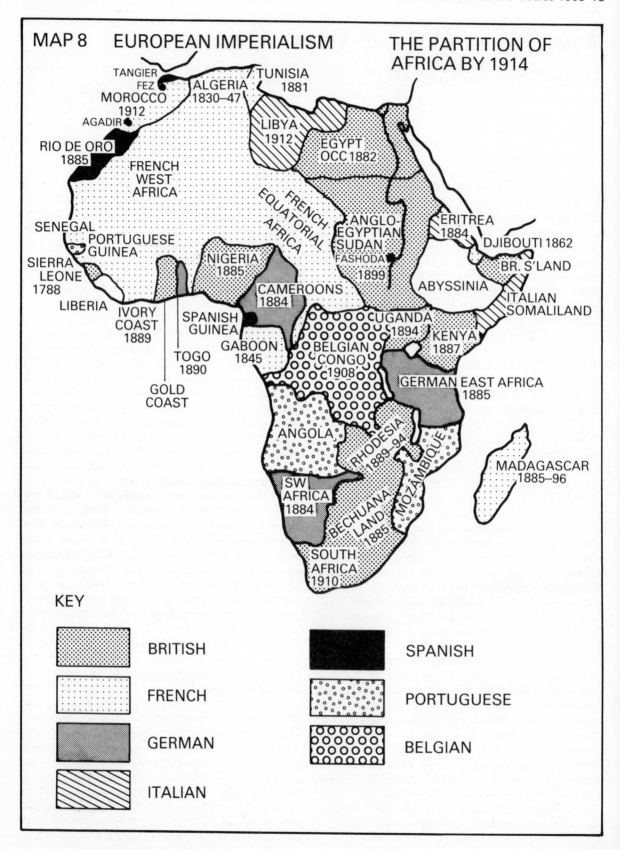

MAP 8   EUROPEAN IMPERIALISM   THE PARTITION OF
                                 AFRICA BY 1914

TANGIER
FEZ   ALGERIA
MOROCCO   1830–47   TUNISIA
1912   1881
AGADIR

RIO DE ORO   LIBYA
1885   1912   EGYPT
                                    OCC 1882
FRENCH
WEST
AFRICA

SENEGAL
         PORTUGUESE
         GUINEA   FRENCH
SIERRA   EQUATORIAL   ANGLO-   ERITREA
LEONE   AFRICA   EGYPTIAN   1884
1788   NIGERIA   SUDAN   DJIBOUTI 1862
                     1885   FASHODA
LIBERIA   CAMEROONS   1899   BR. S'LAND
         IVORY   1884   ABYSSINIA
         COAST   SPANISH   ITALIAN
         1889   GUINEA   UGANDA   SOMALILAND
         TOGO   GABOON   BELGIAN   1894
         1890   1845   CONGO   KENYA
                               1908   1887
         GOLD
         COAST   GERMAN EAST AFRICA
                                                               1885

                               ANGOLA
                                        RHODESIA
                                        1889–94
                                                    MADAGASCAR
                               SW   1885–96
                               AFRICA
                               1884   BECHUANA
                                        LAND   MOZAMBIQUE
                                        1885
                               SOUTH
                               AFRICA
                               1910

KEY

[BRITISH pattern]   BRITISH   [SPANISH pattern]   SPANISH

[FRENCH pattern]   FRENCH   [PORTUGUESE pattern] PORTUGUESE

[GERMAN pattern]   GERMAN   [BELGIAN pattern]   BELGIAN

[ITALIAN pattern]   ITALIAN

by its enormous speed and extent. Although the 'New Imperialism' was not confined to Africa, the 'scramble' for territory in that continent was its most spectacular manifestation. In 1875, only some 10% of Africa was occupied by European states; twenty years later, only 10% remained unoccupied. Table 11.1 indicates the extent of the imperial expansion over the globe as a whole of Europe's major powers between 1871–1900. Taking into account such lesser colonisers as Italy and Belgium, the movement embraced some 20% of the earth's surface, and some 10% of its population. The details of the colonial enterprises of individual states are outlined elsewhere (see Chapter 3, section **q**; Chapter 6, section **n**; Chapter 7, section **n**; Chapter 8, section **o**; and Chapter 10, section **k**). Considering, however, the significance ascribed by some writers to the 'New Imperialism' as a factor in the outbreak of the First World War, it is apt to examine here the phenomenon as a whole, its causes and its consequences.

	Area (million square miles)	Population (million)
Britain	4.25	66
France	3.50	26
Germany	1.00	13
Russia	0.50	6.5

Table 11.1

A popular and widely accepted interpretation of 19th century imperialism has been that which sees it as a natural result of capitalist development in Europe. A pioneer of this view was the English liberal journalist, J. A. Hobson. In *Imperialism: A Study* (1902), he argued from the example of Britain's involvement in South Africa, that the main motive force behind the recent burst of colonisation was the capitalists' desire for the export of surplus capital in the form of overseas investment. The colonies, he argued, satisfied an investment need in capitalists that could not be met by saturated markets nearer home. Secondly, in Hobson's view, imperialism received support from a variety of capitalist interests. These were shipping companies, armament manufacturers, and the administrative professions, which gained occupation and profit from servicing the colonies.

The most influential contribution to the economic interpretation of imperialism was V. I. Lenin's pamphlet *Imperialism, the Highest Stage of Capitalism* (1916). For Lenin, imperialism was the result of the final stages of monopoly capitalism, when domestic markets have been saturated, and resources of raw materials exhausted, by the earlier process of capitalist competition. Colonies represented to these advanced capitalists new markets and new resources, easily defensible against competition. An essential feature of the Lenin thesis was the claim that competition for colonies was bound to precipitate tension and clashes between rival capitalist powers. The First World War, in Lenin's view, had to be seen as just such a clash between states goaded into confrontation by the selfish interests of their capitalists. Its outcome would inevitably be the final exhaustion of the resources of the capitalist system.

(c) The 'New Imperialism': Nationalist Interpretations

Lenin's interpretation was a piece of political invective rather than a reasoned economic or political assessment, and many objections have since been raised to his case and to that of Hobson. In recent years, D. K. Fieldhouse (*The Colonial Empires*, 1966) has led the way in showing how small the extent of investment in the new colonies was, how modest the profits gained by investors were, and how great were the difficulties suffered by some of the new colonial trading companies. Great Britain, for example, invested far more in the USA than in any new acquisition, and Russia remained far more popular with investors, especially French ones, than any African or Asian territory. In 1913, only 3% of Germany's foreign investments were in African or Asian enterprises. One might also object that British investors continued to favour 'safe' dominions, such as Australia or Canada, before less stable colonial gains. Nor is it credible to see certain colonising powers, such as Italy, Russia or Japan, as states that had exhausted their own domestic scope for capital investment. Another line of argument is provided by emerging evidence that the major European powers were by no means locked in cut-throat competition with each other, as Lenin imagined. In particular, R. Poidevin (*Economic and Financial Relations Between France and Germany from 1898 to 1914*, 1969) has shown a remarkable interdependence between the economies of these two arch-rivals. French capitalists had invested some 1.3 billion francs in German enterprises by 1914, and imported some 40% of their fuel, and nearly all of their dyes and chemicals from Germany. Between 1893–1913, French exports to

Germany doubled, while trade in the opposite direction trebled. Poidevin's picture is one of politicians leading reluctant capitalists into confrontation, rather than the other way around, and confirms the earlier conclusion of J. A. Schumpeter (*Imperialism and Social Classes*, 1919) that 'capitalism is by nature anti-imperialist'.

The most serious rivals to the economic interpretations of imperialism have been those which see the phenomenon rather as an extension of European nationalism and national rivalries. 'Imperialism', according to Fieldhouse, 'may best be seen as an extension into the periphery of the political struggle in Europe'. In support of such an argument one might note the example of French expansion in the 1880s which was, both for Jules Ferry and for Bismarck, a deliberate attempt to distract attention from the national humiliation of 1870–71. Two other features of late 19th century expansion have also been cited in support of this view. M. Baumont has stressed the incoherence and illogicality of the 'Scramble for Africa', characterising it as 'taking as much as possible without knowing what to do with it, taking what others want because they want it and to prevent them getting it'. The American commentator, C. J. H. Hayes has emphasised too that support for imperialism was not the preserve of a political or economic elite. On the contrary, he regards widespread popular enthusiasm as a key factor, encouraging governments to seek national unity through a policy of colonial expansion. This tendency might be illustrated by reference both to Disraeli's 'Forward Policy' in Britain in the 1870s, and to German 'Weltpolitik' at the turn of the century. R. Robinson and J. Gallagher (*Africa and the Victorians*, 1961) added a variation to this theme by claiming that the whole concept of a 'New Imperialism' is false, and that governments attached value to colonial expansion throughout the earlier part of the 19th century. What was new in the late 19th century was not the motives of the British colonisers, but the challenges, in the Sudan or in the Boer Republics, for instance, that threatened their interests. Although their argument concentrates upon the example of Great Britain, the thesis of consistent imperialist commitment might be supported from a study of French expansion during, and even before, the Second Empire.

Although they were undoubtedly secondary, a further set of motives should not be overlooked. The idea of imperialism as a moral and humane duty, as the means of spreading western civilisation and Christian values, undoubtedly spurred on many individuals. Equally certainly, this idea did not motivate many governments. Some 60 000 missionaries, two-thirds of them Roman Catholics, were serving in Africa and Asia in 1900, and even socialists sometimes felt the need to take up this civilising mission. The prominent German socialist leader, Eduard Bernstein, voiced the opinion of many when he claimed that 'a certain tutelage of the civilised people over the uncivilised is a necessity'.

In conclusion, some notable individual fortunes were certainly made out of colonial expansion. The friends of Cecil Rhodes benefited substantially from British activities in South Africa, and King Leopold of the Belgians was able to exploit the Congo virtually as a personal fief. There are too many obstacles in the way, however, to allow us to accept imperialism as primarily a plot by European capitalists. Instead, we might accept the compromise proposed by D. Thomson, when he defines imperialism in the late 19th century as 'the combination of novel economic conditions with anarchic political relations'. Similarly, and of more importance for our present purposes, it is hard to accept the colonial movements, for all the tension and ill-will that they occasioned, as primary causes of war in 1914. Indeed, taking account of Britain's chastening experiences in the Second Boer War (1899–1902), the defeat of the Italians at Adowa in Abyssinia (1896), and the victory of Japan over Russia, one could argue convincingly that the 'New Imperialism' was on the wane long before 1914. Referring to one specific European confrontation, R. Poidevin has concluded that 'economic and financial questions are not at the root of Germany's declaration of war on France [in 1914]. It is obvious that political and strategic factors played the decisive role'. To establish the origins of the First World War in a more general context, therefore, a number of such factors demand our attention.

(d) The Moroccan Crisis, 1905–06

Between 1905–14, tensions between the European powers centred upon two disputed areas, the North African sultanate of Morocco, and the Balkan states that had emerged from the wreckage of the Turkish Empire. Attention was first focused upon Morocco by a German initiative that typified the incoherence and illogicality of 'Weltpolitik'. In the course of a Mediterranean cruise, the Kaiser was prevailed upon by his chief ministers to land at Tangier (31st March 1905). There, his public speeches and behaviour implied a recognition of the Sultan of Morocco as an independent monarch, and called into question the recent Anglo-French agreements over the colonial status of these territories. The motives of the Kaiser and his ministers are not altogether clear. They were probably keen to demonstrate, as was now usual, that no international question could be resolved without reference to Germany. They possibly also entertained hopes, by forcing France to give ground, of weakening her credibility as an ally in the eyes of Great Britain and of Russia. The Kaiser's 'coup' was followed by the formal demand that the status of Morocco should be referred to an international conference of the major powers. As that status was formally governed by an international agreement of 1880, Germany looked to be in a strong position, and the prospects of a notable triumph seemed bright. Indeed, when T. Delcassé, France's anti-German foreign minister and architect of the Anglo-French 'Entente', counselled resistance to German projects, he failed to win general support and resigned his office. His resignation was, claims A. J. P. Taylor, 'the greatest German victory since Sedan'.

The outcome of the conference convened at Algeciras (January–March 1906) was, however, very different from that anticipated by Germany. Far more impressed by the bullying and peremptory manner of the Germans than by the justice of their case, Spain, Italy, Russia, Great Britain, and even the USA, all supported French rights in Morocco. Isolated but for the faithful support of Austria-Hungary, Germany had to accept confirmation of French predominance in the sultanate, strengthened now by her control over the Moroccan police.

How significant was the outcome of the Algeciras Conference for the future growth of international tension? A. J. P. Taylor has gone to some lengths to minimise its importance, stressing that no military preparations were made by any power, that British public opinion showed a marked lack of concern over Morocco, and that subsequent Anglo-French military conversations came to nothing. Nevertheless, the impact of diplomatic defeat upon Germany should not be underestimated. It ended Holstein's career and left Bülow in a state of physical collapse. More important, the rebuff did much to confirm German fears that the unreasonable jealousy of her neighbours was leading them to pursue a deliberate 'Policy of Encirclement' ('Einkreisungspolitik'), aimed at stifling her natural growth and vitality. From this point, I. Geiss has claimed, Germany turned her back upon international conferences as a means of settling international disputes.

Lastly, it should be noted that diplomatic co-operation between the French, the British and the Russians at Algeciras also had a number of further side effects. The discussions between the General Staffs of Britain and France were, as has been noted, inconclusive. Colonial discussions between Britain and Russia ended, however, with an agreement (August 1907) that solved many of the outstanding disagreements over rival spheres of influence in Persia. That territory was divided into three zones. British control over south-eastern Persia kept Russia at a safe distance from Afghanistan, and thus from India, and thus did much to remove the Asian tensions that had dogged Anglo-Russian relations at the time of the Russo-Japanese War.

(e) The Bosnian Crisis, 1908–09

By 1908, the Balkans had been free of major political crises for a little more than a decade, despite the emergence of an ambitious and expansionist government in Serbia. In July of that year, however, revolution by the 'Young Turk' movement overthrew the corrupt rule of the Sultan Abdul Hamid and offered the prospect to other powers of easy advantages in the Balkans while Turkey was preoccupied with domestic upheavals. The opportunity coincided broadly with the appointment to high office in Austria-Hungary of men eager to re-establish the prestige of the Dual Monarchy. Conrad von Hötzendorf had been Chief of Staff since late 1906, much more confident than his predecessor, Beck, of the Empire's military capacity. At the same time, A. L. von Aehrenthal had succeeded Goluchowski as Foreign Minister. He too was a more confident man, 'arrogant, vain, impatient, eager for action' (A. J. P. Taylor). Their joint project for the re-establishment of Habsburg prestige was the formal annexation of the Turkish provinces of Bosnia and Herzegovina that had been under Austrian administration since 1878. Certainly this was seen as a counter to growing Serbian influence over the Empire's Slav population, and it may even have been envisaged, as I. Geiss has suggested, as the first move in a programme leading ultimately to the eventual partition of Serbia herself.

In September 1908, Aehrenthal sought the compliance of Russia. Meeting her Foreign Minister, A. Izvolski, at Buchlau, he concluded an agreement whereby Russia would accept the new status of Bosnia and Herzegovina in return for Austro-Hungarian support for Russian designs on the Straits linking the Black Sea and the Mediterranean. By accepting this agreement,

MAP 9   THE BALKANS IN 1914

BOSNIA

BELGRADE

RUMANIA

SARAJEVO

HERZEGO VINA

SERBIA

BULGARIA

SOFIA

SCUTARI

MONTENEGRO

ADRIANOPLE

CONSTANTINOPLE

ALBANIA

SALONIKA

TURKEY

CORFU

JANINA

GREECE

ATHENS

CRETE

KEY

------- NATIONAL BOUNDARIES IN 1914

———— LIMITS OF TERRITORY LOST BY TURKEY IN FIRST
BALKAN WAR

EXTENT OF TURKEY'S EUROPEAN TERRITORY 1877

Izvolski perpetrated a diplomatic blunder of the first order. Evidently he had expected the matter to be referred first to an international conference on the lines of 1878. On 5th October, however, Aehrenthal proclaimed unilaterally the annexation of Bosnia and Herzegovina, leaving Izvolski to seek his part of the bargain single-handed. In this, he not only encountered hostile reactions in London and in Paris, but had his policy disowned by his own Prime Minister as outdated and irrelevant to current Russian priorities. Izvolski's attempts to soften his defeat by demanding that a conference be convened to discuss the annexation, only increased and broadened the international tension. In response, Austria-Hungary sought clarification of the position of their German allies, and received unequivocal assurances of support. 'I shall regard whatever decision you come to as the appropriate one', wrote Bülow to Aehrenthal at the end of October, while Conrad received assurances from his German opposite number that Germany was prepared to mobilise in support of the Dual Monarchy. These assurances represented a significant deterioration in the international situation. Motivated primarily by the hope of humiliating Russia, and perhaps of weakening her links with France, Germany was sacrificing another essential Bismarckian principle by involving herself in the Eastern Question where no fundamental German interest was involved, and where Austria-Hungary had acted without any consultation with her ally whatsoever.

Thus emboldened, Germany and Austria-Hungary felt strong enough to rub both Serbia's and Russia's noses in their defeat by demanding from both a formal acknowledgement of Habsburg authority over Bosnia and Herzegovina. In March 1909, both states gave such an acknowledgement, and the crisis was over. Its legacy, nevertheless, was substantial. Russia suffered a humiliation far greater than that suffered by Germany over the Moroccan question. She could ill afford a further reverse if she was to retain any influence in the politics of the Balkans. Aware of her weaknesses in 1908–09, she was now to embark upon a programme of military reconstruction to ensure that a future confrontation would not find her wanting. Austria's success, and the unconditional nature of German support for her aims, were to embolden her in future Balkan adventures. Serbia's reverse, meanwhile, was to stimulate the growth of nationalist terrorist organisations of the kind responsible for the assassination at Sarajevo in 1914. In all of these respects, although it had given rise to little in the way of serious military preparations, we may accept the logic of I. Geiss'

judgement that 'the Bosnian crisis in the East was a kind of dress rehearsal for the First World War'.

(f) The Agadir Crisis, 1911

In May 1911, the focus of European tension switched once more to Morocco. The cause was the French occupation of Fez, the major city of the territory, a move that was widely thought to indicate that France was preparing to establish an overall protectorate. Given that France was exceeding the limits of her agreed role in Morocco, and that relations between her international partners, Britain and Russia, were once again strained, the prospects for German compensation seemed good. It has been argued that her Foreign Minister, Kiderlen-Wächter, was interested in more than mere compensation. I Geiss has stressed the enthusiasm of expansionist elements in Germany for the establishment of permanent influence in North Africa, and with F. Fischer has attached sinister importance to Kiderlen's apparent willingness to use force to gain Germany's ends. L. C. F. Turner similarly has argued that a great community of interest and aims existed between Kiderlen and the Pan German League.

Whatever its motives, the German Foreign Ministry once more acted aggressively and clumsily. The dispatch of the gunboat 'Panther' to the Moroccan port of Agadir, ostensibly to protect German interests there, immediately resurrected British fears of a hostile naval presence in the Mediterranean, and of a threat to Gibraltar. Unequivocal statements of British support for France, such as that contained in Lloyd George's famous Mansion House speech (21st July 1911), weakened the resolve of the less chauvinistic elements in Germany, including that of the Kaiser himself. A compromise settlement in November did indeed grant Germany compensation in the form of territory in the French Congo. However, the maintenance of French influence in Morocco, culminating in the establishment of a formal protectorate (March 1912), clearly demonstrated that German aims in the crisis had failed.

This second Moroccan Crisis was unlikely to lead to a general war, mainly because of the lack of Russian interest in the affair. 'Russian public opinion', Izvolski informed the French, 'could not see in a colonial dispute the cause for a general conflict'. Nevertheless, the crisis contributed to the likelihood of a future breakdown of international relations in several important ways. Firstly, it worsened relations between Britain and Germany for no good reason, and weakened the support in both countries for reductions in naval building programmes. Indeed, the next two years were to witness the height of the naval 'arms race'. Secondly, French reaction to the compromise settlement destroyed the administration of J. Caillaux (January 1912), whose main aim had been to achieve some measure of reconciliation with Germany. 'The events of 1911', in the opinion of E. Weber, 'persuaded many of the pacific, the hesitant and the indifferent that the threat to France was real and that war was only a matter of time'. The succession of the more aggressively patriotic Poincaré can be seen as the beginning of the 'national awakening' that led France into war by 1914. Thirdly, as a combination of these two factors, especially stimulated by the increased German naval estimates of 1912, the crisis led to a degree of formal military co-operation between Britain and France. This took the form primarily of the naval agreement of March 1912 whereby Britain confided her central Mediterranean interests to the protection of the French fleet, and concentrated her own resources in home waters and at Gibraltar. Such an agreement still did not amount to a formal alliance, but indicated very clearly Britain's awareness of the German threat to her interests. Lastly, the Agadir Crisis dealt a blow to the prestige of the German government similar to that suffered by the Russians in the Balkans. Germany, too, if faced with a similar crisis, might feel that the cost of further compromise might justify the risk of war.

(g) The Balkan Wars 1912–13

The Agadir Crisis brought European politics to a pitch of tension from which it was not released before the outbreak of general war, for its implications spread eastwards down the Mediterranean to affect the other great source of crisis. A direct result of the extension of French influence in Morocco was Italy's attempt in 1911 to improve her own standing in North Africa. To this end she launched an unprovoked attack upon the Turkish possession of Tripoli. This stretching of Turkish resources provided an irresistible temptation to the Balkan states to free themselves forever from the influence of Turkey, and from this temptation there emerged in the early months of 1912 the Balkan League of Serbia, Bulgaria, Greece and Montenegro. Although L. C. F. Turner has stated that 'the Balkan crisis was precipitated by Russia's renewed interest in the region', A. J. P. Taylor has been at pains to clarify Russia's role in the formation of this League. Her main motive, he

stresses, was to free herself from the economic threat posed by Turkey's wartime closure of the Straits. Thus she welcomed the League as a 'buffer' against Austria-Hungary's Balkan ambitions, but had little sympathy with the projects of its members for the partition of Turkey's European territories. In reality, he concludes, the League was far more a vehicle for Serb and Bulgarian ambitions than for Russian expansion.

The First Balkan War, between the League and Turkey, began in October 1912. By the end of that month the Turks had suffered a string of defeats and had been driven out of their European possessions, apart from Constantinople, the peninsula of Gallipoli, and the fortresses of Scutari, Adrianople and Janina. Renewed hostilities in early 1913, however, transferred those last two strongholds to the Bulgarians and the Greeks respectively. Now tension centred upon the division of the spoils. Already in late 1912, Austria-Hungary had attempted to maintain her prestige and security by insisting upon the establishment of an independent Albanian state, and upon the exclusion of Serbia from the Adriatic coastline. L. C. F. Turner has demonstrated in detail how close Russia came to mobilisation in support of Serbia over this matter. More immediate tensions arose, however, between the victors. Serbia, thwarted in her designs on Albania, and acting in partnership with Greece, occupied territory in Macedonia originally earmarked for Bulgaria. Bulgaria's attempts to clear Macedonia of Serbian and Greek forces, in June 1913, precipitated the Second Balkan War. The move was disastrous for Bulgaria. By the Treaty of Bucharest (August 1913) she had to cede territory to Serbia, Greece and Rumania, who had seized the opportunity to intervene. Even Adrianople, won earlier at great cost from the Turks, was now returned to its former masters.

The renewed Balkan crisis of 1912–13 contributed to the advent of general war in numerous important respects. Most obviously, Serbia emerged from these events with both her prestige and her power enormously increased. She had added some million and a half souls to her population, and could now mobilise an army of 400 000 men. Conversely, as A. J. P. Taylor put it, 'the victory for Balkan nationalism was a disaster beyond remedy for the Habsburg monarchy'. Even with Serbia preoccupied, her foreign policy had appeared frozen into inactivity. This was partly due to the indecision of her new Foreign Minister, Count Berchtold, partly to Magyar distrust of actions that might create more Slav subjects for the Monarchy, and partly to uncertainty as to Germany's attitude. By mid-1913 it was clear that the government of Austria-Hungary could afford no further retreat. When, in October, Serbian troops entered Albanian territory to 'mop up' partisan resistance, the Dual Monarchy issued an ultimatum which foreshadowed that of 1914. On this occasion, Serbia yielded and withdrew her troops.

The crisis also had its effect upon official attitudes in both Germany and France. There is much evidence of increased popular willingness in Germany to accept the prospect of war in 1911–12. The government was attacked from all sides in the Reichstag (November 1911) when the compromise settlement over Morocco was debated. The next year and a half saw substantial increases in military estimates. When General Bernhardi published his book *Germany and the Next War* in 1912, it quickly ran to several editions. He claimed that Germany faced the choice between decline and aggressive expansion. In 1912 the government remained reluctant to become involved in Balkan hostilities. 'I will keep out of it', wrote the Kaiser in October. 'Let them get on with their war undisturbed'. The outcome of the Balkan Wars, however, caused a radical reconsideration of Germany's military position and of her relationship with Austria-Hungary. In July 1913, the Reichstag sanctioned the addition of 130 000 men to the army in the biggest army estimate in German history. By October 1913, at the moment of Vienna's ultimatum to Serbia over Albanian independence, the Kaiser was urging his ally to take a firm stance, and assuring her of unswerving German support. He informed Berchtold that month, in a famous and fateful phrase, that 'you can be certain I stand behind you and am ready to draw the sword whenever your action makes it necessary. . . . Whatever comes from Vienna is for me a command'. France, too, had recently ceased to restrain her major ally. During his visit to Russia (August 1912), President Poincaré left Russian ministers in no doubt that, although their formal agreements only committed France to support of Russia if she were attacked by Germany, she could expect French help in the event of a clash with Germany triggered by a confrontation with Austria-Hungary. In the words of E. Helmreich, 'France had virtually given Russia a blank cheque on which she might inscribe whatever she wished'.

In short, by October 1913, all the ingredients of the following year's catastrophe were present. Franco-Russian and Austro-German commitments were tighter than ever, the confidence and daring of Serbia were at a peak, and the prestige of Austria-Hungary and of Russia was at so low an ebb as to make them unable to tolerate any further blow. Only the attitudes of Great Britain and of

Italy were uncertain. In the words of a contemporary French newspaper, 'the state of war in the Balkans constitutes a permanent danger to the peace of Europe. A very fragile thread, which the slightest imprudence may break, supports the sword of Damocles'.

(h) The July Crisis, 1914

'Fifty years', wrote B. Liddell Hart, 'were spent in the process of making Europe explosive. Five days were enough to detonate it'. On 28th June 1914 the final crisis was triggered by the assassination in the Bosnian town of Sarajevo of the Archduke Franz Ferdinand, nephew of the Austrian Emperor. His murderer was one Gavrilo Princip, a member of a Serbian terrorist organisation known as the 'Black Hand'. Although it has proved impossible to establish any clear responsibility on the part of the Serbian government, it is clear that her intelligence chief, Colonel Dimitrievich, played a leading role in the conspiracy, and that her Prime Minister had some foreknowledge of the attempt. Ironically, as N. Stone has pointed out, the death of the Archduke removed one of the strongest influences for peace at the Habsburg court. The opinion was now widespread that Serbian pretensions had to be checked. In this resolution the Dual Monarchy received firm backing from Berlin, a fact which F. Fischer, I. Geiss and others have interpreted as showing the willingness, even the eagerness of the German government to accept the consequences of general war. On the other hand, Germany could hardly accept the further humiliation of her only firm ally, and other authorities have produced evidence to indicate that Germany still hoped that the coming conflict might be confined to the Balkans. Thus encouraged, Austria-Hungary delivered an ultimatum to Serbia (23rd July) 'deliberately framed', as L. C. F. Turner has written, 'in terms that no self-respecting state could accept'. The Serbian government was required, for instance, to suppress all anti-Austrian organisations and propaganda, and to dismiss any officials to whom the Vienna government might object.

Within a week Europe was at war. The first factor determining this outcome was the reaction of Russia. Although Serbia's reaction to the ultimatum was conciliatory, it did not satisfy Austria-Hungary's demands, and she declared war on 28th July. For Russia to remain inactive would have stripped her of any influence in the Balkans, and could have devalued her as an ally in the eyes of France. Thus she chose to mobilise her forces on her southern borders. In so doing, as A. J. P.

Taylor has stressed, the Russians were 'still acting in terms of diplomacy; they were raising their bid, not preparing for war'. Automatically such action triggered the Austro-German alliance, and raised the question of German support for her ally. The escalation of the crisis caused last minute hesitations in Berlin, with the civilian leadership urging caution while the generals advised energetic action. Essentially, German military plans obliged her to act rapidly to deal with France before the Russian machine was fully operative. She thus took three fateful steps. On 31st July, she demanded the suspension of all Russian mobilisation and the following day, when mobilisation continued, she declared war. Lastly, she demanded from France a formal declaration of neutrality, and the surrender of the border fortresses of Toul and Verdun as guarantees. Acceptance would have been quite incompatible with France's 'great power' status, and her inevitable refusal led to a further declaration of war by Germany (3rd August).

Now German diplomacy centred upon attempts to keep Britain out of the war. Bethmann Hollweg had already promised not to annex French territory and to restore the integrity of Belgium after the war. German military strategy, however, depended heavily upon the violation of Belgian neutrality for the purposes of the attack upon France. When she began that violation on 3rd August, Britain's course was decided by her treaty obligations to Belgium, and the following day she, too, entered the war.

Although the victors in 1918 were quick to formulate questions of 'war guilt', the outbreak of the conflict makes much more sense if it is seen as a monstrous combination of miscalculations. The government of Austria-Hungary erred in believing that their clash with Serbia could be settled without wider complications. Russia's partial mobilisation on 30th July was undertaken without sufficient awareness of its effect upon German policy. In Berlin a whole series of misjudgements took place; the hope that an Austro-Serbian clash could be localised; the failure to appreciate that the invasion of Belgium would bring Britain into the war; the long-term failure to anticipate foreign reaction to the bullying tone of 'Weltpolitik'. The further naive supposition that a brief and successful war might ease domestic difficulties was an error shared with Vienna and St. Petersburg. The course of events in 1914 also serves to confirm A. J. P. Taylor's contention that the conflict arose from feelings of weakness rather than from illusions of strength. Russia and Austria-Hungary felt that compromise would destroy their credibility as major powers. France and Germany felt that valuable allies had to be supported lest they

themselves be left in isolation. In the German army, too, the feeling predominated that war in 1914 was preferable to war two or three years later, when the Entente powers would enjoy greater strength. Lastly, all the participants misjudged the nature of the conflict to which they were committing themselves. They anticipated campaigns as sharp and decisive as those of the Balkan Wars, or of the wars of 1859, 1866, or 1870. They anticipated no great strain upon society, and would have been horrified to think that four years of trench warfare, technological revolution and economic attrition were about to tear apart the very fabric of European society.

(i) War Aims

Of the great European powers that entered the war in August 1914, only one had any really clear idea of what they hoped to gain by victory. Austria-Hungary desired to end the challenge of South Slav nationalism, while the other states entered the conflict primarily through fear of the consequences of neutrality. In all other cases, therefore, late 1914 presented the bizarre sight of combatants clumsily formulating war aims after the conflict had begun.

German propaganda portrayed the war as an attempt to escape strangulation by the encirclement policy of jealous and hostile neighbours, and righteously proclaimed that she was 'not driven by the lust of conquest'. On 9th September, however, under pressure from industrial and Pan German interests, and from public opinion inflamed by the early successes of German arms, the Chancellor signed the so-called 'September Programme'. This made it clear that the war aim of achieving 'security for the German Reich in west and east for all imaginable time' involved an unparalleled programme of annexations and expansion. Predictably, the 'September Programme' has provided those historians who have considered Germany guilty of premeditated aggression in 1914, such as F. Fischer and I. Geiss, with their main weapon. Others such as L. C. F. Turner, have preferred to see the programme rather as a chauvinistic response to early German victories. From France, Germany was to demand the fortress of Belfort, the ore fields of French Lorraine, and possibly a strategic coastal strip from Dunkirk to Boulogne. In addition France would pay an indemnity, and accept a disadvantageous commercial treaty. Belgium, by losing Liege, Verviers and possibly Antwerp, would become a German satellite. Luxemburg would become a German federal province. For the east, no such specific details were outlined, but the general principle of the eventual peace settlement was to be to push Russia back 'as far as possible from Germany's eastern frontier'. Germany's conception of security consisted, therefore, of domination of Central Europe (Mitteleuropa), with Austria-Hungary as a junior partner. Also, important controls would be exercised over her western and eastern neighbours. If the war had not begun as a war of conquest, it became one in September 1914.

On the Entente side, the allies were effectively fighting for their survival as major powers, but public opinion demanded the formulation of more appealing war aims than this. As the major threat to their status was the growth of German power, French and British war aims in particular came to concentrate upon the destruction of those forces which made Germany an 'international danger'. Propaganda demanded the elimination of Junker militarism, and of the power of the House of Hohenzollern as essentials for a stable peace, for a Europe 'safe for democracy'. It was not quite consistent with these professions that the material provisions upon which the British were most insistent were the elimination of the German navy, and of her colonial empire. Both were less of a threat to 'democracy' than to British trading interests. The French equivalent was to demand the return of Alsace and Lorraine. It was only indirectly, and over the course of the next year that the dismantlement of the Habsburg Empire and the establishment in its place of independent nation states, also became an article of faith for the allies. Russia had little to gain by defeating Germany, except for more troublesome Polish subjects, and her official war aims soon came to concentrate upon the old attractions of the Straits and Constantinople. In March–April 1915, Britain and France finally agreed that Russia should have these in the event of victory, as long as they were compensated by gains in Egypt and the Near East. In the event of an Entente victory, therefore, the Ottoman Empire, too, was doomed to disintegration.

In the shorter term, both sides sought to strengthen their alliances by tempting neutrals into their 'camps'. The greatest enigma was Italy, formally linked by the Triple Alliance to Germany and to Austria-Hungary, yet set against the latter by all the precedents of 19th century history. Only the Entente could offer Italy the Habsburg territories in the Tyrol and down the Adriatic coast, that her nationalists demanded to complete the process of unification. Thus Italy finally sided with France, Britain and Russia in May 1915. Her war had little to do with the issues that convulsed the rest of Europe, and much to do with the continuation of her anti-Austrian tradition of the 19th century. Among the Balkan states, Russia's growing ambitions facilitated the task of the Dual Alliance powers, and Turkey (December 1914) and Bulgaria (September 1915) both declared war on the Entente. In her turn, Bulgaria's old rival, Rumania, entered the war on the side of the Entente in August 1916, although she declared war only on Austria-Hungary.

(j) The Western Front, 1914–16

On both fronts, at the outset of the war, the combatants anticipated campaigns of movement with the accent on offensive strategies and rapid results. In the west, the French pinned their hopes upon 'Plan XVII'. This dictated a thrust into the Saarland and into Lorraine, with decisive encounters close to the battlefields of 1870, and won by the natural 'elan' or dash of the French soldier. The German High Command had chosen a different geographical location. Their 'Schlieffen Plan' called for a bold sweep by seven-eighths of her western armies through Belgium and Luxemburg, to envelope the French forces, held in check by the remaining German troops. Victory was expected in about six weeks, after which the bulk of the German forces would be free to confront the threat from Russia.

The German plan had considerable weaknesses. It was liable to dangerous delays by the destruction of bridges and railways, not to mention by enemy action. Yet it was very nearly successful. The German offensive commenced on 4th August, took the border fortress of Liege within two weeks, and entered Brussels on 20th August. Meanwhile, the French offensive ran into stubborn opposition in Lorraine and in the Ardennes and began to retreat with heavy casualties. The British Expeditionary Force, after an initially successful delaying action at Mons (23rd–24th August), was also forced to fall back to avoid isolation. Now the German commanders departed from the original plan of von Schlieffen. To avoid creating a break in the German line, Generals von Kluck and von Moltke chose to swing east of Paris to finish off Joffre's retreating Frenchmen, instead of surrounding and capturing the French capital. Between 5th–9th September the invaders and Joffre's brilliantly regrouped armies contested the Battle of the Marne. In a different sense than the combatants had intended, this western engagement did indeed determine the future shape of the war. The allied

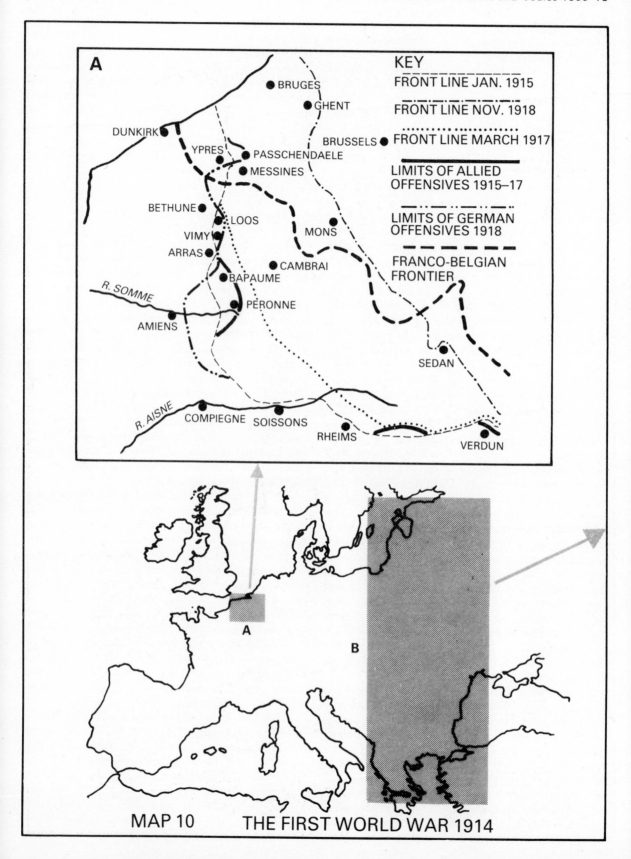

KEY

FRONT LINE JAN. 1915

FRONT LINE NOV. 1918

FRONT LINE MARCH 1917

LIMITS OF ALLIED
OFFENSIVES 1915–17

LIMITS OF GERMAN
OFFENSIVES 1918

FRANCO-BELGIAN
FRONTIER

MAP 10   THE FIRST WORLD WAR 1914

B

KEY

NATIONAL
FRONTIERS 1914

PETROGRAD

RIGA

FRONT LINE DEC. 1917

KÖNIGSBERG

MASURIAN
LAKES

TANNENBERG

MINSK

FRONT LINE APRIL 1915

WARSAW

BREST
LITOVSK

LODZ

PRZEMYSL

CRACOW

LEMBERG

FRONT LINE SEPT. 1916

FRONT LINE DEC. 1916

RUMANIA

BELGRADE

SERBIA

MONT

BULGARIA

ALB

SALONIKA

CONSTANTINOPLE

DARDANELLES

victory ensured that the Schlieffen Plan was a failure, while the Germans' establishment of strong defensive positions along the River Aisne, to check their own retreat, virtually put an end to the 'war of movement' and established the future pattern of trench warfare and siege tactics. The 'war of movement' had one last phase in the west, as both forces attempted outflanking movements to the west of their opponents. When, in mid-November, the rival forces reached the Channel coast, a line of trenches extended unbroken for 450 miles from the sea to the Alps. This stabilisation of the western front was also created by the unprecedented losses of 1914. In some sectors of the front units had lost up to 40% of their strength, and a little over 10% of the entire French officer corps had died. Munition manufacturers, too, had not foreseen a war of attrition, and stocks of shells had been roughly halved. In the last weeks of 1914 both sides were drawing breath and preparing for a form of warfare that neither had experienced.

Where strategy had failed to achieve a decisive breakthrough in 1914, the next two years saw the increasing use of the new technology of warfare to break the deadlock. In April 1915, near the Belgian town of Ypres, the Germans used poison gas for the first time. As anticipated, it caused panic and severe losses and knocked the desired hole in the allied lines, but it also handicapped and delayed the subsequent German advance, and the line was closed up in time. Allied offensives in 1915 preferred the new technology of heavy artillery and prefaced their attacks with enormous bombardments using hundreds of thousands of shells. The subsequent assaults, nevertheless, mostly foundered upon a fully prepared second line of defences, behind the original German trenches. 'The western commanders', M. Ferro has concluded, launched attacks not from any real hope of victory, but 'to keep their troops in a state of alert'. The cost of such a consideration was enormous. The Battles of Artois (May), Loos and Champagne (September) cost 135 000 French dead and 140 000 Germans. This contributed to a total for 1915 on the western front of 400 000 killed or captured, and over a million wounded. Survivors, too, suffered unprecedented hardships. A French officer's description of troops returning from the front conveys their suffering. 'Squads came on, their heads bowed; stricken, sad eyes appearing from beneath field caps; rusty, muddy rifles were held suspended by the sling. Caps and faces were coloured alike by dry mud, and then covered by more mud. The men were now beyond speech; they no longer had strength even to complain; you could see in their eyes an abyss of grief, a petrification through dust and strain. These dumb faces proclaimed a martyrdom of hideous proportions'. 'We are nibbling at them', proclaimed Joffre but, as B. Liddell-Hart has observed, 'such efforts were like mice nibbling at a steel safe'.

The year 1916 was dominated in the west by one enormous engagement, the most terrible of the war. The logic behind German strategy at the Battle of Verdun was that if France was 'militarily and economically weakened, almost to the limit of her endurance', then Britain in turn would find herself isolated and be forced to seek peace. To achieve this, a blow would be struck at a place of paramount strategic importance. This would leave France the alternatives of withdrawal, with its disastrous effect on morale, or resistance, in which case German bombardment would bleed her resources white. The bombardment began on 21st February 1916 and used in all some two million shells. The subsequent infantry advance captured two miles of ground in three days, then General Petain took command of Verdun to conduct one of the great defences of history. French units were rotated regularly so that none would be completely overwhelmed by the dreadful conditions in which it fought. The road from Bar-le-Duc became the 'Sacred Road' ('La Voie Sacree'), over which lorries passed at intervals of 14 seconds to supply the defences. In June the Germans captured one of the foremost defences, Fort Vaux, and plans were prepared for evacuation, yet German resources gave out first and discontinued their offensive in mid-July. French counter attacks in October and December regained virtually all their earlier losses. The massive casualty list of some 700 000 dead was evenly divided between the two sides, but it has been argued that the French suffered a further disadvantage in that the widespread experience of the horrors of this battle did much to breed the pacifism that affected France in the 1930s. 'Troops coming up to relieve the soldiers', writes M. Ferro, 'were often overwhelmed at the horror of Verdun; they saw an implacable fate before them, of digging a grave to stay alive, and then supporting it with their corpses. . . . The only certainty was death—for one, or other, or all'.

Further west, on the Somme, the allies launched their own massive offensive (July–November 1916) in part to deflect German resources from Verdun. Despite a week of preliminary bombardment, the failure of the offensive was evident within minutes of its launching. Failure to admit as much cost 600 000 casualties for no significant gain. Between them, the two monumental failures of 1916 brought an end to the 'war of attrition' on the western front.

(k) The Eastern Front, 1914–16

The Russians, too, expected early results, although less from rapid strategic thrusts than from the huge numbers of peasant soldiers that they could mobilise. On 17th August, far earlier than the authors of the Schlieffen Plan had envisaged, the Russian 'steam roller' entered German territory in East Prussia. Three days later, General Rennenkampf defeated a German force at Gumbinnen. The defeat, however, merely brought on the scene the two most successful German commanders of the war, Paul von Hindenburg and Erich von Ludendorff. In the campaign of the next month, by which they sought to defend the Junker heartland of Prussia, they were aided by a variety of Russian shortcomings and errors. To render maximum aid to the French, the Russian army had attacked before it was fully ready for the task, and the personal hostility between Generals Rennenkampf and Samsonov made co-operation between the two main attacking forces difficult. Furthermore, the Generals allowed the two Russian armies to be separated at the point of contact with the enemy by the 50 mile chain of the Masurian Lakes. As a result, Hindenburg and Ludendorff were able to tackle the two forces individually. Samsonov was defeated in a massive engagement christened the Battle of Tannenberg (26th–29th August) in memory of and in revenge for the defeat of the Teutonic Knights by the Slavs in 1410. Less than two weeks later Rennenkampf's army was similarly defeated at the Battle of the Masurian Lakes (8th–9th September). In the precipitous Russian retreat, the Germans took some 130 000 prisoners.

The two great battles saved Prussia from Russian invasion and established Hindenburg as the major German folk-hero of the war. Their influence on the war in the east as a whole should not, however, be overestimated. Indeed, by forcing the withdrawal of German troops from the western front, the Russian offensive had made no small contribution to the defeat of the Schlieffen Plan. Farther south, against her main rival, Austria-Hungary, Russia secured some notable successes. Lemberg (Lvov), the fourth largest city in the Dual Monarchy, was captured in early September, and the Russians, in B. Tuchman's words, 'accomplished a mutilation of the Austro-Hungarian army, especially in trained officers, from which it was never to recover'.

Hesitant Russian leadership and substantial German intervention in support of the crumbling Habsburg forces then combined to produce two years of fluctuating fortunes on the main eastern fronts. 1915 was marked by a slow and costly rolling back of the the Russian forces beyond their frontiers. The long German campaign in Poland, launched in October 1914, finally achieved its purpose with the capture of Warsaw (August 1915), while a combined Austro-German offensive in the Carpathians (May 1915) had recaptured most of Russia's gains of 1914 by late June. By the end of the year, the Russian lines had withdrawn some 300 miles, leaving behind a million dead and a further million prisoners.

Yet 1916 witnessed the greatest Russian successes of the war. Remarkably, neither her resources nor her morale had been crushed by the earlier reverses. N. Stone has emphasised the upswing in Russian military supplies and production by this point in the war, and J. N. Westwood has stressed that, since 1812, retreat was not necessarily seen as a shameful or dis-spiriting factor in Russian military circles. Urged into action by Russia's allies, to relieve pressure on Verdun and on the Italian front, General Brusilov launched a massive offensive on a wide front in June 1916. Its initial success was startling. Three of the four Russian armies involved achieved an immediate breakthrough, and within five days Brusilov had taken 70 000 prisoners. By early August, however, lack of adequate reserves, political jealousy at headquarters, and a further influx of German support for the wavering Austrians had all brought the 'Brusilov Offensive' to a halt. Nevertheless, the casualties inflicted upon Austria-Hungary, some 340 000 of them, plus another 400 000 men taken prisoner, were more than the Dual Monarchy could stand. The offensive, states A. J. P. Taylor, 'marked the moment when the armies of Austria-Hungary lost their fighting spirit. Unity, cohesion, loyalty vanished; and from this time Austria-Hungary was kept in the war by German power'. It had also marked the last great effort of the Russians, and had not quite achieved its aim of eliminating Austria-Hungary from the conflict. Where victory might possibly have prolonged the life of the Russian monarchy, a further million casualties combined with mounting civilian hardships at home (see Chapter 12, section **b**) to lead the Romanov dynasty into its final crisis.

(l) The Balkans, Gallipoli and the Italian Front

In the Balkans, meanwhile, the issue that had precipitated the whole conflict was largely decided by late 1915. At first, Austria-Hungary's offensive foundered upon stubborn Serbian resistance and suicidal counter-attack. The invaders held the Serbian capital, Belgrade, for just two weeks in December 1915, and were then flung back with 100 000 casualties. Serbian losses were even higher, and her army was further ravaged by disease. In mid-1915, two factors combined to seal her fate. One was the German decision to intervene in the interests of maintaining safe communications with Turkey, and the second was the entry of Bulgaria into the war. The Serbian army was overwhelmed by a joint Austro-German-Bulgarian offensive in October 1915, and allied forces planning to come to its assistance through Greek territory from Salonika were hopelessly delayed by political and geographical obstacles. The remnants of the Serbian army at least saved face by an epic retreat through Albania to the sea. Thence they were evacuated to Greece to continue the struggle, but without conspicuous success. The entry of Rumania into the war on the side of the Entente was a brief and unhappy episode. Badly equipped and poorly led, her army was in precipitous retreat within a month of its first campaign (August 1916), and her contribution effectively ended with the fall of her capital city, Bucharest, to German forces in early December.

The most ambitious undertaking in this theatre of war was the assault by British, Commonwealth, and French forces upon the Dardanelles between February and November 1915. It was motivated primarily by the deadlock on the western front, and was conceived as a combined operation by sea and land forces to capture Constantinople, knock Turkey out of the war, and to re-open secure lines of communication with the hard-pressed Russians. The operation's prospects at the time of the initial naval bombardment of the Turkish defences (February 1915) were bright. The allies had the advantage of surprise, and the Turkish positions were weak. The allied campaign, however, was distinguished, in B. Liddell Hart's phrase, by 'shortsighted lethargy'. Not until April was a landing attempted in strength, and in the ensuing months the allied cause suffered from lack of co-ordinated command, shortage of supplies, delays and elementary tactical errors. The loss of four allied battleships on Turkish mines further dampened the initial enthusiasm of the naval commanders. We may well accept A. J. P. Taylor's judgement that the expedition 'was a terrible example of an ingenious strategical idea carried through after inadequate preparation and with inadequate drive'. When, in November, the operation was finally abandoned, it had cost the allies 250 000 men, dead, wounded, or captured, and had served to convince most allied

commanders that the war could only be settled on the western front.

Meanwhile, to the north west, Italy's entry into the war produced a campaign of attrition grim and fruitless even by the standards established in France. In answer to the Italian strategy of an attack along the line of the River Isonzo in the north-western corner of the country, Austro-Hungarian forces occupied a line of mountainous defensive positions. As P. Pieri has noted, 'the river could not be crossed until the mountains had been seized, and the mountains could not be seized until the river had been crossed'. Thus, between June 1915 and August 1917, eleven separate battles of the Isonzo were fought, costing Italy nearly a third of her original army strength for minimal gains. Even as a diversionary factor the Isonzo front was of little value, tying down only a dozen Austrian divisions. When (October 1917) a breakthrough finally came it was the Italians themselves who fell back in disorder, handicapped by their own low morale and lack of ammunition, in the face of a combined Austro-German offensive at Caporetto. The Italian army had lost over 300 000 men, many miles of territory, and very nearly the war, before her forces were successfully regrouped on the line of the Piave River in November. As in most of her earlier encounters with Austria, the final outcome of the conflict owed more to external factors than to pure Italian prowess. It was an exhausted Austrian army, pressed by allied victories in the Balkans, and disrupted by domestic upheavals, that was finally swept from Italian soil in October 1918 in the Battle of Vittorio Veneto.

(m) The War at Sea

Two decades of escalating naval expenditure, and the development of fleets of fast, heavily-armed 'Dreadnought' battleships, had created the impression by 1914 that the disputes between Britain and Germany would be settled primarily by a major confrontation between their fleets. Ironically, the earliest naval events of the war made it clear that decisive roles would be played by cheaper and less glamorous weapons. On 22nd September 1914 the German submarine *U9* sank three British cruisers within minutes, and a month later the British battleship 'Audacious' was sunk by a mine. It immediately became obvious that it was not possible after all for battle fleets to range freely in search of each other.

In the early months of the war, therefore, German ships were mainly concerned with raiding missions against British and allied commerce on the high seas. The 'Emden' in the Indian Ocean and Admiral von Spee's cruiser squadron in the Pacific did great harm, the latter badly shaking British complacency by destroying a British force off the Chilean coast at Coronel (1st November 1914). Eventually, however, the redisposition of British resources won back the advantage. Von Spee's force was destroyed at the Battle of the Falklands (December 1914), and the sinking of the 'Dresden' in March 1915 effectively ended the threat of German surface raiders. The British navy enjoyed surface supremacy for the rest of the war, a fact of enormous strategic importance. It allowed 8.5 million troops to be mobilised from the Empire, without a single loss at sea; it established and maintained the crippling blockade imposed upon Germany; it facilitated the conquest of all German colonies in the first year of the war, and ultimately made possible the convoy system that helped thwart German submarine warfare, and the transport of American men and equipment to play their decisive role in the European conflict. As J. Terraine has put it, 'the Royal Navy did not win the war; but it is impossible to see how the war could have been won without it'.

Nevertheless, the war produced two more threats to that British supremacy. The first was the Battle of Jutland (31st May 1916), the only major encounter in naval history between massed fleets of 'Dreadnoughts'. It was fought in the North Sea, at the mouth of the Skagerrak. The battle resulted from the eagerness of the new German commander, Admiral Scheer, to tempt sections of the Grand Fleet out of their ports into the open sea where they might be attacked by superior German forces. Owing to the British ability to decipher German radio signals, Scheer had instead to undertake an engagement involving some 250 ships. The German fleet demonstrated superior gunnery and superior ship design, and lost two capital ships, nine lesser vessels and 2500 men, compared to the three capital ships, eleven lesser vessels and 6000 men lost by the British. The arrival of a second British fleet, the failing light, and the clever evasive tactics of the German commanders, all brought the battle to an end without a decisive outcome. Both sides claimed victory, both with some justification, but the fact remained that only the outright crippling of the British fleet would have transferred the strategic initiative to the Germans, and this they failed to achieve.

Although the German surface fleet had no further role to play in the war, her submarines had. Even as the 'Dreadnoughts' were failing to impose a stranglehold on Britain, a dramatic rise was taking place in the amount of British shipping sunk by U-boat action. In February 1917, when Germany adopted unrestricted submarine warfare, Britain lost 464 000 tons of shipping. In April she lost 834 000 tons, and between February and June 1917 one ship in every four dealing with British ports was destroyed. British corn supplies dwindled to the equivalent of six weeks' normal consumption, and defeat seemed near. The adoption of the system of escorted convoys, in the face of much opposition from the Admiralty, did not eliminate the submarine threat. In the first quarter of 1918 Britain still lost over a million tons of merchant shipping. It reduced losses, however, to a level that could be made good by new vessels leaving the shipyards. By the end of the war, the new counter-technology of mines, depth charges and other devices, had destroyed half of the U-boat fleet. Considering, too, the role that German submarines played in bringing the USA into the conflict on the allied side, it becomes clear that their use, although an extremely dangerous tactic, was also ultimately an unsuccessful one.

(n) The Home Front

Quite apart from the new brand of 'total' warfare waged at the front, the First World War was also remarkable for the fact that it was the first to have a substantial impact upon the civilian populations left at home. At first, this impact was wholly unforeseen, and it is impossible to doubt the popularity of the conflict in all the participating states. In France, earlier political differences were submerged in the 'Sacred Union' ('L'Union Sacrée') for the defence of the country. Where a rate of conscientious objection of 13% had been feared by the security services, the actual level was only 1.5% of those summoned to the colours. Germans, similarly, spoke of the 'Burgfriede', the domestic peace that reigns in a besieged fortress. Speaking of mid-1915, A. J. P. Taylor has concluded that 'there was, as yet, hardly a flicker of discontent or discouragement in any belligerent country'.

The first dents to appear in this universal optimism were the results of the rapid spread of economic warfare. Germany's geographical position made her most vulnerable to this form of attack, and her own merchant navy had virtually ceased to function by the end of 1914. Although imports continued to seep in through neutral neighbours, the value of German trade with the USA, for instance, fell from 68 million dollars in December 1914 to 10 million in January 1915. Germany's recourse to submarine warfare later subjected Britain to similar difficulties, and the German occupation of northern France and of Poland deprived France and Russia respectively of important industrial resources. The entry of Turkey into the war aggravated Russia's problems, with domestic results that are outlined elsewhere (see Chapter 12, section **b**). Food supplies were also hit by the mobilisation of large numbers of men and horses as the war progressed. In Germany, it has been estimated, agricultural production fell by 50 to 70%, according to the individual region, while the drop in Russia was 50% and that in France ranged between 30–50%. Germany was the first to introduce rationing, limiting supplies of bread, meat, potatoes and fats, while Turkey, in particular, suffered an alarming rise in the death-rate from such diseases as typhus.

In several respects, the war resulted in the greater subjection of the citizen to central political authority. Germany was the first combatant to take measures to direct and to control resources and production, creating the War Materials Department (Kriegsrohstoffabteilung—KDA) in 1914. All combatant countries, however, soon experienced government pressure to push available labour into war industries. By the end of the war, these employed 76% of all industrial labour in Russia, and 64% in Italy. A further notable result of the war was the substantial employment of female labour in order to release men for the forces. In France, by 1917, one war worker in four was a woman, and Joffre could claim that 'if the women in the war factories stopped for twenty minutes, we should lose the war'. In Britain, too, in A. J. P. Taylor's words, 'by the end of the war, it was no longer true that woman's place was in the home'. Secondly, the citizen felt the influence of central authority in the unparalleled degree of propaganda and censorship to which he was subjected. News of military failures, of heavy casualties, and of anything else that could contribute to 'defeatism' was progressively eliminated from publications. In France, by 1917, claims M. Ferro, 'the press had failed in its purpose, to inform and to discuss. Public opinion, daily anaesthetised by patriotic newspapers, announcements, books, films, and songs, became less and less capable of exercising its civic function'. Thirdly, the enormous losses of the early campaigns made the citizens in most belligerent countries liable for the first time to military conscription. France introduced conscription at an early stage of the war, and lost men at such a rate that those timetabled for call-up in 1917 were called in December 1915. Even Britain, with her relatively modest contribution to the war on land, abandoned the principle of a volunteer army in January 1916.

For the first time, the civilian did not need to go to the front to become a casualty of war. The new and developing technology of the conflict produced at least three means of striking at the enemy's resources and population. Paris was shelled at regular intervals, at a range of 79 miles, by the massive gun christened by the Germans, 'Long Max'. Two hundred and fifty-six Parisians were killed by the 203 shells launched into the city by 'Long Max', and some 600 were injured. London, meanwhile, suffered her first air-raids. Raids in 1915 by Zeppelin airships killed 498 civilians and injured 1236, while in 1917 it was the turn of the 'Gotha' bombers, killing 162 and wounding 432 in a single raid in June. As part of the retaliation demanded by public opinion, British planes in the last year of the war inflicted 24 million marks worth of damage upon German towns and factories.

Eventually the strain of war, at the front and at home, broke down the enthusiastic unanimity of 1914. Isolated socialist and pacifist voices had been raised against the war, and September 1915 had seen the publication of the Zimmerwald Manifesto by international socialists meeting in Switzerland. Even so, discontent was ultimately the result of price rises and of declining living standards, rather than of internationalism. Reliable figures are incomplete, but it is possible to state that in England in 1917 food prices were 70% higher than in 1914, while wages were only 18% up. The figures for France were 74% and 30% respectively, while those for Italy were 84% and 38%. The social impact of the war upon Russia is described in greater detail elsewhere (see Chapter 12, section **b**). The contrast between the figures above and the substantial increases in the profits made by most branches of heavy industry began to trigger off militant action by 1917. Table 11.2 shows the initial fall in strike action at the outbreak of the war, contrasted with the renewal of industrial unrest as the strains of three or four years of total war began to tear at the fabric of society.

	1913	1914	1915	1916	1917	1918
Russia	2404	3534	928	1410	1938	—
Britain	1459	972	672	532	730	1165
France	1073	690	98	314	697	499
Germany	2127	1115	137	240	561	531

From M. Ferro, *The Great War, 1914–18.*

Table 11.2

(o) 1917

After the failure in 1916 of the policy of attrition on the western front, allied commanders could devise no better plan than a return to the optimistic and unrealistic offensive tactics of 1914. Joffre's replacement at the head of the French forces, General Robert Nivelle, was another firm believer in the 'elan' of the French infantryman, and was able to "sell" the idea of a combined allied offensive to the British. However, as the Germans had withdrawn (March 1917) to prepared positions on the so-called Hindenburg and Siegfried Lines, the 'Nivelle Offensive' of April was launched against the best defences that the Germans had so far occupied. Although some objectives were achieved, such as the Chemin des Dames and Vimy Ridge, the casualty list of 118000 losses on the French side alone told a familiar story of wasted lives in return for little gain. In May, a disillusioned Nivelle was replaced by Pétain who, returning to the tactics successful at Verdun, declared himself committed to a waiting game: 'I am waiting for Americans and tanks'. For the rest of the year, British troops bore the brunt of the futile offensives on the western front. The Battle of Messines (June) produced some successes, including the spectacular use of mining operations to blow up German positions, but the 3rd Battle of Ypres, or Passchendaele (July–November) became a bye-word for mud-encumbered deadlock. Three hundred and twenty-four thousand British casualties could not secure any significant advantage. Only the engagement at Cambrai brought promise of an end to the stalemate. There, on 20th November, a massed force of 381 British tanks broke through the German lines and achieved an advance of five miles. Success was only partial. The infantry could not keep up with the advance, and reserves were lacking. Thus German troops had largely repaired the initial damage within ten days. Nevertheless, the world's first true tank action gave a foretaste of the new 'war of movement' that northern France would witness a generation later.

If tanks did not fulfil Pétain's expectations, the year also witnessed a decisive augmentation of allied strength. The isolationism that had so far characterised America's attitude to the war was ultimately overcome by two German errors. The first was the decision to wage unlimited submarine warfare from February 1917, which inevitably involved attacks upon American ships and the loss of American lives. The second was the dispatch of the so-called 'Zimmermann Telegram'. In March 1917, the German Secretary of State authorised his minister in Mexico to offer that country German support in an attack upon the USA, for which Mexico would regain those territories lost to her neighbour in the 19th century. Intercepted, the message had' a predictable effect upon public opinion in the USA. Several authorities have stressed, however, the extent to which the USA was, in any case, committed to the side of the allies by February 1917. American producers had deals to provide copper, cotton, wheat and other commodities, and her bankers had forwarded substantial loans. Thus German submarines, and the threat of ultimate German victory, put substantial American interests at risk. The fall of the Tsar, in early 1917, also removed the last ideological obstacle to American involvement. Having broken off relations with Germany on 2nd February over the submarine issue, President Wilson declared war on 6th April.

In moral terms, American intervention changed the nature of the war. Without any threat to her security, and far removed from the territorial concerns of the European combatants, the USA approached the war as a moral crusade for the preservation of democracy. This was confirmed by Wilson's major statement on his country's war aims in his 'Fourteen Points' (8th January 1918). Some of his demands, for the evacuation of occupied Belgian and Russian territories, the restoration of Alsace-Lorraine to France, the establishment of self-government among the minority peoples of the Habsburg Empire, were fully consistent with earlier allied declarations (see section i). On the other hand, the calls for the abolition of secret diplomacy, for total freedom of the seas, for the abolition of all trade restrictions, for a general reduction in armaments, and for the 'absolute impartial adjustment of all colonial claims', were not at all what the allies had originally had in mind.

Materially, nevertheless, this intervention was unlikely to make an immediate impact. Time was needed for the mobilisation of men and resources, and thus the American declaration was, in A. J. P. Taylor's phrase, 'a promissory note for the future, provided that the allies held on until it could be cashed'. Several factors in 1917 did indeed cast doubt upon the ability of America's partners to survive long enough to benefit from her assistance. On the western front, 1917 saw the French army shaken by a series of mutinies involving 54 divisions, mainly in protest against the murderous strategy of the commanders. Miraculously, Pétain was able to restore order before the Germans realised their opportunity. Some 23000 soldiers were charged as a result, and over 430 sentenced to death, although it now seems that only 50–55 were executed. Meanwhile, the Austrian offensive at Caporetto (see section 1) threatened the continued existence of the Italian front. Most serious of all, the aftermath of the Bolshevik revolution in November saw the total withdrawal of Russia's forces from the conflict. Even at the very end of 1917, therefore, it was far from certain that American involvement would decide the war in the allies' favour.

(p) 1918: Rebellion and Collapse

1918 opened with the dual prospect for Germany of immediate advantages, in the form of men and supplies transferred from the eastern front, but long-term disadvantage from the influx of American resources and the continued effects of the allied blockade. Ludendorff's strategy was thus to throw everything into a final 'Peace Offensive' ('Friedensturm') to drive Britain and France out of the war. Three major offensives, indeed, won the greatest German successes of the western conflict. In March, 35 divisions on the Somme made gains of some 40 miles against the British. In April, in Flanders, a breakthrough was achieved which for a time threatened allied control of the Channel ports. In May, on the Aisne, the French line broke, and German forces once again reached the Marne within 50 miles of Paris. The strategy had not, however, achieved the desired victory. Each advance, as it lost its impetus, left German forces deep in a salient, around which the allies massed their growing forces. Meanwhile Germany struggled to replace her latest 800 000 casualties. Allied forces at last came under co-ordinated control with the appointment of General Foch in April as 'Commander-in-Chief of the Allied Armies in France'. The last German offensive of the war came in July around Rheims. It met stiff opposition and made no significant progress. Instead, the French counter-attack made a breakthrough, and Ludendorff's forces fell back to safer ground.

The 8th August 1918 marked the beginning of the end for Germany. On what Ludendorff dubbed 'The Black Day', a combined allied offensive made the greatest gains achieved since the stabilisation of the front in 1914. A British tank attack east of Amiens, in particular, broke the German line and advanced some six miles. Yet the German resistance did not collapse then, nor during the next allied offensive in mid-September. Their morale, however, suffered a fatal blow. The loss of ground, combined with disappointment with the results of their own earlier 'Friedensturm', states A. J. P. Taylor, 'shattered the faith in victory which,

until that moment, carried the Germans forward. They no longer wanted to win. They wanted only to end the war'.

For at least a year, war-weariness had affected all the belligerent capitals. The 'Union Sacrée' in France had been strained to breaking point by the decision of the socialists to leave the cabinet in September 1917, and as early as November 1916, the Emperor Karl, succeeding Franz-Josef at the head of the Habsburg Empire, had made tentative secret peace proposals to the allies. While the advent of Clemenceau to power in Paris (November 1917) had strengthened the fight against defeatism in France, morale in Germany and Austria continued to decline. By January 1918, the daily flour ration in Vienna had dropped to 165 grams, food trains from the east were plundered, and the incidence of desertion from the forces rose sharply. In June the German Secretary of State, Kühlmann, publicly broached the subject of a compromise peace, but was disowned and forced from office by the military leaders. By early October, however, reverses on the western front and the surrender of Bulgaria (29th September) to the east, had changed their minds. Ludendorff acknowledged the need to accept withdrawal from occupied territories, and to accept Social Democrats into the government in order to mollify the democrats among the allies. On 4th October, the new government led by the liberal Prince Max of Bavaria requested an armistice based upon the 'Fourteen Points'. On 20th October, Germany officially ended submarine warfare. Meanwhile, although the war effort in the west was maintained, that in the east collapsed. Turkey signed an armistice in late October, broken by highly successful British campaigns in the Middle East. At the same time the Austro-Hungarian Empire quietly disintegrated, with the peaceful declaration of independent nationhood by the Czechs, the South Slavs, and the Hungarians (31st October). Three days later, the remnants of the Habsburg armies requested an armistice. The sequence of events in Germany, too, made further resistance impossible. On 29th October, naval crews at Kiel began to mutiny in protest against orders to resume operations at sea. On 9th November, a German Republic was proclaimed in Berlin by Social Democrats, and the Kaiser left his throne for exile in Holland.

The threat of domestic revolution added urgency to the government's quest for peace. Horrified as they were by the severity of the armistice terms dictated by the allies, the German delegation signed them at Compiegne, in northern France, on 11th November 1918. Germany was to hand over her fleet, and vast stocks of war material. She was to evacuate all occupied territories in the west and to permit allied occupation of the left bank of the Rhine. She was to annul the peace treaties made with defeated Russia and Rumania. As a formal, impotent protest, the leader of the German delegation stated that 'a nation of seventy millions suffers, but does not die'. Foch remarked 'Très Bien', and closed the interview that closed the First World War.

The revolutionary nature of the events of the past four years could scarcely be exaggerated. Their most obvious impact is summarised in Table 11.3, showing the human and material cost of the war. Equally sensational was the war's impact upon the future of European politics. With the almost simultaneous collapse of three great Empires, those of Germany, Russia, and Austria-Hungary, the major points of reference in a century of European history vanished. The traditional balance of power was destroyed, and the peace settlement failed to put anything substantial in its place. Indeed, with the unparalleled intervention by the United States, the whole role of Europe in the world had been called into question. A. J. P. Taylor, for this reason, goes so far as to claim that 'in January 1918 Europe ceased to be the centre of the world'.

	Dead (millions)	Financial cost (million £)
British Empire	0.947	6418
French Empire	1.400	5200
Germany	1.800	8300
Austria-Hungary	1.200	4100
Russia	1.700	5060
USA	0.116	2600
Italy	0.650	2400
Serbia	0.048	—

From T. G. Charman, *Modern European History Notes*. Telles Langdon Publications.

Table 11.3

(q) Historiography

Although 1918 marked the end of the military contest, it marked the beginning of the fierce war of words concerning the causes and nature of the conflict, and the apportioning of 'War Guilt'. As victors, the allies produced in the peace treaty itself

their interpretation of the question. Clause 231 forced the defeated Germans to admit that they bore the moral responsibility for the carnage by virtue of their aggressive and militaristic policies before 1914. If the politicians of the Weimar Republic were forced publicly to accept that interpretation, her historians were not. The analysis of German documentary evidence from the diplomatic archives, undertaken to substantiate German claims of innocence, culminated in a vast 40 volume work. It was edited by J. Lepsius, A. Mendelsohn-Bartholdy and F. Thimme, and entitled *The Grand Policy of the European Cabinets, 1871–1914* (1922–27). This massive piece of scholarship was supported in Germany by interpretative works such as those of H. von Delbrück (*The Peace of Versailles*, 1930) and H. Oncken (*The German Reich and the Prehistory of the First World War*, 1932). These stressed Germany's reasons for fearing encirclement, and sought to lay greater emphasis upon French desire to regain Alsace-Lorraine, and Russian designs upon Constantinople. Together, these achieved some international success in vindicating German diplomatic conduct before 1914. In America, a 'school' developed in which H. E. Barnes (*The Genesis of the World War*, 1926) and S. B. Fay (*The Origins of the World War*, 1928) were prominent, that broadly accepted these revised judgements. Even in France, historians of the Left, hostile to Poincaré, and impressed by the evidence of captured Russian documents released by the Bolsheviks, were willing to accept a substantial degree of French and Russian responsibility. By the early 1930s, however, a number of prominent French writers, among them P. Renouvin (*The Immediate Origins of the War*, 1925), J. Isaac (*A Historical Debate, 1914: The Problem of the Origins of the War*, 1933), and A. Fabre-Luce (*The Victory*, 1924), had formulated a compromise that remained the accepted orthodoxy for thirty years. 'The immediate origins', wrote Isaac, '. . . suffice to tilt the balance [of guilt] to the side of the Central Empires. . . . Nevertheless, one does not discern in the other camp any miraculous will for peace. The Central Empires deliberately offered if not imposed war upon the Entente; she then accepted it with a promptness which even surprised her adversaries'. Fabre-Luce was yet more conciliatory. 'Germany and Austria made gestures that made war possible; the Triple Entente made those which rendered it certain'.

Such orthodoxy would not, of course, have been accepted in Marxist circles. Here the favoured interpretation was that put forward by Lenin himself (*Imperialism, the Highest Form of Capitalism,*

1916). His case was that the war was the inevitable result of the development of capitalism into the monopoly stage, wherein capitalists were bound to compete aggressively for limited resources and markets. The theme remains the accepted interpretation in eastern Europe today, and receives wide support in left-wing circles in the west, despite recent work such as that of R. Poidevin (*Finance and International Relations, 1887–1914,* 1970), suggesting links and strong mutual interests between the business communities of the rival belligerent states.

The views widely accepted as orthodox by western historians were dramatically challenged in the 1960s by the work of the German historian, Fritz Fischer. In the first of his two main works, *Germany's Aims in the First World War* (1961), he shifted a great deal of responsibility for the outbreak of war back onto German shoulders with the claim that her leaders had deliberately accepted the risk of war for the furtherance of their political ambitions, during the course of the July Crisis in 1914. Warming to his controversial theme, Fischer later claimed (*The War of Illusions,* 1969) that German actions since 1911 proved a desire, a preparation and a provocation of war. Furthermore, he referred not only to political activities at governmental levels, but to social and economic developments and views throughout German society. Thus he seemed to align himself with such non-German critics as A. J. P. Taylor and E. Vermeil, who claimed to find a continuous theme of aggression and militarism linking the old Reich with the Germany of Hitler.

Naturally, such an interpretation provoked great opposition, especially in Germany, of which only a few examples can be given here. The prominent historian G. Ritter, then completing his masterpiece on German militarism, *The Sword and the Sceptre* (1954–68) pointed out that, while it was sadly true that the civil authorities steadily abdicated their responsibilities in the face of annexationist and military pressures during the reign of Wilhelm II, this did not amount to premeditated aggression. Wilhelmine Germany, he stressed, displayed few of the ideological aberrations of Nazi Germany. Another of Fischer's prominent critics was E. Zechlin (*The Outbreak of War in 1914, and the Problem of War Aims in International Policy,* 1972). He essentially agreed that Germany accepted the apparent inevitability of war in 1914, but sought to acquit her of the charge of provoking it. The aims declared in the 'September Programme', he argued, were the result of the realisation that this war could not be fought on the limited scale of the earlier 'Cabinet Wars' of 1859, 1866 and 1870, and that a

more far reaching strategy was called for. Such aims and such strategy had not, he believes, been considered by the German government before the outbreak of war. In addition, Fischer has been criticised for a line of argument that considers German actions and responsibilities in isolation from those of the other belligerents. In stressing the readiness of the other great powers to use war for the solution of their own immediate political and social problems, L. C. F. Turner (*The Origins of the First World War,* 1970) and others have led the debate back close to the compromise position held by Renouvin, Isaac and their followers thirty years earlier.

Progress Paragraphs

Answer the following questions in about 150 words.

How likely was conflict between the great powers in 1905?   Section (**a**)

What are the arguments for an economic interpretation of imperialism?   Section (**b**)

What objections may be raised to economic interpretations of imperialism?   Section (**c**)

What were Germany's motives in the Moroccan crisis of 1905–06?   Section (**d**)

Why did the Balkans once more become a focus of international tensions between 1908–09?
Section (**e**)

In what ways was international conflict made more likely by the Moroccan and Bosnian crises?
Sections (**d & e**)

In what ways did the Agadir crisis worsen international tension?   Section (**f**)

How did the situation in the Balkans degenerate in 1912–13?   Section (**g**)

How did the Sarajevo assassination lead to general war in 1914?   Section (**h**)

For what were the main combatants fighting in 1914?
Sections (**h & i**)

Why did a military stalemate develop on the western front?   Section (**j**)

What did Russia contribute to the allied cause between 1914–16?   Section (**k**)

What did the allies try to achieve on the lesser European fronts? Why did their efforts fail?
                                                   Section (**l**)

How seriously was British naval supremacy threatened during the war?   Section (**m**)

In what ways were the civilian populations of the combatant powers affected by the war?
                                                   Section (**n**)

Why did the USA enter the war?   Section (**o**)

What were the effects of the entrance of the USA into the conflict?   Sections (**o** & **p**)

Account for the collapse of the German war effort in 1918.   Section (**p**)

12
The Russian Revolutions: 1914–24

(a) War and the Russian Regime

Despite grim forebodings in some informed circles, the declaration of war in 1914 was undoubtedly popular in Russia. Although the former Minister of the Interior, P. N. Durnovo, accurately warned that the main burden of fighting would fall on Russia, and that she was unprepared for a long struggle, voices such as his were drowned in the swell of popular enthusiasm. The immediate voting of war credits by the Duma (8th August), the sacking of the German embassy by patriotic students, and the general acceptance of the government's ban on the sale of vodka, all bore witness to the readiness at first to suspend old animosities in defence of 'Mother Russia'. Even the capital city was renamed, the Germanic sound of 'St. Petersburg' giving way to the Slav 'Petrograd'. Briefly, the Tsar enjoyed more popularity than at any other point in his reign. For once he could pose convincingly as the personification of all the Russians. Yet, within three years he was Tsar no more, his prestige worn away inexorably by a dismal succession of failures and miscalculations. Three interrelating factors stand out as contributing to this last collapse of Tsarist prestige.

Firstly, the patriotic formation of such bodies as the Union of Zemstvos, to provide medical facilities, and the Congress of Representatives of Industry and Trade (August 1914), to co-ordinate production, raised an old and thorny question. How far could representative bodies, and the latter even included representatives of the workers, be allowed to influence the conduct of the war? The attitude of the government was clearly that the autocracy should exercise sole control. A matter of particular controversy was the formation (July 1914) of 'military zones', comprising most of Finland, Poland, the Baltic provinces, the Caucasus, and Petrograd. Within them all civil authority was subordinated to that of the military, and every obstacle was put in the way of would-be civilian participation. By August 1915, the combination of the Kadets, Octobrists and Progressists in the Duma into a so-called

Progressive Bloc, demanding a government 'possessing the confidence of the public' indicated that the old wounds were open once more. The government's answer was to dismiss the Duma (15th September 1915). Between that date and January 1916, the dispute over the conduct of the war brought about the dismissal of many critical ministers including the premier, I. L. Goremykin, the foreign minister, S. D. Sazonov, and the war minister, A. A. Polivanov. To many it seemed that political ideology was becoming more important than the effective prosecution of the war. Tsarist apologists laid the blame at the door of 'disloyal' liberals, but modern commentators are more inclined to blame the Tsar. 'The truth is', states H. Seton-Watson, 'that the insuperable obstacle was his dogmatic devotion to autocracy'.

Secondly, at this tense juncture came the decision of the Tsar to assume personal command as Commander-in-Chief of the armed forces (September 1915) and to take up residence at the front. However understandable in terms of royal duty and military morale, the decision directly identified the Tsar with all future military disasters, and left the government in Petrograd at the mercy of the Empress' infatuations and the schemes of political opportunists.

Most famous, and perhaps most damaging of these factors was the increased influence over the Empress, and thus over government policy, of Grigori Rasputin. Rasputin, a Siberian 'starets' or holy man, had been known to the Imperial family since 1905. His influence over them dated from 1907 when it began to appear that he was able to control the haemophilia, a blood disease, from which the heir to the throne, Alexis, suffered. The means by which he did this have never been satisfactorily explained. With the Tsar at the front, he became the main influence upon the deeply religious and superstitious Empress. The view of contemporary opponents such as the prominent Duma politician M. V. Rodzianko that Rasputin was the supreme evil influence of the government is not always accepted today. Some have seen him rather as the tool of self-seeking schemers. At any rate, contemporaries saw his advice to the Empress as the main force behind the 'ministerial leapfrog' that occupied the year beginning in September 1915. Some ministries had as many as three or four chiefs within the year, most of them nonentities. Rasputin's murder in December 1916 by right wingers came too late. The damage to the government and its reputation was irreparable and many contemporaries, remembering the German origins of the Empress, could not avoid the suspicion of treason.

(b) War and the Russian People

In the final analysis, the collapse of the Romanov dynasty in Russia was not triggered by ideological arguments, but by the sheer suffering imposed by the war upon the Russian people.

The most immediate hardships, of course, were met by those actually serving in the armed forces. Although Russia only mobilised a little less than 9% of her population during the war, compared to roughly 20% in both Germany and France, the size of the Russian population meant that a very substantial number experienced the horrors of the front. The Russian army totalled 5.3 million men after the initial mobilisation (Germany and France mobilised 3.8 million at this point), and a total of 15.3 million Russians had seen military service by the end of hostilities. Numbers, however, were the Russian soldier's only advantage. Compared to his opposite numbers in other armies he was worse armed, worse treated, and worse led. Shortcomings of armament and tactics exposed in the war of 1904–05 were being treated, but had not been overcome by the outbreak of war in 1914. It was still not unusual in 1915 for Russian artillery to be limited to two or three shells a day, and after mobilisation in 1914 the infantry had only two rifles for every three soldiers. Men were sent into battle with instructions to help themselves to the weapons of fallen comrades. Nothing had been done to raise the soldiers' social status. They were still forbidden access to restaurants, to any but third class railway carriages, and to seats on public omnibuses, and forced to suffer many other marks of public disapproval. The formation of a new body under the Ministry of War which was empowered to dismiss incompetent officers had some way to go yet to overcome the problems of favouritism and patronage. Such factors made casualty levels that were in any case horrendous all the harder to bear. By early 1917, Russia had lost 1.6 million dead, 3.9 million wounded, and 2.4 million taken prisoner.

The civilian population also had increasingly daunting problems to face. 1916 was a comparatively good year for military production, with rifle production doubled and that of heavy artillery quadrupled, but these advances were made at the expense of civilian needs. Locomotive production, for example, was halved between 1913–16 with only 67 new engines completed in the latter year. This factor, together with constant military interference with the railway network for strategic purposes, contributed to the semi-breakdown of the communication and distribution system that was the main cause of urban food shortages. There were other factors. Conscription caused a scarcity of both men and horses on the larger estates, and town populations increased as war industries demanded extra labour, but generally there was enough food. It simply was not getting to those who needed it. Indeed, N. Stone has recently shown that military shortages, too, were due less to failures of production than to inefficient distribution. Fuel shortages constituted another consistent problem. Due to the early loss of the Polish coalfields, total coal production in Russia never reached the same level as was achieved in the last year of peace, and an increasing proportion of what fuel there was was channelled towards military uses.

Food prices rose dramatically. On average, and the figures were actually higher for major urban conglomerations such as Petrograd, the price of flour rose by 99% between 1913–16, that of meat by 232%, that of butter by 124%, and that of salt by 483%. Money wages, it is true, rose by 133% over the same period, but this figure has to be set against a drop in the value of the rouble to only 56% of its pre-war value.

(c) The March Revolution

If the World War does not fully explain the collapse of the Tsarist regime, it did act, in Lenin's words, as 'a mighty accelerator' in the process of alienating the Russian people from their rulers. By mid November 1916, the liberal politicians in the Duma had determined upon a more uncompromising attitude towards the government and its failures. On 15th November the assembly heard a famous denunciation of official incompetence by P. N. Miliukov. Questioning whether government policy represented 'stupidity or treason', he concluded that 'we have lost faith in the ability of this government to achieve victory'. By January 1917 some leading members had even prepared provisional plans to force Nicholas' abdication in favour of his son.

If some commentators have stressed the role of the liberals in the final discrediting of the monarchy, there is wide agreement that neither they, not any other organised political group bears responsibility for the events that finally brought it down. 'The collapse of the Romanov autocracy', stated the American commentator W. H. Chamberlain, 'was one of the most leaderless, spontaneous, anonymous revolutions of all time'. The initiative came primarily from the Petrograd workers whose patience with the deprivations of war was nearing exhaustion as 1917 opened. In January, some 150 000 of them had demonstrated on the anniversary of 'Bloody Sunday', and 80 000 had demonstrated support for the reopened Duma in February. International Women's Day (8th March) brought onto the streets tens of thousands of women exasperated by months of food shortages, and the coincidence of this with a wage strike at the Putilov works raised the number of demonstrators on that day to a new 'high' of perhaps 240 000.

The decisive anti-Tsarist factor, however, was the armed forces. The major difference between the events of 1917 and those of 1905 lay in the attitude of the Petrograd garrison. The shooting of 40 demonstrators on 11th March broke the morale of many of the conscript soldiers, and regiment after regiment fraternised with, and then actively supported the strikers. Even the dreaded Cossack regiments refused to obey their officers. By the end of 12 March, at a cost of an estimated 1300 civilian and military lives, Petrograd was in the hands of a revolution without recognised leaders. 'Not one party', wrote the socialist observer N. N. Sukhanov, 'was preparing for the great overturn'.

In the task of filling the power vacuum in Petrograd the liberal members of the Duma had the incalculable advantage of being on the spot. Their attitude, however, was highly ambiguous. They half obeyed the Tsar's order to disperse, by transforming themselves into a Provisional Committee (12th March) and most of those members who supported M. V. Rodzianko's advice to Nicholas to abdicate did so only in the hope of salvaging something of the monarchy by crowning a more popular, constitutional Tsar. That these men ended as the Provisional Government of a republic was largely due to the indecision and fatalism of the Tsar himself.

Having originally dismissed the Duma's pleas for last-ditch reforms as 'some nonsense from that fatty Rodzianko', the Tsar toyed with the idea of military assault upon his own capital. He was dissuaded by the pleas of his generals, notably Brusilov and Ruzsky, who wanted constitutional reform. However, he was unable to the last to compromise his own autocracy, and agreed to abdicate (15th March). The following day his brother, the Grand Duke Michael, refused the crown, leaving Russia a republic after 304 years of Romanov rule. P. Dukes remarks that 'like a good old soldier, the monarchy did not die but rather faded away'. L. Trotsky naturally put a more positive stress upon the role of a limited body of revolutionaries. 'The revolution was carried out upon the initiative and by the strength of one city, constituting approximately one seventy-fifth of the population of the country. . . . The whole country was placed before a *fait accompli*'.

(d) The Provisional Government and the Soviet

The new republic was in the hands of two powers tolerating, but scarcely supporting each other. The Provisional Committee of the Duma formed itself into a Provisional Government (15th March) containing the most notable Kadet and Octobrist leaders. E. E. Lvov was its first premier, with P. N. Miliukov as foreign minister and A. I. Guchkov as minister of the interior. Its rival for influence was the Petrograd Soviet, formed on 12th March, after the model of 1905, by the spontaneous action of workers and soldiers. It was at first an unwieldy body of up to 3000 members, not dominated by any party, but by individuals of various persuasions. Of its leading orators, A. F. Kerensky was a 'Trudovik' Duma member, while N. S. Chkeidze and M. I. Skobelev were Mensheviks.

Lenin was later to accuse the Soviet of a 'voluntary surrender of state power to the bourgeoisie and its Provisional Government'. Such a charge is not strictly fair in that, while the Duma politicians took on the responsibility of government, the support of workers and of soldiers left the Soviet with most of the practical power. Such was its control over post, railway and telegraph services in Petrograd that virtually nothing could be done without its consent. Guchkov himself wrote that 'the Provisional Government possesses no real power and its orders are executed only as this is permitted by the Soviet of Workers' and Soldiers' Deputies.' The Soviet's 'Order Number One' (14th March), moreover, decreed the establishment of soldiers' councils in each regiment of the armed forces, thus extending its influence to the military sector. From May 1917, the Soviet participated more directly in government when six Mensheviks and Trudoviks, including Skobelev (Minister of Labour) and Kerensky (Minister of War), became ministers in the Provisional Government. From July, Kerensky actually led that Government as premier, but failed to bridge the gap of mistrust that separated the bourgeois body from that of the Petrograd workers.

Why was this dual power tolerated? The Provisional Government, of course, had little choice in the matter, but the motives of the Soviet members are more complex. Partly, they tolerated bourgeois leaders because they had none of their own in March, most party activists being in prison, or in exile. Partly, the preponderance of peasant soldiers' representatives, nearly two-thirds of the original Soviet's membership, exercised a relatively moderate influence upon that body. It is also important to note, as J. Carmichael stresses, that Marxists had been taught to expect a bourgeois revolution before its proletarian successor, and thus felt ideologically bound to allow the government formed by the bourgeoisie to run its short course.

(e) The Provisional Government: Search for a Policy

The first steps towards a policy that would be acceptable to both bodies were easily agreed. On its first day in office the Provisional Government decreed an eight point programme that included a complete amnesty for all political prisoners, complete political and religious freedom, and the promise of elections to a Constituent Assembly. Poland's right to independence was at last recognised (30th March) and capital punishment was abolished, even in the armed forces.

Thereafter, the problems of policy became more thorny. Two major tasks confronted the government, the more pressing of which was perhaps that of satisfying the peasants' age old demand for land. Although the government quickly recognised their right to the great landed estates, an official policy of partition was impossible to implement without inviting mutiny and desertion by peasant soldiers 'trapped' at the front while their local estates were distributed among their neighbours. The peasants, however, were unwilling to wait, and thus disorder spread in the countryside as they took the law into their own hands. The government received nearly 700 complaints about illegal attacks upon landed property in June 1917, and over 1100 in July. It was the turn of the peasant now, in L. A. Owen's phrase, to pose as 'the Autocrat of Russia'.

Clearly, a solution to the land problem depended upon a solution to the second problem, that of the World War in which Russia was engaged. The

revolution raised the question of what war aims she should now pursue. The unanimous conviction of the Provisional Government was that the war should be pursued to a victorious conclusion. Miliukov, for one, saw no reason to abandon the original aims of annexations in eastern Europe and in the Turkish Empire, but was in this respect so far out of touch with popular opinion that he was forced to resign (15th May). The attitude of the Soviet was not for immediate peace either, for such a peace might merely put them at the mercy of monarchist Germany. Instead, they rejected the 'policy of annexations' and refused 'to serve as an instrument of conquest and violence in the hands of kings, landowners and bankers'. Compromising between popular pressure and the need to honour obligations to Russia's allies, the Provisional Government accepted (8th April) the prime war aim of 'the establishment of a stable peace on the basis of the self determination of nations'.

The collapse of the war effort, nevertheless, was the first major failure of the new government. Its July offensive in Galicia, aimed at proving the government's worth to allies and Russians alike, ended in the retreat of demoralised and under equipped forces over a large area. In the same month came demands for the autonomy of the Ukraine, to which some ministers seemed ready to agree, while the left wing 'July Rising' led by Bolshevik sympathisers from the Kronstadt naval base further illustrated the precariousness of the government's position. In September, the threat came from the Right. General L. G. Kornilov, appointed by the government to head the armed forces, marched on Petrograd. His primary aim was probably to oust the Soviet which he saw as undermining military discipline, but his actions and pronouncements were such that he could be seen as attempting to impose a counter revolutionary regime. His failure, largely due to the refusal of troops to obey his orders, left the prestige of the government at a new low ebb, and strengthened the hand of the Bolshevik extremists in the Soviet.

The attitudes of historians to the events of June–September 1917 are, of course, deeply influenced by political sympathies that have not yet cooled. The role of the Bolshevik Party in the July Rising has been played down by Soviet writers who portray the events as spontaneous, while many western commentators follow the line of D. Shub, who sees the events as a seriously planned 'coup' from which the Bolshevik leaders retreated at the last moment due to loss of nerve. The truth of the Kornilov incident has been equally difficult to unravel. Most Soviet sources, and some non-Soviet writers such as L. I. Strakhovsky, assert that

Kerensky was using Kornilov (who in Trotsky's phrase had 'the heart of a lion, but the brains of a lamb') for his own anti-Soviet ends. The charge has never been proven, and has been strenuously denied in Kerensky's own writings, with the more recent support of western authorities such as A. Ascher and W. E. Mosse.

(f) Lenin and the Bolsheviks

The major turning point in the destiny of the revolution was the arrival in Petrograd (16th April) of V. I. Lenin, leader of the Bolshevik 'wing' of the Social Democratic Labour Party, and the architect of its strategy (see Chapter 9, section **f**). The Bolsheviks in Russia were, he found, in a sad state. They numbered only 26 000 members, were in a minority in the Petrograd Soviet, and were severely divided on the issue of co-operation with the Provisional Government. On the other hand, they had so far 'kept their hands clean' by avoiding identification with the policies of the new government. The entry of other socialists such as Chernov, Chkeidze and Kerensky into office in the government was shortly to compromise their factions considerably by identification with the administration's failures. The fact that Lenin and his comrades had had their passage from exile in Switzerland arranged for them by the German government was of ambiguous value. It naturally laid the Bolsheviks open to the charge of being German agents. Although Lenin was, of course, serving Germany's purpose by further disruption of the Russian war effort, the charge has not been taken seriously by historians in its literal sense. On the other hand, the allegation that the Bolsheviks subsequently received large sums of German money to further their cause has better foundation. Soviet historians naturally follow the contemporary lead in denouncing what Trotsky called 'the most gigantic slander in world history'. Others, however, have found the case more convincing, and D. Shub for example has produced evidence of transactions which, if genuine, would have given the Bolsheviks a very substantial economic advantage over their revolutionary rivals in Russia.

The programme that Lenin pronounced upon his arrival, and published in *Pravda* in the so-called *April Theses*, was a complete rejection of the co-operation between the Soviet and the Provisional Government that was even advocated by a number of Bolsheviks. The ten points included an appeal for an immediate end to the war, for total withdrawal of support from the government, for the socialisation of the economy, and for the transfer of all state power to the Soviets. Thus Lenin's arrival

marked, in the words of the Bolshevik F. Raskolnikov, 'a Rubicon between the tactics of yesterday and today'.

The slogan 'All power to the Soviets' was not necessarily an immediate demand, for the Bolsheviks were far from controlling those bodies. What was immediate was the need for Lenin to impose his will upon his own party, and the need for constant propaganda to win the support of those alienated by the delays and failures of the Provisional Government. To this propaganda, Lenin himself contributed *The State and Revolution* in which he set forth in the Russian context the Marxist doctrine of the need completely to dismember the bourgeois state before a proletarian society could be constructed. This form of persuasion, which was not actually published until 1918, was of course less effective than the simple slogans ('End the War', or 'Bread, Peace, Land') aimed at less sophisticated political thinkers. 'If the peasants had not read Lenin', Trotsky observed. 'Lenin had clearly read the thoughts of the peasants'.

Meanwhile the Bolsheviks in general accepted Lenin's policy of opposition to and separatism from the Provisional Government. At the First Congress of Soviets in June, where only 10% of the representatives of 305 Soviets were Bolshevik, Lenin unsuccessfully advocated a break with the government. In July, complicity in the Petrograd rising led to an open attack upon the Bolsheviks, and a government attempt to arrest such leaders as Lenin, G. E. Zinoviev and L. B. Kamenev. That Bolshevik support grew in these months was the result of both negative and positive factors. Among the negative factors were the collapse of the government's military offensive, the reaction of Petrograd workers to the Kornilov 'coup', and the suspicion that Kerensky might be willing to abandon Petrograd to the advancing Germans. More positive was the Bolshevik promise to tackle the questions of land and of peace, and the growing support for the party among Petrograd factory Soviets. By August the party had 200 000 members, produced 41 different newspapers, and had recruited a striking force of 10 000 'Red Guards' in the factories, whose workers were often, in Lenin's words, 'more Bolshevik than the Bolsheviks'. When the Petrograd Soviet was re-elected in September, the Bolsheviks held a majority of seats for the first time, a process repeated in Moscow and in other major centres.

(g) The Bolshevik Seizure of Power

The circumstances under which the Provisional

Government lost power during the 'second revolution' of November 1917 were in direct contrast to the circumstances that had brought them to power. True, substantial social and economic problems persisted. Industrial production was badly disrupted. Some plants closed, causing unemployment, and inflation quickly cancelled out any benefit that the workers may have gained in terms of higher wages. The army, meanwhile, came closer to disintegration, demoralised by failure and by Bolshevik propaganda. 'The soldiers', recalled N. Sukhanov, 'flowed through the countryside from the rear and the front, recalling a great migration of peoples'. An estimated two million desertions took place in the course of 1917.

The events of November, however, owed little to spontaneous discontent, and almost everything to the deliberate actions of a tightly-knit group of revolutionary leaders. By late September, Lenin had decided that the circumstances were right for the Bolsheviks to bid for power. The decision had nothing to do with the feelings of the masses. 'We cannot be guided by the mood of the masses', he wrote at the time, 'that is changeable and unaccountable. . . . The masses have given their confidence to the Bolsheviks and ask from them not words, but deeds'. It took over a month for him to convince the party, however, and even then such notable members as Zinoviev and Kamenev stood out against him. His arguments in favour of an immediate insurrection were based not only upon the fear of a 'second Kornilov affair', or of a surrender of Petrograd to the Germans, but especially upon the hopeful signs of unrest in the German forces. This encouraged him to hope for international working class support for a Communist 'coup'. It was also essential to have practical control before the meeting of the next Congress of Soviets, which might be more difficult still to convince of the merits of such an adventure.

The weapon for insurrection also presented itself with the formation (26th October) of the Military Revolutionary Committee by the Soviet, pledged to protect Petrograd against the Germans. With 48 Bolsheviks among its 66 members, it was capable too of being turned against other enemies. The 'revolution' of 7th–8th November (24th–25th October by the existing Julian calender; hence the more familiar title of 'October Revolution') was, in reality, an extremely skilful military 'coup d'état' directed predominantly by Trotsky. Key positions such as railway stations, telephone exchanges, banks and post offices were seized by 'Red Guards' with a remarkable lack of opposition from their opponents. The body assembled at the Tauride Palace to discuss the formation of a Constituent Assembly was dismissed, and late on the 8th the half-hearted defence of the Winter Palace, now the headquarters of the Provisional Government, was overcome. The second Congress of Soviets, meeting that same day in Petrograd, now had 390 Bolshevik representatives, only too eager to accept Lenin's *fait accompli*. For Kerensky, there was no immediate alternative to flight, while the Mensheviks and the SRs, with only 80 and 180 seats respectively in the Congress, had little choice but to accept Trotsky's famous dismissal: 'You have played out your role. Go where you belong: to the dust heap of history'.

What judgement should be made on the Provisional Government that thus fell after eight months in office, and on the reasons why it was the Bolsheviks that supplanted them? The programme and theory of the government were admirable as the most liberal constitution that the continent had yet seen had been created out of Europe's strictest autocracy. 1917, however, was a time for action on pressing problems, not for theory, and 'although noble in intent', as A. Mazour has written, 'the programme was ill defined and poorly enforced'. Kerensky, in his memoirs, lays most of the blame for this upon those who 'betrayed' the government, most notably Kornilov and his supporters. Others, such as D. Treadgold, are inclined to blame Kerensky himself, for whom 'oratory became a substitute for action'.

As for the Bolsheviks, the official Soviet explanation of their triumph lays great stress upon the party's mastery of Marxist theory, which made it 'a revolutionary party of the proletariat, a party free from opportunism . . . and revolutionary in its attitude towards the bourgeoisie and its state power'. To most western commentators it has been difficult to give this credit to the party as a whole. E. H. Carr represents the view of many in writing that 'the triumph of the party seemed almost exclusively due to Lenin's consistent success in stamping his personality upon it and leading his often reluctant colleagues in his train'.

(h) The Foundation of the Soviet State

Lenin's first speech to the Congress of Soviets consisted of the simple statement, 'We shall now proceed to construct the socialist order'. As D. Mitchell has pointed out, however, the business of ruling Russia was not so simple. 'The Bolsheviks had not captured a Ship of State, they had boarded a derelict'.

The priority of the first Soviet government was, therefore, the extension and consolidation of Bolshevik power. In early November, the authority of the administration elected by the Congress extended little beyond Petrograd. V. I. Lenin was Chairman of the Council of People's Commissars, A. I. Rykov Commissar for the Interior, and L. D. Trotsky Commissar for Foreign Affairs. In some cases, as in Moscow, Kiev, Kazan and Smolensk, Bolsheviks had to overcome stern armed resistance. November, nevertheless, saw 15 main provincial towns fall into their hands, followed by 13 in December and further 15 in January 1918. Within the territory thus secured the main constitutional opposition to the Bolsheviks came from the election of the long awaited Constituent Assembly, which gathered in Petrograd with 380 SR representatives as against only 168 Bolsheviks. Lenin, however, was in no mood for constitutional games, and the body was dispersed by force after less than two days. It was, declared Lenin, 'a complete and frank liquidation of the idea of democracy by the idea of dictatorship'.

The Marxist concept of the 'dictatorship of the proletariat' (see Chapter 1, section **k**) also necessitated the formation of two armed forces to destroy the remnants of aristocratic and bourgeois power. A secret police force known as the 'Extraordinary Commission' (but generally known as the CHEKA, from its Russian initials) was formed, in contrast to the leniency of the Provisional Government, in December 1917. Its aim was quite openly proclaimed as the combating of 'counter revolution and sabotage' by means of terror. 'The CHEKA', claimed one of its leaders, 'does not judge, it strikes'. Its chief was F. Dzerzhinsky, a dedicated Polish Bolshevik, but contemporary evidence clearly indicates the role played by Lenin himself in enforcing the policy of terror. In July 1918 he urged that 'the energy and mass nature of the terror must be encouraged' and, a month later, called for it to be extended even 'to execute and exterminate hundreds of prostitutes, drunken soldiers, former officers, etc'. The Imperial family, under arrest at Ekaterinburg, were the most famous victims (July 1918). The official figure for executions in 1918 is 6300, but this must be regarded as a conservative estimate. The use of revolutionary terror has been widely justified from a partisan political point of view. A. Ulam on the other hand has condemned it as an excessively doctrinaire move that ultimately proved counter productive. 'Far from being a regrettable necessity, the extent of the Bolshevik Terror was one of the factors that made their victory in the Civil War more difficult'.

On a more regular basis, the Bolshevik regime, having undermined and dispersed an army upon which it could not depend, now set about the formation of an army of its own. The Red Army was first formed in January 1918, open to all 'class conscious' workers of eighteen years of age or more. The bourgeoisie was banned from membership, but 50 000 former Tsarist officers were retained to train the new force. To oversee them and the force as a whole, political commissars were attached to each unit, responsible for indoctrination and for ensuring that the army remained under Bolshevik control. To ensure reliable discipline, the reforms made since March 1917 were systematically cancelled. The powers of the regimental councils were curtailed, the practice of electing officers was abolished, and the death penalty for deserters was reintroduced. By August 1919 the Red Army numbered 300 000, and by January 1920 it boasted over 5 000 000 members, under the supreme command of L. D. Trotsky.

Meanwhile, the constitution of the state took shape. A series of decrees in February attacked the Church, separating it from the state and banning religious teaching in schools. Another series, between April and June, nationalised banks, mineral resources, industrial concerns and foreign trade, and made the inheritance of property illegal. A formal constitution became law on 10th July 1918. The state was given the name of the Russian Soviet Federated Socialist Republic (RSFSR). It proclaimed itself a classless society, with freedom of worship, no private ownership of property, and based upon the economic principle of 'He who does not work, neither shall he eat'. The electoral system was based upon the unit of the village and city soviets, culminating in the All-Russian Congress of Soviets, the supreme authority in the state. The suffrage was universal, with the exception of former members or agents of the Tsarist government, those who profited from others' labour, those with unearned income, priests, lunatics and criminals.

(i) Soviet policy: Brest–Litovsk and War Communism

In the first days of Soviet power, as their earlier propaganda had obliged them to do, the Bolsheviks produced a 'Decree on Peace' and a 'Decree on Land'. The former called upon all participants in the war to begin immediate peace negotiations, while the latter abolished all landed proprietorship, but encouraged the peasantry to continue the process of carving up the great estates themselves. The actual achievement of such ideals was not, however, such an easy matter.

The new regime formally opened peace negotiations with the Central Powers at Brest-Litovsk in late November, confident in the expectation that the Bolshevik 'coup' would trigger a general European revolution, thus ending the war in any case. When, by early 1918, this had not materialised, and the impatient Germans had pushed deeper into Russian territory, Lenin was eventually able to convince his party that a separate peace was necessary, even at the harshest price. The Treaty of Brest-Litovsk was concluded on 3rd March 1918. From a patriotic point of view, its terms were disastrous. Georgia, the Ukraine and Finland became independent, while, Estonia, Latvia, Lithuania and Poland came formally under German occupation. This meant that, of her pre-war resources, Russia lost 26% of her population, 32% of her arable land, 33% of her manufacturing industry, and 75% of her coal and iron resources. A variety of motives have been suggested to explain and to justify the Bolshevik sacrifice. B. Dmytryshyn is quick to point out that most of the lost territory was not in any case under Bolshevik control, while D. Shub has cited evidence that the Bolsheviks were still in receipt of German funds, and could not risk the exposure of that fact. Above all, the most pressing motive must be recognised as that stated by Lenin himself in 1920: 'we gained a little time, and sacrificed a great deal of space for it'.

The succession of events of which the Treaty of Brest-Litovsk was part soon demonstrated the inadequacy of edicts such as the 'Decree on Land' and the 'Decree on Workers' Control'. The piecemeal division of land by peasant committees and the direction of factories by workers' committees proved wholly unsatisfactory as Russia was stripped of huge agricultural and industrial resources while faced simultaneously with the likelihood of a large scale civil conflict. It was soon evident to Lenin that the intended slow progress towards nationalisation of the 'commanding heights' of the economy, such as fuel, transport and banking, was insufficient. The formation of a Supreme Economic Council (Vesenkha) in December 1917 can be seen as a first step towards the policy established by the 'Decree on Nationalisation' (June 1918), and now known as War Communism.

The main features of War Communism were to be strict centralised state control of all forms of economic production and distribution, the virtual outlawing of all private trade, and the near destruction of the money economy by the printing of vast quantities of banknotes. In January 1918 there was 27 billion roubles worth of notes in circulation, backed by only 1.3 million roubles in gold. Three years later the figures were 1168 billion and 0.07 million.

In the countryside the main manifestation of the new policy was the large scale requisitioning of grain in order to feed the towns. In June 1918 the government formed 'Committees of Poor Peasants' to control the richer peasants, or 'Kulaks', but soon had to resort to direct confiscation of supplies by military force. All food distribution was centralised into the hands of a Commissariat of Food and a Commissariat of Agriculture. These divided the population into four categories, the food ration of each depending upon its contribution to the economy. The highest category had roughly one seventh of the calories received by German workers at the height of the allied blockade, while the lowest had rations insufficient to prevent starvation. The disillusioned peasantry turned, as before, to disorder. Two hundred and forty-nine rural risings were recorded in 1918, and 99 in Bolshevik controlled territory the following year. In the towns the main feature was the wholesale nationalisation, which extended by December 1920 to all enterprises employing ten people or more, a total of about 37 000 enterprises. Accompanying this came the forced mobilisation of unemployed labour to serve essential strategic industries, the outlawing of strikes, and a large scale desertion of the towns in favour of the countryside where food seemed more easily available. Petrograd, with a population of 2.5 million in 1917, boasted only 0.6 million inhabitants three years later.

(j) The Civil War: The Whites

By early 1918, the events of the 'second revolution' had alienated large sections of the Russian population from the Bolshevik government, but without uniting the aims or motives of these opponents. Whereas the 'Reds' fought in the Civil War for very specific aims and Marxist–Leninist principles, albeit with a strong degree of compulsion at times, the 'Whites' formed no such homogeneous grouping. Broadly, the 'White' forces consisted of three main component parts; those attached to other revolutionary groups, hostile to, or rejected by the Bolsheviks; former officers of the Imperial army, usually resentful of the 'betrayal' at Brest-Litovsk; and nationalist groups seeking independence for their particular minority.

The administration that established itself in the Don region of Southern Russia early in 1918 illustrates this diversity. Its military leaders were Tsarist generals, such as A. I. Denikin, L. G. Kornilov and P. N. Krasnov, who had also held office under the Provisional Government and now claimed to fight 'until the Provisional Government

MAP 11   THE CIVIL WAR IN EUROPEAN RUSSIA 1918–21

MURMANSK
BRITISH

ARCHANGELSK
BRITISH
MILLER

FINNS

In Siberia:
BRITISH
AMERICANS
JAPANESE

PERM
CZECHS

PETROGRAD
YUDENICH

UFA

KAZAN

KOLCHAK

ESTONIANS
LATVIANS
LITHUANIANS

MOSCOW

SAMARA

ORAL

DENIKIN

POLES

KIEV

DON
COSSACKS

UKRAINIANS

FRENCH

ODESSA

BRITISH
BAKU

GEORGIANS

ARMENIANS

WRANGEL

KEY

—··—··—   RUSSIAN BOUNDARIES BEFORE BREST–LITOVSK

[FINNS]   NATIONALIST OR INTERVENTIONIST GROUPS OPPOSING
            BOLSHEVIKS

———————   FURTHEST ADVANCE OF ANTI BOLSHEVIK FORCES

YUDENICH   WHITE COMMANDERS OPPOSING BOLSHEVIKS

and order in the nation are restored'. The politicians who joined them, however, were a mixture of Kadets such as P. N. Miliukov, and the SRs such as V. M. Chernov. Other SRs concentrated their forces further north, along the Volga, where they established an administration based at Samara (June 1918). In the Don region, the nationalist element was represented by the Cossacks, whose local ambitions clashed fundamentally with such 'White' slogans as Alexeyev's 'Russia One and Indivisible'.

Already other independent republics had declared themselves, in the Ukraine and in Transcaucasia (November 1917) and in Finland (December 1917). With the collapse of the German war effort in the next year, Estonia, Latvia, Lithuania and Poland all pressed their own claims to independence. The Polish claim was especially complicated for, although both the Soviet government and the victorious allies assembled at Versailles recognised Poland's right to independence, it was not clear whether her eastern borders were to be fixed by the so-called Curzon Line, drawn by the allies around the main areas of Polish speaking population, or by the historic borders of the old Polish kingdom as it had existed before partition in 1772. The difference was considerable, and involved a Polish claim to much of Lithuania, the Ukraine and Byelorussia. The dispute raised tensions between Poland and her new Communist neighbour that were to culminate in war in 1920.

The great catalyst of civil conflict in Russia was the successful revolt of the Czechoslovak Legion. The Legion had been formed in 1917 from Czechs and Slovaks resident in Russia and from prisoners of war, and was dedicated to the fight for independence from the crumbling Austro-Hungarian Empire. After Brest-Litovsk it had placed itself at the disposal of the French, and began a long journey via Siberia and the USA to continue the fight on the western front. In May 1918, a confrontation with Hungarian prisoners at Cheliabinsk led local Soviet officials to attempt to disarm the Legion. Instead they themselves were seized, and when Trotsky ordered military retaliation, the well organised and well equipped Czechs proceeded to seize and occupy all the main towns along the Trans-Siberian railway in the regions of Cheliabinsk, Omsk and Irkutsk. Although the Legion had no specifically anti-Bolshevik aims, its resounding success against Soviet forces provided enormous encouragement for the 'White' cause. By June representatives of the SRs had combined with the Czechs to form a third centre of 'White' administration at Omsk.

(k) The Civil War: Allied Intervention

The motives that led Russia's former allies to intervene in her internal conflicts have been the subject of considerable controversy. The standard interpretation among Soviet historians has reflected the contemporary view expressed by Lenin. Concerned, as J. Bradley has stated, 'with political tactics and success rather than with historical analysis and truth', Lenin portrayed the allied missions as essentially concerned with the suppression of communism. Some sympathetic western commentators have accepted this view. E. H. Carr, for example, describes the allies declared intention of re-opening the World War in the east against Germany as 'a pretext', and speaks of 'the fear and hatred felt by the western governments for the revolutionary regime'. J. Bradley, on the other hand, points to a number of factors that contradict this interpretation. A plan by Marshal Foch for a co-ordinated anti-Bolshevik campaign (January 1919) was rejected by allied leaders at Versailles, and in February 1919, the Americans in particular were proposing negotiations between the 'Reds' and the 'Whites' at Prinkipo Island, near Istanbul. It is also true that Britain and the USA had come close, before Brest-Litovsk, to aiding the Red Army, at Trotsky's request, against the Germans.

Thus there is much evidence that, in its early stages, allied intervention in the Russian conflict must be viewed in the context of the World War. The separate peace made by the Bolsheviks at Brest-Litovsk released huge German forces and resources for use on the western front. It thus became imperative for the western allies to attempt to restart the war in the east or, at least, to prevent Germany from making free use of the Russian, Polish and Ukranian raw materials available to them under the terms of Brest-Litovsk. Furthermore, German success in the east seemed to threaten large concentrations of allied stores supplied earlier to Russia. It is no coincidence that British forces landed first at Murmansk (March 1918), and that British and Japanese forces also concentrated on the distant port of Vladivostok (April 1918) which was far from the Bolshevik 'heartland', but where substantial allied stores were housed. Britain's seizure of Baku, on the Caspian Sea, was also motivated by the desire to keep the local oil resources out of hostile hands.

The end of the World War did not strip the allies of their reasons for intervention. The French, for instance, continued to have a pressing motive in the form of the vast sum of 16 billion francs invested in Tsarist Russia between 1887 and 1917, in enterprises now nationalised without compensation by the Soviet State. Britain and the USA had lesser investments to defend, and Japan, after the hard won gains of 1904–05, found the prospect opening up of substantial territorial gains in eastern Asia at Russia's expense. That they failed to realise these ambitions was due primarily to the presence of American troops in Siberia, probably more concerned with checking Japanese annexations in the east than with combating Bolshevism further west. Nevertheless, by late 1918, as many as 70 000 Japanese troops had occupied Vladivostok, northern Sakhalin, and much of Siberia east of Lake Baikal. Only when the Third Communist International ('Comintern') began in mid-1919 to proclaim the 'overthrow of capitalism, the establishment of the dictatorship of the proletariat and of the International Soviet Republic' did intervention become overtly ideological, and by then allied efforts in Russia had become negligible.

The scale and scope of the intervention were in any case strictly limited. At the end of 1918 there were only about 15 000 troops in northern Russia and these were affected by acute war-weariness after four years of European conflict. The USA sent only about 6000 to the Siberian theatre of war, and then with strictly limited objectives. More important were the substantial sums of money and the large quantities of military stores made available to the 'Whites'. Britain and France both allocated the equivalent of 20 million pounds for this purpose, although R. Luckett has stressed that corruption and inefficiency often meant that relatively little of this aid actually reached the front.

Even more limited was the success achieved by the intervention. The number of troops involved was small, and only in the north, around Murmansk and Archangelsk, did foreign troops really predominate in the 'White' war effort. Aims and motives were all too often at odds, as in Siberia, where the political views of Admiral Kolchak's regime were of such an undemocratic nature that the Americans refused all co-operation with him, and the French could only co-operate with the greatest difficulty. In all, the intervention probably gave far greater assistance to the Soviet authorities who could now draw a veil over domestic disagreements by claiming that they were defending Russia against foreign imperialism. At the conclusion of British involvement, Lord Curzon described it as 'a totally discredited affair and a complete failure'. The same judgement could probably extend to the allied intervention as a whole.

(l) The Civil War: The Campaigns

In the summer of 1918, the combination of forces ranged against the Soviet government seemed overwhelming. To the south, the Volunteer Army under A. I. Denikin, with French and British support, had cleared the Don and Kuban regions of Bolsheviks, and threatened the food and fuel supplies to Soviet controlled areas. To the east, the varied forces occupying Siberia and controlling the Trans-Siberian Railway had at length agreed (September 1918) to the formation of a coalition government, the Directory. To the north, 'White' forces under the Tsarist general E. K. Miller, with British support, controlled the ports of Murmansk and Archangelsk. To the west lay the Germans and a variety of hostile nationalists. Even in central Russia, less organised opposition, especially amongst the peasants and the SRs, led to risings in some 25 towns and cities. There was a rash of assassination attempts that killed M. S. Uritsky, chief of the Petrograd CHEKA, and the German ambassador, and saw Lenin himself seriously wounded.

The first concern of the Soviet government was to tackle the opposition forces centred upon Omsk. Their eventual success on this front owed as much to the short-comings of their opponents as to the efforts of the Red Army itself. Certainly Trotsky's organisation and the military leadership of such commanders as M. V. Frunze were important factors. The Whites, nevertheless, were disunited and quarrelsome. The internal dispute that brought down the Directory (November 1918) resulted in the elevation of A. V. Kolchak, formerly Admiral of the Black Sea Fleet, and a political conservative, to the title of 'Supreme Ruler of All the Russias'. His failure to establish satisfactory understandings with the SRs, the Czechs, or even with some of the allies, contributed to a steady retreat after reaching Perm and Ufa in March 1919. By June, Kolchak's force had been pushed back beyond the Urals, and Soviet forces captured Omsk itself in November. Kolchak suffered the indignity of being handed over to the Red Army by the commander of the local French forces, and was shot (7th February 1920).

In the south and west, similarly, White forces under Denikin and under N. N. Yudenich initially made rapid progress. In two months (August–October 1919) Denikin's forces advanced from Odessa to within 250 miles of Moscow, while Yudenich came within 30 miles of Petrograd in mid-October. In both cases, retreat was as rapid as the advance had been. Stubborn defence, organised by Trotsky, thwarted Yudenich before a counter attack drove him back into Estonia. Between October and December, Bolshevik forces pushed Denikin back until most of the Ukraine had been recaptured from the Whites. From April 1920, only the force in the Crimea under P. N. Wrangel stood between the Red Army and victory. Wrangel was probably the most able of the White commanders exercising strong discipline over his men and with an intelligent agrarian policy to appeal to the peasantry, but he had come on the scene too late. His army won some notable victories while the Red Army was distracted by the Poles, but in mid-November 1920 he, too, with 135 000 soldiers and civilians evacuated the Crimea, the last stronghold of the White cause.

The defeat of the Whites, like that of the Russians in Korea in 1905, was not so surprising as it might at first have seemed. In the south and in the east their armies fought on very wide fronts, often in areas with poor communications and far from major centres of industry. The aims of the military leaders were sometimes at odds with each other, and often at odds with those of the intervening allies. With the exception of Wrangel, none of the military leaders could sympathise with or even understand the hopes and wishes of the peasantry and the national minorities, and became hopelessly identified with the restoration of the landlords and the old regime. The political leaders, meanwhile, who identified themselves with the White cause made almost no impact on policy or on international relations at all. 'They failed to recognise', wrote A. Mazour, 'that they were coping with a great revolution and not an isolated plot'. Methods of operation, as well as aims, were defective. 'I think most of us were secretly in sympathy with the Bolsheviks', wrote a British officer serving with Kolchak's forces, 'after our experiences with the corruption and cowardice of the other side'. The communists, meanwhile, had the benefits of excellent leadership and coherent policy and propaganda. L. Fischer's description of Lenin as 'a one man political–military staff' is inaccurate only insofar as it undervalues the dynamic role played by Trotsky, who made his main contribution to the revolution by his brilliant direction of the war on most of the major fronts.

One anti-Bolshevik force, however, remained undefeated. In April 1920 Poland and Russia had finally resorted to arms to settle the question of the boundaries of the new Polish state (see section **j**). This was far more of a national war than an affair of 'Red' versus 'White' and it, too, brought varying fortunes for the participants. In May 1920 the Poles under Marshal Pilsudski were in Kiev. Two months later the Red Army was within reach of Warsaw. Finally, by August 1920, with moral and material aid from the allies, Pilsudski's counter attack had driven the Red Army almost back to Minsk. The Treaty of Riga (18th March 1921), like Brest-Litovsk, was accepted by Lenin because 'a bad peace seemed to me cheaper than the prolongation of war'. It settled Russia's western borders until 1939 by granting to Poland Galicia and parts of Byelorussia, and by confirming the independence of Estonia, Latvia and Lithuania.

(m) The New Economic Policy

By 1921, social and economic life in Russia had been brought to their knees by an unparalleled series of disasters. The rigours and miscalculations of War Communism combined with the damage caused by the civil war. The number of deaths directly caused by the war has been estimated by R. Conquest as 'no more than a million', but the economic collapse that accompanied war had far more drastic effects. Urban industry declined disastrously. The Russian coal industry in 1921 produced 27% of its pre-war output, a large proportion compared with steel (5.5%), pig iron (2.5%) or copper (1.7%). Inflation had effectively destroyed the rouble, and some 90% of all wages were paid in kind. This was compounded by disastrous famines. Especially serious in the Ukraine and in other parts of southern Russia, the famines probably caused some 5 million deaths. Taking into account associated diseases, the casualty figure for the years between 1917–21 may be as high as 9 million.

Probably as serious from Lenin's point of view was the evidence of political discontent from within the communists' own ranks. The most spectacular example of widespread refusal to tolerate any further the deprivations of wartime came with the revolt at the Kronstadt naval base (February/March 1921), originally a major source of Bolshevik support. The demands of the sailors included freedom of the press, elections by secret ballot, and the release of political prisoners. The rising was brutally suppressed like similar, lesser peasant risings, but it could not be ignored. 'It illuminated reality', stated Lenin, 'like a flash of lightning', and perhaps contributed more than any other single factor to the decision of the government to pursue a New Economic Policy (NEP). Lenin made it very clear that the NEP was another in the series of temporary compromises that communist theory had to make when confronted with adverse circumstances. 'Life has exposed our error', he told the Party. 'There was a need of a series of transitional stages to communism'. NEP was thus a sort of economic Brest-Litovsk and, like that treaty, had to be imposed against fierce criticism from communist purists.

The major features of the new policy were concerned with agriculture. Above all, the government decided to abandon the requisitioning of grain surpluses from peasants and to demand instead a tax paid in food, set at a lower level. Thus the peasant retained some of his surplus which he was now permitted to sell for private profit, and was thus likely to be encouraged to grow more. Although the land remained the property of the state, the peasant was free to hire labour, buy machinery, and so forth. On a secondary level, in industry, freedom of enterprise was restored in a host of small factories and workshops, while the state continued to control the 'dominating heights' of the economy, such as heavy industry, transport and foreign trade. In 1922, 88.5% of all enterprises were privately run, although the smallness of their scale is indicated by the fact that they employed only 12.4% of the work force. The third main feature of the NEP was the restoration of a stable soviet currency. In October 1922 the reconstituted State Bank introduced the reconstituted rouble, backed by precious metals and foreign currency. Early in 1923, savings banks were re-opened.

The path of the NEP was not always smooth. Bad harvests and drought in 1921 nullified most of the benefits to be gained by the peasants, and in 1923 they had to contend with the so-called 'scissors crisis' when declining food prices and the soaring price of industrial goods minimised their gain from free enterprise. The government had to defend itself, right up to the launching of collectivisation in 1928, against the charge that it was defending this 'state capitalism' as a preparation for a return to private capitalism.

Indeed, in 1923 it was true that 75% of Russian retail trade was being handled by the 'Nepmen', the private traders who flourished under the NEP. Thus one of the by-products of the NEP was the strengthening of party discipline to eliminate internal friction. Over 30% of the party's membership was expelled between 1921–24, a precedent that was to have grave implications in the 1930s. Eventually the aims of the policy, the restoration of production and of economic stability, were largely achieved.

Table 12.1 shows that, in most major industries, production figures by 1926 had nearly regained their pre-war levels.

Lenin, however, did not live to see this recovery completed. A series of strokes that began in May 1922 finally killed him in January 1924. His organisational genius and unique blend of determination and flexibility played a greater role than any other factor in the creation of soviet power. Public reaction to his death, represented by the millions who filed, and still file past his embalmed body in its Mausoleum in Moscow's Red Square, showed that the communists now had a saint to venerate, like the Orthodox Church before them. On the other hand, by his insistence upon party power and party discipline, and by his initiation of the policy of terror as a political weapon, he was also the creator of those unacceptable elements in Russian communism that were to dominate its history in the 1930s.

(n) A Cultural Revolution?

The period from 1917 to the end of the NEP expedient was one of unparalleled experiment in Russian culture. Although a large number of artists and writers left the country at the outbreak of revolution, those that remained revelled in the brief freedom from the Tsarist censorship. They accepted

	1913	1920	1921	1922	1923	1924	1925	1926
Factory production (million new roubles)	10 251	1410	2004	2619	4005	4660	7739	11 083
Coal (million tons)	29.0	8.7	8.9	9.5	13.7	16.1	18.1	27.6
Electricity (million kWs)	1945	—	520	775	1146	1562	2925	3508
Steel (thousand tons)	4231	—	183	392	709	1140	2135	3141
Grain (million tons)	80.1	46.1	37.6	50.3	56.6	51.4	72.5	76.8

From A. Nove, *An Economic History of the USSR*, Pelican Books.

Table 12.1

the Soviet doctrine that they, too, were now freer agents, released from the exploitation of bourgeois and aristocratic patrons.

Immediately, however, the revolution raised a new controversy which was eventually resolved by the pressure of the state. Those artists who more keenly supported the new regime, calling themselves 'Constructivists', claimed that art should now serve an active social and political purpose. One of the greatest literary figures of the immediate post revolutionary period was the poet V. V. Mayakovsky, of whom T. Frankel has written 'his every effort was to unify art and life, to enlist art in the service of society'. His work in this period included slogans for political campaigns and posters as well as pro-Bolshevik poetry. Theatre, too, rallied to the new atmosphere of revolution and liberation. The great producer and designer V. E. Meyerhold teamed up with Mayakovsky and the artist K. Malevich to produce the pageant *Mystery Bouffe* (1918) which showed the proletariat defeating its exploiters. In 1920, N. Yevreinov celebrated the third anniversary of the Revolution with a re-enactment of the storming of the Winter Palace, employing a cast of 8000, and founding the tradition of May Day parades in Red Square. The group that formed itself around the journal *Proletarian Culture* (*Proletkult*) also enjoyed brief success between 1918–22 in their efforts to found new literary and cultural forms by workers and for workers.

A more lasting achievement, however, was made by that section of writers and artists in Russia characterised by Trotsky as the 'Fellow Travellers'. In general, these men and women were not communists, but were broadly in sympathy with the ideals of the revolution, and found much fascinating human material in the great events of the revolution and the civil war. Among the leading writers of this tendency were D. A. Furmanov (*Chapaev*), V. V. Ivanov (*Armoured Train No. 14–69*), and M. A. Sholokhov (*Quiet Flows the Don*). Another, E. I. Zamyatin, produced a political satire *We* (1920) in which he showed a regimented socialist society whose inhabitants were identified only by numbers; the forerunner both of Huxley's *Brave New World* and of Orwell's *1984*. In poetry, S. A. Yesenin rivalled Mayakovsky's popularity with work that was highly personal, almost mystical.

'The cinema', Lenin declared in 1921, 'is for us the most important of all the arts'. Naturally, therefore, the new art form found itself constrained at first to serve largely propagandistic purposes. Nevertheless, in the greater freedom of the NEP period, the Soviet cinema produced more than its fair share of the art's early classics, notable examples being S. M. Eisenshtein's *Battleship Potemkin*, A. P. Dovzhenko's *The Land*, and V. I. Pudovkin's *Mother*, which was a film version of Gorky's novel. Music produced only one immediate heir to the great Russian traditions in D. D. Shostakovich. He produced his first symphony in 1926, and the subtitles given to the next two, the *October* and the *May Day* symphonies (1927 and 1929) demonstrated the tight rope that he, too, had to walk between artistic expression and official approval.

The growth of collectivist policies under Stalin (see Chapter 13, section **f**), however, also extended to the arts. Earlier means of artistic control, employed during the civil war, such as the state's monopoly over publishing through the State Publishing Organisation ('Gosizdat') were renewed, and new ones introduced, such as the concentration of artists and writers into official unions. A policy aimed at constraining artists and writers strictly to serve the purposes of government policy saw the collapse of the best elements in the revivified Russian culture. The artists M. Chagall and V. Kandinsky had already chosen in the early twenties to conduct their experiments in surrealist painting in western Europe. Zamyatin followed them in 1931. In 1930 Mayakovsky, who had recently attacked the bureaucracy and narrow-mindedness of Soviet leadership in *The Bedbug* (1929) and *The Bathhouse* (1930), committed suicide, as Yesenin had done five years earlier. Even Gorky, the greatest of the Soviet writers, had protested against the 'disgraceful attitude' of the Soviet leaders 'toward the freedoms of speech and of person'. His own death in 1935 was surrounded by suspicious circumstances and rumours of poison.

The period between 1928–53 was to be the age of 'Socialist Realism' in art, under which Soviet artists and writers were to concentrate upon subjects conducive to the building of a socialist society. Such subjects were defined by B. Dmytryshyn as including 'contented cows, dedicated milkmaids, devoted pig breeders, vigilant party members, and young lovers arguing by the light of the moon about problems of industrial production'.

(o) Historiography

In a sense it is false to talk of a historiography of the Russian Revolution, for no series of events in modern history has been written about with so much partisan enthusiasm and with so little detachment. Political views continue to play a large part in determining historical views on this subject. Much of the work produced in the west may be broadly classified as belonging to the 'liberal school' of interpretation. That is to say that it sees Russia's political history since the mid 19th century, through the Emancipation, the formation of the Zemstvos, and then of the Duma, as a promising progress towards liberal institutions. This progress was then shattered by Russia's disastrous involvement in the First World War, which provided the extremists with their opportunity. Propounded by disappointed Russian liberals, such as P. N. Miliukov (*History of the Second Russian Revolution*, 1921) and M. Florinski (*The End of the Russian Empire*, 1931), this line is, with modifications, that taken up more recently by L. Schapiro (*The Origin of Communist Autocracy*, 1955) and by the English authority H. Seton-Watson (*The Russian Empire, 1801–1917*, 1967).

The 'liberal' school, of course, is in competition primarily with the Marxist interpretation. This rejects the possibility of Russian society settling into a liberal 'middle way', when the laws of economic development and of the class struggle dictate the eventual inevitability of proletarian revolution. In the standard Soviet version, therefore (*History of the Communist Party of the Soviet Union*, 1960), the revolution is explained in terms of the Party's correct and courageous application of Marxist principle, with Lenin playing the vital role of keeping the party to the correct line. A variation of this view has been put forward by socialist commentators unsympathetic to Bolshevism, who claim that Lenin's actions in and after 1917 were premature, and that the revolution was rushed into a socialist phase before a mature bourgeois phase had been achieved, in direct defiance of Marxist principles. This view has been argued by exiled Mensheviks such as V. M. Chernov (*The Great Russian Revolution*, 1936) and T. Dan (*The Origins of Bolshevism*, 1964). Trotsky, with an intimate knowledge of the events, saw the revolution (*History of the Russian Revolution*, 1936) as a series of corrections of course by Lenin, each in keeping with Marxist principles, but carried out in the face of excessively doctrine Marxism on the part of the Party. Indeed, few western writers have questioned the greatness of Lenin. Most, however, have tempered their praise with an awareness of his role in the formation of subsequent communist dictatorship. This approach can be seen in the work of D. Shub (*Lenin: a Biography*, 1948) and A. Ulam (*Lenin and the Bolsheviks*, 1965).

In the interpretation of the Civil War contemporary propaganda is again hard to dispel. The two main Soviet works (*The Civil War 1918–21*, 1929–30, and *A History of the Civil War in the USSR*, 1957–60) predominantly repeat Lenin's interpretations and especially repeat the stress he laid upon the imperialistic nature of the allied intervention. Theirs is a civil war without Trotsky and without numerous other leaders subsequently purged from the Party. In the 1930s, of course, official writers such as S. E. Rabinovich exaggerated and glorified the wartime role of Stalin almost to the exclusion of other commanders. The White viewpoint, equally self-justificatory, has been provided by the memoirs of various surviving leaders such as Denikin (*The White Army*, 1930) and Wrangel (*Always with Honour*, 1957). Only relatively recently has documentary evidence become available to make possible such accounts as those of D. J. Footman (*Civil War in Russia*, 1961) and J. Bradley (*Civil War in Russia*, 1975) which are more balanced in their accounts of Reds and Whites, and tend to diminish the scale and significance of the allied intervention. Among English writings on the revolution as a whole, however, the field continues to be dominated by the massive work of E. H. Carr (*The Bolshevik Revolution*, 1950–54).

Progress Paragraphs

Answer the following in about 150 words

In what ways did government conduct of the war renew political tensions in Russia?

Section **(a)**

What special hardships befell the Russian population as a result of the war?   Section **(b)**

What were the short-term causes of the March Revolution?   Sections **(a, b & c)**

Why was it the Duma politicians who filled the power vacuum left by the abdication of the Tsar?

Sections **(c & d)**

How and why did the Provisional Government and the Petrograd Soviet co-exist between March and November?   Section **(d)**

How successful was the Provisional Government in solving problems (a) of peasant demands for land, (b) of continuing the war effort?   Section **(e)**

In what ways did the arrival of Lenin in Petrograd change the policies and aims of the Bolshevik Party?
Section (**f**)

What factors persuaded the Bolsheviks to seize power in November 1917?   Section (**g**)

What measures did the Bolsheviks take between November 1917 and July 1918 to 'construct the socialist order'?   Section (**h**)

Why, and at what cost, did the Soviet government agree to the Treaty of Brest-Litovsk?
Section (**i**)

What was War Communism, and why was it introduced?   Section (**i**)

What factions made up the 'White' opposition to Bolshevism?   Section (**j**)

Why, and with what effect, did the wartime allies intervene in the Russian Civil War?
Section (**k**)

Why did the Whites lose the civil war?
Sections (**j** & **l**)

Why, and with what effect, did Lenin introduce the New Economic Policy?   Section (**m**)

What were the main effects of the revolution upon the cultural life of Russia?   Section (**n**)

13
Russia Without Lenin, 1924-41

(a) The Succession to Lenin

The paralytic stroke that removed Lenin from active politics (26th May 1922), and which finally killed him (21st January 1924), destroyed the undisputed source of leadership in Russia. 'The impact of Lenin's illness on the Bolshevik leadership can hardly be exaggerated', wrote I. Deutscher. 'The whole constellation ceased, almost at once, to shine with the reflected light of its master mind . . .'. There could be no adequate replacement for Lenin's genius, and the shortcomings of the various candidates had already been aptly summarized in his 'Testament', composed during his last illness. L. D. Trotsky, for all his great intellectual qualities, was guilty of a 'too far-reaching self-confidence and a disposition to be too much attracted by the purely administrative side of affairs'. G. E. Zinoviev and L. B. Kamenev had shown a disturbing hesitancy in the months before the seizure of power in October 1917, and N. I. Bukharin's grasp of theoretical Marxism was regarded as faulty. J. V. Stalin, lastly, offset his great practical abilities with an excessive roughness, impatience and lack of caution and of consideration for his colleagues.

The main feature of the struggle for the succession during the last weeks of Lenin's life was the isolation of Trotsky from the other candidates. In part this was due to his personal arrogance, and in part to the fact that he never quite lived down the lateness of his conversion to Bolshevism. His achievements at the head of the Red Army, furthermore, were offset by the widespread fear that this military leader might turn against the Russian Revolution as General Bonaparte had turned against its counterpart in France. The failure of his campaign for greater democracy in the upper echelons of the party, between October 1923 and January 1924, stressed the narrowness of his support, and his absence through illness from Lenin's funeral badly undermined his credibility as successor in the popular view. On the other hand, the coalition that opposed him, a triumvirate of Zinoviev, Kamenev and Stalin, exerted immense influence. Zinoviev dominated the party organisation in Petrograd (renamed Leningrad in honour of the dead leader in 1924), and was head of the Comintern. Kamenev exerted similar influence in Moscow. Stalin, while occupying the relatively unglamorous post of Commissar for Nationalities, had spent the past years insinuating himself into an impregnable position in the party bureaucracy. Not only was he, like Zinoviev and Kamenev, a member of the party's inner cabinet (Politburo), but was also prominent in the executive bureau (Orgburo) and in the Commissariat of Workers' and Peasants' Inspection, which was responsible for the elimination of economic inefficiency and corruption. Above all, since 1922, he had held the post of General Secretary of the party's Central Committee. This enabled him to exert substantial control over party membership. In terms of the range of political weapons available to him, no other Bolshevik was the rival of Stalin.

(b) Joseph Stalin

The future dictator of the Soviet Union was not Russian by birth, but from Georgia, the province in the Caucasus mountains. She was absorbed by Russia in the 19th century, but had a long, independent culture and history of her own. He was born as Joseph Djugashvili, in the small town of Gori (21st January 1879), the son of a shoemaker and the grandson of serfs. He was thus one of the few true proletarians in the leading ranks of the Bolsheviks. The most significant features in his early life were the harshness and occasional brutality of his early upbringing and the unusual fact that the ambition and devotion of his mother secured for him the rare privilege of eleven years of education (1888–99). Of the former, a boyhood friend later recalled that 'undeserved and frightful beatings made the boy as grim and heartless as the father'. As to the latter, it was significant that the theological seminary in Tbilisi that Djugashvili attended from 1894 until his expulsion five years later, had a history of student unrest and political disloyalty. 'I became a Marxist', its most famous student was later to reminisce, 'because of my social position . . . but also . . . because of the harsh intolerance and Jesuitical discipline that crushed me so mercilessly at the seminary'.

Djugashvili's political stance seems in fact to have developed steadily between 1898, when he joined a social democratic underground group in Tbilisi, and 1904 at which point he clearly identified himself with the Bolshevik faction of the communists. His subsequent career, unlike those of the intellectual Marxists in exile, followed a practical path of strike organisation, agitation, and armed robberies for the benefit of party funds, interspersed with periods of imprisonment and Siberian exile. Sheltering behind revolutionary pseudonyms, he used the name 'Koba' from 1902, and signed himself 'Stalin' ('Man of Steel') for the first time in 1913. From such a childhood and early career can be traced the leading traits of his character; distrust, alertness, dissimulation, endurance and, above all, an intense sense of class hatred that was never for Stalin merely a matter of Marxist theory. 'In Djugashvili', I. Deutscher has written, 'class hatred was not his second nature—it was his first'.

Stalin's reputation in local revolutionary circles expanded to a wider stage between 1905, when he travelled abroad for the first time to attend a Bolshevik conference in Finland, and 1912 when he was appointed by Lenin to the Central Committee of the party. Lenin's choice in this, A. Ulam has suggested, was determined by his desire to leaven the assembly of theoretical Marxists with a rougher breed of active revolutionary, more truly a 'man from the people'. In exile in Siberia at the beginning of 1917, Stalin quickly assumed a number of unobtrusive but influential roles in the revolution. He was editor of the Bolshevik journal 'Pravda', leader of the Petrograd Soviet, and temporary director of Bolshevik strategy until the return of the exiles from abroad. Thus he was, if not a familiar public figure, a man of substantial internal political influence, as the events of the next decade were to demonstrate.

(c) The Consolidation of Power

In 1924 it was widely assumed that the death of Lenin would result in a collective leadership of the Soviet Union. The reasons for the steady decline of that form of political authority, and the emergence of Stalin's undisputed leadership are complex.

Neither the Stalinist explanation, that he offered the only correct analysis of the future course of the Soviet Union, nor Trotsky's bitter reflection that Stalin rode to power on a wave of war-weariness and reaction, is fully satisfactory. In large part the phenomenon must be explained by Stalin's consummate political skill, and by his shrewd handling of the weapons at his disposal. Foremost among these was the party machinery over which he exercised such control, and which he could use to assign supporters of his opponents to remote posts, while admitting to high office those upon whose support he could rely. The promotion to the Central Committee of L. M. Kaganovich (1924) and A. I. Mikoyan (1923) and to the Politburo of V. M. Molotov and M. I. Kalinin (1926) marked the emergence of a new school of 'Stalinist' Bolsheviks. The appointment of S. M. Kirov as head of the party in Leningrad (1926), formerly Zinoviev's stronghold, and of K. E. Voroshilov in Trotsky's former military office (1925), marked the extension of this tactic to key political areas. At this crucial point in the struggle, the Stalinists also enjoyed the support of the 'Rightist' wing of the party, headed by N. I. Bukharin, M. Tomsky and A. I. Rykov.

Secondly, Stalin showed great skill, both in the creation of a cult of 'Leninism', and in the formation of his own image as 'the best, the staunchest, the truest comrade in arms of Lenin'. His stage-management of Lenin's funeral was, in I. Deutscher's words, 'calculated to stir the mind of a primitive, semi-oriental people into a mood of exaltation for the new Leninist cult'. The effect was then compounded by Stalin's foundation of the Lenin Institute (January 1924), and by a series of carefully calculated lectures on 'The Foundations of Leninism' delivered at the Communist University in Moscow (April 1924). Given his late conversion to Bolshevism, Trotsky was at a particular disadvantage in terms of Leninist orthodoxy. Stalin's third great advantage lay in the blameless orthodoxy and simplicity of his former private and political life. His image as the uncomplicated and dedicated peasant, married (1918) to the daughter of an old Bolshevik, contrasted favourably with those of his more sophisticated rivals. As Commissar for Nationalities, moreover, he could claim the successful merging of the national republics into the Union of Soviet Socialist Republics (1922) as one of the greatest achievements of the revolution to date.

Lastly, Stalin benefited from a string of tactical errors by his most prominent opponents. Trotsky's attack upon such elements of Lenin's policy as the New Economic Policy, in his essays 'Lessons of

October' (1924), was a serious miscalculation in the prevailing atmosphere of 'Lenin worship'. The refusal of both Trotsky and Zinoviev to publish Lenin's 'Testament', with its damaging verdict upon Stalin, saved Stalin from the most dangerous threat to his position. Indeed R. A. Medvedev has stressed that in the crucial early stages of the contest, 'Trotsky considered it beneath his dignity to engage actively in a struggle for power'. The belated union of Trotsky, Zinoviev and Kamenev (1926) in the so-called 'United Opposition' to Stalin, was unlikely to increase their credibility in the light of the mutual hostility of a few months earlier.

Indeed, from 1926 onwards, the position of this opposition became more and more hopeless. Isolated and outnumbered, Zinoviev lost his leadership of the Communist International, and all three leaders of the 'United Opposition' were voted from the Politburo by the end of the year. In October 1927, Trotsky and Zinoviev lost their places on the Central Committee, and were expelled altogether from the party a month later, followed by 75 of their supporters. In January 1928, Trotsky began a period of internal exile in Soviet Asia, and was taking the first steps upon a road to banishment that was only to end with his murder in Mexico in August 1940.

(d) Socialism in One Country

The leadership struggle of the late 1920s was certainly in part a clash of powerful personalities. It was also, however, a genuine dispute about the future path of Soviet communism. The candidates, for instance, clashed over the issue of democratic decision making within the party, over the pace at which the economic backwardness of the Soviet Union should be tackled, and over the roles allowed to independent merchants, manufacturers and peasants under the New Economic Policy. Above all, the dispute centred around two alternative views of the future of Bolshevism.

Trotsky and his followers held fast to the theory of the 'Permanency of Revolution'. The revolution in Russia, they claimed, could not be regarded as an end in itself, but only as a vital link in the wider process of European and even world revolution. By its example, and with the continued assistance of the Soviet Union, the revolution would eventually lead to the general destruction of capitalism. Only then could the future of the Soviet system be assured. It was a view closely in accord with the expectations of Lenin right up to his death, but offered a prospect of further struggle that was a bleak one after recent Russian sufferings, and discouraging in the light of recent socialist failures in Germany, Hungary and elsewhere. Although Stalin seems to have subscribed to this view until late 1924, he thereafter formulated an alternative, usually known as the theory of 'Socialism in One Country'. By this he stressed that, despite the Soviet Union's present state of ruin and exhaustion, her immense resources would be sufficient for the construction of a stable socialist society, without external aid. Within two years, 'Trotskyism' was being officially branded as 'a lack of faith in the strength and capabilities of the Russian revolution, and as a negation and repudiation of Lenin's theory of the proletarian revolution'. While Stalin left open the possibility of future Soviet participation in a wider revolution, he made consolidation of the Russian achievement an unalterable priority.

By the last two years of the decade Stalin's thesis had won complete dominance over that of Trotsky as the official view of the Soviet government. Some writers have explained this as the natural consequence of Stalin's political victory within the party. It is now, however, more usual to reverse this reasoning and to see Stalin's political supremacy as the result rather than the cause of the wide acceptance of the theory of 'Socialism in One Country'. The American researcher S. F. Cohen has argued strongly that Stalin's rise depended in large part upon his acceptance by the 'influentials' within the party, and that a majority of them supported him 'less because of his bureaucratic power than because they preferred his leadership and policies. To some extent their choice doubtless expressed their identification with the General Secretary as a forceful practical politician'. Why was the principle so widely accepted? Firstly, whatever its unorthodoxy in pure Leninist terms, it was hard to dispute the practical logic of Stalin's approach in the light of contemporary European developments. Secondly, as I. Deutscher has stressed, it offered the prospect of a future that lay wholly in Soviet hands, and involved little dependence upon forces beyond Soviet control. 'It gave them', he stated, 'the soothing theoretical conviction that, barring war, nothing could shake their mastery over Russia'. Lastly, it offered to the Soviet people as a whole the prospect of relief from the enormous suffering and perpetual struggle of the decade between 1914–24. There was perhaps some justification, after all, in Trotsky's later conviction that the unreadiness of the people to undertake a further era of struggle contributed largely to his defeat in the leadership contest.

(e) The Government of Stalin's Russia

The theoretical heart of Soviet political organisation in 1928 was the constitution introduced in 1924. Confirming the merger of the component national units of the old Empire into the Union of Soviet Socialist Republics (USSR), it left each republic with the theoretical right to secede from the Union if its 'non-Russian working class' so wished, although in reality any such wish would invariably be treated as the counter revolutionary agitation of nationalist, bourgeois elements. At the head of the constitutional structure stood the All-Union Congress of Soviets, with its executive Central Committee, and its elite Presidium, in which all major decisions were made. Below stretched a hierarchy of Soviets at republican, provincial, district and local levels. The right to vote belonged to all adults, except those deprived of citizenship. It extended, however, only to the election of local soviet members who, in turn, selected members for each higher soviet. The system thus constituted a complex filter to test the orthodoxy of each aspiring politician.

The articles of the constitution veiled the three main driving forces of Soviet politics. The first of these was the Communist Party of the Soviet Union (Bolshevik), membership of which was an essential qualification for every political aspirant. It was a body that had undergone substantial changes since the heady days of 1917. A series of purges had by 1922 rid the party of any serious ideological diversity, eliminating the last traces of Menshevik or Social Revolutionary opinion. In the later 1920s two more changes took place. The party grew steadily in size, from 1.3 million members in early 1928 to 3.5 million in January 1933, and it also changed its composition. It became less a party of the workers, who constituted 48.6% of membership in 1930, and more a party of the new, Soviet-educated intelligentsia.

The constitution also failed to indicate the growing importance in the state of the government agencies for internal security. The State Political Administration (GPU or OGPU) was the successor of the CHEKA, the post revolutionary secret police. It was headed by the CHEKA'S founder, F. Dzerzhinsky, until his death in 1926. Its duties were vaguely defined but, as L. Schapiro has noted, 'in practice, it never lacked the power to do whatever it was required to do by the party'. In July 1934, the OGPU was merged into a wider body, the People's Commissariat of Internal Affairs (NKVD). Under the leadership of H. G. Yagoda (1934–36), N. I. Yezhov (1936–38) and L. P. Beria (1938–53), the NKVD was the main tool for the internal policy of the Soviet state. It supervised many of the most important and dangerous projects of the Five Year Plans, including the Pechora railway and the White Sea Ship Canal, played a central role in the purging of the party, and controlled a labour force perhaps as large as ten million in the state's prison camps.

The third element in the practical government of the USSR, the army, was also brought under close party control by the end of the 1920s. Trotsky's hopes of a citizen militia, under direct proletarian control, were killed off by the necessities of the Civil War. Trotsky himself was replaced as Commissar for War by M. V. Frunze in 1925. A series of reforms in 1924–25 placed the political supervision of the army firmly in the hands of the party's Central Committee, and confirmed the system of dual command whereby the military commanders worked alongside Political Commissars who took precedence over them in all political decisions. By 1933, all senior commanders and 93% of divisional commanders were party members. The degree of authority enjoyed by the party was illustrated in October 1925 when Frunze was ordered by his political superiors to undergo a dangerous medical operation from which he died. The influence of the party's leaders was, of course, to be confirmed spectacularly during the political purges of the mid 1930s (see section **j**).

(f) The Planned Economy: Theory

The most dramatic policy decision of the Stalinist establishment was the abandonment of Lenin's New Economic Policy, with its elements of private enterprise, and of Bukharin's policy of 'the creep at a snail's pace' towards socialism. Apart from the obvious ideological hostility within the party to the NEP, it is also true that it had, by 1926, largely achieved its industrial purpose. The toleration of a degree of private economic activity had restored output in most major areas of the economy to pre-1914 levels, and the level of private trading outside agriculture dropped steadily from 42.5% of the total (1924–25) to 22.5% (1928). The alternative of rapid, forced industrial growth through centralised planning and control had been advanced by Trotsky, Kamenev and Zinoviev in the mid 1920s, but had been resisted by Stalin as too great a departure from Leninism. His change of view now involved a predictable break with his former 'rightist' allies within the party. Tomsky's leadership of the Soviet Trades Unions, Bukharin's post at the head of the Comintern, and Rykov's chairmanship of the Council of Commissars

(Sovnarkom), all passed to Stalinists in June 1929. From the public admission by the 'rightists' that their views were erroneous (November 1929) may be dated the beginning of Stalin's undisputed power in the USSR which was to last until his death in 1953.

Why did Stalin now change course so abruptly to embrace the policies of his conquered opponents? Although this has sometimes been seen as a cynical expression of his newfound political security, it is more likely that it was a pragmatic response to the risk of substantial food shortages resulting from the so-called 'Procurement Crisis' of 1927–28. Despite the decline in private industrial trade, the independent peasant continued in 1928 to cultivate 97.3% of the farmland of the Soviet Union. The difficulty in procuring from them sufficient grain supplies for the industrial towns arose in part from the inefficiency of many small, private farms, but also from the peasants' reluctance to deliver precious grain at the artificially low prices offered by the state. The result was a shortfall of two million tons of grain in 1927, potentially disastrous in view of the role played by urban hunger in the events of 1917. Under such circumstances, the policy of 'Socialism in One Country' risked falling at the first hurdle thanks, it was felt, to the greed of the richer peasants, the 'Kulaks'.

The introduction of the first Five Year Plan, to run from 1928–33, committed the USSR to the path of planned and centralised economic policy. A second Five Year Plan followed between 1933–37, while a third (1937–42) was disrupted by the outbreak of war. The overall aim of these plans was to match and to overhaul in the shortest possible time the economies of the advanced capitalist states. 'We are fifty or a hundred years behind the advanced countries', Stalin declared in 1931. 'We must make good this distance in ten years. Either we do it, or we shall be crushed'. In view of the fate that befell the USSR in 1941, the prediction proved uncannily accurate. The main tool of the government in these tasks was to be the Central Planning Committee (Gosplan). In industry, the planned economy meant an expansion of output, an improvement of communications, the discovery and exploitation of new resources, all to predetermined production quotas. In agriculture it meant, not only the forced grain procurements of 1928–29, but a fundamental change thereafter in the agrarian life of the USSR. The way out of Russia's agrarian backwardness, Stalin declared to the party in December 1927, 'is to turn the small and scattered peasant farms into large united farms based upon cultivation of the land in common'. Although it was still stressed that the party should

proceed with caution, and should frown upon coercion, the statement spelled the end of the brief decade of liberation for the Russian peasant, and marked the beginning of the era of collectivisation.

(g) The Planned Economy: Industry

The task of the first Five Year Plan, commenced in 1928, was nothing less than to lay the foundations for the transformation of Soviet society into an industrial force comparable to the United States. Its main emphasis, therefore, fell upon the production of energy and of construction materials, upon coal, oil, electricity, iron, steel and cement. The rate of increase envisaged, averaging out at an annual increase of 20%, was hugely unrealistic, and the declaration (31st December 1932) that the plan had been completed in four years, was wholly a propaganda exercise. Detractors might point to significant shortfalls, as in steel production (where only 62% of the quota was completed), in iron (59%), in heavy metallurgy (67.7%) and in consumer goods (73.5%). A more friendly observer might still conclude that the achievement of 1928–32 was substantial. Machinery output increased four times, oil production doubled, and electrical output in 1932 was 250% of the 1928 figure. Seventeen new blast furnaces were completed and twenty others modernised. Fifteen new rolling mills came into operation with twelve others reconstructed. The plan also produced some notable 'show pieces', such as the new centres of iron and steel production at Magnitogorsk in the Urals, and Kuznetsk in central Siberia. Also there was the building of the Dnieprostroi Dam, the biggest in Europe. Stalin's own criticism of the Dnieprostroi project in the mid-1920s, that it was like a poor peasant spending money on a gramophone instead of buying another cow, remained true, but he was now far more appreciative of the propaganda value of such achievements.

The second Five Year Plan, which ran its full course from 1933–37, avoided some of the mistakes of the first. Its average annual target was a rather more reasonable 14% increase, and by virtue of a more experienced and better trained workforce it avoided at least some of the waste and poor quality of 1928–32. Priority continued to be given to heavy industry, but greater emphasis was now placed upon newer metallurgical resources, such as lead, zinc, nickel and tin. The second plan also concentrated more upon the improvement of Soviet communications. Railways were largely double tracked, and this sphere of activity produced many of the 'showpieces' of this plan, such as the

Moscow–Volga, and Volga–Don Canals and, most famous of all, the palatial Moscow Metro. Before the end of the second Five Year Plan, a new circumstance began to interfere with the projections of the planners as the deteriorating international situation called for more and more state investment to be diverted to rearmament. Whereas this had consumed only 3.4% of total expenditure in 1933, the figure had swollen to 16.1% in 1936, and in 1940, the third year of the third plan, accounted for 32.6% of government investment.

Nevertheless, there can be little doubt that the pre-war Five Year Plans achieved their primary aims. They may indeed be criticised for lack of realism, for administrative inefficiency, and for the human cost that they entailed (see section **i**). Yet the goal of making the Soviet Union an industrial power, and able to withstand conflict with a major capitalist state was, within the short space of ten years, undoubtedly achieved. Table 13.1 illustrates the case.

(h) The Planned Economy: Agriculture

No branch of the Soviet economy was as sensationally affected by the policy of centralisation as was agriculture. In the short term, the 'evils' of small scale farming, inadequate equipment, and low proportions of the harvest reaching the market, were combated by rigorous and often brutal searches for and confiscation of grain stocks by local officials. In the longer term, under the aegis of the Five Year Plan, they were combated by the forceable collectivisation of peasant production. This was not so much a 'war against the peasant', as R. Medvedev has described it, as a 'war between the peasants'. The government's main weapon against the prosperous 'Kulaks', just under a million of the total peasantry, was the jealousy of the seven million 'Bedniaks', or poor peasants, those without livestock or modern implements of

any kind. With the aid of party officials, police and army, a class war was waged in the countryside between late 1928 and March 1930, involving the dispossession, deportation and often murder of those designated as Kulaks. By the latter date, it was announced that 58% of peasant households were 'collectivised', although the term meant little more than that the land, livestock and equipment of the Kulaks had been handed over for communal use by the Bedniaks. The middle peasants (Seredniaks) were not only scared into the collectives by the fate of the Kulaks, but left with no alternative form of livelihood.

Briefly, in 1930, even Stalin seems to have taken fright at the 'pandemonium' reigning in rural Russia and, by blaming local officials for overzealousness, and authorising withdrawal from collectives, produced the sharp drop indicated in Table 13.2. In reality, however, policy remained unchanged. The ruthless elimination of the private farmer continued until, in 1938, the Soviet Union boasted 242 000 collective farms. These farms subdivided into two basic types. The state farm (Sovkhoz) was entirely state property, on which

Year	Proportion of households collectivised (%)
December 1928	1.7
October 1929	4.1
March 1930	58.0
September 1930	21.0
1931	52.7
1932	61.5
1933	65.6
1934	71.4
1935	83.2
1936	90.5

Table 13.2

	1927	1932	(goal)	1937	(goal)
Electricity (million kWh)	505.0	1340.0	(2200.0)	3620.0	(3800.0)
Coal (million tons)	35.4	64.3	(75.0)	128.0	(152.5)
Oil (million tons)	11.7	21.4	(22.0)	28.5	(46.8)
Iron ore (million tons)	5.7	12.1	(19.0)	?	?
Pig iron (million tons)	3.3	6.2	(10.0)	14.5	(16.0)
Steel (million tons)	4.0	5.9	(10.4)	17.7	(17.0)
Labour force (millions)	11.3	22.8	(15.8)	26.9	(28.9)

Table 13.1

peasants worked for wages. The collective farm (Kolkhoz) was, on the other hand, a 'voluntary' co-operative on which land and equipment was collectively owned by the peasantry. Until 1958, no collective farm possessed its own heavy machinery, but were served instead by 'Machine Tractor Stations' whose state owned machinery and state controlled specialists were at the disposal of the peasantry. Each Kolkhoz was committed to deliver a substantial proportion of its produce to the state, while on a Sovkhoz, the produce was, in any case, state property.

It is certain that, as B. Dmytryshyn has written, 'the speed and ferocity with which the mass collectivisation was carried out benefited neither the state, nor the collective farms, nor the peasants'. Destruction by rebellious peasants, the loss of Kulak expertise, and the inexperience of many collective farm managers resulted in a sharp decline in many areas of production. Between 1928–34 the cattle population of the USSR declined from 66.8 million to 33.5 million, the number of sheep and goats fell from 114.6 million to 36.5 million, and the number of horses from 34 million to 16.5 million. Grain shortages, combined with continued forced procurements, led to rural famine. This was especially severe in the Ukraine and the northern Caucasus region, where successive census figures between 1933–38 suggest a death toll of around 5 million people. Only slowly, as a government confident of its victory showed more tolerance towards small-scale private enterprise among the peasantry, did livestock populations and rural living standards rise. Not until 1940 did figures for grain production match those of 1914. What gains there were from collectivisation in the short term were enjoyed by Soviet industry, which benefited from a flow of surplus peasant labour into more attractive factory occupations, and by industrial workers, who gained a reliable, if not always plentiful supply of cheap grain. A crucial part of the basis of Soviet industrial power was thus laid at the cost of the peasantry. Stalin himself would later privately compare this battle with the later struggle for survival against the Germans.

(i) The Planned Economy: Living Standards

Quite apart from the obvious deprivations suffered by much of the peasantry in the course of collectivisation, the Five Year Plans also involved considerable initial sacrifice on the part of many industrial workers. The initial stage of industrialisation rode roughshod over the individual

freedom of the Soviet worker. The government's more ambitious projects might involve the mobilisation of labour to remote areas, working with inadequate equipment and without facilities and comforts of their own,' closely supervised by NKVD 'shock brigades'. Unrealistic production quotas usually meant the neglect of safety precautions, and the ever-present risk of prosecution as a 'saboteur' or 'wrecker', if the targets were not met. The replacement of Tomsky by N. M. Shvernik as head of Soviet Trades Unions (June 1929) turned these bodies into virtual government departments unresponsive to the interests of the individual worker. Similarly, the worker found himself hedged in by a whole new body of Soviet law. Absenteeism from work without due cause became (November 1932) an offence punishable by loss of job, food rations and housing. To prevent the drift of labour from areas of greatest need, the internal passport system of Tsarist days was reintroduced (December 1932). It must be extremely doubtful whether the gradual and irregular introduction of such facilities as subsidised canteen meals and free medical attention fully offset these losses.

Tremendous difficulties confront the historian who tries to make precise judgements about industrial standards of living in this period. The task, writes A. Nove, 'is rendered almost impossible not only by the existence of rationing, price differences and shortages, but also of queues, decline in quality, and neglect of consumer requirements'. These can be little doubt, however, that the first years of collectivisation were accompanied by a wave of rises in food prices. In 1933 alone, official Soviet figures showed rises of 80% in the cost of bread and of eggs, and of 55% in the cost of butter. Nove has been quite uncompromising in his description of the years 1928–33 as witnessing 'the most precipitous decline in living standards known in recorded history'. Although the subsequent years saw a steady improvement in levels of wages and of consumer goods production, western and Soviet research has agreed that 'real' wages in 1937 were not more than 85% of the 1928 level, an indication of how low the level must have been in 1933. The worsening of the international situation after 1938, furthermore, once more limited the production of consumer goods. It caused a tightening of government control over the workforce, and ended the temporary trend towards better living standards. Renewed labour legislation in 1940 lengthened the working week from five days to six, and made absenteeism, which came to include lateness for work by more than twenty minutes, a criminal offence punishable now by imprisonment.

For a select few, the industrial drive could bring recognition and rewards. The abandonment in 1931 of earlier attempts to level wages paved the way for the privileged treatment of the most skilled and productive workers, which culminated in the 'Stakhanovite' movement. This took its name from a Donbas miner, Alexei Stakhanov, who in September 1935 achieved the (probably contrived) feat of cutting fourteen times his quota of coal. Such workers stood to gain rewards in many forms, such as higher salaries, access to better housing, and to scarce consumer goods. For the average worker, however, the 'Stakhanovites' were the cause of greater government pressure for increased production. Thus government decrees of 1936, 1938 and 1939 all demanded the raising of shift production quotas by as much as 50%. In general, it was not until the late 1950s, when the scars of war had been partly erased, that the Soviet government ceased so completely to sacrifice the interests of the individual worker to those of the state.

(j) The Purges: Causes

Between 1934–38, having initiated an economic transformation of revolutionary proportions, Stalin set about the transformation of the Soviet communist party by a series of murderous and far-reaching purges. In seeking to establish his motives we must first realise that purges in themselves were relatively commonplace in Soviet government. In addition to the purges carried out during Lenin's lifetime, 116 000 members had been expelled from the party in April 1929 on charges of 'passivity', 'lack of discipline', or as 'alien elements'. They were followed by another 800 000 in 1933. The Five Year Plan had also brought 'show trials' in its wake, such as the so-called 'Shakhti' trial (1928), in which bourgeois mining specialists and foreign technicians had been accused of sabotage. It is with some justification, therefore, that Z. Brzezinski has referred to Soviet government between the wars as 'the permanent purge'. The 'Great Purge', like London's 'Great Plague', was an extreme example of a well-known phenomenon. It was striking in its extent, and also by virtue of the fact that its victims were not White Guards or Kulaks, but respected communists and comrades-in-arms of Lenin himself.

Nevertheless, Stalin's precise motivation is not easy to establish. The official contemporary claim that the party was infiltrated by 'Trotskyites', 'Zinovievites' and 'Bukharinites' who were all agents of international capitalism, can no longer be taken seriously, even in the USSR. Nor does the claim that Stalin sought scapegoats for domestic economic problems explain the eventual scale of the purges. It is true that there was a strong and growing element of opposition within the party to Stalin's ruthless and divisive policies, especially to the pace and consequences of collectivisation. As Trotsky wrote in March 1933, 'within the party and beyond the slogan "Down with Stalin" is heard more and more widely'. His political opponents still retained some influence. Bukharin for instance was now editor of *Isvestya*, and without doubt the emergence of S. M. Kirov, head of the party organisation in Leningrad, seemed to many to offer a capable and popular alternative to Stalin. The fact that five members of the ten-man Politburo in 1934 (Kirov, Kossyor, Kuibyshev, Ordzhonikidze and Rudzutak) died under various circumstances in the years of the purge, suggests that resistance to Stalin may even have been widespread in the top ranks of government. It is difficult to avoid the conclusion that N. S. Khrushchev was close to the truth when he stated in his famous 'Secret Speech' of 1956 that Stalin had commited his excesses to boost and guarantee his own security, the continuation of his supremacy, and the supremacy of his policies within the Soviet leadership.

(k) The Purges: Course

The course of the Great Purge may be conveniently divided into three stages. The first stage may be precisely dated from 1st December 1934, when the leader of the Leningrad administration, S. M. Kirov, was assassinated at his office. Whether or not Kirov died at Stalin's orders continues to puzzle historians. Official Soviet sources successively blamed the crime on foreign capitalists, on Soviet rightists, and on Trotskyites, while R. Conquest speaks for very many western writers in concluding that Stalin was directly responsible for the murder of a potential rival. I. Deutscher, on the other hand, suggests that Stalin may have been genuinely shocked by the event, but turned it to his own purposes much as the German Nazis had recently exploited the lucky stroke of the Reichstag fire. A feature of this first stage was that the senior ranks of the party remained untouched. The fourteen men executed for Kirov's murder were all minor figures and, although Kamenev and Zinoviev were imprisoned for 'opposition', they were not directly accused of the assassination. Nevertheless, the deaths at this time of Politburo member V. V. Kuibyshev (1935) and of the writer Maxim Gorky

(1936) have never been satisfactorily explained, and may mark the beginning of the elimination of those who opposed Stalin's chosen path. In retrospect, this early stage also saw the establishment of the machinery and personnel necessary for the succeeding waves of purges. By appointing A. A. Zhdanov in Kirov's place in Leningrad, by inserting N. S. Khrushchev at the head of the party in Moscow, and by subjugating the law courts to the influence of A. I. Vyshinsky as Chief Procurator, Stalin ensured reliable implementation of his orders in several vital areas of the administration.

The second stage was triggered in August 1936 by the arrest and execution of Kamenev, Zinoviev and fourteen others. They were charged with plotting terrorist activities, including the death of Kirov, on behalf of 'the Trotskyite-Zinovievite Counter-Revolutionary Bloc'. Their trials produced several features soon to become familiar, notably the confessions of the accused and the implication in those confessions of other prominent figures. Why did such men confess? The application of torture, and of threats to their families undoubtedly explains much. It has also been argued that many of the victims of the purges saw their deaths as a last service to a party to which they had dedicated their lives, and which they genuinely believed to be under attack. 'The loyalty of these men to the idea of "the party"', L. Schapiro has written, 'was in the last resort the main reason for Stalin's victory'. The same writer also stresses the number of accused who refused to confess, and who therefore met their fate under much more obscure circumstances.

Nevertheless, Stalin's control of events was not yet complete, as was demonstrated by the acquital (September 1936) of Bukharin and Rykov on charges arising out of the earlier trial of the 'Sixteen'. This acquital is often seen as the trigger of the third and greatest wave of purges. Among its first victims was Yagoda, head of the NKVD. One of the first tasks of his successor, Yezhov, was the preparation of renewed charges of treason and espionage against Bukharin and Rykov. The fact that the commander-in-chief of the Red Army, Marshal Tukhachevsky, and several other senior officers, were also tried and shot (June 1937) for plotting with Japan and Germany, indicated that the armed forces too were about to be 'cleansed'. The last great series of 'show trials' ran into 1938, involving the condemnation of 21 prominent Bolsheviks including Bukharin and Rykov. These, however, were merely the tip of the iceberg of suspicion and implication that involved the friends, families and subordinates of the accused. Suspicion reached into every area of Soviet life. No reliable figures as to the extent of the purge are possible, of course. It is extremely unlikely that the total number of deaths can be estimated in units less than hundreds of thousands, while the total population of the USSR's penal labour camps by 1940 has sometimes been set as high as ten million.

(l) The Purges: Results

When the great tide of political persecution receded in 1938, ending with the execution of Yezhov and other NKVD functionaries, two major changes in Soviet government were discernable as its results. Firstly, the political position of Stalin himself was absolutely unchallengeable. All possible sources of opposition, in the party, in the armed forces, among economic and political theorists, had been crushed. 'Every man in the Politburo', wrote L. Schapiro, 'was now a tried and proved follower of the leader, who could be relied upon to support him through every turn and twist of policy. . . . Below the Politburo nothing counted'. Secondly, the Soviet communist party, which had borne the brunt of the purges, was transformed. It was not just a matter of personnel, a substitution of Zhdanov, Khrushchev, Voroshilov and Molotov for Zinoviev, Kamenev, Bukharin and Rykov. Stalin had effectively destroyed the revolutionary generation of Russian communists. Of 139 Central Committee members in 1934, over 90 were shot. Of 1961 delegates to the 17th Party Congress in the same year, 1108 were arrested in the purges. Foreign communists living in Russia also suffered heavily, the Hungarian revolutionary leader Bela Kun figuring among the victims of the NKVD. Of Lenin's Politburo, only Stalin and Trotsky remained alive, the latter under sentence of death passed in his absence. Stalin knew, Deutscher has explained, 'that the older generation of revolutionaries would always look upon him as a falsifier of first truths, and usurper. He now appealed to the young generation which knew little or nothing about the pristine ideas of Bolshevism and was unwilling to be bothered about them'. A generation of officials, in short, replaced a generation of revolutionaries.

Apart from the human cost, the whole security of the Soviet Union was nearly undermined as the price of this transformation. The Red Army in particular paid a terrible price for arousing Stalin's mistrust. Three Marshals out of five, and thirteen army commanders out of fifteen died. Ninety per cent of all Soviet generals, 80% of all colonels, and an estimated 30 000 officers below the rank of colonel lost their posts and often their lives. The difficulties experienced in the 'Winter War' with Finland in 1939–40 may be traced directly to the loss of so much military expertise in the purges. The foreign relations of the Soviet Union were also bound to be adversely affected, for foreign powers were offered the alternatives of viewing the Soviet Union as a state riddled with treason, if the charges against purge victims were accurate, or as a power led by a madman if the charges were false. Lastly, the less tangible legacy of the purges may be traced today in the insularity and siege mentality natural in people led to believe that their society was under assault from capitalists, fascists, imperialists and renegade communists alike. This legacy also survived for years in 'a grotesque fear of initiative and responsibility in all grades of the administration' (I. Deutscher). This was a direct result of the personal peril that accompanied any position of responsibility during the years of Stalin's purges.

(m) The 1936 Constitution

'Stalin', Deutscher wrote, 'offered the people a mixed diet of terror and illusion'. Alongside the terror of the purges, indeed, he created the illusion of a true dawn of socialism by the formulation of a new Soviet constitution in 1936. The theoretical basis of the document was the assumption that victory over the Kulaks had ended the decade and a half of class struggle in Russia and that a truly socialist order had now been constructed.

By comparison with its predecessor, the 'Stalin Constitution' extended the jurisdiction of the central, federal government. Moscow now exercised control, through the All-Union ministries, over all important areas of administration, such as defence and foreign affairs, leaving to the constituent republics responsibility for such relatively minor matters as elementary education. The dominance of central government was further confirmed by Moscow's overall control of the budget, and by the pervasive influence of the party. The chief legislative body of the USSR continued to be the Supreme Soviet, whose Presidium continued to exercise all major executive functions of the state. Now, however, the Supreme Soviet was formally divided into two 'houses'. The Soviet of the Union contained one member for every 300 000 citizens, while the Soviet of Nationalities reflected the ethnic composition of the USSR, containing 25 members from each union republic, 11 from each lesser, or 'autonomous' republic, and 5 from each autonomous region. An important innovation since 1924 was that all soviets, to the highest level, were now directly elected. Elections were held every four years, by secret ballot, with citizens qualified to vote from the age of 18 (raised to 23 in 1945). As a further indication of the end of class warfare, clergymen, former Tsarist officials, and so on, now enjoyed full civil rights again. Among the rights now guaranteed to Soviet citizens were the freedoms of speech, of the press and of association, along with the rights to work, to rest and leisure, to education, and to maintenance in old age and in sickness. The constitution stated quite clearly, however, that these rights existed only if exercised 'in conformity with the interests of the working people and in order to strengthen the socialist system'. Similarly, because political parties were an expression of class interests, which no longer existed in the USSR, the constitution recognised only one legitimate party in Soviet government.

Western commentators have usually reacted harshly to the 'Stalin Constitution'. 'It bore much of the outward form of the US constitution', wrote J. N. Westwood, 'but in fact most of its provisions were either meaningless or misleading'. The constitution, concludes L. Schapiro, was 'worthless as a guarantee of individual rights'. Certainly the constitution invited such criticism by using and misapplying familiar liberal terminology. These liberal criticisms were of an illiberal constitution, which in reality, had several aims. Primarily, it sought to protect, not the rights of the individual, but the continuity of the Soviet socialist system. Secondly, it sought to impress foreign opinion at a time when democratic institutions in the west were under severe pressure from fascism, and in this purpose it achieved no mean success. Also, as A. Ulam has pointed out, the constitution should be seen as part of Stalin's desire to show that the USSR had emerged from her period of revolutionary buffetings. 'For him the constitution was a welcome proof that the USSR was becoming a "respectable" state and that the revolutionary mumbo-jumbo of its previous documents was being discarded'. In this respect, of course, the constitution went hand-in-hand with the purges which themselves were discarding so much of Bolshevism's revolutionary past. In these contexts, therefore, the 'Stalin Constitution' was less a fraud than a document of considerable significance, which continued to dictate the shape of Soviet political life until the drafting of its successor in 1977.

(n) Soviet Society: Religion, Education, the Family

In common with other totalitarian regimes, the

Soviet government in the two decades after the revolution grappled with the problems of deep-rooted 'reactionary' elements in the society it now dominated. Just as the 1930s saw the elimination of the first generation of Bolshevik revolutionaries, so it saw the abandonment of many of their initial ideas for Soviet society.

Soviet education, during A. V. Lunacharsky's tenure of office as Commissar for Education (1917–29), saw the rejection of many 'bourgeois' values. There was experimentation with new techniques that owed much to the ideas of the American educationalist J. Dewey. Project work widely replaced the instillation of traditionally 'useful' knowledge, and more 'democratic' ideas on discipline and on pupil–teacher relationships became fashionable. The government's purge of the universities, and subsequent preference for students and teachers of working class origins, combined with experimentation, had a disastrous effect upon academic standards. The impact of this educational decline was felt with the launching of the first Five Year Plan, which found itself struggling against widespread ignorance and lack of basic education and training. Educational policy, therefore, changed direction nearly as sharply as economic policy. A series of government decrees between September 1931 and January 1932 roundly condemned 'irresponsible projectorising and the introduction on a mass scale of methods untested in practice'. They demanded instead the inculcation of 'a strictly defined body of systematic knowledge' (native language, mathematics, physics, chemistry, geography, history). Curriculum changes were matched by the re-introduction of traditional forms of reports, grades, authority and discipline.

Overall, the educational achievement of the Soviet government between the wars was impressive. The introduction of compulsory primary education (July 1930) resulted in the doubling of the Soviet Union's primary school population, from 9 million to 18 million, between 1920–33. Meanwhile, the number of secondary pupils rose from 0.5 million (1922) to 3.5 million (1933). In 1941, the total school population of the USSR was around 35 million. The greatest achievement was the victory over the traditional peasant curse of illiteracy. This afflicted 75% of the population in 1917, but was rare by the outbreak of the Second World War, by which time 70 000 public libraries had opened in the Soviet Union.

Similarly, as social stability became the government's priority, the family began to revert to its traditional role. As an institution it had been under severe pressure in the 1920s, from such revolutionary notions as free love, free divorce and legalised abortions. It was also under pressure from the efforts of such party organisations as the Communist League of Youth (Komsomol), to divert the allegiance of the young. A fall in the birthrate, and a rise in crime figures prompted an official change of course. Decrees such as that which established parental responsibility for the misdemeanours of their children (May 1935), and that which made abortion illegal except upon medical grounds (June 1936), reinstated the family as the basis of society. The role of the mother was also traditionalised by a system of rewards for child-bearing. A mother of five children received the 'Medal of Motherhood', while the mother of ten became a 'Mother Heroine' of the Soviet Union.

The most serious opposition to the Bolsheviks in their attempts to create a new society had come of course from the established religions of the old Empire, especially from the Orthodox Church. Marxists could not easily tolerate a philosophy that stressed the importance of the next world at the expense of material conditions in this one. On the other hand, the creation of martyrs was counter productive. It was assumed that religious belief, being a feature of the old society, would lose all purpose as the new society took shape. The Soviet compromise was thus to strip the Churches of all material trappings and of all state power, but to enshrine in successive constitutions the right to freedom of worship, alongside the right to have no religious beliefs at all. Thus, in 1918 Church and state were formally separated. This involved the confiscation of all Church property, but allowed congregations to lease back buildings from the state, and to maintain priests for their worship. In 1921 public religious instruction was declared illegal for all citizens under 18 years of age, and churchmen were deprived of civil rights as 'non-productive workers'. To counteract the supernatural message of the Church, the so-called 'League of the Godless' was formed in 1925 to propagate atheism through such means as scientific lectures, journals, and exhibitions. Unfortunately, violence and vandalism often played a part in the League's activities too, making life difficult and unpleasant for all adherents to organised worship. There was an initial period of overt resistance, which saw the imprisonment of religious leaders for anti-communist utterances, and for refusal to surrender Church property. After this the Orthodox Church and most other communities settled into a period of uneasy coexistence with the Soviet regime. Undoubtedly the political influence of the Orthodox Church was broken. There is much evidence to suggest, however, that its spiritual influence survived, diminished in extent, but unbroken. The Orthodox Church received its reward for its patience during the war years of 1941–45, when the need for national unity caused the government to restore some of its former autonomy and to extend further gestures, such as the disbanding of the League of the Godless.

(o) The Aims of Soviet Foreign Policy

In the immediate aftermath of the October Revolution, the problems of formulation of foreign policy would not have seemed to many Soviet theorists to have existed. In their view the Russian revolution was the forerunner of the general collapse of capitalism, and of the end of international tensions and disputes which were the product of capitalist rivalries. Instead, in the next three years they witnessed the traumas of civil war and of foreign intervention (see Chapter 12, section **k**). Also there was the total failure of those communists who, in Germany and in Hungary, attempted to follow the Russian example. By the conclusion of the peace treaties in Paris, Russia's international situation was precarious in the extreme. She was isolated, surrounded by hostile powers, and in great economic difficulties. Thus, the central aim of Soviet foreign policy between the wars was simple and singular; it was survival.

Two principle routes to survival suggested themselves in the 1920s. For Trotsky, and for many others on the left of the Bolshevik party, the favoured policy consisted of collaboration with foreign revolutionaries to undermine the strength of the capitalist regimes. The consolidation of Stalin's power, however, saw an irreversible drift away from this internationalism. In foreign as in domestic policies, Stalin saw the best hope for Soviet survival in the development of material strength. Where normal coexistence with capitalist states served Soviet interests, he was quite willing to countenance it. 'One Soviet tractor', he affirmed at the time, 'it worth more than ten good foreign communists'.

The fact remained that the Soviet Union had no natural allies, no states with whom she had an overall community of interests, among the European powers. They remained capitalist powers and, in G. F. Kennan's words, 'the enmity Stalin bore towards the western bourgeois world was no less fierce than that of Lenin'. Thus, Soviet contacts with Britain and with France remained ambiguous. The declaration of G. V. Chicherin, Commissar for Foreign Affairs (October 1921), that Russia was willing to recognise and honour Tsarist debts to other powers, helped to counteract initial hostility. In the years that followed the Soviet government secured several important benefits from the victorious powers. A trade agreement was secured with Britain in March 1921, and official recognition of the Soviet regime was forthcoming from Britain, France and Italy in 1924. Mutual suspicion of long-term motives, however, made closer relations impossible. The incident of the so-called 'Zinoviev Letter', purporting to contain instructions to British agitators for political and economic disruption (October 1924) from the prominent Bolshevik and chairman of the Comintern, showed the fragility of Soviet credibility. Although it was never proved genuine, many conservatives remained convinced that Russia still harboured ambitions for international revolution. Indeed, between 1927–29, all official relations between Britain and the Soviet Union were severed.

Superficially, the greatest successes for Soviet diplomacy were scored in dealings with Germany. In the short term, the signature of the Treaty of Rapallo (April 1922) seemed a triumph. The establishment of full diplomatic relations with Germany ended Soviet isolation and ensured that Germany would drop claims for the repayment of Tsarist debts. The military and economic advice gained from Germany was also invaluable in the post revolutionary chaos. In the longer term, however, the appearance of triumph was deceptive. Rapallo provided a sharp shock to the allies, and their persistent assumption that it concealed a deeper relationship between Germany and the USSR soured Soviet relations with the west until 1941. Furthermore, Rapallo was not an alliance, but merely an arrangement momentarily useful to two isolated and apprehensive states. Russian relations with Germany continued to seesaw for a decade afterwards. Germany's apparent integration into the Versailles 'system', through the Locarno Pact and the Dawes Plan, could be interpreted in Moscow as evidence of growing capitalist solidarity. Conversely, such incidents as the thwarted communist rising in Germany in October 1923 served to renew fears of revolutionary internationalism.

Although, in retrospect, the rise of Adolf Hitler was a turning point in Soviet–German relations, it does not seem that Stalin was immediately aware of the fact. Contemporary Japanese expansion in China probably made it unclear whether the greater threat to Soviet territory lay in the west or in the east. 'To him', I. Deutscher has written, 'Hitler was merely one of the many reactionary leaders whom the political seesaw throws up for a moment, another Brüning or Papen, another Baldwin or Harding'. Nazism, in the view of Soviet theorists, was no new phenomenon. It was the inevitable death agony of capitalism caused by the recent economic crisis. To seek allies among the capitalist powers against a purely capitalist threat would thus be absurd. It is not clear at what point Stalin changed his view of Nazism. Several commentators have attached great importance to the conclusion of the non-aggression pact between Germany and Poland in January 1934. This suggested that, whatever the nature of Nazism, it was making common cause with Russia's enemies to threaten the domestic security of the Soviet Union. Certainly 1934 saw a major change in the tactics of Soviet diplomacy. Firstly, she showed great interest once more in understandings with western states, concluding mutual assistance pacts with Czechoslovakia and with France (May 1935). In the course of these negotiations she also undertook to enter the League of Nations (September 1934). We may conclude that Soviet motives included a desire to scare Hitler into a revision of aggressive plans. They wanted to ensure that, if he did precipitate a conflict, it would be fought on several fronts, and not concentrated against the USSR. Lastly, the nature of Moscow's advice to foreign communist parties changed radically. After a decade in which they had been consistently instructed that socialists and social democrats were capitalist allies and false friends, they now found themselves advised and instructed to form 'popular front' alliances with these parties. This would present more effective opposition to the real enemy, fascism. There can be little doubt that by 1935 the Soviet government had clearly identified the danger of Nazism. They had not, however, identified any reliable ally against it. It is hard to resist the conclusion from a more detailed narrative of Soviet diplomacy in the later 1930s (see Chapter 17), that Stalin sought international security without any real conviction that it could be found anywhere other than in her own industrial and military strength.

(p) Historiography

In forming so much of the modern structure of the Soviet Union, Stalin and his government engineered one of the most monumental achievements of the 20th century. The human cost of that achievement was so high that not even Stalin's successors in power could openly accept it. As a result of this unique combination of factors, historical judgements on Stalin have varied more

widely than those on any other modern political figure. Nowhere has this been more evident than in the USSR itself. During his tenure of office he was of course praised as the all-wise leader, the natural continuator of the ideology of Marx and Lenin, guiding his country through the various perils of the epoch. Much of the history of the revolution was indeed rewritten to support this view, as in Stalin's own work, *Short History of the Communist Party of the Soviet Union* (1938). Much was swallowed wholesale by sympathetic foreign writers such as Stalin's French biographer H. Barbusse (*Stalin: A New World Seen Through One Man*, 1936). Between 1956–61, however, official historiography in the Soviet Union sought to reverse the process entirely. Stalin, it was now declared, had perverted the course of the revolution by allowing the 'cult of the personality' to develop in the 1930s and by taking savage and unwarranted action against other sound communists in the purges. His body was removed from Lenin's mausoleum in Red Square. It was, however, reburied in a place of honour alongside the Kremlin wall. In reality, the approved view of Stalin in the Soviet Union today is probably close to that stated by N. S. Khrushchev in a speech in 1957. 'It is, of course, a bad thing that Stalin launched into deviations and mistakes which harmed our cause. But even when he committed mistakes and allowed the laws to be broken, he did that with the full conviction that he was defending the gains of the Revolution, the cause of socialism. That was Stalin's tragedy'.

The most violent opposition to Stalin in his lifetime and since his death has come, not from the west, but from the followers of L. D. Trotsky. Trotsky's own works, such as *The Revolution Betrayed* (1937), will admit no compromise with Stalinism. Instead, they portray Stalin's whole career in power, the building of the party bureaucracy, the development of personal leadership, the whole concept of 'Socialism in One Country', as a betrayal of the principles of Marx and Lenin. The man responsible for this perversion of the revolution was thus, in Trotsky's famous phrase, the 'gravedigger of the revolution'.

Western commentaries upon Stalin's life and policies have generally been characterised by a mixture of awe and disapproval. They might be roughly divided into two 'schools'. The first is that which views the personality and psychology of Stalin as vital formative factors in the events of the 1930s. This school might be represented by the work of R. C. Tucker (*Stalin as Revolutionary*, 1973). He argues in 'psychohistorical' terms that Stalin's inflated self-image of himself as Lenin's natural successor was a crucial factor in Soviet developments in the 1920s and 1930s, which might otherwise have followed a rather different path. More writers have preferred to view Stalin as the agent of other impersonal forces released, but not mastered in the earlier stages of the revolution. For A. Ulam (*Stalin: the Man and his Era*, 1974), he represents a remarkable continuity with earlier Bolshevism. He was forced to deal with problems created by Lenin's opportunism, and solved them by methods quite consistent with earlier Bolshevik practice. He, rather than Lenin, is the greatest and most successful of the Bolsheviks. For I. Deutscher (*Stalin: A Political Biography*, 1949), it was less the impetus of Bolshevism than that of centuries of Russian history to which Stalin was the heir. His comparison is less with Lenin than with Ivan the Terrible and Peter the Great who similarly forced the inert mass of Russian society and tradition into new paths by extreme and inhuman methods. Deutscher is also one of many writers who have stressed the absence in Russia after the revolution and civil war of the proper economic and social conditions for the development of the free revolutionary society originally envisaged by the Bolsheviks. Similar lines of argument have been followed by A. Nove (*An Economic History of the USSR*, 1969) and by R. Pethybridge (*The Social Prelude to Stalinism*, 1974). They lay their stresses respectively upon the economic and the social backwardness of post revolutionary Russia, which faced Stalin with the alternatives of drastic action or ultimate political failure. By avoiding the latter fate, by whatever means, Stalin stands as a dominant figure in the formation of the modern world.

Progress Paragraphs

Answer the following questions in about 150 words.

What were Stalin's strengths in the struggle for the succession to Lenin?   Sections (**a** & **c**)

Why did Trotsky receive so little support as the successor to Lenin?   Sections (**a** & **c**)

How did Stalin differ from other leading Bolsheviks?
                                             Section (**b**)

How did Stalin and Trotsky differ over the course of Bolshevism after the death of Lenin?
                                             Section (**d**)

Why did Stalin's view of Bolshevism's future win acceptance?   Section (**d**)

Where did real power lie in Soviet government under Stalin?   Section (**e**)

Why was it considered necessary to institute centralised economic planning in the USSR?
                                             Section (**f**)

Was planned industrialisation a success?
                                             Section (**g**)

How successful was the forced collectivisation of agriculture?   Section (**h**)

Did Soviet workers benefit from the economic changes of the 1930s?   Section (**h** & **i**)

Why were the political purges of the 1930s undertaken?   Sections (**j** & **k**)

How were Soviet politics affected by the purges?
                                             Section (**l**)

Did the new Soviet constitution of 1936 really represent a new era of socialist democracy in the Soviet Union?   Section (**m**)

To what extent was there a social revolution in the Soviet Union in the years of Stalin's government?
                                             Section (**n**)

What motivated Soviet foreign policy between the wars?   Section (**o**)

By what different means did the Soviet Union try to achieve her foreign aims between the wars?
                                             Section (**o**)

14
Western Democracy in Crisis: Germany, France, and Spain

The belief and hope of the western allies that the defeat and collapse of three autocratic Empires would create a 'world safe for democracy' was soon to prove an illusion. The end of the World War proved to be the opening of two decades in which parliamentary democracy was to be shaken to its foundations.

(a) Germany: The Birth of the Weimar Republic

Republican government in Germany was born (9th November 1918) under the most inauspicious circumstances. Quite apart from the imminent collapse of the war effort, and the abdication of the Kaiser, the fleet was in mutiny at Kiel and at Wilhelmshaven. Soldiers' and workers' councils had appeared in Berlin, in Cologne, and in Munich where a Bavarian republic was declared. The very name by which the German republic is commonly known derived from the fact that the dangerous condition of the capital in 1919 obliged the newly elected National Assembly to meet in the small provincial town of Weimar. The earlier failure of successive emergency governments, the desire of many conservatives to present a liberal front to the allies, and the radical nature of much anti-government agitation, all placed the Social Democratic Party (SPD) in the van of events. The shape of the Weimar Republic was to be determined by the state and aims of that party.

The German socialist movement was deeply divided. An Independent Social Democratic Party (USPD) had broken away from the SPD (April 1917), and a more extreme Communist Party (KPD) had been formed in November 1918. While the Communists advocated seizure of power and implementation of radical programmes, the SPD followed the lead of its chief, Friedrich Ebert, in preferring peaceful and democratic change through an elected assembly. The non-revolutionary nature of Ebert's government was confirmed on the first day of the republic's life, when he accepted the offer of General Groener of army assistance against the forces of the left. His decision undoubtedly strengthened his government by alliance with such a traditional and respected force. A. J. Nicholls has written that he possibly saved Germany from the intervention of allied troops. It naturally drew, however, fierce criticism from the left. This was increased in the next few weeks when army units, aided by a newly formed Volunteer Corps (Freikorps) bloodily suppressed a communist ('Spartacist') rising in Berlin (January 1919) and dispersed the 'Soviet' that had briefly held power in Munich (April 1919). Thus, while the republic came into existence across the corpses of some of its enemies, it owed that passage to a force that was merely a temporary ally. In the light of subsequent events, it was ominous that Groener had made no promise to protect the Republic from the forces of the right.

The elections to the National Assembly (January 1919) placed the SPD at the head of the poll, but without an overall majority. It was thus obliged to enter a coalition with the Centre Party and the Democratic Party (DDP), which was to characterise the fragmented political life of the Weimar Republic. The constitution drafted by the Assembly (July 1919) nevertheless represented a considerable democratic advance since 1914. It designated the parliament (Reichstag) as the sovereign authority of the state, and decreed that it should be elected every four years by proportional representation, by all men and women over twenty-one years of age. The President, elected every seven years, was to be subject to the authority of the Reichstag, although he also possessed special powers for use in a national emergency. A further outstanding break with the principles of the Bismarckian constitution concerned the powers of the upper house (Reichsrat). This continued to represent the interests of the component parts of the federal state, but was now subservient in all respects to the Reichstag. These component parts, instead of existing as sovereign kingdoms or duchies, were now designated merely as provinces (länder).

A vigorous historical debate has surrounded the

events of 1918–19 and their true significance. For
A. J. Nicholls they represented a true democratic
advance for Germany, bringing peace and a more
genuinely representative system in place of the
parliamentary 'charades' of Bismarck's time. Yet to
G. A. Craig these events constituted an 'aborted
revolution' which failed to change basic political
attitudes and prejudices, and which thus
condemned the Republic to failure in the long run.
J. W. Hiden has compromised between the two
views, seeing the 1919 constitution, like the
preceding events, as 'a synthesis between
progressive political and social ideas and the desire
to protect traditional institutions'.

(b) Germany: The Republic and the Versailles Treaty

As imminent defeat in war brought the Republic
into being, so its most pressing task was the
conclusion of peace. In this task, its freedom of
action was virtually nil. Advised by the military
chiefs that continuation of hostilities was
impossible, and forced to accept the allies' dictated
terms as the only alternative to invasion, the
Republic nevertheless inherited a legacy of
bitterness and resentment at its actions. German
hopes that peace would be based upon Woodrow
Wilson's 'Fourteen Points', and that the
replacement of the Kaiser by social democracy
would incline the allies to leniency, proved wholly
misplaced. The terms (see Chapter 17, section **a**)
that the Republican ministers Müller and Bell
finally accepted caused a wide range of
resentments. It was resented that Germany would
not be accepted into the community of the League
of Nations, that she lost eastern territories to states
that could not pretend to have defeated her, and
that future German industry would pass the fruits
of its labours in the form of reparations to foreign
capitalists. Worse, it was claimed that the German
armies had not been defeated by the enemy at all,
but betrayed by the secret enemy, the socialist and
the Jew, at home. The myth of the 'Stab in the
Back' ('Dolchstoss') was born.

Despite the widespread feeling that 'the true
basis of the Republic is not the Weimar
Constitution but the Treaty of Versailles', it is not
fair to imagine that the regime was doomed by the
circumstances of its birth. For all its losses,
Republican Germany still had potentially the
strongest economy in Europe, and her recovery was
rapid. The political demoralisation caused by
Versailles was more serious, for it not only
guaranteed a constant right-wing opposition to the

Republic, but also undermined the initial
enthusiasm of more moderate patriots for the
regime. The future of the Weimar Republic,
therefore, depended upon surviving long enough for
such passions to cool.

(c) Germany: The Enemies of the Weimar Republic

The passage of the Weimar Constitution by 262
votes to 75, and the success of the centrist parties in
the elections of 1919, should not be allowed to
obscure the substantial hostility that existed in
Germany to the new regime. The election result,
E. Troeltsch has explained, was not really a vote of
confidence, for 'this democracy was in essence an
anti-revolutionary system, dedicated to the
maintenance of order and opposed to the
dictatorship of the proletariat'.

On the left extreme of the Republic's enemies
stood the KPD, separated from the regime by a
gulf of bitterness formed during the risings of 1919,
and by the brutal murders of communist leaders
Karl Liebknecht and Rosa Luxemburg by
'Freikorps' men. By December 1920, when its
decision to join the International (the International
Organisation of Communist and Socialist Parties)
attracted many converts from the Independent
Social Democrats, the KPD could boast a
membership of 400 000 with 33 daily newspapers at
its disposal. Although closely tied to a pro-Moscow
policy by the leadership of Ernst Thälmann (1925–
33), the party pursued a cautious policy, preferring
the steady consolidation of strength, membership
and influence to further adventures on the lines of
1919. Its achievement in this respect was, however,
unimpressive. It failed to win any great influence
among the trades unions, and alienated many
potential supporters by its pro-Soviet stance.
Nevertheless, the hostility between communists and
social democrats went far in the next decade to
explain the failure of the left in Germany to resist
the rise of Nazism.

To the right of the Republic lay a more
daunting array of opponents. The nationalists,
grouped especially around the German National
People's Party (DNVP) represented the brand of
conservatism that hankered after the principles and
institutions of Wilhelmine Germany. The DNVP
had especially influential support in the civil
service, in the judiciary, among industrialists, and
in the Churches. Indeed, the hostility of the legal
system towards the Republic, shown in the lenient
sentences passed against right-wing terrorists and
insurgents, has been described by K. S. Pinson as

'one of the most shameful chapters in the history of that epoch'. The nationalist threat to the regime was, nevertheless, limited by several factors. The leadership of the DNVP was divided over the issue of co-operation with the republican regime, and the whole stress of the party's policies was laid upon principles partly compromised by the defeat of the old Germany in 1914–18.

In the course of the later 1920s the nationalists began to surrender the leadership of the right-wing opposition to the National Socialist German Workers' Party (NSDAP or 'Nazis'), the most successful of the 'völkisch' groups that appeared on the right of German politics. They laid their stress upon the concept of race (volk), preaching the superiority of the German racial characteristics and culture, and the need to protect them against alien influences, especially the insidious influence of the Jews. Founded in 1919 by Anton Drexler, but soon dominated by the determined and brilliant orator Adolf Hitler, the Nazis came close to ruin in their early life by placing their trust in a policy of insurrection (putschism). This resulted in public discredit and the imprisonment of their leaders. Although the subsequent change of emphasis, whereby the NSDAP now sought power by parliamentary means, led to poor results, the party had hidden strengths. Its local organisation, although uneven, was especially strong in Bavaria. Elsewhere it employed some notable local leaders such as Gregor Strasser and Julius Streicher, who ensured tight local discipline. It deployed a powerful para-military force, the Storm Troopers (Sturmabteilung or SA), which proved more than a match for its communist rivals in the street violence that scarred the political life of the Weimar Republic. Lastly, its wide policy appealed to the resentments of the defeated Germans, both 'national' and 'socialist'. Although it had little success in the years of republican prosperity, this policy promised to serve the party well should Germany once more fall upon hard times.

It is open to dispute whether the German Army (Reichswehr), in its reduced post-Versailles form, should be listed among the Republic's enemies. Although it had done much to enable the Weimar government to survive its first weeks of existence, there was much in the principles of the traditional officer class, which still drew 21% of its membership from the nobility, that was at odds with the philosophy of the social-democratic Republic. The view of H. von Seeckt, chief of Army Command between 1920–26, was that the Reichswehr should be an apolitical body, preserving its traditional values above the hurly-burly of party rivalry. Comparison between

Reichswehr action in 1919, and its refusal to act against army veterans in Freikorps units during the Kapp 'putsch' (see section **d**), clearly showed that its attitude towards the regime was merely lukewarm. In the words of J. W. Hiden, it 'would tolerate the Republic for the time being in its own interests'.

(d) Germany: The Years of Crisis, 1920–23

In the first months of its life, the Weimar Republic fought for its life against the hostility of the left, surviving by virtue of its temporary allies. In the next four years, however, there was to be much to maintain the sense of crisis and bitterness. The belated revelation (April 1921) of the magnitude of Germany's commitment in reparation payments to the allies and M. Erzberger's plans to strengthen the national economy by taxes upon war profits and upon inherited wealth, combined to stir special resentment on the right. Such resentment merged with existing nationalist hostility to subject the Republic to increasing right-wing violence. During those stages of the Republic's life, wrote G. A. Craig, 'its normal state was crisis'.

The first of these assaults took the form of the so-called 'Kapp Putsch' (March 1920). Although the attempted coup d'état was a symptom of wider right-wing discontent, the immediate trigger was the government's attempt to disband a Freikorps unit under Captain Ehrhardt at the request of the allies. Ominously, the Reichswehr took up a neutral stance, claiming that 'obviously there can be no talk of letting Reichswehr fight against Reichswehr'. Kapp's plans were frustrated instead by Berlin workers and civil servants who refused the orders of the insurgents and denied them transport and publicity facilities. Unfortunately, this concerted action was not repeated in later moments of republican peril. Meanwhile, Germany experienced political violence and assassination unparalleled in her history. The most spectacular examples were the murders of W. Rathenau, the Foreign Minister (June 1922) and M. Erzberger, former Finance Minister and one of the leaders of the armistice delegation (August 1921). The final drama of this period of right-wing pressure was played in Munich in November 1923 when Hitler and some Nazi followers attempted to exploit a clash between the reactionary government of Bavaria and the federal authorities to institute a 'March on Berlin' after the style of Mussolini. Resolute police action reduced the so-called 'Beerhall Putsch' to fiasco. Taken out of context it would indeed be possible to dismiss the activities of

Kapp and Hitler as, in K. S. Pinson's phrase, 'a ludicrous fizzle'. Nevertheless, the derisory sentences passed on the offenders, five years' imprisonment for Hitler and no punishment for any of Ehrhardt's Freikorps men, made clear the sympathy in high places for their cause. The Reichstag elections held in June 1920 added further indications of the ascendancy of the right.

By the time of Hitler's putsch, the Republic had also to confront a more serious threat from another, international, source. The reasons for, and the course of the Franco-Belgian occupation of the Ruhr in January 1923 have been given elsewhere (see Chapter 17, section **d**). Here we have mainly to consider the domestic effects of that action upon Germany. The most sensational of these was the acceleration of the decline of the Reichsmark that had been in progress since the war. The initial blame lay, not with the French invasion, but with the crippling cost of the war, the pressure of reparation demands, and the sad policy of the Republic of printing money to meet resultant budget deficits. Now, as Table 14.1 indicates, the decline raced out of control. Apart from its role in the origins of the inflation, the government bore some responsibility for not checking it at an early stage. 'Cheap Money' had its attractions for the industrialist who now found plant and wages cheap, and for the landowner whose mortgages were easier to pay off. Some enormous fortunes, of which the greatest was perhaps that of the industrialist Hugo Stinnes, were forged out of the financial chaos. Inflation had no consolations for the small saver or investor whose carefully accumulated sums and guaranteed interest became worthless in a matter of days. The collapse of the value of pensions and savings ruined many, and the

	Value against dollar
July 1914	4.2
July 1919	14.0
July 1920	39.5
July 1921	76.7
July 1922	493.2
Jan 1923	17 972.0
July 1923	353 412.0
Aug 1923	4 620 455.0
Sept 1923	98 860 000.0
Oct 1923	25 260 208 000.0
15th Nov 1923	4 200 000 000 000.0

From G. A. Craig *Germany 1800–1945* OUP
Table 14.1

number of recipients of public relief in 1923 was three times that in 1913. 'Millions of Germans', wrote G. A. Craig, 'who had passively accepted the transition from Empire to Republic suffered deprivations that shattered their faith in the democratic process and left them cynical and alienated'. As a further ominous by-product many trades unions, unable in the crisis to protect their members' interests, suffered a sharp drop in their rolls and in their political influence.

(e) Germany: The Prime of the Weimar Republic, 1924–29

The Weimar Republic not only survived, but launched out upon the most successful period of its life, a period when long-term survival at last seemed possible. Two factors contributed greatly to this recovery. For the first time, the Republic had at its head men who commanded substantial respect. The fall of the broken Chancellor Cuno (August 1923) brought into office the major political figure of the Republic. Gustav Stresemann's political apprenticeship had been served in nationalist and militarist circles but, despite his initial sympathy with the Kapp insurgents in 1920, he had been shocked by the growth of political violence and instability in Germany. He became republican because he was horrified by the alternatives. His political background, nevertheless, made him acceptable to many who could barely tolerate his predecessors. Although Chancellor for only three months, he continued to exert a profound influence upon German politics from the foreign ministry until his death in 1929. The earlier death (February 1925) of Ebert brought to the Presidency of the Republic a man of impeccable patriotic credentials, the wartime hero Field Marshal Paul von Hindenburg. His election was to a large extent a statement of nostalgia for the stability and strength of the 'old' Germany. 'The truth is', stated Stresemann, 'that Germans want no President in a top hat. He must wear a military uniform and plenty of decorations'. Hindenburg, however, wore both his uniform and his office with tact, and effectively defended the Republic from the worst barbs of its right-wing opponents. The second vital factor in the recovery of the Republic was the urgent desire of the former wartime allies to prevent the collapse or political disintegration of Germany. Foreign co-operation was central to the regime's new lease of life.

The first achievements of the revivified Republic were the rescue of the German currency and the regularisation of the reparations question. At the end of 1923, thanks also to the work of H. Luther at the Ministry of Finance, the discredited Mark was replaced by the so-called 'Rentenmark'. In the absence of sufficient gold reserves, the new currency was backed in theory by Germany's agricultural and industrial resources. It was a novel, and largely fictitious form of security, which relied heavily upon foreign goodwill for its general acceptance. Such goodwill was forthcoming in sufficient quantities not only to support the stabilisation of the currency, but also to regulate the question of Germany's reparation payments through the formulation of the Dawes Plan (see Chapter 17, section **e**) in 1924. Outwardly, the German economy presented a picture in the later 1920s of stability and prosperity. The emergence of giant industrial combines such as I. G. Farben and United Steelworks (Vereinigte Stahlwerke) in 1926 seemed to testify to the renewed dynamism of German heavy industry, while in 1927 overall production figures at last matched those of 1913.

Financial stability was accompanied by a greater degree of political stability. Apart from the relative acceptability of Stresemann and Hindenburg, the economic recovery blunted Nationalist opposition to the Republic by appeasing the industrialists who played a substantial role in the DNVP. The armed forces, too, seemed to be on better terms with the Republic after the resignation of von Seeckt (October 1926) as commander of the Wehrmacht. After the appointment of General Groener (December 1927) as Defence Minister, 1928–29 provided two pieces of electoral comfort for the government. The Reichstag elections in May 1928 provided the worst results for a decade for the parties of the political extremes. Between them the DNVP (14.2%), the NSDAP (2.6%) and the KDP (10.6%) secured less than 30% of the popular vote. In December 1929 there was a referendum forced by a coalition of Nationalists and Nazis, trying to condemn the Young Plan and propose treason charges against the government for trafficking with foreign interests. It received only 13.8% of the votes cast.

Yet the Republic still had its weaknesses. It seemed to be winning the public relations battle, but it had established few durable institutions to sustain it in time of crisis. The lukewarm toleration of the regime shown by the Reichswehr was not generally imitated by the civil service, the universities or the schools. K. S. Pinson has described in detail the atmosphere of German education in the 1920s. 'The essential control of both lower and higher education remained in the hands of those who had nothing but contempt for the Republic and who therefore made no effort to

prepare the German youth for republican citizenship. Not a single school text in Weimar Germany presented the true story of German defeat in 1918. German geography texts still inculcated in the minds of the young the definition that Germany was a country surrounded on all sides by enemies'. Neither had the Republic developed a system of parliamentary parties strong enough to give stability to its democracy. The classic Weimar coalition parties, the Social Democrats, the Democratic Party and the Centre Party, remained divided on many points of economic, political and religious doctrine. Their lack of cohesion in the face of the rise of a popular anti-democratic movement would play a major role in the disasters of the early 1930s. Lastly, for all the appearances of superficial prosperity, the basis of the German economy was essentially unsound. Industrial investment and government expenses were not adequately financed from German capital or German profits. More than a third of all capital invested in the late 1920s came from foreign loans. Imports, between 1924–30, were always greater than exports. The total deficit on the German budget over those years amounted to nearly 1.3 billion Reichmarks. It is impossible to deny that, between 1924–29, the Weimar Republic was progressing and achieving some of the attributes of permanency. In that limited period, however, as H. Holborn has put it, 'normalcy was never quite achieved, and even the period when it appeared close at hand proved only a belief interlude between two disasters'.

(f) Germany: The Weimar Republic and Foreign Affairs

German affairs were a central factor in the development of international relations between the world wars, and are thus described in detail elsewhere (see Chapter 17). In the context of the Weimar Republic, however, it is useful to establish separately the essential aims of German policy in the 1920s.

'For most Germans', writes J. Hiden, 'foreign policy meant an unremitting effort to revise the terms of the Treaty of Versailles'. In addition to the material deprivations suffered as a result of that treaty, successive German governments sought also to remedy the dangerous diplomatic isolation that resulted from defeat, and to restore the degree of national independence lost to the allies and their occupation agencies. The first method to hand was the simple tactic of sullen obstruction. Hence the clauses of the treaty aimed against the Kaiser and other alleged war criminals were never effectively enforced. The disbanding of paramilitary organisations was slow and unreliable, and the clauses relating to disarmament and to reparations were implemented only with constant allied supervision. Such a policy could not long be successful against opponents with both the determination and the means to enforce the treaty terms, and could in the long run only lead to potential disasters such as the occupation of the Ruhr. German policy thus changed under the Chancellorship of J. Wirth (May 1921–November 1922) to one of 'fulfilment' ('Erfüllungspolitik'). This apparent co-operation with the allies was one of the greatest causes of bitterness among the right-wing opponents of the regime, and played a direct role in stirring the political violence of the period. It was, nevertheless, a sensible and realistic policy, based upon the realisation that 'the realities of the European situation made patience, ambiguity and opportunism requirements of Germany foreign policy' (G. A. Craig). It was designed to encourage future allied leniency towards Germany. Its introduction coincided with a successful solution to the problem of diplomatic isolation. The conclusion of the Treaty of Rapallo with the Soviet Union in April 1922 (see Chapter 13, section **o**), created investment opportunities for Germany, and opened up substantial prospects for evading the military restrictions imposed at Versailles. It may also be argued that it did much, in combination with the chaos caused by the French occupation of the Ruhr, to frighten the western powers into a more reasonable attitude to Germany.

The greatest successes of 'Erfüllungspolitik' were achieved during Gustav Stresemann's tenure of the Foreign Ministry, during which he combined the broad principles of 'fulfilment' with a distinct attempt to lay the foundations for a revision of the peace treaties. He was portrayed by liberal historians as a 'good European', eager to put co-operation in the place of confrontation, and by historians of the Marxist left as a capitalist joining the Locarno Pact for essentially anti-Soviet reasons. The publication of his official papers has indicated that Stresemann was neither of these things. His primary aim was to rid Germany of foreign restraints, and to regain for her full sovereignty and freedom of political action. Thus the Locarno Pact of 1925 (see Chapter 17, section **f**) guaranteed Germany's western borders against further incursions, without committing Germany to acceptance of the hated territorial settlement in the east. It also paved the way for Germany's acceptance into the international community of the League of Nations. The agreement of the Dawes Plan in 1924 and the Young Plan in 1929 (see Chapter 17, section **e**) were classic examples of the policy of 'fulfilment'. They reduced Germany's total reparation debt, and gained foreign recognition of her difficulties in paying it at all. Steadily, from January 1926, Germany began to reap the fruits of this policy. In that month, British withdrawal from Cologne marked the first major reduction of the occupying forces. This was followed in January 1927 by the withdrawal from Germany of the Inter-Allied Control Commission, the major 'watchdog' of the Versailles terms. Before the fall of the Republic, the evacuation of foreign troops had been completed by the French withdrawal (August 1929). The continuation of reparation payments had been dealt a near mortal below by Chancellor Brüning's successful application to the United States for a 'Moratorium' (June 1931). No area of policy under the Weimar Republic could claim to rival the success of its foreign policy. Its tragedy was that it failed consistently to convince the zealots of the political extremes of the constructive good sense of that policy. When international economic crisis undermined the Republic, its foreign policy of restrained national reassertion was to be one of the first casualties of its collapse.

(g) Germany: The Collapse of the Weimar Republic

'Germany', Stresemann had warned in 1928, 'is dancing on a volcano. If the short-term credits are called in a large section of our economy would collapse'. Indeed, within days of Stresemann's premature death (3rd October 1929), the slump of the Wall Street stock market (24th October 1929) triggered off just such a phenomenon. Germany's foreign capital, which had stood at 5 billion Marks in 1928, dropped by half in 1929, and shrank to a mere 700 million Marks in 1930. Loans began to be called in and bankruptcies multiplied. With the government consistently reluctant to set off a new inflation of the Mark, the crisis manifested itself primarily in the form of massive unemployment. The problem had haunted Germany since the recovery of 1925, with 2 million out of work in the winter of 1925–26 and 1.5 million jobless a year later. The rise towards the catastrophic figures of the Depression began in the summer of 1928. One and a half million were unemployed in mid-1929 and in the following winter the figures soared out of control. Three million were affected in the winter of 1929–30, 5 million by the end of the following summer and 6 million in both January 1932 and January 1933.

The political effect of the economic slump was a substantial revival of extremism. As Table 14.2 indicates, the elections of 1930–32 were marked by the dramatic growth of those parties offering extreme solutions to the contemporary distress. The KPD achieved greater support than it had ever had before, but above all it was the Nazis that benefited from the economic tragedy. The general appeal of the NSDAP is analysed elsewhere (see Chapter 16, section **c**), but there can be no doubt as to the role played by the crisis in its increasing popularity. The research of M. Broszat, for example, has established that, of all the working class recruits into the Nazi party between 1930–33, some 55% were unemployed. As A. Bullock wrote of Hitler, when 'disaster cast its shadow over the land again, the despised prophet entered into his inheritance'. Nevertheless, there was nothing inevitable about the Nazi advent to power. They never represented a majority in the Reichstag and their electoral fortunes were in fact in decline by late 1932. In the event their triumph resulted from the degeneration and miscalculations of republican politics in the years of the economic crisis.

The resignation of Chancellor Müller's cabinet (March 1930), the Republic's last Social-Democrat administration, marked the end of majority government in Germany. As the political parties of the centre continued to place sectional interests before national need, the effective government of the state fell into the hands of President Hindenburg and such advisors as General Groener and General von Schleicher. Their primary aim predictably, was less the protection of democracy and parliamentarianism than the formation of a more authoritative and authoritarian government to face the economic crisis. Their first choice as Chancellor, Heinrich Brüning, therefore had admirable qualifications for office. He was a social, political and economic conservative, a devout

Catholic, a decorated war veteran, and suitably hostile to the principles of Social Democracy. While seeking primarily to cement his administration with some foreign success such as the suspension of reparation payments, he tackled Germany's domestic crisis by orthodox, deflationary economic tactics. Reductions in social services and in unemployment benefits, at the time of greatest need, were unlikely to rally wide support. They led to Brüning's reputation as the 'Hunger Chancellor'. They also played no small part in driving many more unemployed into the ranks of the paramilitary organisations. Meanwhile, military expenditure and subsidies to the Junker farmers were maintained. Brüning's greatest political error, however, was surely the dissolution of the Reichstag (July 1930) in search of a secure majority. Instead, at a time of mounting crisis, he found the political extremism of the streets translated into Reichstag seats. Continued failure to curb economic depression, and to achieve ministerial stability, finally encouraged the President to replace Brüning with Franz von Papen in May 1932. This was the move which, according to the liberal historian E. Eyck, 'killed not only the German Republic but the peace of Europe'.

Papen's responsibility for the advent of Nazism is great. In June, he raised Brüning's ban on the SA. In July he used the resultant street violence, and the spate of deaths in clashes between Nazis and Communists as a pretext to dismiss the Social-Democrat provincial government in Prussia, one of last bastions of democratic government in Germany. Like Brüning before him. his decision to hold new elections (July 1932) played into the hands of the Nazis with their increasing support. Papen's efforts to establish an electoral alliance with Hitler as the junior partner were frustrated, both by Hitler's refusal to accept any office less than that of Chancellor, and by the aged

	Jan 1919	June 1920	May 1924	Dec 1924	May 1928	Sept 1930	July 1932	Nov 1932
NSDAP	—	—	32	14	12	107	230	196
DNVP	44	71	95	103	73	41	37	52
DVP	19	65	45	51	45	30	7	11
Centre	91	85	81	88	78	87	98	90
DDP	75	39	28	32	25	20	4	2
SPD	165	102	100	131	153	143	133	121
USPD	22	84	—	—	—	—	—	—
KPD	—	4	62	45	54	77	89	100

Table 14.2

President's personal and social antipathy to the Bavarian upstart. The government had only one alternative to Hitler. When von Schleicher failed in his brief Chancellorship (December 1932–January 1933) to split the Nazi leadership by negotiating with Gregor Strasser, Hindenburg at last accepted Hitler as the only alternative to political chaos and possible civil war. He thus became Chancellor on 30th January 1933, with a cabinet of three Nazis and ten conservatives, the latter representing the vain hope of the traditional German right that they might still use the dynamic force of Nazism for their own purposes. A seven hour torchlight parade by the SA in the streets of Berlin formed the funeral celebrations of the Weimar Republic.

(h) France: 1918, the Price of Victory

Heavy as the burden imposed by defeat upon the Weimar Republic was, it was hardly as daunting as the price that France had paid for victory. The human cost of the war could not be measured in numbers alone, although the figures of 1 390 000 dead and 740 000 maimed represented the highest proportional loss of any combatant apart from Serbia. The quality of the losses, and their significance for the future were even more crippling, for the vital generation of young Frenchmen had been shattered. Of every ten men aged between 20–40 years in 1914, as G. Dupeux has expressed it, 'two had been killed, one had become a burden upon his fellow citizens, and three had been handicapped whether in the short term or long term'. The result, it has been estimated, was a further loss of 1.7 million French citizens through the decline in the birthrate, and the highest proportion of elderly citizens of any European country.

A further casualty of the war was France's proverbial stability. She had to write off the substantial sums invested in pre-revolutionary Russia, yet remained commited to repay 30 billion francs worth of war debts, owed mainly to the USA. This burden was faced with a level of industrial production reduced by 20% by wartime damage, and with a chronically unstable currency. Fearful of public reaction to higher taxation, and largely sharing the public view that in the long run German reparations would pay for the recovery of France, successive governments resorted to the printing presses for the necessary finances, with predictable inflationary results. The total amount of currency in circulation had risen between 1913–20 from 6 billion francs to 38 billion. For all her private wealth, France now became in the inter-war years, in G. Wright's phrase, 'a wealthy country chronically on the verge of bankruptcy'.

Even the great territorial and national gain of the war held its disappointments. The citizens of Alsace-Lorraine, instead of rushing joyfully into the arms of their liberators, showed wide resentment at the increased central control that France now intended to exert over them. Alsatians resisted attempts to extend anti-clerical legislation to the provinces, and opposed attempts to replace their German-based dialect with French as the language of education and administration. The development of an Alsatian autonomist movement in the mid-1920s was strong enough to alarm Parisian politicians and to precipitate political arrests and trials. In every important respect, therefore, there was an ominous accuracy in the judgement of J. Cambon in 1918 that 'France victorious must grow accustomed to being a lesser power than France vanquished'.

(i) France: Domestic Politics 1919–29; Bloc versus Cartel

Under such unpromising circumstances, the wartime unity of French politics barely survived the armistice. On the one hand, in the words of H. Tint, 'bourgeois France had one supreme ambition: to return to bourgeois comforts'. On the other hand, the French left, active and militant enough in the pre-war decade, was now galvanised by the Russian revolution. They saw the prospect of a real and probable alternative to bourgeois France.

The response of French conservatives to the challenge of communism was the 'Bloc National', a coalition of centre and right-wing political, financial and industrial groups. They were united, as their manifesto declared, by 'the desire to combine in one vigorous group those workers, employers and employees who refuse at all costs to suffer Bolshevik tyranny'. The result of the 1919 elections, 433 seats for the Bloc, 86 for the Radicals and 104 for the Socialists, represented the greatest triumph for the French right since 1871. However, the appearance of national unity and purpose was false. A great part was played in the Bloc victory by a curious new electoral system which distributed seats in each Department according to the proportion of votes cast for each party's list of candidates. It gave all the seats to any party gaining an overall majority. Thus the system favoured such combinations as the Bloc. The euphoria of victory in the world war, and the disunity of the left also served to inflate the Bloc's triumph. Five years later, after a tenure of office dominated by foreign affairs and post-war economic difficulties, the Bloc found that the left too had learned the value of electoral alliances. In 1924, in the aftermath of the occupation of the Ruhr (see Chapter 17, section **d**), it was the turn of the 'Cartel des Gauches', who were an alliance of Radicals and Socialists, to benefit from the electoral system. A very moderate swing in votes, which saw the shares of Radicals and Socialists alike increase by only 0.2%, left their coalition with 266 seats to the Bloc's 229.

Once again, France was to be frustrated in her hopes for stable and successful parliamentary government. The Cartel des Gauches, although it could claim that its conciliatory foreign policy was more successful than the confrontation tactics of the Bloc, suffered from two insoluble problems. The first arose from the position of the Socialists within the coalition. They had suffered gravely from the emergence of communism in France. At the Congress of Tours (December 1920), the French Communists secured a vote to join the 3rd Communist International. In doing so they had stripped the Socialists of some 140 000 party members, much of its administrative machinery, and its daily journal 'L'Humanité'. Although the Communists themselves remained divided and on the fringes of parliamentary politics, the Socialist leader, Leon Blum, controlled a rump of some 30 000 members. Unable to risk the alienation of their remaining followers by supporting the Radicals too enthusiastically, the Socialists refused positions in Herriot's Radical cabinet and contented themselves with lukewarm parliamentary co-operation. There could be no co-operation, however, over the second of the Cartel's problems, which was the increasing weakness of the French currency. On this matter, Socialist and Radical philosophies differed fundamentally. The socialists favoured positive action such as heavy direct taxation. The Radicals, aware of their support among small businessmen, peasant farmers, and so forth, favoured minimal government intervention. This was a recipe for disaster in the economic climate of the mid-1920s. Uncontrolled inflation ravaged the savings of the average Frenchman and undermined the traditional security of the franc. From a value of 90 to the pound (December 1924), the currency slid to 130 to the pound (December 1925), and down to 240 in July 1926. In 1928, price levels were 650% of those in 1914. The impact of this collapse should not be underestimated. 'The collapse of the franc', wrote D. S. Landes, 'after over one hundred years of stability, was utterly demoralising in a society whose greatest economic virtue was thrift'. A return

by Herriot to the outdated policy of anti-clericalism, attempting to break off diplomatic relations with the Vatican and to extend anti-clerical legislation to Alsace-Lorraine, was no longer enough to unite the left. In 1926 the Radicals supported the return of the strong conservative, Raymond Poincaré, to the premiership as a symbol of confidence and stability. After this the Cartel was effectively dead.

The return of Poincaré was at least a financial success. By traditional methods which were largely abhorrent to the left, he had restored the franc to stability by 1928. The currency was revalued at 20% of its pre-war value (1926), and put on the gold standard (1928). The substantial budget deficit was made good by a sinking fund, and by raising an extra six billion francs in indirect taxation. The price paid, however, for three years of apparent prosperity and stability between 1926–29 was the infliction of deep scars upon French parliamentary politics. The advent of Poincaré, with the apparent support of the Cartel des Gauches, convinced many voters on the left that their democratic will would always be obstructed by the 'Wall of Money' ('Mur d'Argent'), and by the vested interests of bankers and industrialists. They felt that other means of political expression might bring better results. In a period of less economic stability it was to become evident that France had all the ingredients of 'veiled civil war' (J. P. T. Bury). Involved were the remnants of wartime nationalism, the rise of communism, the insecurity of small tradesmen and farmers, and the vested interests of financiers.

(j) France: Economic Recovery

While state finance suffered a decade of crisis after the war, the national economy underwent a remarkable recovery that Sir D. Brogan has described as 'the greatest economic achievement of post-war Europe'. To an extent, the economy benefited from the very factors that had afflicted the government. The weakness of the franc favoured French exports, and rising prices were an encouragement to manufacturers to produce more. A further industrial factor was the recovery of the valuable potash and iron-ore deposits of Alsace-Lorraine.

The resurgence of the French economy expressed itself in three main ways. Most spectacular was the successful reconstruction carried out in areas and industries devastated by the war. Of two million hectares of agricultural land left barren in 1918, 95% was under cultivation once more in 1925.

Meanwhile, the investment of 80 billion francs in the mines and factories of the north provided the opportunity for large scale modernisation. Secondly, heavy industries, both old and new, made substantial advances in production. Of the old, coal production increased from 40 million tons in 1913 to 55 million in 1929, while steel production doubled. The most impressive of the new developments was the rise of the French motor industry. With the emergence of such giants as Renault, Citroën and Peugeot, the industry led the world by 1929 with an output of 250 000 vehicles. Lastly, France achieved virtually full employment. In fact, due to wartime losses, she actually suffered from a shortage of manpower which necessitated the importation of 1.6 million foreign workers by 1931.

There were limitations to this economic recovery. Agriculture did not share in the advances of other sectors. Production in 1929 was only 3% higher than in 1913, although considering the wartime loss of 673 000 peasants, that modest figure represented substantially greater efficiency in production methods. The post-war recovery also represented a triumph for the larger industrial and financial combinations, rather than for the smaller producer or tradesman. The years that saw the rise of the giant Kuhlmann and Saint Gobain chemical companies, and of the Monoprix, Prisunic and Uniprix chain stores, still held the prospect of insecurity and low investment for smaller enterprises. G. Wright has stressed how the recovery of the French economy accelerated its division 'into two increasingly divergent sectors; the dynamic and the static'. For the dynamic sector, especially, the successes of the 1920s were about to meet an abrupt end.

(k) France: The Economic Impact of Depression

In October 1929, the collapse of the New York stock market set off the greatest economic crisis experienced by world capitalism. It naturally had its primary effect upon the most industrialised states. France, protected somewhat by the stability and the low value of the franc, enjoyed a period of immunity. By late 1931, however, she too was feeling the effects of the world 'slump'. Depressed foreign markets showed less and less interest in French luxury goods, and home sales too found it hard to compete with cheap foreign goods dumped on the market in a desperate search for sales. Firstly, the slump manifested itself in declining production. Steel production fell by 40% between

1930–35 and aluminium production by 50%. Overall industrial output in France in 1932 was only 80% of the 1928 figure. Secondly, France felt the pressure of unemployment after a decade of labour shortages. Forty thousand jobs per month were lost in the first half of 1931, and although the official unemployment figures for January 1932 were only 250 000, these took no account of departing foreign workers. Taking the latter into consideration, the number of jobs lost by early 1933 would total some 1 300 000.

If France suffered less than other European states from the economic depression, she also suffered longer. Government reaction to the crisis typified the conservatism and lack of imagination of much of French political thinking at the time. Traumatised by the collapse of the franc in the 1920s, the politicians and economists gave undue importance to the preservation of 'sound money'. The franc was one of only four major currencies to remain on the gold standard, while the government sought salvation instead in tariff barriers and quotas imposed upon foreign imports. Thus in France the deflationary spiral continued for a full three years. Not until 1935 did the economy show signs of a recovery, and then of a painfully slow one.

(l) France: The Political Impact of Depression

The political handling of the economic crisis was perhaps made all the worse by the fact that the task fell to a new and comparatively inexperienced political generation. The departures through ill-health of Briand and Poincaré had left among their successors, Laval, Tardieu, Daladier and Chautemps, no figure of comparable national stature. The crisis also hit a country bitterly divided by dogma and ideology. Conservatives sought safety in salary reductions and similar measures wholly intolerable to the left, with their visions of extensive and costly programmes of direct aid and relief. Unable to find either policies or personalities to command general support, French politics lurched into one of its worst periods of administrative instability. Eight different cabinets were formed between that of Tardieu (February 1932) and that of Doumergue (February 1934).

As in Italy and Germany, the weaknesses of French parliamentary politics increased the attractions of extra-parliamentary action. Since the mid-1920s, France had witnessed a proliferation of political 'leagues'. They were determined and often vicious in their opposition to the Republic, and drew support from the same sources as many of the European fascist groupings. The oldest of these was the Action Française which enjoyed considerable support among right-wing writers and intellectuals. Ostensibly Catholic, it was in fact repudiated by the Vatican in 1926. Ostensibly monarchist, it was viewed with great suspicion by the current claimant to the French throne. In reality, it was a classic, backward-looking, reactionary movement which attracted, according to A. Cobban, 'those who saw themselves as an elite under attack from the forces of egalitarian democracy and unegalitarian finance'. The Croix de Feu movement, founded by Colonel de la Rocque (1928), had more direct appeal to ex-servicemen, and put forward a vague and general appeal against socialism and internationalism. Also worthy of note are P. Taittinger's 'Jeunesses Patriotes', with their fascist style in uniforms and their substantial financial backing from the cosmetics millionaire Coty, and the 'Francistes' who were founded by M. Bucard, with a special line in anti-semitic propaganda.

It seems unlikely that the leagues could seriously have aspired to a seizure of power in France such as Mussolini achieved in Italy. It is unlikely that their total membership in early 1934 was much higher than 150000, and it is typical of contemporary French politics that the forces which combined elsewhere into substantial right-wing movements were in France divided among half a dozen different factions. If the capacity of the extreme right to take power was limited, their capacity for political disruption was enormous. Firstly, they exercised that power through journalism. Scurrilous, vicious and sometimes obscene defamation of republican and left-wing figures was the speciality of such papers as *Le Matin, Candide,* and *Je Suis Partout*. A. Cobban has stressed that 'the part played by the journalists of the right . . . in sapping the moral fibre and powers of resistance of the Third Republic can hardly be exaggerated'. Secondly, in a manner reminiscent of the Boulanger Affair or the Panama Scandal, the right was able to take advantage of another political/financial scandal to assault the Republic. The 'Stavisky Affair' centred around a shady financier, Serge Stavisky, arrested 19 times between 1927–33 in connection with various swindles. He was released each time, it was widely supposed, upon the intervention of influential friends. In January 1934, when he was found dead, many disregarded the verdict of suicide, and preferred to believe that his protectors had killed him to cover their tracks. The government's refusal to mount an enquiry was the trigger of France's most serious civil disturbances since the war. Unassuaged by the resignation of Chautemps' government, the leagues precipitated extensive rioting in Paris in February. The death of 15 people and serious injuries to another 328 further enflamed political tempers. The left remained convinced that the leagues had made a serious bid for power. With the resignation of Daladier's short-lived administration they felt no confidence in the power of the regime to keep them at bay.

Were the riots of 6th February 1934 a serious attempt to seize power? It has been the consistent claim of the French left that they were, and as late as 1947 an official enquiry described the events as 'a genuine insurrection, minutely prepared'. Others have seen them merely as a spontaneous outburst of anger and frustration against the 'invertebrate republic'. In R. Brasillach's words the events were 'an instinctive and magnificent revolt'. Whatever the case, the 6th February marked a hardening in the political divisions within the nation, and a significant stage in the decline of the Third Republic.

(m) France: The Popular Front

'The most important consequence of the 6th February', in the judgement of A. Cobban, 'was the traumatic effect it had on the French left'. Nevertheless, the startled awareness of the threat of fascism was only one of several reasons for the increased unity of the left between 1934–37. Equally important were the changed tactics of the communists, now instructed by Moscow to co-operate with social-democratic forces against the common enemy (see Chapter 13, section **o**). Also there was the decreased suspicion in France of Russian motives in the light of improved Franco-Soviet relations. Consequently, by July 1934 the Socialist and Communist parties had decided upon a common course of political action for the 1936 elections, drawing the Radical party into their alliance in the following year. The programme of this 'Popular Front' ('Front Populaire') was based in domestic affairs upon a call for the dissolution of the fascist leagues, and for the destruction of the influence of the 'two hundred families' who were the Regents of the Banque de France, and traditionally supposed by the left to dominate the economic shape of the nation. In foreign affairs, the Front advocated peace through collective security, and the consolidation of the Franco-Soviet Pact.

The elections (April 1936) took place in an atmosphere of high unemployment, deflationary economics and continued street violence, and the results indicated a widespread desire for a new political departure. A gain of 39 seats for the Socialists and a huge advance by the Communists from 10 seats to 72 gave the Popular Front a total of 380 seats. Nevertheless, the parties of the right still won 43% of the vote. This, and the fact that Leon Blum, France's first Socialist Prime Minister was of Jewish origin, did not promise a decrease in political bitterness and division.

In one respect, the short-lived Popular Front administration (April 1936–June 1937) marked an important change of direction in French politics. In two other respects, it represented a sad continuation of the slide towards political disaster. Its greatest achievement was to end the stagnation of French social legislation since the war with a package of important reforms. Prodded into premature action by a wave of strikes and factory occupations with which over a million French workers greeted 'their' electoral victory, the government concluded the 'Matignon Agreements' with representatives of unions and employers in June 1936. The agreements included wage increases of an average of 12%, a forty hour working week, compulsory collective bargaining with unions over future salary settlements, and two weeks' paid holiday per year. Independently, Blum's government took measures to nationalise arms manufacture, to bring the Banque de France under closer government control, and to stabilise the price of wheat.

The Matignon Agreements, although they went far to remedy the long-standing social backwardness of France, served nevertheless to aggravate the nation's two greatest problems. The cost of the policies, the impact of the forty hour week upon production, the apparent confirmation of the fears of industrialists and financiers, and the sporadic continuation of strike action, all served to prolong France's economic problems. The left-wing interpretation of the undermining of the Popular Front, by capitalists exporting bullion and refusing investment, obviously has some validity. The continual stagnation of production, at about 86% of the 1929 level, suggests however that the government was also let down by the very workers that placed such faith in it. Between May and December 1936 prices rose 17%, eroding the value of salary increases and eliminating the possibility of the increased consumption in which Blum had placed his hopes of recovery. In October, Blum was forced to devalue the franc after all by 25%. The government's decision (March 1937) to institute a 'pause' in its social programme, for economic reasons, had a predictable effect upon the unity of the coalition. The refusal of the Senate (June 1937) to allow the government special powers to repay its debts effectively ended its existence.

Secondly, far from bridging the rifts in French political society by the introduction of greater social justice, the Popular Front increased the polarisation of extreme political views. The Communist Party increased its membership from 30 000 to 300 000 between 1933–37. Its credibility was re-established, and it benefited from the failures of Blum's Socialists. The legal dissolution of the fascist leagues by the government resulted either in their re-emergence as legal political parties, such as Doriot's Parti Populaire Français, or in their crystallisation into sinister secret societies such as Deloncle's 'Hooded Men' ('Cagoulards'). Just as the Popular Front had declared fascism to be the true threat to France, so the right now retaliated by claiming that anti-bolshevism was the truest form of patriotism, and coining the insidious slogan 'Better Hitler than Blum'. The optimism and political cohesion of 1936 degenerated into a further flurry of brief ministries, led by Chautemps (June 1937–January 1938), Blum (March–April 1938) and Daladier (April 1938–March 1940). They were able eventually to stabilise the franc, but unable to do the same for French society, at its moment of greatest peril. Unlike the Weimar Republic, the French Third Republic was not destroyed by domestic dissention and extremism. It was, however, drained of its energy by those factors, and of the will to resist an external enemy that threatened to renew the holocaust of 1914–18.

(n) The Aims of French Foreign Policy Between the Wars

The central theme uniting the foreign policies of the inter-war French governments is not difficult to assess. It was the search for that security that the peace of 1918 had failed to guarantee, and the attempt to ensure that German recovery would not again subject France to the sufferings of a world war. The apparent continental dominance of France between 1918–33, with Russia preoccupied and Germany defeated, did not deceive many of the nation's leaders. The precondition upon which they based their policies was that renewed foreign conflict would be ruinous for France, even if she emerged victorious, and thus had to be avoided.

The means by which these aims were to be achieved were less obvious. The most striking feature of France's foreign position by 1920 was her isolation. With Russia defeated and in the throes of civil war, and with the USA turning her diplomatic back on Europe, the alliance that had saved France from defeat lay in ruins. Even the British showed suspicion of French continental power, and returned to Imperial preoccupations. 'England', remarked Clemenceau, 'is the lost illusion of my life'. Several possible remedies suggested themselves, but the tragedy of French foreign policy between the wars resulted from a failure consistently to commit the nation to any one course. The first possibility was to substitute for the vital pre-war alliance with Russia a system of alliances with the eastern European states that had emerged from the collapse of the Habsburg and Romanov empires. Thus France extended material aid and military guarantees (February 1921) to Poland, and concluded similar agreements with the 'Little Entente' of Yugoslavia, Rumania and Czechoslovakia (1922). Considerations of distance, and the comparative weakness of the 'successor states' made it unlikely that these treaties could of themselves form a sound basis for French security. In co-ordination with these anti-German alliances the French government between 1919–24 favoured a policy of 'enforcement'. That is to say, it sought security by ensuring that Germany observed the punitive clauses of the peace treaty to the letter. The culmination of this policy was the occupation of the Ruhr in January 1923 (see Chapter 17, section **d**), an action whose superficial success was offset by the increased international isolation of France which resulted. It marked the last attempt in the inter-war years to conduct a wholly independent French foreign policy.

Thereafter, French statesmen sought security in one form or another of collective security. The 'grand design' of Aristide Briand from 1925 to 1932 was to construct a series of international agreements which would bind the world's major powers to the maintenance of the 'status quo'. To the 'Briand Era', therefore, belong the Locarno Pact, Germany's admittance to the League of Nations, the Dawes and Young Plans, and the apparently naive 'Briand–Kellogg' Pact to outlaw war (see Chapter 17, sections **e** & **f**).

'Briandism' was one of the casualties of the economic crisis of the early 1930s. As her own economy slumped, the USA once again turned her back on Europe, and the collapse of the system of reparations and war debts (see Chapter 17, section **g**) renewed French isolation. Worst of all, the advent to power of rampant nationalism in the form of the Nazis nullified all progress made in Franco-German reconciliation. In the last six years of the Third Republic, France sought security primarily through the construction of traditional alliances with other states alarmed at the rise of

Germany. In doing so, foreign policy could not escape the chronic divisions of domestic politics. The reopening of serious diplomatic relations with the Soviet Union by Louis Barthou caused predictable misgivings on the right. After Barthou's death (October 1934), the foundations laid for renewed Franco-Russian co-operation, notably the Mutual Assistance Pact, were neglected by his successor. Pierre Laval's preference for developing existing Franco-Italian understanding was to founder seriously over the question of Italy's assault upon Abyssinia, and over left wing reaction to Italian involvement in the Spanish Civil War. Meanwhile, French inaction over the German remilitarisation of the Rhineland, and the completion of her Maginot Line fortifications along her eastern and north-eastern borders, seemed to many to betray a purely defensive mentality that promised little to her allies. When Hitler's fortification of the Rhineland further reduced France's capacity for offensive action, she was left largely dependent upon the support and approval of Britain. The only alternative course was that of friendship with Nazism and Italian fascism. This was preached in the immediate pre-war years by Doriot's PPF and other forces of the extreme right, but was later taken up by some parliamentary conservatives, such as Laval and Flandin. From this stultifying combination of factors arose French acceptance of the Anschluss, her non-intervention in the Spanish Civil War, and her participation in the Munich agreement.

The precise cause of France's collapse in 1940 has aroused lively controversy. The theses that ascribe responsibility to the domestic tensions within France, to the indecision of Republican politicians after 1933, and to the enormous economic and political factors outside France that placed obstacles in her path, all have some validity. For our present purposes it is sufficient to repeat that French strength in 1919 was illusory, owing most to the weaknesses of potential rivals. As those rivals recovered in the 1920s and 1930s, the Third Republic could find no agreed formula to combat their challenge.

(o) Spain: The Rival Political Forces

Of the western European nations disrupted by the economic and ideological tensions of the interwar decades, democracy had her weakest roots in Spain. Her decline from the status of a great imperial power had been a long and painful one, ending only in 1898 with the loss of Cuba and of the Philippines. The decline of feudal Spain was not offset as in France by the rise of a powerful industrial or mercantile middle class. Spain had relatively few mineral resources and, with her chronic political disorders in the 19th century, found it hard to attract foreign capital. Thus the political forces of the old Spain, and those of the new Europe, faced each other across a divide of centuries.

Three sources of intense conservatism should be noted in Spain. The aristocracy remained more of an elite and aloof caste than in any other western state, barricaded behind pedigrees and influence accumulated over hundreds of years. Often the prestige of centuries was supplemented by huge fortunes. The Duke of Medinaceli owned 200 000 acres; the Duke of Penaranda owned 125 000; a total of only 50 000 landowners accounted between them for the ownership of half of Spain. Secondly, Spanish conservatism drew support from the Church, staffed in the 1930s by 115 000 priests, monks and nuns. Its influence rested upon an almost complete control of education, and also upon very substantial wealth, acquired not only from land, but from a wide variety of investments. Cardinal Segura, Archbishop of Toledo, represented not only the wealth of the Church, with an annual income of 600 000 pesetas, but also its philosophical outlook. He was, wrote R. Oliveira, 'a thirteenth century churchman, who thought that a bath was the invention of heathens if not the devil himself, and who wore a hair shirt like an early monk'. The spiritual power of the Church was supplemented by the worldly authority of the army. Despite an unenviable record of colonial defeats, the Spanish army maintained a social and political prestige unique in Europe. It was staffed predominantly by the sons of the right, boasting one officer to every six men, and a total of 800 generals. Largely ill-armed, ill-fed and ill-equipped, it was better suited to keep the peace in Spain than to defeat any external enemy. The exceptions to this depressing rule were the elite units stationed in Spanish Morocco, sharpened by recent successful campaigns against the rebel Moorish leader Abd-el-Krim (1921–26).

Three sources of opposition confronted this 'old' Spain. Two of them were centuries old. The first of these was the deadweight of poverty under which so many Spaniards laboured. H. Rabasseire estimated in 1938 that of 11 million Spaniards, 8 million lived at subsistence level. Of these, 4 to 5 million came into the rural categories of agricultural labourers or tenant farmers, the majority owning no land, or plots of up to 2.5 acres. The circumstances of this peasantry varied, but were especially harsh in Galicia, Léon and Old Castile. Worst of all the provinces was Andalusia which, according to P. Broué, 'probably included some of the most wretched people in Europe, and was also the land of class hatred, of the slave ever ready to revolt against his master'. A parallel theme of age-old discontent was provided by regionalism, still unextinguished after more than four centuries of nominal national unity. In the Basque region of the north, and in Catalonia, local language and traditions were guarded with special jealousy, and central government was regarded with special distrust. Barcelona was effectively the capital of Spanish political violence in the first quarter of the 20th century. Between 1919–23 alone, 700 political assassinations were committed in Catalonia, most of them in Barcelona.

The newest, but not the least bitter element in Spanish political divisions was provided by the rise of a divided but intense labour movement. Of the conflicting dogmas that competed for the favour of the Spanish working classes, anarchism had enjoyed the greatest impact. Influenced by French Syndicalism (see Chapter 8, section **m**), and by the theories of the Russian, Bakunin, the movement had enjoyed particular success in Barcelona and in Andalusia. From 1911, it found more coherent expression through the CNT (Confederacion Nacional de Trabajo—National Labour Confederation), whose various wings combined terrorism with revolutionary unionism. Socialism, again largely inspired by the French example, took time to counter the attractions of revolutionary anarchism. The socialist UGT (Union General de Trabajadores—General Workers' Union) boasted on 6000 members in 1899. By 1918, however, it numbered 200 000, especially in Madrid, Bilbao, and the Asturias. They were divided, as were the French socialists, over the question of membership of the 3rd International. The Spanish movement nevertheless produced, in Largo Caballero, the most prestigious leader of Spanish labour between the wars. Communism came late to Spain, and suffered both from that fact, and from internal divisions that reflected those of the Soviet mother-party. Gaining only one parliamentary seat in the 1933 elections, the party was further weakened by the breakaway of the dissident POUM (Partido Obrero de Unificacion Marxista—Workers' Marxist Unification Party) faction, whose influence became concentrated primarily in Catalonia.

(p) Spain: The Rise of the Republic

The Second Spanish Republic was born in 1931, less through the great strength of republican political forces than through the persistent weakness of the monarchy. Alfonso XIII, king since his birth in 1886, had worn the mantle of constitutional monarch uneasily, and not always with good faith. He was perhaps lucky that his reign had not ended ten years earlier. Military disaster in July 1921, when a conscript army of 7000 was massacred by Moorish tribesmen at Annual, in Morocco, had reflected seriously upon the competence of Alfonso. This event had called the future of the monarchy into question. As usual, however, a major political issue was settled by the attitude of the army. The king was saved from a damaging official enquiry by a 'coup' staged (September 1923) by the military commander of Catalonia, M. Primo de Rivera. Profiting from improving economic conditions, Primo de Rivera exercised a 'genial dictatorship' over Spain based, says R. Carr, on 'the Nation, Church and King in that order'. His power lasted until January 1929. In his fall, Primo de Rivera was in part the victim of general economic depression, but to a greater extent was brought down by purely Spanish factors. He had failed to create a 'new legality', that is, to found his regime upon any firm institutional basis. Above all, he had alienated powerful military elements by his attempts to streamline and modernise the army. To some historians, the period of Primo de Rivera's dictatorship was an inept and almost irrelevant interlude. R. Carr, however, has seen it as an episode of the utmost importance in Spain's development, in that it provided 'both a model and a warning to General Franco'. It provided the future dictator with economic, political and institutional ideas, but also convinced him that Spain could only be controlled with a ruthlessness that Primo de Rivera had been unwilling or unable to exercise.

Primo de Rivera's resignation brought Spain little comfort. His greatest failing was, as H. Thomas has noted, that 'he left behind him no basis for a regime'. The monarchy remained more isolated than ever, unpopular with the left for accepting the 'illegal' dictatorship of the last five and a half years, and with some on the right for dismissing it. Doubtful whether Alfonso could continue to represent their interests, the Army and the Church remained lukewarm in their support. Meanwhile, evidence of the revival and growth of republican feeling was provided by widespread student rioting and the so-called Pact of San Sebastian. This was an anti-monarchical agreement concluded by liberal, socialist and Catalan politicians and intellectuals (August 1930). In April 1931, the government decided to hold municipal elections as a means of testing the political

atmosphere. In what was effectively a plebiscite, republican candidates received huge votes of confidence in Spain's major cities. Informed by the army commanders that they would not stand against this clear expression of popular opinion, Alfonso left Madrid for exile on the evening of 14th April.

(q) Spain: The Divided Republic, 1931–36

In a manner reminiscent of 1848, the Spanish Republic came into being, not through the defeat of conservative forces, but through the unwillingness of those forces to defend the old regime. Between 1931–36, therefore, those forces lived in uneasy coexistence with the more radical forces that supported the Republic. Political instability was further guaranteed by the divisions within the Republican forces. While the left-wing groupings looked upon the constitutional change as merely the prelude to far-reaching social transformation, the centre sought an 'open republic', accommodating all Spaniards regardless of class and previous political record. The political fragmentation of contemporary Spain is well illustrated by the presence in the Parliament (Cortes) of 26 different political parties in 1931.

From April 1931 until mid-1933, the Spanish Republic was directed by a progressive alliance of Republicans and Socialists under the premierships of A. Zamora (April–December 1931) and M. Azana y Diaz (December 1931–March 1933). Their policies embraced all the prime problems of Spanish politics, but eliminated none of them. The problem of rural poverty was tackled by an Agrarian Law (1932). This allowed for the distribution to the peasantry of all unworked estates over 56 acres in area. This reform, like others, suffered from the coincidence of social radicalism with international economic depression. With Spanish exports falling by 75% between 1930–34, no funds existed to pay for loans or improvement grants to the peasantry, and the reform changed little. In short, it achieved the worst of both worlds, going far enough to excite conservative fears, but not far enough to prevent the development of frustration and impatience on the left. The projected land reform, concluded E. Malefakis, was the decisive action of the Republic, for it 'seriously threatened the strongest economic class in Spain and awakened the hopes of the impoverished peasantry'. There was much more in the Republican programme to stimulate conservative fears. Anti-clericalism, for example, was a dominant theme. The Church and the State were separated under Article 26 of the new Spanish constitution. The Jesuit order was expropriated and expelled, divorce was legalised, and the Ministry of Justice was granted powers to suppress any other religious orders that it deemed a threat to the state. The worst blow was the reaction of the government to the wave of church burnings that swept Madrid and Andalusia in May 1931. Refusing to use force against the insurgents, Azana remarked provocatively that 'all the convents in Madrid are not worth one Republican life'. Army opinion was offended by the compulsory retirement of 40% of the officer corps, by the appointment of Republican officers, and by the legal reform that made soldiers liable to civil, rather then military law, when they committed civil offences. Nationalists, meanwhile, saw with horror the grants of autonomy to Catalonia (August 1931), which seemed to them to threaten the unity of 'Holy Spain'.

Violence was never far from the surface of contemporary Spanish politics, and could come from either extreme. In August 1932, military unrest was manifested in the unsuccessful 'coup' engineered by General Sanjurjo, specifically in protest against the grant of Catalonian autonomy. In January 1933, on the other hand, an abortive anarchist rising in Andalusia resulted in a massacre of rebels by Civil Guards in the village of Casas Viejas. This was a combination of threatened revolution and savage repression that alienated right and left alike.

As a reaction to Republican policies and to the threat of revolutionary violence, Spanish conservatism presented a more united front at the elections of November 1933, in the form of the CEDA (Confederacion Espanola de Derechos Autonomas—Spanish Confederation for Autonomous Rights). Its leader was J.-M. Gil Robles. Its inspiration was the Catholic Centre Party in Germany, although its enemies saw a greater resemblance to Mussolini's Fascism, and its funds came from the wealth of landowners and of the Church. It marked the beginning of that right-wing solidarity that was to do much to shape the events of the next six years. Although failing to win an absolute majority, CEDA was, as the largest party in the Cortes, able to force a number of members into the successive cabinets of the Premier, A. Lerroux. He was himself the leader of the Radical Party. Between late 1933 and February 1936, therefore, the Republic passed through a phase of conservative government in which the legislative advances of the past three years were slowed and eroded. The salaries of priests, for example, were restored, as was much of the freedom of action of the landowners. The latter

tendency was reflected in a sharp rise in rural evictions, and in an equally sharp drop in rural wages. Predictably, the major outbreaks of anti-Republican violence now originated from the left. Saragossa and Valencia both experienced general strikes lasting for weeks, and numerous incidents and disorders culminated in the attempted national rising of the 'Workers Alliance' in October 1934. This consisted of a combination of Anarchists, Socialists and Communists. Ill-planned and badly-executed for the most part, it led, however, to two weeks of bitter fighting in the Asturias region. It ended in an estimated 3000 deaths, many of them summary executions by the victorious army.

(r) Spain: The Descent into Violence

By the time of the new parliamentary elections of February 1936, the concept of the 'open republic' to serve the interests of all Spaniards was effectively dead. It had been killed by the polarisation of politics that was more evident than ever in early 1936. On the right it was evident in the increasing popularity of the 'Falange Espanol' ('Spanish Phalanx'). This was a nationalist and elitist group founded (October 1933) by José Antonio Primo de Rivera, son of the former dictator. Influenced by the tactics of Nazism, the Falange vied with the CEDA for the leadership of the right, not by achieving electoral success, but by transferring the ideological battle to the streets. 'A mixture of rhetorical poetry and gang warfare', R. Carr has written, 'its most important contribution was to heighten the atmosphere of violence'. On the left, this polarisation was witnessed by the emergence of a 'Popular Front' coalition of Anarchists, Socialists and Communists to fight and win the elections. In fact, these elections witnessed the virtual destruction of the centre parties. They gained only 680 000 votes, against 3.78 million gained by the parties of the right, and 4.21 million polled by the Popular Front.

Although the Popular Front only thinly disguised a 'chaotic incoherence' (R. Carr) of left-wing views, its victory, and the consequences of that victory were sufficient to terrify conservatives. They were further alienated by the opening of prisons in Valencia, Oviedo and elsewhere, without governmental authority, to release those imprisoned in 1934. Also there was the dismissal of the moderate Catholic, Zamora, as President of the Republic (May 1936). Street violence, strikes and lockouts proliferated. By the estimate of Gil Robles, 269 deaths, 1287 serious injuries, and 381 political attacks upon buildings or premises occurred between February and mid-June 1936.

As in 1923 and 1931, all depended upon the attitude of the army. Although military opinion was not united, it now seemed to many officers, and especially to the younger ones, that the whole structure of 'Holy Spain' was threatened by the leftwards lurch of Spanish politics. The resolution of such commanders as General Mola and General Francisco Franco seems to have been strengthened by the murder (13th July 1936) of Calvo Sotelo, Gil Robles' successor at the head of the CEDA. He was arrested and murdered by an official police detachment in Madrid, apparently in retaliation against the assassination of a senior police officer by Falangists. Five days later, General Franco left his remote posting in the Canary Islands to join the army's crack units in Morocco and the 'generals' rising' began. Such 'indiscipline', declared General Mola, 'is justified when the abuses of power . . . lead the nation to ruin'.

Hopes of a neat military 'coup' were frustrated by the prompt reaction of left-wing and Republican organisations throughout Spain. In many places, claimed A. Nin, the army rebellion 'speeded up the revolutionary process by provoking a proletarian revolution more profound than the Russian Revolution itself'. Thus, while Seville and Valladolid fell quickly into military hands, the army rising failed totally in Madrid, Barcelona and Valencia. In late July 1936, therefore, Spain stood divided along class lines, but also along lines of 'geographical loyalty' with Catalonia and the Basque region remaining loyal to the Republic that had given them autonomy.

(s) Spain: The Civil War

The relative strengths of the two sides at the outbreak of war appeared evenly balanced. Many of the Republican strengths, however, were illusory. The Republic certainly benefited from the enthusiasm and dedication of tens of thousands of workers. They were armed by their political organisations and, eventually, by a reluctant government. These were weapons, however, of dubious value. Factional rivalries and ideological disagreements, such as those witnessed in Barcelona by George Orwell, severely reduced the efficiency of these militias as a front line force. Although they often fought bravely in defensive positions, they rarely produced a sustained or co-ordinated offensive. Outbursts of class hatred, and of more positive revolutionary expropriations and collectivisations of estates and factories, completed the alienation of property owners and sent them flocking into Nationalist zones. The task of the Republican leaders was, in Malraux's phrase, 'to organise the Apocalypse'.

The Nationalists, as supporters of the military rebels chose to call themselves, had the best of the troops and the best of the commanders. The African Army formed the cream of the Spanish forces, and they were soon to enjoy the support of substantial foreign interventionist forces. In particular, the latter factor ensured the Nationalists of air superiority. In contrast to the divided leadership of the Republic, the commander of the African Army, General Franco, soon came to exercise an unparalleled political and military authority. He was aided in this by the deaths in action of such potential rivals as Generals Sanjurjo and Mola, and by the execution by the Republicans of the Falangist leader José Antonio Primo de Rivera. He nevertheless owed much to his own political tact which made him broadly acceptable to Catholic, Monarchist and Falangist factions, and in 1937 he was formally designated head of the Nationalist state. In terms of resources, the Nationalists also controlled the main agricultural regions, quickly causing hardship in the industrial cities. The Republicans' initial economic advantage in controlling those cities faded, on the other hand, as resources of raw materials fell into the hands of the Nationalists.

The first blows of the war were struck in the pursuit of the class struggle. In the Republican zone, an estimated 6800 priests were murdered as suspected enemy agents. In Nationalist territory the shooting of working class leaders, and of resisting workers, was a matter of routine. Such events, in R. Carr's words, 'put a river of blood between the working class and the gentlemen'. Strategically, the advantage quickly passed to the Nationalists. Advancing north and west, Franco's troops captured Badajoz (August 1936) and linked up with Mola's forces in the north. Meanwhile, the capture of Irun (September 1936) cut off the Basque region from any hope of relief from the French border. At this juncture, Madrid became the focal point of the war. Advancing along the Tagus valley, Nationalist troops were in the suburbs of the capital by the end of September. They were still there in the spring of 1937, denied by the heroic defence which made Madrid an international symbol of resistance to fascism. Aided by the arrival of the International Brigades, Republican troops won their first major victories against Franco's troops at the Battle of the Jarama (February 1937) and against Italian forces at Guadalajara (March 1937).

Frustrated, Franco turned his attention north to the Basque region. There he gained greater success.

SPAIN: MAIN REGIONS & TOWNS

THE MILITARY SITUATION IN JULY
1936

THE MILITARY SITUATION IN MARCH
1937

THE MILITARY SITUATION IN JULY
1938

MAP 12   THE SPANISH CIVIL WAR

KEY

     NATIONALIST TERRITORY

Bilbao (June 1937) and Santander (August 1937) fell, leaving the socialist strongholds of the north with their rich iron ore deposits in Nationalist hands. By the close of 1937 Franco controlled 62% of Spanish territory and half of the nation's population. Further south, a series of Republican offensives succeeded in keeping the Nationalists out of Madrid, but their forces nevertheless struck an important blow with a drive through Aragon to the sea near Valencia (March 1938) which cut Republican territory in two. Although still capable of bold offensives to harrass Franco's forces, such as that across the River Ebro (July 1938), the Republican cause was now suffering from crippling handicaps. Military inferiority, material shortages, and desertions in the face of defeat were now capped by political divisions and ideological disputes. Republican resistance in Catalonia crumbled in the face of Nationalist offensives in December and January, and Barcelona fell on 23rd January 1939. It was sadly fitting that one of the last acts of the Civil War was an internal feud between Anarchists and Communists that led to the collapse of resistance in Madrid in March 1939, and thus to the end of the conflict.

(t) Spain: The War and Europe

Although essentially Spanish in its origins, the Civil War seemed to many observers to be a miniature enactment of the great contemporary tension in Europe, of the great confrontation between the forces of communism and fascism, or between political freedom and totalitarianism. It became, therefore, a major focus of political and intellectual concern throughout Europe. Its impact upon a generation of western intellectuals was fundamental. It seemed, wrote the English poet C. Day Lewis, to be 'a battle between light and darkness'. Most committed writers would have agreed with him that the Republican cause constituted the 'light'. From the Republican side emerged several masterpieces of literature of which the best known are probably Ernest Hemingway's *For Whom the Bell Tolls* and George Orwell's *Homage to Catalonia*. Perhaps the most famous celebration of the war was a painting, Pablo Picasso's great 'Guernica'. This was an abstract protest at the bombing by German planes of a market town in the Basque region.

The politicians of western European democracies were less committed. Although the French Popular Front government appeared willing to extend aid to its Spanish counterpart in July 1936, its attitude quickly changed. In part this was a reaction to the

demands of her British ally for caution, but in large part was due to right-wing hostility within France to the idea of aid to the Spanish leftists. 'We are reluctant to believe', declared the right-wing *L'Echo de Paris*, 'that the government could commit this crime against the nation'. In Britain, too, the distinct preference of some leading political figures for the politics of Franco, and the desire to avoid further confrontation with Italy, contributed towards the eventual policy of 'Nonintervention'. In theory, this principle became the official policy of 25 powers who accepted the invitation to join and support (September 1936) the International Committee for the Application of Nonintervention in Spain. Three powers, however, were prominent in flouting that principle.

Of these, the most cautious was the Soviet Union. Stalin was torn between his desire to win the trust of the western democracies, and his hostility to Spanish Anarchist and Trotskyite elements and, on the other hand, the need to be seen at the head of world socialism. Thus he committed himself only hesitantly to the Republican cause. Soviet manpower played little part in the war, but her military material was a crucial factor in the Republic's early survival. In March 1937, so American observers estimated, 420 of the Republic's 460 aircraft were Russian. For manpower, however, the Republic had to rely upon the foreign volunteers of the International Brigades. Organised into national units, with Frenchmen and left-wing Italian and German refugees prominent, some 35 000 men fought in Spain from November 1936 onwards. They formed probably the most reliable units of the Republican army, and were prominent in most of the major engagements.

As was the case with most resources, the most valuable foreign aid was available to the Nationalists. Italian aid had been sought as early as 1934, and began to arrive in substantial quantities as soon as Nationalist troops secured their first successes. Mussolini's motives for intervention were complex. While undoubtedly flattered by the apparent expansion of his Fascist creed, his reasons were primarily practical. He wanted to maintain the military prestige of his regime established in Abyssinia, and to strengthen Italy's Mediterranean status by the establishment of a friendly regime, and perhaps of bases, at the western end of that sea. In all, Italy probably contributed some 70 000 men, about 20% of the total Nationalist forces, some 700 aircraft, and 950 tanks to Franco's cause. It is probable that the total cost to Italy of this intervention was some 14 billion lire and some 11 000 casualties. The contribution of Germany was less ambitious both in terms of motive and of scale. There seems little doubt that Hitler was primarily concerned that Spain should serve as a testing ground for Germany's new and untried armaments. The fact that they would be tested against Soviet material, and that the prolonged war in Spain might stir up pacifism in Britain and France only added to the attractions of intervention. Nevertheless, it is unlikely that there were ever more than 10 000 Nazi personnel in Spain. The German government compensated, however, by the quality of its aid. The elite Condor Legion, perpetrators of the infamous aerial attack on Guernica, was the most effective airforce unit in the war. Although equipped at first with older aircraft, such as commercial Junker 52s converted to serve as bombers, they later had, in their Heinkel 111 bombers, and their Messerschmitt 109 fighters, the most advanced planes seen in Spain. It was the Condor Legion that ensured that Spanish civilians were the first in the world to experience the new phenomenon of concentrated aerial bombardment.

The impact of German and Italian aid on the military outcome of the war was fundamental. Its impact on Spain's future political alignment was slight. Although Franco's government concluded economic agreements with her allies, and joined the Anticomintern Pact (March 1939), it steadfastly refused to align Spain with Fascism and Nazism in the coming European conflict. Franco's resistance to Hitler's blandishments at their meeting at Hendaye (October 1940) was so stubborn that the Führer remarked that he 'would rather have three or four teeth yanked out than go through that again'.

(u) Spain: The Price of the War

The changes wrought in Spain by the Civil War were far-reaching. It was, judged H. Thomas, 'the Spanish share in the tragic European breakdown of the 20th century, in which the liberal heritage of the 19th century and the sense of optimism which had lasted since the renaissance, were shattered'. As such, it left scars that time has not yet erased. The most obvious scar was that inflicted by human and material losses. H. Thomas has estimated the total human cost of the war at about 500 000 lives. Of these, not more than 40% died in action. The rest were the victims of bombing, executions, reprisals and malnutrition. The list of material damage is equally eloquent. One hundred and seventy-three towns were so badly damaged as to need substantial post-war government aid for their reconstruction; half a million houses were damaged, half of them so badly as to be uninhabitable; 42% of all railway locomotives and 33% of all merchant shipping was destroyed. War damage rendered economic recovery difficult. The 11 million hectares sown with wheat in 1935, for instance, had been reduced to 8 million by 1939. The advent of European war in the wake of civil war meant, furthermore, that Spain had to continue for another decade in isolation and without hope of aid or recovery. To this must be added the bitterness of exile for many Spaniards. No wholly reliable figures exist for the number of Republicans who sought safety across the French border, but by early 1940 there were some 350 000 in France alone. Others had determined to try their luck in South America or even in the USSR. Some had even risked a return to Spain.

Nationalist Spain, meanwhile, faced the twin problems of a domestic political vacuum, and of diplomatic isolation. In the first respect, General Franco had no serious rivals. The war had wiped out not only the whole spectrum of the Spanish left but many of the leading figures of the right. Sanjurjo, Mola, Sotelo, and José Antonio Primo de Rivera had all met violent deaths. Also, in S. Payne's estimate, 60% of all pre-war Falangists had died in the war. This situation Franco was able to exploit cleverly throughout his 36 years of pragmatic dictatorship. Drawing representatives of monarchist, military, ecclesiastical and financial interests into his cabinets, he succeeded in forming governments of the broad right, where the Republic had never succeeded in uniting the broad left. Compromise with his allies went hand-in-hand with unmitigated hostility to those who opposed him. The Italian foreign minister, Count Ciano, spoke of 'a serious and most rigorous purge' in the years after 1939. In his estimate of wartime deaths, H. Thomas allowed for 100 000 postwar executions. Diplomatic normality came much more slowly. Although a member of the Anticomintern Pact, and recognised after April 1939 by all major powers except the USSR, the allied victory in the Second World War left the Franco regime in renewed ideological isolation. Gradually she was reintegrated into the international community. In 1955 she was admitted to the United Nations, and ten years later benefited from the 'Cold War' between eastern and western blocs by leasing military bases to the USA in return for 1.8 billion dollars in American aid. Only very recently has Spain truly begun to live down the terrible legacy of her civil war, by the proclamation of a constitutional monarchy upon Franco's death (1975), and her application for membership of the European Common Market.

Progress Paragraphs

Answer the following questions in about 150 words.

What major problems did the Weimar Republic inherit in 1918? Sections (**a** & **b**)

In what ways was the Republican constitution more democratic than that of the pre-war years?
Section (**a**)

What alternative political systems were proposed by the enemies of the Weimar Republic? Section (**c**)

Why did right-wing opposition to the Republic fail between 1920–23? Sections (**c** & **d**)

What were the effects on the Weimar Republic of the invasion of the Ruhr? Section (**d**)

Explain the increased stability of the Weimar Republic between 1924–29. Section (**e**)

To what extent, and by what means did the Weimar Republic restore Germany's position in European diplomacy? Section (**f**)

Explain the political success of the NSDAP between 1928–33. Section (**g**)

In what respects was France's victory in 1918 illusory? Section (**h**)

Account for the general success of French conservatism in the 1920s. Section (**i**)

To what extent had France recovered from the economic damage of the war by 1929? Section (**j**)

How did the depression affect the French economy?
Section (**k**)

Account for the growing disillusion with French parliamentary politics in the late 1920s and the early 1930s. Sections (**i** & **l**)

How serious was the threat of right-wing extremism in France in the early 1930s? Section (**l**)

What was the impact of the French Popular Front (a) upon social policy, (b) upon domestic political stability? Section (**m**)

By what different means did French Foreign Ministers seek to ensure national security between the wars?
Section (**n**)

What were the main conservative forces in Spain in 1930? Section (**o**)

What were the main influences on the Spanish left in 1930? Section (**o**)

Why did the Spanish monarchy fall in 1931?
Section (**p**)

Show how the Republican government offended Spanish conservatives between 1931–36.
Section (**q**)

What evidence was there of hardening political attitudes in Spain between 1931–36?
Sections (**q** &

Why did Franco's coup degenerate into civil war?
Sections (**r** & **s**)

What advantages were enjoyed by the Spanish Nationalist forces? Sections (**s** & **t**)

Explain the attitudes of the major European powers to the Spanish Civil War. Section (**t**)

What did Spain lose by the Civil War?
Section (**u**)

15
Fascism and Italy

(a) The Nature of Fascism

Probably no historical term has been so abused and misused as the word 'fascism'. In modern political usage the term has too often become one of crude abuse aimed at any political views to the right of one's own and, as M. Kitchen has pointed out, 'to denounce as "fascist" regimes in Latin America . . . the practices of the Metropolitan Police, or restrictions on the rights and freedoms of homosexuals . . . does nothing to uncover the true nature of the problems under attack'. In the strictest sense, fascism in the 1920s and 1930s could be taken to refer only to the movement led by Mussolini in Italy, which called itself by that name. So many other movements, however, imitated elements of Italian fascism, that it is usual to refer to the fashion for authoritarian right-wing regimes in inter-war Europe as a fashion for fascism. The generalisation, as this chapter will show, is neither wholly valid, nor altogether misleading, and it is in that sense, therefore, that we will employ the term.

During its life, and since its decline, a number of general theories of fascism have been devised. To many Marxist theorists, especially those of the contemporary Third International, fascism was interpreted as the last desperate and violent attempts of capitalism to prevent its own collapse. It is a theory that gains some sustenance from the widespread sympathy of 'big business' for fascist and Nazi policies in Italy and Germany, but which suffers from the fact that it is hard to see Italy, Spain or Portugal as societies in which capitalism in the 1920s had reached its highest point of development. Many western liberals, such as Hannah Arendt and C. J. Friedrich, retaliated in the atmosphere of the east–west 'Cold War' by equating fascism, not with western capitalism, but with Soviet communism. They saw both as manifestations of the wider concept of 'totalitarianism'. Parallels were drawn stressing the common imposition of ideology and a single party system, and the common use of terror as a political tool. This line of approach succeeds as long as one concentrates upon means, but is weaker when one

considers ends. The preconceived end product of the Marxist revolution, the classless society, is clearly stated by communist theorists. The final aim of fascism, where it is possible to find one at all, is certainly not the same.

At the root of this problem of definition lies the essential difference between the histories of Marxism and fascism. The first began life as a theory, subsequently modified and adapted when put into practice. Fascism, on the other hand, existed as an emotional form of political action before theories were devised, as by G. Gentile in Italy or A. Rosenberg in Germany, to justify or to define it. Essentially, for all its claims to the contrary, fascism was a negative phenomenon. It was not a brave new world, but a reaction against certain elements in the contemporary world. Fascism, as H. Trevor-Roper has concluded, 'is inseparable from the special experience of one generation: the generation which flourished—or failed to flourish—between the two world wars'. The great political facts for that generation were those created by the First World War. The collapse of well-established regimes in central Europe left in their place parliamentary regimes often unable to solve the vast economic and social problems they inherited. They were thus unable to command widespread loyalty or respect. The economic collapse that threatened to follow in the 1920s and early 1930s only heightened the sense of insecurity and instability. In specific cases, as in Germany, Hungary and Italy, the peace terms of 1919 left a burning sense of national injustice. On the other hand, the success of the Bolshevik revolution in Russia offered an alternative vision of the future that horrified the bourgeoisie and those members of the working classes that aspired to bourgeois standards. Sometimes, as H. Trevor-Roper has pointed out, response to these factors took the form of a dynamic, if incoherent philosophy, genuinely determined to sweep away existing religious, social and governmental systems, as was the young Mussolini. Sometimes it expressed itself in more traditional conservative forms, such as Franco personified in Spain. Most 'fascist' regimes in the

1920s and 1930s were coalitions of the two responses. Hence their frequent internal tensions and their divergent forms. On a more practical level, the war and subsequent recession left a further element that was to be a prominent feature of fascist movements. The large numbers of ex-servicemen, brutalised by war and apparently robbed of security in peacetime, formed the basis of the characteristic para-military organisations that gave fascism its original physical impact. These were the SA in Germany and the 'Squadristi' in Italy.

Fascism certainly had an ancestry in past political and social philosophy, but it was a confused and incoherent one. In the work of two men we can see the embryos of the authoritarian fascist state and of the charismatic fascist leader. These are Hegel (see Chapter 1, section **e**), with his views on the dominant role of the state, and Nietzsche (see Chapter 7, section **p**), with his belief in the potential of man once freed from the 'slave mentality' of Christianity. Socialism, too, played its role in the genesis of fascism. Mussolini in Italy, Mosley in Britain, Doriot in France, Quisling in Norway, all began their political careers as socialists. On the left of most fascist movements stood men, like the Strasser brothers in Germany, who still cherished ideas of sweeping away the old social and political order, and substituting a new one. This was to be socialist in its social aims, but otherwise still clinging to the principles of nationalism. Indeed, because nationalism was such a strong element in fascism, it was inevitable that each movement broadly termed 'fascist' should be firmly rooted in the specific historical problems of its own country, and should be dedicated to specifically national aims. In this sense, in Mussolini's words, fascism was truly 'not for export'. For all the shared features of the authoritarian regimes of the 1920s and 1930s, it would be wrong to seek in them uniformity of aims. Nevertheless, we can perhaps accept the broad definition proposed by R. A. H. Robinson of fascism as 'a nationalist, anti-Marxist, mass-mobilising political movement, normally headed by a charismatic leader, aiming at the complete conquest of power and seeking the fullest control possible over all aspects of life in a polity by means of a single-party system'.

(b) Italy: the Bankruptcy of Liberalism

Superficially, it might seem surprising that fascism was able to establish itself so firmly in Italy, a state apparently founded throughout its 60 years' existence up to 1920 upon the liberal principles of Cavour and upon the moderate concepts of constitutional monarchy. Behind the achievements of Cavour, however, lurked the illiberal ghost of Mazzini and, as Chapter Four has indicated, the liberalism of Cavour himself was laced with elements of arbitrary government. Since 1870, furthermore, a number of factors had operated to undermine the liberal foundations of the Italian state.

One factor was the debased and often corrupt form of parliamentary government practised in Italy. It was dominated by 'Transformism', the habit first developed by Cavour of welding large and sometimes unlikely coalitions in support of ministries. Thus it lacked true party spirit and principles, and precluded any real clash of alternative party principles. It tended merely to facilitate the personal control of those politicians most skilled at the art, and the three longest serving premiers of the period, A. Depretis (1881–87), F. Crispi (1887–90 and 1893–96) and G. Giolitti (1892, 1903–04, 1906 and 1911), were all masters of the practice. All too often, what was justified as a means to political stability became, in D. Mack Smith's words, 'a common refuge where they laid aside their internal quarrels and joined in parcelling out power and jobbery'. Although this form of administration was not without its legislative successes, such as the various laws for agricultural improvement (1897–1906) and Giolitti's new electoral law (1912), Italy remained a country of enormous social and economic problems. The southern provinces, especially, remained backward and poverty-stricken. The sociologist L. Franchetti described in 1902 how 'peasant risings, which usually lead to bloodshed, are characteristic and normal events in the public life of the south', which was 'without any middle class, even without workers who are above the poverty level and possess a rudimentary education'. Eighty per cent of Sicilians were illiterate in 1900, and 90% of Sicilian army recruits had to be rejected as medically unfit. The general condition of the Italian working classes expressed itself in the 'haemorrhage' of emigration whereby, in 1914, nearly 6 million Italians out of 41 million lived and worked abroad.

Two major interests regarded the liberal state with almost unrelieved hostility. One was the growing force of socialism, stimulated by the industrial growth of the late 1880s and the early 1890s, and developing its political organisation. By the eve of the First World War, it was capturing 25% of electoral votes. As an alternative to liberalism before the war it was weakened by its constant divisions, and by the preference of many of its leaders for reform rather than revolution. Its many off-shoots, such as the anarchists, the syndicalists, who engineered a highly effective general strike in 1904, and the embryonic communist party, represented altogether a substantial number of men in opposition to the whole basis of parliamentarianism. The second hostile force was the Catholic Church. Until the turn of the century the Church maintained the official detachment of Pius IX (see Chapter 4, section **p**). It instructed good Catholics to boycott elections, and scarcely any leading figure in national politics was a practising Catholic. When Pius X officially relaxed this boycott in 1904, it was not out of any increased regard for the state, but from fear of the increasing influence of socialism. The Church, therefore, became the potential ally of the more conservative elements in the state. As such, it was equally likely to be an ally, active or passive, of the anti-Marxist forces that arose in the wake of the First World War.

Lastly, in the years immediately before the war, parliamentary government came under attack from a resurgent nationalist party. Modest in terms of electoral success, this group enjoyed disproportionate intellectual influence, notably from the support of the writer Gabriele D'Annunzio. The residual nationalism surviving from the 'Risorgimento' received great stimulus from the war of 1911–12 in which Italy secured Libya from Turkey, while the mismanagement and huge cost of the war went further to discredit the existing regime. The entry of Italy into the European war in 1915 naturally enhanced the influence of this movement to an extent unprecedented since the capture of Rome in 1870.

(c) Benito Mussolini

Although the rise of fascism in Italy had deeper and more complex causes than the personality of Benito Mussolini, that personality had a profound influence upon the form taken by this alternative to liberalism. Mussolini was born (29th July 1883) the son of a blacksmith, near Forli in the Romagna. In a hard childhood may be found the seeds of his hostility towards bourgeois society, its principles and its standards, which he maintained throughout his political career. In the enthusiastic, republican socialism of his father may be found the impetus that propelled him into the ranks of the socialist party in his early days. In his turbulent, violent personality as a young man may be seen the beginnings of the vigorous, often incoherent

gestures that later characterised so much of fascist policy. The young Mussolini was expelled four times from his various schools for indiscipline and violence. His most recent biographer, D. Mack Smith, has concluded that the innate streak of violence in his character was of as great importance in his development as any of the political philosophers, such as Sorel and Nietzsche, by whom he later claimed to have been influenced.

Failing to find either satisfaction or success in his brief career as a teacher, Mussolini was soon set upon the road of political agitation, organisation and journalism. His success as editor of a provincial socialist journal (1909–12) led to national recognition and to the highly successful editorship of Italy's primary socialist organ *Avanti!* ('Forward!') in November 1912. In his views during this period can be discerned some of the future bases of fascism. Identified with the left wing of Italian socialism, Mussolini was a violent critic of parliamentary government, and of those socialists who sought parliamentary seats. His solutions to the social and economic problems of contemporary Italy were revolutionary solutions, and he was vitriolic in his attacks upon socialists such as Turati and Bissolati who sought change by moderate reform. Alongside such views, however, stood others that are difficult to square with the subsequent policies of fascist Italy. The man who dismissed the notion of the "Fatherland' as 'a fiction, a mystification, a conventional lie', and who condemned imperialist ambitions in North Africa as 'a mad adventure', seems far removed from the nationalist leader of the 1930s and from the conqueror of Abyssinia.

Mussolini's conversion from internationalism and left wing socialism shortly followed the outbreak of war in 1914. By condemning the Italian policy of neutrality in a sensational editorial in *Avanti!* (18th October 1914), he not only flew in the face of accepted socialist policy, but effectively turned his back on the party for ever. His change of heart has been interpreted in a variety of fashions. His former socialist colleagues, in their sense of betrayal, brought charges of foreign bribery. Other critics have seen the reversal of policy as a cynical acknowledgement that, with his recent election defeat in Forli (October 1913) and the collapse of the revolutionary 'Red Week' riots (June 1914), the political future of socialism seemed bleak. C. Hibbert has been more generous in his view that Mussolini was attracted to intervention in the war by the anticipation that it would bring nearer the revolutionary upheaval for which he hoped. There is also much to be said for the interpretation of S. W. Halperin, who has ascribed Mussolini's warlike stance to 'his temperamental incapacity to abide a neutral stance, to remain a mere spectator, in the midst of world-shaking events'.

Although fascist historians later invented a number of heroic exploits for Mussolini, his military service seems to have been relatively uneventful, apart from an injury received during a training exercise. When he returned thereafter to civilian life, to journalism, the editorials of his new journal *Il Popolo d'Italia* ('The Italian People') were distinguished by views easily recognisable as those of embryonic fascism. Prominent among them were the demand that post-war Italy should be governed by those who had fought for her, and the resentment that Italy should be cheated of such fruits of victory as Fiume by the vague idealism of President Wilson.

(d) The Rise of Italian Fascism

The immediate post-war period held considerable promise for such an ambitious and flexible politician. The frustrations of the peace treaty, the economic difficulties that produced two million Italian unemployed by November 1919, and the subsequent disillusionment of many ex-servicemen, reduced the prestige of the liberal regime to a new low ebb. The political format by which Mussolini hoped to exploit this discontent became evident with the formation in Milan (March 1919) of the first 'Combat Group' ('Fascio di combattimento'). The name of the group, and of the movement, was derived from the 'Fascio'. This was a bundle of rods with an axe at its centre, that formed the insignia of the lictors of ancient Rome, and was a symbol of unity and strength. Initially, the programme proposed by these 'fascists' showed the continuing influence of left wing politics, and especially of French syndicalism (see Chapter 8, section **m**). They proposed a republic, the decentralisation of government, the abolition of conscription, the closure of all banks and of the stock exchange, profit sharing and management participation by the workers, and the seizure of Church lands. For Mussolini, however, as D. Mack Smith has stated, 'fascism was not a system of immutable beliefs but a path to political power'. When the party only polled 4795 votes in the Milan elections of November 1919, fascist policy began a steady movement to the right.

From 1920 the stress of fascist policy fell instead upon the twin themes of nationalism and anti-Bolshevism. Fervent support for D'Annunzio in his spectacular, illegal seizure of the city of Fiume for Italy (September 1919) seemed almost to annex

him to the fascist cause. Meanwhile, the anti-communist violence of the fascist action squads (Squadristi) and the new party line in favour of free enterprise went far to reassure the middle classes. The change of direction was a substantial success. Big business was eager to subsidise this valuable anti-communist force, and substantial contributions from such sources as the Fiat motor company, the Pirelli tyre company and the Italian Banking Association put the fascists on a firmer financial footing than most of their rivals. By late 1921 the party claimed 320 000 members. Of these 18 000 were landowners, 14 000 were small tradesmen, and 4000 were industrialists. However, many were peasants (36 000) or members of the urban working classes (23 000) seeking a refuge from what they saw as the twin evils of ruthless capitalism and doctrinaire socialism.

The spectacular growth of this faction made it a natural candidate for a place in one of the government's 'Transformist' coalitions: Giolitti had already aided the growth of fascism by turning a blind eye to the excesses of the Squadristi when, in May 1921, he accepted Mussolini's offer of an electoral pact. As part of a government alliance, the fascists won 35 parliamentary seats in the elections of that year. This was a small start in a house of 535 seats, but a substantial advance that gave Mussolini and his fellow deputies, as D. Mack Smith has pointed out, 'a new authority, a new respectability and a valuable freedom from arrest'.

(e) The March on Rome

It was neither probable, nor desirable to many in the fascist movement, that they should come to power by these parliamentary means. Mussolini himself found his style of oratory ill-suited to parliamentary debate, while other fascist deputies showed their contempt for the institution by brandishing pistols in the chamber and assaulting socialist deputies.

In the event, the crisis in Italian politics continued to operate to the advantage of the fascists. A general strike called by the socialists in August 1922 gave the 'Squadristi' a golden opportunity to pose as the country's sole protection against the imminent 'red' threat. The strike, badly organised and ill-led, collapsed within 24 hours. This created the impression that the nation had been saved while the liberal regime stood helplessly by. In reality, the events of August illustrated the weaknesses both of the liberals and of the socialists, as well as the pro-fascist sympathies of many police and army officers, and indicated that the time was ripe for ambitious action. Simultaneously with the formulation of a plan for the seizure of strategic points in Milan and other major cities, and for a subsequent march on Rome, Mussolini sought to reassure influential sectors of Italian opinion of fascism's regard for the monarchy and for economic liberalism.

The 'coup d'état' began on 27th October 1922. In many cities, the active or passive support of local government guaranteed success, but it seemed unlikely that the 26 000 fascists converging on Rome could succeed against the regular troops in their path. Success was, however, guaranteed by the surprising refusal of King Victor Emmanuel to sign his prime minister's decree of martial law. Historians seeking to explain this fateful timidity have variously stressed the degree of pro-fascist feeling in court circles, and the effect of veiled fascist threats to replace the king with the Duke of Aosta. 'Temperamentally', wrote D. Mack Smith, the king 'was drawn to anyone who would take firm decisions and control domestic unrest'. The result was the cutting of the ground from beneath the feet of the liberal ministers. Losing all doubts, Mussolini exploited his position of strength and had, by 29th October, received a royal summons to form a ministry as the youngest prime minister in Italian history.

It was in the nature of fascism that its official historians should portray the events of October 1922 as a glorious national revolution. More recently it has become fashionable to belittle the fascist insurrection and to stress the surrender of the regime through panic, weakness or self-interest. The truth lies between the two extremes. The insurrection was, indeed, a bold stroke, a substantial risk by its leaders, and carefully and intelligently prepared. On the other hand, it was resistable. Fascism owed its triumph ultimately, not to fascists alone, but to the mass of conservatives, businessmen, army officers, small traders and peasants, who saw Mussolini as the alternative to anarchy. This was regardless of the fact that the anarchy was largely the responsibility of the fascists in the first place.

(f) The Growth of Fascist Dictatorship

It was never likely that the fascist leadership would be content merely to capture the machinery of the liberal state. Despite an initially conciliatory attitude to other non-socialist parties, therefore, the first years in power were dedicated to the steady destruction of parliamentarianism in Italy. Such had been the success of the party's black-shirted 'Squadristi' in the early years of the movement, that Mussolini now transformed them (December 1922) into an official paramilitary body called the Volunteer Militia for National Security. Their wholesale use of violence and intimidation was to be a prominent feature of Italian elections in the 1920s. A prime minister also had more subtle means at his disposal. The new electoral law drafted by G. Acerbo (July 1923) aimed to transform fascism's minority status by proposing that any party gaining more votes than any of its rivals, providing that it gained at least 25% of the total, would be entitled to two-thirds of the seats in the assembly. This was in the interests of political stability. It should be noted that this law, like others in the early days of Mussolini's power, became law with the help of liberal votes. This mutilated form of parliamentarianism limped on for five years, until a further electoral law (September 1928) decreed that the whole composition of parliament should be determined by the Fascist Grand Council headed by Mussolini. This body would formulate a list of 400 nominees which the electorate would then be invited to accept or reject 'en masse'. Given the means of intimidation in the government's hands, it is perhaps surprising that as many as 136 000 voters rejected the list in 1929. By 1934, however, the number of rejections had fallen to 15 000.

The Acerbo electoral law and the violence of the 1924 elections also precipitated the decisive clash with the party's major rivals, the socialists. A socialist deputy, Giacomo Matteotti, showed great courage in his open defiance and criticism of fascist methods. The result was his kidnap and subsequent murder by fascist thugs. Whether or not he had directly encouraged or ordered the crime, Mussolini clearly bore the moral responsibility for it, and his political position became extremely vulnerable. Two factors aided his survival. Once again, the political tactics of the socialists were naive. Their reaction to the death of Matteotti was to leave parliament in protest. This action became known as the 'Aventine Secession', in commemoration of an incident in ancient Roman history. Their eloquent gesture merely left the fascists in fuller control. Secondly, King Victor Emmanuel, the only man with the constitutional power to dismiss Mussolini, once again shirked a hard decision and accepted the argument of force.

Initially shaken by the Matteotti crisis, Mussolini now seemed to exploit the new-found strength of his position, although F. W. Deakin has stressed the role played in this process by nominal subordinates. Of special importance was the work of the new party secretary, R. Farinacci, in overhauling and centralising the party machinery for the tasks of national government. The first months of 1925 saw a miniature 'reign of terror' characterised by house searches, closures of hostile newspapers, harassment of political opponents and constant attacks upon freedom of association and of speech. In November, a plot against Mussolini's life by a former socialist deputy, Zaniboni, provided the pretext for the official suppression of the socialist party. A series of decrees to strengthen the powers of provincial fascist officers, a formal decree (October 1926) banning all other political parties, and the formation (September 1926) of a secret police force, the OVRA, completed the apparatus of political dictatorship.

(g) The Fascist State: The Corporative Theory

The years 1923–25 formed a period of ambiguous policy statements designed to attract the widest possible support, and of negative assaults upon existing institutions. Only very slowly did the outline of a fascist 'new order' emerge. In theory, this 'new order' owed much to the ideas of syndicalism, but in Italian hands the theories of Sorel had changed significantly. From being a means towards the revolutionary overthrow of capitalism, the 'corporative' system in Italy posed as a solution to the problems of class warfare. It also posed as a bridge between the factions of workers and employers in the interests of the fatherland.

The suppression of existing Socialist and Catholic trades unions paved the way for the so-called Rocco Law of April 1926. While outlawing both workers' strikes and employers' lockouts, the law gave legal recognition to the fascist syndicates. Although these syndicates consisted exclusively either of workers or employers, the law provided for corporations, or 'central liaison organs', to mediate between the two. The actual implementation of this new order was extremely slow. Only in March 1930 was a National Council of Corporations created as an advisory body on the development of the system, and not until 1934 were the Corporations actually brought into existence. By 1936 there were 22 of them representing all the major branches of industrial, agricultural, artistic and professional life in Italy. Now Mussolini claimed to see in these institutions the logical successors to the parliament whose very 'raison d'étre' had ceased to exist, he claimed, with the death of the multi-party system. Indeed, in 1938–39, the parliamentary system was abolished in name as well as in practice, and replaced by a so-called Chamber of Fasces and Corporations.

In theory, therefore, the government of Italy moved towards a decentralised state in which the varying interests of workers and employers were directly represented through their corporations. In reality, in the words of the contemporary historian G. Salvemini, corporatism was 'an elaborate piece of imposing humbug'. For all their activity in an advisory capacity, the corporations had no role in the formulation of economic policy, which remained firmly in the government's hands. In each corporation, furthermore, the representatives of employers and workers were joined by officials of the Ministry of Corporations, whose task was to ensure that the government's view prevailed. The theory of decentralisation barely masked the reality of rigid fascist control. As S. W. Halperin has concluded: 'In the last analysis, the principal mission of the corporative machinery was to lend an air of decentralisation and democratic spontaneity to a decision-making process that was completely dominated by the dictator and his associates. . . . The disparity between pretence and practice could hardly have been greater'.

(h) The Fascist State: The Reality

If corporativism did not dominate the Italian state under fascist rule, then what did? As we have seen, much fascist energy in the early years of power was poured into the task of disarming other existing sources of influence such as the other political parties and parliament (see section **f**), the trades unions (see section **g**) or the Church (see section **i**). The powers of the monarchy, already limited, were further restricted by laws that gave Mussolini the power to make laws by decree (January 1926), and deprived Victor Emmanuel of the right to select the prime minister (December 1928). On a local level, elected mayors were replaced by nominated fascist officials known as 'podestà'. Even the local powers of the fascist 'Ras', the local party leaders taking their nickname from the semi-independent chieftains of Abyssinia, found themselves subjugated to central authority. They were unable to resist largely because their intense rivalry with each other made them so easy to isolate.

Apart from the corporations, the major new constitutional feature of the 1920s was the Fascist Grand Council. This was a body of 56 hierarchs (gerarchi), later reduced to 30, whose functions as an organ of state came to include determining the succession both to the throne and to the premiership. Even so, the powers defined for it by the laws of 1928–29 make it clear that the Grand Council, too, played only a secondary role. Its membership, times of meetings, even the agenda that it should discuss, all remained the firm prerogative of the 'Duce'. In short, the end product of the fascist revolution was the personal dictatorship of Benito Mussolini. Two factors help to explain his success in this respect in the 1920s and 1930s. One is the comparative mediocrity of other leading fascists. 'Most of them', wrote D. Mack Smith, 'were unintelligent, grasping, jealous and incompetent, and jockeyed for place by telling tales against their rivals'. Of the men closest to the 'Duce' some, like R. Farinacci and I. Balbo, were glorified street fighters, lacking Mussolini's political flair. Some, like D. Grandi, were too obsequious to consider firm opposition. Others, like the future foreign minister G. Ciano, who married Mussolini's daughter in 1930, had tied their own fate too closely to that of their leader to risk toppling him. Italian fascism produced no Goering, no Himmler, and certainly no Röhm. The second factor in Mussolini's favour was his own enormous talent for self-advertisement. Exploiting his journalistic talents to the full, he not only convinced very many Italians that 'Mussolini is always right', but created an image, very far from the truth, of a man who possessed all the talents. The controlled press portrayed him as an excellent violinist, fine horseman, daring pilot, bold war hero, and as an intellectual who had mastered all the major philosophies of the day and had found time to memorise whole cantos of Dante. This very mastery of publicity, which made him a genius at the art of seizing power, goes far to explain the disappointing record of the fascist government. D. Mack Smith has summarised Mussolini's failings as an administrator admirably. 'Mussolini's own mental processes never ceased to be governed by slogans and eight-column headlines. He preferred to argue and speechify rather than to penetrate behind words to reality, and so never properly dissected a problem. Fascism, which affected to despise speeches and talk, was itself essentially rhetoric and blather'.

(i) State and Church

One influential element in Italian life could not be subdued or suppressed by threats and violence. Relations between fascism and the Catholic Church remained complex and ambiguous throughout the 1920s. While Mussolini and other fascist leaders never lost their fierce anticlericalism, and while the two forces remained especially divided over the

question of the education and indoctrination of youth, in other respects they shared common ground. Ever the realist, Mussolini never seriously imagined that he could govern Italy successfully in the teeth of Catholic opposition. The Papacy, for all its reservations, still saw fascism as the only alternative to the godless doctrines of socialism.

Despite an interlude of tension in 1927, when the state dissolved the Catholic boy scout movement, Church and state extended olive branches to each other. Gentile's education act (February 1923) restored the compulsory religious education that the liberal regime had abolished in elementary schools. The following year, the Pope did fascism a singular service by withdrawing his support from the Catholic Popular Party, a substantial electoral rival. Always too progressive for the tastes of Pius XI, the party could not survive the blow, and Mussolini was left free of major parliamentary rivals.

These signs of mutual respect reached fruition with the signature of a batch of agreements known as the Lateran Accords (February 1929). On the side of the Church, the Accords settled most of the outstanding conflicts between the Papacy and the Italian state. By creating the tiny state within Rome, known as the Vatican City, the state restored a face-saving vestige of the Papacy's temporal authority. Furthermore, it confirmed catholicism as 'the only state religion', extended compulsory religious education to secondary schools and outlawed divorce. Lastly, the Papacy received a substantial financial compensation, amounting to some 1750 million lire, for its losses since the Italian seizure of Rome in 1870. Mussolini's gains from the Accords were less tangible, but were perhaps greater. By linking his administration in the popular mind with the immense moral influence of the Church, he entered upon a period of unprecedented national popularity. The Lateran Accords thus represented the greatest political success of his career and, as E. Wiskemann has pointed out, the most lasting impact of fascist government on modern Italy.

It should not be imagined that the agreements of 1929 represent a surrender by either party. Mussolini immediately reminded parliament that the Italian state 'is Catholic, to be sure, but it is above all fascist . . . exclusively, essentially fascist'. In 1931 a further crisis illustrated the lines beyond which neither side would step. In that year, Mussolini declared the disbanding of the youth and student groups affiliated to Catholic Action, an educational and moral organisation highly prized by Pius XI. In the face of a fierce Papal counter-attack Mussolini replaced the dissolution order with lesser limitations on the groups' activities. The incident illustrated the limitations upon fascist absolutism in Italy, the value of even tacit Catholic support to the government and, thereby, the shrewdness of the understandings reached in 1929.

(j) Education and Culture in the Fascist State

In common with the contemporary Soviet government, fascist Italy demanded in theory that all aspects of the cultural life of the society should support and sustain the regime. For the first time in western Europe, a government attempted to turn the considerable communications machinery of a modern state to a co-ordinated political purpose. The press was steadily subjected to the party line by the suppression of political papers such as *Avanti!* and consistent pressure upon other editors and owners. By 1926 there was no opposition press in Italy, so that E. R. Tannenbaum has referred to the fascist decades as 'the rule of the journalists'. Radio, on the other hand, was more slowly exploited. This was partly because its use was not yet widespread in Italy, and partly because Mussolini judged with some reason that his style of oratory was less well suited to that medium. An embryonic cinema industry was tentatively utilised, but produced few good films that were directly fascist.

The control of education was, of course, considered essential by the fascist regime. In the classroom, the 'fascistisation' of youth was sought by the strict control of textbooks and of curriculum, and by the removal of teachers critical of fascist principles. The primary purpose of the school came to be the inculcation into the young of the fascist virtues, such as manliness, patriotism and obedience. 'A child who asks "Why?"', declared a textbook approved for eight-year-olds, 'is like a bayonet made of milk. "You must obey because you must", said Mussolini, when explaining the reasons for obedience'. Glorification of the 'Duce' was, of course, another pervasive element. Outside the school, Italy set a pattern for other authoritarian regimes by the law (April 1926) which introduced a system of compulsory youth organisation to coax the male child into the required fascist path. From four to eight he would belong to the 'Sons of the She-Wolf' ('Figli della Lupa'), from eight to fourteen to the 'Balilla', and to the age of eighteen to the 'Vanguard' ('Avanguardisti'). From 1937, the best graduates of this system might join the 'Young Fascists' ('Giovani Fascisti') until the age of twenty-one. Whatever the political success of the

system, the fascist years marked no great advance in conventional educational areas. Illiteracy, which stood at 48.5% in 1901, had been reduced by the liberals to 30% by 1921, but still stood above 20% in 1931.

Sport, too, was highly prized by the regime, both as a breeder of fascist virtues and as a source of nationalist propaganda. On a popular level, the 'Dopolavoro' organisation was formed in May 1925. It hoped to provide for 'the healthy and profitable occupation of the workers' leisure hours', by means such as cheap holidays, libraries, lectures and theatrical entertainments. On a more elite level, several major sports had their organisation reorganised and centralised, and their international successes exploited by the state. In soccer, the 1934 World Cup competition was held in, and won by, Italy. She retained the trophy in 1938, to the great satisfaction of the regime. As boxing was naturally regarded by Mussolini as 'an essentially fascist method of self-expression', the triumph of Primo Carnera (1933) in the World Heavyweight Championship was hailed as a further proof of fascist virility.

Like its ambiguous relationship with the Church, fascism's failure to dominate Italian cultural life illustrates the limits of its absolutism. Although the movement had a considerable appeal in intellectual circles in its early days, this was partly dissipated by its later authoritarianism. The conductor, A. Toscanini, a fascist candidate in 1919, left Italy for America in the 1920s. He was followed by the historian G. Salvemini in 1925, and the physicist E. Fermi in 1938. Italy's greatest intellectual figure, the philosopher and historian B. Croce, was an opponent of the regime from 1925, when he organised an anti-fascist manifesto. Yet he not only remained in the country throughout Mussolini's years in power, but continued to produce liberal historical works, and to publish his liberal review *La Critica*. Although usually cited as an example of fascist weakness, this might possibly be ascribed to fascist tolerance of an influential rival, putting Croce in the same bracket as the Pope. Certainly, he would not have survived either in Nazi Germany or in Stalin's Russia. A greater failure was the inability to found any true 'fascist culture'. Although Nobel Prizes for literature went to G. Deledda (1926) and to L. Pirandello (1936), neither was truly a fascist. Despite the much publicised foundation of the Royal Academy of Italy (October 1929), the literature and art encouraged by the regime remained, in E. R. Tannenbaum's words, 'conformist, old-fashioned and lifeless'. Only in the less directly political fields of engineering and music did names of international repute, such as P. L. Nervi and O. Respighi, emerge during the two decades of fascist Italy.

(k) The Fascist Economy: Policy

Upon its advent to power, Italian fascism inherited a depressing range of economic problems, including a sizeable budget deficit and a total of some 500 000 unemployed. Its most consistent success in tackling these was achieved between 1922–25 when, largely for reasons of political expediency, the Ministry of Finance was in the hands of the liberal economist, A. De Stefani. His measures included the abolition of price-fixing and of rent controls, and the reduction of government expenditure wherever possible. His achievements included a budget that was in surplus for the first time since 1918, and a total of unemployed reduced to only 122 000.

Mussolini's motives for departing from this policy, and for replacing De Stefani with the financier and industrialist G. Volpi, have been the subject of debate. To Marxist commentators, of whom the contemporary French journalist D. Guerin was an extreme example, the reversion to protectionism was proof that Mussolini was doing the bidding of Italian capitalism. Heavy import duties were imposed, for example, upon grain, sugar and milk. D. Mack Smith, however, is adamant that 'Mussolini was no mere instrument of business and agrarian interests'. He does concede that 'his ignorance of economics and human nature left him an easy target for sharks who wanted protective duties or who extracted money from the state for quite impossible schemes of industrialisation'. An explanation wholly consistent with other areas of fascist policy is that Mussolini was influenced by considerations of political prestige. Certainly, the revaluation of the lire (August 1926) at 90 to the pound, gave it an artificial impression of strength. The immediate result of this swing to protection was that the Italian economy ran into difficulties long before the Wall Street Crash. The low exchange rate of the lire deterred tourist traffic and damaged trade in luxury commodities.

By 1930 the government, tempted by the prospects of domestic prestige and foreign military adventures, had adopted the principle of autarky, that is of economic self-sufficiency. The policy bred some impressive successes, such as the five-fold increase in electricity production between 1917–42, and the spectacular rise in motor production by 1941, when an estimated 34 000 cars were completed. In typically ostentatious fascist fashion,

however, the policy was constructed around three great national 'struggles'. The 'Battle for Grain', officially inaugurated in 1925, was superficially successful. Production figures that had been steady at 40 million 'quintals' since 1870 rose to 60 million in 1930 and to 80 million by 1939. It has been pointed out by agricultural authorities that the official fixation with grain damaged other forms of agricultural output, and kept the relative cost of Italian grain production high. The 'Battle for Land' was also marked by notable successes. Most famous of the land reclamation schemes was that which drained the Pontine Marshes near Rome to provide hundreds of thousands of acres of new farmland. Much of it, unfortunately, was lost again between 1943–45 due to the ravages and neglect of war. It is also well worth noting, as E. Wiskemann does, that fascist attentions to southern Italy resulted in a more effective control of Mafia activities than was achieved before or since. Also in the same vein of public works, which combined public utility with political propaganda, was the construction of motorways ('autostrada') between Italy's main urban centres, and the electrification of some 5000 kms of Italy's railway system.

Least necessary, and least successful, of the fascist 'struggles' was the 'Battle for Births'. Imagining that an increased population would provide proof of Italian virility and would support her claims for colonies, Mussolini demanded a rapid rise in the birthrate. Parents of large families were rewarded, while bachelors, with the exceptions of priests and maimed war veterans, were penalised by high taxes (1926). Abortion and contraception, of course, were outlawed. In this aim, so foolish in relation to Italy's limited resources, the Duce suffered bitter disappointment. Although the Italian population rose from 37.5 million (1921) to 44.4 million (1941), two quite different factors were primarily responsible. These were the fall in the death rate, and the restrictions placed upon immigration by the USA.

(l) The Fascist Economy: Social Impact

The 'balance sheet' of the policy of autarky was not altogether negative. It produced some durable monuments, and served Italy well when the League of Nations imposed sanctions upon her in the course of the Abyssinian War. In general, its narrow political motives made the period from 1925–40 one of the most stagnant in Italy's economic history, in terms of industrial growth. In those years the annual growth in productivity was only 0.8%, compared with 3.8% between 1901–25 and 3.5% between 1940–52. Cut off from the mainstream of world economics, Italy suffered recession earlier than other European powers, yet drew little benefit from the steady world recovery of the mid-1930s.

The fascist 'revolution' in Italy failed to transform the lives of the ordinary Italians as many of its early supporters had hoped. The 'Battle for Land', although a potent political symbol, fell far short of any substantial change in the pattern of land ownership in Italy. In 1930, the peasant smallholder still constituted 87.3% of the farming population, yet held only 13.2% of the farmland. The richest 0.5% of the landed population, on the other hand, still farmed 41.9% of the available land. No significant change occurred in these proportions in the next decade. Smallholders and small businessmen alike found survival increasingly difficult, with an annual average of 7000 small farms passing to the exchequer as a result of their owners' failure to pay land tax.

Naturally, the fascist period was for most Italians one of stagnant or declining living standards. The task of penetrating fascist statistics is a complex one, and researchers have differed in their conclusions. They have not disputed about improvement or decline, but merely about the rate of decline. Professor Chabod has claimed that the Italian farm labourer lost half, and in some cases more, of the real value of his wages, while C. Vannutelli has claimed a drop in the average 'per capita' income of the Italians from 3079 lire (1929) to 1829 (1934). The figures have to be set against a falling cost of living and a subsequent rise of the 'per capita' income to return to the 1929 level by 1937. One should also note the range of social benefits that the workers' syndicates secured, most of them late in the fascist period. Sick pay was first introduced in 1928, followed ten years later by a 'package' comprising end-of-year bonuses, paid holidays and severance pay. Although it is possible that the lot of the worker in fascist Italy may have been less severe than it has been painted, the abolition of the right to strike, the failure of the government's 'Charter of Labour' (1927) to guarantee a minimum wage, and an unemployment figure that rose from 110 000 (1926) to over a million (1933), and then levelled off at around 700 000, all show that the years 1923–40 marked little tangible improvement in the worker's life.

(m) The International Influence of Fascism

Considering the steady collapse of liberal democratic modes of government throughout Europe in the 1920s and 1930s, it would be tempting to see Mussolini as he sometimes pictured himself. This was as the founder of the conquering political creed of the era. By the end of the 1930s, indeed, authoritarian government had been established in Germany, Spain, Portugal, Hungary, Austria, Rumania, Yugoslavia and Poland. Even in France democracy was under severe strain. One should not exaggerate, however, the international influence of the Italian fascist form of government which Mussolini himself had declared earlier in his career was 'not for export'.

Many apparent similarities between fascism and these other movements result, not from conscious imitation by the latter, but from common features in the movements' origins. Hungary, like Italy, received a strong nationalist impulse from the supposed injustices of the peace treaties, and the short-lived socialist regime of Bela Kun (1919) left an even stronger anti-communist feeling than that which had helped Mussolini to power. The threatening proximity of the Soviet Union also stimulated anti-Marxist passions in Hungary, Poland, Finland and Rumania alike. The influence of such writers as Nietzsche, whom Mussolini claimed as a primary inspiration, can be seen quite independently in the thought of 'fascists' elsewhere, notably in that of the National Socialists of his native Germany. Other stimulants, such as the economic depression, obviously operated throughout Europe quite independently of Mussolini.

When Italian fascism did directly influence her 'sister' movements, it was in the one area where Mussolini showed true mastery, in the tactics of the seizure and consolidation of power. There can be little doubt of the direct influence upon Hitler of the fascist use of salutes, uniforms and rallies as means of fascinating the public, and of the use of organised violence to terrorise one's enemies. In Germany, however, these remained means to other ends, whereas in Italy they too often appeared as ends in themselves. Much later, Hitler remained fond of referring to Mussolini as 'his only friend', and of claiming that it was the Italian's example that had given him the initial courage to pursue his own political ambitions. In Hitler's consolidation of power many elements, such as the suppression of the press and of the trades unions, had close parallels in Italy. Throughout Europe, especially where fascistic movements still struggled to achieve power, the superficial paraphernalia of Italian fascism was imitated. This occurred in Mosley's British Union of Fascists, among the French 'Cagoulards', and in the Rumanian Iron Guards.

Direct imitations of Italian ideology or methods of government are, however, harder to detect. Corporativism appeared in the right wing programmes of Salazar in Portugal and of Dollfuss in Austria, while the Italian 'Charter of Labour' (1927) found echoes in Spanish 'Falangist' policy and in Portugal. Neither had any parallel in the Nazi movement. The French 'Cagoulards' and the Austrian 'Heimwehr' were rare in having direct contact with the Italian government. In many cases it is easier to pick out direct contrasts with Italian fascism. The Catholicism that Mussolini tolerated because he could not defeat it was a central factor in the authoritarianism of Dollfuss in Austria and of the Spanish 'Falange'. The Greek Orthodox Church played an equally strong role in the thought of Codreanu, creator of the Rumanian Iron Guard movement. Where Italian fascism had made a virtual prisoner of the monarchy, the Spanish dictator Primo de Rivera was largely motivated by an unswerving loyalty to the crown. Totalitarianism, to which Mussolini aspired, but which only Hitler perfected, was not seriously sought by Primo de Rivera, by Dollfuss, or by Pilsudski in Poland. Their opponents continued to operate in public, albeit often under difficult conditions. In short, it is easy to over-estimate the international influence of Italian fascism, as it is to exaggerate the united nature of right wing politics as a whole in inter-war Europe. As E. Wiskemann has remarked, 'Italian fascism was not the conquering creed of the twentieth century', but merely in some superficial respects 'led a political fashion for two decades'.

In fact, by the late 1930s, there was increasing evidence that fascism itself was coming strongly under the influence of more dynamic forces. Several of the means by which Mussolini sought to revivify his regime appeared, although he strongly denied it, to be reflections of German practices. The Ministry of Popular Culture (Minculpop) set up in June 1937 played much the same role as Goebbels' Propaganda Ministry. Above all, the range of anti-semitic legislation which successively forbade foreign Jews to enter Italy (September 1938), and banned Italian Jews from public, academic and party posts (November 1938), seemed incongruous in a country with so little previous history of anti-semitism. It could only be seen as an imitation by Mussolini of his more forceful partner. Such a trivial matter as the introduction of the 'goosestep' into the Italian army, under the new title of the 'Roman Step' ('Passo Romano'), convinced many of the extent to which, as E. Wiskemann put it, 'fascism in Italy lost its character and became a poor imitation of German National Socialism'.

(n) The Aims of Fascist Foreign Policy, 1922–34

Although the details of fascist Italy's international dealings are to be found elsewhere (see Chapter 17), it is apt to consider here the broader principles that shaped those dealings.

Foreign policy played a leading role in the government of fascist Italy. Not only did the aggressive poses consistently struck by Mussolini and his followers make it essential to pursue a 'dynamic' policy, but there were many in Italy in the 1930s who believed that the government used foreign affairs as a convenient distraction from the stagnation of domestic policies. A leader who declared, as Mussolini did, that 'it is a crime not to be strong', was committed to seek national prestige wherever it could be found. There can be found no parallel in Italian foreign policy, however, to the programme of 'Mein Kampf'. Many commentators have concluded that fascist policy was merely incoherent, based upon an opportunistic seeking of advantage wherever it could be found. Those who have seen more consistent purpose in it have usually agreed with the contemporary English statesman, Lord Halifax, who saw in Mussolini's aims 'the classic Italian role of balancing between Germany and the western powers'.

Certainly, Mussolini carefully pointed out to parliament upon coming to office (November 1922) that, although Italy had 'no intention of abandoning her wartime allies', she did not accept the peace treaties as permanent or perfect. She would not hesitate to seek revision 'if their absurdity becomes evident'. Neither France nor Britain was a 'natural' ally for fascist Italy. Both were liberal democracies, often highly critical of Mussolini's domestic policies or methods. Also, both had considerable interests in the Mediterranean which, Mussolini told the Italians in the style of the Roman Empire, was 'Mare Nostrum' ('Our Sea'). Between Italy and France, the old territorial claims to Corsica, Nice and Savoy, lost in the days of Italy's weakness, still rankled. The years of the Ruhr occupation, of economic crisis, and the consolidation of the Soviet Union were no time, however, to desert such apparently powerful allies.

Italian relations with Germany remained even more ambiguous. The rise of Nazism excited two conflicting emotions in Mussolini. On the one hand, he was enormously pleased at the triumph of 'his' doctrines in so powerful a state. For many years, furthermore, he badly underestimated the German leader. 'In politics', he told an associate in the early 1930s, 'it is undeniable that I am more intelligent than Hitler'. On the other hand, the prospect of resurgent German nationalism creating a 'Greater Germany' on Italy's borders horrified him. Austria, indeed, provided one of the keys to Italy's alignment in the 1930s. By 1922, Italy's traditional enemy had been reduced to the status of a weak 'buffer' state between Italy and Germany. Her territory in the South Tyrol had been ceded to Italy and the fascist government had pursued a brutal policy of 'Italianisation'. She forbade the use of German, and changed place names and personal names in what now had to be referred to as the 'Alto Adige'. The prospect that Austria might become a province of a dynamic German state, committed to rule over all German territories, was the greatest problem facing Italian diplomats between 1925–35. The protection of Italy's frontier on the Brenner Pass was Mussolini's main motive in his co-operation with France and Britain in the Locarno Pacts (see Chapter 17, section **f**) and in the subsequent Four Power Pact, and Stresa agreement. By way of unilateral action, Mussolini sought to prop up Austria by subsidising, from 1930, the anti-Nazi 'Heimwehr' militia. She also concluded the Rome Protocols (March 1934), an agreement to promote trade between Italy, Hungary and Austria.

Meanwhile, unwilling to accept the international repose envisaged by the peace treaties and the League of Nations, Italy sought to improve her influence and status in traditional areas of involvement. The first of these was on the east coast of the Adriatic. There in 1923 Mussolini defied the League of Nations by an invasion of the Greek island of Corfu to exact compensation for the murder of Italians engaged on League business. The eventual withdrawal from Corfu was followed by more permanent gains. Agreement with Yugoslavia (January 1924) allowed Italy to acquire Fiume, designated a 'free city' by the peace treaties. In November 1926, a pact with Albania tied that state to close economic dependence upon Italy. By the time of the conclusion of Mussolini's treaty with Hungary (April 1927), supplying arms and aid to the chief revisionist state in eastern Europe, Mussolini had seemed to become, in the words of E. Wiskemann, 'the chief anti-democratic conspirator of Europe'. Also, he had established a strong position as patron of the minor states of eastern Europe.

The second area of ambition was Africa. Mussolini's main justification was that imperialism provided relief for Italy's problems of overpopulation. D. Mack Smith has dismissed this as bogus, preferring to see African expansion as a means of rivalling the Mediterranean influence of Britain and France. Thus, much of the 1920s saw a brutal colonial war in Libya, and a systematic build-up of arms and resources in Somalia. The latter policy betrayed the plans that Mussolini was nursing even then for his major colonial project, the acquisition of Abyssinia (see Chapter 17, section **j**).

Superficially, the confused and hesitant nature of western diplomacy in the 1930s seemed to offer great hopes for this policy of opportunistic aggrandisement. That it ultimately brought disaster was due to three main factors. From 1932, Mussolini was in personal control of foreign policy, free from the restraints of traditional diplomats, and frequently the prisoner of his own rhetoric. He had dismissed D. Grandi as foreign minister, first taking over the duties himself, and then transferring them to his compliant son-in-law, Count Ciano. Secondly, he badly underestimated Hitler, and by his own destabilisation of European politics, helped to further the projects of the man who was ultimately to destroy fascist Italy. Lastly, for all his warlike slogans, Mussolini totally failed to provide Italy with the means to fight and to win a modern war although he was head of the armed forces by 1932. In 1939, when the Versailles peace finally collapsed, writes D. Mack Smith, 'the prosaic truth turned out to be that only ten divisions were ready to fight and these were understrength, with antiquated and inadequate equipment'. The air force, which Mussolini had boasted would 'darken the sky', was described by a contemporary aviation expert as 'irremediably out of date'.

(o) Historiography

Attempts to explain the phenomenon of Italian fascism have been many and varied and were especially numerous in the two decades that followed the collapse of the regime. Dominating the controversy has been the enigmatic figure of Mussolini himself, and much of the debate attempted precisely to establish his role in the development of the doctrine and the movement. Here, the necessity in Italian writing in the fascist era to emphasise the personal importance of the 'Duce' still exercises some influence. 'Hero worship' was of course the central theme of contemporary Italian works such as those by A. Beltramelli (*The New Man: Benito Mussolini*, 1923) and G. Prezzolini (*Benito Mussolini*, 1924). It was carried over into some foreign accounts, such as that by the American V. de Fiori (*Mussolini: the Man of Destiny*, 1928). Their view, that the doctrine of fascism and its salvation of Italy from economic disaster and

Bolshevism owed everything to the genius of one man, did not die altogether after the war. In a more moderate and rational version of the theme, G. Pini and D. Susmel (*Mussolini: The Man and His Work*, 1953–55) continued to view fascism as containing and achieving much of value, at least until the mid-1930s, when the disastrous entanglement with Hitler destroyed the true purpose and nature of the regime.

A variation of this 'Duce orientated' theme has been the post-war tendency to view fascism not as the product of Mussolini's genius, but of his fatal weaknesses. G. Dorso (*Mussolini to the Conquest of Power*, 1949) interpreted the rise of fascism as the result of Mussolini's 'vulgar opportunism' in exploiting contemporary political trends, while P. Monelli (*Mussolini the Petit Bourgeois*, 1950) dwelt upon the middle class mediocrity of the supposed 'revolutionary'. Fifteen years later, S. W. Halperin (*Mussolini and Italian Fascism*, 1964) could still write that 'fascism was fundamentally nothing but Mussolinianism. . . . Fascism's identity with Mussolini gave the movement tremendous rhetorical dash . . . but also accounted for its extraordinary intellectual poverty'.

Many writers, on the other hand, have seen Mussolini as the product of fascism rather than the reverse. R. de Felice, in his four volume political biography of the leader (1965–74), wrote 'Mussolini was doubtless a very important component of fascism, but to equate fascism with Mussolini would be absurd. Fascism was much more than its Duce, who indeed was often driven by it into positions that he would have preferred not to take'. From that point, arguments as to the nature of the Italian movement tend to reflect the wider debate over the nature of fascism in general. As early as the mid 1920s, the movement was placed convincingly in the context of Italy's recent past by L. Salvatorelli (*National Fascism*, 1925), and by G. Salvemini (*The Fascist Dictatorship in Italy*, 1927). Salvatorelli's stress was upon the peculiar combination of economic depression with post-war nationalist disillusionment, while Salvemini emphasised a longer term conjunction of developing capitalism with wartime militarism. He stressed the violence that the author felt to be an integral part of fascism from the outset. The role of capitalism in the development of Italian fascism is, of course, a theme eagerly taken up by most Marxist interpreters of the subject. P. Alatri (*Biographical Profile of Benito Mussolini*, 1956) may stand as a representative example of the school of thought that sees Mussolini as, at every turn in his political career, the tool of the interests of monopoly capitalism.

Progress Paragraphs

Answer the following questions in about 150 words.

What influence had the events of 1914–18 upon the rise of fascism in post-war Europe?   Section (**a**)

How real was the apparent strength of Italian liberalism in 1914?   Section (**b**)

What elements in Mussolini's boyhood, and early socialism, helped to form the future fascist leader?
Section (**c**)

To whom did fascism appeal in post-war Italy?
Sections (**d & e**)

How did the existing ruling classes contribute to the success of fascism?   Sections (**d & e**)

By what stages was parliamentary democracy undermined in Italy?   Sections (**f & g**)

With what was parliamentary democracy replaced in Italy (a) in theory, and (b) in practice?
Sections (**g & h**)

Explain Mussolini's personal influence over fascist government.   Section (**h**)

What did the fascist state and the Catholic Church gain from the Lateran Accords?   Section (**i**)

By what means did Mussolini seek to 'fascistise' Italian youth?   Section (**j**)

How successful was fascism in its attempts to turn sport and culture to the ends of the state?
Section (**j**)

Why did Italy pursue a policy of autarky under fascist government?   Section (**k**)

What did Italy and the Italians gain or lose by this policy of autarky?   Sections (**k & l**)

How great was the influence of fascism on other European movements between the wars?
Section (**m**)

What causes were there for rivalry between Italy and (a) France, (b) Germany between 1922–34?
Section (**n**)

In which areas did Italy seek expansion and prestige between 1922–34?   Section (**n**)

16
The Third Reich

(a) Adolf Hitler

The tenure of national power of the man who assumed the office of Chancellor in January 1933 lasted only twelve years. His tenure of real international power was shorter by half. That his is undoubtedly the best known face, and his the best documented political career of the century, bears witness to the extraordinary impact of the man. Yet Hitler's origins were unremarkable in the extreme. Born in the small Austrian town of Braunau am Inn (20th April 1889), he was the son of a customs official already well into middle age. His mother was a young peasant girl to whom Hitler remained so attached that he was later to link her death with Germany's defeat in the First World War, as the two great tragedies of his life. Academically and socially, the young Hitler was a failure. His inability to gain admission to the Academy of Fine Arts in Vienna (1907) formed the prelude to 'five years of misery and woe' in the Austrian capital, living by odd jobs and occasional artistic work.

Hitler's 'Greater German' nationalism was already formed then, and he later claimed that it was in Vienna that he first formulated the intense and obsessive hatred of Jews and Judaism that was thereafter a central feature of his political beliefs. Convinced of the decadence of the Austro-Hungarian Empire, and of the invincibility of the racially more pure German Reich, Hitler evaded Austrian conscription in 1914 to serve in a Bavarian regiment. After a creditable military career at the western front, the sudden collapse of the German war effort in November 1918 provided Hitler with perhaps the most traumatic blow of his early life. For him, there could be no other explanation than that the Reich, and all patriotic Germans, had been vilely betrayed by the socialists, Marxists and Jews prominent in the November 'revolution' and in the subsequent Weimar Republic. In subsequent years, Hitler propagated the myth of the 'stab in the back', not because of its propaganda value, but because he was personally convinced of its truth. His natural place thereafter was in the ranks of the extreme nationalist opposition to the Republic. In September 1917 he joined the tiny German Workers' Party which shortly afterwards changed its name to the National Socialist German Workers' Party (NSDAP). By July 1921 Hitler was its chairman.

Hitler's primary qualification for a political career was his extraordinary talent as an orator. In part, this was based upon careful study of all the elements of public speaking, and brilliant mastery of the tactics of dogmatic assertion, sarcasm and emotional appeal. As W. Carr has written, 'a Hitler speech was superb theatre. . . . Hitler was his own script writer, choreographer and actor-manager all rolled into one'. His success was not wholly explained, however, by contrived effects, but was largely due to the intense sincerity of his nationalistic outrage, and by his ability to communicate thereby with the outrage and frustration of millions of Germans. Otto Strasser described the effect of a speech as follows. 'He enters a hall. He sniffs the air. For a moment he gropes, feels his way, senses the atmosphere. Suddenly he bursts forth. His words go like an arrow to their target; he touches every private wound on the raw, liberating the mass unconscious, expressing its innermost aspirations, telling it what it most wants to hear'. Such skills were more than adequate for one who saw himself at first only as a 'Drummer' preparing the way for a greater leader, a John the Baptist, smoothing the way for Germany's true saviour. The stage at which he came to believe in himself as that saviour is unclear; perhaps as he reformulated his political views after the failure of the Munich 'putsch' of 1923 (see Chapter 14, section **d**). The years after 1923, however, certainly saw the emergence of Hitler as unchallenged party leader.

He achieved and fulfilled this role in an unorthodox fashion, for his were not the usual talents of political organiser and administrator. Lazy, and often bored by practical detail, he has been called by W. Carr a 'chronic procrastinator', while K. S. Pinson has gone so far as to declare that 'mediocrity was Hitler's most distinguishing characteristic'. Administrative mediocrity, however, was wholly outweighed by a remarkable political instinct, an unconquerable will-power and self-confidence, total ruthlessness, and a talent for winning the dogged devotion of individuals. It is indeed quite probable that he even cultivated his disinterest in detail and practicalities to maintain party unity, and to present the image that he maintained so well throughout his career as the demi-god, the man of destiny, far above the petty wrangling that disfigured and corrupted mundane politics. Above all, as Hjalmar Schacht described him, Hitler was 'a mass psychologist of really diabolical genius'. These were the talents that transformed Adolf Hitler from the 'nobody of Vienna' into the most dynamic and fateful figure in German history.

(b) National Socialism: Its Doctrine

The origins of the Nazi Party and its first disastrous bid for power in 1923 have been noted elsewhere (see Chapter 14, section **d**). What concerns us here are the structure and aims of the party as it renewed itself in the decade between 1923–33.

The intellectual antecedents of Nazism must be sought in a bewildering variety of locations. Essentially a distillation of resentments and fears, it was philosophically an incoherent rag-bag of elements borrowed from most of the major political tendencies of the last century. From Germany alone it borrowed the conservative 'realpolitik' of Bismarck, the nationalism of Fichte, and the godless humanism of Nietzsche. Its racial theories leaned heavily upon those of Houston Stewart Chamberlain (*Foundations of the 19th Century*, 1899) and of the Comte de Gobineau (*Essay on the Inequality of the Human Races*, 1855), who had argued from the lunatic fringes of Darwinism that the key to human development lay in the inevitable triumph of the Aryan races over the 'lesser varieties of mankind'. From further afield, and more recently, came the practical examples provided by Italian fascism with its attractive trappings, and its bold seizure of national power. Also there was the ruthless example of Stalin in his consolidation of power in the Soviet Union. Distanced as he was from Stalin's political aims, Hitler himself could only feel the greatest respect for his coldly logical methods. 'Stalin and I', he was to declare, 'are the only ones who see the future'.

Some semblance of cohesion and consistency was given to this variety of influences by the initial programme of the National Socialist Party (February 1920) which predated Hitler's dominance over the party and, more importantly, by Hitler's own political testament *My Struggle* (*Mein Kampf*). This was written during his imprisonment after the failure of the 1923 coup, and published in 1925. A rambling and highly personal work, *Mein Kampf* provided no precise manifesto for future government, but made clear the essential precepts upon which the Nazis and their leader intended to proceed. Central to Hitler's argument was the conviction that the only true basis of the state was, not that of class interest (an invention of Marxism and Judaism) or of community of economic interest, but that of race. It was thus the primary duty of the German state to unite within its borders all those of common racial origin, and to eliminate alien elements that might weaken or corrupt the ethnic community (Volksgemeinschaft). In the case of Germany, this meant the elimination of the influence of world Jewry. In Hitler's view their international conspiracy bore the responsibility for all Germany's recent ills. Subsequently, the major duty of the state would be the provision of adequate resources and 'Living Space' ('Lebensraum') for the population that dwelt by right within its boundaries. As the preservation of its people was the very reason for the state's existence, it was not only permissible, but positively desirable for the state to acquire this 'Lebensraum' by means of struggle against neighbouring races. Nor did Hitler attempt to dodge the implications of this doctrine in the specific case of Germany. 'History proves', he declared in *Mein Kampf*, 'that the German people owes its existence solely to its determination to fight in the east and to obtain land by military conquest. Land in Europe is only to be gained at the expense of Russia'.

To provide the dynamism and the unity of purpose necessary for the achievement of such a visionary programme, Nazism defined the 'Leader Principle ('Führerprinzip'). Thereby, each level of Nazi organisation was committed to unquestioning obedience to its chief, with ultimate allegiance owed to the man at the apex of the pyramid of command, the Führer. This was to form an essential feature of Nazism. This was not only because of the appearance of consistency that it lent to a divided movement, or because of its importance in ensuring Hitler's personal authority, but also because of its eventual appeal to millions of Germans for whom representative democracy seemed a short road to economic ruin and to national humiliation. Through this principle, the Nazis posed not merely as the latest candidates for party political power, but as the appointed guardians of the destiny of the whole German nation. 'The Führer', wrote the Nazi theorist Ernst Huber in 1933, 'is the bearer of the people's will; he is independent of all groups, associations, and interests. . . . In his will the will of the people is realised'.

For all this, the views of prominent party members at the time of the advent to power as to Nazi priorities were by no means unanimous. To such men as the brothers Otto and Gregor Strasser, and to many of the ex-soldiers who filled the ranks of the SA, the socialist element, the desire to overturn the great capitalist enterprises that had made such a contribution to the economic hardships of the past decade was central to National Socialism. 'We are enemies', Gregor Strasser had written, 'deadly enemies of the present day capitalist economy with its exploitation of the economically weak, with its unjust wage system, with its immoral evaluation of the individual according to property'. To Hitler such doctrine was divisive, and alienated forces without which German national greatness could scarcely be restored. For him, it remained essential to concentrate upon such vague and emotive concepts as 'Fatherland', 'Volk', 'loyalty' and 'sacrifice'. While one can appreciate the reasons, however, for the judgement of D. Schönbaum that Nazism was 'a conglomerate of disparities and contradictions', the movement, like fascism in Italy, retained an element of negative cohesion in its agreement as to the prime objects of Nazi hate. The Versailles Treaty, the Weimar Republic, parliamentary liberalism in general, Marxism, and Judaism, all condemned and execrated, were the objects that united the Nazi movement in 1933.

(c) National Socialism: Its Support

To whom, therefore, did Nazism appeal and for what reasons? An analysis by M. K. Kater of 4800 party members in 1923 shows 60% of them to originate from the lower middle, or skilled working classes. These were men who had established some small stake in the world and feared that social and economic chaos would drag them back to the bottom of the ladder. Shopkeepers and small tradesmen (14%), clerks and minor officials (17%), skilled craftsmen (20%) and specialist workers (9%), were prominent on party lists. Two major modifications to this pattern of support had occurred in the years between 1930–33. The first was the emergence of the Nazis as the prime representatives of nationalist politics. This occurred by the so-called Harzberg agreement (October

1930) with the Nationalist Party, based upon a common anti-republican campaign in opposition especially to the Young Plan. The co-operation of such Nationalist figures as the industrialist A. Hugenberg, H. Schacht (head of the Reichsbank) and F. Seldte (head of the 'Stahlhelm' veterans' organisation) extended Nazi influence into spheres where it could scarcely have hoped to have penetrated before. Secondly, came the party's remarkably successful campaign to win peasant support, and to infiltrate existing agrarian organisations. H. Gies has shown that the Nazi share of the rural vote rose from 22.6% (1930) to 52.4% (1933), while their share of the urban vote never rose higher than 39.6% (1933).

It is not difficult to understand, therefore, why both party membership and electoral support stagnated during the relative stability of 1924–29, to be regenerated by renewed economic crisis in the wake of the Wall Street 'crash'. In 1928, the party had 40 000 members, received about 1.03 million votes, and won 12 Reichstag seats. Between 1931–32, those figures rose to 800 000, 16.5 million, and 230 respectively. The motives of these new adherents were undoubtedly similar to those that moved Albert Speer after his first exposure to Hitler's oratory in 1931. 'Here it seemed to me was hope. Here were new ideals, a new understanding, new tasks. The perils of communism could be checked, Hitler persuaded us, and instead of hopeless unemployment, Germany could move towards economic recovery. . . . It must have been during these months that my mother saw an SA parade in the streets of Heidelberg. The sight of discipline in a time of chaos, the impression of energy in an atmosphere of universal hopelessness, seems to have won her over too'.

(d) The Consolidation of Power: Legislation

Despite their popular pose as a revolutionary party, the Nazis had come to power by wholly constitutional means (see Chapter 14, section **g**). It would not be excessive, however, to claim that the years after 1933 witnessed an adaptation of the German state to Nazi needs that was truly revolutionary. Like Mussolini in 1923, Hitler was never likely to be satisfied with power limited by a constitution and by the presence in the state of parties and interests potentially hostile to his own. At first, his tactics for strengthening his position centred upon the Reichstag election to be held in March, for which he prepared with a massive propaganda campaign that stressed the continuity between Nazism and other forms of German conservatism, and by practical measures such as Goering's rapid extension of Nazi control over the police and civil service in Prussia. The result still left the Nazis with the direct support of only 43.9% of the population, but by then a whole new range of possibilities had opened up for Hitler.

The fire that destroyed the Reichstag building (27th February 1933) provided such a convenient crisis for the Nazis that it was supposed for many years that their agents had started it. It now seems, as F. Tobias has demonstrated, that van der Lubbe, the unbalanced Dutch communist who was accused of the crime, really did commit it. The government may merely have exploited the happy coincidence. This powerful illustration of the 'Communist Threat', upon which Nazi propaganda had long insisted, went far to ensure public acquiescence in the arrest of communist deputies and in the passage of two measures central to the collapse of German democracy. The arrests themselves strengthened Hitler's position in the Reichstag. The 'Decree for the Protection of People and State' (28th February) suspended the essential freedoms of the individual, giving the state unprecedented rights of search, arrest and censorship. The 'Enabling Law' (23rd March), which only the SPD opposed, transferred full legislative and executive power to the Chancellor, Hitler, for a period of four years. Undoubtedly, although German democracy was done to death by Hitler, he was greatly abetted in the crime by so-called democrats who lacked the determination to keep liberty alive.

Long before the expiry of that four year period, Hitler had destroyed or neutralised all those groups and institutions in a position to impose limits upon his power. This policy was referred to by the euphemism 'Co-ordination' ('Gleichschaltung'). In some cases, the weapon used was the naked exercise of state or party power. Thus, the KPD and the SPD were formally outlawed and their property seized, while by the 'Law against the New Formation of Parties' all other political parties except the Nazis were declared illegal. By accepting this law such well-established organisations as the Catholic Centre Party effectively dissolved themselves and accepted Nazi dictatorship. In January 1934, after preliminary tampering with their constitutions, Hitler abolished the provincial assemblies of the Länder. In their places he put Nazi governors (Reichsstatthalter), and made Germany a centralised, unitary state for the first time. Other institutions weakened their positions by attempts to compromise with the new government. The socialist trades unions had already guaranteed their non-intervention in political questions. They had also accepted the supervision of a Nazi Reichskommissar when (2nd May 1933) Storm Troopers occupied their offices throughout Germany, dissolved them, and began the enrolment of all labour into a German Labour Front. Other institutions lost their independence by a process of subtle infiltration. The Prussian civil service was brought under firmer control by the dismissal of nearly 30% of its officers on racial grounds or on grounds of 'incompetence'. The legal and academic professions became subject to Nazi 'Fronts' or 'Academies' outside which there was little hope of practice or of professional advancement.

(e) The Consolidation of Power: Industry, Church and Army

Three major elements in German society were too powerful to be directly coerced, and perhaps bear more guilt for the accommodations that they reached with Hitler. The support of German industry for Hitler had got seriously underway in 1928–29, when his disciplining of the Strasser 'wing' of the party, and his subsequent alliance with the conservative Nationalist Party had convinced its leaders that the Nazis were not, as the contemporary joke had it, 'like a beefsteak, brown on the outside but red in the middle'. At this early stage substantial financial contributions to the party were forthcoming from a variety of banking and mining interests, headed by the great steel magnate F. Thyssen. Hitler's consistent policies of anti-socialist legislation and subsequent rearmament earned much wider support in these areas in the years immediately after the seizure of power.

The Catholic Church, too, was quick to seek an arrangement with the new regime, which now found it convenient to play down its essentially anti-Christian nature. The Concordat (July 1933) that it concluded with the Nazi state in an attempt to preserve educational and similar privileges undertook to dissuade Catholic priests from political activity, and did much to hasten the collapse of the Centre Party. Unlike the Lateran Pacts (see Chapter 15, section **i**) concluded with Mussolini, the Concordat represented an almost complete surrender to the new political leadership. Certain elements in the Lutheran Church, by agreeing to the formation of a Reichs Church (Reichskirche), surrendered in similarly abject fashion. In this case, however, a breakaway Confessional Church managed with difficulty to survive as a symbol of Christian opposition to Nazism.

Like the major industrialists, the German Army (Reichswehr) shared a community of interest with the Nazi Führer. Its commanders had little objection to his declared nationalist aims, while the realisation of those aims seemed unlikely without heavy industry to produce weapons and without soldiers to use them. Although elements of suspicion remained, the army accepted in general the promises as to its future role made to it in February and March 1933. While this gave Hitler the support of the army, he had to wait longer for any substantial element of direct control. The death of President Hindenburg (February 1934) not only made possible the combination of the offices of President and Chancellor in the new office of 'Führer and Chancellor', but gave Hitler the chance to revise his relationship with the army. By imposing a new oath of allegiance upon all ranks (August 1934), he ensured their commitment, not to their superior officers, nor to the Fatherland, but directly to 'the Führer of the German Reich and People, Adolf Hitler'. The later dismissal of the War Minister, General von Blomberg (January 1938), over the scandal of his marriage to a former prostitute, and of the Commander-in-Chief of the Army General von Fritsch (February 1938), over trumped-up charges of homosexuality, merely consolidated and reinforced Hitler's control over the army at a time of increasing foreign commitment.

(f) The Consolidation of Power: The Night of the Long Knives

For all these successes in 'co-ordinating' influential elements in the state into the Nazi system, Hitler could not feel wholly secure by the beginning of 1934. Ironically the greatest surviving threat to him and to his policies came from within the Nazis' own ranks. The paramilitary SA (Sturmabteilung) had been formed in the early days of the movement to provide physical protection for Nazi meetings and to disrupt those of their opponents. Its attraction for disorientated former soldiers, as well as for simple hooligans, was enormous, and by late 1933 its numbers had swollen to some 2.5 million men. To its leader, Ernst Röhm, it represented the central weapon of the Nazi Revolution, the German equivalent of Trotsky's Red Army. It would guarantee the radical transformation of German society and, by taking over the functions of the Reichswehr, would guarantee the Nazification of the state. To Hitler, in the words of A. Bullock, the SA was an 'embarrassing legacy of the years of struggle'. It had fulfilled its street-

fighting purpose and served now only to scare industrialists and conservative army officers by its radical posturing. Besides, with the SA under his command, Röhm stood as the only man in the Nazi Party realistically able to challenge the power of Hitler.

There is much dispute over the process by which Hitler reached the decision to eliminate the threat of the SA. J. Fest and M. Broszat have pictured him upon a deliberate collision course with Röhm since the beginning of 1934, while A. Bullock is inclined to believe that Hitler would have been willing to delay, had it not been for mounting pressure from the Reichswehr. The ill-health of Hindenburg, moreover, made it imperative for Hitler to enjoy full Reichswehr support when the opportunity arose for him to take over the dead President's functions. In any case, the decision had been taken by late June when Hitler unleashed the purge known since as the 'Night of the Long Knives' (30th June 1934). This was in response to bogus SA 'revolts' in Berlin and Munich staged by Himmler, Goering and their agents. The estimates of those murdered by SS squads with material support from the Reichswehr range from a low of 77 to a high of 401. The bulk of these were SA men, including Röhm himself and most of his hierarchy, shot in prison without trial. The opportunity to settle diverse scores with old rivals was, however, too good to miss. The dead also included General von Kahr, who had deserted Hitler in the 1923 'putsch', Gregor Strasser, who had long opposed him within the party, and a number of other non-Nazi political figures.

The 'Night of the Long Knives' was Hitler's most spectacular and probably his most successful piece of 'realpolitik'. For all the initial shock that it caused, it had eliminated the threat from the left of the party and assuaged important conservative interests outside the party. Less than three weeks after the event, 38 000 000 Germans gave their tacit support by accepting in a plebiscite vote Hitler's assumption of the office of 'Führer and Chancellor'.

(g) The Nazi State

In theory, the far-reaching process of 'Gleichschaltung' transformed Germany into a state dominated by its single political party. 'The party', declared Hitler in mid-1933, 'has now become the state', and that principle was legally enshrined in the 'Law to Ensure the Unity of Party and State' (December 1933). In reality, as G. A. Craig has put it, 'the smoothly functioning Nazi state was never much more than a myth', for government consisted largely of a jostling for influence between the old ministerial hierarchies and a variety of party bodies that sought to supervise or to control them. In several cases, ministers who were Nazis only in the sense of collaboration such as von Krosigk at the Ministry of Finance and Schacht at the Ministry of Economics, were highly successful in preserving the traditions of their departments. On the other hand, the Minister of the Interior, W. Frick, a Nazi himself, ultimately failed to prevent the infiltration of his department by the Party Chancellery under Martin Bormann. The Foreign Office found itself in competition with the Nazi Bureau for Foreign Affairs, headed by A. Rosenberg, and with the specialist agencies headed by J. von Ribbentrop, before he himself became Foreign Minister in 1938. The pattern of 'dualism, struggles over competence, and duplication of function' was repeated at local government level between local administrators and Nazi provincial chiefs (Gauleiter). In all cases, a high price was paid in terms of administrative efficiency.

Some have claimed that this confusion arose from Hitler's great failings, his boredom with administrative detail, and his preference for wider questions, especially in foreign affairs. D. Irving has even gone so far as to describe him as 'probably the weakest leader Germany has known this century'. More likely Hitler saw the departmental in-fighting as a deliberate means of maintaining his personal power, being the great arbiter in any such dispute. He was satisfied with a system that enabled him to block and nullify any initiative or individual unacceptable to him.

The Nazi state had two great cohesive agents, both directly responsible to the Führer. One of these was the Ministry of Propaganda under the guidance of Joseph Goebbels. This reached new heights of sophistication through more complex and powerful media than had been available a generation earlier. The second body was the SS (Schutzstaffel—Protection Unit), with its secret police offshoot, the 'Gestapo' ('Geheime Staatspolizei'—Secret State Police). Founded in 1925, but transformed four years later with the appointment of Heinrich Himmler as its commander, the SS differed from the SA in several important respects. Whereas the SA was a mass organisation, relying upon force of numbers for its effect, the SS was an elite force, under Hitler's direct control. As such, its role extended rapidly once the Nazis were in power. From 1932 it dominated the party's intelligence work, from 1934 it had effective control of the nation's police system, and under the emergency laws of 1933, the SS controlled the concentration camps which sprang

up to receive political opponents of the regime. If there ever was such a thing as a Nazi state, it was primarily an organism for ensuring the maintenance of power, and the SS was at its centre. Surveying the general incoherence of Nazi administration, G. A. Craig has concluded that 'the force that prevented the regime from dissolving into chaos was terror, and its instrument was the SS'. As war increased the need for cohesion in Nazi policy after 1939, so the activities of the SS expanded further. Its members dominated the administration of the occupied territories, and its military wing, the 'Waffen SS', sought to exert more and more influence over military affairs, resurrecting the threat that the army appeared to have conquered in the 'Night of the Long Knives'.

Thus, as was the case in fascist Italy, the varied and conflicting postures of Nazism amounted in practice in domestic policy to a mechanism for the maintenance of one man's power. The Reichstag after 1934 performed merely formal functions, and the cabinet rarely met. The Nazi theorist Ernst Huber admitted as much in his definition of the Nazi constitution in 1939. 'We must speak, not of state power, but of Führer power, if we want to describe political power in the national Reich correctly. . . . The Führer power is not hemmed in by conditions and controls, and jealously guarded individual rights, but is free and independent, exclusive and without restriction'. It cannot be doubted that this power was hugely effective in the negative sense of destroying opposition. What it succeeded in creating now remains to be seen.

(h) The Nazi Economy

Whatever the effects of terror and propaganda, the Nazi regime depended for its survival upon the solution of the monstrous economic problems that had caused so many voters to turn to the party in 1929–32. Yet at no time, as K. D. Bracher has written, 'did National Socialism develop a consistent economic or social theory'. In place of such a theory, Nazism had a set of fixed and sometimes contradictory commitments. Within the context of those commitments, its economic achievements were considerable.

Firstly, to maintain popular sympathy and industrial support, an expansion of industrial activity and a dramatic reduction of unemployment were necessary. Without departing from the essential principles followed by Papen and Schleicher, the government poured money into public works, the most spectacular example of which was the construction of 7000 kilometres of motorway (Autobahn). Aided by the recruitment of many unemployed into the Reich Labour Service, the unemployment figures fell from nearly 6 million to 2.5 million within 18 months of the Nazis' advent to power. With the subsequent expansion of heavy industry to meet the needs of re-armament, and the re-introduction of military conscription (1935), the Nazis could claim almost complete success in this field by 1939, when unemployment figures stood at less than 200 000.

The second range of commitments was met with less consistency and with less obvious success. To preserve the German peasantry from the twin curses of rising industrial prices and falling prices for their agricultural produce, a complex programme of legislation was introduced. All peasant debts, totalling 12 billion Reichsmarks, were suspended between March–October 1933, and many imported foodstuffs were subjected to higher tariffs. The Hereditary Farm Law (October 1933) gave the smaller farmer security of tenure by forbidding the sale, confiscation, division or mortgaging of any farm of between 7.5 and 10 hectares, owned by farmers of Aryan stock. While ensuring the permanence of the peasant food producer, the very foundation of the German race in the view of many Nazi theorists, the law militated against the development of larger farming units, against the development of new farming methods, and thus ultimately against the self-sufficiency that was a major economic aim of the Nazi state. By 1936 the price of many basic foodstuffs had increased by up to 50% since the Nazi advent to power.

The urban equivalent of the peasant, the small trader or business man, gained still less from the regime that he had helped to bring to power. A number of tentative laws, such as the Law for the Protection of the Retail Trade (May 1933) which was designed to protect the trader against the influence of the larger concerns, were far outweighed by the continued advance of 'Big Business'. This was witnessed by the formation of over 1500 new cartel arrangements between mid-1933 and the end of 1936. R. Grunberger has estimated that, whereas only 40% of German production was in the hands of monopolists in 1933, the proportion had grown to 70% by 1937.

Ultimately the regime would support the larger enterprises, given that its long-term priority was re-armament and the achievement of self-sufficiency in all strategic products. This was perhaps the only economic goal towards which Nazi Germany moved with any consistency in the 1930s. The first phase of the policy was supervised by Hjalmar Schacht as President of the Reichsbank (from May

1933) and Minister of Economics (from June 1934). His major achievement was to limit the drain of Germany's foreign exchange by paying foreign debts in Reichsmarks. Also there was a series of trade agreements notably with Balkan and South American states, whereby Germany paid for her purchases in Reichsmarks, thereby also encouraging her trade partners to purchase German goods in return. 'His creation of credit', wrote W. L. Shirer, 'in a country that had little liquid capital and almost no financial reserves, was a work of genius'. Schacht's great weakness from the Nazi point of view was his financial orthodoxy. His reluctance to spend more than Germany was earning threatened to put the brake on the process of re-armament. It thus became necessary, by the announcement of the Four Year Plan (August 1936), which was entrusted to the direction of Herman Goering, to devise machinery for this task which was directly under the control of the Führer. The primary aim of the Four Year Plan was to achieve self-sufficiency in strategic industrial and agricultural products, either by increasing production, or by developing synthetic substitutes. The plan had its important 'showpiece' successes, such as the Hermann Goering Steelworks erected at Watenstedt-Salzgitter. It established a complicated system of controls over prices, and the distribution of raw materials, but in some important respects, in fuel, rubber, and light metals, Germany remained well short of self-sufficiency in 1939.

By most orthodox economic criteria, the economy of Nazi Germany was chaotic. Her reserves of foreign currency remained low, and her balance of payments remained dramatically in deficit. K. D. Bracher and others have painted a picture of the ruination of the economy by Nazi exploitation. On the other hand, B. H. Klein has denied that preparation for war totally dominated German economic activity, stressing that production of consumer goods rose steadily right up to the eve of war in 1939. Certainly, by a mixture of Schacht's clever financing and 'windfalls' such as the confiscation of Jewish property and the seizure of Austrian assets after the 'Anschluss', the economy produced impressive results. Table 16.1 indicates both those results, and the economic priorities of the Nazi government, which those results reveal.

Marxist historians have usually been eager to portray the Nazi regime as a 'front' for the more effective pursuit of the aims of Germany's capitalists. By this theory, the suppression of trades unions and the expansion of heavy industrial output were among the 'tasks allotted by finance–capital to its fascism' (D. Eichholtz). T. W. Mason,

	Unemployed (millions)	Coal (m. tons)	Iron ore (m. tons)	Pig iron (m. tons)	Steel (m. tons)	Arms expenditure (billion RM)
1932	6.042 (Jan.) 5.392 (July)	118.6	2.6	6.1	8.2	1.9
1935	2.974 (Jan.) 1.754 (July)	143.0	6.0	12.8	16.2	6.0
1938	1.052 (Jan.) 0.218 (July)	186.4	12.4	18.1	21.9	17.2

Table 16.1

on the other hand, speaks for a substantial school of thought in arguing the 'primacy of politics'. He has shown convincingly that, although there was a genuine degree of co-operation between industry and Nazism up to 1936, thereafter all major decisions were taken with the regime's political objectives in view. Often these decisions involved consequences of which the business community heartily disapproved, as in the case of attacks upon Jewish financial and industrial institutions. The decline of Hjalmar Schacht's influence, culminating in his resignation from the Reichsbank (January 1939), typifies the dominance of Nazism in its grim alliance with capitalism. K. D. Bracher has supported these views in his conclusion that 'the basic principle of National Socialist economic policy was to use the traditional capitalist structure with its competent economic bureaucracy to move towards its prime objective: acceleration of rearmament'.

(i) Nazi Society: Workers and Women

Promise of radical social change probably ranked only a little lower than the prospects of economic recovery and national resurgence as a vote winner for the Nazis in 1929–32. In the event, hopes of a 'social revolution' were frustrated. The dominant classes continued in most cases to exercise their social and economic functions and the Nazi advocates of radical change were eliminated. What change did occur served, not as a revolutionary end in itself, but as a means towards the broader Nazi aims of the consolidation of power and the preparation of the nation for war.

The emptiness of Nazi promises of a 'social revolution' should not lead one to suppose that German workers gained nothing from their industrial co-operation with Nazi strategy.

Although many contemporary commentators, such as R. A. Brady and F. Neumann, stressed the class nature of the Third Reich, seeing it primarily as a middle-class mechanism for the exploitation of the working class, more recent authorities, such as D. Schoenbaum, have indicated instead the solid benefits that accrued to many German workers during this period. Although they lost important rights such as that of union representation, maybe they were awarded prosperity as a consolation prize for the loss of political freedom, as were French workers under Napoleon III. Their greatest gain was, of course, employment. Arguments about the wage levels of the Third Reich are, as G. A. Craig has stressed, academic in view of the fact that six million workers were not receiving a salary of any sort in 1932. In any case there is evidence that, although average wages remained around the 1932 levels, those of skilled workers and workers in strategic industries such as metallurgy, engineering and building benefited markedly from Nazi industrial expansion with wage increases of up to 30%. Production and sales figures for consumer goods in the immediate pre-war years suggest a distinct rise in the standard of living. Nor should the activities of the 'Strength through Joy' ('Kraft durch Freude') programme, for all their propaganda content, be dismissed solely as 'window dressing'. In 1938 alone, 180 000 Germans enjoyed holiday cruises under its auspices, while 10 million took holidays of one kind or another. Its activities also extended to evening classes, and a large variety of cultural and sporting activities. Material rewards, however, were often offset by declining conditions of employment. Above all, the German worker frequently put in far longer hours than any of his counterparts in western Europe or the USA. The industrial demands of the regime made 10% increases in hours commonplace, with rises of 25% in some specialised areas of employment. The national average working week lasted 49 hours in 1939, rising to 52 by 1943. Linked closely with these increases was a 150% increase in the number of industrial accidents between 1933–39, and a 200% increase in the occurrence of occupational diseases. Whether motivated by material gain or by patriotism, it can scarcely be doubted that, as R. Grunberger has put it, 'the working class that Karl Marx had seen as being in the van of the proletarian revolution . . . significantly extended the lifespan of the Third Reich by exertions that came very close to giving it victory'.

A significant feature of Nazi society in the 1930s was its reactionary view of the place of women. The duties of women were defined by the party's propaganda in the glib slogan 'Children, Church, Kitchen' ('Kinder, Kirche, Küche'), and every effort was made to eliminate them from leading roles in political and economic life. To an extent this was an ideological aim, based upon the mystical Nazi regard for the breeding and rearing of a pure race. As R. Grunberger has observed, 'women basked in Nazi esteem between marriage and menopause'. It also had a practical element, in that the removal of women from the competition for jobs would make easier the full employment of the male population. Thus by 1936 only 37 of Germany's 7000 university teachers were women, while married women were banned by law from the legal and medical professions, from the civil service, and from higher office in the Nazi party. On the other hand, interest free loans were made available to newly-weds who undertook that the wife would not seek employment outside the home. The birth rate did indeed rise, from 1 200 000 births in 1934, to 1 410 000 in 1939. While the Nazis claimed this as a success for their methods, T. W. Mason has more recently suggested that it may simply have arisen from the improving economic circumstances in contemporary Germany. In the Nazi attitude to women, as in other areas of Nazi policy, the necessities of politics came eventually to triumph over ideology, and the industrial expansion of the Four Year Plan once more made female employment unavoidable. Although professional posts remained closed to them, therefore, women once more constituted 33% of the total German workforce by 1939.

(j) Nazi Culture

With the advent of the Nazis to power, one of the most exciting, experimental periods in Germany's cultural history gave way to one of the most stagnant. The 1920s had witnessed a period of unparalleled innovation and experiment in German art. In the aftermath of the collapse of the 'old' Germany, many of the cultural values of that 'old' society were challenged and re-interpreted. The dramatic work and production of Berthold Brecht, the music of Kurt Weill, and the architecture of the 'Bauhaus' movement are only random examples of the inventiveness of 'Weimar' culture. It was immediately evident that artistic freedom played little part in Nazi philosophy and that cultural activity, like all other social and economic functions, was to be 'co-ordinated' to the needs of the regime. This view was aptly summarised by Goebbels in a speech of December 1934, with the judgement that art 'remains free within its own laws of development but it is bound to the moral, social and national principles of the state'. Official 'taste' in the Third Reich had three main distinguishing features. The first was the rejection of 'internationalism', the response to cultural stimulae from abroad that had characterised the art of the Weimar period. Secondly, in its place, it demanded a stress upon and a glorification of those values that Nazism preached in other areas of policy. Thirdly, it was frequently dominated by a conservatism, often a philistinism, that was apolitical but spoke eloquently of the intellectual mediocrity of many of Germany's new leaders.

As in all other areas of activity, the Nazis quickly devised a complex machinery to implement this 'co-ordination'. The Reichs Chamber of Culture (Reichskulturkammer—September 1933), under the presidency of Goebbels, was the central body outside which no 'maker of culture' could legally practise his or her craft. Political undesirables and non-Aryans were automatically excluded. Cruder tactics were necessary to deal with the works of art already executed. 'Exhibitions of Shameful Art' ('Schandausstellungen') were held, notably in Karlsruhe (1933) and in Munich (1937), with the works of Expressionists, Cubists, and other modern movements prominent. The destruction of rejected books and paintings by fire was widespread. In one conflagration alone, in Berlin in 1939, over 1000 paintings and 3700 drawings by leading modern artists were destroyed.

The result of this cultural persecution was to rip the heart out of German art, literature and music. The list of those who abandoned their country to work abroad includes such novelists and playwrights as Thomas and Heinrich Mann, Stefan Zweig and Berthold Brecht, the painter Kokoschka, and the masters of the new art of cinema, Sternberg and Fritz Lang. The majority of those who replaced them were nonentities. In the words of G. A. Craig, most of the products of this cultural 'revolution' were 'of a quality so inferior as to be embarrassing. What passed for Nazi art, when it was not a mere disguise for propaganda, was a reflection of the aesthetic ideals of a culturally retarded lower middle class, full of moral attitudinising and mock heroics and sentimentality and emphasis upon the German soul and the sacredness of the soil'. In literature one might refer to the books of Werner Beumelburg, a specialist in glorifying the spiritual experience of war, or of Hans Blunck, with his emphasis upon Nordic legend. In sculpture, the gigantic evocations of teutonic manhood which were the specialities of Professor Thorak and Arno Breker found particular favour with the Führer himself. Musical taste, of course, was dominated by the German 'giants' of the classical past, by Beethoven and Mozart, and of course by the German epics of Wagner.

In one discipline alone did the products of the Third Reich transcend mediocrity. Although the film industry constituted in Goebbels' view 'one of the most modern and scientific methods of influencing the masses', he used it sparingly and intelligently. The most famous films of the era, such as *Hitler Youth Quex* (1933), *The Jew Süss* (1940), and *Ohm Krüger* (1941), an exposé of British atrocities during the Boer War, all had clear political points to make. Yet these were subtly conveyed, and the films were not without artistic merit. The most famous of contemporary German directors, Leni Riefenstahl, showed in her major works, *The Triumph of the Will* (1935), portraying the 1934 Nazi party rally at Nuremberg, and *Olympia* (1937), on the Berlin Olympic Games, that an obvious propaganda message could be conveyed with flair and originality.

The theme of mediocrity is evident once more, however, in the story of German education under Nazism. The creation of a centralised Reich Education Ministry (May 1934) involved no substantial change in the structure of the educational system, but led to a radical revision of syllabuses. Great stress was now laid upon History, Biology, and German as the media by which the philosophy of Nazism could best be put across, while the stress upon physical fitness and development raised the gym teacher to a higher level of prestige than he had ever previously enjoyed. University teaching, too, was subject to haphazard adjustments, such as the dismissal of 'unreliable' teachers, and the banning of such 'Jewish' theses as Einstein's Theory of Relativity. Forty-five per cent of all university posts changed hands between 1933–38. As Nazi agencies competed with established bodies in other spheres, so too in education, youth organisations sought to ensure the indoctrination of the young, to the great detriment of academic standards. From December 1936 it was compulsory for boys to serve in the 'Jungvolk' organisation, paralleled by the 'Jungmädel' organisation for girls, between the ages of 10 and 14. Thereafter, the boys graduated to the 'Hitler Youth' ('Hitlerjugend') and the girls to the 'German Girls' League' ('Bund Deutsche Mädchen') until the age of 18.

(k) Nazism and the Jews

Almost alone among the domestic ideological stances struck by Nazism before its advent to power, anti-semitism was not sacrificed to the practicalities of power politics. Some writers have tried to see in Nazi anti-semitism a tool for the achievement of other aims, as in A. J. P. Taylor's phrase 'a showy substitute for social change'. But the consistency of Nazi policy, even when it appeared ill-advised in terms of foreign relations or of the economy, can leave us in little doubt that hatred of Jews was central to Hitler's beliefs. 'The Jews', wrote L. Dawidowicz, 'inhabited Hitler's mind. He believed that they were the source of all evil, misfortune and tragedy'. Such views, although of unprecedented viciousness, appealed to a long tradition of German anti-semitism deriving from economic envy of Jewish commercial success. To this was added intellectual opposition to such 'modern' notions as parliamentarianism and liberalism, through which some Jews had reached political and social emancipation in recent decades.

This is not to say, however, that Nazi anti-semites had any clear idea in 1933 as to how they would tackle the Jewish 'menace'. Their reasoning dictated that Jews should be excluded from positions of social and political influence, and thus a series of laws (April 1933) banned them from the civil service, the universities and from journalism. Popular emotion, often orchestrated by the SA, led to incoherent outbreaks of violence against Jewish businesses, to the horror of more orthodox nationalists, fearful of foreign reaction and of the breakdown of law and order. For economic reasons, however, Jewish activity in stockbroking and banking remained unimpaired until 1937.

From 1935, with increasing domestic security and greater foreign success, the confidence of the Nazis grew. By the Nuremberg Laws (September 1935) and the National Law of Citizenship (November 1935), all marital and sexual contact between Jews and Aryans was outlawed, and Jews were stripped of their nationality by the stipulation that only Aryan blood entitled one to membership of the German nation. In August 1936, Hitler dictated the principle that the whole Jewish community would be held responsible for the misdeeds of any of its members. The most spectacular application of this principle came on the night of 9th–10th November 1938 (Krystallnacht) when, in a major 'pogrom' following the murder of a German diplomat by a Jewish student in Paris, 7000 Jewish businesses were attacked, about 100 Jews were murdered, and thousands more beaten and intimidated. On Krystallnacht, as R. Grunberger has it, 'Germany had passed the point of no return on the path of regression to barbarism'. Subsequently Nazi policy escalated to include the removal of Jews from the economy and, if possible, from the country itself. The 'Decree on Eliminating Jews from German Economic Life' (November 1938) made it illegal for them to work in sales, services, crafts or management. In January 1939 a Reich Central Office for Jewish Emigration was established to arrange for the expulsion of those with adequate funds and with somewhere to go.

The advent of war in 1939, however, left the majority of Germany's 500 000 Jews stranded without livelihood or political rights in a country that had disowned them. Hitler's apparent conviction that foreign opposition to Germany was part of an international Jewish plot, left them in an even more perilous position. 'If the international Jewish financiers in and outside Europe', he had told the Reichstag in January 1939, 'should succeed in plunging the nations into a world war, then the result will be . . . the annihilation of the Jewish race in Europe'. True, for once, to his propaganda, the war years were to witness the formulation at last of a 'final solution' to the 'Jewish problem' (see Chapter 18, section **j**).

(I) Nazi Foreign Policy: Aims and Motives

The details of German foreign policy between the wars dominate the narrative of Chapter 17. Here we aim only to consider the broad principles that motivated that policy in the Nazi era.

For Hitler and for many in his party it is probable that foreign affairs represented the true purpose of the Third Reich. The domestic transformation of the first years of Nazi power was primarily carried out to fit Germany for the performance of her international tasks. 'Before conquering the external enemy', Hitler had written in *Mein Kampf*, 'the enemy at home would have to be eliminated'. It has nevertheless become a matter of some controversy whether the foreign policy of Nazi Germany really did represent a radical change of direction, or whether, in essentials, Hitler merely continued well established traditions of German power politics. The latter view has been put forward by a number of distinguished German historians, such as F. Meinecke and A. Hillgrüber, and has received the most enthusiastic support in this country from A. J. P. Taylor. 'In one sphere alone', writes Taylor of Hitler, 'he changed nothing. His foreign policy was that of his predecessors, of the professional diplomats at the foreign ministry, and indeed of virtually all Germans'. For this school of thought, the terms imposed upon Russia in the Treaty of Brest-Litovsk in 1917 (see Chapter 12, section **i**) provide strong evidence of Germany's eastern ambitions long before the advent of Hitler. On the other hand, many contemporaries, as well as more recent writers such as H. A. Jacobsen, saw in Hitler, in his racial doctrines, and in his professions in *Mein Kampf*, a new and more dangerous force. 'This is not a man of the past', declared the French ambassador in 1933, 'and his objective is not to restore purely and simply, the state of things in 1914'.

The aims laid down in *Mein Kampf* and elsewhere, whether or not they should be regarded as a premeditated and serious programme for Nazi foreign policy (see Chapter 17, section **q**), in fact constitute a combination of familiar projects and new twists. Firstly, as any diplomat of the Weimar Republic would have agreed, Hitler stated the necessity to overturn the Versailles settlement, to destroy the inequalities of Germany's position with regard to armament and reparations, and to regain for Germany those portions of her population separated from the Reich by the peace terms. Secondly, he was determined to unite with the Reich those Germans who had previously not been part of it, his fellow Austrians for example, or the Sudetenlanders. This was a deliberate departure from Bismarck's 'Lesser Germany' in favour of the 'Grossdeutschland' that Bismarck had feared and rejected. Thirdly, this 'Grossdeutschland' would require 'living space' to provide agricultural and industrial resources for its population, a dangerous and explosive combination of Wilhelmine expansion and newer racial determinism. A. Bullock has argued further that such an outwardly coherent programme can be further reduced to one simple factor. 'Hitler had only one programme', he wrote, 'power without limit, and the rest was window dressing'.

The implications of such a programme as *Mein Kampf* contained for Germany's future foreign relations were clear. For Hitler, Russia was the natural enemy, with its combination of inferior Slavic culture, detested Bolshevism, and he thought, Jewish dominated government. France, too, although a declining power, would be a certain opponent for the future. She was the staunchest supporter of the hated Versailles system, was patron and protector of several of the detested eastern European states, and would have to be dealt with to avoid once more running the risk of war on two fronts. Britain, an essentially maritime and colonial power, and Italy, fascist and with primarily Mediterranean interests, were not natural enemies of Germany. At an early stage in his career, Hitler envisaged fundamental departures both from Nazi ideology and from traditional German policies, to ensure the acquiescence of Britain and Italy in his general plans. In the case of Britain he showed himself willing to renounce the lost German colonies, subject of so much propaganda after 1919, and in the case of Italy, refrained from claiming the Germans of the South Tyrol as subjects of 'Grossdeutschland'.

(m) Nazi Foreign Policy: Methods

For all the dispute over the originality of Germany's international aims during the Nazi period, there is general unanimity as to the masterly flexibility with which those aims were pursued. The diplomatic methods of the Nazi era fall broadly into two sections. The first three years from 1933 formed a period of caution, dictated by domestic weakness and by widespread foreign distrust. Germany successfully avoided commitments to such international bodies as the League of Nations and the Disarmament Conference, which might have compromised her future freedom of action, and made headway with the disruption of the French system of eastern European alliances, while consistently re-assuring foreign opinion as to her peaceful intentions. Through that period, too, ran the theme of re-armament. The re-introduction of conscription (1935), the agreement with Great Britain over the reconstruction of the German Navy (1935), and the steady re-building of an airforce (Luftwaffe) that already boasted 2000 aircraft by late 1934, all illustrate this theme.

Although the phenomenon has been variously explained, as a reaction to greater domestic security, or as a response to evident weaknesses in the diplomacy of Hitler's adversaries, the years 1936–37 undoubtedly witnessed a switch to the offensive. If the introduction of the Four Year Plan (see section **h**) prepared the way, the so-called 'Hossbach Conference' (November 1937) is often

seen as, in the words of C. Thorne, the 'significant moment in the development of Nazi expansionism'. There, in a meeting with the heads of the armed forces and of the Foreign Ministry, the subject of which is known to us through the minutes recorded by one Colonel Hossbach, Hitler defined the immediate principles of his policy. Repeating the principle of 'Lebensraum', he noted that Germany's present military superiority over her rivals could not be expected to last beyond 1943–45. Thereafter, the obsolescence of German material, and the re-equipment of other armed forces would narrow the gap. Therefore, the minutes report, 'it was his unalterable resolve to solve Germany's problem of space at the latest by 1943–45'. Although the timetable retained some flexibility, the subsequent expansion of armament production, and the removal from office of such 'doubters' as von Blomberg, Schacht and Neurath, clearly indicate that the threats made to the future peace of Europe were not idle.

(n) Historiography

The volume of literature on the Third Reich, in the form both of general interpretations and of more specialised studies, is enormous, and its fascination shows little sign of diminishing. Through the complexity a number of consistent themes of interpretation may be distinguished. The debate upon the nature of the regime's foreign policy has already been outlined in this chapter (see section **l**) and elsewhere (see Chapter 17, section **q**). The nature of National Socialism itself, however, has provoked lively controversy, and four main explanations have been proposed as to the ease with which the German people succumbed to the doctrines of the movement.

Firstly, arising in part from wartime hostility towards Germany, came the view that Nazism was a logical development of the authoritarianism and nationalism evident throughout the previous century or ' more of German history. As an extension of the unhealthy respect for power evident as early as 1848, Nazism was a specifically German phenomenon. This argument was put forward in England by R. Butler (*The Roots of National Socialism*, 1941) and in France by E. Vermeil (*Germany: An Explanatory Essay*, 1945), and is prominent in W. L. Shirer's best-selling *Rise and Fall of the Third Reich* (1960). Similarly, in one of the most popular summaries of modern German history (*The Course of German History*, 1945) A. J. P. Taylor wrote that 'during the preceding eighty years the Germans sacrificed to the Reich all their liberties; they demanded as reward the enslavement of others'.

Naturally, such an interpretation of Germany's past has not proved popular with her own writers. In direct contradiction to Taylor, G. Ritter wrote that 'there is no doubt that the majority of educated Germans were very distrustful of the Hitler propaganda. Very many felt at the time of Hitler's victory that his political system was foreign to them'. Ritter (*The Historical Foundations of the Rise of National Socialism*, 1955) and E. Nolte (*The Three Faces of Fascism*, 1966) were thus among those who favoured the view of Nazism, not as the product of German history, but as the product of the unprecedented social and economic pressures upon Europe in the 1920s and 1930s. Its roots were also those of Italian fascism, and of similar movements in France, Spain and elsewhere. Another prominent German authority, K. D. Bracher (*The German Dictatorship*, 1969), actually combines both schools of thought by insisting that 'past research has made clear that an examination of the roots of National Socialism must be conducted simultaneously on two levels; the German and the over-all European'. Relatively close to the 'European' view of Nazism is the Marxist interpretation of the movement proposed in the 1930s and still persisting in some left-wing circles today. In the Marxist view, Nazism should be seen as the last resort of embattled and besieged capitalism in the aftermath of the Russian Revolution and of the Great Depression. As representatives of this school, one might quote the work of F. L. Neumann (*Behemoth: The Structure and Practice of National Socialism*, 1944) and of R. A. Brady (*The Spirit and Structure of German Fascism*, 1937), both of whom viewed Nazism as a mass middle-class movement confronting and defeating a mass working class movement.

A fourth and common approach to the history of the Third Reich is that which concentrates predominantly upon the personality of its founder and leader, Adolf Hitler, and which sees him as the evil genius primarily responsible for the disasters of the 1930s and 1940s. Hitler has indeed been the subject of an unprecedented volume of psychological and psychohistorical works, investigating the intricacies of his family relationships, or his sexual makeup, to explain the mentality and motivation of the man. Of these, R. G. Waite (*Adolf Hitler. The Psychopathic God*, 1977) and W. Langer (*The Mind of Adolf Hitler*, 1972) may serve as examples. Although such an approach devalues many important factors in the rise of the Third Reich, it is difficult to explain the events of that rise in isolation from Hitler's dynamic

personality. A. Bullock (*Hitler: A Study in Tyranny*, 1952) is undoubtedly justified, therefore, in his conclusion that 'the evidence leaves no doubt that no other man played a role in the Nazi revolution or in the history of the Third Reich remotely comparable with that of Adolf Hitler'.

Progress Paragraphs

Answer the following questions in about 150 words.

How would you explain the emergence of Adolf Hitler as a major force in German politics?
Section (a)

What were the central tenets of Nazism on (a) the role and nature of the state and (b) the exercise of political power within the state?   Section (b)

On what issues did Nazis disagree up to 1934?
Section (b)

Who supported the Nazis in 1933 and why?
Section (c)

What limitations were there on Nazi power in 1933, and how had they been eliminated by the end of 1934?   Sections (d & e)

Why did Hitler receive support from industry and from the army?   Section (e)

Why was the SA purged in 1934?   Section (f)

Suggest reasons for the complexity of German administration under the Nazis.   Section (g)

What was the role of the SS in the Nazi state?
Section (g)

By what means and with what success did Hitler tackle the economic problems that faced him in 1933?   Section (h)

What were the primary aims of German economic policy after 1936?   Section (h)

What did German workers lose and what did they gain under the Third Reich?   Section (i)

By what means did the Nazis attempt to eliminate (a) women and (b) Jews from positions of influence?
Sections (i & k)

What did the Nazi regime demand from its artists and writers, and what did it get? Section (j)

What was new and what was unoriginal about German foreign policy under the Nazis?
Sections (l & m)

17
1919-39: The Twenty Years Truce

(a) The Treaty of Versailles: Motives and Terms

November 1918 brought a mere armistice rather than a definitive peace. Some of its terms, however, such as the withdrawal of German forces beyond the Rhine, and the internment of her fleet, made it a foregone conclusion that Germany would be unable to recommence hostilities. In effect, therefore, the leaders of the four main allied powers, France, Britain, the USA and Italy, were concerned during their six months of deliberation (13th January–28th June 1919) with the preparation of the terms for peace that would eventually be dictated to the representatives of Germany when at last they were allowed to appear in France. Rarely has the preparation of peace been attended by such high hopes and rarely has the feeling been so quickly apparent that the outcome of negotiations had fallen far short of initial expectations. 'We arrived', wrote the British historian and diplomat H. Nicolson, 'determined that a peace of justice and wisdom should be negotiated: we left it conscious that the treaties imposed upon our enemies were neither wise nor just'. Others saw the price that Europe would pay for the shortcomings of the peace. 'This is not peace', Foch is reported to have exclaimed when he heard the terms, 'it is a truce for twenty years'.

The first problem for the leaders of the allied powers was that they were not always free agents. Lloyd George was in the process of fighting a general election in which popular anger gave rise to such emotive slogans as 'Hang the Kaiser' and 'Squeeze the German Orange until the pips squeak'. Clemenceau had to contend with an even more volatile combination of anger and anxiety that the losses of the war should never be repeated. Nor were the delegates united in their purposes. French policy was dominated by an overwhelming desire for future security, for the achievement of which almost no imposition upon the German aggressor would be too great. Britain's view was moderated by a number of considerations. The scuttling of the German fleet at Scapa Flow (31st June 1919) guaranteed her own national security, and her traditional concern with the balance of power on the continent made her wary of weakening Germany excessively, especially as it became ever clearer that the Soviet regime in Russia was there to stay. Both sets of vested interests, however, were likely to be overridden by the American President, Woodrow Wilson. He hoped to replace the outdated and corrupt criteria of European diplomacy with a lasting and just peace, based upon the satisfaction of justifiable national claims, and outlawing selfish motives. He hoped, in his famous phrase, for 'a peace without victory'. Wilson was the central figure of the peace conference, partly because the USA alone had the manpower and financial resources to continue the struggle if necessary, and partly because of the enormous popularity that he enjoyed as 'the prophet of peace'. He could not, however, expect to impose his views upon the hard-bitten statesmen of Europe. 'Mr. Wilson bores me with his 14 points', Clemenceau complained. 'Why! God Almighty only has 10!' The terms that emerged from six months of negotiation were thus a confused mixture of idealism, fear, anger, and national self interest.

The 440 clauses that constituted the peace treaty between the allies and Germany may be briefly summarised under four general headings. Firstly, although the Treaty of Versailles made allowance for eventual general disarmament, the disarmament of Germany was to be immediate. As her armed forces in future were to cater merely for the defence of her own territory, she was restricted to an army of 96 000 men and 4000 officers, all serving for a period of 12 years, to prevent the building up of experienced reserves. These armed forces were forbidden the use of all purely offensive weapons, of tanks, heavy artillery, powered aircraft, submarines and capital warships. Secondly, the boundaries of the Reich were adjusted to satisfy the demands of the nationalities that shared her borders. In the west, Alsace-Lorraine returned to France, and the small regions of Eupen and Malmedy became Belgian territory. Ideally France would have

MAP 13   TERRITORIAL CHANGES IN EUROPE 1919–24

NORWAY

SWEDEN

ESTONIA

LATVIA

LITHUANIA

DENMARK

DANZIG

GERMANY

SCHLESWIG

POLISH CORRIDOR

HOLLAND

POLAND

BELGIUM

MALMEDY

GALICIA

CZECHOSLOVAKIA

BESSARABIA

ALSACE LORRAINE

FRANCE

SWITZERLAND

AUSTRIA

HUNGARY

RUMANIA

SOUTH TYROL

YUGOSLAVIA

ITALY

BULGARIA

ALBANIA

GREECE

KEY

- - - NATIONAL BOUNDARIES 1924

TERRITORY LOST BY GERMANY

TERRITORY LOST BY AUSTRIA HUNGARY

TERRITORY LOST BY RUSSIA

wished to make greater inroads for her future security, either to advance her own border to the Rhine, or to create in the Rhineland an independent and neutral state. Both plans met the ideological and pragmatic opposition of Britain and America, and France had to be satisfied with a three-point settlement; a temporary allied occupation of the Rhineland, the permanent banning of all German forces from the Rhineland, and a proposed guarantee of British and American aid in maintaining that settlement. To the north and east, Germany suffered further losses. North Schleswig once more became Danish territory, and territory in Posen and West Prussia was transferred to Poland, notably the infamous 'Polish Corridor' giving the new state access to the sea. At the end of the 'Corridor', the distinctly German city of Danzig became a 'Free City' with Poland granted the use of its port facilities, her only access to the sea.

Central to Germany's resentment of this imposed peace was Clause 231 which forced Germany to acknowledge that the guilt and responsibility for the outbreak of the war was hers. Without this 'War Guilt Clause' there would have been little moral justification for the fourth imposition upon Germany. The question of reparation payments to the victor by the vanquished had a long tradition in European warfare, but never before had any war been fought on such a scale. Now the allies proposed to charge Germany for the material damage done to them during the hostilities, a very considerable figure in the case of France, and for their future expenses on such items as pensions for their widows and war wounded. This last item alone constituted nearly half the total bill of £6600 million which was handed to the Germans when the huge task of estimation was eventually completed (May 1921).

Lastly, although the peace settlement with Germany naturally dominated the attention of European statesmen, it must not be forgotten that it was accompanied by a collection of other treaties with Germany's erstwhile allies, with Austria at St. Germain en Laye, with Hungary at Trianon, with Turkey at Sèvres, and with Bulgaria at Neuilly. Central to these was the disappearance of that dominant feature of central Europe for five centuries, the Habsburg Empire. In its place stood the rump German state of Austria, specially forbidden by the treaties to associate with their fellow Germans to the north, and a number of new states, Yugoslavia, Czechoslovakia and Poland, representing the fulfilled national aspirations of nearly a century. In the cases of Yugoslavia and Czechoslovakia the delegates around Paris had been able to do little but accept the actions of national leaders such as Masaryk, Beneš and Trumbić who had seized their opportunities with the collapse of the Austro-Hungarian war effort. Hungary, after a century of increasing national fulfilment, now found herself stripped of Croatia, Slovenia, Slovakia and Ruthenia by these new states. Her resentment of her losses was also to be a significant factor in the politics of central and eastern Europe over the next two decades.

(b) The Treaty of Versailles: Implications

Patently, the peace settlement of 1919 was unsuccessful. A. J. P. Taylor's blunt judgement that 'the second world war was, in large part, a repeat performance of the first' conveys clearly the extent to which the problems of 1919 were left unresolved. In part, its failure may be ascribed to the enormous complexity of the problems facing the delegates. In 1815 at Vienna the Empire of Napoleon had collapsed. In 1919 at Versailles, the Empires of Germany, Turkey, Austria-Hungary and Russia were in ruins. Several other distinct weaknesses in the final drafts of the treaties must, however, also be identified.

The prime problem that was to haunt Europe for the next two and a half decades was that of German resentment of the terms imposed upon them. Although on the verge of military defeat in November 1918, German lines were still on foreign soil, and their representatives had approached the allies confident that a settlement would be offered based upon the Fourteen Points. Instead Germans found themselves presented with a dictated peace which stripped the Reich of 25 000 square miles of territory and 7 000 000 inhabitants, about $13\frac{1}{2}\%$ and 10% of her respective totals. She found, furthermore, that in many cases Germany was treated according to principles quite different from those that governed the settlements with other states. Nationality was the proclaimed principle behind most territorial settlements, yet union between Germany and the German-speakers of Austria was specifically forbidden. Germany was disarmed and stripped of her colonies, while the victors retained their weapons and in some cases actually added to their colonial empires. Yet, while Germany was treated as a defeated power, she retained the means once more to become a great force in the world. She was not partitioned, as she was eventually to be in 1945, and she retained nearly 90% of her economic resources. Although deprived of her weapons now, she retained the potential to produce modern replacements at a later date. As early as 1925, Germany's production of steel, for instance, was twice that of Great Britain. Her relative position in the European balance of power had hardly suffered, furthermore, by the development that left a collection of relatively weak 'successor states' on her eastern borders.

Given this German resentment, the treaty would need to be enforced. Yet, already in 1918, the alliance that had fought the war was in the process of disintegration. By 1920 it was in ruins. Firstly, the great power of Russia, a key factor in the considerations of 1914, was quite excluded from the deliberations of 1919. Not only did the Soviet revolution of 1917 remove Russia temporarily from the diplomatic scene, but its eventual success, and its brief imitations in Hungary (March 1919) and Bavaria (April 1919), had profoundly shocked the governing classes of Europe. Their attitudes towards Germany often became, as a result of the revolution, highly ambiguous. With Germany defeated, might not communist Russia now be seen as the major threat to Europe's stability and security? And if a relatively strong, conservative Germany was not preserved as a bulwark in central Europe, what would prevent the westward flow of the communist tide? By mid-1919 it was clear that the United States would not fulfil this role, for she had turned her back on Europe as abruptly as she had intervened in the first place. The considerable prestige of President Wilson at Versailles had hidden the true weakness of his domestic position. Involvement in Europe had never been universally popular, and the prospect of a permanent peacekeeping role there was quite unacceptable to the Senate, which accordingly refused to ratify the treaties that Wilson had negotiated (November 1919). A year later, Wilson's party was out of power, and America was once again firmly on the path of isolationism. In short, the implementation of the peace treaty had to be undertaken from 1919 without the participation of either of the powers who were to decide Europe's fate in 1939–45.

On none of the foregoing points has there been serious historical dispute. The same cannot be said, however, for the third area of objection that was quickly raised to the peace terms. In an influential work, *The Economic Consequences of the Peace* (1920), the English economist J. M. Keynes denounced what he saw as the folly of the treaty's reparations clauses. By putting such intolerable pressure on the German economy, he concluded, the allies threatened the stability of the whole European economy of which it was part. 'This treaty', he argued, 'ignores the economic solidarity of Europe, and by aiming at the economic life of Germany, it threatens the health and prosperity of the allies

themselves'. Although influential in Britain and in the United States, Keynes' arguments incited great opposition in France, the country most in need of reparations. There they were most effectively answered by E. Mantoux (*The Economic Consequences of Mr. Keynes*, 1944). The crux of his argument was that the productivity of German industry in the 1930s, especially as regards armaments manufacture, showed that the levels of reparations set in 1921 were, after all, within Germany's capacity.

Mantoux's work is, in fact, part of a substantial literature since the 1939–45 war which has modified the earlier condemnation of the Versailles treaty. Where Winston Churchill saw 'a turbulent collision of embarrassed demagogues', where Keynes saw profound economic ignorance, and where Nicolson saw a sad failure to stick to original high ideals, more recent writers have often cited extenuating circumstances. The Frenchman, M. Baumont, has stressed that the shortcomings that survived the peace conference should not blind us to the fact that 'as a whole the treaties righted age-old wrongs', especially with regard to the subject nationalities of central Europe. A. Adamthwaite has claimed that the main fault in 1919 lay, not with the terms of the treaties, but with the hopes that preceded them, so high that they were bound to be disappointed. 'No peace settlement', he writes, 'could have fulfilled the millenial hopes of a new heaven and a new earth. It was the destruction of these Utopian hopes that provoked the denunciations of the settlement'. Perhaps the most relevant judgement, however, comes from another Frenchman, J. Néré, who finds the fault of the treaty not in its terms but in the failure of its enforcement. 'Ultimately the preservation of peace depended on a close and permanent understanding between France, Britain and the USA'. In the failure of the victorious wartime alliance to continue its co-operation to maintain the hard-won peace lies the real tragedy of the 1920s and the 1930s.

(c) The League of Nations

Central to Woodrow Wilson's ideas on the establishment and maintenance of European and world peace was the concept of an international organisation able to transcend the selfish motives and the misunderstandings which, in Wilson's view, were the root causes of international conflict. In general, the idea of a 'League of Nations' was greeted with enthusiasm by the nations represented at the peace conference. Two distinct schools of thought developed, however, as to the form it should take. France took the realistic view that such a body could only be influential if equipped with sufficient armed force to enforce its decision. Such a view encountered opposition from Great Britain, uneasy at the idea of an international armed force possibly under French command, and from other states who baulked at the idea of portions of their own forces coming under international control. Above all, President Wilson refused to allow his 'brain child' to become simply another weapon of traditional power politics, or a weapon with which the victors could torment the defeated. Thus, the body whose Covenant, or constitution, was written specifically into each of the peace treaties, and which met for the first time in Geneva in December 1920, was primarily a forum, or agency, to which nations in dispute could bring their problems for advice and settlement.

The Covenant of the League of Nations defined four main aims for the organisation. It sought to prevent future wars by peaceful settlement of international disputes, to promote disarmament, to supervise territories referred to it by the peace treaties, such as the former German colonies and the Saarland, and lastly to promote general international co-operation by means of its various organisations for social and economic work. Its powers and the obligations of its members in these tasks were also clearly defined. Members in dispute with one another were obliged to refer their differences to one of three processes provided by the League, to the Permanent Court of International Justice, to arbitration, or to enquiry by the Council of the League, its executive committee. Failure to do so, or failure to take reasonable account of the resulting decisions rendered offending members liable to sanctions. So impressed had the allies been by the effect of economic embargoes employed against Germany in the war, that economic sanctions were chosen as the League's main weapon. The possibility of military sanctions was admitted, but their extent was left undefined, and they could only ever be applied if a member state agreed to put its own forces at the disposal of the League. In its twenty year life, the League never once sought to apply military sanctions. Among the 42 states originally subscribing to these terms, there were some notable absentees. The United States, because of the Senate's refusal to ratify the peace terms, was never a member of the organisation inspired by her President. Soviet Russia did not become a member until 1934, the year after Japan left the League. Germany was a member only between 1926–33, her initial absence confirming the impression that, for all Wilson's claims to the contrary, the League in essence stood for the preservation of the 'status quo' established in 1919. None of the several powers dissatisfied with either the terms or the principles of the peace settlement could happily accept or further the aims of the League of Nations.

Yet the League was not a total failure. When states accepted its mediatory functions it could and did reach notable settlements, as over the Åland Islands claimed by Sweden and Finland (1921), and its border disputes between Greece and Bulgaria (1924) and between Hungary and Yugoslavia (1934). When European statesmen such as MacDonald, Stressemann and Briand worked with it in the late 1920s, it seemed at the centre of European diplomacy, and its international bodies such as the Health Organisation and the Advisory Committee on Traffic in Women and Children, still function today, as the World Health Organisation and UNICEF. That it failed in its primary task, to prevent further war, was due to the fact that the League represented a new concept of international relations in a world where most major powers were content to stick to the old selfish methods of force and 'Realpolitik'. In the major confrontations of the inter-war period the League failed, not because it could not find common ground between disputing parties, but because it was totally ignored by one or more of those parties. In the case of Polish seizure of the town of Vilna (1920), Japanese aggression in Manchuria (1931), Italian attacks on Abyssinia (1935), and all of Hitler's expansionist moves, the League was bypassed. It had no means in its Covenant to prevent that. Two contemporary verdicts illustrate well the League's weakness in the face of selfish acts of aggression. In all the cases just mentioned the judgement of Lord David Cecil held good that 'the League of Nations has not been tried and found wanting; it has been found inconvenient and not tried'. Prominent among those who found the 'peacemongering' of the League inconvenient was Mussolini. He fully appreciated that, especially in the 1930s, the machinery of the League appealed only to those nations too weak to look after their own interests. 'The League is all right', he declared, 'when sparrows quarrel. It fails when eagles fall out'.

(d) The Occupation of the Ruhr

In the years immediately after the conclusion of peace, the maintenance of the treaty's terms was primarily a problem for France. For her, the questions of reparation payments, of post-war reconstruction and of German economic potential were not questions of morality or theory, but of national survival. By 1920, however, the bases of French security proposed at Versailles lay in ruins. America had withdrawn from European involvement, Britain showed little interest in continuing the co-operation of wartime, and domestic developments in Germany (see Chapter 14, section **d**) offered little prospect of her willing acceptance of the settlement. Most serious for France's recovery and prosperity, Germany showed increasing reluctance to maintain her reparation payments. By the Wiesbaden Accords (October 1921), France agreed to facilitate German payments by accepting a proportion in raw materials and industrial produce, rather than in cash, but in the next year, these payments in kind had also slipped steadily into arrears. Faced with the choice of using conciliation or confrontation to exact her due from Germany, public and political opinion in France inclined more and more toward the latter solution, the more so with the appointment of Raymond Poincaré as Prime Minister (January 1922). Poincaré was a hard headed and determined politician, a native of Lorraine, who remembered Germany's past offences towards his home region, and was determined that she should not escape her due punishment.

The crisis in French–German relations erupted in November 1922 when Germany requested a suspension of her payments for up to four years in the light of domestic economic difficulties. It was her third such request in three years and strongly suggested that the whole question of adherence to the Versailles settlement was at stake. It was thus this vital issue, rather than the trivial pretext of non-delivery of a batch of telegraph poles, that prompted France, with support from Italy and Belgium, to send troops across the Rhine into the industrial heartland of the Ruhr (January 1923). Protesting, with justification, that the invasion of her sovereign territory was against the terms of the peace treaty, the German government of Chancellor Cuno appealed with great success for a policy of passive resistance in the Ruhr. In February 1923, coal production there fell to 2.5 million tons, where 90 million had been mined in 1922. Three iron smelting furnaces operated in March, where 70 had worked the previous year. Occasional terrorist attacks on troops, and military action against German demonstrators raised the overall tension. To overcome the effects of strikes and passive resistance, Poincaré appealed, with equal success, for unemployed Frenchmen and Belgians to operate mines, furnaces and railways in the Ruhr. Faced with the success of this ploy, with the total collapse of the German currency (see

Chapter 14, section **d**), and with the ominous spread of separatist movements in Germany, the government conceded defeat. Although it never became official French governmental policy, commanders in the Ruhr certainly showed some sympathy to political movements that proposed the establishment of an independent Rhineland state. With the very existence of united Germany at risk, G. Stresemann replaced Cuno as Chancellor in August and decreed the end of passive resistance within a month.

What, then, had Poincaré achieved in the Ruhr? Economically, he seemed to have triumphed, with France guaranteed 21% of the region's production up to December 1923 and 27% thereafter. Against this, however, Poincaré had reinforced the mistrust and apprehension of his former allies as to the French threat to the balance of power, and had made difficult, if not impossible, any future co-operation between France and Germany. 'France', wrote the Italian minister Count Sforza, 'has committed the supreme error of polarising against her the hostility of all the patriotic elements in the Reich'. The economic gains, important as they were, were largely nullified by France's subsequent political isolation. In his own country Poincaré came under attack, from the left wing for high-handed action in the interests of French capitalists, and from the right, for once more withdrawing when the chance existed finally to break the unity and economic backbone of Germany. In terms of its political consequences it must be considered highly doubtful whether the Ruhr gamble was worth the cost.

(e) Conciliation: The Dawes Plan and the Young Plan

At least France learned her lesson from the Ruhr adventure. The hostility of British and American reaction, the dramatic decline in the franc (from 70 to the £ in 1922 to 240 to the £ in 1926), and the defeat of the National Bloc in the 1924 elections, all brought home the point that she could not safely rely upon unilateral action. The agreement between France, Britain and the United States (November 1923) to replace the reparations question upon an international footing, represented not only French misgivings, but British and American fears as to where unilateral action might lead.

The result of this decision was the formation of the commission, chaired by the American economist C. C. Dawes, which produced in April 1924 the so-called 'Dawes Plan' for the future regulation of redemption payments. By the Dawes Plan, which was to operate for five years, reparation payments would be guaranteed by two mortgages, one on Germany's railways, and the other on certain German industries, supplemented by deductions from certain German taxes. An American 'General Reparations Agent', Parker Gilbert, was to be installed in Germany to supervise payments. The amounts to be paid by Germany were substantially reduced, but this was outweighed in the French view by the facts that much of her post-war reconstruction was nearing completion, and that the plan once more involved her wartime allies in the collection of reparations. Thus, France accepted the Dawes Plan. The five years of the Plan's operation have been described as the 'Golden Age' of reparations, with the allies receiving payments, in cash and in kind, with far greater regularity than ever before. It was, however, a temporary expedient, and was still accompanied by German complaints both at the level of payments and at the fact that no definite date had been fixed for their end. From the allied point of view, the plan also failed to provide any link between German payments and their own repayment of war debts to the United States.

The Young Plan (June 1929), proposed to succeed the Dawes Plan, set out to tackle all these questions. Although it further reduced the total to be paid by Germany, it linked French and British debts to the level of German payments, and set 1988 as the final year of reparation payments. It also continued American commitment and involvement in this vital area of European politics. Therein, in both the Dawes Plan and the Young Plan, lay the fatal weakness of these reparation solutions. The operation of both was very largely dependent upon the large sums of foreign capital, two-thirds of it American, that was in the late 1920s being invested in Germany to stimulate and sustain her industries. J. M. Keynes had already written in 1926 that the duration of these arrangements was 'in the hands of the American capitalist'. Within three years, the great crisis of American capitalism was finally to wreck these hopeful prospects of economic reconciliation.

(f) Conciliation: The Locarno Pact

For the German government, the primary objects of their agreement to the reparations plans were to clear their territory of foreign troops and to guard against their return. The first aim was only partially achieved for, although French and Belgian troops had withdrawn from the Ruhr by August 1925, allied troops remained in other Rhineland cities, such as Cologne, under the direct terms of the peace treaty. To complete the process, and to guard against the dangers of separatism in the Rhineland which he took very seriously, Stresemann approached the allies with the boldest proposal of his political career and one that was by no means universally popular in Germany. At a meeting in Locarno, in Switzerland (February 1925), he proposed a voluntary German guarantee of her Western borders. For France and Belgium, this meant that Germany freely gave up her claims to Alsace and Lorraine and to Eupen and Malmedy. For Germany, it meant that France would no longer be able to use the weapon of invasion, or harbour hopes of an independent Rhineland state, factors which also made the proposals highly acceptable to Britain. There were, however, shortcomings in the 'package' from the French viewpoint. Would Germany similarly acknowledge her eastern frontiers? Would she acknowledge the peace treaties as a whole? Italy, also a party to the proposals, was equally keen that Stresemann should acknowledge Germany's southern border with Austria. The German government would not go so far, and the Locarno Pact agreed by Germany, France, Britain, Italy and Belgium (October 1925), apart from guaranteeing the current western borders of Germany, merely recognised France's treaty commitments to Poland and Czechoslovakia. France would find these commitments very hard to carry out without violating Germany's western frontiers.

The judgements of historians upon the Locarno Pact have differed according to the relative stress they have placed upon its literal terms, and upon the new spirit of diplomacy which some, at least, of its authors hoped that it represented. The contemporary judgement of the British Foreign Secretary, Sir Austen Chamberlain, that the Pact was 'the real dividing line between the years of war and the years of peace' proved, of course, to be premature. Nevertheless E. Wiskemann could still describe much more recently the relationship between the French and German ministers, Briand and Stresemann, as 'an involvement which . . . did not spell hostility towards others and which thus had genuinely fertile possibilities'. To E. H. Carr and A. Adamthwaite, on the other hand, the promise of Locarno was an illusion. Carr points out that, welcome as it was at the time, Locarno undermined both the Versailles Treaty and the League of Nations. It showed that further action, and action involving major powers, was necessary to guarantee peace. For Adamthwaite, the illusory success of the Pact was due to the fact that 'it had meant different things to different statesmen. For Gustav Stresemann, Locarno was the first step towards treaty revision; for Aristide Briand, it was the first step on the road to compliance; for Austen Chamberlain, it was an assertion of British detachment'.

It must be understood, however, that the French government accepted the Locarno terms, not because it misunderstood their implications, but because its foreign policy had deliberately rejected attempts to control Germany in favour of attempts to draw her into international undertakings guaranteed by other powers. Locarno has to be seen as part of that programme. Germany's entry into the League of Nations (September 1926) was another essential element in the same programme. So, too was the so-called 'Briand–Kellogg' Pact (August 1928) whereby the French Foreign Minister and the American Secretary of State agreed to 'the renunciation of war as an instrument of national policy'. Sixty-two of the 64 states invited to subscribe to this agreement agreed, Brazil and Argentina being the exceptions, and although it has been widely attacked for its apparent naivete, it was interpreted at the time as an important commitment to the principle of peace by the world's leading powers.

By the summer of 1929, when a conference at The Hague reached agreement on the evacuation of the Rhineland, five years earlier than envisaged at Versailles, the policy of reconciliation seemed largely vindicated and its future prospects engendered confidence. Locarno and German membership of the League of Nations seemed to create political stability in Europe; the Dawes Plan and its successor seemed to prove that reparations could be paid on a regular basis; the consultative spirit of the League of Nations seemed to be accepted by all major powers. The disintegration of this reassuring 'scenario' was brutally abrupt. In July, the retirement of Poincaré removed the major source of stability in French politics. On 3rd October, Stresemann died of a heart attack, aged 51, and exactly three weeks later, on 'Black Thursday', share values on the Wall Street Stock Market went into a disastrous decline. The 'Great Depression' had begun.

(g) Economic Crisis and the End of Reparations

Details of the impact of the 'Great Depression' upon the individual European states belong elsewhere (see Chapter 14). The large-scale withdrawal of American capital from European investment, and the general fall in prices of industrial and agricultural goods, however, also had overall implications in terms of international relations. Any spirit of international co-operation that may have been in the process of formation gave way to a desperate sense of 'every man for himself'. Nation after nation, for example, abandoned the gold standard, and most hurriedly enclosed themselves behind tariff barriers in an attempt to minimise the effects of the crisis upon themselves. By 1931, only France, Italy and Poland of the major European states continued to base their currencies upon gold. We have already seen (Chapter 14, section **g**) the direct role played by the economic crisis in the rise of the Nazi party to power in Germany between 1930–33, but quite apart from aiding the spread of fascism and self-interested nationalism, the depression also prepared the ground for international appeasement of those forces. As Britain, America and other states slowly recovered, they sought safety in economic entrenchment and carefully balanced budgets. There seemed no room, at the time of careful housekeeping, for heavy arms expenditure, and the expense of another war was unthinkable. Besides, as the domestic affairs of France and Spain showed clearly, the apparent failure of existing regimes to cope with the ills of capitalism caused many to entertain thoughts of Bolshevism or of Fascism as an alternative. France, Spain, Belgium and even Britain were not immune from the forces that had engendered fascism in Germany.

A direct casualty of the economic catastrophe was the Young Plan for reparation payments. In October 1930, German representatives had approached President Hoover of the United States, as the peace treaty entitled them to do, to request a suspension (or 'moratorium') of reparation payments in the light of increasing economic difficulties. The resultant Hoover Moratorium covered all inter-state debts from mid-1931 to mid-1932. By December 1931, however, it was clear that Europe was not experiencing the 'relatively short depression' for which a moratorium was designed. In that month the powers involved with the Young Plan met in Basle to consider the reparations question and concluded that 'an adjustment of all intergovernmental debts . . . is the only lasting measure which is capable of restoring . . . economic stability and true peace'. The Lausanne Conference (June 1932) agreed that reparation should be ended by a lump-sum payment of 3000 million marks, relieving Germany of 90% of her outstanding debt. To the anger of the United States, however, her European debtors insisted that their war debt repayments should also end. Even the last payment proposed by the French premier was vetoed by the Assembly. Thus, the financial clauses of the Treaty of Versailles ceased to exist, and if France had gained 'tit for tat' on an economic level, her diplomatic account was left badly in debit by renewed isolation from the United States. The final lump sum payment by Germany, incidentally, was never made.

(h) The Failure of Disarmament

The principle of international disarmament was the second major casualty of the early 1930s. It will be recalled that, in theory, the disarmament of Germany was merely a preliminary to a general disarmament. Not until 1926, however, did a 'Preparatory Commission' meet in Geneva, and not until February 1932 did the conference finally gather there to begin serious deliberation. On the surface, the prospects seemed relatively bright, for the renunciation of expensive armaments made good sense at a time of dramatic recession. France, consistently one of the most positive members of the conference, explored three different routes to the goal. The original plan proposed by A. Tardieu was to the effect that each nation should submit its major offensive weapons, planes, capital ships, heavy artillery, to the control of the League of Nations, to provide a force to oppose aggression. It was, in short, a revival of the 1919 idea of a 'League with Teeth', and fell foul of the same objections about the infringement of national sovereignty. In the face of division among the wartime allies, Germany played her 'trump' card, demanded equal treatment with the allies on the question of armaments, and withdrew from the conference. So pointless was the idea of an agreement without Germany that France effectively conceded the radical idea of German equality in her new 'Constructive Plan' (November 1932). This combined the idea of a League of Nations force with the maintenance of national defensive militias, of which Germany was entitled to as large a one as any other state. The principle of German equality was also specifically acknowledged within 'a system which would comprise security for all nations'. Germany returned to the conference but, with Italy, showed little interest in the Constructive Plan. After the failure of a British plan to establish a common limit of 200000 men on the forces of France, Germany, Italy and Poland, the third French plan came close to success (June 1933). She suggested an eight year period, during the latter half of which the continental armies would conform

to the figures suggested by the British. With Britain, France, Italy and the USA in agreement, and Germany in danger of becoming trapped, Hitler, now in power, withdrew finally from the conference (October 1933). Within five days he turned his back finally on international co-operation by quitting the League of Nations.

Although the conference sat until April 1935, it could achieve nothing without Germany, as Hitler well knew. A second major element in the Versailles peace plans was now a dead letter.

(i) The Failure of 'Great Power' Security

The collapse of two essential bases of the collective security envisaged at Versailles caused the major powers of Western Europe to turn to the alternative form of security already explored with some success at Locarno, the security of traditional pacts and alliances. The initiative this time came primarily from Mussolini who, in separate conversations with British and French ministers (March 1933), proposed the idea of a joint undertaking by Italy, France, Germany and Britain to take no unilateral action that might disturb the peace of Europe. The motives of the four powers in following up the suggestion were various. Britain, in the words of then Foreign Secretary, Sir John Simon, saw Italy as 'the key to European peace', and was willing to work with her to maintain a traditional balance of power. France shared these motives to an extent, although opinion there was by no means united as to the value of such a pact. Germany, at this delicate stage so soon after Hitler's advent to power, was happy to take any step that reassured European opinion while she solved her domestic problems. Only in the case of Italy has there been real disagreement among historians. Those who have generally regarded Mussolini as altogether cynical have seen his proposals as a means of separating France from her allies in eastern Europe, where Italy of course had ambitions, and perhaps from Britain. Others, following E. Wiskemann, have regarded Mussolini as genuinely perturbed by the resurgence of Germany. They saw his proposals in 1933 as a genuine attempt to appease Hitler, by recognising Germany's great power status, while restricting her freedom of action by international guarantees.

The Four Power Pact concluded in July 1933 committed the contracting states to co-operation for a period of ten years to preserve the peace of Europe. But, as a further step away from the Versailles settlement, it acknowledged the principle of 'reasonable revision' of the peace treaties. In fact, the pact was a 'dead letter' almost as soon as it was agreed. In October Hitler already felt confident enough to leave the Disarmament Conference and the League of Nations. Within 18 months (March 1935) he had re-introduced conscription in Germany, which promised little for his desire to co-operate with his neighbours. In the light of these events, the Four Power Pact was never ratified by the other powers. Its effects, therefore, were wholly negative, providing a nasty shock for the eastern European states who now found themselves excluded from an apparent great power 'club'. Russia's reaction was to enter negotiations with France for a mutual assistance pact, possibly with a view to splitting this new capitalist 'bloc'. Poland, apparently let down by France, reacted differently and concluded a non-aggesssion pact with Germany in January 1934.

Italy, France and Britain did not yet despair of combined action to preserve their security. Contacts between Mussolini and the pro-Italian Foreign Minister of France, Pierre Laval, fuelled by an attempted Nazi 'coup' in Austria (July 1934) resulted in a set of Rome Agreements (January 1935) in which the parties seemed to have reached an understanding on European security and Italian colonial ambitions. With Britain drawn in once more, the Stresa Conference (April 1935) produced a three-sided agreement to oppose 'by all practical means, any unilateral repudiation of treaties, which may endanger the peace of Europe'. In theory, this 'Stresa Front', formed by the leaders of the three powers, was an imposing structure. In reality, it had a number of weaknesses. In effect, far from girding up their loins to fight Hitler, all the members hoped rather that the very existence of the 'Stresa Front' might deter the German dictator from dangerous adventures. 'In truth', as A. J. P. Taylor has written, 'each of the three powers hoped to receive help from the others without providing any in return'. Secondly, Mussolini, although his concern at the rise of Germany was undoubtedly genuine, quite specifically desired this agreement to gain such European security as would enable him to pursue Italy's 'Imperial destiny'. The reaction of his Stresa partners to his colonial policy was shortly to put this final attempt at a great power equilibrium to the test.

(j) The Abyssinian Invasion

In October 1935, Italian forces began the pursuit of Mussolini's colonial plans by an open assault upon the East African state of Abyssinia (also called Ethiopia). The long-term motives for this attack reached back to the 19th century when Italy had marked out this region as her sphere of influence in the general 'Scramble for Africa', and had suffered the humiliation of defeat at the hands of Abyssinian tribesmen at Adowa (1896). Not only did national pride demand some compensation for Adowa, but the aggressive nature of Italian fascism demanded, in Mussolini's words, 'war for war's sake, since fascism needs the glory of victory'. Besides, since Britain and France showed no signs of liquidating their empires, was not Italy entitled to equal colonial status? Although evidence suggests that Mussolini had determined his course by 1932, the precise timing of his attack was dictated by several factors; by the rate of military preparation, and especially by Mussolini's conviction that his agreement with France and Britain at Stresa had ensured that Hitler would take no revisionist initiatives while his back was turned.

The new phase of Italian policy opened with a border incident at Wal-Wal (November 1934) and proceeded with a steady and obvious build-up of arms in Italian Somalia and Eritrea. On 2nd October 1935 Italian troops invaded Abyssinia on the pretext that they were 'restoring order in a vast country left in the most atrocious slavery and the most primitive conditions of existence'. When local geography and the courage of the local tribesmen caused temporary embarrassment, Mussolini poured huge resources into the fray. Four hundred thousand men fought in Abyssinia, and the full weight of modern weaponry, aerial bombardment and the use of poison gas, was brought to bear. The flight of the Abyssinian Emperor, Haile Selassie, and the capture of his capital, Addis Ababa, confirmed Italy's victory in May 1936.

The implications of the conquest of Abyssinia were not, however, confined to East Africa. Unfortunately for Italy, Abyssinia, despite her vague boundaries and semi-feudal government, had been admitted to the League of Nations in 1923 and demanded that that body apply the prescribed economic sanctions against the aggressor. Britain and France thus found themselves committed, with differing degrees of enthusiasm, to a boycott of all Italian goods and to a ban on exports of arms, rubber, and metal ore to Italy. The attempts of their foreign ministers, Hoare and Laval, to buy-off either Mussolini or Haile Selassie ended in embarrassing failure, and their apparent 'double game' of applying sanctions and negotiating at the same time behind the back of the League of Nations effectively dragged down both the League and the Stresa Front. Furthermore, the sanctions were largely ineffective. The vital commodity of oil was not among the prohibited items and, in any case, non-members such as Germany, Japan and the United States were not committed to sanctions. Although his most recent biographer, D. Mack Smith, draws the conclusion that Mussolini's whole policy over Stresa and Abyssinia was one of calculated duplicity, it seems likely that he was genuinely shocked by the imposition of economic sanctions. His assumption that Laval had granted him a 'free hand' by the Rome Agreements seemed confirmed by British and French silence at Stresa on the Abyssinian question, despite the contemporary build-up of Italian forces in Africa. Surely this had indicated their acquiescence? To Mussolini, a League of Nations that allowed the Japanese to escape unpunished for the aggression in China, and then turned on Italy, was a 'front of conservation, of selfishness, and of hypocrisy'.

Whatever their limitations, the 1935 agreements between France, Italy and Britain perished, not necessarily because of Mussolini's deviousness, but because of the extraordinary confusion of British and French foreign policy. In the overall context of European politics, the invasion of Abyssinia was a chapter of errors. Although victory cemented Mussolini's personal prestige at home, Italy gained little or nothing from it in material terms. The damage done, meanwhile, to the prestige of Britain, France and the League of Nations was irreversible. The only winner in the whole sorry episode was Adolf Hitler.

(k) The Remilitarisation of the Rhineland

The Abyssinian crisis preoccupied European statesmen for eight months (October 1935–May 1936), during which time Hitler struck his first blow at the territorial clauses of the Treaty of Versailles. On 7th March 1936, he ordered a force of 22 000 men into the Rhineland in direct defiance of those treaty terms which declared it a demilitarised zone. As pretext, he claimed that the French pact with the Soviet Union had breached the Locarno understanding. A more realistic explanation of his timing would, of course, take into account Italy's colonial involvement and the resultant weakening of the Stresa 'Front'.

Europe was taken by surprise, not by the fact of remilitarisation, but by the method. Diplomats had expected Hitler to negotiate; instead he took swift, decisive action, and offered negotiations afterwards, a method soon to become familiar. The operation succeeded through a combination of Hitler's boldness and French miscalculations. France's military leaders estimated that up to 295 000 German troops were available to Hitler and that

their intervention would lead to a major conflict. Her political leaders thus concluded that they could intervene only with British aid. It is now known that the German forces were under direct orders to withdraw if they met resistance. No British aid, however, was forthcoming. In Britain and France alike much public opinion felt that confrontation with Germany and Italy at the same time was folly, that French friendship with the Soviet Union was unwise and that, in any case, as a taxi driver remarked to the British Foreign Secretary, 'Jerry can do what he likes in his own back garden'. In short, Hitler's move did not cause widespread popular outrage because, in the words of the French historian M. Baumont, 'a blow had been aimed, not at French territory, but only at the Treaty of Versailles, in which no one believed any longer'.

The implications of the remilitarisation were substantial and complex. In combination with the Abyssinian affair, it seemed to show that the western powers were as unwilling as the League of Nations was unable to act against unilateral revision of the treaties. The effect on France's strategic position was disastrous. Not only did Hitler's action provide further disillusionment for such nations as Poland and Czechoslovakia, but the rapid fortification of Germany's frontiers now made it extremely difficult for France to fulfil her eastern pacts by attacks against Germany in the west. French reluctance to act alone also provided proof that she had become the junior partner in her relationship with Britain. Lastly, Hitler's bold gamble, like that of Mussolini in Abyssinia, was invaluable in strengthening his prestige and authority at home, especially in military circles. If Abyssinia destroyed the League of Nations, the remilitarisation of the Rhineland destroyed Locarno, and the way was thus open to the disaster of 1939.

(l) The Formation of the Rome–Berlin Axis

The key feature of European diplomatic relationships, and a major factor in the collapse of the balance of power in Europe after 1935, was the movement of Italy out of the orbit of London and Paris and into that of Berlin. Superficially appealing as the attraction of one fascist dictatorship for another may have been, the coming together of Italy and Germany had little to do with ideology. In the words of M. Baumont, Mussolini 'wanted to be on the side of power, the only decisive attraction for him'. In this context of power politics, he had drawn four lessons from the events of 1935–37. Firstly, it had become clear that the statesmen of Britain and France, and still less those of the League of Nations from which Italy withdrew in November 1937, had neither the will nor the means to check the resurgence of Germany. Secondly, it was evident that Italy could not pursue her interests in Abyssinia and in Spain and, at the same time, guard her security in central Europe. Thirdly, involvement in Spain (see Chapter 14, section **t**) had badly weakened Italy's international position. It had shown up weaknesses in her army, absorbed half of her foreign currency reserves, and established a gulf between Mussolini and the democrats without guaranteeing any gain or support from General Franco. Lastly, and perhaps most important, just as he became disgusted at the weakness of the western powers, so Mussolini was at once seduced and horrified by the power of Germany. After a relatively unsuccessful visit to Rome in 1934, Hitler had spared no effort to demonstrate German military strength when Mussolini came to Berlin (September 1937). To quote Baumont once again, 'Mussolini gave way to the magnetism of strength. He was astounded by the spectacle of German strength, and he found himself seized beyond hope of return, subjugated by a master'. The fact that there seemed to be no essential clash between Italian interests in Africa and the Mediterranean, and those of Germany in eastern Europe, merely hastened the process of alliance.

This alliance had its origins in the so-called 'October Protocols' signed by Count Ciano in Berlin in 1936. They contained little but vague anti-Bolshevik phrases, but gave the relationship the name by which it is known to history, by declaring that the Berlin–Rome line was now 'an axis around which can revolve all those European states with a will to collaboration and peace'. In November 1937, shortly after Mussolini's fateful visit to Germany, this 'Axis' took on wider implications when Italy subscribed to the Anti-Comintern Pact, originally concluded between Germany and Japan (November 1936) to present a united front against Bolshevism. The Anschluss of March 1938, and Italy's meek acceptance of it, did not so much mark a further step towards alliance, as indicate the extent to which Italian policy was already subject to that of Germany. Within two months, Hitler began to pressurise the Italian government to accept a full military alliance. Mussolini's initial reluctance to commit himself was worn down by May 1939, when he allowed Ciano to conclude the alliance, known as the Pact of Steel, which committed both sides to aid each other in the event of one of them becoming 'involved in warlike complications'. The terms made no pretence to be merely defensive. The Pact of Steel constituted a triumph for Hitler in his re-orientation of European diplomacy, and completed Mussolini's loss of control over his own policy. 'In point of fact', as E. Wiskemann has written, 'by underwriting all future German schemes, 'Mussolini gave Hitler "carte blanche" to attack Poland and to plunge into the Second World War.

(m) The Anschluss

The question of union (Anschluss) between Austria and the German Reich was nearly a century old when Hitler came to power. It had its roots in the 19th century contest for German leadership, seemingly settled by the triumph of Bismarck's Prussia and his careful exclusion of Austria from the German state. The loss of Austria's non-German territories in 1919, and the rise of an ardent Pan Germanist in the person of Hitler, raised the question anew. In favour of Anschluss at the beginning of the 1930s were the long-established factors of language and the memory of centuries during which Vienna had been the chief of the German cities, and the more modern consideration that many Austrians would undoubtedly be economically better off as part of a greater state. Against Anschluss were the remains of the old spirit of Austrian independence, still resenting the ascendancy of Berlin over Vienna, and the implacable hostility of the Versailles allies, especially of France and Italy. The project for a Customs Union between Germany and Austria (March 1931) had foundered upon the rock of French suspicion. 'They must take us for asses', wrote the French politician, E. Herriot, 'if they think that we are able to forget that the political union of Germany was reached by way of a customs union'. The mismanaged 'coup' by Austrian Nazis, with the knowledge of Hitler (July 1934) which ended in the murder of the Austrian Chancellor, E. Dollfuss, foundered upon the prompt action of Mussolini, mobilising the Italian army on the Austrian frontier.

This alignment of obstacles had, however, been much altered by the end of 1937. French inactivity over the advance of German troops to her very frontiers did not suggest that she would act energetically over Austria. Indeed, beset with domestic problems, British and French diplomats had even indicated to their German counterparts that they had 'no objection to a marked extension of German influence in Austria obtained through evolutionary means'. Most significant was the changed attitude of Italy. Deeply committed to intervention in the Spanish Civil War, deeply impressed by the shows of military power staged for him in Germany, Mussolini had already begun his drift into Hitler's wake. Count Ciano, his son-in-law and Foreign Minister, expressed the hopelessness of Italy's position over Austrian independence: 'What in fact could we do? Start a war with Germany? At the first shot we fired every Austrian, without exception, would fall in behind the Germans against us'.

Despite this, and despite the fact that the very first page of *Mein Kampf* makes clear Hitler's attachment to the principle of German–Austrian unity, A. J. P. Taylor has forwarded a convincing argument to suggest that Hitler did not deliberately set out to absorb Austria in 1938. Although he had hoped to be able to deal first with the question of the Sudetenland, his hand was forced by two factors. Firstly, by continuing agitation on the part of Austrian Nazis led by A. Seyss-Inquart, and secondly by the rash decision of the new Austrian Chancellor, K. von Schuschnigg, to confront Hitler and force him to disown the agitators. If Schuschnigg and Seyss-Inquart precipitated the crisis, Hitler nevertheless acted brilliantly to exploit it, partly in the interests of Anschluss, but partly to distract attention from contemporary domestic disagreements. In a violent interview at Berchtesgaten (12th February 1938) Hitler accused Schuschnigg of racial treason, and demanded that Seyss-Inquart be admitted to the Austrian government. Although accepting this demand, Schuschnigg attempted to defend his position by holding a referendum on the question of union with Germany. Unable to risk an anti-German vote, Hitler's hand was now forced. Successively, the German government demanded the postponement of the referendum, the replacement of Schuschnigg by Seyss-Inquart, and finally threatened military intervention. On 11th March, the Austrian Nazi leader, having formed a 'provisional government' of very doubtful legality, requested the dispatch of German troops 'to restore order and save Austria from chaos'. Even so, it is doubtful whether Hitler envisaged more than a 'puppet' government under Seyss-Inquart. On 13th March, however, encouraged by the enthusiastic reception accorded him by Austrian crowds at Linz, and by Mussolini's meek acceptance of the principle of Anschluss, Hitler proclaimed the formal union of his native Austria with the German Reich.

The Anschluss marked a clear escalation in Nazi policy, in that it involved the actual obliteration of an independent state set up by the peace treaties. Still, however, Hitler's action did not excite united European condemnation. The approval registered in the referendums now held by Hitler, 99.08% in Germany and 99.75% in Austria, probably had a sound basis in Pan-German feeling. Nevertheless, they were obviously in part the result of pressure and fear. 'In Austria', claimed Goering at Nuremberg in 1945, 'we were not met with rifle shots and bombs; only one thing was thrown at us, flowers'. The British government merely made a formal protest. There was no French government. Chautemps had resigned four days earlier and Blum had yet to take office. Once again, rapid and risky action had reaped a rich reward. Hitler's confidence in such action was now to put the peace of Europe in increasing danger.

(n) The Sudeten Question and the Fate of Czechoslovakia

If Hitler was serious in his desires either to unite all Germans in a single Reich, or to expand the territories of that Reich eastwards, the state of Czechoslovakia constituted a substantial obstacle in his path. She possessed a mountainous and easily defensible frontier with Germany, an army of 34 divisions well supplied by the giant Skoda arms factories at Pilsen, and enjoyed membership of a diplomatic system comprising France, Britain, Poland and the Soviet Union. She also, however, had her weaknesses. She was, for instance, a state of minority groups. Apart from the uneasy union of Czechs and Slovaks at the heart of the state, Hungarians, Poles and Ukrainians had been placed under the authority of Prague to give the new creation territorial and economic viability. Thirty-five per cent of the population, in fact, was neither Czech nor Slovak. The greatest of these minorities were the Germans of the Sudetenland. As A. J. P. Taylor has pointed out, the Sudetenland was actually a false concept, not a coherent geographical region at all, but an irregular ribbon of territory around the northern, western and southern periphery of Bohemia and Moravia. Spread through these regions, however, lived 3.25 million Germans, resentful that they no longer enjoyed the privileges that had been theirs under the Habsburg rule, and regarded with suspicion by the Czech government. Furthermore, the events of the mid-1930s isolated Czechoslovakia and increased her vulnerability. She had no border with friendly states such as France and the Soviet Union, could expect no help from Italy, if Austria had received none and, after the Anschluss, had a southern border with the enlarged Reich devoid of any natural defences.

As in the case of Austria, Hitler did not so much cause a crisis over Czechoslovakia, as exploit a crisis that was already developing. A key factor in this was the Sudeten Party, formed in 1935 by Konrad Henlein, whose political demands had escalated by the time of Henlein's 'Karlsbad Programme' (April 1938) from a claim for equal treatment with the Czechs to a demand for full independence from Czechoslovakia. Still relatively confident of French and British backing, the Czech President, E. Benes, was happy to confront and defy the Sudeten Germans. Hitler, more confident than ever after his Austrian successes, had no objection to confrontation, and was greatly aided by a new turn in British and French policy.

Britain and France were committed by the second half of 1938 to a policy of persuading Benes to grant Sudeten demands. They were convinced by the events in Austria and by rumours of German troop movements (May 1938) that, if Hitler was determined to support Henlein, the choice lay between Czech concessions and a general war. Henlein's policy, however, and that of Hitler, was to 'demand so much that we never can be satisfied'. When the Czech President conceded the principle demands of the Sudeten Germans, their leaders precipitated unsuccessful risings in Karlsbad, Eger and other centres (13th September) to sustain the tension. The danger that Hitler would intervene as he had in Austria broke the British and French nerve and their respective premiers, Chamberlain and Daladier, plunged into direct negotiations with Hitler. At Berchtesgaten (15th September) and at Bad Godesberg (22nd September), Chamberlain heard Hitler's demands escalate through direct German annexation of the Sudetenland, to immediate military occupation. Dramatically, six days later, Hitler agreed to a conference between himself, Chamberlain and, Daladier, to be held in Munich with Mussolini as mediator. It has been variously suggested that he had become aware of the lack of enthusiasm in Germany for a military solution, that he was disturbed by Mussolini's reluctance to give military support, or simply that he now knew that his shaken opponents were willing now to allow him the bulk of his demands. Certainly the Munich Conference (29th–30th September 1938) granted Hitler far more than he had been demanding a few weeks earlier. It was agreed between the powers that, although Germany would receive all Czech territory where Germans were in a majority, the transfer would be by stages, and under international supervision. In none of these negotiations was the Czech government consulted or allowed to participate. It was simply presented with the alternatives of acceptance or single combat with Germany.

Both morally and practically, the implications of the Munich agreement were enormous. The allies, especially the French with their direct treaty obligations, had betrayed Czechoslovakia. Although Britain, France, Italy and Germany all formally guaranteed her remaining territory, the state was in fact doomed, by the loss of her defensible frontier, by the loss of 70% of her iron and steel resources, by the loss of the Skoda works, and by the encouragement that Sudeten success gave to other separatists. Hungary and Poland both revived claims to Czech territory, and the cause of Slovak separatism took on a new lease of life. In March 1939, having failed to cause the collapse of Czechoslovakia by the Sudeten crisis, Hitler was to precipitate a new crisis over the Slovak demands, and to force the Czechs to accept a German 'protectorate' over Bohemia and Moravia, while Hungary, Poland and the Slovaks achieved their desires. Czechoslovakia, therefore, like Poland in the past, died of partition. From the viewpoint of Britain and of France, Munich could be seen in two ways, as the great achievement of the policy of appeasement, or as the test that revealed the fatal weaknesses of that policy. The tremendous popular relief in those countries at the avoidance of war was short-lived, and certainly did not survive Hitler's seizure of Prague in March. Despite the weakness displayed at Munich, and despite the loss of Czechoslovakia's 34 divisions to their cause, the subsequent military co-ordination between Britain and France, and their renewal of guarantees to Poland, Greece and Rumania (March–April 1939) strongly suggested that the next crisis would be confronted with greater resolution.

(o) The Ribbentrop–Molotov Pact

An undoubted casualty of the Munich surrender was the relationship between the western democracies and the Soviet Union. That relationship had suffered for a decade from mutual suspicion; suspicion on the Soviet side that the British and French secretly preferred German resurgence to the existence of a stable Soviet regime; suspicion in London and Paris either that Stalin still favoured the international spread of communism, or that his vicious domestic purges (see Chapter 13, section **k**) had destroyed Russia's viability as an ally. The Munich agreement, made without any reference to the Soviet Union, showed at best that the diplomacy of the western powers was incapable of checking German ambitions, and at worst represented a tacit agreement to Germany's quest for 'living space' in eastern Europe. Either way, the Soviet Union could no longer trust for her security to Paris and London. 'We nearly put our foot on a rotten plank', declared a prominent Soviet diplomat. 'Now we are going elsewhere'.

The first Soviet overtures for a more positive relationship with Nazi Germany came in May 1938, when the new ambassador to Berlin, A. Meretalov, received instructions to press for better commercial relations. At a time when he was increasingly pre-occupied with the problem of Czechoslovakia, Hitler reacted favourably to anything that might separate the Soviet Union from his immediate enemies. In July, the governments reached an oral agreement on the ending of their mutually hostile press campaigns. With the allied abandonment of Czechoslovakia, the Soviet government began to knock harder on Germany's door. The replacement of M. Litvinov as Commissar for Foreign Affairs by V. Molotov (May 1939) was invested by foreign observers with great significance. Molotov, as a member of the Politburo, had the necessary power to engineer major policy changes. Litvinov, on the other hand, had been a persistent advocate of collective security, and was furthermore a Jew. Nevertheless, it was widely agreed that Stalin at this stage was still merely keeping open his option of choosing between Germany and the western democracies. It was in mid-August, when British–French–Soviet military negotiations in Moscow collapsed over the reluctance of Poland to allow Soviet troops to cross her territory in the event of an attack on Germany, that Stalin and his advisors drew the conclusion that they had but one remaining option for their national security. Hitler responded far more rapidly and favourably than the allies had, for his short-term purposes were also served by a change of policy. With his eyes now turned towards Poland, and with Britain and France renewing their pledges to the Poles, it was an urgent priority to ensure that his ambitions would not encounter Soviet opposition. From this desire, and from Stalin's desire for greater security for the Soviet frontiers, sprang the startling agreement reached after only one day's negotiation in Moscow between Molotov and the German Foreign Minister, J. von Ribbentrop (23rd August 1939).

To the outside world, the Ribbentrop–Molotov Pact took the form of a non-aggression treaty lasting ten years. Secretly, however, it divided the territories between the German and Soviet borders into 'spheres of influence', that of Germany comprising Poland, west of the rivers Narew,

Vistula and San, and part of Lithuania. The Soviet zone comprised the rest of Poland and Lithuania, and the states of Estonia, Latvia and Finland. Germany, furthermore, expressed her disinterest in the Balkans and recognised Russia's interest in the Rumanian territory of Bessarabia. Hitler, in short, received tacit Soviet approval to fulfil his designs on Danzig and the Polish 'corridor'. In return, Stalin not only triumphantly reversed the losses suffered by Russia during the Revolution and Civil War twenty years earlier, but seemed to have won a breathing space in terms both of time and of territory. With the Soviet occupation of their sphere of influence between June–August 1940, the amount of territory between a future invader and the vital centres of Leningrad and Moscow was increased by some 200 miles.

To western commentators, as to M. Baumont, this was seen as 'one of the most cynical treaties in world history', a complete reversal of the ideologies of both states. As A. J. P. Taylor has commented, however, 'it is difficult to see what other course Soviet Russia could have followed' in the light of western indifference. It was difficult, too, to see why their part in the destruction of Poland was worse than that of the allies in the destruction of Czechoslovakia. Doubtless both Hitler and Stalin believed that the pact ensured that the Polish question could now be solved without general war. In the event, by giving Hitler the confidence to attack Poland, without diverting Britain and France from their renewed guarantees, Stalin's signature made war in Europe virtually inevitable.

(p) Poland and the Coming of War

The collapse of Czechoslovakia left, in the German view, one major limiting element of the Versailles Treaty standing in eastern Europe. Antipathy between Germans and Poles had a far longer history than the life of the post-war Polish state, but the treaty had created a new focus of hostility in the forms of the 'Free City' of Danzig, and the 'Corridor' of territory transferred in 1919 from Germany to Poland to connect Danzig with the Polish heartland. Although the treaty gave the Poles complete control of its docks, its customs duties, its railway system and foreign relations, Danzig was undeniably a German city, inhabited by 400 000 Germans and without a name in Polish until 'Gdansk' was invented for it in 1919. Similarly, the 'corridor' contained the homes of one million Germans. It was not a settlement that the majority of Germans were willing to tolerate freely. The contemporary historian, Professor Lenz, spoke for many of his countrymen when he wrote that 'we had to suffer the greatest and most unbearable ignominy at the hands of the Poles . . . these Sarmatians who never were able to create anything out of their own strength. That we shall never forgive or forget'.

Successive Polish governments remained fully aware of this hostility. She was trapped between an unforgiving Germany to the west and a resentful Russia to the east, from which she had newly won her independence (see Chapter 12, section **1**). Her apprehension was heightened by the Russo-German agreement at Rapallo and the failure of the Locarno Pact to guarantee Germany's eastern borders. Thus Poland sought security through her own armed forces and through her treaties with France. By the mid-1930s, however, her international position had been greatly complicated by the rise of Hitler, the bankruptcy of French policy towards eastern Europe, and the entry of the Soviet Union into the diplomatic arena. In general, under the direction of General J. Beck between 1932–39, the Polish foreign ministry proceeded upon the assumption that the Soviet Union posed the greater threat to Poland. 'With the Germans', he reputedly declared, 'we risk losing our liberty. With the Russians we lose our souls'. From this line of thought sprang the Polish–German non-aggression pact of 1934 and the persistent refusal to allow passage to Soviet troops across Polish territory in the event of war. Overestimation of his nation's strength, furthermore, led Beck in 1938–39 into the cynical policy whereby Poland participated in the partition of Czechoslovakia, gaining the region of Teschen (March 1939) and staking an unsuccessful claim to Slovakia.

Throughout this period Danzig, its local government in the hands of the local Nazi party since May 1933, remained a canker in Polish–German relations. From the completion of his destruction of Czechoslovakia, the signs accumulated that Hitler intended next to turn his attentions towards Poland. As in the cases of Austria and Czechoslovakia, his initial policy was that of a war of nerves. In April 1939, Hitler not only repudiated Germany's non-aggression pact with Poland, but renewed German claims to Danzig. In May, the 'Pact of Steel' agreement committed Italy to follow Hitler's path, and by August he was assured that the Soviet Union would not stand in his way. Meanwhile, the German press conducted a persistent campaign of accusations concerning alleged persecution of Poland's German minority. Surely, under these circumstances, Britain and France would not risk themselves on Poland's behalf?

The last week of August 1939 was, indeed, occupied by Anglo-French efforts to persuade Poland to sacrifice Danzig. This time, however, the situation differed in important respects from that pertaining at Munich. Poland, aware that surrender had not saved Czechoslovakia, refused now to compromise her national sovereignty. The two democratic governments, although eager to avoid war, refused to repeat their Munich performances. Perhaps they were encouraged by increasing evidence of Mussolini's un-fascist reluctance to commit himself to war. Perhaps, as A. J. P. Taylor has stressed, the political conservatives of Britain and France, rather than being terrified by the Russo-German agreement, became more hostile to Hitler now that he no longer posed as a bulwark against communism. Maybe Chamberlain and Daladier merely recognised the futility of their Munich policy. General war, in the event, resulted from the conviction of both sides that the other was bluffing. 'The men I met at Munich', Hitler declared to his generals, 'are not the kind to start another world war'. Thus, on 1st September, German troops invaded Poland on the false pretext of Polish border violations. Only two days later did Britain and France issue separate ultimatums for German withdrawal, perhaps encouraging Hitler by their delay. Nevertheless, upon the expiry of the ultimatums, both powers declared war on Germany, ending almost exactly to Foch's prediction, the 'Twenty Year Truce'.

(q) Historiography

Although the first decade after the conclusion of the Second World War saw a considerable volume of writing on the war's origins, not much of it could really be described as detached and analytical history. Its arguments tended to reinforce the arguments of wartime and the general conclusions drawn from it were consistent and predictable. In general, it took one of two forms. One form was that of accounts by participants in the war, often members of the defeated sides seeking to set themselves right in the eyes of posterity. The posthumously published work of Count Ciano (*Diary*, 1947) or of von Ribbentrop (*Memoirs*, 1954), both written in prison cells under sentence of death, may stand as representatives of a substantial literature of this kind. Secondly, came official documentary collections, most frequently edited and published by the victors, which naturally, as in the case of the work of E. L. Woodward and R. Butler (*Documents on British Foreign Policy*, 1946 onwards), tended to present a relatively favourable view of the policy of the state concerned. Hence E. M. Robertson's characterisation of many of the earlier historians of the origins of the war as 'Intelligence NCOs in plain clothes'. The conclusions reached during this decade varied little. The war was precipitated by a German government dedicated to the principle of overturning the Versailles settlement and fulfilling the racial claims of its leader. T. D. Williams, commenting in 1958 on the work of Sir L. Namier (*In the Nazi Era*, 1952), stated that 'he has proved that Hitler wanted war. Nobody would, on the whole, now contest this fact'.

In 1961, however, in *The Origins of the Second World War*, A. J. P. Taylor did, indeed, contest the fact. Briefly summarised, his view was as follows. Refusing to see in *Mein Kampf* anything more than the daydreaming of a frustrated revolutionary, Taylor stressed the continuity between Hitler's foreign policy aims and those of earlier German politicians. Refusing to attach any great importance to the alleged statement of war aims to his generals reported in Colonel Hossbach's memorandum (November 1937), he dismissed the notion of a masterplan for conquest. He viewed Hitler's achievement in 1938–39 primarily as a skilful exploitation of openings offered to him by the errors and hesitations of British, French and Italian leaders. War, in Taylor's view, did not result from Hitler's long-term determination to begin one, but from his short-term miscalculation of allied reaction to the Polish crisis. Although many writers have agreed that Taylor's work has shed important light on details of some of the individual crises that preceded the Second World War, his overall thesis has provoked widespread controversy. It has been argued that his presentation has dangerous political implications, in that it could cast doubt on the legitimacy of the verdicts passed on Nazi War Criminals at Nuremberg, and could provide encouragement for neo-fascist groups in Germany and elsewhere. It has also been criticised on grounds of historical method. H. Trevor Roper, in an article in the magazine *Encounter* (1961), refused to accept Taylor's dismissal of *Mein Kampf* and the Hossbach Memorandum, and argued that Hitler considered himself not merely a practical politician, but 'a thinker, a practical philosopher, the demiurge of a new age of history', and did therefore conceive of a long-term future programme. E. H. Carr (*The Twenty Years Crisis*, 1958) and E. Wiskemann (*Europe of the Dictators*, 1966) see *Mein Kampf* as a much more systematic and preconceived plan for national and racial expansion. Others, such as T. W. Mason (article in *Past and Present*, 1964) and

A. S. Milward (*The German War Economy*, 1965) stressed that Taylor's preoccupation with diplomacy blinded him to the steady economic and social progress towards a war footing made since 1933. It is interesting to note that much recent German scholarship has tended to suggest that the direction of German policy depended upon more than the will of the Führer. H. A. Jacobsen (*National Socialist Foreign Policy*, 1969) has shown the extent of nationalist demands even among Germans who were not strictly Nazis, and H. Krausnick (*Anatomy of the SS State*, 1968) has demonstrated the depth of popular anti-semitism in contemporary Germany.

Important as the controversy over the Taylor thesis is in terms of detail, it is still possible to find a synthesis of agreement on the broad causes of the Second World War. The responsibility of expansionist elements in German policy has not seriously been questioned, and the less the outbreak is attributed directly to the 'evil genius' of Hitler himself, the more the historian is bound to concentrate on the continuous theme of expansion in recent German history and thought. This theme occupies much of the attention of the American journalist W. L. Shirer in his massive *Rise and Fall of the Third Reich* (1962). Returning finally to Hitler's aims and motives in the late 1930s, sound conclusions, compromising between those of Taylor and those of his opponents, have been drawn by A. Bullock (*Hitler, A Study in Tyranny*, 1962) and E. M. Robertson (*The Origins of the Second World War*, ed., 1971). On the question of a Nazi masterplan for aggression and aggrandisement, Bullock concludes that 'Hitler's foreign policy . . . combined consistency of aim with complete opportunism in methods and tactics'. The weakness of his opponents, that is, dictated the timing, but not the initial conception of Hitler's policy. On the specific problem of the outbreak of hostilities in 1939, Robertson has tried to resolve the question 'Did Hitler want war?' by the plausible conclusion that he did indeed desire an armed clash with Poland. Where the element of miscalculation and accident occurred was that he had not expected the forceable destruction of Poland to involve him in a general European war with Britain and France.

Progress Paragraphs

Answer the following questions in about 150 words.

What forces shaped the Treaty of Versailles?

Section (a)

By what means did the allied powers seek to limit Germany's future power in the Treaty of Versailles?

Section (**a**)

What main weaknesses were there in the treaties of 1919?

Section (**b**)

Did France gain more than she lost by the occupation of the Ruhr?

Section (**d**)

How well suited was the League of Nations to the task of keeping the peace after 1919?

Section (**c**)

Why were the Dawes Plan and the Locarno Pact accepted (a) by France, and (b) Germany?

Sections (**e & f**)

In what ways was the Versailles Treaty undermined between 1930–33?

Sections (**g & h**)

What motivated the formation of the Four Power Pact, and why did the Pact achieve so little?

Section (**i**)

Why did Italy invade Abyssinia in 1935?

Section (**j**)

What effects did the Anglo-French response to the Abyssinian crisis have upon great power relations in Europe?

Section (**j**)

Why was Hitler able to get away with the remilitarisation of the Rhineland?

Section (**k**)

What factors attracted Mussolini into the orbit of Berlin?

Section (**l**)

Why did Germany absorb Austria into the Reich in 1938?

Section (**m**)

Why did Britain and France tolerate German annexation of the Sudetenland?

Section (**n**)

What were the consequences of the Munich agreement?

Section (**n**)

Did the Ribbentrop–Molotov Pact represent a reversal of Soviet foreign policy?

Section (**o**)

Account for German hostility towards Poland.

Section (**p**)

18
The Second World War

Unlike the conflict of 1914–18, the war that began in 1939 was truly to become a World War. The First World War was, in fact, global mainly in the sense that the imperialist interests of some of the combatants caused European powers to clash in distant regions. The Second World War was to include campaigns in the Pacific and in East Asia in which European power was indirectly concerned, if at all. These conflicts, however, must remain beyond our present scope, and the aim of this chapter will only be to describe and explain those elements of the Second World War that had the most direct impact upon the political, social and economic structure of the continent of Europe itself.

(a) The State of the Powers, 1939

The relative strengths of the major European powers in 1939 may be judged from Table 18.1. Such figures tell part of the story accurately enough, but they do not tell the whole story. As the lessons of the 1914–18 war should have taught, the importance of the 'big battalions' was now outweighed by the factor of technical and tactical superiority. In these respects German leadership was indisputable. Under the influence of such commanders as Guderian and Rommel she had

adopted the principles of mechanised warfare, of rapid thrusts against a slow-moving enemy to cut his lines of supply and of retreat, far more effectively than her opponents. In the areas vital to this 'Lightning War' ('Blitzkrieg'), in the design and deployment of her tanks and the use of aerial support, Germany enjoyed a distinct advantage. She had turned her enforced disarmament of 1919 to her own ends, building modern weapons now while her opponents laboured under the weight of obsolete equipment. The most modern of the Luftwaffe's planes were faster and more manoeuvrable than anything possessed by the French or the Poles and, although her 3200 tanks did not represent a numerical superiority, models such as the PkwIII and the PkwIV were superior to their counterparts.

Despite the entreaties in the earlier 1930s of a young tank officer, Colonel de Gaulle, French military commanders continued to think of the tank as a form of mechanised horse, supporting the all-important infantry advances. Neither they nor their allies appreciated the value of the weapon used in massed formations. Their plans and their armies proceeded at the pace of the foot soldier in a military world dominated by the internal combustion engine. Most ominous of all for the allies' immediate prospects in the autumn of 1939 were the weaknesses of the Polish armed forces,

	Army divisions	Air strength	Capital ships	Submarines
Germany	125	4210	5	65
Italy	73	1531	4	104
USSR	125	3361	3	18
France	86	1234	7	78
Great Britain	4	1750	15	57
Poland	40	500	—	—

Source: A. Adamthwaite, *The Coming of the Second World War.*

Table 18.1

largely unchanged since their successes against the Russians twenty years before. In the damning summary of P. Calvocoressi, 'their mobilisation was slow, their communications flimsy, their reserves thin, their aircraft obsolete and their tactics—cavalry charging tanks with the aim of dashing into Germany—hopeless'. Upon such a force the European balance of power depended in September 1939.

(b) Blitzkrieg and Phoney War

'Although Hitler blundered', wrote A. J. P. Taylor, 'in supposing that the two western powers would not go to war at all, his expectation that they would not go to war seriously turned out to be correct'. Poland received no material support from her allies and the tactics of all three powers contrasted starkly with those of the invaders. Poland became the first victim of the Blitzkrieg perfected by the German forces as, pitching armoured columns and overwhelming aerial superiority against an army that continued to trust in the mobility of large cavalry forces, the Wehrmacht made rapid progress eastwards, encircling the defending forces in a great pincer movement. On 17th September the fate of Poland was sealed when Soviet forces began their occupation of her eastern regions. Within ten days these forces and those of Germany had reached the line agreed in the Ribbentrop–Molotov Pact, and the Polish state had ceased to exist.

In the west, meanwhile, a very different kind of war was being waged. The leading contemporary military historian, Sir B. Liddell Hart, has argued strongly that the allies, with 85 French divisions alone, could have taken effective action against a German frontier guarded by only 43 divisions, without tanks, aircraft or substantial supplies. Yet nothing positive was done. This was largely due to the outmoded thinking of the French commanders, still wedded to the defensive strategy of the previous war, but also in part to the hesitations of political leaders who had still not wholly overcome the appeasement mentality of the last decade. Thus, when allied bombers did fly over German industrial towns, it was to drop propaganda leaflets rather than bombs. This curious state of suspended hostility was christened the 'Phoney War'. To the Germans it became the 'Sitting Down War' ('Sitzkrieg') in ironic contrast to the more effective tactics of the eastern front.

Illogically, the attention of allied strategists during this 'Phoney War' turned towards Scandinavia. There, in the mines of Sweden and Norway, lay the source of 51% of Germany's supplies of iron ore. That, in itself, provided a sound justification for allied attempts to entice Norway and Sweden into the war on their side. However, with the opening of the Soviet Union's 'Winter War' with Finland (November 1939–March 1940), it is hard to resist the conclusion that the allied governments continued to be as much concerned with the Soviet threat as with that posed by Germany. Similarly, French actions in the Middle East against Hitler's Caspian oil supplies were as much anti-Soviet in conception as anti-German. Once more, allied action proved hesitant and half-hearted. While they debated the mining of neutral Norwegian waters to prevent the passage of ore to Germany, Hitler ordered the extension of operations to Scandinavia to safeguard his supplies. The invasion of Denmark (April 1940), necessary for purposes of communication, was an immediate success, but the simultaneous assault on Norway encountered stiffer resistance aided by allied forces. By the end of June, nevertheless, all allied forces had been forced to withdraw leaving that state, too, in German hands.

(c) The Fall of France

The 'Phoney War' ended abruptly on 10th May 1940 with the launching of the German offensive into France and the Low Countries. Despite the months that had been available for preparation, the defending forces were taken largely unawares, not only by the speed and power of the German attack, but also by its strategy. Expecting an offensive like that of 1914, based upon a drive through central Belgium, allied strategy centred upon an advance into Belgium to check the enemy's right wing short of the French frontier while the rest of his forces dashed themselves against the defences of the Maginot Line. Indeed, until January 1940, Belgium had played a leading role in Wehrmacht plans. Only then, upon the suggestion of General von Manstein, had a daring new strategy been introduced. Aware that the allies regarded the hilly and wooded region of the Ardennes, beyond the flank of the Maginot Line, as virtually impassable, and that it was thus only lightly defended, Manstein proposed a massive armoured attack across the River Meuse and into this weakest sector of the allied line.

In the event, the German offensive contained both elements. For the first ten days Holland and Belgium bore the brunt of aerial bombardment and assault by infantry, artillery and airborne troops. In particular, the bombing of Rotterdam, where

MAP 14   THE SECOND WORLD WAR IN EUROPE

FRONTIERS 1939

MAGINOT LINE

MAIN GERMAN OFFENSIVE 1940

OCCUPIED ZONE

'FREE' ZONE, UNTIL 1942

ALSACE-LORRAINE ANNEXED 1940.

ANTWERP

BRUSSELS

DUNKIRK

PARIS

BORDEAUX

A. THE FALL OF FRANCE

GERMANY AND ALLIES

OCCUPIED TERRITORIES

FRONTIER OF GREATER REICH

FURTHEST ADVANCE 1942

1939 FRONTIERS

USSR

FIN

NOR

SWE

LENINGRAD

EST

MOSCOW

LAT

LITH

IRE

GB

H

B

GER

POL

FRA

CZ

STALINGRAD

KIEV

SW

AUS

HUN

ITA

RUM

SP

YUG

BUL

A

GR

TURK

B. EXTENT OF GERMAN DOMINATION 1942

MAP 14 Continued.   THE SECOND WORLD WAR IN EUROPE

C. THE WESTERN FRONT 1943–5

————— D-DAY BEACHES

.... ALLIED FRONT LINE
AUG. 1944

—··—··— ALLIED FRONT LINE
DEC. 1944

ARNHEM

SIEGFRIED LINE

CAEN

PARIS

R. RHINE

MILAN

GOTHIC LINE

GUSTAV LINE

AMERICAN
LANDING
AUG. 1944

ROME

NAPLES

SICILY

D. THE EASTERN FRONT 1943–5

MINSK

BERLIN

WARSAW

KHARKOV

PRAGUE

KIEV

VIENNA

BUDAPEST

—··—··— FRONT LINE
OCT. 1943

————— FRONT LINE
OCT. 1940

.... BORDER OF SOVIET
ZONE 1945

– – – – – NATIONAL
FRONTIERS 1945

– – – – AREA UNDER GERMAN
CONTROL MAY 1945

nearly 1000 civilians died within a few minutes, was unparalleled in European experience and created a profound psychological impression. The Dutch government capitulated on 15th May. The breaching of Belgium's defences drew British and French forces onto her territory to check the German advance and when, on 12th May, the massive armoured force under General von Kleist broke through the Ardennes and breached the French line near Sedan, these advanced allied forces were threatened with encirclement. This breakthrough, although it did not end the battle for France, effectively decided its eventual outcome. Faced with the alternatives of evacuation or annihilation, the British forces, with some 10 000 French troops, retreated to the Channel at Dunkirk. Here, by a combination of heroism, good fortune and puzzling German tactics, they were transported back to Britain by a fleet of 860 assorted vessels hastily assembled for the task (26th May–4th June). The operation owed much, perhaps everything to Hitler's curious decision to hold back tanks and aircraft that could have destroyed the allied forces and their rescuers on the beaches. Variously explained as a temporary loss of nerve, or as evidence of a continuing hope that Britain would still conclude a separate peace, Hitler's decision allowed an escape which, in the popular mind, did something to obscure the magnitude of the allied defeat.

The new French line, along the Rivers Aisne and Somme, was attacked on 5th June and broke two days later. Thereafter, disaster piled upon disaster. The government abandoned Paris for the safety of the south (9th June). Any remaining hope of national survival vanished the following day when, with the main fighting done and the spoils there for the taking, Mussolini judged the moment ripe for Italy, too, to declare war on France. From their retreat near Bordeaux the French government, now led by the hero of the First World War, Marshal Philippe Pétain, rejected the option of flight to Africa and requested Germany's terms for an armistice. Considering the extent of the military defeat the terms dictated at Rethondes (21st June), in the very railway carriage used for the German surrender in 1918, were moderate. In 46 days of fighting, France had lost 84 000 men dead, 120 000 injured and 1 500 000 taken prisoner. Yet, with the exception of strategic areas in the north and along the Atlantic coast, French officials were to be allowed to retain responsibility for civil administration while the French government retained complete sovereignty over the southern 40% of the country free from German military occupation. No territory was earmarked for annexation by Germany, although Italy claimed the return of Nice and Savoy, and France kept control of her fleet and of her Empire. The fact remained, as the future would show, that with total military domination, Hitler could take what he did not now claim whenever he felt the need.

The astonishing collapse of France had many causes, among which the confused foreign policy of the last two decades, the deep domestic divisions of recent years, and the extraordinary incompetence of commanders who neglected airpower, mechanised forces and modern communications, are prominent. Although the transformation of this European conflict into a true World War was eventually to reverse the decision of 1940, the significance of the German victory in purely European terms must not be underestimated. A nation that had held the first place in the affairs of the continent for three centuries had been rendered impotent within five weeks, and the rise of German power, checked at great cost in 1918, seemed after all to have reached its logical conclusion. P. Calvocoressi has summarised the impact of these events in his judgement that 'the fall of France opened an abyss of uncertainty for the whole continent and shook the imagination as perhaps nothing had shaken it since the victory of the Turks at Mohacs in 1526'.

(d) The Battle of Britain

The collapse of France seemed likely to end the war in western Europe. Britain's chances of continuing the war seemed hopeless. Her land forces, although extricated from Dunkirk, had lost most of their equipment, and the defence of 2000 miles of coastline posed enormous problems. Yet, stiffened by the extraordinary leadership and resolution of the new Prime Minister, Winston Churchill, Britain did not sue for peace. Instead, Churchill announced his determination that 'we shall fight on the beaches, we shall fight on the landing grounds, we shall fight in the hills; we shall never surrender'.

Hitler's response to this decision seems to have been conditioned by three factors. Firstly, although it is unlikely that Britain could have resisted an invasion, no definite plans had been prepared for one, so sure was the German High Command that the fall of France would end the western campaign. Secondly, Hitler professed a persistent reluctance to treat a 'Germanic' civilisation in the same way that he had treated the Poles. 'He astonished us', wrote General Blumentritt in the last days of the French campaign, 'by speaking with admiration of the

British Empire. . . . He compared the British Empire with the Catholic Church, saying that they were both essential elements of stability in the world. He said that all he wanted from Britain was that she acknowledged Germany's position on the continent'. Lastly, if Britain still needed to be prodded towards peace, the commander of the Luftwaffe, Hermann Goering, was determined that his forces should be allowed to demonstrate their effectiveness.

Unlike the Battle of France, therefore, the Battle of Britain took the form of a concentrated aerial attack, firstly upon Britain's airfields, to gain total air supremacy, and then upon London and other centres, in order to break the resistance of the civilian population. Neither effort was successful. The numerical superiority of the Luftwaffe, about 1200 bombers and 1000 fighters based in France to some 900 British fighters, was offset by several factors. The relatively light German bombers such as the He.111 and the Do.217 were vulnerable without substantial fighter support, and the range of such fighters as the Me.109E was only sufficient to give them a few minutes of combat over British targets. On the British side, the Spitfire and Hurricane fighters were formidable weapons, fast, manoeuvrable, heavily armed, and with the advantage of fighting over their own territory. The rapid development of Radar and its establishment along the southern and eastern coasts provided valuable early warning of the bombers' approach. Thus, in the main phase of the engagement (early August–late September 1940), the Luftwaffe lost over 1100 aircraft, against a British loss of 650. Half-hearted in his campaign from the outset, and impatient to turn against his 'real' enemy in the east, Hitler suspended the plan for invasion on 17th September, and reduced Luftwaffe operations over Britain at the end of the month. Although decided as much by German errors and miscalculations as by British strengths, the Battle of Britain represented a first checking of Germany's triumphant military progress, and the beginning of that overstretching of her military resources that was to be her downfall.

(e) The Conflict Spreads

In mid-1940, the conflict that we now call the Second World War was a strictly limited one, tightly confined to areas of western and northern Europe. The failure of Germany in that summer to eliminate British opposition began a process of proliferation which transformed this into a truly global war. Firstly, after the failure of aerial warfare, the Atlantic Ocean became the major theatre of Anglo-German conflict as the German navy sought, with submarines, surface raiders and mines, to cut British supply lines. Secondly, the entry of Italy into the war inevitably spread the conflict to those areas that Mussolini considered to be his sphere of influence, to the Balkans, the Mediterranean, and North Africa. That these regions came to involve German troops was the result of two factors. The failure of Italian forces to sustain their offensive against Greece (October 1940) and the British decision to send aid to the Greeks seriously threatened interests that Germany had carefully built up in that region. By a mixture of bullying and diplomacy, Hitler had ensured that Hungary, Rumania and Yugoslavia would remain sympathetic to German ambitions in eastern Europe, valuable sources of strategic supplies and potential assembly areas for anti-Soviet forces. The hope that General Franco might repay his debt from the Spanish Civil War by supporting Axis interests in the Mediterranean collapsed in a series of discussions in October and November in which the Spanish leader made it very clear that his priority was domestic consolidation and reconstruction. Thus, with Italian forces checked in Greece and later in North Africa, and with the pro-German government of Yugoslavia overthrown by a 'coup d'état' (March 1941), Hitler found himself forced into large-scale intervention. Although militarily successful, with Greece cleared of hostile troops by late April, and the island of Crete captured in May, the commitment of 28 divisions to the Balkans and of several mechanised divisions to North Africa forced a postponement of the planned Russian offensive and the establishment of a costly and lasting 'side show' for the German forces.

Of far greater significance, however, was the gradual involvement of the United States in the conflict. American isolationism, re-established by the Senate's refusal to ratify the Versailles Treaty, and confirmed by three Neutrality Acts (1935–36–37), was only slowly eroded by the influence of Churchill's close personal relationship with President F. D. Roosevelt, and by a growing public awareness that events in the world were beginning to pose a direct threat to American interests. The fall of France, for instance, presented the prospect of an Atlantic ocean dominated by hostile fleets at the same time as Japanese influence spread in the Pacific Ocean. The Battle of the Atlantic, with its extensive German submarine actions, not only confirmed this prospect, but posed a definite danger to American shipping. Thus there was sufficient support in the United States for the

'Destroyer Deal' (September 1940), which placed 50 older ships in British hands, and for the more important 'Lend-Lease' agreement (March 1941), whereby British purchase of war materials from American companies was financed by the American government regardless of Britain's current dollar reserves. By late 1941, therefore, the United States, largely due to the influence of Roosevelt himself, had taken up an ambiguous position. She was clearly sympathetic to Germany's opponents, but not openly committed to war.

This position was changed dramatically on 7th December 1941 by the Japanese air attack upon the American Pacific fleet at Pearl Harbour. The American declaration of war upon Japan was followed almost immediately (11th December) by Hitler's declaration of war upon the United States. Many have since followed A. Bullock in regarding this declaration as 'the greatest single mistake of his career'. P. Calvocoressi and others have, on the other hand, noted Hitler's previous efforts to avoid provoking the United States into intervention in Europe, and have interpreted his declaration of war as a simple acceptance of American hostility to Germany. While allowing Hitler to take overt action against American supplies to Europe, the declaration now involved hostilities in four continents. In December 1941, the Second World War truly began.

(f) The Invasion of the Soviet Union

Although increasingly committed to secondary theatres of war, Hitler would not postpone the major element in his policy, the assault upon Soviet Russia, beyond June 1941. Although such an assault was dictated by long-term hostility to Bolshevism and by theories of 'Lebensraum', there were also logical short-term factors that dictated its timing. An attack now upon the Soviet Union would leave Britain with no prospect of future support in Europe, and would leave Japan without any distraction in her impending confrontation with the United States. Besides, Hitler was convinced that his successes in eastern Europe would, sooner or later, cause Stalin to take action to redress the balance, and it made no sense to delay until the Soviet Army had had time to fortify the territories occupied in 1939. Thus on 22nd June 121 divisions of the Wehrmacht, with massive aerial support, were launched across the frontier. Dismissing his generals' insistence upon a direct assault upon Moscow, Hitler made the Soviet capital only one of three objectives for his army. In addition, an attack upon Leningrad would secure his Baltic flank with Finnish aid, while a thrust into the Ukraine would secure valuable industrial and agricultural resources.

Although German forces were no greater than those that faced them, indeed the Red Army had more men, more tanks, and more aircraft, the invaders enjoyed several substantial advantages. They enjoyed a great element of surprise, for Soviet propaganda had allowed no word to escape of worsening German–Soviet relations. They attacked an army which, although it had learned much from the difficult war with Finland a year earlier, had not yet had time fully to implement the necessary improvements in command and materials. The Red Army, uncertain which enemy constituted the greater threat, still divided its forces between its frontier with the Germans and that in the east with Japan.

Thus, the initial success of the German offensive was staggering. Brave as Soviet resistance always was, it lacked the co-ordination to contain the enemy advance for any considerable period. In the north, Leningrad found itself surrounded and besieged by September. In the south, a Soviet force of 600 000 was surrounded and the key Ukrainian city of Kiev fell in the same month. By mid-October the Wehrmacht had pushed over 400 miles into central Russia and was within 50 miles of the Soviet capital. Soviet losses had been huge; perhaps three million men and 18 000 tanks in three months. Ominously, however, the rate of German casualties, some 750 000 of them, was also far higher than in any previous campaign.

(g) Moscow, Leningrad, Stalingrad

Great as these successes were, none of the objectives of the invasion had been completely secured by the beginning of the autumn, and the first signs were evident that the tide was turning. The first factor in the Soviet recovery, as in the Napoleonic invasion of 1812, was the weather. Heavy rain in October blocked the German advance with seas of mud, and heavy frosts in November exposed them to all the horrors of a winter campaign in Russia. Frostbite claimed 100 000 victims. Aircraft, tanks, lorries and guns could not operate for want of antifreeze, and men were reduced to stuffing their uniforms with paper to keep out temperatures as low as 40° below freezing. Secondly, the German forces encountered astonishing resistance from military and civilians alike. Although reinforced by fear of retribution from their own side, from the NKVD, this resistance was primarily a manifestation of intense patriotism, of reaction to ill-advised German behaviour in the territories they occupied, and of an acute awareness of the nature of the German threat. In his first wartime address to the nation, Stalin declared that the enemy 'is out to seize our lands watered by the sweat of our brows, to seize our grain and oil, secured by the labour of our hands . . ., to restore the rule of the landlords'. For all their recent differences with the Soviet government, the reaction of millions of Soviet subjects showed that they appreciated the broad truth of these statements. Thirdly, in the respite afforded by the weather, Soviet forces were reinforced, re-equipped and re-organised. The defence of Moscow was strengthened by troops and aircraft hurriedly switched from Siberia and Mongolia, the former specifically equipped for winter warfare. The Soviet counter-attack in December eased the pressure upon the Soviet capital and, at great cost, wrested the strategic initiative for the first time from the Wehrmacht.

In the north, too, German plans were narrowly frustrated. Of the seven Soviet cities awarded the title 'Hero City' after the war, none deserved it more than Leningrad. The siege, a product of Hitler's determination to destroy the cradle of Bolshevism, lasted from September 1941 to January 1944. Desperately short of food and precariously supplied by routes built over the ice of Lake Ladoga and by rail routes open to constant German attack, the inhabitants suffered constant bombardment and the permanent threat of starvation. It is possible that the total casualty figures for the siege may have been as high as 1.5 million, most of them civilians. That Leningrad never fell was due to the heroism of the inhabitants, to the shrewd defensive organisation of the greatest Soviet soldier of the war, G. K. Zhukov, who was backed by the local party machinery, and to the eventual need of the Wehrmacht to divert substantial resources of men and material to the south-west of the USSR.

This region was the key theatre of the European war in 1942. Given the industrial potential of the world's largest state (see section **h**) and the failure of the 1941 campaign to crush her resistance, time was against Hitler. It was essential that Germany should complete her conquest of the oil-rich regions between the Black Sea and the Caspian as quickly as possible. In a fateful strategic decision, Hitler resolved to divide his southern forces between a drive against the Caucasian oilfields to the south and an assault upon the important communications centre of Stalingrad, on the Volga River, to the east. The personal links between Stalin and the city that bore his name gave the ensuing battle special significance in the eyes of both sides. From

September 1942 until January 1943, the streets, houses and factories of the city were the scene of constant and bitter fighting. This continued until the German Sixth Army, surrounded since November but specifically forbidden to retreat by Hitler, finally submitted. The battle cost the Wehrmacht 70 000 casualties, over 100 000 prisoners and vast quantities of guns and vehicles. The Soviet victory forced the retreat of those German forces further south that now faced the danger of being cut off. Worst of all, the invincible reputation of the Wehrmacht and the impetus of two years of Blitzkrieg campaigns in the east also died at Stalingrad.

(h) The New Balance of the Powers, 1942–45

In this transformed war, in which Germany and her allies no longer faced an Anglo-French alliance, but a coalition that included the world's two largest states, the balance of industrial and economic forces would now only admit one eventual outcome.

The Soviet Union brought to the last three years of European war not only enormous industrial resources but a centralised political authority uniquely capable of mobilising and directing them. In the Kremlin, a frantic revision of pre-war principles was now undertaken in the interests of national unity, that included the rehabilitation of the Orthodox Church, and the re-introduction of the privileges of higher military ranks to ensure their undivided loyalty in the struggle. Industrially, the Soviet Union had lost much in the early months of the war, including some 60% of her coal and iron production and as much as 25% of her workforce. The process of industrial re-organisation had been begun before the war, however, when the Third Five Year Plan had dictated the establishment of many new industrial concentrations in the region of the Ural Mountains and in Siberia. Happily these plants remained beyond the reach of German attacks. Now they were supplemented at remarkable speed by the transfer of factories from the vulnerable western regions. One thousand three hundred and sixty factories moved eastwards in 1942 and 2250 new units of production arose there between 1942–44. The astonishing nature of this achievement is conveyed by this description by P. Calvocoressi. 'At the new sites wooden structures were thrown up to house machinery, but there was often neither time nor materials to build houses for the workers . . ., they slept on the floor by their machines. Mortality was high, output poor. The wonder is that they were not worse'. Eventually, results were outstanding in regions old and new. The Moscow coalfield, reduced to an output of 590 tons per day in January 1942, was back to its pre-war norm of 35 000 tons per day by the following October. The trans-Ural regions, at their peak, were producing at 2.5 times the rate of the whole of Soviet industry in 1940. Russian military production overhauled that of Germany in 1943 to reach a peak of 30 000 tanks and 40 000 aircraft in that year.

The merest glance at the industrial capacity of the United States suffices to show the vital role that that nation played in the outcome of the Second World War. American increases in armament production in the war years were prodigious, from 6000 aircraft in 1940 to 96 000 in 1945, from under a thousand tanks in 1940 to 21 000 in 1943. Much of this went, of course, to fight the war in the Pacific, but the American contribution to the European theatre of war remained invaluable. On D-Day the British army operated 3300 Sherman tanks and 86 000 American motor vehicles. Some 20% of the RAF's strength in 1943–45 was also made up of American planes. The USSR benefited largely from 'Lend-Lease' agreements (October 1941 and June 1942) similar to that negotiated with Britain, and which provided 2000 tanks and 1300 planes by mid-1942 at the height of the Soviet crisis. At the peak of its output, American industry in 1943–44 was producing a ship per day and one aircraft every five minutes.

Nor was the contribution of Great Britain herself negligible. Like the Soviet Union she had won time to mobilise her resources and she did so effectively. Having had four divisions ready for combat in 1939, she could count on 60 by mid-1941, 20 of them from the Empire and Dominions. Domestic resources were also fully exploited. Between 1940–42 British aircraft production was actually higher than that of Germany, and by the time Germany regained the lead in 1944, American and Soviet production had already put the issue of industrial supremacy beyond doubt.

Against these overwhelming forces, the German economy performed miracles, but laboured under a variety of insuperable obstacles. It had never been geared for a long war, only for the production of materials for 'Blitzkrieg', and Germany needed to undergo a miniature 'industrial revolution' to meet its new crisis. Central figures in this process were Fritz Todt, Minister of Armaments and Munitions until his death in February 1942, and his successor, Albert Speer. As a relatively civilised and realistic figure surrounded by Nazi extremists, Speer has since received lenient treatment both from the Nuremberg judges and from historians, but his role

in equipping Germany to fight the war between 1942–45 was of great importance. Aircraft production reached a peak of 25 285 in 1944, as against 3744 in 1940, and the rebuilding of factories to protect them from air raids was so effective that 5000 new aircraft were still produced in the first four months of 1945 even as the allies were in the process of over-running Germany. Speer could not, however, overcome Germany's severe political and geographical disadvantages. She was subjected to bombing from two sides while American and Siberian factories lay beyond her reach. There was in Germany no central authority to co-ordinate production. While Hitler specialised in oratory, Speer had frequently to struggle against the influence of Goering, the chiefs of various state agencies, and the local jealousies of the Gauleiters, over questions of policy and resources. Resources, such as the coal and iron of the Ruhr and of Silesia, shrank as allied forces advanced. Lastly, Germany suffered severely from labour shortages. Nazi social doctrine militated against the mass employment of women, as practised by the allies, and although the total labour force rose from 5.6 million in May 1940 to 9.5 million in 1943, much of it consisted of conscripted foreign labour from occupied territories, which clearly had a limited value.

(i) Hitler's New Order

For four years, Nazi Germany dominated the mainland of Europe more completely than it had ever been dominated before. In the west, in France, Norway, and Denmark, 'puppet' governments were installed, checked at every turn by German military commanders and representatives of the security forces, to ensure that German interests were served. Puppet governments also operated in the Balkans, in Greece, in Yugoslavia and in Rumania. In eastern Europe, where the Slavs could not be afforded even this limited freedom, direct German government was the rule. Poland was placed under the arbitrary authority of a German Governor General (Hans Frank), and Bohemia and Moravia under that of a Protector (first Neurath, then Heydrich, then Frick). The territories of Ostland and the Ukraine, created from captured Soviet territory, came under the authority of the Reichsminister for the East, the fanatical Nazi theorist Alfred Rosenberg.

The 'New Order' that these regimes advertised and imposed had a dual nature. In Nazi propaganda, especially in western Europe, it took the form of a gigantic union of European states to combat the alien menace of Judaism and its political offshoot, Bolshevism. It was a highly successful interpretation which found a living expression in the many international units assembled in occupied countries, such as the French 'Legion of Volunteers Against Bolshevism' and the Belgian 'Flemish Legion', to join the Wehrmacht on the eastern front. In reality, of course, the 'New Order' took the form of a colossal plundering of European resources for the exclusive benefit of Germany. In part this could be explained as a necessity imposed by the continuing war, but in large part that was how it had always been envisaged by Nazi theorists. Hitler's aims in the Soviet Union were not merely to defeat its communist leadership, but to 'Germanise the country by the settlement of Germans and treat the natives as redskins'. Germany would provide the industrial heartland of this new Europe, and would in turn be fed by the less developed, largely agricultural territories that surrounded her.

To the occupation administrations, therefore, fell the two main tasks of the economic exploitation of the conquered territories for the war effort, and the breaking of local political and intellectual structures. The first function was dominated by two central figures, Hermann Goering, as Commissioner of the Five Year Plan, and Fritz Sauckel, the official responsible for the supply of labour to German industries. It took a number of forms, including the exploitation of local resources, such as the coal deposits of Silesia, the adaptation of local plant to German requirements, the transfer of some of that plant to German factories, and the recruitment of foreign labour for service in Germany. In the west, this last task was often tackled by means of relatively subtle enticements, such as the promise of higher wages or the placing of obstacles in the way of local employment, but in eastern Europe sheer physical force was the norm. Seven million foreign workers had been transferred to German factories by 1944, not more than 200 000 of them as volunteers, and foreign resources in the same year supplied some 20–25% of the rations consumed by German civilians. Although effective in terms of quantity, however, the system had its drawbacks. Forced labour was bound to be unreliable, especially in more skilled jobs, and the system provided tremendous problems for a transport network also committed to supplying troops on several fronts. As N. Rich has pointed out, the two tasks of the occupation administrations frequently clashed with each other, when the military advantages of a friendly local population were sacrificed to the economic and ideological demands for suppression and exploitation.

Terror, of course, was a standard feature of the 'New Order'. Sometimes it was deliberately applied as a matter of policy, as by the special SS squads (Einsatzgruppen) whose specific task in some eastern areas was to carry out a purge of undesirable groups. The 33 000 Jews murdered at Babi Yar in the Ukraine (September 1941) were some of the victims of these groups. Sometimes, atrocities occurred as a means of reprisal following local opposition or resistance. Proclaiming that 'wars are not won by the methods of the Salvation Army', Hitler fully approved of General Keitel's infamous 'Night and Mist' ('Nacht und Nebel') order (December 1941) which prescribed death as the automatic punishment for any act of sabotage or resistance, and advised summary execution. Most occupied territories suffered some example of the German tactic of destroying whole communities, often at random, as reprisals for attacks upon German personnel. The deaths of nearly 200 innocent civilians at Lidice in Czechoslovakia (May 1942) and of 642 at Oradour-sur-Glane in France (July 1944) are the most notorious examples. To the list could be added Palmiry, near Warsaw, Televaag, in Norway, Boves, in Italy, and Putten, in the Netherlands.

(j) The Fate of the Jews

The unprecedented domination that Nazi Germany enjoyed over the continent also provided her with the opportunity to give prolonged attention to the obsessive anti-semitism of the Nazi movement. Hitler's anti-semitism, like his foreign policy, was a mixture of unswerving principle and uncertain means. For all his hostility towards them, Hitler still had little clear idea in 1939 what he intended to do with the Jews. The most likely official plan was that which called for the shipment of European Jews to the island of Madagascar in the Indian Ocean, which would be demanded from France for that purpose after that nation's defeat. The first two years of warfare, however, caused the rethinking of this plan. Firstly, although France was defeated, the continuing hostility of Britain made regular sea access to Madagascar difficult. Secondly, the fall of Poland amplified the Jewish 'problem' dramatically. Whereas the Reich in 1939 had a Jewish population of about 357 000, the large number of Polish Jews multiplied by ten the number of Jews in the Greater Reich in 1940. Between the invasion of Poland and that of the Soviet Union concentration camps, not exclusively for Jews, but also for Poles, communists, gypsies, and others, were established in Poland at Auschwitz, Chelmno, Treblinka, Sobibor and Belsec. Even so, it was not until 1941, when continued Soviet resistance ruled out the interim plan of dumping the Jews in Siberia, that it was officially resolved that the 'Final Solution' to the 'Jewish Question' was to consist of wholesale and systematic extermination.

The insane intensity of this anti-semitism is illustrated, not only by the scale of the slaughter, but by the fact that, while locked in an increasingly unsuccessful war, the German government still saw fit to devote substantial resources of manpower, communications and technology to this horrible task. In the midst of the eastern campaigns in 1942, trainloads of Jews from France, Belgium and the Netherlands were being shipped the length of Europe to the eastern camps. In 1943 and 1944, the SS was still expanding its programme to deal with Greek and Hungarian Jews. Only in October 1944, with the Red Army threatening to over-run the camps, did Himmler give the order for them to cease their dreadful routine.

Between 1941–44, however, with the aid of technological refinements such as the special Cyclon-B gas and specially designed ovens for incineration, that routine proceeded with awful efficiency. Chelmno, with 1000 victims a day in late 1941, was outrun by Treblinka which managed up to 6000 a day at its peak, while Auschwitz was responsible for the murder of some 3 million people in the course of three years. The German government declared in November 1943, although it was not entirely correct, that there were no Jews left in the Greater Reich. By the end of the war, 50% of Belgian Jews, 66% of Rumanian Jews and 75% of the Dutch community were dead. The best records for the protection of Jews were those of Denmark and of France, although in the latter case the government only preserved the lives of French Jews by assisting the capture and deportation of those who were not French citizens. G. Reitlinger, in his standard history of this genocide, has settled upon a figure between 4.2 million and 4.6 million as the final toll of Jewish victims. Nor should it be forgotten that some 3 million non-Jews, mainly Slavs, and political opponents of Nazism, also died in extermination camps. These camps were responsible for the destruction in the most horrible circumstances, of some 7.5 million human lives. Such, ultimately, is the monument to the 'New Order' of Nazism.

(k) Collaboration

Of the possible reactions to this Nazi 'New Order',

resistance, especially in the first two years of the war, remained the prerogative of a brave but very small minority. The apparent finality of the German victories up to the end of 1941 dictated that the main problem of the conquered was how to live with the conquerors. In general, as N. Rich has concluded, 'the response of the European peoples to Nazi dominion reflects an instinct of people everywhere to cling to life and to seek physical and economic security for themselves and their families'.

This process was especially evident in France where Pierre Laval, Foreign Minister from October 1940 and Premier from April 1942, showed particular enthusiasm for co-operation with Germany. Although this made him the special butt of allied propaganda and led to his execution in 1945, Laval's fault was really short-sightedness, an inability to appreciate the international extent of the conflict, rather than any true sympathy with Nazi aims. 'In the circumstances', writes his biographer G. Warner, 'it is more than unfair that he has gone down in history with the reputation of a devious intriguer, for the greatest flaw in his character was not deviousness, but a frightening tendency towards over-simplification'. Laval's motives were, indeed, simple. They were to save France from the fate of Poland, from dismemberment and disintegration, and to do this it was necessary to co-operate with the new masters of Europe. Others had more positive motives, springing from an actual sympathy with the aims of Nazism, sometimes anti-semitic, sometimes anti-British, often anti-communist. The writer, A. Fabre-Luce, declared that 'inexorably, Europe is coming into being . . . a world revolution is on the march . . . of which France forms an important part'. His colleague, Drieu la Rochelle, referred to Hitler as 'he whose genius alone, at the cost of a torrent of German blood, has preserved Europe from a dreadful fate'. Thirdly, of course, many collaborated simply because the Germans were the winners, with the money, the resources, business contracts and influence that men still sought in war as in peace.

Although France provided a rare example of an established government, staffed by credible pre-war politicians, collaborating enthusiastically with the Germans, western Europe provided many other examples of puppet administrations and national fascist bodies willing to co-operate for opportunist or ideological reasons. The Netherlands had a Nazi party, under A. A. Mussert, which claimed a membership of 50000 during the war, and Belgium had its Flemish nationalists under Staf de Clercq, who saw collaboration with the Germans as a means of breaking the power of the French-speaking Walloons. In Norway, the government of Vidkun Quisling, whose name gave a new word to the English language to describe such collaborators, enthusiastically supported the ideology of Nazism, but generally failed to convince the Norwegian people of its value. In all of these cases, the relationship with Germany ended in frustration as it became clear that Hitler sought, not ideological support, but unconditional domination.

If open collaboration was rarer in eastern Europe, it was because Nazi theory generally forbade co-operation with the 'sub-human' Slavs. Some such co-operation, however, still existed. Even in the USSR racial minorities such as Tartars and Chechens sought German aid against Soviet oppression, and a Russian Liberation Army under General A. A. Vlasov numbered 50 000 men by the end of the war. Similarly, the anti-communist attitudes of D. Mihailovic and his 'cetnik' force, and of A. Pavelic in Yugoslavia offered possibilities for the German and Italian occupiers, which were generally thrown away because of the brutal and callous attitudes of Nazism towards the Slavs.

The fruits of collaboration varied from case to case. In France, the policy of Laval bore little fruit. It did not greatly hasten the return of prisoners of war, did not prevent a 50% rise in the mortality rate due largely to cases of malnutrition and did not save France from total occupation when German interests demanded it (November 1942). On the other hand, it served the Germans well. Thirty-seven per cent of all German materials and finances from foreign sources came from France, tanks and army trucks rolled off the production lines of Renault and Berliet, and 45 000 Frenchmen joined the paramilitary 'Milice' force that combated the resistance and attempted to maintain domestic stability in the last years of the occupation. Elsewhere, the results were sometimes better. N. Rich has cited the cases of Slovakia, which was spared a German occupation by the co-operation of Tiso's government, while Admiral Horthy ensured that Hungary escaped quite lightly from the war. Denmark succeeded in preserving its monarchy, part of its army, and even most of its Jews. In short, it was sometimes possible after the war to justify collaboration in terms of short-term local successes. In the wider context of Nazi inhumanity, the policy was always much harder to justify.

(l) Resistance

The motives that led a select and highly honourable minority into resistance to the Nazi 'New Order' were many and complex. Perhaps a simple national pride was at the basis of the other motives. 'They resisted', wrote A. Werth of the French movements after 1941, 'because it was a matter of ordinary self respect to do so. They were unwilling to accept that while London was "taking it", or that while the Red Army was fighting the Battle of Stalingrad, France was doing nothing.' Secondly, the brutality of German policy in the occupied territories convinced many of the need for resistance. This was especially true in the eastern territories, where the callous recruitment of forced labour, and the determination to 'treat the natives like redskins' made resistance the surer means towards survival. In France, too, it was the recruitment of labour that drove many young men into the countryside, where their groups took their names from the shrub-like bushes that gave them shelter, the 'Maquis'. Thirdly, the entry into the war of the Soviet Union played a dual role. Not only did it make resistance a more attractive prospect by offering some alternative to a German victory, but it set the communist parties of the occupied countries, previously nonplussed by the Russo-German Pact of 1939, in opposition to the invaders. In September 1941, General Keitel, as chief of staff, ordered that all acts of resistance or sabotage should be ascribed to communists and that batches of alleged communists should be executed as reprisals. Communists, or those likely to be suspected of party membership thus had little to lose by active resistance.

Resistance, similarly, took many forms. The most simple, and the safest, was the refusal of social contact with the occupier. The most famous novel to emerge from the occupation of France was Vercors' *The Silence of the Sea* ('Le Silence de la Mer') in which a father and daughter, forced to accept a German officer in their house, make their feelings clear by a sustained silence. Norway provided a fine example of passive resistance when her bishops and High Court judges resigned 'en masse'. The dissemination of war news and propaganda was another important, but highly dangerous function. In Belgium alone some 300 illegal journals were published, and over 1000 such papers appeared in France between 1940–44. Belgium was also the centre of a complex network of groups specialising in the sheltering of allied airmen shot down over Europe, and in smuggling them back to home bases. Some 10 000 individuals were involved, and the number of aircrew thus returned to active service numbered about 3500. Similar networks in Poland and in Czechoslovakia did valuable work by providing intelligence on German troop movements to allied forces. Next came acts of violence against specific German targets or personnel. Such activities, however, entailed costs out of all proportion to their strategic value. The assassination of R. Heydrich, 'Protector' of Bohemia and Moravia, for example, was paid for with 1500 Czech lives and with the destruction of the villages of Lidice and Lezaky.

It was with the weakening of the German war effort, and in co-operation with advancing allied forces, that resistance groups achieved their greatest impact. By mid-1942 there were an estimated 150000 partisan fighters operating behind German lines in the Soviet Union, disrupting communications and tying down large numbers of regular troops. In the west, resistance actions delayed and weakened important German units moving to combat the Normandy landings. Finally, with the German disintegration, these forces formed the basis of resurgent national armies. Sixty thousand Czech partisans fought with the Soviet Army, the French FFI (Forces Francaises de l'Interieur) played a role in the liberation of several French cities and in the final thrust into Germany, and partisan forces played a major part in the liberation of Belgrade, and of many of the cities of northern Italy.

In an area that has proved of great interest to recent historians, disagreement has arisen as to how much was actually achieved by the various resistance movements. A. S. Milward has put forward the view that in no case did a resistance movement seriously defeat German intentions. The crushing of the Warsaw Rising (August 1944) and the heavy losses of the French resistance at Vercors (June 1944) showed the relative impotence of resistance forces when not backed by allied troops. The price exacted by the Germans in the form of reprisals leads Milward to his conclusion that resistance 'seems to have been seldom effective, sometimes stultifying, frequently dangerous, and almost always too costly'. M. R. D. Foot, although not seriously challenging this view of the strategic contribution of the resistance movements, detects a wider value in their activities. 'The greatest good that resistance did', he concludes, 'lay in the hearts of the people who took part in it'. The greatest contribution of resistance, in other words, lay not so much in what it achieved during the war, as in the contribution that it made after the war to the re-establishment of national self-confidence and self-respect in such a country as France, where the traumatic shock of defeat and occupation had been devastating, and where its scars still exist.

(m) The Collapse of the Axis: Italy

The clearance of German and Italian troops from

North Africa by combined British and American forces by May 1943 left exposed the southern flank of fascist Europe. The daunting task of renewing the offensive against 'Fortress Europe' began (10th July 1943) with an allied assault upon Sicily, at the southern tip of Italy, which was not strongly resisted by the Axis forces. Within six weeks the island was in allied hands. The decision to proceed from Sicily to the Italian mainland was an unpopular one with Stalin, who preferred an attack upon German forces in France, to relieve pressure upon the Soviet Union, but it was based upon sound strategic sense. Italy was clearly the weakest point of the Axis, and by her elimination from the war the Mediterranean could be secured, and bases could be won for a future assault upon Germany.

The capture of Sicily precipitated the final crisis for the fascist government of Italy, and transformed the position of Italy in the war. Having joined Hitler's war effort when success seemed certain, Mussolini now faced an invasion of Italian territory, deprived of the services of 200000 troops killed or captured in North Africa, and of a further million committed to distant theatres of war. Resistance to the allies would now be possible only at the cost of turning the country over to the Germans, clearly a terrible price to pay, and a negation of all that fascist nationalism had stood for. Mussolini's failure to extricate himself from the disastrous German alliance caused the collapse of his political position which was wrecked by strikes and demonstrations, by the withdrawal of the support of the Fascist Grand Council (24th July 1943), and by his dismissal as Prime Minister by the King (25th July). Briefly, fascist government survived the fall of Mussolini, under the leadership of Marshal Badoglio. His government had two primary aims, to maintain the credibility of fascism, and to lead Italy into the allied camp without substantial German reprisals. On both counts it failed. While anti-fascist partisan forces reduced parts of Italy to a state of virtual civil war, and while Italian forces disintegrated in the confusion as to their present role, the German High Command took the decision to defend as much of the country as possible from the allied forces now (9th September 1943) landed on the mainland.

Defending first the Gustav Line, midway between Naples and Rome, then the Gothic Line 120 miles farther north, the Wehrmacht ensured that the allies would have to fight for every foot of Italian soil. Mussolini, sensationally rescued from his imprisonment, and installed as head of the 'Italian Social Republic' in the north, found himself reduced to the 'puppet' status of many would-be allies of Germany. It was perhaps the logical outcome of his 'savage friendship' with Hitler. Rome, expected to fall by the end of 1943, was not occupied by the allies until 4th June 1944, and German troops continued to resist in Milan and other northern cities long after allied troops had crossed the Rhine.

If the price paid by the allies for the eighteen months of warfare in Italy was high, for Italy herself that period constituted the final disaster of fascism. A further 100 000 Italians died in military action and bombing raids not only added high civilian casualties, but caused great damage to the cultural heritage of the nation. The destruction of the great Benedictine monastery of Monte Cassino was only the worst example of many. Inflation and the cost-of-living index soared, the latter from a base of 100 in 1938 to 5313 in October 1947. On top of this came political collapse. Badoglio's government collapsed in June 1944 and King Victor Emmanuel III abdicated in May 1946. Forty-three days later a referendum in favour of a republic ended 85 years of Italian monarchy. Mussolini did not live to see all this. Captured by partisans as he tried to flee into Switzerland, he was shot without trial, and his body hanged from a meathook in a Milan square (28th–29th April 1945). Fascist government in Italy had directed so much of its energy to preparing the nation for war, and now collapsed totally because of its failure in the war that it had helped to bring about.

(n) The Collapse of the Axis: The Western Front

By the beginning of 1944 the British and American commanders were able to concentrate men and materials for their greatest undertaking, the re-invasion of France. The technical difficulties facing 'Operation Overlord' were enormous, including the laying of oil pipelines across the Channel, and the designing of artificial 'Mulberry' harbours to provide anchorages for subsequent supply ships. The hopes of resisting the invasion, on the other hand, depended entirely on checking it on the landing beaches themselves. That they failed to do so owed much to the element of surprise, for the High Command had judged an invasion more likely in the region of Calais, rather than in Normandy, and to the enormous air superiority of the allies. Beginning on 6th June 1944, D Day, the allies landed 326 000 men in six days along a 50-mile beachhead. Within a month, a million men had landed, suffering only 9000 fatal casualties. Stiff German resistance around Caen and Falaise could not be sustained after a further American

landing in the south (15th August) and the collapse of German control of France was subsequently rapid. Paris was occupied, appropriately by Free French forces, on 24th August, Brussels and Antwerp were liberated in the first week of September, and by the onset of autumn, German forces were manning the defences of the Siegfried Line on their own frontiers.

German resistance, however, was not quite exhausted. Sir B. Liddell Hart has laid stress upon the decision of the allies to demand unconditional surrender. He claims that this was a factor that made it easier for Hitler, even after such defeats, to rally stiff defence. In the last days of 1944 the Wehrmacht enjoyed its last successes on the western front, defeating an allied attempt to outflank the Siegfried Line at Arnhem (17th–24th September), and temporarily regaining ground in the Ardennes by the counter attack known as the 'Battle of the Bulge' (16th December 1944–13th January 1945). The first months of 1945, however, were a period of steady disintegration. The Wehrmacht had to make good its losses by the conscription of raw teenagers, fuel supplies were on the brink of exhaustion, and the Luftwaffe had finally lost the struggle for air supremacy. Brilliant new weapons, such as the Me262 jet fighter and the V1 and V2 rockets, came too late to save the Reich.

The surviving German units proved quite insufficient to prevent an allied crossing of the Rhine (7th–23rd March 1945), and thereafter the main cities of Germany fell regularly to the advancing allied forces until (25th April 1945) advanced units of the American forces made contact with the Soviet army at Torgau in Saxony. Hitler's vision of a defeated Germany destroying itself in a Wagnerian 'Twilight of the Gods' came to nothing. Civilian morale was severely strained by the 'Thousand Bomber' raids on Dresden (13th–14th February). Also the planned yard-by-yard resistance of the German 'Home Guard' ('Volkssturm') failed to materialise, and local and central officials at last showed open defiance of Hitler's will by disobeying orders to destroy strategic buildings and important industrial plant.

(o) The Collapse of the Axis: The Eastern Front

A major contribution to the rapid allied successes in the west was, of course, made by the heavy German commitment to the Russian front. There, the campaigns of 1943 continued to be fought deep into Soviet territory, but with the Soviet army steadily developing both numerical and technical superiority. A German counter-attack at Kharkov (February 1943) achieved considerable success, but could not be sustained, and an attempt to force back Soviet forces at Kursk (July 1943) was thwarted in the biggest tank battle of the war. In the south, the Soviet army's own counter-attacks after the Battle of Kursk drove the German forces back to the River Dnieper and cut off those units occupying the Crimea.

In 1944 it was the turn of the northern units of the Wehrmacht to feel the weight of the Soviet offensive. In 1943 they had held a defensive line from Orel to Leningrad relatively confortably, an illustration perhaps of the error of Hitler's offensive strategy in the south. Now, a series of massive Soviet campaigns finally broke the encirclement of Leningrad (January 1944), re-occupied Minsk in White Russia (July), and drove into Poland and the Baltic territories (August), capturing 30 German divisions in the process. In the second half of the year southern offensives cleared Soviet soil of German troops and caused the surrender of Germany's Rumanian (August) and Bulgarian (September) allies.

In the east too, the beginning of 1945 saw allied troops poised for the final thrust into the Greater German Reich. Although more heavily manned and equipped than in the west, Germany was similarly in no shape to resist. Hitler himself was now ravaged by nervous disease, in a state where, as A. Bullock describes him, 'his orders became wilder and more contradictory, his demands more impossible, his decisions more arbitrary. His answer to every proposal was; No withdrawal'. He himself had shattered his own High Command. Such able generals as Manstein and Rundstedt had been dismissed for their failures to carry out impossible tasks, and Kluge and Rommel had both committed suicide when their roles in an officers' plot to murder Hitler and set the war upon a sounder footing (July 1944) were discovered. The final assault, by four armies on a front from the Baltic to the Carpathian mountains, thus made rapid progress. In March, Soviet forces crossed the River Oder, driving beyond Berlin to ensure that it was their forces, and not those of their allies, that occupied the German capital. Although he has been much criticised for it since, the commander of the western forces, General Eisenhower, adhered strictly to the spheres of influence agreed by the political leaders (see section **p**) and there was no race for Berlin.

The week from 30th April to 7th May 1945 witnessed the last rites of the Third Reich. Fulminating against the incompetence of his generals, and repeating his doctrines of anti-semitism and of the German need for 'Lebensraum', Hitler killed himself on 30th April and had his body burned to ensure that it could not be treated as that of Mussolini had been. On 7th May, after several unsuccessful attempts to negotiate separate peace treaties and so to divide the allies, the German government, now in the hands of Admiral Doenitz, surrendered unconditionally to the combined allied forces, thus ending the war in Europe.

(p) Teheran to Yalta: Allied War Aims

Although Germany and her allies entered the war with complex but quite well-defined aims, her opponents, especially Britain and the Soviet Union, fought originally for no other reason than that war was forced upon them by German aggression. At first, their war aims were simple and largely negative; to survive, and to destroy Nazism as a means to survival.

Only in 1942 did it become practical and practicable to consider in detail the settlement that the allies should pursue in the event of their victory. In the diplomatic discussions that followed, three main European issues were at stake; the treatment of Germany after her defeat, the fate of eastern Europe, and the means of ensuring future stability. General principles 'for common action to preserve peace and resist aggression in the post-war period' had been laid down in an Anglo-Russian treaty of May 1942, and by British agreements with America. Only in November 1943 did the allied leaders, Churchill, Roosevelt and Stalin, meet at Teheran in Iran, to begin to define details. Although the Teheran meeting was preoccupied with military strategy against Germany, it contained the seeds of the post-war settlement and gave early indications of Soviet ambitions. Roosevelt suggested that post-war Germany be divided into five sectors, with her industrial heartlands of the Ruhr, the Saar, Hamburg and the Kiel Canal, placed under international control. Stalin, determined that the Soviet Union would no longer be threatened by the instability of her immediate European neighbours, produced a 'shopping list' that stipulated future Soviet influence in East Prussia, and in most of those territories gained as a result of the 1939 pact with Germany.

The next meeting of the allied leaders was over a year later, at Yalta in the Crimea (4th February 1945). By then, German resistance was on the verge of collapse, and much of eastern Europe was, in any case, in the hands of the Soviet Army.

Roosevelt and Churchill have since incurred much criticism for their apparent acquiescence in the establishment of a substantial Soviet sphere of influence, but the considerations behind the creation of such a sphere were primarily practical. Only by force could eastern Europe be wrested from Soviet control, and even then it seems unlikely that forceful tactics could have succeeded. Thus, Stalin emerged from Yalta with confirmation of his dominance in Rumania, Bulgaria, Hungary and Poland. The lesser degree of Soviet influence in Yugoslavia, and its absence in Greece, also resulted from practical considerations, for their Mediterranean position made them as much subject to Anglo-American sea power as to Soviet land power. In return for this agreement, to which the Soviet Union has since adhered quite closely, Stalin agreed wholesale to American proposals for a four zone occupation of Germany, with a zone allocated to the French, and for the establishment of a United Nations Organisation. The last great tripartite meeting, at Potsdam (July 1945), was mainly concerned with the detailed implementation of the Yalta agreements.

The broad concept of a 'World Organisation' to replace the League of Nations had arisen at Teheran, and at a separate meeting of foreign ministers in Moscow (November 1943). Its specific format was thrashed out at an interallied conference at Dumbarton Oaks, Washington, in August–October 1944 where, among other decisions, it was agreed that the major powers sitting permanently on the central Council of the organisation could employ a veto over any measure that displeased them. Between April and June 1945 delegates of 50 nations met in San Francisco to draft what has become the United Nations Charter. The decision that the seat of the United Nations Organisation should be in New York was perhaps symbolic of the fact that Europe was no longer the focal point of world politics.

(q) The Nuremberg Trials

In addition to these other war aims, it had been established as early as 1942 that the allies would bring war criminals to account at the end of hostilities. This was decided in the light of the unparalleled ferocity exercised by the Germans in their conquests and in their occupation policies. The official policy of the American, British and Soviet governments was to hand over such criminals as local Nazi governors, local SS chiefs and so on, to the governments of the countries where their crimes had been committed. Those

leaders whose responsibility was wider were to be tried by an International Military Tribunal. The trials begun by this tribunal at Nuremberg (November 1945–September 1946) constituted the tip of a pyramid of trials that spread through the zones of occupation within Germany, and into other parts of Europe.

The Nuremberg Trials considered the cases of 22 leading figures of the Third Reich. Twelve of the accused received death sentences, including central political figures such as Goering and von Ribbentrop, military leaders such as Jodl and Keitel, and some of the most notorious local administrators such as Frank, Frick and Seyss-Inquart. All of the death sentences were carried out by hanging, except that upon Goering, who committed suicide in prison. He thus used the means of escape already exploited by Hitler, Himmler and Goebbels. Other sentences ranged from life imprisonment to terms of ten years. Similarly, in the lesser trials in the former occupied countries, which condemned Laval, Quisling and many lesser collaborators to death, the enemies of Nazism declared and defined its unacceptability in modern civilisation.

Legal objections have been raised to the trials by legal theorists. The principal of trial of the vanquished by the victors is a doubtful one, and little or no international law existed to cover the charges against the Nazi leaders. But however shaky their purely legal foundations, in a broader moral context the war crimes trials fulfilled a necessary and valuable purpose. In the words of P. Calvocoressi, 'the Nuremberg trial and its aftermath were an attempt to establish that war is not so much a visitation like a plague or an act of state like a treaty of alliance . . ., but pre-eminently a crime and a punishable one'.

(r) Consequences

The continuing fascination with the Second World War, manifested in films, novels, military and social history, testifies to its magnitude as an historical event. Its impact upon the next generations of Europeans was twofold, in the form of unparalleled physical and economic destruction, and in the form of revolutionary political change.

Table 18.2, including non-European powers for purposes of comparison, indicates the enormous cost of the war.

Comparisons with the war of 1914–18 may be fruitful. The human losses of the USSR alone in 1941–45 were equal to the total casualty toll of the earlier conflict, and German losses were double

	Probable military casualties	Probable civilian casualties	Probable financial cost (million £)
USSR	13 600 000	7 700 000	23 253
Germany	3 480 000	3 890 000	53 084
Japan	1 700 000	360 000	10 317
Great Britain	452 000	60 000	12 446
Italy	330 000	85 000	5 267
USA	295 000	—	62 560
France	250 000	360 000	27 818
Poland	120 000	5 300 000	not known

From T. G. Charman, *Modern European History Notes*, Telles Langdon Publications.

Table 18.2

those of the first war. The nature of the warfare in the Second World War meant that British and French losses were lighter than in the first war, but the devastation of those areas that saw the bulk of the fighting exceeded all precedents. Again, the Soviet Union and Germany suffered most. In the USSR between half and three quarters of all living quarters in the theatre of war were destroyed. In addition to her casualties, Europe faced the problem between 1939–47 of some 16 million refugees rendered homeless by the fighting.

Although the war made no such impact upon the map of Europe as the Napoleonic Wars and the First World War had done, its effect upon the political balance of the continent was revolutionary. Fascism and Nazism, proclaimed by Mussolini and Hitler as the dominant doctrines of the next millenium, vanished and have made no significant reappearance. They were discredited for ever, it is to be hoped, by the mediocrity of one dictator and by the bestiality of the other. N. Rich has provided an apt epitaph to these 'philosophies'. 'In the end, one of the saddest features of the Nazi experience is that out of all the suffering, the bloodshed and the destruction which Nazism inflicted on the world, the Nazi movement contributed nothing whatever to human culture and civilisation. Nothing except a terrible lesson about how fragile and vulnerable human civilisation is'.

Even more remarkable was that Germany, the central feature of the last century of European history, also vanished. She was replaced by two states, the Federal Republic of Germany and the German Democratic Republic, both closely tied to one of the two power blocs that now dominate world politics. The dominance that Germany had

long aspired to and had briefly enjoyed now clearly passed to the Soviet Union. Although not dominating the eastern European states in the same fashion as Germany had done, her military and economic superiority over the socialist republics that arose with direct Soviet assistance in Czechoslovakia, Poland, Hungary, Bulgaria and Rumania, has survived intact with only two serious challenges. Although Yugoslavia avoided such direct influence from Moscow, her socialist philosophy has affiliated her, too, to this formidable eastern bloc.

Indeed, the Soviet Union may claim to have emerged from the war, not only as the main European power, but perhaps as the only European power of world stature. The intercontinental empires of Britain, France, Italy, Belgium and the Netherlands were racked with difficulties before 1939, but the defeats of these powers, or the vast economic strain of their eventual victories, has meant that the post-war history of these empires has been one of steady liquidation. As a result, the whole nature of political confrontation in the world has changed. It no longer centres around the economic and political ambitions of a few European states, but rather around the different conceptions of human freedom and democracy represented by the two great world powers, one created by refugees from Europe, the other as much Asian as European in its culture and history. A history of Europe between 1848–1945 touches upon many of the issues that affected the lives of people all over the globe. A history of Europe after 1945 would be an altogether more parochial story, for European global dominance was one of the major casualties of the last great European war. At the heart of this new confrontation lies another great product of this war. The nuclear arms race dates from the dropping by the United States of the first atomic bomb on the Japanese city of Hiroshima (6th August 1945), the culmination of the increasing sophistication of weaponry during the war. In so many respects we may truly paraphrase Guérard's judgement on 1848, and conclude that 'our world begins in 1945'.

Progress Paragraphs

Answer the following questions in about 150 words.

Summarise the military advantages enjoyed by Germany in 1939. **Section (a)**

Why did Germany invade Denmark and Norway in 1940? **Section (b)**

How complete was German success in France in 1940? **Section (c)**

Why was the German offensive against Britain less successful than that against France? **Sections (c & d)**

Suggest reasons for the spread of the war to include (a) the Balkans and (b) the United States **Section (e)**

Why did Hitler invade the Soviet Union in June 1941? **Section (f)**

What factors prevented the German offensive against the Soviet Union from achieving total success in 1941? **Section (g)**

What were the consequences of Germany's failure to achieve a quick victory against the Soviet Union? **Sections (g & h)**

What were the material consequences of America's entry into the war? **Section (h)**

Suggest reasons for Germany's failure to match the material resources of her opponents. **Sections (h & i)**

What role did Hitler envisage for the conquered territories of the east? **Section (i)**

What was the 'Final Solution' to the 'Jewish Question' and what did it achieve? **Section (j)**

Compare the main motives for collaboration with or resistance to German occupation. **Sections (k & l)**

How effective were European resistance movements? **Section (l)**

Why did Mussolini's government collapse in 1943? **Section (m)**

What were the main features of allied war aims by early 1945? **Section (p)**

What price did Germany pay for the Second World War? **Sections (o, p, q & r)**

What price did Europe pay for the Second World War? **Section (r)**

Appendix One   Glossary of Terms

This appendix does not include terms that are described in detail in the text.

Anarchism Greek 'Anarchia'—'Non Rule'. Political doctrine advocating abolition of organised authority, and regarding all forms of government as oppressive.

Anti-clericalism Social/political view based upon hostility to the organised Church, and especially to the power and privileges of the clergy.

Anti-Semitism Hostility to Jews.

Autarky (or Autarchy) Economic policy aiming at national self-sufficiency in terms of raw materials and other essentially economic resources.

Authoritarianism Political system favouring or enforcing obedience to state authority, to the detriment of personal liberty.

Autocracy Absolute government in which ruler or rulers are not limited by constitutional rights of the governed.

Blitzkrieg German 'Lightning War'. War decided by rapid and devastating strategic blows.

Bolshevik Member of that branch of the Russian Communist movement favouring the form of strictly organised, élite political party advocated by V. I. Lenin.

Bonapartist Supporter of Napoleon Bonaparte or subsequently of Napoleon III. Broadly in favour of stable prosperous government, preserving the moderate gains of the French Revolution, but resisting the dangers of more radical social reconstruction.

Bourgeoisie The propertied section of the population, owning the means of economic production and distribution.

Capitalism Economic system under which social/political influence lies largely in the hands of the social class controlling the means of production and distribution.

Cartel Organisation of manufacturers with a view to the control of production, marketing, prices, etc.

Comintern International organisation of Communists founded in Moscow in March 1919 to exert Russian Soviet influence over international socialism.

Concordat Agreement or treaty between the Papacy and a secular government.

Corporativism System of government in which trade and professional organisations, or corporations, are the basis of society, and of political activity.

Coup d'état Sudden change of government by force, brought about by those already holding some political or military power.

Duma The semi-constitutional assembly in existence in Russia between 1905–17.

Entente French—Understanding, i.e. an agreement between two states which falls short of a formal alliance.

Franchise The right to vote.

Free trade Economic policy which does not protect home industries against foreign competition, but allows free import and export of all goods.

Führer German—Leader.

Gold standard Currency system whereby money is exchangeable for a fixed weight of gold.

Grossdeutsch Great German, i.e. that view of Germany as a state including all those of the German race.

Imperialism The practice by a country of acquiring economic and political power over other territories, usually with a view to commercial/industrial expansion.

Informal Empire Form of imperialism in which the imperial power does not directly rule the colonised territory, but leaves it nominally independent while pursuing economic penetration and exploitation.

Junker Hereditary Prussian aristocrat, dominating army and civil service positions from basis of landed wealth.

Kadets Russian political group of liberal tendencies, supported by progressive landowners, middle classes and intellectuals.

Kleindeutsch Little German, i.e. that view of Germany as a state comprising only a section of the total German speaking population of Europe. In practice this came to mean a Germany dominated by Prussia rather than by Austria.

Kulak Russian—Fist. A prosperous peasant, regarded by communists, and sometimes by fellow peasants as flourishing at the expense of his poorer fellows.

Lebensraum German—Living space. That foreign territory regarded by extreme German nationalists as necessary for the proper maintenance of the German people.

Legitimist Monarchist supporting the claim of a dynasty which he regards as having a divine right to rule, e.g. a supporter of the Bourbon dynasty in France.

Levant Eastern part of the Mediterranean, with its islands and neighbouring countries.

Luftwaffe German air force.

Menshevik Member of that branch of the Russian communist movement favouring a more popular, loose-knit form of party organisation and discipline, with more democratic leadership.

Octobrists Russian political group favouring limited political reform within the framework of Nicholas II's October Manifesto.

Orleanist French monarchist supporting the claim to the throne of Louis Philippe and his descendants.

Ottoman The ruling dynasty of Turkey. Hence Turkey was frequently referred to as the Ottoman Empire.

Pangermanism The political belief that all German-speaking peoples should be brought together in one political unit.

Panslavism The belief that all Slav peoples should be brought together in one political unit under the protection of Russia.

Papal infallibility The belief that, due to his position as God's representative on Earth, the Pope enjoys a total supremacy in all matters of Church doctrine and government.

Particularism Political view stressing the independence of smaller political units within larger ones, e.g. the independence of the smaller German states within the German Confederation.

Politburo The committee of ministers responsible for policy making in the Soviet Union.

Populism Russian social and political movement based upon an appeal to the peasantry, which it saw as the only viable basis for a socialist society.

Positivism Philosophy preaching that all true knowledge is scientific.

Protectionism Economic policy whereby a state's industries are protected from foreign competition by high tariff barriers.

Putsch German—'Coup d'état'.

Realpolitik Realistic politics, i.e. policies not guided by moral considerations, but by practical applications of available means.

Reichsfeind German—'Enemy of the Empire'. Term applied to a party or group identified as a threat to the state, and used by the state power as a rallying point to unite other groups.

Reichstag Imperial German parliament.

Reichswehr Imperial German army.

Reparations Payments made by a defeated state to compensate victorious state for damage or expenses caused by war.

Serfdom A form of servitude in which a landowner physically owns peasants on his estates, and can dispose of their labour and of their persons at will.

Slavophilism Russian social doctrine preaching the superiority of Slav (and especially of Russian) institutions.

Soviet Russian—'Council'. Thus applied to communist form of government based upon representation of the people through a hierarchy of local councils.

Syndicalism Militant trade union movement aiming at the transfer and control of the means of production, not to the state, but to the unions themselves.

Totalitarianism A form of government centred upon a dictatorial, single-party system, extending its influence over all areas of private and public life in the society.

Ultramontanism Political attitude of subordinating the interests of one's own state to the interests of the Papacy.

Wehrmacht Official designation of the German army under the Third Reich.

Weltpolitik German—'World policy'. Policy pursued by government of Kaiser Wilhelm II, insisting that German influence should extend to all world issues, and not be limited to continental affairs.

Zemstvo Elective rural council established in Russia as part of the reforms of Tsar Alexander II.

Zollverein German—'Customs Union'. The customs union established between various German States under the presidency of Prussia in 1834.

Appendix Two   Further Reading

The Historiography section appended to most chapters gives details of influential works published in various languages on each topic. The following list contains suggestions for further reading, currently available in English. Those titles marked with an asterisk contain selections of contemporary documents, such as may be used in the document-based questions now widely favoured by examiners.

General

(a) France

A. Cobban *History of Modern France* Penguin 1957–65
J. P. T. Bury *France 1814–1940* Methuen 1969
G. Wright *France in Modern Times* Norton 3rd. ed. 1981

(b) Italy

D. Mack Smith *Italy: A Modern History* Ann Arbor 1969

(c) Germany

W. Carr (ed) *A History of Germany 1815–1945* Arnold 1969
G. A. Craig *Germany 1866–1945* Oxford 1978
H. Holborn *A History of Modern Germany* Eyre and Spottiswoode 1965
E. J. Passant *A Short History of Germany* Cambridge 1966

(d) Russia

H. Seton-Watson *The Russian Empire: 1801–1917* Oxford 1967
J. N. Westwood *Endurance and Endeavour: Russian History 1812–1980* Oxford 2nd ed 1981

(e) Austria–Hungary

A. J. P. Taylor *The Habsburg Empire: 1809–1918* Hamish Hamilton 1960
C. A. Macartney *The Habsburg Empire: 1790–1918* Weidenfeld and Nicolson 1971

By Chapter

Chapter One

J. Droz *Europe Between Revolutions* Fontana 1967
E. Kedourie *Nationalism* Hutchinson 1960
H. Kohn *Nationalism* Van Nostrand 1965
N. MacKenzie *Socialism: A Short History* Hutchinson 1949

G. Lichtheim *Marxism* Routledge and Kegan Paul 1971
E. Wilson *To the Finland Station* Fontana 2nd ed 1960
D. S. Landes *The Unbound Prometheus* Cambridge 1970

Chapter Two

P. Robertson *Revolutions of 1848: A Social History* Princeton 1952
F. Eyck *The Revolutions of 1848–1849* Oliver and Boyd 1972
*R. Price (ed) *1848 in France* Thames and Hudson 1975
G. Duveau *1848: The Making of a Revolution* Routledge and Kegan Paul 1967
*P. Jones *The 1848 Revolutions* Longman 1981
R. J. Rath *The Viennese Revolution of 1848* University of Texas 1957

Chapter Three

J. M. Thompson *Louis Napoleon and the Second Empire* Blackwells 1954
J. P. T. Bury *Napoleon III and the Second Empire* English University Press 1964
M. Howard *The Franco-Prussian War* Fontana 1967
T. Zeldin *The Political System of Napoleon III* Macmillan 1958

Chapter Four

*M. Salvadori *Cavour and the Unification of Italy* Van Nostrand 1961
D. Mack Smith *Victor Emmanuel, Cavour and the Risorgimento* Oxford 1971
*D. Beales *The Risorgimento and the Unification of Italy* Allen and Unwin 1972

Chapter Five

O. Pflanze *Bismarck and the Development of Germany: The Period of Unification: 1815–1871* Princeton 1963
E. Eyck *Bismarck and the German Empire* Allen and Unwin 1968
W. N. Medlicott *Bismarck and Modern Germany* Hodder and Stoughton 1967

A. J. P. Taylor *Bismarck: The Man and the Statesman*
NEL 1968
*W. M. Simon *Germany in the Age of Bismarck*
Allen and Unwin 1968
T. S. Hamerow *The Age of Bismarck: Documents and
Interpretations* Harper & Row 1973

Chapter Six

W. Bruce Lincoln *Nicholas I* Allen Lane 1978
W. Mosse *Alexander II and the Modernisation of Russia*
English University Press 1958
*B. Dmytryshyn *Imperial Russia: A Source Book*
Dryden Press Illinois 1974

Chapter Seven

As for Chapter Five

Chapter Eight

A. Horne *The Fall of Paris* Macmillan 1965
D. Thomson *Democracy in France Since 1870* Oxford
1969
D. W. Brogan *France Under the Republic: 1870–1939*
Harper 1940
J. D. McManners *Church and State in France:
1880–1914* SPCK 1972
T. Zeldin *France 1848–1945* Oxford 1973

Chapter Nine

R. Charques *The Twilight of Imperial Russia*
Oxford 1958
D. W. Treadgold *Lenin and His Rivals*
Methuen 1955
T. G. Stavrou (ed) *Russia Under the Last Tsar*
University of Minneapolis 1969
M. E. Falkus *The Industrialisation of Russia:
1700–1914* Macmillan 1972

Chapter Ten

*J. A. Nichols *Germany After Bismarck: The Caprivi
Era: 1890–1894* Cambridge 1958
G. A. Craig *The Politics of the Prussian Army:
1640–1945* Oxford 1955
M. Balfour *The Kaiser and His Times* Cresset Press
1964
A. J. P. Taylor *The Habsburg Empire: 1809–1918*
Hamish Hamilton 1960
C. A. Macartney *The Habsburg Empire: 1790–1918*
Weidenfeld and Nicolson 1971

Chapter Eleven

A. J. P. Taylor *The Struggle for Mastery in Europe:
1848–1918* Oxford 1971

D. K. Fieldhouse *Economics and Empire* Weidenfeld
and Nicolson 1973
K. W. Koch *Origins of the First World War*
Macmillan 1972 (which contains a good
second-hand account of the arguments of Fischer,
Geiss and their opponents)
L. C. F. Turner *The Origins of the First World War*
Arnold 1970
A. J. P. Taylor *The First World War: Illustrated
History* Penguin 1966
B. H. Liddell Hart *The History of the First World
War* Pan 1972

Chapter Twelve

E. H. Carr *A History of Soviet Russia: 1917–1929*
Penguin 1966
M. Ferro *The Russian Revolution of February 1917*
Routledge and Kegan Paul 1972
C. Hill *Lenin and the Russian Revolution* English
University Press 1970
B. D. Wolfe *Three Who Made a Revolution* Penguin
1966
D. Shub *Lenin* Penguin 1966
J. Bradley *Civil War in Russia: 1917–1920* Batsford
1975
R. Luckett *The White Generals* Longman 1971
*A. Wood *The Russian Revolution* Longman 1979

Chapter Thirteen

*B. Dmytryshyn *The USSR: A Concise History*
Scribners 3rd ed 1978
I. Deutscher *Stalin: A Political Biography* Penguin
1966
A. Ulam *Stalin* Allen Lane 1973
L. Schapiro *The Communist Party of the Soviet Union*
Methuen 1970
*M. McCauley *Stalin and Stalinism* Longman
1983
A. Nove *An Economic History of the USSR* Penguin
1969

Chapter Fourteen

A. J. Nicholls *Weimar and the Rise of Hitler*
Macmillan 1968
*J. Hiden *The Weimar Republic* Longman 1974
G. Chapman *Why France Collapsed* Cassell 1968
D. W. Brogan *The Development of Modern France:
1870–1939* Hamish Hamilton 1967
R. Carr *Spain 1808–1939* Oxford 1966
H. Thomas *The Spanish Civil War* Penguin 1968

Chapter Fifteen

S. J. Woolf *European Fascism* Weidenfeld and
Nicolson 1970

*S. W. Halperin *Mussolini and Italian Fascism* Van
Nostrand 1964
E. Wiskemann *Fascism in Italy: Its Development and
Influence* Macmillan 1969
E. R. Tannenbaum *Fascism in Italy: Society and
Culture 1922–1945* Allen Lane 1973
D. Mack Smith *Mussolini* Weidenfeld and
Nicolson 1981

Chapter Sixteen

A. Bullock *Hitler: A Study in Tyranny* Penguin
1962
K. D. Bracher *The German Dictatorship* Peregrine
1978
M. Broszat *The Hitler State* Longman 1981
R. Grunberger *A Social History of the Third Reich*
Penguin 1974
K. Hildebrand *The Foreign Policy of the Third Reich*
Batsford 1973

Chapter Seventeen

A. Bullock *Hitler: A Study in Tyranny*
Penguin 1962
A. J. P. Taylor *Origins of the Second World War*
Penguin 1964
E. Wiskemann *Europe of the Dictators: 1919–1945*
Fontana 1966
E. M. Robertson (ed) *The Origins of the Second
World War* Macmillan 1971
*A. Adamthwaite *The Making of the Second World
War* Allen and Unwin 1977
*G. F. Kennan *Soviet Foreign Policy 1917–1941* Van
Nostrand 1960

Chapter Eighteen

P. Calvocoressi and G. Wint *Total War* Penguin
1974
G. Wright *The Ordeal of Total War* Harper 1968
N. Rich *Hitler's War Aims* Andre Deutsch 1973
M. R. D. Foot *Resistance* Methuen 1976

Index